What readers are saying about *Deploying Rails Applications*

Deploying Rails Applications is a fantastic and vastly important book. Many thanks!

> ▶ **Stan Kaufman**
> Principal, The Epimetrics Group LLC

I've used the section on setting up a virtual private server to get up and running on three different VPS instances in less than thirty minutes each. Your book has saved me days of time preparing servers, letting me focus instead on writing code. Your book also has the best Capistrano tutorial I've ever read. It's no longer a mystery, and I'm now writing custom deployment tasks. I can't wait to get my final copy!

> ▶ **Barry Ezell**
> CTO, Balance Engines LLC

Prior to buying this book, I had to spend hours scouring the Web to find this kind of information. Having it all in one place (and correct!) helped me deliver a successful Rails project. Thank you!

> ▶ **Eric Kramer**
> Programmer, Nationwide Children's Hospital

Deploying Rails Applications

A Step-by-Step Guide

Deploying Rails Applications

A Step-by-Step Guide

Ezra Zygmuntowicz

Bruce A. Tate

Clinton Begin

with Geoffrey Grosenbach

Brian Hogan

The Pragmatic Bookshelf

Raleigh, North Carolina   Dallas, Texas

Many of the designations used by manufacturers and sellers to distinguish their products are claimed as trademarks. Where those designations appear in this book, and The Pragmatic Programmers, LLC was aware of a trademark claim, the designations have been printed in initial capital letters or in all capitals. The Pragmatic Starter Kit, The Pragmatic Programmer, Pragmatic Programming, Pragmatic Bookshelf and the linking *g* device are trademarks of The Pragmatic Programmers, LLC.

Every precaution was taken in the preparation of this book. However, the publisher assumes no responsibility for errors or omissions, or for damages that may result from the use of information (including program listings) contained herein.

Our Pragmatic courses, workshops, and other products can help you and your team create better software and have more fun. For more information, as well as the latest Pragmatic titles, please visit us at

http://www.pragprog.com

ISBN-10: 0-9787392-0-5

ISBN-13: 978-09787392-0-1

Printed on acid-free paper with 50% recycled, 15% post-consumer content.

P1.0 printing, April 2008

Version: 2008-4-21

Contents

## Chapter 1

Introduction

Building Rails apps brings the joy back into development. But I, Ezra, have a confession to make. There was a brief moment that I didn't like Rails at all.

I'd just graduated from the five-minute tutorial to developing my first real Rails application. The helpers, plug-ins, and generators reduced the amount of code I needed to write. The logical organization and layout of the files let me painlessly find what I needed, and the domain-specific languages in Active Record let me express my ideas with simplicity and power. The framework bowed to my will, and aside from a few trivial mistakes, I finished the app. Pure joy washed over me.

But then, it was time to deploy. Deployment means moving your application from a development environment into a home that your customers can visit. For a web application, that process involves choosing a host, setting up a web server and database, and moving all your files to the right places with the right permissions.

I quickly discovered that after the joy of development, deployment was a real drag. All those waves of euphoria completely disintegrated against the endless stream of crash logs, Rails error pages, and futile install scripts. I spent hours wading through the Rails wikis, blogs, and books for answers, but each one gave me a mere fragment of what I needed. Much of the information I found was contradictory or flat-out wrong.

Deployment also involves making the best possible environment for your customers, once you've settled into your new home. There, too, I failed miserably. When I finally made my site work, it was too slow. Stumbling through page caching seemed to make no difference, and my end users watched the spinning (lack of) progress indicator in frustration. I struggled to fix memory leaks, broken database migrations, and worthless server configurations until eventually my site purred in appreciation. Then came success, which means more visitors, followed by more failure. I screamed some choice words that would make a sailor's dead parrot blush. No, at that moment, I really didn't like Rails.

I'm not going to sugarcoat it. If you don't know what you're doing, Rails deployment can stretch the limits of your patience, even endurance. What's worse, Rails deployment suffers especially in areas where Rails development is easy:

- You can always find plenty of Rails development documentation, but when it's time to deploy, you can often find only a fraction of what you need. People just seem to write more about development than deployment.
- You can choose your development platform, but you can't always choose your deployment platform. Most hosts with Rails support run some variant of Linux; others run FreeBSD or Solaris. And the software stack for different hosts can vary wildly, as can application requirements.
- When your development application breaks, you can find mountains of information through breakpointing, rich development logs, and the console. In production, when things go south, there are fewer sources of information, more users, and more variables. You might encounter a problem with the operating system, your application server, system resources, plug-ins, your database server, or any one of dozens of other areas. And your caching environment works differently than your development environment.
- Rails is an integrated platform that narrows the choices. You'll probably use Active Record for persistence and Action Pack for your controllers and views. You'll use Script.aculo.us and Prototype for Ajax. But your deployment environment will require many choices that are not dictated by Rails, including the most basic choice of your web server.

But I'm living proof that you can learn to master this beast. Over time, I've come to understand that my approach to deployment was rushed, as well as a little haphazard. I found that I needed to approach deployment in the same way that I approached development. I had to learn how to do it well, effectively plan each step, and automate as much as possible so I left little to chance. I needed to plan for problems so

I could anticipate them and get automatic notification at the first sign of trouble. At my company, Engine Yard, I support some of the largest and most popular Rails sites in the world. I want to help you learn to do the same.

Because Rails is so new, some people question whether *anyone* can deploy a sophisticated, scalable, and stable Rails application. Based on my experience at Engine Yard, I'd like to first debunk a few myths:

Myth: The Ruby on Rails development framework is much more advanced than the deployment framework.

That's false. Deployment tools for Rails get much less attention, but they are also growing in form and function. If you know where to look, you can find deployment tools that are proven, effective, and free to use. These tools use techniques that are every bit as advanced and functional as those used by the most mature Java or C# development shops. Ruby admins can deploy a typical Rails application with one command and move back to a previous release should that deployment fail, again with one command. You can deploy Rails to simple single-server setups or multiserver sites with very few changes. And if you now copy PHP files to your server by hand or rsync Perl scripts to multiple machines, your life is about to become a lot easier (and yes, you can use some of these same tools as well). I'll show you how to do these things in Chapter 5, *Capistrano*, on page 85.

Myth: Rails is too new to have any large, sophisticated deployments.

That, too, is false. Ruby on Rails is in use on very large sites that are spread across multiple machines. Some of those applications require many full servers just to serve their full feature set to their community. And the list of large Rails sites grows daily. Twitter, Basecamp, and 43 Things are all multiserver large Rails sites. Many more enter production every month.

Myth: The Ruby language is inherently unstructured and is poorly suited for web applications.

That's mostly false. Ruby is an interpreted, dynamically typed language that presents real challenges in high-volume production settings, but the Rails framework has features and strategies that mitigate many risks associated with these challenges. The Rails caching model and performance benchmarking tools help developers to build high-performance sites. The Rails testing frameworks, sometimes in combination with other Ruby testing frameworks, help developers catch errors that a compiler might catch in a statically typed language. And the Rails shared-nothing architecture, like many of the highest-volume Internet sites in existence, allows Rails sites to scale by adding additional hardware. You'll learn how to cluster in Chapter 7, *Scaling Out*, on page 137.

Myth: Rails can get you into trouble, if you don't know what you're doing.

That one is true. If you want to stay out of serious trouble, you need to know how to wield your chosen tools. No development language is immune to bad design. And a poor deployment strategy will burn you. You must always arm yourself with knowledge to protect yourself. In this book, I hope to help you do exactly that.

Rest assured that the Rails deployment story is a good one. You *can* learn to predictably and reliably deploy your applications. You *can* use repeatable techniques to understand what the performance characteristics of your system are likely to be. And you *can* improve the stability and scalability of your system given knowledge, time, and patience. I'm going to start quickly. I want to walk you through the same deployment road map that every Internet application will need to use.

1.1 The Lay of the Land

Web 2.0, the new buzzword that describes a new class of web applications, sounds like a daunting mix of new technologies that radically change the way you think about the Internet. But when you think about it, from a deployment perspective, Web 2.0 doesn't change much at all:

- The Internet still uses the same communication protocols and the same type of web servers.

- You still scale Internet applications the same way, by clustering.

- You can even use some of the same servers, and the new ones work mostly like the old ones.

- You still keep your source code in source control.

- The operating system is still usually Unix-based.

For all the talk about the way your applications may change, deployment remains *precisely the same*. Think of the Internet as a road map.

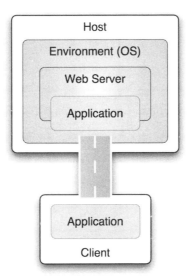

Figure 1.1: BASIC DEPLOYMENT MAP

The buildings and places are servers, browsers on clients, routers, fire-walls, and balancers. The roads are the networks between them and the various communication protocols those networks use. I like the map analogy because when all is said and done, the Internet is all about moving data from one place to another.

When you deploy, you're using the Internet to move your application from one place to another. You can think of every deployment story as a map. In fact, every deployment story in this book will come with a map. A generic version of the simplest possible deployment story is shown in Figure 1.1.

Look at the components of that figure. First, you have a host with an environment. I'll spend much of this book showing you how to build the environment that will host your application. The environment, in this case, includes all the different components that an Internet application needs. You'll learn to build each of these pieces yourself or rely on another vendor to build those pieces for you. Those pieces will include the operating system, the Ruby language, the Rails framework, and the various pieces that will tie them together. The host represents where your customers will go to find your application. As you can well imagine, that host image will get much richer as I take you through the various pieces of this book.

You also see a development client. My machine is my trusty MacBook Pro, but I've also developed on the Windows platform. You might think that this book is about the road that goes from the application on the client to the server. And I'll start the book that way. The basic deployment map (shown in Figure 1.1, on the previous page) will use plain old FTP to move your application from the client to the server.

Deployments are rarely as simple as the one you see in Figure 1.1, on the preceding page. You're going to find that shared hosting is a little limited. And you probably know that plain old FTP may be simple, but it will not handle the demands of effectively managing the site. You will need better deployment tools. You will want to throw a source control repository into the mix. If you're lucky, one web server may not be enough. You'll wind up with a more sophisticated map, like the one in Figure 7.1, on page 140.

In the complete map, you see a vastly different story. What may appear as one site to the user has its own environments. The first change is the website. You can no longer assume a single host. Those environments might be virtual environments that all reside on a single machine, or each individual environment could have its own hardware. Your deployment strategy will have to install your application into each Rails environment. You will need to configure the pieces to work together. And that's the subject of this book.

In the first few chapters, you might think that we're oversimplifying a little bit. Don't worry. You're not going to be using FTP or shared hosting by the time you finish this book. I'll get to the second map. I'll just build it slowly, one piece at a time. We'll keep extending the map throughout the book until you get to your eventual goal. In the next section, I'll walk you through what you can expect in the chapters to follow.

1.2 Finding a Home

You've seen that our maps have one goal in mind. They want to get your development code to its eventual home in the best possible way. By now, you also know that the type of map you need depends on where your application is going to live. You can't adequately understand deployment unless you understand where you're going to put your code, but finding a platform for your Rails code is hard. The process feels like finding a home without a real estate agent, the Internet, or any consolidated home buyer guides. Over the course of this book, I'd like to take you into that hidden universe. You will learn how to:

- develop Rails applications with painless deployment in mind;

- choose between shared hosts, virtual private servers, or dedicated servers;

- understand the software stack that the pros use to deploy Rails for high performance;

- build and configure your web servers and other services;

- stress your application before your users do; and

- streamline your application in production using advanced strategies such as caching so your site can scale.

Throughout this book, I'll treat deployment like buying a new home for your application. Through each of the chapters, you'll learn to pick and prepare your home, streamline your stuff for everyday living, and even move up into wealthier neighborhoods, should you ever need to do so. Let me take you on a guided tour of the book:

Packing up: tending to your application. Before you can move, you need to pack up. If you want a good experience, you need to organize your stuff to prepare for your move. On Rails, that means minding your application. You will need to prepare source control. You will also need to make some important decisions that will have a tremendous impact on your production application, such as the structure of your migrations and your attention to security. This chapter will add source control to your map.

Finding a starter home: shared hosting. Not everyone can afford a house. When most of us leave home, we first move into an apartment building or a dorm. Similarly, most Rails developers will choose some kind of shared hosting to house that first application: a blog or a simple photo log. Shared hosting is the first and cheapest of the hosting alternatives. Setting up shared hosting involves many of the same steps as moving into your first apartment: find a home that meets your requirements, set up your address so that others can find you, and customize your home as much as possible. Like apartment living, shared hosting has its own set of advantages and disadvantages. Shared hosting is cheap, but you need to learn to be a good citizen, and you'll also likely encounter those who aren't. In this chapter, you'll learn to find and make the best use of your first home. The deployment will be simple. You'll need a shared host, a simple application, and a simple mechanism such as FTP to ship your code up there.

Moving up: virtual and dedicated hosting. After you've lived in an apartment for a while, you might decide to move up to your own home or condo. Your virtual world is the same. When shared hosting isn't enough, you can move up to virtual and dedicated hosts. Moving up to a home carries a whole new set of benefits and responsibilities: you get more freedom to add that extra closet you've always wanted, but you also have to fix the toilet and mow the lawn yourself. Dedicated and virtual hosts are like your own home or condo. These plans are typically more robust than shared hosts, but they also require much more knowledge and responsibility. When you set up your own host, you take over as landlord. You need to know how to build and configure your basic software stack from your web server to the Rails environment. This chapter will walk you through building your hosting platform. Your map will get a little more complicated because you'll have to build your environment, but otherwise, it will be the same.

Moving in: Capistrano. After you've chosen and prepared a place, you can move in. Unlike moving in your furnishings, with Rails you will probably move in more than once. You'll want to make that move-in process as painless as possible, automating everything you possibly can. Capistrano is the Rails deployment tool of choice. In this chapter, you'll learn to deploy your application with Capistrano using existing recipes with a single command. You'll also learn to roll back the deployment to the previous version if you fail. You will also see many of Capistrano's customization tools. This chapter will change your map by building a better road between your application and the deployment environment.

Adding on: proxies and load balancing. When your place is no longer big enough, you need to add on or move up. Since we have already covered moving up, this chapter will cover adding on through clustering. One of the most common and effective ways to remodel a Rails deployment without buying a bigger plan is to separate the service of static content and application-backed dynamic content. In this chapter, you'll learn to reconfigure your production environments to handle more load. I'll show you setups with Apache and nginx serving static content and dynamic content with Mongrel. You'll also learn how to distribute your applications across multiple servers with a rudimentary load-balanced cluster. I'll also walk you through potential database deployments. The host side of your deployment map will get much more sophisticated because you'll be deploying to a cluster instead of a single host, but with Capistrano already in the bag, you won't have to change the client side at all.

Planning for the future: benchmarking. As you grow older, your family may grow. Without a plan, your house may not be able to accommodate your needs a few years from now. In Rails or any other Internet environment, capacity planning becomes a much larger problem, because your home may need to serve hundreds of times the number of users it does today. To get the answers you need, you have to benchmark. After you've chosen your stack and deployed your application, you'll want to find out just how far you can push it. In this chapter, you'll learn to use the base Ruby tools, and a few others, to understand just what your environment can handle. You'll also learn a few techniques to break through any bottlenecks you do find. The deployment map won't change at all.

Managing things: monitoring. As you live in your new home, you'll often find that you need help managing your household. You might turn to a watchdog to monitor comings and goings, or you might want to hire a service to do it for you. With the many Rails configuration options, you'll be able to manage some of your installation yourself. You can also use an application called Monit to automatically tell you when a part of your system has failed or is about to fail. You will make only subtle adjustments to your map to allow for the additional monitoring of the system.

Doing windows: deploying on Windows. Homeowners hate doing windows. Rails developers often do, too. But sometimes, you don't have a choice. When you do have to deploy on Windows, this chapter will walk you through the process. We'll keep it as simple and painless as possible. This chapter will focus on the host side of the map to offer the Windows alternative as you build out your environment on Windows.

When you've finished the book, you'll know how to pick the best platform for you. You'll understand how to make Capistrano finesse your application from your development box to your target environment. And you'll be able to configure a variety of deployment scenarios from the inside out. If you've built up any resentment for Rails because of deployment problems in the past, this book should get you back on the path to enjoying Rails development again.

1.3 Conventions

Throughout this book, you'll see several command-line terminal sessions that show various deployment, setup, and configuration tasks. You'll need to make sure you type the right command in the right place. You wouldn't want to accidentally clobber your local code or accidentally load your fixtures to your production database (destroying your data in the process!). To be as safe as possible, I will follow a few conventions with the command-line prompts to make it easier to follow along.

On most Unix-like systems, when the command-line prompt is the number sign (#), it is letting you know that you are logged in as root. When the prompt is the dollar sign ($), you are logged in as a regular system user. These are the conventions for the Bourne Again Shell (bash). If you are running another shell, you might have slightly different indicators in your prompt, and you should adjust accordingly. On the Ubuntu system we are about to set up, the default shell is bash.

The following prompts show how you should log in to run the various shell commands we use in the book. When you should be logged in as root, the prompt will look like this:

```
root#
```

When you should be logged in with your regular user account, the prompt will look like this:

```
ezra$
```

When you should be running a command from your local computer and not the server, the prompt will look like this:

```
local$
```

1.4 Acknowledgments

Collectively

We'd like to thank DHH and the Rails core team for giving us Rails, because none of this would have been possible without their innovations. We'd also like to thank the Rails and the Ruby community as a whole. We send thanks to the Capistrano and Mongrel teams for advancing the early deployment story for Rails. This is one of the friendliest and most helpful communities that we have had the pleasure of knowing. Above all, thanks for the generosity of Brian Hogan and Geoffrey Grosenbach for your invaluable contributions to this book.

Clinton Begin

"I promise, I'll never write another book." That's what I told my wife, Jennifer, after my first book. So, I'd like to start out by thanking her, both for accepting my apology and for her selfless support throughout this process. Being a part-time author robs us dads of valuable family time and mothers of much-needed break time. After a few trial-by-fire experiences, I can attest to the fact that Stay-at-Home Mother is a far tougher job title than any I've ever held. I'd also like to thank my two sons, Cameron and Myles, for teaching me more about myself each and every day.

Outside of my family, I'd like to thank Bruce and Ezra for inviting me to work on this book with them. It was an opportunity to tackle a very important subject that most Rails books gloss over and simply run out of space in their attempt to cover it. I'd also like to thank Thought-Works, as they helped launch my career and gave me my first opportunity to work with production Rails deployments. ThoughtWorks has some of the brightest Ruby and Rails minds out there, including Alexey Verkhovsky and Jay Fields. Finally, I'd like to thank Dave Thomas. Three years ago I challenged him by asking cockily "What does Ruby have over other toy languages?" In a way that only Dave Thomas could respond, he simply didn't and mailed me a book instead.

Bruce Tate

I never thought I'd be writing a book on Ruby on Rails deployment. My gift is as a programmer. As a manager and programmer on larger Internet projects, I simply give the deployment task to others. Thanks to Dave, Andy, and Ezra for the invitation to help tackle this important gap in Rails literature. Thanks also go to my boss, Robert Tolmach, who has become one of my best friends who trusted me to make some radical bets with his money. He shared some time with me to make this book possible so that others may benefit from what we've learned at WellGood LLC with ChangingThePresent. Thanks go out especially to Clinton Begin, who jumped into this project at the very last minute and wrote the most important chapter in the book, giving us a much-needed jolt of productivity when we most needed it.

If these acknowledgments read like a broken record, it's only because those we love make extreme sacrifices to satisfy our addiction to writing and technology. Thanks to Maggie, Kayla, and Julia for sharing me with the written word. This is far from the first book, and with luck, it won't be the last. My love for each of you grows always.

Ezra Zygmuntowicz

I'd like to thank my wife, Regan, for being so understanding and supportive. There were many weekends and evenings that I should have spent with her but instead worked on the book. I'd also like to thank all the folks who helped proofread and critique the content as it changed and morphed into the final result. I'd also like to thank all of my wonderful coauthors for their contributions; I truly could not have done this without all of the help. Special thanks go out to François Beausoleil who helped me with some early svn stuff way back when we started pulling this book together. And thanks to Geoffrey Grosenbach for all of your critical early contributions.

Brian Hogan

I first need to thank Ezra for the opportunity to contribute to this book and Bruce for introducing me to Ruby at a point in my life when I was about to quit programming because of frustration. Without their help and guidance, I would not be where I am today. Zed Shaw deserves credit as well because he challenged me to make it work on Windows, and Luis Laverna is my hero for making Mongrel run as a Windows service, which made my job a lot easier.

I would also like to thank my wife, Carissa, for her support, Her constant patience with me throughout this project (and many others) is truly wonderful. Thanks to Ana and Lisa, my two girls, for being so patient with Daddy. Thanks also to my mom and dad for teaching me to work hard and to never give up no matter how hard I thought something was. I am extremely lucky and blessed to have such a wonderful family.

Finally, thanks to Erich Tesky, Adam Ludwig, Mike Weber, Chris Warren, Chris Johnson, and Josh Swan. You guys are the best. Thanks for keeping me going.

Chapter 2

Refining Applications for Production

Before you can move into your new house, you need to pack up. With Rails, you need to do the same thing: prepare your Rails application for deployment.

You'll need to organize your code and prepare it for production. Specifically, you'll need to think about a few things:

- Making your source code repository work smoothly with your production setup to make your deployments go smoother and be more secure

- Strengthening your brittle migrations to save you from models that change and developers who collide

- Locking down Ruby, Rails, and Gems code to a single, stable version

Fundamentally, you want to build every application with deployment in mind. The earlier you think about deployment issues, the better off you'll be.

I'm not saying you need to make early deployment decisions at demand time. You just need to make sure you build intelligent code that is less likely to break in production situations. Your first order of business is to simplify your Subversion setup.

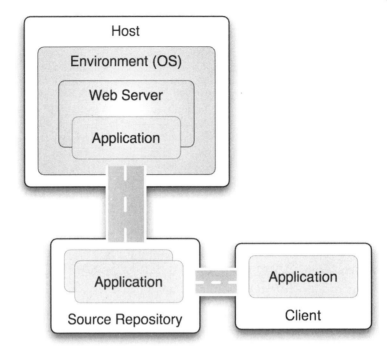

Figure 2.1: APPLICATION MAP

2.1 The Lay of the Land

The first enhancement to the basic deployment map is shown in Figure 2.1. The following list explains what you'll need to accomplish in this chapter:

- Set up source control. If you haven't already done so, setting up source control will make the rest of your deployment picture much simpler and will improve your development experience as well.

- Prepare your application configuration and performance. You will make some simple changes to your application or, better yet, build it right the first time.

The three Rails environments—development, test, and production—will make it easy for you to isolate configuration for deployment. The rest is just common sense. It all starts with source control.

2.2 Source Code Management

Good deployment strategies always start with a good foundation. I want to be able to deploy the same application to my servers with identical results every time. That means I need to be able to pull a given version of the application from a central source. Anything less won't give me dependable, repeatable results. Luckily, Rails will automate a whole lot of the deployment scripts, but only if you use the common infrastructure that other Rails developers do.

Unless you have a strong reason to use something else, you'll want to use Subversion for your application's source code control. The majority of Rails developers use it, the Rails team uses it for Rails, and the Rails plug-in system also uses it. *Version Control with Subversion* [PCSF04] is a great book about Subversion. You should also check out *Pragmatic Version Control* [Mas05] for a pragmatic view of source code control in any language. For this chapter, I'm going to assume you already have Subversion installed and running.

Subversion on Rails

The keys to using Subversion with Rails are maintaining the right structure. You want to keep the right stuff under source control and keep the wrong stuff out. Setting up your application's repository right the first time will save you time and frustration. A number of items in a Rails application do not belong in source control. Many a new Rails developer has clobbered his team's database.yml file or checked in a 5MB log file. Both of these problems are with the Subversion setup, not with Rails or even the Rails developer. In an optimal setup, each developer would have their own database.yml file and log files. Each development or production instance of your application will have its own version of these files, so they need to stay out of the code repository. You might already have a Subversion repository already, but I'll assume you don't and walk you through the entire process from scratch.

Repository Creation

Start by creating a new Subversion repository for your Rails project. Log in to the server that will have your Subversion repository. Create a directory for your repository, and let Subversion know about it:

```
$ svnadmin create /home/ezra/svn
```

The authors of Subversion recommend creating all repositories with three folders at the root: trunk, tags, and branches. This setup works best

if you have one project per repository.[1] You don't have to create the
top-level folders for Subversion to work, but I suggest you do so. The
better Subversion repositories I have seen adhere to this convention,
and if you have only one project in your repository, this approach will
let you tag and branch at will. These commands will build your initial
directories:

```
$ svn mkdir --message="Initial project layout" ←
    file:///home/ezra/svn/trunk file:///home/ezra/svn/tags ←
    file:///home/ezra/svn/branches
Committed revision 1.
```

Importing a Simple Rails Application

I suggest you practice with an empty Rails project first. Create the Rails
application as usual:[2]

```
$ rails ~/deployit
    create
    create  app/controllers
    ...
```

At this point, you could do an svn import and put the whole directory tree
in the repository. I recommend against doing so. If you use the "in-place
import" procedure instead, you can selectively commit the pieces you
want, not the whole tree. See Subversion's "How can I do an in-place
import" FAQ for the full details.

Start your in-place import by checking out trunk into the folder you want
to import:

```
$ svn checkout file:///home/ezra/svn/trunk ~/deployit
Checked out revision 1.
$ cd ~/deployit
```

Next, add the whole tree to the working copy. The results are no different from svn import initially, except all changes are local to the working
copy and you can selectively revert the files and folders you do not want
in the repository before committing. The end result is more convenient
control over what actually becomes part of the repository. We use svn
import with the --force option because otherwise Subversion will fail with
an error indicating that the current directory is already under version
control.

---

1. This is explained in more detail in "Choosing a Repository Layout" in the Subversion
book.
2. If you have an existing project you want to import in Subversion, simply skip this
step. All other steps are identical.

Now, add your Rails project like so:

```
$ svn add . --force
A           app
...
A           README
```

The Rails command helpfully creates most of the tree. Since I will later use migrations in all my Rails projects, I immediately create the db/migrate folder. Rails also creates a tmp folder when it needs it. For completeness sake, I will create both folders immediately:

```
$ svn mkdir db/migrate tmp
A           db/migrate
A           tmp
```

Removing the Log Files from Version Control

At this point, Subversion would helpfully track all changes to the log files. Then some following Friday at 6:30 p.m., some poor, harried developer would then accidentally check in an obscenely large log file, and the rest of the developers would complain that the checkout was taking way too long. To ease our burden, the easiest thing is to tell Subversion to ignore any log files:

```
$ svn revert log/*
Reverted 'log/development.log'
Reverted 'log/production.log'
Reverted 'log/server.log'
Reverted 'log/test.log'

$ svn propset svn:ignore "*.log" log
property 'svn:ignore' set on 'log'
```

That's all there is to it. Next stop: database.yml.

Managing the Database Configuration

Since database.yml file might be different for each developer, you do not want to create havoc by accidentally committing database.yml. Instead, you'll have a sample of the file in the repository so each developer will have their own safely ignored database.yml file. These commands do the magic:

```
$ svn revert config/database.yml
Reverted 'config/database.yml'

$ mv config/database.yml config/database.yml.sample
$ svn add config/database.yml.sample
A           config/database.yml.sample
```

```
$ svn propset svn:ignore "database.yml" config
property 'svn:ignore' set on 'config'
$ cp config/database.yml.sample config/database.yml
$ svn status --non-recursive config/
A       config
A       config/routes.rb
A       config/database.yml.sample
A       config/boot.rb
A       config/environment.rb
A       config/environments
```

Newer Rails versions might already have some of these files. Use svn add with the --force option for files you want to replace that might already be under version control. If you use this approach, you'll need to be sure you communicate.

Since you'd make any changes to database.yml.sample, other developers might not notice the changes. Most of the time, though, the sample file will not change, and leaving it "as is" is OK. Alternatively, you can call the sample file database.sample.yml so your editor can pick up syntax highlighting.

Database Structure Dumps During Testing

When you run the tests, Rails will dump the development database's structure to db/schema.rb.[3]

Managing tmp, documentation, scripts, and public

Rails 1.1 and above now have a tmp folder. This folder will hold only temporary files such as socket, session, and cache files. Ignore anything in it:

```
$ svn propset svn:ignore "*" tmp
property 'svn:ignore' set on 'tmp'
```

The doc folder holds many subfolders: appdoc and apidoc among others. To keep things simple, just ignore any "doc" suffix:

```
$ svn propset svn:ignore "*doc" doc
property 'svn:ignore' set on 'doc'
```

Subversion also has a property to identify executable files. Set the property on files you might run from the command line.

---

3. If the Active Record configuration variable named config.active_record.schema_format is set to:sql, the file will be named development_structure.sql instead. Simply replace schema.rb with development_structure.sql in the commands.

Joe Asks. . .

What About the Deployed database.yml File?

Using the template file technique means the database.yml file is not under version control on your production server. Here are some solutions to this problem:

- Use a branch to deploy, and keep database.yml under version control in the branch. See Section 2.2, *Using a Stable Branch for Deployment*, on page 21 for how to do that.

- Have Capistrano copy the file forward on every deployment. I discuss this solution in Section 5.5, *Using the Built-in Callbacks*, on page 105, and I discuss Capistrano in Chapter 5, *Capistrano*, on page 85.

- You can leave the database.yml file on the server in the shared directory. You can then create a symlink to that file. It's best to create this symlink in an after_update_code Capistrano task. We'll talk more about Capistrano later, but for now, have a quick look at the following Capistrano task just to whet your curiosity:

```
task :after_update_code, :roles => :app,
    :except => {:no_symlink => true} do
  run <<-CMD
    cd #{release_path} &&
    ln -nfs #{shared_path}/config/database.yml ↩
      #{release_path}/config/database.yml &&
    ln -nfs #{shared_path}/config/mongrel_cluster.yml ↩
      #{release_path}/config/mongrel_cluster.yml
  CMD
end
```

> \|/ Joe Asks. . .
> ˆ·ˆ
> ~   **What If I'm Using Rails Engines?**
> ───────────────────────────────
> Rails Engines copies some files to public on startup. Since you do
> not want to see those files on svn status, you should ignore them:
>
> ```
> $ svn propset svn:ignore "engine_files" public
> property 'svn:ignore' set on 'public'
> ```

On *nix, you will have to name each file on the command line:

```
$ svn propset svn:executable "*" ↩
    `find script -type f | grep -v '.svn'` public/dispatch.*
property 'svn:executable' set on 'script/performance/benchmarker'
...
property 'svn:executable' set on 'public/dispatch.fcgi'
```

On Windows systems, do this instead:

```
C:\deployit> svn propset svn:executable  script\performance\* ↩
            script\process\* script\about script\breakpointer ↩
            script\console script\destroy script\generate script\plugin ↩
            script\runner script\server public/dispatch.*
property 'svn:executable' set on 'script/performance/benchmarker'
...
property 'svn:executable' set on 'public/dispatch.fcgi'
```

Since I will deploy on Unix/Linux machines, it makes sense to have
the dispatchers use a proper line ending. To do so, set svn:eol-style
to native to let Subversion manage the line ending according to local
conventions:

```
$ svn propset svn:eol-style native public/dispatch.*
property 'svn:eol-style' set on 'public/dispatch.cgi'
...
```

Last but not least, projects usually have a default home page served
by a Rails action. This means building a route and removing public/
index.html:

```
$ svn revert public/index.html
Reverted 'public/index.html'

$ rm public/index.html
```

> ### Capistrano and Stable Branch Deployment
>
> We'll be dealing with Capistrano in detail later in the book. But for now, know that Capistrano can indeed deploy from the trunk or any branch. For example, this is what the repository line of deploy.rb would look like with a stable branch deployment:
>
> ```
> set :repository,
>     "http://yoursvnserver.com/deployit/branches/stable"
> ```

Saving Your Work

After all these changes, commit your work to the repository:

```
$ svn commit --message="Initial project checkin"
Adding          README
...
Adding          vendor/plugins
Transmitting file data .............................
Committed revision 2.
```

Using a Stable Branch for Deployment

Many simple applications simply run off the trunk. Others will feel more comfortable deploying from a stable branch. Several great books address this topic better than I possibly could, but I do want you to get a feel for what's involved. For detailed information on this topic, you should read *Pragmatic Version Control* [Mas05].

The changes you do on trunk might not be fully tested, or you could be in the middle of a major refactoring when an urgent bug report comes in. You need to have the ability to deploy a fixed version of the application without having to deploy the full set of changes since the last deployment. In Subversion, you can copy a branch of development to another name, and you can set up Capistrano to deploy from your stable branch instead of your development branch. Developers call this technique *stable branch deployment*.

Let's create the stable branch, which will be a copy of trunk:

```
$ svn copy --message "Create the stable branch" ↩
    file:///home/ezra/deployit/trunk          ↩
    file:///home/ezra/deployit/branches/stable
Committed revision 234.
```

When you are ready to merge a set of changes to the stable branch, check the last commit message on the branch to know which revisions you need to merge:

```
$ svn log --revision HEAD:1 --limit 1 ↩
    file:///home/ezra/deployit/branches/stable
----------------------------------------------------------------
r422 | ezra | 2007-05-30 21:30:27 -0500 (30 may 2007) | 1 line

Merged r406:421 from trunk/
----------------------------------------------------------------
```

Using the information in the log message, you can now merge all the changes to the branch:

```
$ svn merge --revision 422:436 ↩
    file:///home/ezra/deployit/trunk .
A    app/models/category.rb
M    app/models/forum.rb
A    db/migrate/009_create_category.rb
...
```

Finally, commit and deploy:

```
$ svn commit --message "Merged r422:436 from trunk/"
A    app/models/category.rb
...
Transmitting file data ....
Committed revision 437.

$ cap deploy_with_migrations
...
```

You now have a good Subversion repository, and you can use it to deploy. You've ignored the files that will break your developers' will or just your application, and you've used common Rails conventions. Still, you should know a few things about developing with Subversion with successful deployment in mind. I'd like to walk you through some tips you can use when you're using Subversion with Rails.

2.3 Subversion Tips

Now that your repository is off and running, I'll cover a few quick tips for using Subversion for your day-to-day coding. I'll teach you how to link to Edge Rails with an external link, how to generate code that's automatically checked in, and how to do a few other tricks as well.

Running Edge Rails

If you are like me, you enjoy keeping up with the latest changes in the Rails trunk or Edge Rails. Get the latest and greatest features right as they are added by using svn:externals.

You can get Edge Rails to automatically update when you update your working copy by setting the vendor directory's svn:externals property by running this command:

```
$ svn propedit svn:externals vendor
```

When your editor opens to allow you to set the svn:externals property, add this line:

```
rails http://dev.rubyonrails.org/svn/rails/trunk/
```

The next time you update,[4] Subversion will download the entire Rails trunk directory to vendor/rails for you.

If you want to negate that option, you can use the following as of Subversion 1.2: [5]

```
$ svn update --ignore-externals
```

Edge Rails has all the greatest features but is sometimes unstable. Make sure you have a fairly wide set of unit, functional, and integration tests to catch any bugs Edge Rails might introduce. Don't forget to report any breakage to the Rails-core mailing list and/or to create a ticket on the Rails Trac (http://dev.rubyonrails.org/). When reporting a bug, you should always report which revision of Rails you were using at the time:

```
$ svnversion vendor/rails
4077
```

Checking in Generated Code

During normal Rails development, you will use generators to create many new files. Some generated files should not go into the repository. As a general rule, if Rails generates a file from scratch at run time, you will not want to check it in. If you will edit a generated file, you'll want to check it in.

---

4. If you set svn:externals before the first commit, the update will not fetch the external source code.

5. http://subversion.tigris.org/svn_1.2_releasenotes.html

Whenever you build a scaffold, you'll want to add the generated files to Subversion. You can save time by adding them as they are created. Rails makes this easy when you use the script/generate command to create new files. Just add the --svn flag. Rails will generate the files and then automatically svn add them for you, like this:

```
$ script/generate scaffold --svn Post
      exists  app/controllers/
      exists  app/helpers/
      create  app/views/posts
A           app/views/posts
      exists  test/functional/
  dependency  model
      exists    app/models/
      exists    test/unit/
      exists    test/fixtures/
      create    app/models/post.rb
A           app/models/post.rb
...
```

2.4 Stabilizing Your Applications

Rails is a fairly forgiving application framework in development mode, with one user. When you push your application up to a production server, it becomes real production software, whether it's ready or not. This section will walk you through a few things you can do to stabilize your application.

Locking Down Plug-ins and Gems

You probably install third-party gems once on your local machine and forget about them. You don't need to do anything unless you want a later gem that fixes a bug or you need features of a new gem.

Shared hosts are a different story, because they often upgrade gems without your knowledge, which could hose your application at the most embarrassing moment conceivable. To prevent this unfortunate circumstance from happening to you, copy each dependency to vendor. Unpack each gem to vendor like this:

```
$ cd vendor
$ gem unpack money
Unpacked gem: 'money-1.5.9'
$ ls
money-1.5.9  plugins  rails
```

Gems all reside in a lib folder. To move your gem to version control, you just need to copy the contents of that lib folder to vendor, like this:

```
$ cp -R money-1.5.9/lib/* .
$ cp money-1.5.9/MIT-LICENSE LICENSE-money
$ rm -Rf money-1.5.9/
$ ls
LICENSE-money  bank  money  money.rb  plugins  rails  support
```

Make sure you abide by your license agreements, too. For example, to comply with the previous gem's license, you also need to copy the license along with the code. Next, add and check in the new files:

```
$ svn add --force *
A          LICENSE-money
...
A          support/cattr_accessor.rb


$ svn commit --message="Imported Money library 1.5.9"
Adding           LICENSE-money
...
Transmitting file data .......
Committed revision 4.
```

Upgrading an Unpacked Gem

When you are ready to integrate a new version of the gem into your application, you essentially follow the same procedure:

```
$ gem unpack money
Unpacked gem: 'money-1.7.1'
$ cp -Rf money-1.7.1/lib/* .
$ cp -f money-1.7.1/MIT-LICENSE LICENSE-money
$ rm -Rf money-1.7.1
$ svn status
M       money/core_extensions.rb
M       money/money.rb
X       rails
$ svn commit --message="Upgraded Money to 1.7.1"
Sending         money/core_extensions.rb
Sending         money/money.rb
Transmitting file data ..
Committed revision 5.
```

If the library provider deleted or moved files around, you need to do the same thing too. Check the library's release notes to learn about any requirements for backward compatibility. A great tool that automates importing new releases of a library is svn_load_dirs.pl (http://svn.collab.net/repos/svn/trunk/contrib/client-side/).

Freeze the Rails Gems

Even new versions of Rails can break backward compatibility. Bruce's shared host once upgraded to Rails 1.1 while he was in Spain to give a Ruby talk at a Java conference. The new version immediately broke his blog, which was bad enough. As you can imagine, the broken blog made it nearly impossible to extol the virtues of Rails.

After several decades of intense therapy, he has finally recovered from this incident and is a better person because of it. You can protect yourself against this possibility by freezing a copy of the Rails libraries to your app's vendor directory. Your application will use the exact version of Rails that you:

- *considered when you designed your application.* Some versions of Rails have philosophical differences between other versions, such as the new forms model introduced in 1.2, not to mention significant changes in Rails 2.0.

- *used to test your application.* If you don't freeze your Rails gems, you're fundamentally saying that you don't need to test how thousands of lines of code will work with your application. If you make such a choice, I wouldn't recommend any long trips to London.

- *understand.* Rails is an active framework. You need to make sure you have a good grasp on changes in the framework before you deploy.

When you upgrade to a newer version of Rails, you can integrate your application, test, and then refreeze it to the vendor directory:

```
local$ rake rails:freeze:gems
```

If you've come from a C, Java, or C# platform, you may be surprised the Ruby gems often break backward compatibility. In truth, this decision is a double-edged sword. If you don't respect backward compatibility, your applications can break, but there's a benefit. Breaking backward compatibility allows your framework to evolve much more quickly and cleanly, without the risk of framework bloat. (See Enterprise JavaBeans or XML for two examples.) Ruby and especially Rails developers value a cleaner code base more than backward compatibility. As more enterprise developers use Rails, you may see a change, but don't ever rely on a future that lets your application run safely without your own version of Rails. With versioned code and gems in hand, you can move on to organizing your migrations.

2.5 Active Record Migrations

Migrations, a Rails feature that lets you express your database tables in Ruby instead of SQL, are a great way to manage your database schema throughout your development process. You can quickly create, change, or delete tables and indexes. If you are already using migrations, I'll show you how to whip them into shape for your production environment. If you're deciding whether to use them, you should know the strengths and weaknesses of the approach.

Migration Strengths and Weaknesses

On the plus side, migrations generally provide a more comfortable environment and ease the process of keeping your production schema up-to-date. More specifically:

- *Migrations let you express database-independent code in Ruby instead of SQL.* Because you're working in Ruby, you can often express your ideas in a cleaner, simpler way.
- *Migrations integrate with Rake (and Capistrano to a lesser extent).* You can call Rake commands to move your migrations up to a precise level or move your schema back to a point in time. You can also ask Capistrano to run your migrations automatically when you deploy.
- *Migrations deal with data.* Some database schema changes require changes in data. Migrations can handle both, since they are Ruby scripts. Setting the data for new columns, selectively adding or deleting rows, or defining lookup tables are all examples of dealing with data in migrations.
- *Migrations simplify backing up.* Rails developers make just as many mistakes as any others. If your latest build is a stinker that also changes the schema, migrations can allow you to back up quickly.
- *Migrations make it easy to change schemas without losing data.* Since migrations use the ALTER TABLE command rather than CREATE and DROP table, you can easily make changes to the schema without worrying about losing production data. Also, you can use the same tools to manage your development and production schemes.

Keep in mind that migrations are not a silver bullet. Some teams can make them work, and others can't. In general, small teams with a simple deployment strategy will work great with migrations.

Large teams, teams that manage multiple releases, or teams that refactor model code on a regular basis and simultaneously use data migrations will struggle. These are some of the disadvantages of migrations:

- *Migrations do not integrate with Subversion.* If an older migration depends on a particular model and that model no longer exists, it will break. The source code history in Subversion has no effective link to the database schema history that lives in your latest Subversion version.

- *Migrations have some curious defaults.* By default, columns allow null. My experience shows that most developers don't think about null columns until it's too late, leading to database integrity problems later.

- *All developers depend on a unified numbering scheme but have no tools to manage them.* If you create a migration and your friend creates one at the same time, they will both have the same number, and they will fail.

- *Branches are tough to manage.* If you want to add a major branch, perhaps to develop a major new feature without deploying it to the public until it is stable, you will effectively have to write your own migration support to do so, because each part of the application will need its own migrations.

- *Components have a tough time depending on migrations.* Try to integrate an existing blog to an existing application, and you'll see what I mean. Migrations don't provide a good default to deal with this problem.

For the most part, I like migrations. They are quick and convenient most of the time, and if you can make them work with your team's model, you'll usually be glad you did. If you've already committed to migrations, make sure you look at the disadvantages and understand them. You will want to solve the problems you're likely to face before a migration blows up in production.

First Look at Migrations

Regardless of whether you have a schema defined already or you are starting a new project, you can easily start using migrations. If you already have a schema in place, you'll find Rails has some good tools that will help you convert them.

Assume you have a forums table defined in a MySQL database and that the SQL looks like this:

```
CREATE TABLE `forums` (
`id` int(11) NOT NULL auto_increment,
`parent_id` int(11) NOT NULL default '0',
`title` varchar(200) NOT NULL default '',
`body` text NOT NULL,
`created_at` datetime default NULL,
`updated_at` datetime default NULL,
`forums_count` int(11) NOT NULL default '0',
PRIMARY KEY (`id`)
) TYPE=InnoDB;
```

To start using a pure-Ruby schema, Rails includes a handy Rake task to kick start your migration (pun intended). Run this command from your application's root:

```
$ rake db:schema:dump
```

This command will create a schema.rb file that looks like this:

before-category-migration/db/schema.rb

```
# This file is autogenerated. Instead of editing this file, please use the
# migrations feature of ActiveRecord to incrementally modify your database, and
# then regenerate this schema definition.

ActiveRecord::Schema.define() do

  create_table "forums", :force => true do |t|
    t.column "parent_id", :integer, :default => 0, :null => false
    t.column "title", :string, :limit => 200, :default => "", :null => false
    t.column "body", :text, :default => "", :null => false
    t.column "created_at", :datetime
    t.column "updated_at", :datetime
    t.column "forums_count", :integer, :default => 0, :null => false
  end

end
```

With db/schema.rb in place, you can start writing migrations. Rails will apply each change to your initial schema.rb file. You will never need to edit this file directly because Rails generates a fresh one after each migration of your schema. Initially, you will need to copy the initial file to your test and production environments.

db/schema.rb serves as the starting place for each migration. The file holds your entire database schema at any point in time in one place for easy reference. Also, migrations create a table called schema_info. That table holds a single version column, with one row and a single number: the version number of the last migration that you ran. Each migration is a Ruby file beginning with a number. The migration has an up() method and a down() method. Migrating up starts with schema.rb and applies the migrations with higher numbers than the number in schema_info, in order. Migrating down will apply the migrations with lower numbers, greatest first.

So now that you have a schema.rb file, you have everything you need to create migrations at will. Your first migration will create schema_info for you. I don't want to teach you how to build a Rails application here, because the Rails documentation is fairly complete. I do want to make sure you know enough to stay out of trouble.

Putting Classes into Migrations

Good Rails developers generally don't depend on domain model objects in migrations. Five weeks from now, that Forum model might not even exist anymore. Still, some data migrations will depend on a model, so you need to create model instances directly inside your migration:

after-category-model/db/migrate/005_cleanup_forum_messages.rb

```ruby
class CleanupForumMessages < ActiveRecord::Migration
  class Forum < ActiveRecord::Base
    has_many :messages, :class_name => 'CleanupForumMessages::Message'
  end

  class Message < ActiveRecord::Base
    def cleanup!
      # cleanup the message
      self.save!
    end
  end

  def self.up
    Forum.find(:all).each do |forum|
      forum.messages.each do |message|
        message.cleanup!
      end
    end
  end

  def self.down
  end
end
```

Notice that I declare each class I need in the migration itself, which acts like a module.

Make sure that you use the :class_name feature of has_many( )has_one( ), belongs_to( ), and has_and_belongs_to_many( ) because Rails uses the top-level namespace by default, instead of the current scope, to find the associated class. If you do not use :class_name, Rails will raise an AssociationTypeMismatch when you try to use the association.

The solution is not perfect. You're introducing replication, and some features such as single-table inheritance become troublesome, because you need to declare each and every subclass in the migration. And good developers can hear the word DRY—"don't repeat yourself"—in their sleep. Still, your goal is not to keep the two versions of your model classes synchronized. You are merely capturing a snapshot of the important features of the class, as they exist today. You don't necessarily have to copy the whole class. You need to copy only the features you intend to use.[6]

More Migrations Tips

You should keep a few other things in mind as you deal with migrations. These tips should improve your experience with them:

- *Keep migrations short.* You shouldn't group together many different operations, because if half of your migration succeeds, it will be too hard to unwind. Alternatively, you can include your migrations in a transaction if your database engine supports DDL statements like CREATE and ALTER TABLE in a transaction. PostgreSQL does; MySQL doesn't.

- *Make sure you correctly identify nullable columns.* Columns are nullable by default. That's probably not the behavior you want for all columns. Rails migrations probably have the wrong default.

This list of tips is by no means an exhaustive list, but it should give you a good start. Now, it's time to shift to looking at improving the rest of your application.

2.6 Application Issues for Deployment

Rails is a convenient framework for developers. Sometimes, the convenience can work in your favor. You can build quickly, and Ruby is

---

6. Thanks to Tim Lucas for the original blog post: http://toolmantim.com/article/2006/2/23/ migrating_with_models.

malleable enough to let you work around the framework. But if you're not careful, all of that flexibility can bite you. In this section, I'll walk you through some common security problems and a few performance problems as well.

Security Problems

Rails has the security characteristics of other web-based frameworks based on dynamic languages. Some elements will work in Rails favor. You can't secure something that you don't understand. The framework is pretty simple, and web development experts already understand the core infrastructure pretty well. But Rails has some characteristics you'll have to watch closely.

Rails is a dynamic, interpreted language. You need to be sure you don't evaluate input as code and that you use the tools Rails provides that can protect you.

Using View Helpers

You likely know how Rails views work. Like most web frameworks, Rails integrates a scripting language into HTML. You can drop code into Rails by using<%= your_code_here %>. Rails will faithfully render any string that you may provide, including a name, helpful HTML formatting tags, or malicious HTML code like this:

```
<img src='http://porn.com/some_porn_image.jpg' />
```

You can easily prevent this problem by using the template helpers. If you surround your code with <%=h your_code_here %>, Rails will escape any HTML code a malicious user may provide.

Don't Evaluate Input

At the same time, you need to be sure not to evaluate any code that any user might type as input. Ruby is a great scripting language, but you should be careful anytime you try to evaluate any code, and you should *never evaluate user input*. For example, consider the following code that assumes you're picking the name of an attribute from a selection box:

```
def update
  ...
  # Don't do this! Potential injection attack
  string = "The value of the attribute is " +
          "#{Person.send(param[:attribute])}"
  ...
end
```

That code would work just fine as long as the user cooperated with you and picked "first_name" or "email" from a selection box. But if a Rails developer wanted to exploit your system, he could send data to your controller by opening a curl session and posting his own data. Or, if you don't verify that the command is a post, he could simply key the following into a URL:

```
your_url.com/update/4?attribute=destroy_all
```

Assume all user input is tainted. Not all metaprogramming is good. Don't ever evaluate any data that comes from a user unless you've scrubbed it first.

Don't Evaluate SQL

You can make a similar mistake with SQL. Say you want to look up a user with a user ID and a password. You could issue the following Active Record command:

```
# Don't do this!
condition = "users.password = #{params[:password]} and
             users.login = #{params[:login]}"
@user = find(:conditions => condition)
```

And all is well. At least, all is well until someone types the following instead of a password:

```
up yours'; drop database deployit_production;
```

The first semicolon ends the first SQL statement. Then, the cracker launches some mischief of his own, dropping the production database. An alternative would be to try to create a user with enhanced permissions. This type of attack, called *SQL injection*, is growing in prominence. You can easily prevent the attack by coding your condition like this:

```
conditions = ["users.login = ? and users.password = ?",
              params[:login], params[:password]]
@user = find(:conditions => conditions)
```

This form of a finder with conditions allows Rails to do the right thing: properly escape all parameters and input that Active Record will pass through to the database.

Check Permissions

Rails gives developers plenty of help when it comes to building pretty URLs. The bad news is that others who would attack Rails also know this. Consider the following action, which is commonly created through scaffolding:

```
def destroy
  Person.find(params[:id]).destroy
  redirect_to :action => 'list'
end
```

To secure the command, you decide to add before_filter :login_required to the top of your controller, meaning people need to log in before accessing the destroy() method. For an application where only admins can delete, that protection is enough. But if any user can create an account and log in, that protection is not nearly enough. Any user can create an account and start deleting records by sequentially typing ID numbers into the browser:

```
/people/destroy/1
/people/destroy/2
/people/destroy/3
/people/destroy/4
/people/destroy/5
/people/destroy/6
/people/destroy/7
...
```

Worse yet, a bot could log in and delete all your records. You need to check that the logged-in user has permission to delete the file within the controller action. Assume that each Person object is associated with the User who created it. Also, assume current_user returns the current logged-in user. Then, you could protect destroy() like this:

```
def destroy
  person = Person.find(params[:id])
  person.destroy if current_user == person.user
  redirect_to :action => 'list'
end
```

Logging in is not enough. You must scope individual destructive actions to one user. That covers the most common security flaws. There are others, such as exposing your .svn directories to the Web. The easiest way to get around this one is to do an svn export instead of an svn checkout when deploying your code to production. This will export your code without the Subversion metadata and keep prying eyes away.

If you take heed of these various issues, then your Rails application should be nice and secure. Do make sure you keep up with the main Rails blog; see http://weblog.rubyonrails.org/ for any security updates or warnings.

Database Performance Problems

Active Record belongs to a family of database frameworks called *wrapping* frameworks. A wrapping framework starts with a single table and places a wrapper around it to allow object-oriented applications to conveniently access rows in the table. The performance of wrapping systems like Active Record is highly dependent on you, the programmer. The biggest thing you can do is benchmark your application. We'll discuss benchmarking in Chapter 9, *Performance*, on page 217. In the meantime, I'll show you the most common problem you're likely to see.

The N + 1 Problem

Active Record makes it easy to retrieve a given object and access its attributes. Bad things happen when those attributes are lists of other Active Record objects. Let's say you're building the next great social networking site. You have a Person that has_many :friends. To populate a list of friends, you write some harmless code that looks like this:

```
friends = Person.find(:all, :conditions => some_friend_conditions)
@friend_addresses = person.friends.collect {|friend| friend.address.street }
```

To be sure, that code will work, but it's also horribly inefficient and will get worse as the list of friends grows. You're actually running an Active Record query for the list of friends and another for every address you need to fetch. You can fix that problem by using *eager associations*, meaning you'll tell Active Record what to load in advance with the :include option:

```
friends = Person.find(:all, :conditions => some_friend_conditions,
                      :include => :address)
  @friend_addresses = person.friends.collect {|friend| friend.address.street }
```

This code works in the same way to you, but the performance will improve dramatically. Active Record will load all people and their addresses instead of just loading people in the first query and addresses as you touch them the first time.

Indexes

Rails lets database developers get pretty far without knowing anything about the database underneath or even the theory surrounding relational databases. If you trust Active Record to take care of you, it's likely that you and your users will be disappointed. One of the easiest things to forget when you're coding Rails is to create indexes. For any large tables, make sure you create an index on any column you need to search. And periodically, you should run statistics so the database optimizer knows when to use indexes. Database administration performance techniques are beyond the scope of this book.

Chapter 3

Shared Hosts

Finding a host for your first Rails app is a lot like finding your first home. When I left home the first time, I wanted to move right into a castle, but real life doesn't work out that way. Most people first move into an apartment or dorm room. True, apartments don't come with their own throne room and servants' quarters, but they do have their advantages. You're sharing common resources and infrastructure with many others, so you wind up paying less. You don't have to mow the lawn or paint the fence. For most people, the first Rails app runs in modest quarters for many of the same reasons: shared infrastructure, lower costs, and help with the maintenance. In this chapter, you'll learn how to pick and prepare a shared host.

3.1 The Lay of the Land

Many Rails apps start life on a shared server, as shown in Figure 3.1, on the next page. You'll buy one slice of a larger server that will have the ability to serve your Rails application and static content. You will control only a few directories for your application. You'll use Subversion to install your application while you set up your initial infrastructure, until you're ready to automate with Capistrano. For a few dollars a month, you'll have your own domain name, access to a database server, several email accounts, and maybe even a Subversion repository. For many people, this setup is enough for a blog, a site prototype, or even a bug-tracking system.

If you can cache your application, and sometimes even if you can't, you can serve hundreds of users daily without needing to pay US$100 per month for a dedicated server. Your hosting company will fix intermittent problems, occasionally upgrade your machine, and keep things running

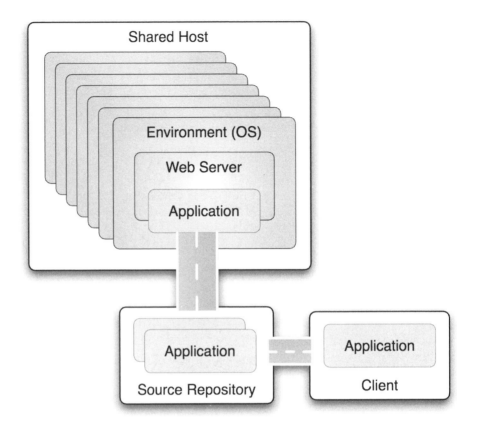

Figure 3.1: MAP FOR A SHARED SERVER

smoothly. When you are ready to move on to a more powerful dedicated machine or a cluster of servers, you can upgrade within your hosting company or transfer to a colocation facility.

At least, that's the theory. Shared hosting is not all sunshine and roses. You may be sharing a single server with more than 1,000 other websites. I've received more than my share of "nasty grams" telling me that my app's memory was out of control or that my unstable app crashed the whole server. I've been on the other end of the equation, too. I've been the good citizen, but someone else ran a script that monopolized the server's resources and slowed my application to a belly crawl. I've also had my site become wildly popular and subsequently gotten a bill for US$500. (I am much happier now that I am on the sending end of those bills!) A good host will keep tabs on these statistics and will notify you if you are using more than your share. Most will even give you a little grace period and eat small overages for short periods of time.

All things considered, you *can* do almost anything on a shared server that you can do on a dedicated server, but you'll have more resource constraints. If you are just learning how to develop a database-driven website, you can focus on the mechanics of your application instead of worrying about the details of configuring DNS, daemons, and disk partitions. Even so, I recommend you treat a shared host as a starting point, not as the final destination for your application. If you are earning more than US$30 per month from your site or if your business depends upon it, you should upgrade to a virtual private server or a dedicated server.

When you look for a new home, you can't do it all at once. You'll have to consider the time it takes to pick a place, change your address, bribe the landlord, and decide whether you'll keep or throw out all that fine stuff like your old Commodore 64. Moving takes time, and things go more smoothly when you plan. Treat setting up a shared host the same way. You have one goal—making your application run on a shared host—but it's best to define a few discrete steps to get there:

1. Find the right place. Pick the plan that works best for your application and your pocketbook.
2. Tell the world where you live. On the Web, that means updating your DNS entries.
3. Move in your stuff. For Rails, that means installing your application. Later, I'll help you automate this step.
4. Set up your utilities. In the web world, that means configuring your web server and database server to work with your Rails app.

When all is said and done, your setup might not work the first time. That's OK. I'll walk you through the process of pulling it all together. When you're done, you'll have a slice of a common server, a Mongrel web server, and a database-backed Rails application.

3.2 Choosing a Shared Host

Way back at the dawn of Rails history (aka the fall of 2004), only a few hosts officially supported Ruby on Rails. That number increases every day as Rails becomes better known. There are many capable hosts, so

I won't recommend any single provider, but you should look for several critical features in a shared host.

Basic Requirements

At minimum, the host you choose must have the following features:

- *Ruby 1.8.6 and Rails 1.2.6 or Rails 2.0.*

- *Mongrel support.* Some shared hosts don't yet support Mongrel, but there are plenty that do, and Mongrel is rapidly emerging as the de facto standard within the Rails community.

- *The ability to specify the web server's document root directory.* There are ways to get around this, but it is much easier if the host provides an interface where you can point the web server to your preferred directory, perhaps one like /home/ezra/brainspl.at/current/ public.

- *SSH access.* This is crucial for troubleshooting your installation and is required for deploying with Capistrano. Some very inexpensive hosts allow you to transfer files only by FTP, so choose one that has SSH as an option.

- *A database server and the required Ruby gems to connect to it.* MySQL and PostgreSQL are popular, but you can use file-based database managers such as SQLite just as easily.

For the optimal Rails setup, I recommend these features:

- *OS-dependent gems, such as RMagick.* These gems let you easily generate graphics, make thumbnails of photographs, and do other useful tasks. You can copy pure-Ruby gems into your Rails application's lib directory, but you really want your hosting provider to install gems requiring compilation and C libraries because building and installing these gems takes more authorization than your account will typically have.

- *Subversion repositories that are accessible over HTTP (or secure HTTPS).* Whether you are a professional programmer or a hobbyist, you should be using source code control. With a source code control system, you can deploy with Capistrano or publish Rails plug-ins that other Rails developers can install with the built-in ./script/plugin mechanism. You can use Subversion in countless other ways, but HTTP access is the most versatile in the context of a Rails application.

The Core Rails Libraries

If you were paying attention, you saw that an installation of the core Rails libraries was missing from both lists! In fact, you will experience more stability if you use the built-in Rake rails:freeze:gems command to save a specific version of Rails to your application's vendor directory. You can find more about this in Section 2.4, *Freeze the Rails Gems*, on page 26. If your host decides to upgrade to a blazingly fast new version of Rails in the middle of the night—one that might break your application—your application will still run with the older version residing in your vendor directory. When you have tested your app against the newer version of Rails, you can again call rake rails:freeze:gems to upgrade.

The adventurous can use rake rails:freeze:edge to use a copy of the development version of Rails (commonly called the *trunk* version or *Edge Rails*). Even though Rails is almost three years old, development continues at a rapid pace. Edge Rails users get to use newer Rails features before the general public. Early use is a double-edged sword. With the benefits you get with the early use of new features comes the potential for API change and bugs. Both problems are inherent in using early software.

You can also tie your application to the newest Rails trunk so it is updated every time the development branch of Rails is updated, but I don't recommend doing so because that strategy adds another unknown element into your deployment process. The Rails core team is very active, and updates to the Rails trunk are made several times a day. Your application might work at 8:05, but an update made at 8:06 could break your app when it is deployed on the server at 8:07. Keeping a consistent version of Rails will let you decide when to upgrade, on your schedule.

If you have installed other third-party libraries or plug-ins, they may use undocumented features of Rails that could change without notice. Well-behaved plug-ins will be more stable, but no authorized group of developers certifies plug-ins. By using a consistent release (or edge) version of Rails in conjunction with a thorough test suite, you can guarantee that the combination of code libraries in your application passes all your tests.

Whether you choose to live on the edge or use an older version of Rails, freezing the libraries within your application will help you simplify your deployment and maintenance in the long run. Next, I'll walk you through some of the intangible factors you should consider when selecting a shared host.

Intangible Factors

Shared hosts have variable reputations. You'll want a shared host with a good reputation for support and one that runs a tight ship. You may not like that nasty email from the overzealous, pimple-ridden admin that threatens the life of your firstborn because your application is taking more than its share of resources, but he's exactly who you want running your server. He will keep all the *other* apps on that shared host in line too. You'll also want a company with enough experience to give you a little grace if your traffic spikes once in a while and won't simply kill your Mongrels without any notification when things step out of the common parameters. System maintenance such as regular backups and cycling log files is a plus because you won't have to do them yourself.

The best way to measure intangibles is to ask around. Good Rails programmers will know who the good vendors are. I won't list any here because I am such a vendor, but be forewarned. The best shop today— one with good deals and good admins—could experience unmanageable growth, could lose that key admin who made everything run like a Swiss watch, or could just get lazy. Ask around and keep up. You'll be glad you did. You can start with the excellent Ruby on Rails wiki[1] or by chatting with Rails developers on IRC.[2]

After you've done your homework and picked your host, you'll want to start setting things up. But first things first. You'll need to tell the world where your application lives. That means you'll need a domain name, and you'll need to configure DNS.

3.3 Setting Up Your Domain and DNS

Any home you choose will need an address so people can find you. On the Internet, you'll have two addresses: the one with numbers and dots is your IP address, and the name with a .com or .org on the end is your domain name. The IP address contains four numbers, each with values from 0 to 255, separated by periods. Since memorizing up to twelve

---

1. http://wiki.rubyonrails.org/

2. http://wiki.rubyonrails.org/rails/pages/IRC

digits is hard, most of your users will refer to your site by its domain name instead. You will buy your domain name from a domain name service such as GoDaddy, Network Solutions, or Enom, and you'll get your IP address from your hosting service. Under the covers, Domain Name System (DNS) will associate your name with your IP. The Internet has several public domain name registries that associate IP addresses with domain names. So to establish your address, you need to do the following:

1. Buy a domain name. They will give you a name and a way to configure the IP address.
2. Pick a shared host. They will give you your IP address.
3. Associate your name with your IP address.

You can easily buy a domain name for as little as US$10, which means the hardest part is picking a name to use! I recommend choosing something that is easy to remember and easy to spell. (I hope your name is simpler than EzraZygmuntowicz.com!) You can use a site such as Instant Domain Search[3] to help find a name that's not already in use.

Most domain name registrars will also give you a web page to configure your DNS settings. If you cannot easily find any place to make DNS changes, contact your providers support system to ask about DNS settings. You want these to point to your shared hosting company's servers so the domain name server will forward requests for your domain name to your specific server.

DNS stands for Domain Name System. It is responsible for resolving a domain name and returning an IP address where the service really lives. Your shared hosting provider will have its own name servers. When you sign up, ask the provider to give you its DNS name server addresses. They will be something like ns1.foobar.com and ns2.foobar.com. Take note of these addresses, go to your domain name registrar where you registered foobar.com, and click the section for DNS or name servers for your domain. They will have multiple form fields you can fill out. Most hosts will give you two name servers, but they may have more. Once you enter these details and save the results, it will take twelve to seventy-two hours for the name servers all across the world to propagate your new records. Once DNS is propagated, you can type foobar.com in your browser, and the domain name service will find the server's IP address and route your request to your domain.

---

3.   http://instantdomainsearch.com

> ### Using Hosting Company Subdomains
>
> Some shared hosts also provide you with a subdomain to use while you are setting up your site. This might be something like http://ezmobius.myhost.com. I strongly recommend against this approach because it looks less professional and requires that you use a third-party service for your email.
>
> Also, if you switch to a different host, you will have to inform all your visitors that your address has changed. When using your own domain name, you can switch from one host to another with fewer consequences, and your customers never need to know.

You may be able to see your new application before the bulk of your customers, depending on where you live and the DNS services near you. Propagation time can range from less than an hour to a couple of days, so plan in advance. While you're waiting for the DNS changes to take hold, you can switch gears and focus on configuring the shared host.

3.4 Configuring Your Server

Configuring your server is surprisingly easy when you follow a simple plan. It really amounts to providing access to your server through SSH and your document root and creating your application's database. If you do these steps correctly, you'll have a good foundation for the easy deployment of your web server and Rails app.

First, you'll want to determine your application's root directory. If you don't know exactly where to put your application, ask. Most host accounts will create this directory for you and set permissions appropriately. In the rest of this chapter, I'll refer to that directory as the *application root*. This is the top-level directory for your Rails project. Your document root is the root directory for your web server and will hold your static files. Usually, you'll put your Rails project in a directory called current, meaning your document root will be current/public. From here on out, I'll refer to that directory as the *relative root* (/current).

Server Setup: Document Root and SSH

To prepare your shared host for your application, you're going to need a way to talk to it securely (SSH). You will also need a new user account on the shared server. Many shared hosts provide only one SSH user per account, and your hosting company may have created one for you already. If not, each hosting company has a different web interface, but the process is usually simple. Just read the documentation the host provided.

After you've created an account, try it. If you're running Windows, you'll need to set up your SSH client. PuTTY is a good one. There are several free clients, and you'll find plenty of documentation for them. If you're running a Unix derivative, you'll have a much easier time. Usually, you won't even need to install anything. Open a terminal, and type ssh username@hostname, using the information from your hosting provider. If you have any trouble, ask your hosting provider. Make sure you get your SSH connection working, because it's your secure window into the system for all your deployment, maintenance, and debugging.

While you are logged in, you will want to change the site's document root, also called the *web root*, to /current/public. Check the control panel for your site for the right place to configure your document root. The tool to change it will vary based on your provider. Shortly, you'll upload your Rails application to the current directory. The public directory has your application's public directory, which hosts static resources for your application. Capistrano, the Rails utility for deployment, will use the current directory to always hold the most recent version of your site.

3.5 Server Setup: Create a Database

The final task to do on the server is to create a database. Again, the means for doing this depends on your hosting provider. As you know, when you created your Rails application, you gave it a name, for example, rails ezra. By default, Rails will use three databases for each of the test, development, and production environments. The default database name for each environment is the name of the Rails project, followed by an underscore, followed by the name of the environment. For example, for an application called ezra, Rails would generate ezra_development for the development database. In practice, many developers omit the _production for their production database.

Normally, your hosting provider will require that you share your database with other users. They will likely give you a user ID and password to access your own database namespace. You'll use that ID to create your database. Whichever name you choose, make sure to keep the database name, combined with an admin-level username and password, in a safe place for use later. Here's an example on MySQL that creates a database called ezra and grants all the appropriate privileges. Your setup may vary.

```
mysql> GRANT SELECT,INSERT,UPDATE,DELETE,CREATE,DROP, ALTER, INDEX
mysql> ON ezra.* TO 'ezra'@'hostname' IDENTIFIED BY 'password';
mysql> FLUSH PRIVILEGES;
mysql> CREATE DATABASE ezra;
```

If you want to peek ahead, the production section of your Rails application's config/database.yml file will look like this:

```
production:
  adapter: mysql
  database: ezra
  username: ezra
  password: password
  host: brainspl.at # provided by your shared host provider
```

At this point, you'll want to make sure your database is running and you can access it. Just using the database and showing the list of tables is enough for now:

```
mysql> use ezra;
Database changed
mysql> show tables;
Empty set (0.00 sec)

mysql>
```

Now, you should have a working domain that's pointed to your hosting provider, you should be able to reach your server through SSH, and you have created and accessed a database on the server. With all that background work out of the way, it's time to configure your web server.

3.6 Installing Your Application

Even before I knew how to write a single line of PHP, I could copy a basic PHP script to a server and run it. Deploying Rails is not that easy. You need to have at least a basic idea of what files and folders are used by Rails when it runs.

Fortunately, Ruby has excellent tools that let you deploy your application easier than PHP. The main one is Capistrano, which you'll see in Chapter 5, *Capistrano*, on page 85. When we're done, your Capistrano script will check your application directly out of your Subversion repository and put it exactly where it needs to be. But you need to walk before you can run.

I'm going to take you through the installation process manually. That way, you'll see where everything goes, and you'll have a greater appreciation of what Capistrano is doing for you. Don't worry, though. I'll walk you through automating the works soon enough.

Your first job is to put your Rails application on your shared host. You should name your root project directory current. (As we mentioned earlier, that's the name that Capistrano will use when you automate your deployment.) Since you have SVN installed, you can use svn export to copy your application to your server, like this:

```
$ svn export your_repository_url ~/webroot/current/
```

You've already done some work to prepare your application for deployment. Even so, you'll often want to build a tiny working application to figure out your deployment story before your full application enters the picture.

If you decide to take this approach, you can build a tiny Rails app in a couple of minutes. You'll create a Rails project, generate a model, create your migration, and configure your database. I'll walk you through that process quickly so you'll have a starter application. If you already have a starter application, skip the next section.

Creating a Starter Application

When you are testing a deployment configuration, you'll often want an application simple enough for your grandmother to build. You'll want this simple application to do enough with Rails so you can see whether your production setup works. You don't want to have to debug your deployment environment and your application at the same time.

With Rails, you can take five or ten minutes and build a dead-simple starter application. Once you have that working, you can move on to your real application.

You'll want to do all the following steps on your development machine, not your shared host. Your goal is to build a Rails application that exercises Rails models, views, and controllers. Since the default Rails project already tests the controller and views by default, you need to worry only about a primitive model.

Run the commands rails ezra, cd ezra, and ruby script/generate model person. (You don't need the ruby on some platforms). You'll get results similar to the following:

```
~ local$ rails ezra
    create
    create  app/controllers
    create  app/helpers
    ... more stuff ...


~ local$ cd ezra/

~/ezra local$ script/generate model person
    exists  app/models/
    exists  test/unit/
    exists  test/fixtures/
    create  app/models/person.rb
    ... more stuff ...
```

These steps give you a project and a model, but one without database backing. The last command also generated a migration that you can use to create your database-backed model. Edit the file db/migrate/001_ create_people.rb. Add a column called name, like this:

```
class CreatePeople < ActiveRecord::Migration
  def self.up
    create_table :people do |t|
      t.string "name"
    end
  end

  def self.down
    drop_table :people
  end
end
```

Create a MySQL database called ezra_development, which you can access with a user called *root* and no password. (If your database engine, user, or password are different, you'll simply have to edit database.yml to match.) Run the migration with rake db:migrate, and create a scaffold with script/generate scaffold person people.

You have everything you need to test your Rails setup:

```
~/ezra local$ mysql -u root
Welcome to the MySQL monitor.  Commands end with ; or \g.
Your MySQL connection id is 33 to server version: 5.0.24-standard

mysql> create database ezra_development;
Query OK, 1 row affected (0.02 sec)

mysql> exit
Bye
~/ezra ezra$ rake db:migrate
(in /Users/batate/rails/ezra)

== CreatePeople: migrating ========================================================
-- create_table(:people)
   -> 0.1843s
== CreatePeople: migrated (0.1844s) ===============================================

~ezra ezra$ script/generate scaffold person people
    exists  app/controllers/
    exists  app/helpers/
    create  app/views/people
    exists  app/views/layouts/
    ... more stuff ...
```

If you've done any Rails development at all, you know these commands create your database, create your initial table for your Person model in a Rails migration, and create a simple scaffolding-based application that you can use to test your simple production setup. Next, you'll move on to the web server configuration. Later, I'll use this starter application to make sure things are working.

3.7 Configuring Your Web Server

On most shared hosts, Rails can run with either the Apache or the lighttpd web server with FastCGI, but I recommend Mongrel behind Apache, nginx, or lighttpd instead if your host supports it. We will cover how to use a proxy in front of a Mongrel cluster later in the book. For this chapter, we will cover configuring Mongrel as well as Apache or lighttpd with FastCGI. As you will see, the Mongrel configuration is trivial, and that's exactly the point of using it. If you're on a hosting provider that forces you to use FastCGI, you can still grin and bear it. I'll help you get set up regardless of web server.

Configuring Mongrel

Your shared host likely has Mongrel already installed. You'll be amazed at how simple configuration, startup, and shutdown can be. Mongrel is a web server written by Zed Shaw in 2,500 lines of Ruby and C. Mongrel is custom-tailored to running Ruby web applications like Rails. Since Mongrel is an HTTP server in its own right, you gain the ability to use it with a wide variety of preexisting tools built to work with HTTP. Here is what Zed has to say about it on the project's home page:[4] "Mongrel is a fast HTTP library and server for Ruby that is intended for hosting Ruby web applications of any kind using plain HTTP rather than FastCGI or SCGI."

Mongrel is truly one of the best weapons in your arsenal when it comes time to deploy your application. It also makes for a great development server environment. Mongrel uses the best of both the Ruby and C worlds. Internal HTTP parsing is done in C, and the API for configuration and application interface is done with Ruby. This C foundation gives it very good speed, and the clean Ruby wrapper provides a familiar Ruby interface for configuration and extension.

Mongrel offers huge deployment advantages because it breaks away from opaque protocols like FastCGI or SCGI and uses plain HTTP for its transfer mechanism. HTTP is a proven, well-tooled, transparent protocol that all sysadmins know well. Because of the affinity to HTTP, you will have a lot of options for integrating Mongrel into your production environment. With Mongrel, you can interrogate individual Rails processes with simple command-line tools like curl or by using a browser and adding the individual Mongrel port number to the URL. By contrast, Apache and lighttpd use FastCGI, so there is no way to communicate with your Rails process without going through your front-end web server.

If your hosting provider has already installed Mongrel for you, you can take your new dog for a walk. Fire up one of your Rails applications on Mongrel. Navigate to your project directory, and type the following:

```
ezra$ cd ~/webroot/current/
ezra$ mongrel_rails start -d
```

That command will start a Mongrel daemon running in the background on port 3000. That port is fine for your development machine, but your

---

4.   http://mongrel.rubyforge.org

shared host can't have everyone on port 3000. Find out which port you should use. You'll have to start Mongrel on your preassigned port with the -p extension:

```
ezra$ mongrel_rails start -d -p 7011
```

It is just as simple to restart or stop the Mongrel server:

```
 ezra$ cd ~/webroot/current
 ezra$ mongrel_rails restart
Sending USR2 to Mongrel at PID 27033...Done.
 ezra$ mongrel_rails stop
Sending TERM to Mongrel at PID 27037...Done.
```

And that's it. You can use the -p 8080 option to specify port 8080 and -e production to specify the production environment. In Chapter 4, *Virtual and Dedicated Hosts*, on page 65, you'll learn more about configuring Mongrel for more advanced needs. In the meantime, your hosting provider probably has some documentation for their policies for dealing with Mongrel. Look them over, and follow them closely. You can point your browser at your domain name and see the starter application you built earlier. You will probably not have to specify your port number, assuming you're following the port allocation and other instructions that your hosting provider gave you.

If you're working with Mongrel, you're done. Whistle a happy tune, and skip ahead to Section 3.8, *Application Setup: Rails Config Files*, on page 53. You can skip ahead while I appease the poor pitiful sots who must deal with lighttpd or Apache.

Apache + FastCGI

All kidding aside, Apache is a great general-purpose web server. In a Rails environment, Apache works best for serving static content. Serving your Rails application will take a little more time to configure. To use Apache, you'll have to configure Rails to run using FastCGI. Then you'll tell the server to forward your request to those Rails FastCGI processes. For security's sake, most shared hosts control the majority of the configuration options for the Apache web server. However, you can specify some directives that will make your Rails application run more smoothly.

By default, Rails provides an .htaccess file for Apache in the public directory of new Rails apps. By default, this will run your application in normal, syrup-slow CGI mode. If you chose a quality shared host with FastCGI support, you should turn on FastCGI in .htaccess. You'll do so by editing the public/.htaccess file in your Rails project to look like the following:

```
# Make sure the line that specifies normal CGI
# is commented out
# RewriteRule ^(.*)$ dispatch.cgi [QSA,L]
# Make sure this line is uncommented for FastCGI
RewriteRule ^(.*)$ dispatch.fcgi [QSA,L]
```

You can include many other directives in the .htaccess file. I won't walk through all of them right now, but one important one is specifying a few custom error pages. No one wants to see "Application error (Rails)."

Even though it is not turned on by default, Rails provides a 404.html file that you can customize to gently inform the visitor that a page could not be found. To use these static error pages, make sure you remove any default error directives and use the following instead:

```
ErrorDocument 404 /404.html
ErrorDocument 500 /500.html
```

You can even write a custom Rails controller that handles 404 (Page Not Found) errors and provides a search box or a list of popular pages:

```
ErrorDocument 404 /search/not_found
```

You will need to verify that you have the correct path to the Ruby interpreter for your host's servers in your dispatch.fcgi file. The path to Ruby in your dispatch.fcgi file will be set to the location of Ruby on the machine you used to generate your Rails application. The easy way around this problem is to use following line instead:

```
#!/usr/bin/env ruby
```

That line will load the environment to set the $PATH variable and then find the Ruby binary by looking at the path. This makes it portable across most Unix-like operating systems.

All in all, Apache + FastCGI is a pretty decent general-purpose Rails platform, but you'll need to watch a few quirks. You'll need to make sure that Apache creates no rogue FastCGI processes. I'll walk you through that process in Chapter 6, *Managing Your Mongrels*, on page 117. I'll walk you through these items and a few others in the sections to follow.

That's pretty much the story for configuring your Rails application with Apache and FastCGI. If you don't need lighttpd, you can skip the next section.

lighttpd

The lighttpd web server runs independently of the other websites on your shared server, so you must include a complete lighttpd.conf file to start it. If you have installed lighttpd on your development machine, Rails will copy a minimal config file to the config directory that you can use as a reference. This file is also located inside the Rails gem in the rails<version>/configs/lighttpd.conf directory.

If you are running several domains or subdomains with one instance of lighttpd, you should keep the lighttpd.conf file in a directory outside any specific Rails application. A good place might be ~/config or ~/lighttpd in your home directory.

I wrote a specialized Capistrano recipe that builds a lighttpd.conf file customized for running lighttpd on TextDrive. It could easily be customized to use the file paths of other hosts as well. You can find it at the Shovel page.[5]

3.8 Application Setup: Rails Config Files

A freshly generated Rails application needs only a minor amount of customization to run in production mode.

config/database.yml

First, make sure you have edited config/database.yml with the appropriate information for the database you created earlier:

```
production:
  adapter: mysql
  database: db_production
  username: db_user
  password: 12345
  host: my_db.brainspl.at
```

In my experience, you can omit the socket attribute for most shared hosts. Some shared servers are configured to use localhost as the host, where others require you to create a separate subdomain for your database. Finally, be sure you use the correct username for the database. It may be different from the account you use to SSH to the server.

---

5. http://nubyonrails.com/pages/shovel

For the most security, you shouldn't keep this file under source code control. A common technique is to copy this file to a safe place on your server and add an after_update_code() task to Capistrano that copies it into the live application after it is deployed. (See Chapter 5, *Capistrano*, on page 85 for more details.)

RAILS_ENV

Rails was intelligently designed to run with different settings for development, test, production, or any other environment you define. It will use the "development" environment unless told otherwise. When running on your shared server, you will want "production" mode to be in effect.

There are at least three ways to set the RAILS_ENV for your application, each with different repercussions. The goal is to set it in a way that will take effect on the server, but not on your local development machine.

Option 1: Set the Environment in Your .bash_login File on the Server

The best way is to set the actual RAILS_ENV environment variable. Rails and Capistrano work best with the bash shell.

```
ezra$ ~/.bashrc
export RAILS_ENV="production"
```

This is the most comprehensive way since migrations and other scripts will also use that environment. Keep in mind this works only if your SSH user runs your web server. If not, you'll need to use one of the following approaches.

Option 2: Set the Environment in Your Web Server Config File

If you can't set the Rails environment variable in your shell, you must look for another way to do it. The next best place is in your web server configuration. Most shared hosts won't let you set environment variables from a local .htaccess file. You must use one of the other options if you are using Apache.

However, you can set the environment if you are using lighttpd.

Edit the bin-environment directives in the FastCGI section of your server's lighttpd.conf:

```
fastcgi.server = ( ".fcgi" =>
  ( "localhost" =>
    (
      "min-procs" => 1,
      "max-procs" => 1,
      "socket"    => "log/fcgi.socket",
      "bin-path"  => "public/dispatch.fcgi",
      "bin-environment" => ( "RAILS_ENV" => "production" )
    )
  )
)
```

This setup can work well even if you use lighttpd locally for development. When you start ./script/server for the first time, Rails creates a file in config/lighttpd.conf that sets RAILS_ENV to development. When you start your local server with ./script/server, that script then uses the lighttpd.conf file to start lighttpd. If you put your shared server's lighttpd.conf in a different location, you will have harmony between your local and remote environments.

In practice, most seasoned Rails developers run lighttpd this way, since most people want to run several domains or subdomains with one lighttpd server. Your lighttpd.conf is usually located somewhere in your home directory, and your Rails applications are located in a subdirectory (such as sites). Even though each Rails application may have its own lighttpd.conf file, these will be ignored on the production server, exactly as they should be.

Option 3: Edit environment.rb

The final way to set the environment for a shared host is to uncomment the following line at the top of environment.rb:

```
ENV['RAILS_ENV'] ||= 'production'
```

Normally, Rails defaults to development mode, expecting other environments to specify a different RAILS_ENV if necessary. Uncommenting this line changes the default to production. In practice, production is a much better default. If you use lighttpd for development, Rails will make a lighttpd.conf file for you that explicitly specifies development mode. WEBrick will use development mode unless explicitly told to do otherwise. Either way, you get the right environment.

3.9 The Well-Behaved Application

The shared hosting environment is a jungle of constantly changing elements. One of the otherwise peaceful coinhabitants of your server may momentarily take the lion's share of resources. Your host may upgrade software or hardware for maintenance or out of necessity. Your host may enforce resource limits and kill your application if it bogs down the CPU for too long. By following a few simple guidelines, you can make your application behave as well as possible and also protect yourself from other poorly behaved applications.

One Rails App per User

Some shared hosts allow you to create several user accounts, and each user account has its own memory allowance. So, you will benefit if you run one Rails application per user account. If you need to run another application, you should create a new user account and run the app under that user.

Be Miserly with Memory

A bare Rails application with no other libraries will use 30MB to 50MB of memory. Adding the RMagick image manipulation libraries can easily push that to more than 100MB. Unlike VPS servers, shared servers don't usually sell plans where a fixed amount of memory is guaranteed to your application. However, there is a fixed amount of total memory available to all applications on the server, and some shared hosts will periodically kill processes that use more than their share, usually about 100MB.

This practice of killing processes is especially problematic if you are trying to run the lighttpd web server. If the host's maintenance bot kills your lighttpd daemon, lighttpd will not restart itself automatically. To make matters worse, some hosts restrict the use of automated scripts that restart dead or zombified FastCGI processes. Even though the Apache web server can leak memory when running FastCGI processes, it will automatically restart them if they have been killed. The bottom line is that you need to conserve memory and make sure you don't have any leaks. Rails doesn't have any silver bullets for dealing with memory leaks, but I'll tell you what I know throughout the chapters that follow.

The cruel reality is that a Rails app can outgrow the shared server environment. I wrote an application for a client that used several large libraries including RMagick and PDF::Writer. The overall memory requirements meant that the app was too large to run reliably within the constraints of a shared host. Both are useful libraries, but if they cause your app to use too much memory, you must either reconsider your choices or move to a virtual private server. I'll walk you through memory in Chapter 9, *Performance*, on page 217.

In all likelihood, you already know that some applications just won't work in a shared hosting environment. If you're ramping up the scalability curve on the next Facebook application, you already know that shared hosting is not the ultimate answer. And if you have applications with intense number crunching, your shared hosting provider and anyone on your box will curse you until you give up. As a hosting provider, I'm watching you. Do the right thing.

3.10 Troubleshooting Checklist

Rails deployment means more than dropping in a JAR file or a PHP file. Even if you follow the previous instructions precisely, your installation may not run smoothly. Here are some common problems and ways to easily fix them.

Look at the Web Server Error Logs (in Addition to Rails)

One of the best places to start troubleshooting are the web server's error logs, especially when you are initially debugging your configuration. Rails can't start writing to production.log until it has launched, so Rails logging can't help you if your initial setup has critical problems. File permission problems and other errors will show up in the web server's access_log and may give you clues about what is going wrong.

The tail command is often the most useful way to view your logs. Normally, tail shows the last ten lines of a file. You can ask for more lines with the -n argument (for example, tail -n 50 access_log). For real-time output, the -f argument will continue to print new lines as the web server writes them. On Unix-based systems, you see this kind of output when you run the Rails script/server command during development.

With some versions of the tail command, you can even tail several logs simultaneously. If your operating system doesn't include a capable version of tail, you can download a version written in Perl by Jason Fesler.[6]

---

6.   http://gigo.com/archives/Source\%20Code\xtailpl_tail_multiple_files_at_once.html

In any case, find where your host keeps the httpd logs, and tail them all:

```
ezra$ tail -f log/production.log log/fastcgi.crash.log ↩
      httpd/error_log httpd/access_log
```

Refresh any page of your site, and you should see some kind of output in the logs:

```
[Mon April 17 11:20:20 2007] [error] [client 66.33.219.16]
FastCGI:server "/home/ezra/brainspl.at/public/dispatch.fcgi"
stderr: ./../config/../app/helpers/xml_helper.rb:11:
warning: Object#type is deprecated; use Object#class
```

A common error is Premature end of script headers, which is quite vague and usually signals a problem that needs to be debugged separately. However, file permission errors will show up with the full path to the file or folder that has the problem.

Do Files Have the Correct Permissions?

Rails has to write to several kinds of logs, so those files and folders need to be writable by the user who runs the FastCGI processes. Usually this login is the same as the user account used to SSH to the server, but it might be different. If you have other FastCGI processes or Mongrels already running, you can run the top command and see what user is running them:

```
ezra$ top
  PID USER  PR NI  VIRT  RES  SHR S %CPU %MEM  TIME+   COMMAND
25698 ezra  11 2 22072 21m 2288 S 0.0 1.1 0:03.30 dispatch.fcgi
```

Here are a few important files and the permissions they must have:

- The log directory and files must be writable by the user running the FastCGI or Mongrel process. With Capistrano, the logs directory is a symbolic link to the shared/logs directory. Make sure both, and the files inside, are writable.

- The public directory must be writable by the user running the FastCGI or Mongrel process if you are using page caching. Rails will run if the public directory is not writable but will not use caching.

- Capistrano makes a system directory inside public. It also makes links from this directory to the shared directory holding the core Rails logs, including production.log. The benefit is that you can store uploads and other files there, and they will remain between deployments. If you keep the page cache or uploads there, the folder (and the link) must be writable by the FastCGI user.

- dispatch.fcgi must be executable, but not writable by others. Properly configured web servers will refuse to execute files if dispatch.fcgi is writable by the general public. dispatch.fcgi is the main file that handles requests and fires them off to the controllers in your application, so it must be executable.

If you have permission problems with any of these files, you can remedy the problem with the Unix chmod command. The chmod command has many capabilities that are beyond the scope of this book. You can read about it in excruciating detail in the Unix manual page by running the command man chmod:

```
ezra$ chmod 755 public/dispatch.fcgi
ezra$ ls -l public/dispatch.fcgi
-rwxr-xr-x 1 ezra group 855 2006-01-15 02:03 dispatch.fcgi
```

The rwx means that ezra can read, write, and execute the file. The first r-x means that only others in the same group can read and execute the file. The last r-x means anyone can read and execute but not write the file. This permission set is the proper setup for the dispatch.fcgi file.

Did You Specify the Correct Path to the Ruby Executables?

When generating a new Rails application, Rails uses the location of your local Ruby executable to generate the dispatch scripts in the public directory and all the scripts in the script directory.

Your shared server may not have a copy of Ruby in the same location. For example, I used MacPorts to build a fresh copy of Ruby on my development machine, so my local copy of Ruby is located at /opt/local/bin/ruby. Even though I made a symbolic link from /usr/bin/ruby, Rails builds all my script files like this:

```
#!/opt/local/bin/ruby
# ERROR: Incorrect for most production servers!
```

If you've already generated your application, you need to manually edit your configuration files, including possibly dispatch.fcgi and others, to match the actual location of Ruby on your shared server. You can find this information by connecting to your server via SSH and issuing this command:

```
ezra$ which ruby
/usr/local/bin/ruby
```

Note the path returned by the which command. If you know this information before you start building your application, you can send it to Rails as you generate your application:

```
ezra$ rails my_rails_app --ruby /usr/local/bin/ruby
```

Be careful! Make sure you substitute the Ruby install path you noted earlier for /usr/local/bin/ruby. All the relevant files will then start with the correct location:

```
#!/usr/local/bin/ruby
```

If your development machine doesn't have a link to Ruby in that location, you can make one to match your production server:

```
# Link to the actual location of Ruby from an aliased location
ezra$ sudo ln -s /opt/local/bin/ruby /usr/local/bin/ruby
ezra$ sudo ln -s /opt/local/bin/ruby /usr/bin/ruby
ezra$ sudo ln -s /opt/local/bin/ruby /home/ezra/bin/ruby
```

Now I can set the application's shebang[7] to the location on the remote server, but the application will still run on my development machine.

Does the Sessions Table Exist in the Database?

Some of the most baffling errors happen when Rails can't save its session data. I've gotten a completely blank page with no errors in any of the logs. Often, the problem is an unwritable /tmp folder or an absent sessions table. Fortunately, Rails 1.1+ has been enhanced to give a more informative message when this happens.

By default, Rails stores user sessions in cookies. Cookie-based sessions are fast, requiring no server-based disk access. This session storage solution scales well because the server has very little overhead for each additional client. There are a couple of limitations, though. Sessions are limited to roughly 4,000 characters. Also, Rails stores cookie session data without encryption so it is not secure. If you need large sessions or secure sessions, databases may be the way to go. If you are storing user sessions in the database, you may have started by creating the sessions table in your development database like this:

```
ezra$ rake db:sessions:create
```

This command will create a numbered migration file that can be run against the production database to add a sessions table. Then, you'll

---

7. *shebang* refers to the #! characters. The #! characters specify the interpreter that will execute the rest of the script.

have to add the database sessions to your environment by the line config.action_controller.session_store = :active_record_store to environment.rb.

Are Current Versions of Necessary Files Present?

Rails is a complete framework and expects to find files in certain places. It is common to omit core files with the svn:ignore property while developing. However, those files must be included in your build process on the production server.

A common example is database.yml. For security reasons, people don't want to have their name and password flying all over the Internet every time they check out the code for a project. But if it isn't on the production server, Rails won't be able to connect to the database at all.

A solution is to save it to a safe place on the server and make an after_update_code() task to copy it into the current live directory. (See Chapter 5, *Capistrano*, on page 85 for a detailed example.)

If you have saved a copy of the core Rails libraries to the vendor directory, your application will not run unless all the libraries are there. And like the rest of Rails, filenames and directory names matter. I once saw an odd situation where the built-in has_many() and belongs_to() methods were causing errors. The rest of the application ran fine until the programmer asked for data from a related table. We discovered that the actual filenames in ActiveRecord had somehow been truncated and were causing the error.

Is the RAILS_ENV Environment Variable Set Correctly?

One of the most common problems during deployment is an incorrect RAILS_ENV. For your production server, RAILS_ENV should be set to production.

There are several ways to set RAILS_ENV and several ways to determine the current setting of RAILS_ENV. The only thing that really matters is the value of RAILS_ENV inside your Rails application, and there is no direct way to test that (apart from a fully running application).

This can also be confusing since some scripts don't tell you what environment they are using, and others don't tell you what environment they are using until they are running properly.

However, you can use the following troubleshooting tools to find out what RAILS_ENV might be.

The about Script

Rails 1.0 and above ship with a script that prints useful information about your configuration. Unfortunately, this will not be accurate if the environment was set in lighttpd.conf.

```
ezra$ ./script/about
About your application's environment
Ruby version            1.8.6 (i686-linux)
RubyGems version        1.0.1
Rails version           2.0.2
Active Record version   2.0.2
Action Pack version     2.0.2
Active Resource version 2.0.2
Action Mailer version   2.0.2
Active Support version  2.0.2
Application root        /Users/ez/brainspl.at/current
Environment             development
Database adapter        mysql
Database schema version  3
```

Echo

If you have set the environment in your shell, you should be able to SSH to your shared server and print it out like this:

```
ezra$ echo $RAILS_ENV
production
```

It should also take effect when you start the console:

```
ezra$ ./script/console
Loading production environment.
>>
```

Is the Database Alive and Present?

Although Rails can run without touching a database, most applications use the database in some way. If the database doesn't exist, your application will not run and will show errors.

You can test the database independently of the rest of your application. Call up the console in production mode, and you should be able to send simple queries to the database:

```
ezra$ ./script/console production
Loading production environment.
>> User.find 1
=> #<User:0x263662c @attributes=...
```

If this doesn't work, one of the following may help:

- Can you connect directly to the database with a command-line client such as mysql or psql? If not, the database may be down or may not be accessible from your shared server. This method is not always conclusive. I have used hosts where the command-line MySQL client cannot connect to the server but the Rails application runs without any problems.

- Do you have the proper database, username, password, host, and port specified in the production section of config/database.yml?

Has the Database Been Migrated to the Correct Version for Your Application?

You may have run your migrations, but was the right database affected? If RAILS_ENV is missing from the shell, you may have migrated your development or test database instead of the production database.

The easiest way to discover your current schema_version is to use the ./script/about command. Newer versions of Rails will display the schema version on the last line:

```
ezra$ ./script/about RAILS_ENV=production
About your application's environment
Ruby version            1.8.6 (i686-linux)
RubyGems version        1.0.1
Rails version           2.0.2
Active Record version   2.0.2
Action Pack version     2.0.2
Active Resource version 2.0.2
Action Mailer version   2.0.2
Active Support version  2.0.2
Application root        /Users/ez/brainspl.at/current
Environment             development
Database adapter        mysql
Database schema version 47
```

If this doesn't show the version you expect, you may need to run your migration again or check your other database connections to make sure the correct database is being addressed. To reapply the migration manually, issue this command:

```
ezra$ rake db:migrate RAILS_ENV=production
```

3.11 Conclusion

When possible, I run applications on a VPS or dedicated server. However, I still have several shared-hosted applications that run with an acceptable degree of reliability. By following the steps mentioned here, you can also run small applications reliably on an inexpensive, affordable shared host.

In this chapter, you learned to set up a typical shared hosting Rails environment. You also learned that you can't push shared hosts too hard, and you can't rely on them for perfect service. In the next chapter, you'll see the alternative: virtual and dedicated hosting. If you're bursting at the seams and hearing your neighbor through paper-thin walls, it's time to move up. Read on.

Chapter 4

Virtual and Dedicated Hosts

Most shared host plans are roughly equivalent to a 7-by-7 apartment with a shared bathroom and no kitchen. After a little time on that shared host, it may start to feel pretty cramped. When you come to a point where you are pushing the limits of your shared host, it's time for your own virtual private server or dedicated server. You will be able to stretch out and take over the whole environment without worrying about fighting others for your CPU time and memory. You're probably thinking to yourself, "Ah, the good life."

Not so fast. With your newly found space and flexibility comes great responsibility. No one else will hold your hand and watch over your server, unless you're willing to pay big bucks for a fully managed server. You will have to decide whether that extra cost of disk redundancy through RAID is worth it; you will be responsible for backing up your system and restoring the data should something go wrong. For better or worse, you are living the great American dream: full home ownership. This chapter will walk you through the move-in.

4.1 The Lay of the Land

In this chapter, I'll show you how to build out a server from scratch. You'll first build and install your operating system. Then, you'll build some of the tools that you will need to build the Ruby stack. You will move on to build out the Ruby stack, including Ruby, Rails, RMagick, and Mongrel. You will also install a database and your web server, though you won't integrate your web server until Chapter 7, *Scaling Out*, on page 137. You'll have a working Rails installation like the one in Figure 4.1, on the next page.

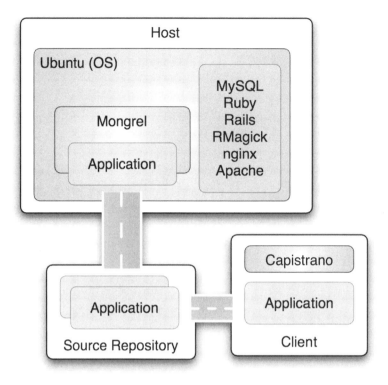

Figure 4.1: DEDICATED SERVER MAP

In practice, the setup will not work much differently from the one you saw in Chapter 3, *Shared Hosts*, on page 37. You will serve each request with a single Mongrel. That architecture will not scale, but your emphasis is on building a workable foundation that you can use as a foundation. In later chapters, you'll cluster your Mongrels, and then if your application requires it, you'll scale out using one of the options in Chapter 7, *Scaling Out*, on page 137. For now, focus on building all the pieces that you'll need through the rest of the book.

Introducing Your Own Host and Administrator

As if deploying a Rails application to someone else's server wasn't enough fun, now you're ready to build your own machine. Whether you want the role or not, you're an administrator. You earned that rank the moment you built your own environment. I recommend you take your new role seriously. As an administrator, you have many responsibilities—topics that other books will do a better job of exhausting. You can group your responsibilities into these categories:

- Security and stability

- Configuration and upgrades

- Documentation

Keeping your server secure and stable is a tough business and is a subject I won't even attempt to tackle in this book. Managing configuration and upgrades can be a weekly occurrence, and patching the system is an important security practice. But the one that I really want to drive home is documentation. Developers have a bad habit of avoiding documentation. Programmers I know use insanely creative rationalizations. Here are some of the best:

- "You may not think you have the time or skill to pull it off, but you'll pay with your time now or later."

- "You might think that documentation is always out-of-date and unable to keep up with changes in code, but I'm not talking about code."

- "The configuration won't change as fast as code, and even if it does, that's all the more reason to document it."

None of the old arguments against documentation work for infrastructure. As system administrators, we have to document our configurations. The following tips will help with managing documentation:

- Keep a server journal next to the machine or in a common place if there are multiple administrators or remote servers. Treat it like the conch from *Lord of the Flies*: only the person with the journal can modify the server configuration. In the journal, record and date which changes were made and why.

- Keep a directory containing dated session logs in a well-known directory. If at all possible, comment the logs with "why?" questions. It's often easy to see what someone did with the logs, but the "why?" needs to be filled in to communicate with others.

- Update formal documentation once per week or anytime a major change is made. Formal documentation includes simple diagrams and organized sections of documentation for key infrastructure components.

- Make sure everyone reads the documentation. Let people know when you update the documentation, and walk them through it over coffee. These practices will ensure that they understand the system and also encourage discussion and questions about the system.

When you must move to multiple servers, you will need to do your best to keep the configurations in sync. And by "in sync," I mean preferably identical. You will want to try to automate differences in configuration by your application or even Capistrano, and your service provider will manage others for you. To keep your configurations identical, you will need good organization and up-to-date documentation. I've preached enough for now. Roll up your sleeves, and let's get to work.

4.2 Virtual Private Servers

Even after you've decided that shared hosting is not enough, one size does not fit all. Before you decide to spring for that dedicated host package, take a deep breath and look at another attractive alternative first. The virtual private server, or VPS for short, is the first logical step up from a shared server plan. Some hosts might call these virtual dedicated servers (VDSs). These type of servers run in a virtual machine. Multiple VM instances run on one physical hardware server. Before you run away shrieking in horror, you need to know that a VPS is not a shared server package. You will get complete root access to your VPS, and often you'll even pick your operating system from some Linux distribution or FreeBSD.

Your host may run one of quite a few different server virtualization software packages. Out of all of these that I have tried, Xen is my favorite. Xen is a relative newcomer to the virtualization scene, but the open source package is built right into certain Linux kernels, so the virtualized server processes run a little closer to the metal. Xen also offers superior disk I/O, which is a big issue for anything that deals with many files. And guess what? The majority of the time, a web application does nothing more than deliver file after file to the user. More and more web hosts are making Xen-based virtual servers available to hosting clients, so it shouldn't be hard to find one.

Once you acquire your own VPS, it acts like a dedicated box. You have full root access to install or remove anything you need. On a Xen-based VPS, you could even recompile your own kernel if you wanted to (but you should ask your host provider first). Since most virtual servers will run on high-end hardware, you can get very good performance. Of course, the more VPSs that your host tries to squeeze onto one physical box, the less resources there are to go around. It is a good practice to ask the provider about the hardware setup and exactly how many virtual machines it runs per box. Generally speaking, bigger slices on bigger boxes are better. If you need help interpreting the numbers, ask an expert. You might pay one if you have a lot of money riding on the answer, or you might simply post the question on one of the many excellent Ruby on Rails forums.

Memory

Usually, your performance bottleneck will not be processing power but memory. Some shared hosting providers oversell their hardware in the hopes that not everyone will be running full blast at once. When too many customers need too much, your VPS can easily run out of memory and start swapping out memory pages to disk. To understand the impact on performance, imagine an Olympic sprinter running at full speed in perfect conditions and then plunging him into water up to his chest to finish the race. But with Xen-based VMs, the memory allocation you get for your server is your memory only. A Xen-based architecture will not allow a hosting provider to oversell the memory of the physical box, and your application can run in the clean air of memory instead of the quagmire of disk swapping. Products like Virtuozzo and OpenVZ are a few to investigate.

Depending on what you're doing, I'd recommend a minimum of 160MB to 256MB of RAM on your VPS. This amount of memory will allow you to run one or two small Rails sites, depending on the application's resource usage. But you can be more precise. Rather than take a blind guess, you can estimate how much you will need based on one critical question: how many Mongrels or FastCGI listeners will you need?

One or two back-end processes is plenty for many Rails applications. A typo or Mephisto blog that gets a medium amount of traffic will usually be fine on one process. A typical Rails process can take anywhere from 35MB to 120MB, but some Rails application may take more. Keep in mind there are always exceptions to the rule, and you should test locally to see what your memory consumption is before you order your VPS. I'll show you how in Chapter 9, *Performance*, on page 217.

Even if you get your initial memory size wrong, a VPS system is very easy to upgrade. If you need more RAM, disk space, or other resources, usually all you have to do is request these from your host and reboot your VPS. When it comes back online, you will have the new resources available without the need to change anything in your settings to take advantage of them. Another benefit of the virtual server approach is the ability to easily migrate your entire server to another physical box or host when the time comes. If you choose the right provider, upgrading with your traffic should happen smoothly.

Using Lightweight Web Servers

Mongrel is emerging as the de facto method of deploying a Rails application on a VPS. You can run a blog or smaller apps on one Mongrel alone. Should you need another web server in front of Mongrel for static content, using nginx or lighttpd can be a huge win. These servers use fewer resources than Apache and are very fast. If you want an alternative to Mongrel, nginx and lighttpd have FastCGI support that is top-notch and stable.

Most hosting providers offer a number of Linux distributions to choose from. Primarily, you want a distribution with a minimal footprint. When you run on a smaller memory system, make sure to install only what you need and no more. From there, you should build only what you need. In the end, you will come out with a leaner, faster server.

The instructions for setting up a VPS are basically the same as setting up a dedicated server. You'll need to know a little more about dedicated hosting before I move into the setup tutorial.

4.3 Dedicated Servers

Say you have written the latest popular Rails web 2.0 application and a shared host is no longer enough. Your shared host admin is screaming at you about resource usage, he's not responding to your requests for support quickly enough, and you've decided to either challenge him to a duel or switch to a higher plan. It's time to move. You're ready for root, and your customers are ready to see your fabulous content without the dreaded spinning globe, or whatever icon their browser is spinning these days.

With a dedicated server, you don't have to worry about memory constraints or disk space as much. A good starting system would have a modern processor, 512MB to 1024MB RAM minimum, and a spacious hard drive. A system like this will let your application service a lot of traffic and concurrent users. I'm not going to bore you with statistics here because there are too many variable factors to weigh, but once you're on a dedicated box, if your application keeps growing to the point where you need to start thinking about a cluster, you will be ready.

Typically dedicated boxes cost more than VPS systems. A starter VPS can run you US$25 to US$60 per month, whereas a starter dedicated box is usually closer to US$150 to US$300.

Even if you do get your own dedicated box, you may want to consider using Xen. In the real world, Xen offers acceptable performance and gives you a nice long-term solution for scaling your system out as you grow. Installing and configuring Xen is out of scope for this book, but it is definitely worth your time to investigate this alternative. You trade a small percentage of raw performance for ease of administration and scalability. With Xen you can partition your dedicated server into a number of targeted VPS servers that you can easily move to other boxes as you grow. I'll tell you how to do exactly this in the Chapter 7, *Scaling Out*, on page 137.

4.4 Setting Up Shop

Building a deployment environment is not for the impatient, but with a good knowledge of the command line and a willingness to google, you should be able to build your own setup for running Rails applications in production. I'll spell out the rest for you. This is all well-traveled territory, so if things go wrong and you can't find the answers here, don't be afraid to go searching for answers. I'll show you many of the answers that you need, and Google can help you find the rest.

Regardless of whether you decide to go with a VPS or dedicated server, your Rails setup will be the same. I'll use Ubuntu Linux 7.10 Server Edition, but don't worry if your favorite server platform is OS X, BSD, or another Linux distribution. Everything pertaining to web server and Rails configuration will work pretty much the same way on any Unix-like operating system.

I like to build from scratch using Ubuntu Gutsy Gibbon Server. You can get the download image and instructions online.[1] In all likelihood,

---

1. http://www.ubuntu.com/getubuntu/download

you won't wind up building your own system. Almost any virtual or dedicated hosting provider offers this as an option when you set up your account with them. If not, just ask them to install the Server version of Ubuntu for you. They will also set up the basic network interface to work with their network and data center.

From here on out I'll assume you are starting from a working install base with the right network install. If you are installing on your own server at home or work, you can get detailed Ubuntu Server installation instructions online.[2]

Any virtual host provider will have some version of SSH installed and configured, but you may need to install OpenSSH2 if you're building your own host locally. Use the ssh install package by typing sudo apt-get install ssh to get things working.

I can't possibly cover all the details for securing a Linux server, but I'll give you a few important tips along the way. Here's the first. Use ssh and sftp or scp, not ftp or rsh. If you don't, all your communications will be in the clear, directly readable at any of the intermediate hosts between your local machine and server. To use SSH, you will need SSH on both the client and the host. I've already told you about the host system, so shift your attentions to the client. If you are on OS X, Linux, or BSD, you undoubtedly have a client installed, but if you run Windows locally, you will want to install PuTTY. The Windows de facto standard, PuTTY is an excellent and free SSH program you can find online.[3] Follow the instructions you find there, and you'll be ready for the rest of this book.

Building your production setup is not a trivial exercise. Here is the rundown of the whole list you'll be installing:

- *Gnu Compiler Collection (GCC for short) and associated tools.* You'll use it to build several components including RubyGems and the RMagick plug-in.

- *Ruby and RubyGems.* You'll get the latest stable version of Ruby and the RubyGems third-party library packing and distribution system.

- *Rails.* After installing the operating system and RubyGems, installing and configuring Rails will be surprisingly easy.

---

2.   https://help.ubuntu.com/
3.   http://www.chiark.greenend.org.uk/~sgtatham/putty/download.html

- *MySQL and the mysql-ruby bindings.* You can use a variety of different database servers, but I'm going to go with the most popular Rails database engine.

- *Subversion.* Capistrano will check out your code right out of your Subversion repository.

- *Mongrel and dependencies.* Mongrel is rapidly becoming the de facto standard for serving Rails applications.

- *ImageMagick and RMagick.* Many modern web applications allow the uploading of images. RMagick can help by automatically creating thumbnails and cropping images.

- *FastCGI Developers Kit and the Ruby FastCGI bindings.* If you're running Apache or lighttpd instead of Mongrel, you will want to replace the slower, default CGI right away.

- *nginx.* This tiny web server is lightning in a bottle, making it a good substitute for Apache with many installations. Installing it is easy if you want to go that route.

With these elements, you will have the basic stack that will serve as the basic foundation for all we do in the remainder of the book. We will cover optimizing the individual web server configurations in other chapters in the book. Once you've completed the steps in this chapter, you will be able to run a basic production Rails application.

I'm going to break a cardinal publishing rule here and repeat some details from Chapter 1, *Introduction*, on page 1. I'm doing so not to pad the book but to protect you from major havoc. You're going to issue commands against your local box and remote servers, with user permissions and root permissions. You'll need to understand where you are at all times and how much power (and potential for damage) you have at any given time. Moving files around and installing software can destroy lots of work if you're not extremely careful, so look for the clues that tell you where and how you're logged in.

If I'm logged on to my production system, the login will begin with ezra. If I'm logged in locally, the login will begin with local. In the bash shell on *nix systems, the # command-line prompt tells you that you are logged in as root, and a $ means you are logged in as a regular system user. I'm going to use bash. If you want to use a different shell, make sure you understand the prompt indicators for your system.

Configuring the Server

It's time to get started. I'm going to name my virtual server *«tracklayer»*. Whenever you see *«tracklayer»* in the commands, replace it with the IP address or domain name of your server.

You'll need a root user and a regular user. Admins usually set up Ubuntu with a normal user account instead of a root account only. If you are configuring most other Linux distributions, you will need to make a normal user and add yourself to the /etc/sudoers file.

If you have a normal user account, use it to log in and skip past the next two session listings. If you have only root, you'll need to create a normal user. SSH in to your new account's IP with your root user and password:

```
local$ ssh root@tracklayer
root@tracklayer password: <enter your password>
```

If all is well, create your normal user account:

```
root# adduser ezra
Adding user `ezra'...
Adding new group `ezra' (1001).
Adding new user `ezra' (1001) with group `ezra'.
Creating home directory `/home/ezra'.
Copying files from `/etc/skel'
Enter new UNIX password:
Retype new UNIX password:
# you will be asked a few more questions,
# fill them out however you like.
```

Be careful with root. After you've established your account, always log in to your machine as your own user instead of root. Simply use su or sudo to gain root privileges as needed. su stands for *super user*, and sudo stands for *super user do*. If you're not logged in as root, become root now:

```
$ su -
Password:
root#
```

Now edit /etc/sudoers. You should use a program called visudo to edit the sudoers file because visudo won't let two people edit at the same time.

```
root# visudo
```

Use your arrow key to move the cursor down, and add this line at the end of the file:

```
yourusername  ALL=(ALL) ALL
```

Securing SSH

Most experienced *nix admins tend to run sshd on high port numbers. Here's why. Crackers commonly create automated attacking programs called *bots* that crawl the Net, visiting one machine after the next to find machines with a running SSH daemon. Then, the bot uses an automated script with a dictionary to try many combinations of usernames and passwords. The attacks are so prevalent that these days most servers on the Internet will experience this kind of attack with some frequency. If you have a weak login/password combination on a live SSH port, you're toast, especially if sshd is on the standard port 22. Since most of these attack bots will not scan ports higher than 1024, you should always assign sshd to a free port above 1024.

Modify the port for sshd by editing /etc/ssh/sshd_config. Edit the line that looks like this:

```
Port 22
```

Change it to this:

```
Port 8888 # or any unused port above 1024
```

Then save the file and quit the editor. And don't forget to restart the SSH server daemon.

Now press the Escape key, and type :wq. This means write file and quit.

For security's sake, you don't want to allow SSH root logins because an unauthorized login would be disastrous. Edit /etc/ssh/sshd_config, replacing this line:

```
PermitRootLogin yes
```

with this one:

```
PermitRootLogin no
```

Now reload its /etc/ssh/sshd_config to pick up the new settings:

```
root# /etc/init.d/sshd reload
 * Reloading OpenBSD Secure Shell server's configuration sshd   [ ok ]
```

For security and to make things easier on yourself, using SSH keys instead of passwords for logins is a great technique. Let's create a pair of public/private keys and get them installed on our new server; the key generation is done on your local machine:

```
local$ ssh-keygen -t dsa
```

This will prompt you for a secret passphrase. If this is your primary identity key, make sure to use a good passphrase. When this is done, you will get two files called id_dsa and id_dsa.pub in your ~/.ssh directory. Note that it is possible to just press the Enter key when prompted for a passphrase, which will make a key with no passphrase. This is a Bad Idea™ for an identity key, so don't do it! You will learn how to achieve passwordless logins in a secure manner shortly.

Now we need to place your public key on the server. Here is a nice bash function that will do this for us; place this in your ~/.bashrc or ~/.bash_profile depending on the type of computer you are using locally. (The function assumes you've already created the .ssh directory, so if you haven't done so, create it first.)

```
function authme {
    ssh $1 'cat >>.ssh/authorized_keys' <~/.ssh/id_dsa.pub
}
```

Once that is in your shell's rc file, you will need to start a new shell or source the file:

```
local$ . ~/.bashrc
```

With this all in place, we can now use the authme command to place your new keys on the server (replace tracklayer with your IP or hostname):

```
local$ authme tracklayer
```

You will be prompted for the password, and your key will be placed on the server. Now you will want to enter a new shell with your SSH keys loaded. This will allow you to start a shell and enter your passphrase for your private key only once, and then you will be able to ssh to anywhere your key is placed without entering the passphrase again:

```
local$ ssh-agent sh -c 'ssh-add < /dev/null && bash'
```

Now you can ssh to your new server with no passphrase entry:

```
local$ ssh tracklayer
```

Install the GCC Tool Chain

You will need to install a compiler tool chain to build and install many elements including RubyGems. The build-essential package has everything you need to build the components you'll need to install later. Install it on Ubuntu like so:

```
root# apt-get install build-essential
```

Install Ruby and RubyGems

By default, Debian and Ubuntu have five package repositories called *main*, *restricted*, *universe*, *multiverse*, and *commercial*. For the setup in this chapter, you will need the universe package repository. By default, it is not enabled. Fix that by editing the /etc/apt/sources.list file, and uncomment the following two lines:

```
deb http://us.archive.ubuntu.com/ubuntu/ gutsy universe
deb-src http://us.archive.ubuntu.com/ubuntu/ gutsy universe
```

Now, update your apt-sources file, and install Ruby and friends. You should have least Ruby 1.8.6 and Rails 1.2.*x* or 2.0.*x*.

```
root# apt-get update
root# apt-get upgrade
root# apt-get install ruby ri rdoc irb ri1.8 ruby1.8-dev libzlib-ruby zlib1g
...
root# ruby -v
ruby 1.8.4 (2005-12-24) [i486-linux]
```

Ruby is live. If you want to verify that fact, run irb, and type a few commands, but for now, I'll press onward. Install RubyGems. You really don't want to install Rails without it. Ubuntu and Debian do not officially package RubyGems, so you will need to build it from source. Go to RubyForge,[4] download the latest stable version, and then build and install it like this:

```
root# wget https://rubyforge.org/frs/download.php/29548/rubygems-1.0.1.tgz
...
root# tar xvzf rubygems-1.0.1.tgz
...
root# cd rubygems-1.0.1/
root# ruby setup.rb
   ---> bin
   <--- bin
     ...
     Successfully built RubyGem
     Name: sources
     Version: 0.0.1
     File: sources-0.0.1.gem
   Removing old RubyGems RDoc and ri...
   Installing rubygems-1.0.1 ri...
   Installing rubygems-1.0.1 rdoc...

   As of RubyGems 0.8.0, library stubs are no longer needed.
   Searching $LOAD_PATH for stubs to optionally delete (may take a while)...
   ...done.
   No library stubs found.
```

---

4. http://rubyforge.org/projects/rubygems/

Building the Latest Ruby from Source

Ubuntu and Debian releases often do some strange things with Ruby. A given release may break Ruby up into tiny pieces or install some earlier release of Ruby. If you want Ruby-1.8.6, you will need to build from source.

The first step is getting the latest stable release of Ruby. In your web browser, go to the Ruby home,* and download the desired release. I'm going to install Ruby-1.8.6.

```
ezra$ wget ftp://ftp.ruby-lang.org/pub/ruby/1.8/ruby-1.8.6.tar.gz
```

Now, unpack, build, and install Ruby:

```
ezra$ tar -xvfz ruby-1.8.6.tar.gz
  ...
  ezra$ cd ruby-1.8.6
  ezra$ ./configure && make && sudo make install
  ...
```

You will need to make sure your $PATH has /usr/local/bin in it:

```
ezra$ echo $PATH
 /usr/local/sbin:/usr/local/bin:/usr/sbin:/usr/bin:/sbin:/bin
```

If you don't have /usr/local/sbin:/usr/local/bin in your $PATH, then you will need to add it. Open /etc/profile with your editor, and add the following line:

```
export PATH=/usr/local/sbin:/usr/local/bin:$PATH
```

Those are the basic steps required to build Ruby from source. Please note that if you choose to build your own Ruby, it will not work with the Ruby packages in Ubuntu. You will have to install the mysql and rmagick gems through Ruby Gems and not through apt-get.

---

*. http://www.ruby-lang.org/en/

Remember to clean up after yourself. Delete the RubyGems source files:

```
root# cd ..
root# rm -rf rubygems-1.0.1*
```

Now you are ready to move into some more familiar territory. You have already installed Rails on your development machine, and now you will do the same thing for your production setup. The component version numbers will probably be higher by the time you read this, but the following command will install the latest stable version of Rails. The include-dependencies option will make sure you have all necessary dependencies:

```
root# sudo gem install rails --no-rdoc --no-ri
Successfully installed rake-0.8.1
Successfully installed activesupport-2.0.2
Successfully installed activerecord-2.0.2
Successfully installed actionpack-2.0.2
Successfully installed actionmailer-2.0.2
Successfully installed activeresource-2.0.2
Successfully installed rails-2.0.2
```

Usually, your server-side installation won't need the documentation, so the --no-rdoc --no-ri flags will skip them and keep your installation lean.

Mongrel is next. If you have suffered through building and installing Apache, you'll really appreciate the following command:

```
root# gem install mongrel mongrel_cluster ↩
     --include-dependencies --no-rdoc --no-ri
            Select which gem to install for your platform (i486-linux)
            1. mongrel 1.0.1 (ruby)
            2. mongrel 1.0.1 (mswin32)
            3. mongrel 1.0 (mswin32)
            4. mongrel 1.0 (ruby)
            5. Skip this gem
            6. Cancel installation
     ...
```

When multiple versions of a gem are available, RubyGems will prompt you for the version and platform you want. I'm on Ubuntu, so choosing 1 gives me the latest compatible version. Most of the time, Mongrel is enough. If I need more performance, I put a proxy in front of Mongrel to serve static content. I'll talk more about that in Chapter 7, *Scaling Out*, on page 137. But now, it's on to the database.

Install MySQL

Next, you will install MySQL and the MySQL-Ruby bindings. You don't have to use MySQL—several available database engines work quite well with Rails. PostgreSQL is another popular choice. You will also install the zlib1g-dev package because it is a requirement for RubyGems and a few other things you will need along the way:

```
root# apt-get install mysql-server-5.0 mysql-client-5.0 ↩
    libmysqlclient15-dev libmysqlclient15off zlib1g-dev ↩
    libmysql-ruby1.8
```

You've installed the database server, but don't forget to set the root password:

```
root# mysqladmin -u root password <your password here>
```

You can easily verify that the MySQL-Ruby bindings work correctly with a simple require command in irb:

```
root# irb
irb(main):001:0> require 'rubygems'
=> true
irb(main):001:0> require 'mysql'
=> true
irb(main):002:0> exit
```

This require command tells Ruby to load the mysql library that provides basic Ruby support for MySQL. Since Rails uses the same bindings, if the require returns true, Rails will probably work too.

So far, you've installed Ruby, Ruby on Rails, RubyGems, Mongrel, and MySQL. I'm going to walk you through installing nginx and FastCGI as well. You'll need nginx if you want to use nginx for load balancing and static content. FastCGI is a good alternative to Mongrel, should you ever need an alternative. If you want, you can skip these steps and pick them up later.

Install nginx and FastCGI

This book will concentrate on clustering with Mongrel and Mongrel cluster. If you want to use FastCGI instead, you can install it now. Install libfcgi-dev and libfcgi-ruby1.8 like this:

```
root# apt-get install libfcgi-ruby1.8 libfcgi-dev
```

To check that fcgi-ruby works, make sure neither installation returns any errors. You want to be sure you successfully installed the C extension version of ruby-fcgi and not just the pure-Ruby version. The C extension is much faster then the pure-Ruby version.

Just as you did with MySQL, you'll use a require statement to make sure you have the right libraries installed:

```
root# irb
irb(main):001:0> require 'fcgi.so'
=> true
irb(main):002:0> require 'fcgi'
=> true
irb(main):003:0> exit
```

If both requires returned true, you're ready to proceed. You need the Perl Compatible Regular Expression Library (or libpcre) for the rewrite module in nginx to work properly. You also need the OpenSSL library and development package for SSL support in nginx:

```
root# apt-get install libpcre3-dev libpcre3 openssl libssl-dev
```

Now, the bad news: nginx does not have the latest Ubuntu package at this time, so you'll have to build it from scratch. Get the latest release[5] (nginx 0.5.33 at the time of this writing), and build it like so:

```
root# wget http://sysoev.ru/nginx/nginx-0.5.33.tar.gz
...
root# tar xzvf nginx-0.5.33.tar.gz
...
root# cd nginx-0.5.33
root# ./configure  --with-http_ssl_module
...
root# make
...
root# make install
...
```

That's it for nginx. As always, clean up after yourself and add nginx to the $PATH:

```
root# cd ..
root# rm -rf nginx-0.5.33*
```

The default nginx installation directory is /usr/local/nginx, so you need to add /usr/local/nginx/sbin to the $PATH. Open /etc/profile with your editor, and add the following line:

```
export PATH=/usr/local/nginx/sbin:$PATH
```

Check that nginx is working and in your $PATH. The version command option should do the trick:

```
root# nginx -v
nginx version: nginx/0.5.33
```

---

5. http://www.nginx.net/

Install ImageMagick and RMagick

You've installed a pretty good stack. Many Rails applications will also need ImageMagick and RMagick to process image upload and manipulation. This set of libraries gives everyone a little trouble, so pay close attention:

```
root# apt-get install imagemagick librmagick-ruby1.8 ↩
    libfreetype6-dev xml-core
```

Check to see that RMagick works. Put an arbitrary image file called test.jpg in your current working directory for a test, and run the following command:

```
root# irb
irb(main):001:0> require 'RMagick'
=> true
irb(main):002:0> include Magick
=> Object
irb(main):003:0> img = ImageList.new "test.jpg"
=> [test.jpg JPEG 10x11 DirectClass 8-bit 391b]
scene=0
irb(main):004:0> img.write "test.png"
=> [test.jpg=>test.png JPEG 10x11 DirectClass 8-bit]
scene=0
irb(main):005:0>
```

RMagick should now work fine, but it is notorious for being hard to install. If you run into any issues getting RMagick working, you can look at the Install FAQ on the website.[6]

Installing Subversion

To get things ready for Capistrano, you'll need to install Subversion. Let's install it now:

```
root# apt-get install subversion subversion-tools
```

When you install subversion-tools, it will pull in the exim SMTP server as a dependency. Configuring your mail server is beyond the scope of this book, but during the install you will be prompted to choose the general type of mail configuration you want. Choose the option that says "internet site; mail is sent and received directly using SMTP."

You will need to create new Subversion repositories that you can reach from your development machine. If you don't have Apache installed, the best way to run Subversion over the network is with svnserve or

---

6. http://rmagick.rubyforge.org/install-faq.html

over Subversion and SSH. See the Chapter 2, *Refining Applications for Production*, on page 13 for instructions on setting up and using Subversion for your Rails projects.

Test It!

Now you should be in great shape for Rails deployment. Generate a skeleton Rails app, and fire it up with Mongrel to make sure everything is working fine. Switch to your normal user now because you don't need root for Rails development:

```
root# su yourusername
ezra$ cd ~
ezra$ rails test
```

Take it for a test-drive:

```
ezra$ cd test
ezra$ ruby script/server
 => Booting Mongrel (use 'script/server webrick' to force WEBrick)
 => Rails application starting on http://0.0.0.0:3000
 => Call with -d to detach
 => Ctrl-C to shutdown server
 ** Starting Mongrel listening at 0.0.0.0:3000
 ** Starting Rails with development environment...
 ** Rails loaded.
 ** Loading any Rails specific GemPlugins
 ** Signals ready.   TERM => stop.  USR2 => restart.  INT => stop (no restart).
 ** Rails signals registered.  HUP => reload (without restart).
 **     It might not work well.
 ** Mongrel available at 0.0.0.0:3000
 ** Use CTRL-C to stop.
```

The script/server command will start Mongrel instead of WEBrick. If the server starts OK, point your browser at http://tracklayer:3000. Remember to replace tracklayer with the IP or domain of your server.

You should see the "Congratulations, you've put Ruby on Rails!" page, so we are done with the basics for our sweet Rails server stack! You're the captain of your own ship now.

4.5 Conclusion

Running your own Rails server is a rewarding experience. With this basic stack in place, you can start to build your empire and tweak it to your every desire. With nginx and Mongrel installed, you have many configuration options to try on your new server.

Now that the basic building blocks are in place, you're ready to use the techniques you'll find in the rest of this book to make your deployment scale—and make it screaming fast.

In this chapter, you've walked through building your basic installation. You have the components to run Ruby via Mongrel or another web server. In the chapters that follow, you'll put each of those components through their paces. You'll start by building some scripts to repeatedly and reliably deploy your applications. If you're excited and ready to move in to this new home, read on. Moving in with Capistrano is next.

Chapter 5

Capistrano

If you've ever rented an apartment or bought a house, you know that the financial transaction is only the first tiny step. Moving in comes next, and the process can be, well, overwhelming. In the previous chapters, you used FTP, SFTP, or Subversion to install your application onto the shared host. You simply found the files you needed to copy, and you used Subversion or FTP to push the whole Rails project directory up to your sever, wholesale. But this limited approach presents several important problems:

- *It's not scalable.* Once you move beyond a single server, your deployment will get much more complicated.
- *You need to schedule downtime.* While you're copying your application, the app is in an inconsistent state, with some of the files from your old application and some from the new.
- *If something goes wrong, it's hard to backtrack.* You would need to put the old version of your application back. Doing so means more manual work or more guesswork.
- *For FTP, you need to handle source control manually.* Unless you're living in the dark ages, you're keeping your code base in a source control system. Most Rails developers use Subversion.[1]
- *The deployment process is not automated.* You have to do it by hand, which leaves room for error. Laziness may be one of the programmer's greatest virtues, but it doesn't make for perfect execution when many steps are involved.

---

1. If you're not using some form of source control, put this book down and run, don't walk, to pick up *Pragmatic Version Control* [Mas05]. Running without version control these days is madness.

You might decide to use an existing tool, such as rsync. The rsync open source utility provides fast, incremental file transfer, meaning it copies only those files that change between one invocation and the next.

This method works a little better than plain old FTP because you don't move all the files at once, but it still has most of the same problems. rsync is usually faster than plain FTP, works better with multiple servers, and works without any additional modifications to your server's configuration. If you are in a situation where you have little control over the rest of the server, this might be an acceptable solution. But as a programmer who aspires to do great things, you want more than just the *acceptable* solution, don't you?

5.1 The Lay of the Land

So far, you have an application that's ready for deployment and served from a common repository and a host. To move in with style, you need some software to manage your move. That's Capistrano. As you see in Figure 5.1, on the next page, the Capistrano tool sits on the developer's client. Think of Capistrano as the moving company that orchestrates your move to make sure your application makes it to the server in an orderly and repeatable manner. You just call them up from any phone, give the command, and they do the work. Capistrano works the same way. You can direct any deployment from the comfort of your development client, without needing to log onto the deployment servers at all.

For the same reason the company wrote Rails, 37signals created Capistrano to solve actual business problems. As its Rails deployments became more regular and more complex, the growing company needed an automated solution to handle complex application deployments. This typically entailed deploying code updates to at least two web servers and one database server. Any solution would need to do at least the following:

- Securely update multiple web and database servers from a central source code control repository.
- Be sensitive to errors, and roll back any changes if necessary.
- Work with the Rails file layout and allow logging to happen without interruption.
- Operate quickly and reduce the need for downtime.
- Work well with Ruby on Rails.

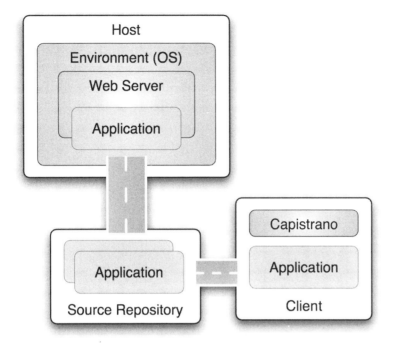

Figure 5.1: CAPISTRANO MAP

In the early stages of Rails development, Jamis Buck wrote an application named Capistrano to solve this problem. Like Rails, Capistrano is opinionated software and assumes that you do the following:

- Deploy to a dedicated server.
- Use a Unix-like operating system and file system on the server.
- Have SSH access to that server.
- Use Subversion or some other form of source code control.
- Have the ability to run commands as root with the sudo command.
- Deploy to a web server, an application server, and a database server (on one or more machines).

Fortunately, you can still configure Capistrano if these assumptions don't hold in your particular situation. Shared hosting is such a situation, and I will show you how to set up a rock-solid recipe for Capistrano later in this chapter.

5.2 How It Works

You will need to install the Capistrano gem and its dependencies. The recipes in this chapter use Capistrano 2.0, so install it now. Remember, local$ is the prompt on your local development machine, and ezra# is the prompt on your development server:

```
local$ sudo gem install capistrano
```

Always keep in mind that Capistrano runs on your local machine. It uses Net::SSH and Net::SFTP to connect to your remote servers and run shell commands on them. This means you do not need to install Capistrano on your remote servers, only on the machines you want to use to trigger a deploy.

Once you've configured Capistrano with a few variables, called a *recipe*, you can deploy with the following simple command (some initial setup is required, which I'll cover next):

```
local$ cap deploy
```

This unassuming command does everything you need to reliably deploy your application. Rather than tell you what's happening in English, you can just look at the Ruby deploy task:

```
task :deploy do
  transaction do
    update_code
    symlink
  end

  restart
end
```

That's a pretty simple block of Ruby code. Capistrano uses a Rake-like syntax for defining tasks that will execute on the server. Each task has a name, followed by a code block. This task, named deploy, does the following:

1. Before either of these lines is executed, Capistrano connects to your server via SSH.
2. The code begins a transaction. That means that all the code will happen in the scope of a transaction. If any part of the transaction fails, the whole transaction will fail, triggering a rollback. I'll cover rollbacks later in this chapter.

3. The first step in the transaction, update_code, does a Subversion checkout to load a full copy of your Rails application into a dated release directory on the remote server. For example, a cap deploy might create a directory called releases/20070416190111. The number 20070416190111 is actually a time stamp for 7:01:11 p.m. on April 16, 2007.

4. The next step in the transaction, symlink, links the log directory for your Rails application to a shared log directory. symlink then links your application's folder to the current directory so the web server can find it.

5. The task finally restarts any active Mongrel or FastCGI processes.

Each of these steps is a critical component to a secure, successful deployment. Using Subversion ensures that Capistrano will always get the right code base. SSH provides the necessary security so your files cannot be compromised in transit, and the symlinks force an instantaneous conversion. The symbolic link also lets you revert to an older version of the code if your code is bad or Capistrano encounters an error. Finally, Capistrano restarts any active Mongrels or FastCGI processes, and the new code goes live.

The Capistrano deploy task is certainly better than rsync, but the automation comes at a cost. You'll need to do a little more setup, but not too much. Before I walk you through the gory details, let's take a look at Capistrano's file organization.

Capistrano's File Organization

37signals built Capistrano specifically to deploy Rails applications, but you can configure it to work with other types of applications too. The default recipe assumes you have a log directory for log files and a public directory for the web server's public files.

Every time you deploy, Capistrano creates a new folder named with the current date and then checks out your entire Rails app into that folder. Next, it wires the whole thing together with several symbolic links. The directory structure is shown in Figure 5.2, on the following page. Notice the current directory doesn't have the physical file structure underneath it. current directory is only a link into a specific dated folder in the releases directory. The result is that current will always hold the current active version of your application. For your convenience, Capistrano also creates a public/system folder and links it to the shared/system directory, helping you retain cache files or uploads between deployments.

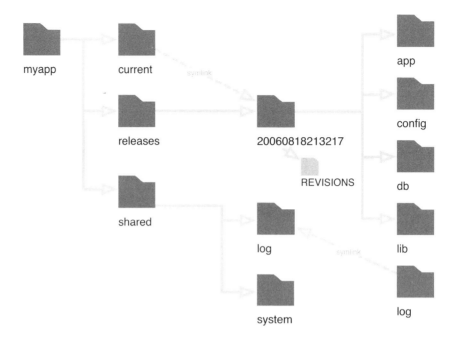

Figure 5.2: THE CURRENT DIRECTORY WITH SYMBOLIC LINKS TO RELEASES

5.3 Local and Remote Setup for Rails

Capistrano configuration isn't too difficult, but you will need to do a few steps on both your development machine and the remote server. I'll list the steps and then go through each in detail. First, on your local machine you'll need to do the following:

1. Install the Capistrano gem.
2. Tell Capistrano about your application so it can add the necessary files to it.
3. Customize config/deploy.rb with your server's information.
4. Import your application into Subversion.

Those local changes prepare your development machine to deploy your code base from Subversion. Next, you'll need to make the following changes on your server:

1. Set your web server's document root to current/public.
2. Do a checkout of your app so Subversion will cache your login information.

> **Practice with a Blank Rails Project**
>
> If you are using Capistrano for the first time, it might help to make a blank Rails project and practice a simple deployment on your server. You don't need to write any code or even create a database. Just use a new project with the default index.html page that is generated by Rails. To create the default project, just type rails projectname.

When you've completed these steps, you can run the cap deploy:setup and cap deploy tasks. Next, I'll show you each independent step in more detail.

Install the Capistrano Gem

You need to install Capistrano only on your development machine, not the server, because Capistrano runs commands on the server with a regular SSH session. If you've installed Rails, you probably already have RubyGems on your system. To install Capistrano, issue this command on your local machine:

```
local$ sudo gem install capistrano

Attempting local installation of 'capistrano'
Local gem file not found: capistrano*.gem
Attempting remote installation of 'capistrano'
Successfully installed capistrano-2.0.0
Successfully installed net-ssh-1.1.1
Successfully installed net-sftp-1.1.0
Installing ri documentation for net-ssh-1.1.1...
Installing ri documentation for net-sftp-1.1.0...
Installing RDoc documentation for net-ssh-1.1.1...
Installing RDoc documentation for net-sftp-1.1.0...
```

While you are installing gems, install the termios gem as well. (Sorry, termios is not readily available for Windows.) By default, Capistrano echoes your password to the screen when you deploy. Installing the termios gem keeps your password hidden from wandering eyes.

Reinstalling Ruby on Mac OS X

Capistrano relies heavily on Ruby's ability to communicate over SSH, which does not work properly with the default Ruby interpreter included with Mac OS X for versions before Leopard. The C bindings do not always work correctly. (Leopard includes Capistrano, Ruby version 1.8.6, and Mongrel.) If you have one of these versions of OS X, you can fix this problem in a couple of ways:

- Install the MacPorts package management system, and let it install Ruby for you. You can download MacPorts* and then run this command:

  ```
  local$ sudo port install ruby
  ```

- Install Ruby from source. Dan Benjamin has step-by-step instructions.† You can find a shell script that automates an installation of Ruby using Dan's instructions online.‡

---

*. http://macports.org/
†. http://hivelogic.com/narrative/articles/ruby-rails-mongrel-mysql-osx
‡. http://nubyonrails.com/pages/install

To install termios, type the following:

```
local$ sudo gem install termios

Attempting local installation of 'termios'
Local gem file not found: termios*.gem
Attempting remote installation of 'termios'
Building native extensions.  This could take a while...
ruby extconf.rb install termios
checking for termios.h... yes
checking for unistd.h... yes
...
Successfully installed termios-0.9.4
```

Generate an Application Deployment File

A deployment file brings together all the Ruby scripts and configuration parameters that Capistrano needs to deploy your application. Just as the Rails script/generate command generates some default application code that you later modify, Capistrano has a special flag to copy a few Rake tasks and a sample deployment file to the proper locations inside your Rails application.

Generate your deployment file now by typing the following command:

```
local$ cd my_rails_app
local$ capify .
[add] writing `./Capfile'
[add] writing `./config/deploy.rb'
[done] capified!
```

Let's break down what just happened.

capify is the Capistrano script. The dot tells it to install in the current directory. Alternatively, you can provide the full or relative path to your Rails app. The command creates a config/deploy.rb file, which contains the deployment hosts, and Capfile, which tells Capistrano to load its default deploy recipes and where to look for your deploy.rb when you run cap deploy from inside your Rails application.

Customize config/deploy.rb

Here is a first glance at the default deploy.rb recipe file that the capify created for you:

```
set :application, "set your application name here"
set :repository,  "set your repository location here"

# If you aren't deploying to /u/apps/#{application} on the target
# servers (which is the default), you can specify the actual location
# via the :deploy_to variable:
# set :deploy_to, "/var/www/#{application}"

# If you aren't using Subversion to manage your source code, specify
# your SCM below:
# set :scm, :subversion

role :app, "your app-server here"
role :web, "your web-server here"
role :db,  "your db-server here", :primary => true
```

There's no rocket science in deploy.rb. The :application symbol defines the deployment target application's name. The :repository symbol defines the Subversion repository for the application. The next three roles then define the machines that serve as the web, application, and database servers for your application. Most applications will need to set a few variables depending on the installed location of the application, the user deploying the app, and the web servers involved.

Here is a slightly more customized deploy.rb file:

```
# Customized deploy.rb
set :application, "brainspl.at"
set :repository, "http://brainspl.at/svn/#{application}"
set :scm_username, 'ezra'
set :scm_password, proc{Capistrano::CLI.password_prompt('SVN pass:')}
role :web, "web1.brainspl.at", "web2.brainspl.at"
role :app, "app1.brainspl.at", "app2.brainspl.at"
role :db,  "db.brainspl.at", :primary => true

set :user, "ezra"
set :deploy_to, "/home/#{user}/#{application}"

set :deploy_via, :export
```

The most obvious differences in the default file and the customized file are the roles and the few lines below that. Roles are groupings of machines that handle different tasks for your application. The key roles are the web server (Apache), application server (Mongrel), and database server (MySQL). Now, look at the next few lines below the roles.

Capistrano lets you customize many different elements related to your servers, your application, authentication, and Subversion. The previous script customizes the deployment directory, the system user, the :scm_username command, the :scm_password command, and the command used to access Subversion.

In Capistrano 2.0, Subversion is the default SCM module. The user and password used to connect to your Subversion repository are defined as :scm_username and :scm_password. If you use a different source code repository, then you can set the :scm variable in your deploy recipe. For example, if you use Darcs instead of Subversion, it would look like this:

```
set :scm_username, 'ezra'
set :scm_password, proc{Capistrano::CLI.password_prompt('Darcs pass:')}
set :scm, 'darcs'
```

You will notice that we have something different going on for the :scm_password variable. Since we don't want to hard-code the password in our deploy recipe, we have asked Capistrano to prompt us for the password every time we run a deploy.

If you're running a shared host, you can't run with root access, so you'll need to handle restarts a little differently.

Setup Apache or lighttpd to Use the Maintenance Page

The deploy:web:enable task assumes your server will serve the public/system/maintenance.html page instead of the real site, if the maintenance page exists. Add the following Rewrite directive to your Apache config or your local .htaccess in order to make deploy:web:disable work correctly:

```
RewriteCond %{DOCUMENT_ROOT}/system/maintenance.html -f
RewriteCond %{SCRIPT_FILENAME} !maintenance.html
RewriteRule ^.*$ /system/maintenance.html [L]
```

This rewrite rule says that if there is a file called %{DOCU-MENT_ROOT}/system/maintenance.html, rewrite all requests to /system/maintenance.html. With that rewrite rule in place, if the maintenance page exists, the web server will deliver it to satisfy any requests to this application regardless of what URL they requested.

In the following code, I use a script called the reaper that does the trick:

```
set :use_sudo, false
set :run_method, :run

namespace(:deploy) do
  desc "Restart with shared-host reaper"
  task :restart do
    run "#{current_path}/script/process/reaper --dispatcher=dispatch.fcgi"
  end
end
```

Notice that the :restart is defined inside the namespace(:deploy) block. Capistrano 2 has an organization concept of namespaces. Namespaces let you collect related concepts into a central grouping of names. The method namespace takes a single parameter, defining the namespace, and a code block. All of the Capistrano tasks in the code block will be part of that namespace. In this case, I'm adding the :restart task to the default namespace. I'll create all the deploy-related tasks inside that namespace. To call this restart task in the deploy namespace, you need to specify the namespace, like this:

```
local$ cap deploy:restart
```

Import Your App into Subversion

In Chapter 5, *Capistrano*, on page 85, you learned how to place your code under source control, if you were not already doing so. Capistrano works with several source code control systems, but Subversion is the most common. Many shared hosts offer Subversion hosting, or you can install the Subversion server on your own dedicated or VPS server (see Chapter 4, *Virtual and Dedicated Hosts*, on page 65).

You will save configuration time by creating a repository named for your deployment domain. For example, the brainspl.at repository stores the Rails app that powers the Brainspl.at site.[2] To import the project for the very first time, issue the following command:

```
ezra$ svn import brainspl.at http://brainspl.at/svn/brainspl.at
```

brainspl.at is the local directory containing the application. The source control server is brainspl.at. The repository on the server is also named brainspl.at.

After importing a project for the first time, you must check out a new copy. The new copy will have all the extra files Capistrano needs to keep everything synchronized. To edit the code for development, you can issue this command:

```
local$ svn checkout http://brainspl.at/svn/brainspl.at
```

To prevent confusion, it's a good idea to use a separate password for checking out code on your server instead of the one you use for your local workstation. From this point, you can make changes to the source and synchronize it with the server by issuing the svn commit command:

```
local$ svn commit --message "Bugs have been fixed!"
```

Setting Your Public Document Root

The document root is a directory your shared host uses to serve all your static web pages. Rails will manage all the dynamic content. The local host uses a web server such as Apache to serve your static content—images, HTML pages, JavaScripts, and style sheets. In Rails, the public directory holds all static content. Since the current directory points to your Rails application, you need to set your document root to current/public. Just how you do so will depend on whether you have a shared or dedicated host and on the web server you're using. Your hosting provider will tell you how to set that document root appropriately.

---

2. http://brainspl.at

Cache Your Password on the Remote Server

Subversion clients cache login credentials for convenience and performance. But remember, Capistrano runs commands in a shell on the server, not your local host. To make things work smoothly, you need to log in to Subversion at least once from the remote server so the remote server's Subversion client caches your username and password. When you deploy, the server will use the cached information to do checkouts from the repository. An easy way to invoke Subversion is to request a listing from your repository from any directory on the remote server, like so:

```
ezra$ svn list http://brainspl.at/svn/brainspl.at
Password: ******
Rakefile
app/
config/
db/
doc/
lib/
log/
public/
script/
test/
vendor/
```

After you type the command, Subversion will prompt you for your password and then show a list of the folders in the repository. More important, the remote server will be able to cache your username and password for subsequent Capistrano commands.

Run the setup and deploy Tasks

You are nearly done! Capistrano needs to create a few directories on the remote server for organization, so run the setup task:

```
local$ cap deploy:setup
 * executing `deploy:setup'
 * executing "umask 02 && mkdir -p /home/ezra/brainspl.at/releases
 /home/ezra/brainspl.at/shared /home/ezra/brainspl.at/shared/system
 /home/ezra/brainspl.at/shared/log /home/ezra/brainspl.at/shared/pids"

    servers: ["brainspl.at"]
Password: ******
    [brainspl.at] executing command
    command finished
```

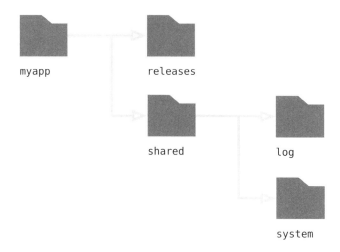

Figure 5.3: DIRECTORY LAYOUT ON THE SERVER AFTER SETUP

---

setup creates the releases and shared directories on the remote server as in Figure 5.3. No current directory exists yet since you've not yet deployed. You're finally ready to remedy that. Run the deploy task for the first time:

```
local$ cap deploy
```

If you have a standard setup, you should have a running application, but you should be aware of a few variations on the plain deploy task. If you're running FastCGI and no listeners are running now, you may need to run the deploy:cold task instead so Capistrano knows to start FastCGI listeners. Also, if your application has new migrations and you haven't run them yet, you should run cap deploy:migrations to populate your database with the initial schema.

If all has gone well, you will be able to see your new site in a web browser. If not, see the troubleshooting sections in Chapter 4, *Virtual and Dedicated Hosts*, on page 65 and Chapter 3, *Shared Hosts*, on page 37.

You've spent a little time getting your deployment right, but you should already be seeing the benefits. You now have a deploy command that is also secure, integrated with source control, informative to your users, and completely automated. True, I've shown you only the most basic setup so far, but in the rest of the chapter I'll walk you through a few more scenarios. First, let me lay a little foundation for customization.

Under the Hood

By now you should understand the basics of Capistrano. Before you start to customize it, I should provide a little more detail about how Capistrano executes tasks. Take a look under the hood.

Capistrano Runs Locally

Some developers get a little confused with where and how Capistrano works. In principle, Capistrano is a client-side tool that issues remote commands via SSH. From that point, the commands run within the bash shell just as if you had logged in to the server and typed them manually. So, the remote server doesn't need to know anything about Capistrano, and you don't even need to install the Capistrano gem there, but you do need the bash shell.

Code Synchronization Happens from Subversion

Local changes to your copy of the source don't affect the code on the remote server! Capistrano synchronizes the remote server from the remote repository, so you must commit any code changes that you want deployed.

I just lied a little, but only a little. One piece of code does not come from Subversion: deploy.rb. All changes to deploy.rb will take effect during deployment whether those changes have been checked in or not. You already know why: that's the script that runs Capistrano, including the code that exports the current version of your app. It's still a good idea to keep your deploy script under source code control with the rest of your project.

Now, you've seen the basic Capistrano deploy script in action, but only in the default configuration with very few customizations. In the sections that follow, I'll show you how to create your own Capistrano tasks and customize your existing tasks to handle more demanding scenarios. First, you'll see some tasks, called *recipes*, that handle some common tasks.

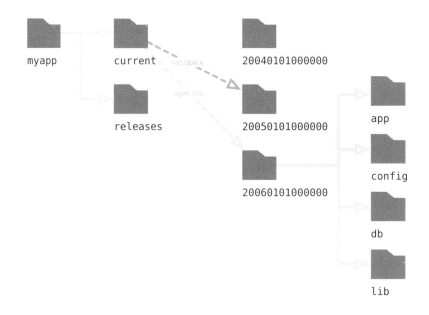

Figure 5.4: THE ROLLBACK TASK

5.4 Standard Recipes

Developers across the globe continually enhance Capistrano. To see the name and description of the current built-in tasks, use the cap -T command. As an added bonus, cap -T shows any of your own custom tasks too, as long as they have a description. From the root of your Rails application, do this:

```
local$ cap -T
```

Here are a few useful tasks:

cap deploy:migrate Use the power of the Rails migration system to update your database or manipulate data. This task will migrate the currently deployed code, so use deploy first, or use the composite deploy:migrations task to keep everything synchronized.

cap deploy:rollback Houston, we have a problem! Something went wrong, and you need to revert to the previous version of your code. Running this task activates your previous release. You can run this several times in a row to continue rolling back to older and older versions as shown in Figure 5.4. Remember that this uses only the versions that you've previously deployed to the server, not older tagged versions from the repository. This task does not touch the database. If older versions of your code require downward migrations, you will have to revert to a previous migration manually.

cap deploy:cleanup deploy:cleanup deletes older versions from the releases folder. By default, cleanup leaves the five latest versions, but you can configure this number with the :keep_releases variable in your recipe. You could set an after "deploy", "deploy:cleanup" callback task to run deploy:cleanup automatically, but remember that you won't be able to deploy:rollback further than the number of releases currently on the server.

cap invoke COMMAND='uname -a' Run a single command on the remote server. invoke is useful for doing one-time tasks such as executing Rake tasks.

cap deploy:web:disable This command copies a file called public/system/maintenance.html with messages when your site is down. Using deploy:web:disable requires you to first set up your web server to use a static error page if it exists. deploy:web:disable simply copies that file to the public/system directory, which your web server will show to any clients, thus bypassing the web server when your Rails site is down for maintenance.

cap deploy:web:enable The opposite of deploy:web:disable, deploy:web:enable deletes the temporary maintenance file created by the deploy:web:disable task.

When you call the deploy:web:disable task, you can pass in two environmental variables, UNTIL and REASON. Capistrano will render these into the maintenance.html page that your web server displayed while your site is down for maintenance. Here is an example call:

```
local$ cap deploy:web:disable UNTIL='4:30pm' ↩
       REASON='We are deploying new features,↩
       please check back shortly.'
```

5.5 Writing Tasks

Capistrano is even more powerful when you start writing your own tasks. Jamis Buck used Ruby's metaprogramming capabilities to write Capistrano. If you've used Rake (written by Ruby's metaprogramming master, Jim Weirich), you'll understand the general format of a Capistrano task, with a few minor differences that you can find in Section 5.5, *Like Rake, Not Exactly*, on page 110.

Capistrano has many built-in tasks and capabilities that are always evolving. As with Rails itself, it is being developed at a rapid rate, and this chapter has been rewritten several times as new features have been added. Even now, Capistrano developers are discussing plans that would drastically change the internal organization of Capistrano, but the external interface and operation of existing tasks should remain the same. For the most current information on Capistrano's built-in methods and variables, see the online documentation.[3]

Setting Variables

The standard deploy task uses several user-customized variables in order to find the server, repository, and remote directory in which to deploy an application. If you are writing your own recipes, you can also create variables with the set() method:

```
set :food, "chunky bacon"
```

The food variable becomes a local variable for any task, on either side of a standard assignment. I can then use the variable as follows:

```
set :breakfast, "a hot slab of #{food}"

task :serve_breakfast, :roles => :web do
  run <<-CMD
    echo "Are you ready for #{breakfast}?"
  CMD
end
```

This important task prints "Are you ready for a hot slab of chunky bacon?" You can also use the set() method with an array, a hash, or any other kind of object. You can even assign the variable to the output of any method, like so:

```
set :projects, ['todo_list', 'lib/payment_library']

desc "Update remote folders from the repository"
task :update_projects do
  projects.each do |project|
    run "svn update /home/ezra/#{project}"
  end
end
```

---

3. http://capify.org/

In the previous code listing, I set the projects variable to an array value. I reuse that variable in a task that Capistrano runs on the remote server.

Lazy Evaluation of Variables

Sometimes you want to define a variable that uses other variables that haven't been defined yet. No problem. You can enclose your variable within {}, and Capistrano will use lazy evaluation. For example:

```
set(:released_stylesheets_dir) {"#{release_path}/public/stylesheets"}
```

In the previous example, Capistrano will evaluate #{release_path} when it uses the string. Lazy evaluation lets you wait to bind a given variable to a value, increasing your flexibility.

Standard Variables and Their Default Values

Capistrano has many different predefined variables. You can set them to configure different tasks in different ways. Capistrano creates them for use with your tasks or within other custom variables that you set. These are some of the predefined variables and their associated uses:

- :application has no default. This variable has the name of your application. Other variables such as deploy_to use this variable. You will probably want to set this to the domain name of the application you are deploying or to the preferred nickname for your application.

- :repository has no default. This variable defines the address of your Subversion repository containing the code you want to deploy.

- :user defaults to the currently logged-in user. This variable defines the SSH user Capistrano will use to deploy the application. If your username on your deployment machine is the same as your SSH username, then you can use the default value. This user account will also be used to check out code from the repository and perform sudo commands during the deployment process.

- :deploy_to defaults to /u/apps/#{application}. This variable defines the target deployment directory.

- :use_sudo defaults to true. Capistrano often needs to run commands under the root user. You can suppress this behavior by setting use_sudo to false.

- :run_method defaults to :sudo. Capistrano uses this option to determine whether the cap deploy:restart should run under the current user (specify the :run value) or root (specify the :sudo option).

- :password has no default. This parameter defines your password for SSH authentication. If you leave this blank, Capistrano will prompt you for the password when you try to deploy.

- :deploy_via defaults to :co. This command defines which Subversion command Capistrano should use to check out your application from your repository. Most Rails developers now use :export instead in order to avoid displaying .svn directory information via the Web.

- :shared_path, :release_path, and :current_path all point to the various directories in your environment, as I've described in this chapter.

Defining Tasks

Now that you've seen a few existing Capistrano variables and tasks, it's time to build your own. Tasks consist of a description, a name, and a list of applicable roles. They are similar to Rake tasks (Section 5.5, *Like Rake, Not Exactly*, on page 110).

Any custom tasks you write that are used during your deployment process should be put in the :deploy namespace. For the following tasks, we will assume they are being defined inside the namespace.

Here is a simple task:

```
desc "Delete cached files"
task :sweep_remote_cache, :roles => :web do
  run "cd #{release_path}; rake sweep_cache RAILS_ENV=production"
end
```

The sweep_remote_cache command runs the Rake task called sweep_cache. The benefit of building a Capistrano task to do this job is that I can run the task from my development machine. Take a look in greater detail:

- desc is a short description Capistrano will show when anyone runs the cap -T command. This tag is optional, but it's a good idea to use it since your tasks will not show up when you run cap -T unless they have a description defined.

- task identifies the name of the task.

- :roles limits the task to certain groups of servers. The most common roles are :app, :db, and :web. You can define your own roles and subroles should you have the need.

The rest of the script contains more conventional Ruby code. Capistrano provides these methods to make custom task-writing easier:

- run and sudo: Most tasks will use one of these methods. Each sends shell commands to the remote server, but sudo runs the commands as root. See the Capistrano page at the Ruby on Rails site[4] for more details.

- put: This uploads a file to the remote server.

- delete: This forcibly deletes a file on the server.

- on_rollback: This executes whenever you explicitly issue a cap deploy:rollback or when a cap command within a transaction fails.

Here is the definition of the deploy:web:disable task from Capistrano's default recipes:

```
namespace :web do
  task :disable, :roles => :web, :except => { :no_release => true } do
    require 'erb'
    on_rollback { run "rm #{shared_path}/system/maintenance.html" }

    reason = ENV['REASON']
    deadline = ENV['UNTIL']

    template = File.read(File.join(File.dirname(__FILE__), "templates", ↩
      "maintenance.rhtml"))
    result = ERB.new(template).result(binding)

    put result, "#{shared_path}/system/maintenance.html", :mode => 0644
  end
end
```

This demonstrates the proper use of the on_rollback and put tasks available to any Capistrano recipe file.

Using the Built-in Callbacks

If you want to add functionality to the standard deployment process to run a Ruby script when you deploy your application, the best way is to use the built-in callback system. For every task, Capistrano looks

---

4. http://manuals.rubyonrails.com/read/chapter/104

> ## Use the cap Shortcut for Custom Tasks
>
> The easiest way to run custom tasks is to use the cap command-line tool. Capistrano will automatically discover the config/deploy.rb recipe file and will run actions that are passed as arguments. It does this by looking for a Capfile in the current working directory that tells it which deploy.rb to load.
>
> ```
> # With cap command and arguments
> local$ cap -f config/deploy.rb  my_custom_task
>
> # The same command, but even simpler!
> local$ cap my_custom_task
> ```

for a before and after task and calls each one at the appropriate time if it exists. This was how you would write callbacks in Capistrano 1.*x*. In Capistrano 2, there is a more event-driven callback mechanism with methods called before() and after().

I mentioned earlier that the deploy task calls three other tasks. This gives you a total of four tasks that you can hook in to. If you write a task named before_deploy, Capistrano will execute it in advance of the rest of the deployment process. Similarly, after_deploy will run after the deployment task.

Here is a short bit of pseudocode that illustrates how this works:

```
--> before_deploy
deploy do
  --> before_update_code
  update_code
  --> after_update_code
  --> before_symlink
  symlink
  --> after_symlink
  --> before_restart
  restart
  --> after_restart
end
--> after_deploy
```

In addition, Capistrano automatically creates callbacks for each of your own tasks, opening a world of possibilities.

For any task you define, you automatically get a before and after task:

```
task :global_thermonuclear_war do
  ...
end

task :before_global_thermonuclear_war do
  kiss_your_butt_goodbye
end

task :after_global_thermonuclear_war do
  paint_the_house
end
```

At this point, I'm sure your mind is racing with the possibilities. Need to check out code and run the test suite before every deployment? Check. Want to send email to admins after every deployment? Yup. Give yourself a raise in after_symlink? Possible, but not likely. With before and after tasks, you can extend the right task at exactly the right time.

Now, you *can* take things too far. Let your mind wander a little bit, and you'll see what I mean. If before_deploy is also a task, you could conceivably write a before_before_deploy task. In fact, you can write an action as convoluted as before_before_after_before_deploy, which looks like something out of a Monty Python skit. I said you could do it, not that you should do it. In fact, I'd like a deployment without so much before in it!

I hope you never write such a task. Still, imagine with me a little bit longer. A task without any roles will be executed on all servers and all roles, no matter what the parent task is. It seems that before_wash_dishes should happen only on the kitchen server if wash_dishes was defined as a task that happens on the kitchen server. Not so! You must explicitly specify :role => :kitchen for any task that needs to be restricted to the kitchen server:

```
role :kitchen, "kitchen.ezra.com"
role :home_theater, "theater.ezra.com"

# Executed on all servers!
task :before_wash_dishes do
  ...
end

# Executed only on the servers that have the :kitchen role
task :wash_dishes, :roles => :kitchen do
  ...
end
```

```
# Here's the right way to limit this to one group of servers
task :after_wash_dishes, :roles => :kitchen do
  ...
end
```

Having taken that trip down the rabbit hole, it is usually better to refactor your tasks and give them self-documenting names. A make_dinner task makes much more sense than a generic before_wash_dishes task. Here's the revised code, with a better name:

```
desc "Perform household maintenance."
task :maintain_house, :roles => :estate do
  mow_lawn
  prepare_soap_bucket
  wash_car
  wax_car
  make_dinner
  wash_dishes
end
```

Defining callbacks by making tasks named after your tasks with before_ or after_ prepended is still a valid method of using callbacks in Capistrano. But there is also new syntax for defining callbacks that are a bit cleaner. For example:

```
desc "Perform household maintenance."
task :maintain_house, :roles => :estate do
  mow_lawn
  prepare_soap_bucket
  wash_car
  wax_car
  make_dinner
  wash_dishes
end

before "deploy", "maintain_house"
```

As you can see, this new notation allows you to name your tasks whatever you desire and still be able to hook them to certain events.

Consider a more practical problem. If your database.yml file is not under source code control—remember, database.yml has your password—you need to use another method to copy it to your server when you deploy. Writing an after callback task is a perfect way to solve this problem.

When you run cap deploy, Capistrano calls other tasks that you can define without having to override the built-in tasks. To build such a task, you would save the appropriate password information to a file in shared/config/database.yml. The shared folder is made by Capistrano when you run the deploy:setup task, but you will have to make the config folder manually. If you have a cluster of servers, you will have to do this on each of your servers. The following task shows how. Add it to deploy.rb:

```
desc "Symlink the database config file from shared
      directory to current release directory."
task :symlink_database_yml do
  run "ln -nsf #{shared_path}/config/database.yml
      #{release_path}/config/database.yml"
end

after 'deploy:update_code', 'symlink_database_yml'
```

Because we did not specify any roles, Capistrano will run the task on all the servers in the cluster (:app, :web, :db, and any others you define). Anytime you deploy, your script will symlink database.yml to the config folder in the current release directory. It's just so easy!

Using Roles

By default, Capistrano executes tasks in parallel on all the servers defined with the role command. You can limit the scope of a command by explicitly specifying the roles for that task. It is also important to note that Capistrano also runs tasks in parallel, but not concurrently. Imagine three tasks and three servers:

```
role :web, ['one', 'two', 'three']

task :daily do
  wash_dishes
  mow_lawn
  learn_japanese
end
```

The tasks would be executed like this:

```
local$ cap daily
* wash_dishes on server one
* wash_dishes on server two
* wash_dishes on server three

* mow_lawn on server one
* mow_lawn on server two
* mow_lawn on server three

* learn_japanese on server one
* learn_japanese on server two
* learn_japanese on server three
```

Like Rake, Not Exactly

Earlier I told you that Capistrano was almost exactly like Rake. I'm sure you noticed the *almost*. I'll point those differences out now.

Tasks Are Methods

Unlike Rake, other tasks can call Capistrano tasks directly, just as if they were methods. Rake tasks can call other Rake tasks only as tasks, but not as methods. Capistrano uses this feature internally, but you can use it in your tasks, too. For example, here is a simple task:

```
desc "Play a war game"
task :play_global_thermonuclear_war do
  ...
end
```

play_global_thermonuclear_war is a Capistrano task, but you can call it from another task like a normal method:

```
desc "Play several games"
task :play_games do
  play_global_thermonuclear_war
  play_llor_dot_nu
end
```

This strategy lets you run a task alone or together with other tasks. For example, you could call a :rotate_logs task from a task called :weekly or alone.

You Can't List Other Tasks as Dependencies of a Capistrano Task

With Rake, you can pass the name of a task as a hash where the key is the task name and the values are the other tasks that must be run before the current task. Capistrano doesn't use this syntax. Instead, you must call other tasks as methods or write before and after callbacks, as mentioned previously.

You Can Override Capistrano Tasks

Rake lets you define tasks in stages, so it is not possible to override an existing Rake task. Capistrano gives you the ability to override tasks. If you don't like the behavior of a built-in task, you can redefine it. For example, if you are deploying to a shared host, you might need to send a special argument to the reaper script in order to restart your FastCGI processes.

To do this, define your own restart task as if it had never been written:

```
namespace(:deploy) do
  desc "Shared host restart"
  task :restart do
    run "#{current_path}/script/process/reaper --dispatcher=dispatch.fcgi"
  end
end
```

Other built-in tasks such as deploy will now use this task instead of the built-in deploy:restart task.

Capistrano Tasks Aren't Automatically Available as Rake Tasks

Even though Capistrano tasks look like Rake tasks, they are part of a separate system. Rake doesn't know about Capistrano tasks, even though older versions of Capistrano tried to bridge that gap. The approved way to call Capistrano tasks is with the cap command. It will automatically discover recipes in config/deploy.rb (depending on the contents of Capfile):

```
local$ cap deploy
```

5.6 A Little Extra Flavor

In this section, I'll walk you through the topics that will make your Capistrano experience a little sweeter. You'll sometimes want to see extra output or speed up your checkouts. These extra touches can really improve your overall experience.

Stream

Capistrano has a built-in helper called stream. You can use this helper to stream information such as log files and other stats from your remote servers to your local terminal.

You can use a task like this to tail the log files of your server:

```
capistrano/recipes/stream.rb
```

```
task :tail_log, :roles => :app do
  stream "tail -f #{shared_path}/log/production.log"
end
```

You can also continuously monitor the output of a shell command with Capistrano's streaming callbacks.

For example, to get the output of the rails_stat log parser, you would use something like this:

```
capistrano/recipes/stream.rb
```

```ruby
desc "Watch continuous rails_stat output"
task :rails_stat, :roles => [:app] do
  sudo "rails_stat /var/log/production.log" do |channel, stream, data|
    puts data if stream == :out
    if stream == :err
      puts "[Error: #{channel[:host]}] #{data}"
      break
    end
  end
end
```

In this task, you can see that the sudo method takes a block with three parameters: channel, stream, and data. The channel is the raw SSH connection, the stream is equal to either :out or :err, and the data is the output from the server.

This produces the following output on my blog:

```
~ 0.4 req/sec, 2.6 queries/sec, 6.7 lines/sec
~ 0.3 req/sec, 1.4 queries/sec, 4.3 lines/sec
~ 0.6 req/sec, 0.6 queries/sec, 4.2 lines/sec
~ 0.5 req/sec, 0.5 queries/sec, 3.5 lines/sec
~ 0.2 req/sec, 0.2 queries/sec, 1.4 lines/sec
```

Run Solo

Capistrano can do any kind of task that can be run over SSH, and it can be used with other technologies such as PHP, Perl, or Python (I've used it to deploy a web app written in Perl). I run my blog off the Typo trunk but use a separate theme that is stored in my own repository. To easily update it on the remote server, I use a custom recipe kept in its own deploy.rb file within the theme directory:

```ruby
set :application, "example.com"
set :user, "ezra"
role :web, application

desc "Update the theme and delete cached CSS files."
task :theme_update, :roles => :web do
  run "svn update #{application}/themes/nuby"
  run "rm #{application}/public/stylesheets/theme/*.css"
end
```

What's happening here? I use Capistrano's built-in capability to connect to a remote server and execute commands. By specifying a :role for the task, it knows that it should connect to all the :web servers and run the svn update and rm commands. I also used its ability to set local variables like :application to simplify the recipe. I keep the files in a folder with the name of the domain, which makes it simple to specify a path to the theme folder and the cached style sheets.

To deploy, you could call it from the command line like this:

```
local$ cap -f /path/to/deploy.rb theme_update
```

Since deploy.rb is in a nonstandard location, use the -f argument to specify the location on the file system. Then you need to specify the task to run with theme_update. This makes it easy to address deploy recipes anywhere on your computer rather than only those in the standard locations.

Capistrano will prompt you for your password and will execute the actions, showing the output as it happens. It will not do the standard deploy:update_code, deploy:symlink, and other tasks. Those are only part of the deploy task. If you write your own tasks, they will be executed independently.

You could also use Capistrano in a similar fashion to do maintenance tasks built into Rails, including log rotation and session sweeping:

```
desc "A Capistrano task that runs a remote rake task."
task :clear_sessions, :roles => :db do
  run "cd #{release_path}; rake db:sessions:clear RAILS_ENV=production"
end
```

Do a Push Deploy Instead of Pull with a Custom Deployment Strategy

Capistrano is a great system by default. But some people would rather push a tarball of their application code base to the servers rather than let the servers pull the application from Subversion. Luckily, Capistrano 2.0 has different deployment strategy, and it's easy to change the deploy to work via push instead of pull:

```
set :deploy_via, :copy
```

Just changing the :deploy_via variable to :copy will alter the behavior of your deploy. Now instead of logging in to your servers and doing an svn export, Capistrano will now do a local Subversion checkout to a temporary location on your local machine. It will then compress and create a gzipped tarball of your application. Once it has the tarball, it will upload it to the server and create a new release directory. The rest of the deploy tasks will remain unchanged, and all your symlinks and callbacks will fire like usual. This is extremely useful if you can access your Subversion repository only from inside your office building but not from your servers. Now you can deploy via push to avoid this issue.

5.7 Troubleshooting

Since Capistrano executes remotely on the target server via SSH, debugging can be difficult. These tips can help you troubleshoot your scripts when things go wrong.

The current Directory Can't Exist as an Actual Folder

Capistrano is a tremendously convenient tool, but it's part of your infrastructure. As with Rake or other Rails scripts, you might find debugging Capistrano recipes a little intimidating. Take heart, though. It's all Ruby code.

Shared hosts often give you a directory called current as part of the overall setup process. The recipes that I've shown you will create that directory for you. You'll want to delete the host's version.

Migrations Out of Sync with Code Base

Capistrano usually makes it easy to deal with migrations if you follow the precautions I lay out in Chapter 2, *Refining Applications for Production*, on page 13. That chapter laid out what you should do to keep your migrations well behaved. If you've gotten yourself into trouble, keep these tricks up your sleeve to get you back out.

One problem can occur with partially completed migrations. If a migration has a bug in the up() or down() method, your migration might leave your database in an inconsistent state, or you may be lucky and need only to set the version number correctly. If your version number is wrong, you need to reset it with a SQL query.[5] You can easily do so in the console or from the Rails script runner. Say Rails crashed in migration 44 before setting the version in the schema information, so your migrations are always crashing on number 43. You can set the version

---

5. Alternatively, you can use the transactional_migration plug-in at http://www.redhillonrails. org/#transactional_migrations.

column of schema_info to 44 with this command: ruby script/runner 'Active Record::Base.connection.execute "update schema_info set version=44"'.

You may also have a situation where Rails is breaking because the version of code your migration needs is inconsistent with an earlier migration. (If you put your models in your migrations, this problem won't occur.) You can solve the problem by deploying an earlier version by running your migrations (on the server) up to a specific version like this: rake db:migrate VERSION=42.

Then, you can simply run cap deploy:migrations to deploy your current code base with the rest of your migrations.

Only the Contents of log and public/system Will Be Kept Between Deployments

Each time you deploy, Capistrano makes a time-stamped release directory. If you have user-generated file uploads that end up in public, they will disappear the next time you deploy. This is because Capistrano made a new release directory and symlinked to it. My favorite way to fix this is to make an after 'deploy:update_code'() hook task to symlink your own folders into public from the Capistrano shared directory.

Assume you have a public/avatars directory where you store uploaded avatars. You want this directory to persist between deployments and not get overwritten. You need to create an empty avatars directory in the Capistrano shared directory and then have it get symlinked into the proper place each time you deploy:

```
after 'deploy:update_code', 'deploy:link_images'
namespace(:deploy) do
  task :link_images do
    run <<-CMD
      cd #{release_path} &&
      ln -nfs #{shared_path}/avatars #{release_path}/public/avatars
    CMD
  end
end
```

User Permissions

The user performing the SSH deployment will own all your files. You need to remember that the web server user must be able to read and write to all of the appropriate files. Most Rails shops use a single deployment ID to deploy. If you must change permissions as part of a Capistrano script, use an after task to change permissions if necessary.

Keep in mind that any cron runner or email-receiving task should also have write access to the appropriate log file.

5.8 Conclusion

In this chapter, you've taken a pretty deep stroll through Capistrano. You can now deploy your application in a repeatable, reliable way. You've also learned to extend Capistrano using recipes or callbacks.

In the chapters to come, I'll shift the focus to your application. You now know the basics for Rails deployments. It's time to read about the finer points. In the next chapter, you will learn to build applications that are friendlier to your production environment. Read on.

Chapter 6

Managing Your Mongrels

By now, you've located a good home and moved in. If you've chosen to manage your own deployment and followed the steps in this book, you have a single Mongrel running your application. Things will start happening very quickly now. The next step is to make sure your house is running smoothly and that it is safe. Part of that job will be clustering and configuring Mongrel. Next, you'll want to get a watchdog to help keep an eye on things. In this chapter, you'll learn Mongrel configuration, clustering, and monitoring.

6.1 The Lay of the Land

Clustering Mongrel is the first step to achieving better scalability with Ruby on Rails. You'll find the process amazingly easy to do. First, you'll build a customized configuration file that will let you predictably and reliably restart Mongrel with an automated script. Then, you'll use a Mongrel cluster to launch more than one Mongrel so that your installation can share many simultaneous requests.

After you have a working cluster, you will place that cluster under a monitoring process called Monit. This watchdog process will take action when rogue Mongrel processes take up too much memory, stop responding, or misbehave in other ways. The Mongrel cluster under management from Monit is shown in Figure 6.1, on page 119.

6.2 Training Your Mongrels

You've seen how easy it is to use a Mongrel server in its default configuration. In practice, you're often going to need more flexibility than the default configuration can provide. You will want to cluster your Mongrels and probably run them as a service. Fortunately, configuring Mongrel and even enabling Mongrel clusters is surprisingly easy. As you recall, to start Mongrel, you want to run the following commands:

```
ezra$ cd /path/to/railsapp
ezra$ mongrel_rails start -d
```

That command starts a Mongrel daemon running in the background on port 3000. It is just as simple to restart or stop the server. You'd use mongrel_rails restart to restart and mongrel_rails stop to stop. But these commands simply take your dog for a walk. You are ready to teach your dog a few more advanced tricks. You can train your dog with much more control through a variety of command-line options and configuration files.

The mongrel_rails command-line tool contains explanations for all its options. To access this embedded documentation, use the -h flag:

```
 ezra$ mongrel_rails start -h
Usage: mongrel_rails <command> [options]
    -e, --environment ENV    Rails environment to run as
    -d, --daemonize          Whether to run in the background or not
    -p, --port PORT          Which port to bind to
    -a, --address ADDR       Address to bind to
    -l, --log FILE           Where to write log messages
    -P, --pid FILE           Where to write the PID
    -n, --num-procs INT      Number of processors active before clients denied
    -t, --timeout TIME       Timeout all requests after 100th seconds time
    -m, --mime PATH          A YAML file that lists additional MIME types
    -c, --chdir PATH         Change to dir before starting (will be expanded)
    -r, --root PATH          Set the document root (default 'public')
    -B, --debug              Enable debugging mode
    -C, --config PATH        Use a config file
    -S, --script PATH        Load the given file as an extra config script.
    -G, --generate CONFIG    Generate a config file for -C
        --user USER          User to run as
        --group GROUP        Group to run as
        --prefix PATH        URL prefix for Rails app
    -h, --help               Show this message
        --version            Show version
```

Keep in mind that this list will doubtlessly change as Mongrel grows and improves. For a detailed explanation of every command-line option, refer to the great online how-to.[1] You can also find excellent documentation at the Mongrel website.[2]

---

1. http://mongrel.rubyforge.org/docs/howto.html
2. http://mongrel.rubyforge.org/docs/

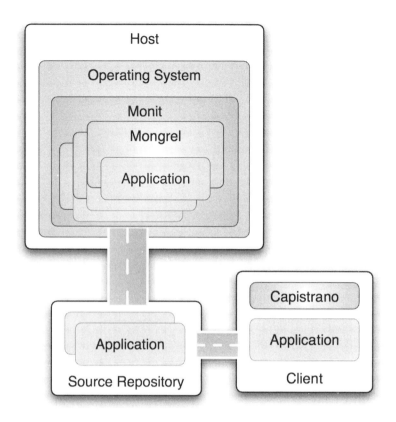

Figure 6.1: DEPLOYMENT MAP FOR SCALING OUT

You can specify all these options on the command line each time you start mongrel_rails, but if you need anything more than the most basic configuration, flags will quickly get tedious. This is where the Mongrel configuration file comes into play. The -G or --generate option will create a config file for a given set of command-line flags. Once you have a command line with all the options you desire, you can save them to disk for later use. From the root of your Rails application, run the following command:

```
ezra$ mongrel_rails start -G config/mongrel_7000.yml ↩
      -e production -p 7000 -d
** Writing config to "config/mongrel_7000.yml".
** Finished.  Run "mongrel_rails -C config/mongrel_7000.yml"
** to use the config file.
```

The previous command generates a file called mongrel_7000.yml in the config/ directory of your Rails application:

```
ezra$ cat mongrel_7000.yml
---
:config_file:
:daemon: true
:cwd: /Users/ezra/railsapp
:includes:
- mongrel
:environment: production
:log_file: log/mongrel.log
:group:
:config_script:
:pid_file: log/mongrel.pid
:num_processors: 1024
:debug: false
:docroot: public
:user:
:timeout: 0
:mime_map:
:prefix:
:port: "7000"
:host: 0.0.0.0
```

That file has a lot of options. Thankfully, you don't usually need all these settings, so you can trim the file down quite a bit, like so:

```
---
:daemon: true
:cwd: /Users/ezra/railsapp
:environment: production
:log_file: log/mongrel.log
:pid_file: log/mongrel.pid
:docroot: public
:port: "7000"
:host: 0.0.0.0
```

Now you can make changes to your Mongrel configuration without typing them on the command line each time you want to start a Mongrel server. To start Mongrel with your shiny new config file, use the -C flag:

```
ezra$ mongrel_rails start -C config/mongrel.yml
```

If you aren't sure what options you want yet but you want to generate a config file to start with, you can use the -G option without any other arguments:

```
ezra$ mongrel_rails start -G config/mongrel.yml
```

When you run Mongrel on any Unix-like operating system, you can control it with signals similar to WEBrick or FastCGI.

The signals that Mongrel understands include the following:

TERM   Stops Mongrel and deletes the PID file.

USR2   Restarts Mongrel (new process) and deletes the PID file.

INT   Same as USR2. This command is a convenience because
        Ctrl + C generates an interrupt signal and Ctrl + C is used in
        debug mode.

HUP   Internal reload. This command might not work well because
        sometimes doing an internal reload will not reload all the code
        in the system. You are safer if you do a real USR2 restart.

You can send these signals with the kill command:

```
ezra$ kill -HUP 27333
```

Configuring a Cluster

You've seen how to configure a single Mongrel instance. Your next step
is to build a more flexible configuration for a cluster. First, you need to
generate your mongrel_cluster.yml file. Let's configure a cluster of three
Mongrels by running the following command from the root of your Rails
application directory:

```
ezra$ mongrel_rails cluster::configure -p 8000 ↩
     -e production -a 127.0.0.1 -N 3
Writing configuration file to config/mongrel_cluster.yml.
ezra$ cat config/mongrel_cluster.yml
---
port: "8000"
environment: production
address: 127.0.0.1
pid_file: log/mongrel.pid
servers: 3
```

You just built a minimal, but working, mongrel_cluster.yml file to run a
cluster. The port option is a little different from the port option you used
when you configured a single Mongrel instance. For a cluster, port specifies the first port number for your first Mongrel. Each subsequent Mongrel starts on the next port. These Mongrels will start on ports 8000,
8001, and 8002. You also specified the Rails environment for your Rails
application. Normally, you'll run a single Mongrel in development mode
and a cluster for production. Mongrel will listen on the hostname or
IP address specified by the address option. The pid_file option specifies
the location for Mongrel's PID files, and servers specifies the number
of Mongrels you want in the cluster. The previous file configures three
Mongrels running on ports 8000, 8001, and 8002. Next, customize this
config file a bit to take advantage of a few more attributes:

```
---
port: "8080"
cwd: /Users/ezra/railsapp
log_file: log/mongrel.log
environment: production
address: 127.0.0.1
pid_file: log/mongrel.pid
servers: 3
docroot: public
user: ezra
group: ezra
```

It's a good idea to set cwd (current working directory) to the root of your Rails application. I also added the log_file, docroot, user, and group settings. Configuring the user and group will make Mongrel run under that user and group even if you accidentally start it with sudo. It is always a good idea to run web applications as a normal user instead of root, just in case your application has a security breach. We know all applications have security holes.

To start and stop your Mongrel cluster, you still use the mongrel_rails command, but you gain a set of cluster commands to use with it. Try it now from the root of your Rails app:

```
ezra$ mongrel_rails cluster::start
Starting 3 Mongrel servers...
ezra$ mongrel_rails cluster::restart
Stopping 3 Mongrel servers...
Starting 3 Mongrel servers...
ezra$ mongrel_rails cluster::stop
Stopping 3 Mongrel servers...
```

You've just tidied up your Mongrel configuration. Next, you can work on running Mongrel as a service.

Running Mongrel as a Service

Using the mongrel_rails command from your local directory is fine for playing around on your local machine or for staging environments. But in a production environment, it's nice to configure Mongrel more like Apache and MySQL. The service configuration keeps things consistent. The operating system will include Mongrel when automatically starting services each time your server starts or restarts. The service configuration works much like the Mongrel configuration you've already built.

You'll need to ensure that you have the mongrel_cluster gem installed first. Once it is, you simply need to create a file at /etc/mongrel_cluster/ myapp.conf. I recommend you replace myapp with the name of your application, but you can use anything you like. If you're running multiple applications on one server, you can have multiple Mongrel cluster configuration files. In the file, you configure your Mongrel cluster with a few simple options. They are documented with inline comments in the following example configuration file:

```
# /etc/mongrel_cluster/myapp.conf

# The user and group with which to run Mongrel
user: deploy
group: deploy

# The location of our Rails application
# and the environment to run within
cwd: /home/deploy/apps/myapp/current
environment: production

# The number of servers in the cluster
servers: 4

# The starting port
# e.g. with 3 mongrels would bind ports 8000-8002
port: "8000"

# The IP Addresses allowed to connect to Mongrel
# If your web server proxy is separate from your app server,
# put its IP address here instead of the localhost IP address
address: 0.0.0.0

# The location of the process ID files relative to the rails app above
pid_file: log/mongrel.pid
```

With that configuration file in place, you can now start, restart, or stop Mongrel using the following simple command from any current working directory:

- mongrel_cluster_ctlstart will start a Mongrel cluster from scratch.
- mongrel_cluster_ctlrestart will restart a running Mongrel cluster.
- mongrel_cluster_ctlstop will stop a Mongrel cluster.

Now that you have your cluster of Mongrels happily running as a service, you can turn your attention to managing the Mongrel server. The Monit tool will let you handle scenarios where your Mongrels might run out of memory or experience any other problems.

Starting Mongrel Cluster on Boot

You can get your Mongrel cluster to start at boot time, and it should be fairly simple with most Linux distributions. The Mongrel cluster comes with a script ready to go. Installing it is simply a matter of finding it and copying it to the /etc/init.d/ directory. On my setup, the mongrel_cluster script file is located at the following location: /usr/lib/ruby/gems/1.8/gems/mongrel_cluster-<VERSION>/resources/mongrel_cluster.

Simply copy it to /etc/init.d/, and make it executable like this:

```
ezra$ sudo cp \
  /usr/lib/ruby/gems/1.8/gems/mongrel_cluster-1.0.5/resources/\
  mongrel_cluster \
  /etc/init.d
ezra$ sudo chmod +x /etc/init.d/mongrel_cluster
```

Now your Mongrel cluster is configured to load on boot, just like Apache and MySQL. As an added bonus, you can now also use /etc/init.d/mongrel_cluster [start|restart|stop] anywhere you read mongrel_cluster_ctl [start|restart|stop]. This is nice because it's very familiar to anyone who has used other service scripts like those for Apache and MySQL.

You might need to make a few changes to the PATH variable inside the script depending on your specific setup, Linux distribution, and hosting provider's custom configuration. Check with your host provider or the documentation for your Linux distribution in case yours is a little different.

6.3 Configuring the Watchdog

Monit is a simple utility used to manage files, processes, and directories on Unix. You can configure Monit to split your logs if they get too big, start and stop processes, and also keep tabs on resources. Monit can notify you if your memory use gets out of control and actually do something about it. You may want Monit to restart one of the Mongrels in your cluster or restart your nginx web server, if someone changes your configuration file.

For starters, you're going to use Monit to make sure your Mongrels keep running at peak efficiency. You'll need to do three things to get the management process running:

- You will need to install the right version of mongrel_cluster. The minimum version of Mongrel you will want to run is 1.0.1.1.

> ### Building Monit on RHEL or CentOS
>
> You need to install a few dependencies before you can get Monit to build on Red Hat or CentOS distributions. Use rpm or yum to search for and install the following packages: flex, bison, and byacc. Once you have these prerequisites installed, you can build Monit with the same instructions shown for other systems.

Earlier versions do not support the --clean option. This is important because Mongrel 1.0+ will not start if there is a process identification (PID) file sitting on disk. So if your server crashes and has to be rebooted, Mongrel tries to start up and fails because there was a leftover PID file. The --clean option deletes leftover PID files if they exist.

- You need a good mongrel_cluster.yml file. You've already built one earlier in this chapter, and that one should work fine.
- You need a Monit configuration file, called mongrel.monitrc. This configuration file will tell Monit what to do for each Mongrel on your system.

The first order of business is to install Monit. Most Linux distributions will have a Monit package available in their package managers. On Debian/Ubuntu you can run sudo apt-get install monit, and on Gentoo you can run sudo emerge monit. If you cannot locate a package for your preferred Linux, don't sweat it, because you can build Monit from source, like this:

```
ezra$ wget http://www.tildeslash.com/monit/dist/monit-4.9.tar.gz
  ...
ezra$ tar xzvf monit-4.9.tar.gz
  ...
ezra$ cd monit-4.9
ezra$ ./configure && make && sudo make install
  ...
```

Next up you need to install the correct version of mongrel_cluster. You will want the latest version from RubyForge. It is important to clean up older versions of mongrel_cluster if you had any installed:

```
    $ sudo gem install mongrel_cluster ↩
&& sudo gem cleanup mongrel_cluster
```

After you've set that up, you are ready to configure Monit. I like to create a separate configuration for each Mongrel cluster. You'll add the following configuration to mongrel.monitrc, which you'll keep in Monit's directory, in our case, /etc/monit.d:

```
check process mongrel_deployit_5000
  with pidfile /data/deployit/shared/log/mongrel.5000.pid
  start program = "/usr/bin/mongrel_rails cluster::start -C ↩
              /data/deployit/current/config/mongrel_cluster.yml ↩
              --clean --only 5000"
  stop program = "/usr/bin/mongrel_rails cluster::stop -C ↩
              /data/deployit/current/config/mongrel_cluster.yml ↩
              --only 5000"
  if totalmem is greater than 110.0 MB for 4 cycles then restart
  if cpu is greater than 80% for 4 cycles then restart
  if 20 restarts within 20 cycles then timeout
  group deployit
```

Notice that you will need a block for each process that you want Monit to monitor. The previous configuration is for one Mongrel only. The first directive, check_process, identifies a process to monitor. I have skipped that directive in favor of the alternative with pidfile option that tells Monit which process file to monitor. Recall that each Mongrel instance has a file stored in the log/mongrel.port.pid file. The next two directives tell Monit how to start and stop Mongrel. The last three directives tell Monit what to do when certain pathological conditions exist. This configuration will restart Mongrel instances if the memory exceeds a threshold (110.0MB in the previous configuration) or the CPU is too busy for a process. These directives also can take more extreme measures, such as timing out and notifying administrators. Keep in mind that all this is fully automated and requires notification only in extreme circumstances.

Keep in mind that Monit will start your Mongrels with a completely clean shell environment. This means your normal $PATH will not be set up. You will need to use the fully qualified path to your mongrel_rails command. In the previous config I used /usr/bin/mongrel_rails, but you may need to adjust this path depending on where your system installed the command. You can figure out where the command was installed like this:

```
ezra$ which mongrel_rails
     /usr/bin/mongrel_rails
```

A final configuration provides the general setup for Monit, including the configuration for the mail server and alerts. This file is located at /etc/monit/monitrc.

```
set daemon  30
set logfile syslog facility log_daemon
set mailserver smtp.example.com
set mail-format {from:monit@example.com}
set alert sysadmin@example.com only on { timeout, nonexist }
set httpd port 9111
    allow localhost
include /etc/monit.d/*
```

This config is fairly straightforward, but there are a few things to note. set daemon 30 tells Monit how often to check processes, in this case every 30 seconds. I have found that 30 seconds is perfect for this setting. You need to set your own SMTP server and email addresses for alerts. The last two directives turn on Monit's built-in HTTP server on port 9111, making it viewable only from the localhost, and sets /etc/monit.d to be the directory from which to include config files.

When you're done, you can try a couple of commands. You can actually start and stop Mongrel cluster instances through Monit. First you need to make sure Monit has your latest configuration loaded:

```
ezra$ sudo /etc/init.d/monit restart
```

When Monit starts, it will automatically boot your Mongrels. Then you can restart the Mongrels by their groups through Monit:

```
$ sudo monit restart all -g deployit
```

Or restart one single Mongrel by its name:

```
$ sudo monit restart mongrel_deployit_5000
```

To see the current status of your Mongrels, use the status command:

```
$ sudo monit status
  The monit daemon 4.9 uptime: 4d 2h 27m

  Process 'mongrel_deployit_5000'
    status                        running
    monitoring status             monitored
    pid                           20467
    parent pid                    1
    uptime                        55m
    childrens                     0
    memory kilobytes              50432
    memory kilobytes total        50432
    memory percent                12.8%
    memory percent total          12.8%
    cpu percent                   0.0%
    cpu percent total             0.0%
    data collected                Sun Jul  1 14:38:26 2007
```

You may be asking yourself "Who monitors Monit?" That is a great question. Monit is usually very stable, but certain conditions such as "out of memory" can cause Monit itself to crash. If you want to prevent this from happening, you can put Monit under the control of init. On a Linux system, init is responsible for running all the scripts in /etc/init.d. init can also respawn daemons if they die. The first step is to remove Monit from the /etc/init.d scripts. Consult the documentation for your system for information on how to remove a start-up script from the default run level. On Gentoo, you would do it by running rc-update del monit. The next step is to edit /etc/inittab and add the following lines near the bottom of the file:

```
mo:345:respawn:/usr/bin/monit -Ic /etc/monitrc
m0:06:wait:/usr/bin/monit -Ic /etc/monitrc stop all
```

Now you can have init to watch Monit. The first step is to stop Monit. Then you tell init to spawn Monit and keep it alive:

```
ezra$ sudo /etc/init.d/monit stop
ezra$ sudo telinit q
```

Now that Monit runs under init, the /etc/init.d/monit command will not work to start and stop the Monit daemon. Instead, you will have to kill Monit and let init pick it back up again, like this:

```
ezra$ sudo killall -9 monit
```

You will need some custom Capistrano tasks now that you are using Monit to watch your Mongrels. When you use Monit, you do not need to use mongrel_cluster/recipes in your deploy recipe. Instead, you will set the Monit group of the Mongrels you are targeting with this line in your deploy.rb file:

```
set :monit_group,  'deployit'
```

Now you need to add the following tasks to your deploy recipe:

```
desc <<-DESC
Restart the Mongrel processes on the app server by
calling restart_mongrel_cluster.
DESC
task :restart, :roles => :app do
  restart_mongrel_cluster
end

desc <<-DESC
Start Mongrel processes on the app server.
DESC
task :start_mongrel_cluster , :roles => :app do
  sudo "/usr/bin/monit start all -g #{monit_group}"
end
```

```
desc <<-DESC
Restart the Mongrel processes on the app server by
starting and stopping the cluster.
DESC
task :restart_mongrel_cluster , :roles => :app do
  sudo "/usr/bin/monit restart all -g #{monit_group}"
end

desc <<-DESC
Stop the Mongrel processes on the app server.
DESC
task :stop_mongrel_cluster , :roles => :app do
  sudo "/usr/bin/monit stop all -g #{monit_group}"
end
```

Now you know how to use Monit to keep a leash on your Mongrels. Monit can be a lifesaver for your production Rails applications, and I highly suggest using it whenever you deploy Mongrels.

6.4 Keeping FastCGI Under Control

Our primary focus has been on Mongrel. I'm going to dedicate the rest of the chapter to FastCGI. If you should find yourself deploying with FastCGI, you'll want to read the next few sections. Otherwise, feel free to skip ahead to Section 6.5, *Building in Error Notification*, on page 131.

Zombie FastCGI Processes

During the dog days of summer in 2005, I noticed that one of my Rails apps was running a little slower than expected. Confident in my debugging abilities, I fired up my SSH client and logged into my shared server. Almost immediately, the server kicked me out with an odd "resource unavailable" error.

After three more tries with the same result, I emailed the customer support team. It turns out that I had fifty processes running, the maximum allowed for any single user! Every one of those processes was a zombie, aimlessly occupying my process allocation but unable to do anything useful. Like a bad horror sequel, one of my Rails apps on a completely different host had the same problem a few days later.

The Apache web server is famous for producing these zombies when running with FastCGI, causing many developers to favor Mongrels or nginx instead. The good news is that a few simple cron tasks can keep zombies from getting out of hand, making the difference between a smoothly running site and one that dies daily. I'll discuss them in *The Reaper* below.

The conclusion to the story is that the sysadmin at the shared host killed the zombie processes, and things began working again. I learned to start a daily cron task that cleans out zombies and gives my server a fresh start. Some people restart their dispatch processes every single hour. You will have to experiment with your specific situation and see what works best.

The Reaper

The reaper is not a black-hooded messenger of doom; he is your best friend. The reaper command reliably prunes back FastCGI processes. Capistrano uses it to restart your Rails app after a fresh deployment. You can also use it to restart processes on a regular schedule.

The reaper is a script you run on the command line. By default it restarts FastCGI dispatch processes for your application only, so you won't disrupt other applications running under the same user account. You can fire off other actions with the reaper as well:

- restart: Restarts the application by reloading both application and framework code (the default). Send the USR2 signal to each dispatch.fcgi process belonging to the current application.

- reload: Reloads only the application, not the framework (like the development environment). Reload sends the HUP signal.

- graceful: Marks all the processes for exit after the next request. Graceful sends the TERM signal.

- kill: Forcefully exits all processes regardless of whether they're currently serving a request. kill sends the -9 signal. Use this only if none of the other signals is successful.

You can run the reaper without any arguments or request one of the previous actions such as the following:

```
ezra$ ./script/process/reaper --action=graceful
```

In my experience, the defaults don't work on most shared hosts because their output doesn't match the reaper's expectations. The good news is that you can send an extra argument to match the specific output of your host.

Let me show you how I fine-tuned this on one of my shared hosting accounts. First, I tried to run the dispatcher normally. Even though I knew that there were several dispatch.fcgi processes running at that very moment, the reaper couldn't find them.

```
ezra$ ./script/process/reaper
```

```
Couldn't find any process matching:
/data/deployit/releases/20060224192655/public/dispatch.fcgi
```

Reading through the reaper code revealed the exact command that the reaper used to find the list of running processes. I called that command manually:

```
ezra$ ps axww -o 'pid command'
```

```
  PID COMMAND
 4830 /usr/bin/ruby dispatch.fcgi
18714 /usr/bin/ruby dispatch.fcgi
 2076 /usr/bin/ruby1.8 dispatch.fcgi
12536 -bash
 5607 ps axww -o pid command
```

I could then see what was happening. The reaper was looking for the full path to the dispatcher, but the ps command on my server returned a shorter version of the current process list. Consequently, the reaper could not find the full path, so I can't restart this application independently of the others running under that same user account. As configured, the reaper was all or nothing!

Running the same command on my local Mac OS X machine shows the entire path to the dispatch.fcgi script, as it should. A fact of shared hosting is that you can't control systemwide settings, so you may have to adjust your scripts to match.

With this information in hand, I could send a more general argument to restart all dispatch processes running under that user account in order to keep things fresh and zombie-free:

```
ezra$ ./script/process/reaper --action=restart --dispatcher=dispatch.fcgi
```

```
Restarting [4830] /usr/bin/ruby dispatch.fcgi
Restarting [18714] /usr/bin/ruby1.8 dispatch.fcgi
Restarting [2076] /usr/bin/ruby1.8 dispatch.fcgi
```

6.5 Building in Error Notification

With a Mongrel cluster in place, your setup has greater scalability, and you should be able to sustain minor failures. With Monit in place to manage your Mongrel clusters, you have the capability to take preemptive action when a single Mongrel cluster fails or when resources get scarce.

But most of the time, your failures will come from plain old human error. If you want a good management story, you are going to have to deal with your programmer's mistakes. Usually, Rails errors will generate an application error, the dreaded 500 error page. With Ruby, it's fairly easy to intercept the default error behavior to, for example, send email notifications. And that is exactly what the exception_notification plug-in does.

You can read about the exception_notification plug-in at the Rails wiki (http://wiki.rubyonrails.org/rails/pages/ExceptionNotification). To install it, simply run the installation script like this:

```
ezra$ ruby script/plugin install exception_notification
```

Next, to build notification into a particular controller, include the error notification module. I like to include error notification in application.rb so I'll get email notification when any user of any controller encounters an error that I failed to handle correctly, like so:

```
class ApplicationController < ActionController::Base
  include ExceptionNotifiable
  ...
end
```

Next, configure the email addresses that should get notified of Rails exceptions. Put the notification in config/environment.rb:

```
ExceptionNotifier.exception_recipients = ←
  %w(you@yourdomain.com another@yourdomain.com)
```

Now, if any error should occur, you'll get an error notification like the following:

```
A ActionView::TemplateError occurred in drives#edit_comment:

  undefined method `title' for nil:NilClass
  On line #5 of app/views/drives/edit_comment.rhtml

    2: <%= error_messages_for 'gift' %>
    3: <!--[form:drive]-->
    4:
    5: <h1><%= @drive.title %></h1>
    6: <div>
    7:
    8: <table><tr>

  #{RAILS_ROOT}/app/views/drives/edit_comment.rhtml:5:in ←
    `_run_rhtml_47app47views47drives47edit_comment46rhtml'
  #{RAILS_ROOT}/vendor/rails/actionpack/lib/action_view/base.rb:326:in ←
    `compile_and_render_template'
```

```
#{RAILS_ROOT}/vendor/rails/actionpack/lib/action_view/base.rb:301:in ↩
  `render_template'
```
...


```
------------------------------
Request:
------------------------------

  * URL: http://changingthepresent.org/drives/edit_comment/65?donate=true
  * Parameters: {"donate"=>"true", "action"=>"edit_comment", ↩
                 "id"=>"65", "controller"=>"drives"}
  * Rails root: /home/deploy/importantgifts/current


------------------------------
Session:
------------------------------

  * @write_lock: true
  * @session_id: "875ce6f70cb9b8e9348a72147999303c"
  * @data: {"flash"=>{}}
  * @new_session: true


------------------------------
Environment:
------------------------------

  * GATEWAY_INTERFACE   : CGI/1.2
  * HTTP_ACCEPT         : */*
  * HTTP_ACCEPT_ENCODING: gzip
  * HTTP_CONNECTION     : Keep-alive
  * HTTP_FROM           : googlebot(at)googlebot.com
  * HTTP_HOST           : changingthepresent.org
  * HTTP_USER_AGENT     : Mozilla/5.0 (compatible; ↩
    Googlebot/2.1; +http://www.google.com/bot.html)
  * HTTP_VERSION        : HTTP/1.1
  * HTTP_X_FORWARDED_FOR: 66.249.72.161
  * HTTP_X_TEXTDRIVE    : BigIP
  * PATH_INFO           : /drives/edit_comment/65
  * QUERY_STRING        : donate=true
  * REMOTE_ADDR         : 66.249.72.161
  * REQUEST_METHOD      : GET
  * REQUEST_PATH        : /drives/edit_comment/65
  * REQUEST_URI         : /drives/edit_comment/65?donate=true
  * SCRIPT_NAME         : /
  * SERVER_NAME         : changingthepresent.org
  * SERVER_PORT         : 80
  * SERVER_PROTOCOL     : HTTP/1.1
  * SERVER_SOFTWARE     : Mongrel 1.0

  * Process: 1620
```

```
      * Server :

      ------------------------------
      Backtrace:
      ------------------------------

      On line #5 of app/views/drives/edit_comment.rhtml

          2: <%= error_messages_for 'gift' %>
          3: <!--[form:drive]-->
          4:
          5: <h1><%= @drive.title %></h1>
          6: <div>
          7:
          8: <table><tr>

      #{RAILS_ROOT}/app/views/drives/edit_comment.rhtml:5:in ←
        `_run_rhtml_47app47views47drives47edit_comment46rhtml'
      #{RAILS_ROOT}/vendor/rails/actionpack/lib/action_view/base.rb:326:in ←
        `compile_and_render_template'
      #{RAILS_ROOT}/vendor/rails/actionpack/lib/action_view/base.rb:301:in ←
        `render_template'
      #{RAILS_ROOT}/vendor/rails/actionpack/lib/action_view/base.rb:260:in ←
        `render_file'
  ...
```

Voila! This email message is an actual email notification that helped solve a production problem in the code at ChangingThePresent.[3] The email contains a full complement of debugging information, including a full trace and back trace, the contents of the session, the offending view code, and the full environment for the HTTP request.

You can configure a few other options as well. Configure the sender with ExceptionNotifier.sender_address, and append a string to the subject line (to help with email filters) with ExceptionNotifier.email_prefix. This plug-in will send email notifications only when the address is not local. You can configure which IP addresses should be considered as local with ExceptionNotifier.consider_local.

With this solution, Rails will notify you whenever your application experiences an exception. You can configure it to work well with your email clients, and because it's plugged directly into Rails, as long as Rails does not fail completely and your network and email keep working, you'll get a notification.

---

3. http://ChangingThePresent.org

6.6 Heartbeat

The exception_notification plug-in is a great way to understand, when your application has errors, whether the errors are consistent or inter-mittent. It's not a complete management solution, though. For larger or more critical production systems, you also need to verify that the system is running at all.

A heartbeat service will tell you when your application fails. I find that a simple script running on a separate host works better than cus-tom solutions because it's easy, infinitely customizable, and deployable on any host with your scripting language. The following script detects when one of four pages is down at ChangingThePresent:

managing_things/heartbeat.rb

```ruby
#!/usr/local/bin/ruby

require 'net/smtp'
require 'net/http'
require 'net/https'
require 'uri'

urls = %w{
  http://www.changingthepresent.org/
  http://www.changingthepresent.org/nonprofits/show/23/
  http://www.changingthepresent.org/causes/list/
  https://www.changingthepresent.org/
}

from = 'system@importantgifts.org'

recipients = %w{development@changingthepresent.org}

errors = []

urls.each do |url|
  begin
    uri = URI.parse(url)
    http = Net::HTTP.new(uri.host, uri.scheme == "https" ? 443 : nil)
    http.use_ssl = (uri.scheme == "https" ? true : false)
    http.start do |http|
      request = Net::HTTP::Get.new(uri.path)
      response = http.request(request)
      case response
      when Net::HTTPSuccess, Net::HTTPRedirection
      else
        raise "requesting #{url} returned code #{response.code}"
      end
    end
  end
```

```
    rescue
      error = "#{url}: #{$!}"
      errors << error
      puts error
    end
end

unless errors.empty?
  msg = "From: #{from}\n"
  msg += "Subject: ChangingThePresent.org is down!\n\n"
  msg += errors.join("\n")
  puts "sending email to #{recipients.join(', ')}"
  Net::SMTP.start('localhost', 25, 'localhost') do |smtp|
    smtp.send_message(msg, from, recipients)
  end
end
```

The four URLs are not haphazard. They represent a secure page, a page-cached page, a fragment-cached page, and a standard dynamic page. The admin team executes this script once every five minutes via a cron job. The script notifies all the developers on the project via an email address that is forwarded to all developers whenever the site is down.

The script counts redirects and success as a successful contact. Anything else is a failure. Timeouts will also trigger a notification.

6.7 Conclusion

The management strategies in this chapter don't cost anything, but they are surprisingly robust. Building repeatable Mongrel configurations rather than command-line options is easy and enables consistent clustering. Configuring your Mongrels in a cluster gives you good performance and some failover. Clustering Mongrel is important because of the Rails shared-nothing strategy.

Clustering is only the beginning of your managing strategy. To run production Mongrels, you need information and control. By using Monit, you get a watchdog that will automatically kill and restart any rogue Mongrels. By using the various email notification features, the scripts will notify the recipients of your choice when the server is down or when anyone encounters a Rails error.

Still, our error recovery solutions are not yet complete. You will need a better handle on monitoring resources and on performance before you have a complete strategy. Read on.

Chapter 7

Scaling Out

You will often want your website to grow. When you can't fit into your existing home anymore, you have to find some way to move up or to add on. The Rails model for scaling will take you beyond the single home owner and into the realm of a real estate developer or community planner. This chapter will examine scaling out.

7.1 The Lay of the Land

I'm going to put down my real estate agent hat for a little while and put on the hat of a community planner. If you own a house near a congested city and work in its busy downtown core, you're all too familiar with multilane highway traffic that travels at times as fast as a cheetah and other times as slow as a statue of a cheetah. Presented with this problem, you might start with one of the following two solutions to the problem:

- Increase the speed limit.
- Increase the number of lanes.

These solutions sound obvious and you have probably heard similar analogies before, but there's a lot more to it. Natural and political laws place a limit on how fast cars can travel safely, and you can add only so many lanes to a highway. These constraints effectively limit how effective either solution can ultimately be.

Sometimes, these solutions are not even attacking the right problem. The obstacles to effectively moving people aren't always speed limits or lanes. You need to consider interfaces—on-ramps and merges—that can slow traffic down. Entrances force lane changes and slowdowns, exits double the problem, and accidents or construction projects force lane closures. The biggest bottleneck of all, though—and the one that's responsible for the others—is the destination. Not only are all the cars on the same road, but they're all heading to the same place. The problem is the *city center itself*. You can only hope that there are enough parking spaces and office space available once you finally reach it!

Your computer infrastructure isn't much different. Each lane of the highway is a network connection to some service provided by the application. The city center is the resource pool. Every ramp is a client node. Each car is a user request headed downtown to do some business. The idea of adding lanes and increasing speed limits is effectively a way of "scaling up." You can scale up by upgrading hardware such as CPUs, memory, disks, and network bandwidth. That strategy works sometimes, but upward scaling has its limits. There are only so many CPUs, so much memory, so many disks, and so much bandwidth that you can jam into a single box. These limits will likely never allow your application to meet the demands of the global crowd.

The low ceiling isn't the only problem with scaling up. As your business grows, the cost of failure becomes greater too. You'll need redundant systems and hot backups to handle failure and even the occasional hardware upgrade. Ultimately, scaling up is harder, with a lower ceiling.

Most successful web businesses scale up, not by chance or even necessity but by preference. I won't completely write off scaling up. I'll touch upon it when I address the database because scaling up has some real advantages in that space.

7.2 Scaling Out with Clustering

Scaling out means adding more servers, complete with their own dedicated CPUs, disks, memory, and network bandwidth. Think back to the traffic analogy for a moment. The ultimate problem was that everyone was heading to the same city center. Scaling out adds a second city center so half the travelers that day would suddenly be on a different road and heading toward a different city center. Imagine what your daily commute would be like tomorrow if half the city's population were simply not on your road! Scaling out certainly yields greater rewards. But what about cost, complexity, and maintainability?

Scaling out to hundreds of servers can cost you plenty in dollars and complexity, but you don't have to pay all the price at once. Conveniently, scaling out lets the complexity scale with you. In the beginning, designing to scale outward costs little, but your preparations will position you for bigger challenges to come. You can deal with new performance demands later by doing a little prep work today. To get ready, you'll prepare a few key elements of infrastructure. The trick is to get your scaling right early so you can avoid surprises later.

Keep in mind that you'll still have to get your performance right. Even if you plan to scale by throwing money and hardware at the problem, you'll want to save enough time to address performance. I'll talk more about performance in Chapter 9, *Performance*, on page 217.

From a deployment perspective, you're looking at a map something like Figure 7.1, on the next page. You'll have two or three different virtual hosts that may or may not reside on the same servers. Each Mongrel cluster is a separate city center. One server will use Apache or nginx as a static proxy and load balancer. The other two will serve Rails applications through Mongrel clusters. You'll use Capistrano to deploy to each of them. The next few sections will help you set up a simple architecture that can easily grow from a single dedicated server to around five servers with minimal changes to your application. In the sections that follow, I'll walk you through the following:

- Adding multiple virtual machines to your environment

- Setting up subdomains for your cluster using CNAMEs with your DNS provider

- Ensuring your Mongrel servers are deployed as clusters and as services

- Setting up a load-balancing proxy web server with Apache or nginx

- Configuring multimaster and master/slave MySQL clusters

I'll start with the simplest Rails deployment and slowly grow the server into a scaled-out model ready to handle your angry mob of Web 2.0 users. When I'm done, you will have a web server that serves as a static proxy and a load balancer that serves content to one or more Mongrel clusters. This system will serve a typical request as shown in Figure 7.2, on page 141. The user makes a request to a gateway server. If it's a static request, the gateway server simply serves up the static content, and you're done. If not, the gateway server will forward the request to one of several Mongrel clusters. The Mongrel clusters forward the request to an individual Mongrel server.

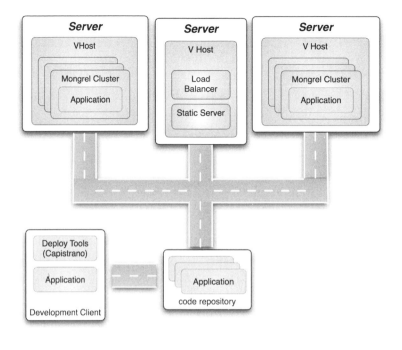

Figure 7.1: DEPLOYMENT MAP FOR SCALING OUT

Prerequisites

If you don't have access to a hosted virtual private server (VPS), you can set a couple of virtual machines up on your desktop. For Windows users, both VMware and Microsoft Virtual PC are free for non-commercial use. Linux users have commercial and free options including VMware, Xen, or OpenVZ. Mac users can use Parallels or VMware, neither of which is free. Check for free trials if you're not sure which one to buy. I prefer VMware, but any one of them will work.

These virtual machine technologies work in a similar way to what a VPS host will provide. They will allow you to install an entirely separate operating system in a contained environment that acts like a computer within your computer. In fact, if you're considering a VPS hosting service and aren't sure how much memory or disk space you need, you can test various configurations with these "home versions" to artificially constrain system resources. Try running your application in a 256MB VMware virtual machine before committing to 12 months of a 256MB managed Xen VPS.

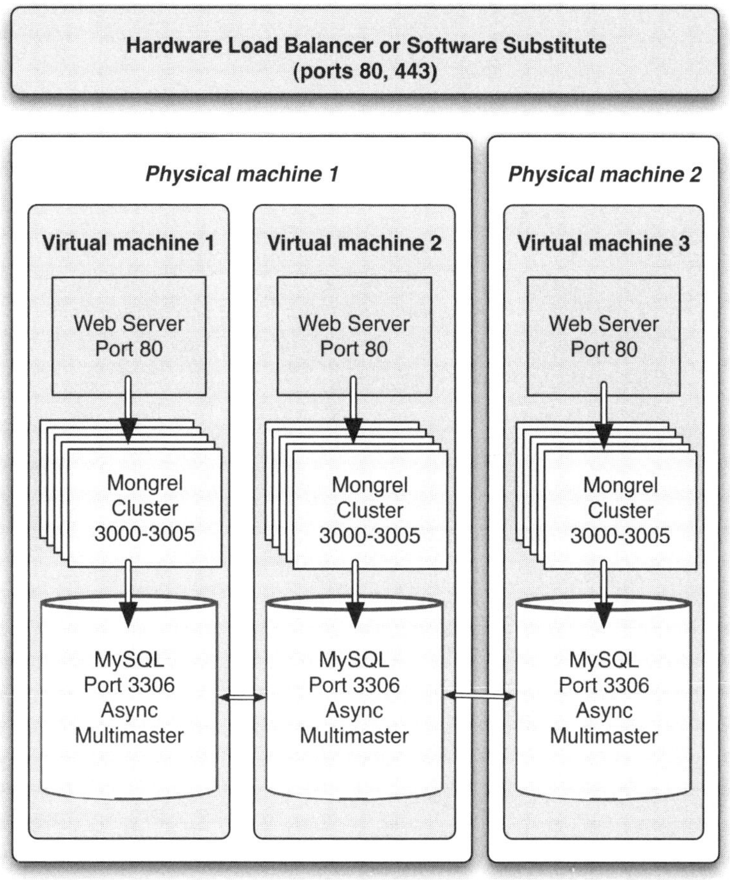

Figure 7.2: TYPICAL RAILS CLUSTERED DEPLOYMENT SETUP

You can use any Linux distribution, but I've always found the Red Hat–derived ones like CentOS and Fedora to be the most friendly. They are similar to what many VPS hosting providers will offer (RHEL and CentOS are very popular). There are a lot of Linux package dependencies to get your Rails application up and running. At a minimum, you will need a C/C++ compiler, Ruby and gems related to your app, Subversion, Apache httpd, MySQL Server, and your favorite text editor, be it vi or emacs. Sometimes you can build out a system by just installing your Linux distribution with its "web server" and "developer" options. However, it's not terribly hard to install everything from a minimal installation, especially given the documentation in Chapter 4, *Virtual and Dedicated Hosts*, on page 65.

\\//
›ƒ **Joe Asks...**
ζ̃
Why Bother with Virtualization for Scaling Out?

Virtualization has many advantages for scaling out. Primarily, you can configure your application to scale out sooner. You can probably get at least two or more virtual private servers for the same price as a single dedicated server. You gain most of the advantages of redundancy and increased performance sooner, and you can always switch to a dedicated box later, with a reduced impact to your configuration and less down-time. Personally, I choose to run virtualized environments even on a dedicated server. I find them far easier to manage and configure. Advances in hardware and software have made virtualization technology fast, and the benefits far outweigh any marginal performance cost.

You will need two virtual machine instances. With most of the software technologies mentioned earlier, you can build one and simply copy the virtual machine files, changing only some identification information such as the IP address and the hostname.

Once you have your virtual machines up and running, create the database and deploy your application with Capistrano to one of them using the techniques you learned in the earlier chapters. You can deploy your application in its simplest form so you can at least start up Mongrel and access your application via a web browser by hitting the Mongrel server directly.

Any application will do, but it should be more than an empty Rails app. If you need a application to work with, try using the example from *Agile Web Development with Rails* found at http://www.pragprog. com/titles/rails2/source_code.

You can find entire books about the administration of Linux, Apache, and MySQL. I may skip some steps here and there to keep your focus on topics specific to Rails deployment. When I do, I'll try to direct you to other resources when necessary to further tighten security or tweak performance.

7.3   Mirror Images

Your server farm will have a number of servers across many roles. Try hard to keep servers in the same role configured identically. Your life will be easier, you will experience fewer surprises, and you'll have less documentation to write. If identical configurations sound like too much work, you're going to love virtualization.

Virtual servers are like files that sit on your hard drive. You can move them, copy them, delete them, and back them up. When it comes time to keep configurations the same, the easiest thing to do is just make a copy. Here are a few strategies for ensuring configuration consistency across your VMs, depending on the size and timing of the change.

Cold Copy It

When you're first setting up your environment, just configure one virtual server. Get that server to the point where all the software, patches, dependencies, and configurations are in place so you can run a single instance of your app. Then, make one copy for each server role, including application servers, web servers, and database servers.

Automate It

You can often automate a change in configuration with Capistrano. You have seen that Capistrano scripts do a good job, use Ruby code, and can distinguish between server roles for different configurations.

Hot Copy It

Larger, more serious configuration changes may require you to shut down the server. The cool thing about VMs in this case is that you can use the copy strategy. Simply pull one server out of your cluster, make your changes to it, and then copy it to replicate all the other servers in the farm. This hot copy approach lets you introduce a new server into the farm to handle additional load. Be careful. You will want to always be able to uniquely identify each server. Whenever you make a copy, you have to be sure to properly set the IP address, hostname, and any other unique information for each server. If possible, automate such a thing with a script common to each of the servers. Remember to document the process!

Just Do It

If you can't justify automating a change or don't want to shut down servers, you might just have to walk through the servers and make the change. Remember to keep organized and document your steps, though—it will make a world of difference.

Keep Offline Master Copies

A master copy is an offline configuration that has never been deployed or exposed as a server to the public Internet. You will use it the first time for your cold copy. After you build your initial VM, you can use that copy as an online master copy. Whenever you need to make configuration changes, you can change this master copy. Most important, this is the copy you can safely deploy should your servers become compromised because of a security breach. Once a server has been compromised, it is hard to ever trust it again. You'll have enough to worry about regarding potential threats to your data, let alone the nightmare of trying to clean out your server farm. Having offline master copies allows you to patch the security hole in the offline copy that has never been exposed to the network and redeploy each of the server roles to the farm.

Use Third-Party Tools

So far I've discussed only custom brute-force approaches to managing these configurations. Third-party tools that can do the same might even be included with your virtual machine software or by your VPS provider. Shop around and talk to your service and software providers.

7.4 Domain Names and Hosts

When you have multiple servers in your environment, managing their names becomes important. You'll manage domain names through the web-based user interfaces you used in Chapter 3, *Shared Hosts*, on page 37, as well as in Chapter 4, *Virtual and Dedicated Hosts*, on page 65. Remember, changes to the domain name configuration can take hours or even days to propagate fully throughout the Internet. Managing these details for a cluster is a little tougher than managing a single web server, but you can usually get by knowing only a few more concepts:

A records The default configuration for most domain name services is to support brainspl.at in addition to www.brainspl.at. The primary

> \\\// Joe Asks...
> ꙮ **So Do I Use an A Record or a CNAME?**
>
> When I researched the A record vs. CNAME issue for myself, I remember coming across debates over various uses and abuses of CNAME records and advantages and disadvantages of different configurations. My conservative nature led me to avoid playing games, so I generally follow the rules:
>
> • Use A records for mappings of names to IP addresses.
>
> • Use CNAME records to alias A records.

domain (brainspl.at) is an A, or address, record in DNS terms. This record maps brainspl.at directly to your IP and is the lowest-level mapping.

CNAME records CNAME records are like aliases for an A record, be it one of your own or someone else's. Aliases usually indicate the kind of service that a server provides. For example, www.brainspl.at is an alias to brainspl.at that indicates interest in the HTTP server, and ftp.brainspl.at indicates interest in the File Transfer Protocol. Keep in mind that longstanding conventions exist, and you should follow them where you can.[1]

What Names Do I Need?

Armed with your new knowledge of domain name configuration, you now need to decide what names you will need. Try to name all your site's publicly available nodes, including the load balancer and the nodes that it balances. You'll probably have a firewall installed too. Getting your names and visibility right in a real production environment can require some advanced firewall setup, which is beyond the scope of this book. For simplicity, I'll let the web server act as the load balancer and remind you later that a hardware load-balancing solution is definitely a must-have for the most serious websites.

Imagine that you have a configuration involving a load balancer, two web servers, and a database server. You will expose the load balancer

---

1. See http://en.wikipedia.org/wiki/Domain_name_system for more.

to the network but not the database. So, you'll need a name for the load balancer. The database server may have a name on your local intranet, but it will not have a name in the domain name service (so there will be no db.brainspl.at). The load balancer will distribute requests between the two web servers. They will also need names because you'll eventually need to access individual web servers directly or redirect a request to a specific server—for debugging, configuration, or testing, if nothing else. I see three A records and one CNAME because the load balancer will map to the load balancer IP address, and each of the web servers will also have an IP address. I'll use a CNAME for the www alias that visitors use. I'll throw in an extra CNAME for a potential caching service. The final table looks like this:

A Records

- brainspl.at => 999.999.999.100—load balancer

- www1.brainspl.at => 999.999.999.101—first web server

- www2.brainspl.at => 999.999.999.102—second web server

CNAME Records

- www.brainspl.at => brainspl.at—alias to the load balancer

- content.brainspl.at => content.contentcache.com—alias to the content caching service

That last CNAME is to a third-party A record that provides caching of large content such as music, images, and videos.

When setting up both A records and CNAMEs, you need to set the or time-to-live (TTL) parameter. This value will determine how often name servers return to your configuration to check for changes. Setting this value a low value, such as 30 minutes, will give you a little more flexibility to change your configuration with minimal impact to your site. Setting it to a higher value, such as seven days, will provide better performance of your site because client software like browsers will have to do fewer name lookups. I recommend setting it low to start so that you can make a few mistakes with minimal impact. Then once you're comfortable with your configuration, return and increase the values for all A and CNAME records to at least twenty-four hours.

Now that you have named servers, you can start deploying your application to them.

7.5 Deploying to Multiple Hosts

With Rails and Capistrano, you have a lot of deployment options. Capistrano supports three server roles right out of the box:

- The web role points to servers responsible for static content. Apache or nginx lives here.

- The app role points to the server that will run your Rails application. Mongrel lives here.

- The db role points to your database server. MySQL lives here.

Capistrano deploys the right files to each server. If you need to do so, you can override its behavior. With only one server, you generally deploy all roles to that one server. The following Capistrano script is an example of a single-server configuration. I'll reference parts of it for the remaining examples in this section.

```
# Customized deploy.rb
set :application, "brainsplat"
set :user, "ezra"
set :repository, "http://brainspl.at/svn/#{application}"
set :deploy_to, "/home/#{user}/#{application}"

role :web, "www1.brainspl.at"
role :app, "www1.brainspl.at"
role :db,  "www1.brainspl.at", :primary => true
```

Options for Clustering

Given two servers, you now have a decision to make. The three following options are the most reasonable.

Isolate the database: This first option is simple and may offer the best performance for an individual request depending on the application. If your application is transaction heavy and depends on a lot of dynamic data, then this option might be the right choice. With this configuration, the database alone is separate, so it has fully dedicated access to the server resources, which should include lots of fast disks. You will also have the added security of keeping the database further away from the public network interface. You would configure the isolated database option like this:

```
# Relevant lines of deploy.rb
# ...
role :web, "www1.brainspl.at"
role :app, "www1.brainspl.at"
role :db,  "internal.brainspl.at", :primary => true
```

> ∖⎸⟋ **Joe Asks...**
> ᳵ⏝ **Why Not Just "Scale Up" the Database?**
>
> You absolutely could "scale up" the database. The database server is a good candidate for scaling upward, because it is often a bottleneck and can benefit from ultra-fast disks and lots of memory. You can also put redundant disks in a RAID-1, RAID-5, or RAID-10 configuration that would offer a similar level of redundancy as a software cluster and would probably perform better. Do not underestimate the costs of such hardware, and remember the limitations and consequences of a scale-up approach. They still apply!

Isolate the web server: The second option is to isolate the web server so it can concentrate on caching and serving static pages with lots of memory and a fast network connection. If your application is heavy on static content and wants a chance at surviving the Digg effect, you might want to choose a dedicated web server. The application and database are isolated on a second internal server. Conveniently, you still have the security advantage of keeping the database away from the web server. However, deploying the web server and application server to a separate machines loses the benefit of directly serving cached pages that Rails creates on the fly. Clustered or shared file systems, or another web server on the app server, may solve the problem. In any case, the isolated web server roles look like this in a Capistrano configuration:

```
# Relevant lines of deploy.rb
# ...
role :web, "www1.brainspl.at"
role :app, "internal.brainspl.at"
role :db,  "internal.brainspl.at", :primary => true
```

It's a subtle difference that has huge consequences. The type of application you're running and the hardware available to you will dictate the right option. If you plan on quickly growing beyond the capacity supported by either of these options, then you might want to consider a third option, because you'll likely end up there anyway.

Cluster: This third option has both servers running all the roles: web server, application, and database. It offers the benefit of full redundancy. You can lose one entire server, and the site will keep running with data intact. The site may well perform better under certain kinds of load. Given two users, each will have a full application stack and dedicated hardware ready to serve the individual request. However, the option is somewhat less secure because the database lives in the same environment as the web server, fully exposed to web-related bugs and security risks.

This configuration can be a bear to set up, especially with regard to the database. Separating reads and writes to different databases with a single master/slave configuration won't do you much good if either one crashes.

If you want full redundancy, you need to implement a synchronous database cluster that supports reading and writing to either database instance. I've dedicated a full section to it in Section 7.8, *Clustering MySQL*, on page 172. For now, I'll assume it's already set up. The following Capistrano configuration makes use of it:

```
# Relevant lines of deploy.rb
# ...
role :web, "www1.brainspl.at"
role :app, "www1.brainspl.at"
role :db,  "www1.brainspl.at", :primary => true

role :web, "www2.brainspl.at"
role :app, "www2.brainspl.at"
role :db,  "www2.brainspl.at"
```

Combining Approaches with More Servers

Capistrano and Rails are flexible enough to support a great number of server configuration options. As soon as you scale beyond two servers, you have many, many more options. The following sections highlight a few of the more popular options.

Four Servers: Clustered Database

This configuration has a clustered database with separate web and app servers. This configuration emphasizes transactions and dynamic data. If your database is the bottleneck or you need to add failover at the database level, this configuration is a good place to start:

```
# Relevant lines of deploy.rb
# ...
role :web, "www.brainspl.at"
role :app, "app.brainspl.at"
role :db,  "db1.brainspl.at", :primary => true
role :db,  "db2.brainspl.at"
```

Five Servers: Clustered Web Servers

This configuration uses clustered web servers, a separate app server and a scaled-up database. The emphasis for this solution is on static content, but it has extra muscle in the database server to handle load.

```
# Relevant lines of deploy.rb
# ...
role :web, "www1.brainspl.at"
role :web, "www2.brainspl.at"
role :web, "www3.brainspl.at"
role :app, "app.brainspl.at"
role :db,  "bigdb.brainspl.at", :primary => true
```

Ten Servers

This configuration, shown in Figure 7.3, on the next page, supports a full cluster with no specific emphasis. Two large database servers support the application as clustering a database to more than two servers starts to yield fewer benefits with each server. If you want to cluster the database server more broadly, consider sharding, which I discuss in more detail in Section 7.8, *Challenge 3: Clustering vs. Sharding*, on page 173.

```
# Relevant lines of deploy.rb
# ...
role :web, "www1.brainspl.at"
role :web, "www2.brainspl.at"
role :web, "www3.brainspl.at"
role :app, "app1.brainspl.at"
role :app, "app2.brainspl.at"
role :app, "app3.brainspl.at"
role :app, "app4.brainspl.at"
role :app, "app5.brainspl.at"
role :db,  "bigdb1.brainspl.at", :primary => true
role :db,  "bigdb2.brainspl.at"
```

Web Servers vs. Application Servers: What's the Difference?

At this point you've heard a lot about web and app roles. I've also hinted that Mongrels may not make the best web servers. It's time to drill down a little deeper.

The Web Server

The web server is good at quickly routing requests, serving static file content, and caching, so it makes an excellent proxy that sits in front of the application server. After briefly flirting with lighttpd, the Rails community seems to have settled on one of two servers that are preferred in the web role: Apache and nginx. Apache is a scalable, full-featured,

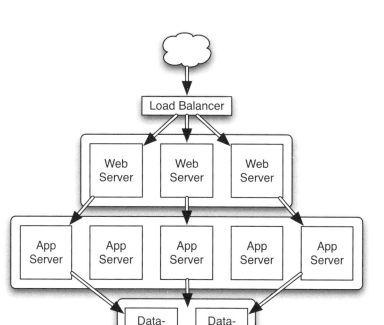

Figure 7.3: A TEN-SERVER CLUSTER

and extremely reliable web server. But with Apache, you may get more than you want and may suffer with having to configure it regardless. Enter nginx. This Russian creation is very capable and well suited to sitting in front of a Mongrel cluster. However, nginx has a simpler configuration, is very fast, and uses minimal system resources. It makes a great candidate for virtual hosting services where memory is limited and software efficiency is key.

The Application Server

The application server is a container focused on securely executing code and managing the runtime environment. For Rails, a single runtime environment is not enough because Rails uses a single-threaded architecture. One Mongrel can serve only one request at a time. Because of its share-nothing architecture, each concurrent user request to a Rails application requires an isolated runtime environment.

The Rails application server architecture has two challenges:

- Mongrel is not optimized for serving static content, and doing so puts unnecessary load on the Rails controller.
- In a production environment, you will have multiple application servers on different ports, so you need a router of sorts to distribute requests among them.

You'll need a web server optimized for routing requests, serving static content, and caching. You can also see the need for an application server optimized for serving Rails requests. Mongrel is by far the most preferred server for Rails content because of its performance, stability, and security. FastCGI is also an option and is marginally faster than Mongrel. But because of stability problems and configuration headaches, few would choose FastCGI over Mongrel.

At this point, make sure your Mongrel instance is working as a cluster and running as a service. In the sections to come, I'll lay out the other side of this equation: the static web server.

7.6 Apache

Apache may be the most successful open source project ever created. Apache powers some of the biggest Internet sites in the world and has a huge community. Apache also has an official 501(c)(3) nonprofit behind it—the Apache Software Foundation. Apache is a safe bet to remain the de facto standard web server for a long time to come.

Despite its success, Apache is not always easy to install, configure, or manage. Like anything, it's a matter of perspective and opinion. Some people believe Apache is complex and hard to set up. Others believe it is one of the easiest because of its incredible flexibility. Regardless of which one is true, if you choose to run Apache, you'll want to set it up properly now. You don't want to hammer in a simple configuration and then be a slave to that configuration later. Before you roll up your sleeves, you should have a more detailed picture of what Apache will do for you.

Separation of Concerns: Web Server Style

I'm going to take a little bit of a different approach to configuring Apache here. I'm going to use more virtual host proxies than usual.

I'm going to do this for a few reasons:

- To better isolate various configuration elements to make it easier for you to read and follow.
- To separate the concerns and responsibilities into different virtual servers.
- To mock the behavior of infrastructure components that would be hard to demonstrate while you follow through these examples on your own—unless you happen to have a hardware load balancer on hand to distribute requests between your virtual machines. I don't, so I'll use Apache.

That last point is especially important. You normally would have a hardware load balancer distributing requests to the web servers on each of your virtual machines, which would then either serve up some static content or forward the request to one of the Mongrels in your cluster. You can already begin to imagine the layering of responsibilities. Initially, Apache serves as a web server, taking all incoming HTTP requests. Then, Apache serves as a static proxy, serving static pages as requests come in. Then, when dynamic requests come in, Apache serves as a load balancer that forwards requests to the appropriate web server.

However, in the absence of a hardware load balancer, you'll set up a couple of Apache virtual servers to handle the following tasks:

- Load balancing between the virtual machines
- Forwarding HTTP requests on port 80 to the web server on one of those virtual machines
- Forwarding secure HTTPS/SSL requests on port 443, possibly just to a regular nonsecure HTTP web server on port 80 within our intranet

Prerequisites

Before we start, you'll need to ensure that Apache is installed on your server. If you are hosting with a managed VPS host, your provider may have installed Apache by default. I recommend using Apache 2.2, and that's what I'm going to configure here. You'll also need mod_ssl installed to handle HTTPS requests on port 443. If you don't have these installed, it's usually a simple matter. On CentOS or Fedora, use yum install httpd and yum install mod_ssl. On Debian or Ubuntu, use apt-get install apache and apt-get install libapache-mod-ssl. You can also compile Apache from source, but for that I suggest buying an Apache book.

To fully simulate a load-balanced environment on your local machine, you'll need three (yes, three) virtual machines. Now would be a good time to make copies of your virtual machine image and configure their hostnames and IP addresses so that you have three uniquely identifiable machines.

Apache as a Load Balancer

Using Apache in place of a hardware load balancer may not yield the best performance, but it will give you an opportunity to explore the proxy balancer features that Apache provides in a simpler context. In essence, you have two virtual machines, and you want to distribute evenly between them. How evenly depends on the load balancer implementation, and Apache's is fairly simplistic, but it will do for now.

Apache's configuration starts with one file found at one of two locations depending on your Linux distribution:

- *Debian, Ubuntu*: /etc/apache2/conf/apache2.conf
- *Fedora, CentOS*: /etc/httpd/conf/httpd.conf

The contents of the files are similar. From here on in, we'll refer primarily to the apache2-based names. On some Linux distributions, there will be an empty httpd.conf file besides the apache2.conf file. Ignore it.

I've noticed that some VPS service providers like to break the configuration file up into pieces and customize it quite a bit. You should leave the configuration as intact as possible because it's likely optimized for the limitations of your VPS. Also, they may already have a directory for you to place your own custom site configurations in. Be sure to read the specific documentation for your VPS host. Different Linux distributions may already have a directory for you to place your own site configurations in. So again, be sure to check with the documentation for your specific Linux distribution. Usually the only thing that is different is the specific directory locations. They will always be fairly obviously named, derived from either apache or httpd, with custom app directories named sites and apps.

Fedora and CentOS have a fairly simplistic directory structure that you will need to customize for yourself. Ubuntu has a nice default directory structure that can be easily imitated on Fedora and CentOS. However, it's bad enough the Apache configuration files are named differently and are in different locations. So, to make this discussion as easy to follow as possible, we'll make a new directory for our Rails applications so we can all be on the same page.

First let's orient ourselves. Navigate to the Apache 2 configuration directory, which again will be either /etc/apache2/conf or /etc/httpd/conf. Then at the command line, enter tail apache2.conf or tail httpd.conf. At the bottom of the file, you will notice that it probably "includes" a couple of other directories, for example:

- Include /etc/apache2/conf.d/
- Include /etc/apache2/sites-enabled/

The first conf.d/ directory is for common or reusable snippets of configuration. Think of it like a lib directory of sorts but for configuration. We won't be using it here. The second should appear on most Ubuntu or Debian Linux distributions. Your Linux distribution may differ, or your VPS host provider may have included some other directories, which you're free to use instead of those we'll suggest here. For simplicity, let's add a new included configuration directory. At the very end of the file—below the other Include statements—add the following:

```
Include conf/applications/*.conf
```

This line simply includes your private configuration file, giving you a place to work. It can be any directory you like. You can now add your own *.conf files to the /etc/apache2/conf/applications/ subdirectory, which act like extensions to the master configuration file. The other 990 lines of apache2.conf (aka httpd.conf) are beyond the scope of this book to discuss in detail. The good news is that the vast majority of those lines are actually inline documentation! The Apache developers do a good job of documenting the configuration file, or at least the basics of it. Take a look and read it. While you're there, as an exercise, find some of the following pieces of information: the document root, the user and group to run the processes as, the number of worker processes, the listening port, the log file locations, and the virtual host example. Here's a bonus question: if you have mod_ssl installed, how is the SSL configuration loaded? I'll touch upon that in a bit.

The Apache configuration file looks kind of like XML, but it uses number (#) signs to comment lines. Once you are a little more familiar with the Apache configuration files, you can start to create your own. You're going to be configuring virtual hosts, which will in some cases override some of the configurations you saw in apache2.conf. Most notably, the root directory will no longer point to the document root that you found. Your virtual host will handle the routing of those requests instead.

Configuring the Load Balancer VM

You're going to create three files to cleanly separate concerns. All of them should be placed in the /etc/apache2/conf/applications directory included in the apache2.conf file you edited earlier. If the /etc/apache2/conf/applications directory doesn't exist yet, create it now.

- cluster.conf will define a load balancer that will distribute requests across two or more machines.
- http_proxy.conf will define a virtual host that will proxy typical HTTP requests on port 80 to the load balancer.
- https_proxy.conf will define a virtual host that will proxy secure HTTPS requests on port 443 to the load balancer.

Let's start with cluster.conf, into which you'll put the following:

```
# cluster.conf
<Proxy balancer://mycluster>
  BalancerMember http://10.0.0.102:80
  BalancerMember http://10.0.0.103:80
</Proxy>
```

This file defines the cluster definition itself. The Proxy stanza defines the load balancer named *mycluster*. You are free to name the cluster whatever you like, and it should probably be something meaningful to your environment or application.

The balancer includes two BalancerMember entries—one for each of our virtual machines. Here I'm using the IP address and specifying the port explicitly. In certain cases, you may have different servers running on different ports, and Apache lets you fully map requests received on port 80 of the proxy to any port on the balancer members. You'll see an example of that later when we map requests to our Mongrel cluster.

By itself, cluster.conf would not impact your site very much. You need to somehow tell the server to use the balancer, which brings us to the next step: defining the virtual host to proxy the requests. The file you'll use to do that is http_proxy.conf:

```
# http_proxy.conf
<VirtualHost *:80>
  ServerName brainspl.at
  ServerAlias www.brainspl.at
  ServerAlias 10.0.0.101 # if you don't have a hostname yet
```

```
  ProxyPass / balancer://mycluster/
  ProxyPassReverse / balancer://mycluster/

  ErrorLog logs/http_proxy_error_log
  TransferLog logs/http_proxy_access_log
  LogLevel warn
</VirtualHost>
```

The first three lines, ServerName and ServerAlias, tell the virtual server which hostnames to intercept. These commands allow you to host multiple websites with different domain names on a single server easily. That's pretty nice stuff. I generally map the A record from my DNS configuration to the ServerName property if I can and then map any relevant CNAME records in the ServerAlias. That implementation is clean and consistent with our DNS configuration.

The next two lines, ProxyPass and ProxyPassReverse, tell Apache to map the root path (/) of this virtual host to a load balancer called mycluster.

Finally, you'll configure the location and name of our error and access logs, as well as set the log level, which is pretty self-explanatory.

Next, I'll dive a little deeper and configure a secured port just like this. I'll put this configuration in a file called https_proxy.conf. It starts out exactly like the HTTP version but then gets a little more complicated. Here is what the file should look like:

```
# https_proxy.conf
NameVirtualHost *:443
<VirtualHost *:443>
  ServerName brainspl.at
  ServerAlias www.brainspl.at
  ServerAlias 10.0.0.101 # if you don't have a hostname yet
  ProxyPass / balancer://mycluster/
  ProxyPassReverse / balancer://mycluster/
  ErrorLog logs/https_proxy_error_log
  TransferLog logs/https_proxy_access_log
  LogLevel warn

  RequestHeader set X_FORWARDED_PROTO 'https'

  SSLEngine on
  # The following line was broken to fit the book.
  # Don't break it when you type it!
  SSLCipherSuite  ALL:!ADH:!EXPORT56:RC4+RSA:
+HIGH:+MEDIUM:+LOW:+SSLv2:+EXP:+eNULL
  SSLCertificateFile /etc/apache2/conf/ssl/crt/server.crt
  SSLCertificateKeyFile /etc/apache2/conf/ssl/key/server.key
```

```
  <FilesMatch "\.(cgi|shtml|phtml|php)$">
    SSLOptions +StdEnvVars
  </FilesMatch>
  <Directory "/var/www/cgi-bin">
    SSLOptions +StdEnvVars
  </Directory>
  BrowserMatch ".*MSIE.*" \
    nokeepalive ssl-unclean-shutdown \
    downgrade-1.0 force-response-1.0
</VirtualHost>
```

The first line tells Apache that you want to access your virtual host by names based on the URL of the incoming request. Without this, your server would likely never be invoked because the default handler will grab all the incoming requests. With this enabled, when it sees the server name or one of the server aliases in the URL, it knows that this is the virtual host to use.

The next seven lines of https_proxy.conf look very much like its HTTP counterpart. In fact, you could have created an include file for the first four lines to avoid the duplication.

However, I chose to duplicate it for readability and because it's four lines in two files in the same directory. I'll warn you that there's a nice balance somewhere between excessive duplication and excessive hierarchies of include files. Both can be overdone.

The rest of the file is quite different, starting with RequestHeader called X_FORWARDED_PROTO. Recall that in your cluster configuration, both of your balancer members used basic, unencrypted HTTP on port 80. Without forwarding the protocol, your Rails application would be unaware that the request actually came through over a secure connection. This information is important to e-commerce applications that might redirect the user to a secure page when necessary. X_FORWARDED_PROTO tricks Rails into thinking that it was directly requested via an HTTPS protocol.

The rest of the lines are awkward to the extreme. This confusion loses friends for Apache. But there is good news. Luckily, the mod_ssl installation or VPS host probably created a default SSL configuration file, usually called ssl.conf. On Fedora and CentOS it is located in /etc/apache2/conf.d/. On Ubuntu and Debian, it is located in /etc/apache2/mods-available. Also, on Ubuntu/Debian you should also see a symbolic link to ssl.conf in /etc/apache2/mods-enabled. If you do not, you need to enable the module by typing on the command line: a2enmod ssl. Even though it sounds annoying, Ubuntu's a2enmod/a2dismod and a2ensite/a2dissite are worth looking into.

Regardless of where ssl.conf is located, in it you'll find all the same lines that are listed earlier (and more). I certainly won't try to increase our page count by repeating the file here, so you should go give it a quick read if you have it.

There are two options that I should mention, though: SSLCertificateFile and SSLCertificateKeyFile. These two lines specify the location of your private key file and your certificate. SSL and public key cryptography is another one of those subjects that would double the size of this book. I'll settle for giving you enough information to set up your test environment, but you should definitely research this topic further for your production environment. Luckily, most hosting providers will help you out here and may even properly set up the keys up for you. You do have to pay for these keys to be signed by a certificate authority for them to be valid. You don't have to do that with your test certificates, but realize that they won't be secure, and your user's browsers will tell them so with an irritating warning.

Here's how to generate the test certificates:

```
#root> # Generate a private key file with a passphrase
#root> openssl genrsa -des3 -out server.key 1024

#root> # TEST ONLY: Remove the passphrase to make
#root> # our test environment easier to manage
#root> # DO NOT do this in production. The *.pem
#root> # file is the key file without the passphrase
#root> openssl rsa -in server.key -out server.pem

#root> # Generate a certificate signing request.
#root> # Answer aquestions as accurately as you can for test environment
#root> openssl req -new -key server.pem -out server.csr

#root> # TEST ONLY: Self sign the key.
#root> # In production the Certificate Authority's signature is what matters.
#root> openssl x509 -req -in server.csr -signkey server.pem -out server.crt
```

An alternative to generating them is to just use the examples that Apache created when you installed mod_ssl. You can check the default ssl.conf I mentioned before to find the locations of those example files.

In a true production situation, you'll want keep the key file encrypted and lock down the file itself so that only root has access to it. If you lose this file or if it is compromised by a malicious party, you will have to buy a new certificate and immediately revoke the old one.

With that, your Apache-based software load balancer is done. You can now test it by starting Apache on all three virtual machines. You can start, restart, stop, or test the Apache configuration as follows:

- sudo /etc/init.d/apache2 start

- sudo /etc/init.d/apache2 restart

- sudo /etc/init.d/apache2 stop

- sudo /etc/init.d/apache2 configtest

The configtest option will often give some insight into any problems if the server is failing to start.

To test the cluster and see how it behaves, you should put something interesting and uniquely identifiable in the /var/www/html/index.html file of your balancer members. That way, you can watch how your balancer distributes requests between them by refreshing the balancer URL. If everything is working properly, you should see the page alternating between the two balancer members.

You're not here to serve static index.html pages, though. It's now time to set up the balancer members with your Rails application! The cool thing is that it's really no different from what you've seen so far. It's just another proxy balancer on another server. You already know most of what you need, but let's step through it together.

Apache as a Mongrel Proxy

As you recall, Mongrel is a cool little web server that's custom-tailored to serve up a single request through the Rails share-nothing architecture. Therefore, you need to run multiple Mongrels to allow multiple users of our application to use your site concurrently. Otherwise, your users would all be waiting in line for a single Mongrel server. You've just learned in the previous section that Apache can balance requests across multiple servers, so let's do that for Mongrel now.

First remember that you're no longer on the same virtual machine as before. You're done with the software load balancer and are now working on one of the balancer members.

On each balancer member, you're going to create two files, only to keep the concerns separated as before. These files will also reside in /etc/apache2/conf/applications/, and you'll need to remember to add the Include conf/applications/*.conf to /etc/apache2/conf/apache2.conf. These are the files you'll need:

- mongrel_cluster.conf will define a load balancer that will distribute requests across two or more Mongrel servers.

- mongrel_proxy.conf will define a virtual host that will proxy typical HTTP requests on port 80 to the Mongrel cluster.

Note the lack of a secure SSL configuration. The reason for that omission is that our software load balancer configured in the previous section will take care of that for us. A hardware load balancer would do the same. Secure requests are proxied through to a basic HTTP service on port 80 of our balancer members, which are inside our firewall. This keeps the configuration of the balancer members far cleaner. The exception is if you do want to expose your balancer members directly (for example, www1.brainspl.at), then you may need additional configuration in the load balancer to support SSL for each one.

The Mongrel cluster configuration contained in mongrel_cluster.conf will look very familiar:

```
# mongrel_cluster.conf
<Proxy balancer://mongrelcluster>
  BalancerMember http://0.0.0.0.8000
  BalancerMember http://0.0.0.0.8001
  BalancerMember http://0.0.0.0.8002
  BalancerMember http://0.0.0.0.8003
</Proxy>
```

This time, you'll notice that we're not balancing to a different server. Recall our Capistrano roles. In this case, it's clear that this one server is filling both the web and app roles. If we wanted to separate the web and app roles, we'd run the Mongrels on a different server, and the IP addresses in the cluster would be to a remote server. For example:

```
# Alternative mongrel_cluster.conf
# with separated web and app roles
<Proxy balancer://mongrelcluster>
  BalancerMember http://10.0.0.104.8000
  BalancerMember http://10.0.0.104.8001
  BalancerMember http://10.0.0.104.8002
  BalancerMember http://10.0.0.104.8003
</Proxy>
```

Also remember that in our /etc/mongrel_cluster/myapp.conf file, there was a line restricting the IP address allowed to access the Mongrel servers:

```
# Partial /etc/mongrel_cluster/myapp.conf
# ...
address: 0.0.0.0
# ...
```

If you're running both on the same server, you can use the IP address 0.0.0.0 or 127.0.0.1. If you've separated the web and app roles, this address line will have to match the web server/Mongrel proxy—the server you're working with now (for example, 10.0.0.101). Note that these are all internal IP addresses we're using here, not public IP addresses exposed to the Internet.

Also recall the following two lines from /etc/mongrel_cluster/myapp.conf:

```
# Partial /etc/mongrel_cluster/myapp.conf
# ...
servers: 4
port: "8000"
# ...
```

These two values will determine how many balancer members you will have and what their port numbers will be. In this example, there would be four servers ranging from port 8000 to 8003. Thus, that's our balancer configuration.

The second file that you need on each balancer member, and the final Apache configuration file we'll deal with, is mongrel_proxy.conf. If you're keen, you are probably thinking you already know the answer here, because you can just add a virtual host that routes all requests to the balancer. That does indeed work, and the configuration would look nearly identical to the virtual hosts we defined on the load balancer:

```
# A very simple mongrel_proxy.conf
<VirtualHost *:80>
  ServerName www1.brainspl.at
  ServerAlias 10.0.0.102 # if you don't have a hostname yet
  RequestHeader set X_FORWARDED_HOST 'www.brainspl.at'

  ProxyPass / balancer://mongrelcluster/
  ProxyPassReverse / balancer://mongrelcluster/

  ErrorLog logs/mongrel_proxy_error_log
  TransferLog logs/mongrel_proxy_access_log
  LogLevel warn
</VirtualHost>
```

I have added only one new element here. Did you spot it? The X_ FORWARDED_HOST header is there to trick Rails into thinking the hostname is one thing, even if it is actually something else. The reason for this is that after all of this proxying and indirection, the original hostname will likely be lost in the shuffle. This trick just makes it easier for Rails to do things like redirect to its own server, without having to worry about unintentionally getting an internal hostname instead of the public web address.

The disadvantage here is performance. This configuration would have Mongrel serving up static content and images, as well as all cached Rails pages. You didn't go through all this work just to be as slow as Mongrel! You want to leverage the Apache web server and have it serve up the static stuff. The unfortunate solution here is yet another configuration that will have you turning up your nose a bit. It is not a trivial or easily digestible approach. Luckily, once again, you can pretty much take it line for line and use it in your own applications.

There is another approach that does away with the ProxyPass and ProxyPassReverse configurations and replaces them with a number of URL-rewriting statements. The advantage is that Apache will serve static content directly, which is far faster and leaves your Mongrels available for more important work that actually requires application code to run. The following listing contains the mongrel_proxy.conf file in its entirety. I've numbered the sections for later discussion and identified the purpose in capital letters where relevant. Look through it, and then I'll walk you through it:

```
# A full featured mongrel_proxy.conf
<VirtualHost *:80>
  ServerName www1.brainspl.at
  ServerAlias 10.0.0.102 # if you don't have a hostname yet
  RequestHeader set X_FORWARDED_HOST 'www.brainspl.at'

  ### New configuration elements begin here. ###

  # 1. Document root specified to provide access to static files directly
  DocumentRoot /home/deploy/applications/myapp/current/public
  <Directory /home/deploy/applications/myapp/current/public>
    Options FollowSymLinks
    AllowOverride None
    Order allow,deny
    Allow from all
  </Directory>

  RewriteEngine On
```

```
# 2. SECURITY: Don't allow SVN directories to be accessed
RewriteRule ^(.*/)?\.svn/ - [F,L]
ErrorDocument 403 "Access Forbidden"

# 3. MAINTENANCE:  Temporary display of maintenance file if it exists
RewriteCond %{DOCUMENT_ROOT}/system/maintenance.html -f
RewriteCond %{SCRIPT_FILENAME} !maintenance.html
RewriteRule ^.*$ /system/maintenance.html [L]

# 4. PERFORMANCE:  Check for static index and cached pages.
RewriteRule ^/$ /index.html [QSA]
RewriteRule ^([^.]+)$ $1.html [QSA]

# 5. OTHERWISE:  If no static file exists, let Mongrel handle the request
RewriteCond %{DOCUMENT_ROOT}/%{REQUEST_FILENAME} !-f
RewriteRule ^/(.*)$ balancer://mongrel_cluster%{REQUEST_URI} [P,QSA,L]

# 6. PERFORMANCE:  Compress text output for compatible browsers
AddOutputFilterByType DEFLATE text/html text/plain text/xml
BrowserMatch ^Mozilla/4 gzip-only-text/html
BrowserMatch ^Mozilla/4\.0[678] no-gzip
BrowserMatch \bMSIE !no-gzip !gzip-only-text/html

### End new configuration elements, logging below is the same. ###


ErrorLog logs/mongrel_proxy_error_log
TransferLog logs/mongrel_proxy_access_log
LogLevel warn
</VirtualHost>
```

The first thing you'll notice is a fairly typical-looking web server document root stanza (#1). This is what allows static content to be served. However, before it attempts to serve any file, Apache must execute a number of rewrite rules. These rules are based on regular expressions that check for some condition and then rewrite the request to modify the resulting behavior. For example, the first rewrite rule (#2) blocks access to .svn directories that Capistrano tends to leave behind. The next group of rules form a maintenance (#3) rule that lets you gracefully respond to visitors while your site is not available. But the next rules (#4) demonstrate the overall goal: better performance. They look for static index pages when no file is specified in the URL and also serve up cached Rails pages if they exist. If Apache can't find a static file matching the request, Rails handles the request through the last pair of rewrite rules (#5). Finally, to speed up network transfers at the expense of some processing power, you can optionally enable the mod_deflate output filter (#6) to compress outbound text data.

These are huge performance advantages for high-traffic sites. Not only is Apache faster at serving static content, but it keeps unnecessary load off of the Mongrels so they can efficiently handle only Rails requests.

You can now start up Apache and the Mongrel cluster on your balancer members. Better yet, have Capistrano do it! After all, that's what Capistrano is for. Also, you have only a single database so far, and therefore you have to configure it to accept connections from remote servers. This database configuration is usually a simple matter of granting permissions to remote users (for example, 'deploy'@'10.0.0.102') on your database. I'll cover more advanced MySQL topics later in this chapter.

Congratulations! You have now configured a highly flexible and high-performance clustered server architecture. If you look back and consider some of your options, you can scale this out to six servers quite easily: the software load balancer, two web proxy servers, two application servers, and a database server. You can play around with your local virtual machines to try adding another web server or to try separating the web and app roles onto different hosts. Otherwise, if you've found all this to be a little overbearing, with too much unneeded flexibility and indirection, or if your server is strictly limited to low resources, you might need an alternative to Apache. In that case, there's nginx.

7.7 nginx, from Russia with Love

nginx (pronounced "engine-x") is a fast, lightweight web server written by Igor Sysoev. It is extremely well suited as a front-end server for Mongrel clusters. Out of the box, some find that nginx serves static files faster and under heavier load than Apache, often using a fraction of the resources under similar work loads. Where Apache focuses clearly on modularity and flexibility, nginx focuses on simplicity and performance. That's not to say nginx isn't feature rich, because it has nice built-in rewrite and proxy modules and a clean configuration file syntax that makes it a pleasure to use.

The proxy module has similar capabilities to mod_proxy_balancer in Apache, so it works great for fronting clusters of Mongrels. Conditional if statements and regular expressions matching allow precise control over which requests get served as static content and which dynamic requests nginx will proxy through to a Mongrel back end.

nginx is surprisingly full-featured considering how fast and efficient it is. It has support for SSL, HTTP AUTH, FastCGI, gzip compression, FLV streaming, memcached, and many other modules, so you'll be able to handle the more advanced topics in this book such as caching and clustering. The nginx wiki (http://wiki.codemongers.com/nginx) is the definitive place go for nginx documentation.

nginx can do everything you configured Apache to do in the previous section: software load balancing, acting as a Mongrel proxy, and serving static content. If you repeated everything all over again with nginx, you'd probably find it quite repetitive. Instead, I'll show you the nginx configuration and separate the concerns as before. That should give you enough knowledge to configure nginx as we did Apache or however you like. I think you'll agree that the simplicity of the nginx configuration will make it quite a bit more straightforward compared to Apache.

Starting, Stopping, and Reloading

If you haven't already noticed, nginx has a more hard-core feel to it. Case in point: you have to compile it from source, and even after it's installed, it doesn't come with all the user-friendly service scripts that Apache comes with. You've already installed nginx in Chapter 4, *Virtual and Dedicated Hosts*, on page 65. To start it, you'll be running the executable directly, and to stop or restart it, you'll be using the kill program to send signals to the process. This sounds like it could get messy, but luckily the basics for using it are pretty simple. To start the server, run the command /usr/local/nginx/sbin/nginx as root. That command will load the configuration file at/usr/local/nginx/conf/nginx.conf. To load or test other configuration files, you'll need a couple of options:

-c filename Load the configuration file named filename instead of the default file.

-t   Don't run the server. Just test the configuration file.

As with other *nix applications, you can control nginx through the use of signals. To use signals, you'll need the process ID. Use this version of the ps command to get it (output truncated to fit the book):

```
ezra$ ps -aef | egrep '(PID|nginx)'
UID     PID PPID .. CMD
root    6850    1 .. nginx: master /usr/local/nginx/sbin/nginx
nobody 6979 6850 .. nginx: worker
nobody 6980 6850 .. nginx: worker
nobody 6981 6850 .. nginx: worker
nobody 6982 6850 .. nginx: worker
```

The master process PID is 6850, as you can see in the Parent Process ID (PPID) column of the output. nginx is architected as a single master process with any number of worker processes. We are running four workers in our configuration. You can stop the master process with the kill 15 signal (kill -15 6850), which will also kill the worker processes. If you change a configuration file, you can reload it without restarting nginx:

```
ezra$# The -c option is only needed if your .conf file is in a custom location.
ezra$ sudo /usr/local/nginx/sbin/nginx -c /etc/nginx/nginx.conf
ezra$ sudo kill -HUP 614
```

The first command sets up the new configuration file. The second sends a kill signal with HUP. The HUP signal is a configuration reload signal. If the configuration is successful, nginx will load the new configuration into new worker processes and kill the old ones. Now you know enough to run the server, stop the server, and configure the server. The next step is building a configuration file.

Configuring nginx

nginx has a master configuration file that includes a number of other files, including our virtual host configurations. The master configuration file is stored at /usr/local/nginx/conf/nginx.conf. We're going to add a line to the end of that file to include our virtual host configurations. You're going to add only one line, but it's important to put it in the right spot. You want it in the http block:

```
# Partial nginx.conf
# ...
http {
  # ...
  # Include the following line at the end of the http block
  include /etc/nginx/vhosts/*.conf;
}
```

Be sure to create the vhosts directory for yourself. This should seem familiar, because it is very much like the approach you saw when setting up Apache. However, the nginx master configuration file is not well documented with inline comments, so I've done that for you in Appendix A, on page 251. Please take this time to refer to the nginx.conf file on your server, using Appendix A as a guide.

There is a default virtual host built into the master configuration file that you should remove. As you'll see in the next section, you'll be replacing the default virtual hosts with your own. You'll keep it in a separate file for cleanliness, though.

Virtual Host Configuration

The nginx virtual host configuration is similar to the Apache equivalent but with less noise. The syntax is more like that of a domain-specific language than a structured file format, which is more comfortable for Ruby programmers. You'll find most of the configuration elements familiar from our earlier discussions of the Apache configuration, but I'll go through each just to be sure.

The first thing you'll do in your virtual host configuration is set up a load-balancing cluster for your Mongrels. You'll then configure some typical HTTP details such as the server name, port, root directory, error files, and logs. Finally, you'll set up the URL-rewriting rules to make sure you get the most out of nginx by having it serve static files and cached Rails files and to help keep unnecessary load off your Mongrels.

Take a look at an nginx virtual host configuration file now. I'll name mine after my site and call it brainspl.at.conf:

```
# brainspl.at.conf
# nginx virtual host configuration file
# to be included by nginx.conf

# Load balance to mongrels
upstream mongrel_cluster {
  server 0.0.0.0:8000;
  server 0.0.0.0:8001;
  server 0.0.0.0:8002;
}

# Begin virtual host configuration
server {
  # Familiar HTTP settings
  listen 80;
  server_name brainspl.at *.brainspl.at;
  root /data/brainspl.at/current/public;
  access_log  /var/log/nginx/brainspl.at.access.log  main;
  error_page   500 502 503 504  /500.html;
  client_max_body_size 50M;

  # First rewrite rule for handling maintenance page
  if (-f $document_root/system/maintenance.html) {
    rewrite  ^(.*)$  /system/maintenance.html last;
    break;
  }
```

```
  location / {
    index   index.html index.htm;

    # Forward information about the client and host
    # Otherwise our Rails app wouldn't have access to it
    proxy_set_header  X-Real-IP  $remote_addr;
    proxy_set_header  X-Forwarded-For $proxy_add_x_forwarded_for;
    proxy_set_header Host $http_host;
    proxy_max_temp_file_size 0;

    # Directly serve static content
    location ~ ^/(images|javascripts|stylesheets)/ {
      expires 10y;
    }
    if (-f $request_filename) {
      break;
    }

    # Directly serve cached pages
    if (-f $request_filename.html) {
      rewrite (.*) $1.html break;
    }

    # Otherwise let Mongrel handle the request
    if (!-f $request_filename) {
      proxy_pass http://mongrel_cluster;
      break;
    }
  }
}
```

The upstream block defines a load-balancing cluster of three Mongrel
servers, which in this case happen to be on the same host as the nginx
server. You can, of course, separate the Mongrels onto their own application server and then simply specify a remote IP address here.

You can define as many clusters like this as you need, but be sure to
name each one uniquely and descriptively. In this case, I named it fairly
generically as mongrel_cluster.

The server block is the virtual host directive. You will need one server
block for each Rails app you want to run; pair it with a cluster as
you did in your upstream block. If you have only a single virtual host
accessing the cluster, you might as well keep it in the same file. But if
you have two or more virtual hosts accessing it, you might want to put
the upstream block in its own include file. That way, it's easier to find,
and you can maintain your separation of concerns as before.

The contents of the server block begins with some basic HTTP configuration. This HTTP configuration is quite self-explanatory, a result of the simplicity of the nginx configuration syntax. Read through it now. First, I'm configuring nginx to listen on the standard HTTP port 80. The server is named brainspl.at, and I've also aliased all subdomains (*.brainspl.at). I've set the document root to the /public directory of my Rails application, which was deployed with Capistrano. I pointed the main access log at a file specific to this server and set the default error page for 50x-class error codes. Finally, for security reasons, I've limited the maximum response size to avoid attempts to overload the server.

Just below the basic HTTP configuration, you'll see the first rewrite rule. You're already familiar with rewrite rules from the Apache configuration; however, I think you'll agree that these are cleaner and easier to read. That first rewrite rule checks for the existence of a maintenance.html file and displays it (and only it) if it exists. This rule allows you to gracefully respond to your visitors while you are making changes requiring an application shutdown.

The location block allows nginx to set custom configuration options for different URLs. In this default configuration, I'm setting configuration options for the root (/) . The index directive tells nginx which file to load for requests like / or/foo/. Here I'll use the standbys index.htm and index.html.

Next you'll see a group of proxy_* directives that forward information about the client and spoof information about the host to help hide the nginx proxy from the Rails application. This way, Rails has all the information it would normally have if it were serving requests directly to the user from one of the Mongrel servers. The forwarded information includes the IP of the client and the hostname we want Rails to see (for example, www.brainspl.at instead of the internal address of our Mongrel server). This is important for the request objects to work properly.

The sections immediately after the proxy_* directives are the meat of the URL rewriting. The expires directive sets the Expires header for any URLs that match images, JavaScripts, or style sheets. This rule will make the client download these respective assets only once and then use their local cached versions for ten years from the first download. When Capistrano deploys Rails apps, Capistrano appends a time stamp to the URL so that clients will think they are new assets and download them again. This allows you to push changes to the same filename and properly invalidate the cache.

Next, if the requested filename exists on disk, just serve it directly, and then finalize the request by breaking out of the block. If the static file doesn't exist, Rails then checks for the requested filename with .html appended. In other words, it checks for a cached Rails view. So when a user requests a URL such as /post/foo, nginx will check for /post/foo.html and serve it directly instead of proxying to Rails for a dynamic page.

Finally, if none of the other rules matched, the config then proxies the request to one of the Mongrels defined in the upstream block.

Secure Connections

To use SSL with nginx, you use a configuration that matches the server block as shown earlier but with the following differences:

- The secure HTTPS/SSL server will normally listen on port 443.

- SSL needs to be enabled.

- You need to create secure certificate and private key files and put them in the appropriate directories, just as we did with Apache.

- You need to forward one more header to ensure Rails knows when we have a secure connection.

You can put the configuration in another configuration file called brain-spl.at.ssl.conf. Remember to consider putting the upstream block from the non-SSL configuration into its own file and include it in the nginx. You can add the relevant lines like this:

```
server {
  listen 443;
  ssl on;
  # path to your certificate
  ssl_certificate /etc/nginx/certs/server.crt;
  # path to your ssl key
  ssl_certificate_key /etc/nginx/certs/server.key;

  # put the rest of your server configuration here.

  location / {
    # set X-FORWARDED_PROTO so ssl_requirement plugin works
    proxy_set_header X-FORWARDED_PROTO https;

    # standard rails+mongrel configuration goes here.
  }
}
```

Notice I didn't define the Mongrel cluster again. I can use the same one.

Taking It to the Next Level

You can get more life out of your web tier by first introducing hardware load balancing to replace the Apache-based load balancer you built earlier. Hardware load balancers offer many of the same features plus more, including enhanced security, proxying HTTPS/SSL requests, and server affinity (sticky load balancing).

Another excellent enhancement is to offload serving of large static content from your own web servers and instead employ a content delivery service. These services will cache images, videos, music, PDF files, and any other large files that you need not bother your own servers with. It doesn't make your application any faster, of course, but it certainly will reduce the load on your web server's network, memory, and disks.

7.8　Clustering MySQL

I've shown how you might cluster multiple web and application servers behind a software load balancer, but a single database on the back end can take you only so far. The database would be thrashed severely if you had ten servers all vying for its time and resources, so you need some solution to allow for multiple databases in your application infrastructure. I should warn you that you must customize clustering solutions to fit the application that you are building, considering carefully the balance of performance against data integrity concerns.

The Challenges with MySQL Clustering

In this book, I've chosen MySQL because it is by far the most common and best supported database for Rails applications. Truth be told, for the most extreme scalability problems, there are better databases on the market that offer more powerful clustering features. As it turns out, MySQL is actually not a very good candidate for clustering at all, because of some challenges.

Challenge 1: The Relational Database

MySQL is a relational database. Relational databases do not scale well to super-high loads like those experienced by Google and Facebook. Instead, such sites will often use simpler, faster systems such as the Oracle Berkeley DB, which is an in-process nonrelational data storage solution that offers far better performance and stability, even in a distributed environment. Others may use in-memory object-oriented databases or even flat files! Each of these has their pros and cons, but the relational database can actually be among the slower options, often favoring features over performance.[2]

Challenge 2: Asynchronous vs. Synchronous Replication

MySQL supports only asynchronous replication. Under this scaling model, you will have a lag between the time a transaction completes on one of the databases and when MySQL replicates that row to all the others in the cluster. This lag time can cause you pain when you are dealing with unique indexes such as the primary key. It's especially challenging with other unique indexes. Say that a given user must have a unique login. If two users took the same name at the same time, you'd have inconsistent data. The only solution is often your own custom algorithm for guaranteeing uniqueness. A few ambitious developers have formed projects to implement a synchronous clustering solution for MySQL, one that would eliminate the time-lag problem. One such project called google-mysql-tools includes a feature called SemiSyncReplication. Another is solidDB for MySQL, by Solid Information Technology. It also offers synchronous replication and other high-availability features. If you're serious about clustering MySQL, you should watch these projects.

Challenge 3: Clustering vs. Sharding

Clustering in general doesn't perform well enough for the most extreme database loads. Even if you do manage to get a synchronous cluster set up, certain kinds of transactions must update all the databases before completing. This limitation means that if you have ten database servers in your synchronous cluster and update a number of records that are centrally dependent to your system, your transaction will need to write to all ten servers! Your database cluster can easily become more of a hindrance than a help. Furthermore, it's hard to cluster in a geographically diverse way, so it becomes difficult to put one server in Japan and another in Canada and have them belong to a cluster. The performance implications of synchronizing a database across a wide network is not at all practical, regardless of the other benefits. So as an alternative to clustering, many modern high-load websites use an approach called *sharding*.

Sharding means splitting your database up into groupings of cohesive data, such that all the data that a certain user or function requires

---

2. See http://www.oracle.com/database/berkeley-db/index.html for more.

is colocated in one database, and data for other users or functions is stored in another database. For example, you might choose to store all the users whose names start with A–L in one database and M–Z in another. Or, you may choose to keep records based on geography, so you could store Japanese records in a database in Japan and Canadian records in a database located in Canada. Perhaps you can easily organize your database by data and time: a news site may store the most recent articles on one server and older archived ones on another. Sharding is highly application dependent, so I can't really do a good job of discussing approaches in a generic way within the scope of this book. You can imagine how complex this may make your application, though.

Challenge 4: The Official MySQL Cluster Is Limited

So far I've been using the term *cluster* in a pretty generic sense and will continue to do so because it's simply the best word to use for this situation. However, MySQL does distinguish between replication and clustering, and they're right to do so. In this book, the way that we implement the cluster is through MySQL replication features. Recall that the replication features are asynchronous and are not really meant to be used to create a cluster. Unfortunately, the fact is that the official MySQL cluster will not satisfy the requirements for most projects because of a number of limitations. As we'll soon see, MySQL replication simply works better to create a "poor man's cluster."

The official MySQL cluster feature uses a different data store called NDB. Like ISAM and InnoDB, NDB changes the way MySQL works and has its own advantages and disadvantages. Unfortunately for most people, the disadvantages and limitations will significantly outweigh the advantages. In my opinion, NDB borderlines on useless for most applications. If one of the replication approaches presented here doesn't work for you, then you're far better off seeking a commercial synchronous clustering/replication technology for MySQL. It is possible you might need to seek out a different RDBMS altogether. For more about the limitations of the NDB data store, see http://dev.mysql.com/doc/refman/4.1/en/mysql-cluster-limitations.html.

As you may be thinking by now, a scale-up approach for the database may be an easier solution. After all, you can buy a monstrous database server with sixteen cores, 16GB of RAM, four independent network interfaces, sixteen SCSI drives, and a RAID controller with a battery backup and 64MB of cache RAM. But that sounds expensive, and this is not a hardware book! So, pretend that you're a start-up with a Rails application experiencing medium to high load and that you have made an informed decision to cluster your MySQL database despite these challenges.

Separating Reads and Writes

The first approach to scaling out your database would be to separate the reads from the writes. MySQL has decent support for this model through its master/slave replication. The idea here is that all data is written to one of the single databases, the master, while all data reads occur on the slave. This strategy lets you optimize the databases more specifically for read or write performance and split the database up on to separate servers.

Configuring MySQL Master/Slave Replication

I have kind of a conservative nature, so I don't like to mess around with existing data too much. So, regardless of whether I have an existing database, I take the same approach to introducing the master/slave configuration to my environment. I will take the time to build a new master and slave virtual server from scratch. I find it less risky because I can work offline and less problematic because I am not balancing between old and new configurations. Once I've prepared the new master/slave servers, it's simply a task of dumping your data from the old database and uploading to the new one. Then, I can shut down the old server and introduce the new one into the environment. This approach may sound like you would have a lot of downtime, but really, you need to be down only for as long as it takes to dump the old data and import it into the new database. You won't have to rebuild your database infrastructure very often.

To set this up, you'll need two MySQL 5.0+ database servers, on separate virtual machines. The first thing you'll need to do is give each of your servers an identity. On the master machine, open /etc/my.cnf, and add the following two lines to the [mysqld] section:

```
# /etc/my.cnf on MASTER
# These lines added below the [mysqld] section
log-bin=mysql-bin
server-id=1
```

The first line, log-bin, tells MySQL to log activity in a binary format file using the prefix specified on the right side of the assignment. This binary logging needs to be done only on the master, and it's what the slave will read from when replicating data. The second line, server-id, is a unique identifier for the server, in this case, 1. Restart the master server using this:

```
# Restart MySQL -- My conservative nature leads
# me to avoid restart scripts for major changes.
/etc/init.d/mysqld stop
/etc/init.d/mysqld start
```

Next, set up the slave, which is even easier. You don't need to use the binary logging on the slave. Add the server ID to the slave, choosing a different ID, of course, and then restart the slave as you did the master:

```
# /etc/my.cnf on SLAVE
# Following line added below the [mysqld] section
server-id=2
```

You should now log into the master server as root and query the replication status using SHOW MASTER STATUS, which produces output like the following. The important bits to note are the file and the position. You'll need those to configure the slave.

```
mysql> # ON MASTER;
mysql> SHOW MASTER STATUS\G;
*************************** 1. row ***************************
            File: mysql-bin.000001
        Position: 98
    Binlog_Do_DB:
Binlog_Ignore_DB:
1 row in set (0.00 sec)
```

Now log into the slave and set the master using CHANGE MASTER TO. I usually use the same user as my Rails app, because it would normally have all the necessary permissions (ALL PRIVILEGES). You'll need to grant privileges to the remote user, though (for example, 'deploy'@'10.0.0.3'). Notice that I used the name of the file and position that I retrieved from the master server in the previous step.

```
mysql> # ON SLAVE;
mysql> CHANGE MASTER TO
    ->    MASTER_HOST='10.0.0.3',
    ->    MASTER_USER='deploy',
    ->    MASTER_PASSWORD='deploypassword',
    ->    MASTER_LOG_FILE='mysql-bin.000001',
    ->    MASTER_LOG_POS=98;
Query OK, 0 rows affected (0.04 sec)
```

You can now start the slave by using the START SLAVE command and stop it using STOP SLAVE. Stopping is more like pausing: when you start it up again, MySQL will catch up on anything it missed while it was stopped.

It can be frustrating if you make a mistake, which is another reason why I start with a fresh server. If you make a mistake and somehow the servers get out of sync and become deadlocked, you can start over. Simply use RESET MASTER and RESET SLAVE. The slave should be stopped, before resetting them. You should requery the master status with SHOW MASTER STATUS and rerun CHANGE MASTER TO to reconfigure the slave before restarting it. It's a worthwhile exercise to tinker around with this on a couple of test database instances and make mistakes on purpose to see how to get yourself out of them. If you have data to import, you can simply run your dump script against the master once everything is set up correctly. The slave should replicate all the imported data, assuming it's all set up correctly.

You can also set up multiple read-only databases. If your application is far heavier on reads than writes, then you may want more than one read-only database. The cool thing is that adding more read-only slaves can be a simple matter of stopping the slave temporarily, copying the slave virtual machine, and of course configuring the machine's identity. Recall that this includes the hostname, the IP address, and also the MySQL server ID! Don't forget that. You can then start up the slaves again, and the new one will pick up as if it had always been there.

To test your configuration, connect to the master server, create a database, create a table, and write a row or two to it. Then log onto the slave server to see whether the changes were replicated.

Configuring Your Rails Application

Now that you have two databases, one for writing and one for reading, you need to tell Rails how to use them. Unfortunately, Rails does not support this out of the box. So, you can write something yourself to override the finders and which database they can connect to, or you can search for something that someone else has already built.

I did, and I found something I really like acts_as_readonlyable (yes, that's the name). You can find it at the longest URL I've ever had to put in a book (but Google works too): http://revolutiononrails.blogspot.com/2007/04/plugin-release-actsasreadonlyable.html

Names aside, acts_as_readonlyable uses a very clean syntax and simple configuration for dealing with separate read and write databases. Follow the instructions on the website for installation. At the time of this writing, it was simply a script/plugin install with their most current release tag in their Subversion repository.

Once it's installed, you can configure additional read-only databases in your database.yml file:

```
production:
  database: my_app_master
  host: master_host

read_only_a:
  database: my_app_slave
  host: slave-a

read_only_b:
  database: my_app_slave
  host: slave-b
```

Applying the plug-in to your model classes is straightforward, and when you do so, your finders will behave differently. They will use the read-only databases specified in the parameter of the declaration. So, for example:

```
class Product < ActiveRecord::Base
  acts_as_readonlyable [:read_only_a,:read_only_b]
end
```

Here I've chosen to use two read-only databases. However, I think we can do one better. We can use this approach to achieve a sort of "poor man's sharding," by simply being selective about which read-only database is used by each model. For example:

```
# partial database.yml
#...
read_only_products:
  database: my_app_slave
  host: slave-products
read_only_articles:
  database: my_app_slave
  host: slave-articles

# product.rb
#...
class Product < ActiveRecord::Base
  acts_as_readonlyable [:read_only_products]
end

# article.rb
#...
class Article < ActiveRecord::Base
  acts_as_readonlyable [:read_only_article]
end
```

You can also get a little extreme and just apply the plug-in to all your model classes and cross your fingers, like this:

```
# environment.rb
# not recommended....
class << ActiveRecord::Base

  def read_only_inherited(child)
    child.acts_as_readonlyable :read_only
    ar_inherited(child)
  end

  alias_method :ar_inherited, :inherited
  alias_method :inherited, :read_only_inherited

end
```

I highly recommend against this. Because of the asynchronous replication in MySQL, there will be certain data you'll always want to read from the master database. Rails sessions are a good example of where lag between the write and read may create instability in your application. Also, beware of anything to do with money!

You've seen how to enjoy multiple read-only databases but are still constrained by being able to write to a single database only. It's time to enable two read/write databases.

Multimaster, Read/Write Clustering

The advantages to having two or more databases that accept writes are mostly stability and redundancy. Performance isn't greatly improved, because eventually the data does have to be written to each database in the cluster. But if you lose a server to a catastrophic failure, you can rest assured that your data will be mostly intact. I say "mostly" again because of the asynchronous replication. There is still a slight chance that data will be lost in a crash, before it can propagate throughout the cluster.

Now that we'll be reading and writing to the cluster, the challenges of asynchronous replication is doubled. Not only do we have to worry that the data may not be there when reading, but we also have to worry that it might already be there upon writing! If somehow a duplicate value was written to the same primary key column in two databases within the cluster, we'd have a real problem. MySQL allows us to configure offsets to keep autogenerated primary keys unique. Server 1 could have odd keys, and server 2 could have even keys, for example. But if you have any other unique indices on your tables, you will have to find your own solution for preventing conflicts.

Configuring the Asynchronous Multimaster MySQL Cluster

The configuration doesn't look much harder, but it can definitely be frustrating initially. So if you're going to try this, definitely bring a full bag of patience. Since you're already familiar with the my.cnf file, I'll spare you some time and tackle both master configurations in one shot. The following configuration files have comments identifying each server:

```
# /etc/my.cnf on FIRST MASTER
# These lines added below the [mysqld] section
    server-id=1
    log-bin=mysql-bin
    log-slave-updates
    replicate-same-server-id=0
    auto_increment_increment=10
    auto_increment_offset=1

# /etc/my.cnf on SECOND MASTER
# These lines added below the [mysqld] section
    server-id=2
    log-bin=mysql-bin
    log-slave-updates
    replicate-same-server-id=0
    auto_increment_increment=10
    auto_increment_offset=2
```

Notice the differences compared to the master/slave configuration we discussed before. Of course, you still need the server-id to identify each server. The first difference, though, is that both servers now use log-bin to enable binary logging. Each server will produce its own binary log and read the binary log from the other server. The log files allow each server to pick up the writes from the other server. It's the same concept as master/slave, but done twice over. You're using the same file prefix for the binary log files, but you can use whatever you like. The server name works perfectly well.

The log-slave-updates option ensures that if you chain more than one slave together in a circular arrangement, MySQL will forward along all updates received from other servers. Since you don't want to send the same update around in an infinite replication loop, the next option, replicate-same-server-id, tells a server to ignore its own updates.

Finally, the last two lines of each file help MySQL deal with asynchronous autoincrement key generation. The first, auto_increment_increment, tells MySQL to increment autoincrement fields by ten each time, essentially dividing the total number of possible keys a server can generate by ten. The auto_increment_offset command is basically added to the increment. By making this offset different for each server, you will avoid key collisions. The first master will generate keys such as 1, 11, 21, and 31, and the second master will generate keys like 2, 12, 22, and 32. Having an increment level of 10 basically leaves room in the keyspace for ten servers in your cluster. You can tune it higher or lower depending on the number of servers you expect to have, but I don't think introducing more than ten servers in an asynchronous cluster is practical. In fact, I probably wouldn't do more than two or three and would favor a hardware solution or replacing MySQL with a more capable clustered database solution.

The remainder of the configuration is the same as for the master/slave setup, but doubled up. As before, execute SHOW MASTER STATUS, but on each server. Take the values from each master, and use them in the appropriate file and position parameters of the CHANGE MASTER TO statement, on each slave. Then, use START SLAVE on both servers to bind them to each other. Refer to these steps in the earlier master/slave discussion for more details.

Testing your work is pretty straightforward. Create a database and some tables, and insert some rows on each server to ensure that MySQL updates both databases. It's pretty cool when you get it up and running. However, as you'll see in the next section, it's not all sunshine and roses.

Configuring Your Application for the Multimaster Cluster

The good news about a multimaster, read/write cluster is that you may not have to change your application at all. You won't need any plug-ins or special software. Your application sees a fully functional database and is unaware of the cluster. This transparency is nice, especially compared to handling the clustering by hand. But remember, being explicit with each update has advantages too, along the lines of the sharding solutions I presented earlier.

The multimaster approach has its own challenges, serious challenges indeed. Again, because of the asynchronous nature of the replication, you really have to be careful when you write sensitive data. In addition, you have to be aware of situations where a single user may make multiple requests in rapid succession, perhaps without even knowing it.

One of my favorite web application patterns is the Redirect-After-Post pattern. Posting is annoying because when the user hits the Back button in their browser, they get prompted to resend the data. However, if you redirect them after they post a form of data, their Back button behaves nicely, and their overall experience is improved. However, this pattern results in a very quick update to the database in one request and then a subsequent read within a second or two from the redirected request. Often, the very next request will query for the data that you just wrote.

In the case of a multimaster cluster, if the user posts to one server and is then redirected to a query for the same data on another server, that data may not have been written yet! This inconsistency could cause random instability in your site that's hard to track down. So when you use a multimaster cluster, use sticky load balancing to ensure that a given user remains on the same server for the duration of their browser session. Sticky balancing is not the best performing solution, but I'll always choose stability over performance.

Most web servers and hardware load balancers offer support for sticky load balancing. With Apache, the configuration is simple. Recall the Apache cluster definition from our software load balancer solution earlier in this chapter. It looked like the following, but we've made some changes:

```
# cluster.conf
<Proxy balancer://mycluster> lbmethod=byrequests stickysession=BALANCEID
  BalancerMember http://10.0.0.102:80 route=www1
  BalancerMember http://10.0.0.103:80 route=www2
</Proxy>
```

Did you spot the changes? In the first line I added lbmethod to tell the balancer to load balance every request, alternating the members between them. However, the stickysession option overrides the default behavior if it finds a cookie called BALANCEID with a valid route value. If the value of BALANCEID matches any of the route values of any balancer members, then it will ensure to balance only among balancer members with the same value. It basically locks a user's browser session into a specific balancer member or group of balancer members (yes, multiple balancer members can have the same route value).

You're not quite done yet, though. Your software load balancer itself does not set the cookie, so you need to ask your web servers to do that for you.

Luckily, it's a one-liner, an ugly line, but one line nevertheless:

```
# Partial mongrel_proxy.conf
# on 10.0.0.102
#...
RewriteEngine On
RewriteRule .* - [CO=BALANCEID:balancer.www1:.brainspl.at]

# Partial mongrel_proxy.conf
# on 10.0.0.103
#...
RewriteEngine On
RewriteRule .* - [CO=BALANCEID:balancer.www2:.brainspl.at]
```

Writing the cookie makes use of the rewrite engine, as you should recall from our earlier Apache discussions. The cookie value is balancer.www1, where the www1 matches the route of the appropriate balancer member. Note that we set the domain explicitly to .brainspl.at so that the cookie can be read, written, or overwritten from any server on our domain.

Combining the Approaches

There just isn't any pleasing some people, so you may want the redundancy and failover capabilities of a multimaster cluster, as well as the performance of read-only databases in master/slave configuration. This is entirely possible. However, you will be inheriting not only the benefits of both, but also the challenges of both. Getting a configuration like this right will take time, patience, and some documentation on your part. Don't build something like this and expect everyone to understand it at a glance. So, draw a picture of your environment, and include some high-level documentation.

I won't go through the step-by-step configuration details all over again, because they're the same as they were earlier. Essentially, what you'll do is build a multimaster cluster with sticky load balancing. But each balancer route will lead to an set of application and database servers that includes one master database server from the master cluster and a number of read-only slave servers dedicated to that master server in particular.

Don't forget that in addition to the sticky load balancing, you will also have to use the acts_as_readonlyable plug-in or a similar solution to handle the read-only databases. If you follow all the rules, you shouldn't get bitten by the asynchronous bug too hard or too often. If your environment is getting this complex, then you might want to seriously start considering an alternative to MySQL or perhaps do away with the relational database entirely.

7.9 Summary

If I haven't exhausted the subject of scaling out, then at the very least I must have exhausted you. In this chapter, I gave you a number of tools to build convincingly high-performance infrastructure for Ruby on Rails. You learned to configure A records and CNAMES for a cluster. Then, you learned to dabble in virtualized servers with VMware and Parallels. You also learned to deploy to those virtual servers with Capistrano.

Next, you learned to build both Apache and nginx servers to serve as load balancers, secured servers, and static proxies. Apache demonstrated its flexibility and modularity as a Mongrel proxy and load balancer. For those interested in simplicity and performance, nginx shines brightly. With some better documentation and a few more battle scars, nginx looks like it could become a popular alternative to Apache and possibly the new king of lightweight web servers.

Finally, I tackled one of the more daunting tasks of Rails deployments: clustering a MySQL database. Although there are more powerful databases for clustering, MySQL ultimately handles the job effectively, if not gracefully. I'm happy to have MySQL despite its shortcomings, because it makes up for them in spades in other areas, including community and Rails support. And you can't beat the price.

Before I move on, I should warn you that you can find books about most of the topics in this chapter. If you're a developer, I encourage you to explore each one more deeply if you're serious about deploying a massively scalable website. Stepping out of your developer shoes and dealing with operational tasks will grow you as a person and a developer. Or at the very least, you'll be a little nicer to your system administrator because of your new appreciation for the role. And if you're an admin, you can better understand the foundations of your deployment. I've really just scratched the surface.

In the next chapter, I'll dive into some basic performance topics. You'll learn how to benchmark and profile systems for performance. You'll also see some solutions to common Rails bottlenecks such as caching and eager loading.

Deploying on Windows

If you asked for a show of hands of how many people had ever deployed Rails on Windows at a Ruby conference, you would get almost no one to admit to that crime. The truth is something very different. Microsoft has sold a bunch of copies of Windows to someone, and many companies and educational institutions simply don't have access to other platforms for deployment. For many companies, bringing in a Linux-based server isn't an option because of politics, a lack of experience, or the perceptions of management. If you are deploying small departmental applications in such a company, Windows may be your best bet.

This chapter explores a few strategies that you can use to get a Rails application deployed within a Windows server environment. I've used each one of these methods at various times to serve applications to various audiences. I'll cover using single instances of Mongrel, load balancing with Pen or Apache, and finally, a strategy to integrate Rails apps into an existing IIS web server using a special ISAPI filter and custom Rails plug-in.

8.1 Setting Up the Server

To serve Ruby on Rails applications in our Windows environment, you need to do a few things to get your machine ready. You have to install Ruby, Gems, and Rails, as well as Subversion. I'll also demonstrate how to get your Rails application talking to a Microsoft SQL Server.

Installing Ruby on Rails

Getting Ruby, Gems, and Rails on a Windows server is extremely easy thanks to the work done by Curt Hibbs. His One-Click Ruby Installer package makes installing Ruby and Gems painless.

Just do the following:

1. Download the One-Click Ruby Installer from RubyForge.[1] Download version 1.8.6 or higher, because previous versions had issues with security and lacked proper debugging support.

2. Double-click the One-Click Ruby Installer to install the package, and accept all the default settings.

3. Open a command prompt, and run the following command:

```
C:\>gem install rails --no-rdoc --no-ri
Successfully installed rake-0.8.1
Successfully installed activesupport-2.0.2
Successfully installed activerecord-2.0.2
Successfully installed actionpack-2.0.2
Successfully installed actionmailer-2.0.2
Successfully installed activeresource-2.0.2
Successfully installed rails-2.0.2
```

The gem install rails command installs the latest version of Rails on your system. As before, we'll skip the documentation for our server installation with the --no-rdoc and --no-ri flags. Next, I'll show you how to install Subversion.

Installing Subversion

You will need to have the Subversion client tools installed on your machine in order to install the necessary Rails plug-ins. If you use Subversion to manage your projects, you can easily copy your applications to your production server. You can find a handy Windows installation of Subversion at Tigris.[2] Download the most recent Windows installer.

The Subversion installation alters your PATH environment variable to include the path of the Subversion executables. You do not have to restart your machine for these path changes to take effect, but you will need to close any open command windows.

Configuring Ruby on Rails to Use Microsoft SQL Server

Microsoft SQL Server doesn't work with Rails without some tweaking. You will have to take a few minor steps to establish a successful connection. If you don't plan to use SQL Server with your Rails applications, you can safely skip this section.

---

1. http://rubyforge.org/projects/rubyinstaller/
2. http://subversion.tigris.org/servlets/ProjectDocumentList?folderID=91

Virtualization to the Rescue...Again?

If you have worked with Ruby on Windows before, even just for development, you know that it's slow. Very, very slow. On Windows Vista, based on my own personal (daily) experience, it is even slower. Simply running unit tests can be orders of magnitude slower than running the same tests on Linux. Believe it or not, it's so slow that it might be faster to run your Rails applications in a virtual Linux machine on Windows using VMware Server or similar software. Modern virtualization software combined with multicore CPUs has made virtualization extremely fast. Thus, Rails on Linux, on VMware, and on Windows should actually perform quite well. The only way to know for sure is to try it for yourself. Build a simple Rails-capable virtual Linux server with VMware, and run your unit tests (see Chapter 7, *Scaling Out*, on page 137). Compare it against the time it takes to run the tests on Windows natively. If you see a huge difference, then try performing some load tests (see Chapter 9, *Performance*, on page 217) against your application to see whether it's truly faster running on a virtual machine.

Performance isn't the only benefit of running in a virtual machine. Recall our discussions from Chapter 7, *Scaling Out*, on page 137, about how virtualization simplifies a great number of deployment issues and can help you scale out faster.

I can think of only one good reason why virtualization may not be a practical choice for your Rails application: integration. If your Rails application needs to integrate with native Windows services or other applications that would not be accessible from within a virtual machine, then the rest of this chapter will become very important to you.

> ### ∖∣∕ Joe Asks…
> ### What About InstantRails, Apache, and FastCGI?
>
> I won't discuss InstantRails, a popular and easy way to get started with Rails development on Windows, in this chapter because it's really not meant to be a production deployment solution. Some people claim to have deployed applications with it to varying degrees of success, but the lack of load balancing and the inability to run as a service disqualify it as a good solution.
>
> I also won't discuss the setup of Apache and FastCGI in this chapter. There are many issues with using this method on Windows including random server errors, poor performance, and really long start-up times for Apache.
>
> I'll stick to the deployment options that will give you the best possible chance of success.

1. Download the latest stable version of Ruby-DBI.[3] Look for a file with the name dbi-0.1.0.tar.gz or something similar. Extract this file to a temporary location like C:\TEMP.

2. Grab one file from that archive called ADO.rb. If you have extracted the files to C:\TEMP, you can find the file in the folder C:\TEMP\lib\dbd.

3. Copy this file to C:\ruby\lib\ruby\site_ruby\1.8\DBD\ADO. You will need to create the ADO folder, because it won't exist.

4. Please see the Rails wiki[4] for more information on using SQL Server with your Rails applications.[5]

While Microsoft SQL Server is a common database for the Microsoft platform, it's not the only popular choice. You can also use several of the popular open source databases with Rails, including MySQL, SQLite, and Oracle.

---

3. http://rubyforge.org/projects/ruby-dbi/
4. http://wiki.rubyonrails.org/rails/pages/HowtoConnectToMicrosoftSQLServer
5. You can also use ODBC DSNs to connect to SQL Server from Rails, but there are some tricky permissions issues with ODBC and Mongrel as a service, so I don't typically recommend going that route.

MySQL on Windows

If you intend to use MySQL instead of SQL Server, you'll be happy to know you can do so easily. I'm going to assume you already have MySQL installed and working. Rails has built-in support for MySQL, but to avoid potential problems such as speed and performance, you'll need to install the MySQL/Ruby for Windows adapter. You will see better performance when using this C-based library instead of the pure-Ruby library. Until recently, installing MySQL/Ruby was a pain, but the gem now comes complete with a binary version for Windows. Installing it is as simple as opening a command prompt and installing the gem:

```
C:\>gem install mysql
Bulk updating Gem source index for: http://gems.rubyforge.org
Select which gem to install for your platform (i386-mswin32)
 1. mysql 2.7.3 (mswin32)
 2. mysql 2.7.1 (mswin32)
 3. mysql 2.7 (ruby)
 4. mysql 2.6 (ruby)
 5. Skip this gem
 6. Cancel installation
> 1
Successfully installed mysql-2.7.3-mswin32
Installing ri documentation for mysql-2.7.3-mswin32...
Installing RDoc documentation for mysql-2.7.3-mswin32...
While generating documentation for mysql-2.7.3-mswin32
... MESSAGE:   Unhandled special: Special: type=17, text="<!-- $Id: README.html,
v 1.20 2006-12-20 05:31:52 tommy Exp $ -->"
... RDOC args: --op c:/ruby/lib/ruby/gems/1.8/doc/mysql-2.7.3-mswin32/rdoc --exc
lude ext --main README --quiet ext README docs/README.html
(continuing with the rest of the installation)
```

Be sure to select the highest-numbered version for Windows.[6] That's really all there is to it. You have the prerequisites installed. It's time to turn your attention to the server you'll use to serve your Rails application. I'll first show you Mongrel and then a few tricks you can use to enhance the installation.

8.2 Mongrel

As with *nix platforms, if you're running Ruby applications, Mongrel is usually the way to go. Not only is Mongrel relatively fast, but it's also extremely easy to install and use. You can install the Windows version of Mongrel as a Windows service. There's no mongrel_cluster for Windows yet, but don't worry. I will show you how to manually build a cluster of Mongrels.

---

6. Future versions of RubyGems will automatically install the correct version for you.

Installing Mongrel

Installing Mongrel on Windows is easy. Open a command prompt, and install Mongrel with the gem command. Choose the highest-numbered Win32 option.[7] The latest version is always at the top of the list, so pay close attention to both the version number and the platform, like this:

```
C:\>gem install mongrel --include-dependencies
Select which gem to install for your platform (i386-mswin32)
1. mongrel 1.1.1 (ruby)
2. mongrel 1.1.1 (jruby)
3. mongrel 1.1.1 (mswin32)
4. mongrel 1.1 (mswin32)
5. mongrel 1.1 (ruby)
6. mongrel 1.1 (jruby)
7. Skip this gem
8. Cancel installation
> 3
Successfully installed mongrel-1.1.1-mswin32
Successfully installed gem_plugin-0.2.2
Successfully installed cgi_multipart_eof_fix-2.3
Installing ri documentation for mongrel-1.0.1-mswin32...
Installing ri documentation for gem_plugin-0.2.2...
Installing ri documentation for cgi_multipart_eof_fix-2.3...
Installing RDoc documentation for mongrel-1.0.1-mswin32...
Installing RDoc documentation for gem_plugin-0.2.2...
Installing RDoc documentation for cgi_multipart_eof_fix-2.3...
```

Next, install the Mongrel Service plug-in. This plug-in provides the necessary commands to get Mongrel installed and running as a Windows service. To do so, just run the following command:

```
C:\>gem install mongrel_service --include-dependencies
Select which gem to install for your platform (i386-mswin32)
 1. mongrel_service 0.3.3 (mswin32)
 2. mongrel_service 0.3.2 (mswin32)
 3. mongrel_service 0.3.1 (mswin32)
 4. mongrel_service 0.1 (ruby)
 5. Skip this gem
 6. Cancel installation
> 1
Select which gem to install for your platform (i386-mswin32)
 1. win32-service 0.5.2 (ruby)
 2. win32-service 0.5.2 (mswin32)
 3. Skip this gem
 4. Cancel installation
> 2
Successfully installed mongrel_service-0.3.3-mswin32
Successfully installed win32-service-0.5.2-mswin32
```

---

7. RubyGems version 0.9.5 lets you skip the platform selection step.

```
Installing ri documentation for mongrel_service-0.3.2-mswin32...
Installing ri documentation for win32-service-0.5.2-mswin32...
Installing RDoc documentation for mongrel_service-0.3.2-mswin32...
Installing RDoc documentation for win32-service-0.5.2-mswin32...
```

Watch closely for the gem for the win32-service file. The *win32* version is not always at the top of the list like it is for mongrel_service. Whenever installing gems, always take note of the version number and the platform to make sure you get the right version; the *ruby* ones won't install on Windows when you're using the One-Click Ruby Installer's Ruby interpreter.

Test Mongrel

Now that you've installed Mongrel, you should test it against your application to ensure that Mongrel can serve pages. I typically test Mongrel like this:

1. Create a folder on your hard drive called c:\web.

2. Open the command prompt, and navigate to c:\web.

3. Create a new Rails application in that folder:

   ```
   C:\web>rails mytestapp
          create
          create  app/controllers
          create  app/helpers
          create  app/models
          create  app/views/layouts
          create  config/environments
          ...
          create  doc/README_FOR_APP
          create  log/server.log
          create  log/production.log
          create  log/development.log
          create  log/test.log
   ```

   If you have a working Rails application you want to try, you should place that in a subfolder of c:\web and then reference that path in all future steps. Also, make sure the database configuration for the production environment is correct before proceeding. Review config/database.yml to ensure that your production database is defined properly.

   To test your application, execute the following command:

   ```
   C:\web\mytestapp>mongrel_rails start -e production -p 4001
   ** Starting Mongrel listening at 0.0.0.0:4001
   ** Starting Rails with production environment...
   ```

```
** Rails loaded.
** Loading any Rails specific GemPlugins
** Signals ready.  INT => stop (no restart).
** Mongrel available at 0.0.0.0:4001
```

This command starts Mongrel on port 4001. Navigate to http://localhost:4001, and make sure that your application works before continuing.

If you do not get a response, make sure port 4001 is not being blocked by Windows Firewall or by your router.

Once you know your application works in production mode, stop the server with `Ctrl`+ `C`.

Install Mongrel as a Windows Service

Now that you know your application works and that you have Mongrel installed correctly, you can install your application as a Windows service. You'll install this application using production mode, so make sure your database.yml file points to a working production database if you're using your own application with this tutorial.

1. Stop Mongrel by pressing `Ctrl`+`C`.

2. Execute the following command in order to install the application as a service:

```
C:\web\mytestapp>
    mongrel_rails service::install -N MyTestApp_4001 -p 4001 -e production

** Copying native mongrel_service executable...
Mongrel service 'MyTestApp_4001' installed as 'MyTestApp_4001'.
```

This command creates a new Windows service with the name MyTestApp_4001, which you can view in the Control Panel Services applet, as shown in Figure 8.1, on the facing page.

3. You can start the service from the Services applet or from the command line by executing the following command: mongrel_rails service::start -N MyTestApp_4001.

   - To stop the service from the command line, use mongrel_rails service::stop -N MyTestApp_4001.

   - Later, you can remove the service at any time using mongrel_rails service::remove -N MyTestApp_4001.

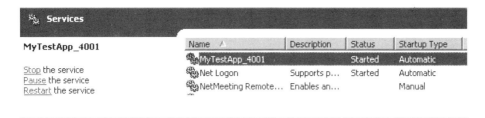

Figure 8.1: MONGREL AS A WINDOWS SERVICE IN THE SERVICES APPLET

Adding the port number to the service name is a really helpful way to keep track of the ports you've used. As you add services, the port number becomes even more useful. It's not a requirement, but it's a good convention to follow.

Creating a Second Instance of Mongrel for Your Application

Your application is now hosted by Mongrel, running as a service. Now, it's time to kick up your feet and pop open a tall frosty one, right? Be careful, though. One Mongrel is not likely enough. Rails is not always the fastest available framework, and a single instance of Mongrel can handle only one request at a time. As load increases, you need to add more instances of Mongrel and then balance the requests.

Those lucky *nix guys get to use a tool called mongrel_cluster, which can start and stop multiple instances of Mongrel with ease. Windows doesn't have mongrel_cluster yet, so you'll need to improvise. You can just create another instance of Mongrel as a service that points to the same Rails application. You can then use a load balancer to distribute traffic to each instance.

Creating your custom cluster manually is not as hard as it sounds. You'll create another service that points to the same application, but this time use port 4002 by running the following commands:

```
mongrel_rails service::install -N MyTestApp_4002 -p 4002 -e production
mongrel_rails service::start -N MyTestApp_4002
```

If you look in the Control Panel under Services, you will see both services running. Adding the port number to the service name makes it easier to remember which port each service uses. If you look at Figure 8.2, on the next page, you will see an example of both services installed.

Figure 8.2: BOTH MONGREL INSTANCES AS SERVICES

Keep in mind that these services aren't set to automatically start when you reboot the server, so your app isn't going to be available after a restart. Let's remedy that. Configure each service to start up automatically by right-clicking each service name and setting the start-up type to Automatic.

Test each address to make sure the requests work and that the services are in fact serving your web application. http://localhost:4001 and http://localhost:4002 should both be serving the same application.

So, you have two instances of your application running on different ports. That's better than one, but the setup is not that useful yet; you need to load balance them, and you make that happen by using Pen or Apache.

8.3 Mongrel and Pen

Pen is a nice, simple way to load balance an application without having to do too much setup. Pen is great for small sites without a huge number of expected connections, and it's great because you don't have to spend a lot of time learning how to configure it. Pen handles reverse-proxying and balancing very well, but it isn't a web server, which means you can't serve static content with it. Your static content will be served by your back-end Mongrel services. For small apps with more than a couple of users, this setup should work just fine.

You can download a Windows binary of Pen from ftp://siag.nu/pub/pen/pen-0.17.1.exe.

Pen supports SSL, but its support is very experimental, so if you need to host a secure site, you'll have to use some sort of proxy server in front of this setup.

Figure 8.3: Required files to run Pen

Setting Up Pen

Create a folder to store Pen. C:\pen will do just fine. Save the file you just downloaded in this folder, and rename it to pen.exe so it's easier to call. To run Pen on Windows, you'll need to download the file cygwin1.dll[8] and place it in C:\pen. The file is compressed, so unzip it first.

Figure 8.3 shows the files required to run Pen. Once you've downloaded both of them, you can give Pen a quick test, but first make sure your Rails app is running with Mongrel as described previously. Open a command window, and navigate to C:\pen. Execute the following command to start Pen:

```
pen -f 80 localhost:4001
```

This tells Pen to listen on port 80 and forward all requests to localhost: 4001. If your Mongrel service is still running there, this command will make your application available on port 80.

Now open http://localhost in your browser, and you should see your Rails app. It's just that simple. The -f switch keeps Pen from going into the background. If you forget this switch, then you'll have to kill Pen using the Windows Task Manager.

Use Ctrl + C to stop Pen and return to the command prompt.

Load Balancing with Pen

Load balancing with Pen is as easy as adding each remote host and port to the command line. If you had two Mongrel instances running, one on port 4001 and the other on port 4002, you would use the following command:

```
pen -f 80 localhost:4001 localhost:4002
```

8. http://www.dll-files.com/dllindex/dll-files.shtml?cygwin1

Installing Pen as a Service

If you decide that Pen is right for you, you should install it as a service so you can have it automatically start just like your Mongrel services do. There's a relatively easy (and free) way to do that.

1. Download the Windows 2003 Server Resource Kit from Microsoft,[9] and install it.

2. Open a command prompt, and run the following command:
   ```
   "C:\Program Files\Windows Resource Kits\Tools\instsrv.exe" Pen
   "C:\Program Files\Windows Resource Kits\Tools\srvany.exe"

   The service was successfully added!

   Make sure that you go into the Control Panel and use
   the Services applet to change the Account Name and
   Password that this newly installed service will use
   for its Security Context
   ```
   The commands in the following list will create a new registry entry containing the configuration for your new service.

3. Open regedit, and locate the key HKEY_LOCAL_MACHINE\SYSTEM\CurrentControlSet\Services\Pen.

4. Create a new key beneath that key called Parameters.

5. Select the Parameters key, and create a new string value with the name Application. Enter c:\pen\pen.exe for the value.

6. Create another string value called AppParameters. Enter -f 4000 localhost:4001 localhost:4002 for the value.

7. Create a third string value called AppDirectory. Enter c:\pen for the value.

8. Close regedit, and open a command prompt.

9. Start the service by typing the following command:
   ```
   C:\>net start pen
   The Pen service is starting.
   The Pen service was started successfully.
   ```
   You can stop the Pen service just as easily:
   ```
   C:\>net stop pen

   The Pen service was stopped successfully.
   ```

That's it. This setup should work well for single applications that need to handle a lot of users. Though you see a lot of steps, they take only about fifteen minutes from beginning to end. If you decide that this

---

9. http://www.microsoft.com/downloads/details.aspx?familyid=9d467a69-57ff-4ae7-96ee-b18c4790cffd

method is not for you, you can remove the service with the command sc delete pen.

Before moving on, you should know that a single instance of Pen is going to work for only one Rails application. If you are trying to serve multiple Rails applications with Pen, you'll need to copy pen.exe to another file like my_app_name_pen.exe and then set up the service with a new name. You could end up with quite a few services if you're serving lots of apps.

So, Pen works great for small apps that need a bit of load balancing help, but what do you do when you have to handle a *lot* more requests? You're going to have to use what some Windows system administrators refer to as "the A word."

8.4 Using Apache 2.2 and Mongrel

If you need to handle load, there's no better solution on Windows than Apache 2.2. Not only can you load balance with relative ease, but you can also make Apache serve all the static content such as cached pages, CSS, JavaScript, and images. If you're taking advantage of page caching (and you should if you're doing a public site), then Apache is going to be your best bet for high performance.

Another great advantage of using this approach is that you can "borrow" a lot of configuration files from the *nix guys.

Install Apache

Download the Apache 2.2 Windows binary from Apache.[10] Be sure to grab the latest release.

Install Apache 2.2 using the installer you downloaded.

The wizard should be pretty easy to handle. I'll just walk you through a few of the highlights. Most important, be careful when you pick a port. I usually choose to install Apache for a single user on port 8080 to prevent conflicts with IIS on port 80. I'll install the Windows service manually later. Also, make sure you don't install Apache as a web service, as shown in Figure 8.4, on the next page.

Install Apache to c:\apache or some other directory you can easily find later. The Apache configuration should complete without any problems.

---

10. http://httpd.apache.org/download.cgi

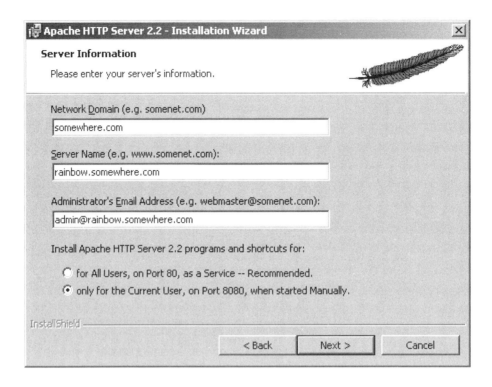

Figure 8.4: ENSURE THAT YOU'RE NOT INSTALLING APACHE AS A SERVICE.

Configuring Apache to Serve Your Rails Applications

Apache uses the file httpd.conf to hold all the configuration settings. You know the drill. I'm not going to talk about them all, only the ones you will need to know for this Windows installation. You can always consult the excellent documentation to learn more. In fact, I recommend you familiarize yourself with the contents of that file before you roll out into production. Apache is big, it has lots of options, and you really want to make sure you don't have any gaping security holes.

Locate the httpd.conf file. It's in the folder C:\apache\conf.

First, locate the section of the file that starts with this:

```
# Dynamic Shared Object (DSO) Support
```

This section contains all the modules that can be loaded by Apache. Each hash mark (#) means that the line is commented out.

Uncomment the following lines to activate the proxy balancer:

```
LoadModule proxy_module modules/mod_proxy.so
LoadModule proxy_balancer_module modules/mod_proxy_balancer.so
LoadModule proxy_http_module modules/mod_proxy_http.so
```

You also need to enable URL-rewriting support by uncommenting this line:

```
LoadModule rewrite_module modules/mod_rewrite.so
```

Next, you'll want to enable the deflate module to allow your content to be compressed as it is served:

```
LoadModule deflate_module modules/mod_deflate.so
```

Finally, add this line to the bottom of the file:

```
Include conf/httpd-proxy.conf
```

This allows you to split up your configuration for your application into another file. At this point, you should save the httpd.conf configuration file. Create a new file in C:\Apache\Apache2.2\conf called httpd-proxy.conf with the following contents:

```
<VirtualHost *:8080>
    ServerName yourdomain.com
    DocumentRoot c:/web/mytestapp/public

    <Directory "c:/web/mytestapp/public">
      Options FollowSymLinks
      AllowOverride None
      Order allow,deny
      Allow from all
    </Directory>

    # Configure mongrel instances

    <Proxy balancer://mongrel_cluster>
      BalancerMember http://127.0.0.1:4001
      BalancerMember http://127.0.0.1:4002
    </Proxy>

    RewriteEngine On

    # Uncomment for rewrite debugging
    #RewriteLog logs/your_app_deflate_log deflate
    #RewriteLogLevel 9

    # Check for maintenance file and redirect all requests
    RewriteCond %{DOCUMENT_ROOT}/system/maintenance.html -f
    RewriteCond %{SCRIPT_FILENAME} !maintenance.html
    RewriteRule ^.*$ /system/maintenance.html [L]
```

```
# Rewrite index to check for static
RewriteRule ^/$ /index.html [QSA]

# Rewrite to check for Rails cached page
RewriteRule ^([^.]+)$ $1.html [QSA]

# Redirect all non-static requests to cluster
RewriteCond %{DOCUMENT_ROOT}/%{REQUEST_FILENAME} !-f
RewriteRule ^/(.*)$ balancer://mongrel_cluster%{REQUEST_URI} [P,QSA,L]

# Deflate
AddOutputFilterByType DEFLATE text/html text/plain text/xml
BrowserMatch ^Mozilla/4 gzip-only-text/html
BrowserMatch ^Mozilla/4\.0[678] no-gzip
BrowserMatch \bMSIE !no-gzip !gzip-only-text/html

# Uncomment for deflate debugging
#DeflateFilterNote Input input_info
#DeflateFilterNote Output output_info
#DeflateFilterNote Ratio ratio_info
#LogFormat '"%r" %{output_info}n/%{input_info}n (%{ratio_info}n%%)' deflate
#CustomLog logs/your_app_deflate_log deflate
ErrorLog logs/your_app_error_log
CustomLog logs/your_access_log combined
</VirtualHost>
```

Save the file, and double-check to make sure it's in the same folder as httpd.conf.

Explaining the Proxy

The important part of the file is this section:

```
# Configure mongrel_cluster
<Proxy balancer://mongrel_cluster>
  BalancerMember http://127.0.0.1:4001
  BalancerMember http://127.0.0.1:4002
</Proxy>
```

This section is the load balancer configuration. Each BalanceMember points to one of your back-end instances of Mongrel. This configuration supports only two back ends, but you can easily add more. Keep in mind that changing this configuration file requires a restart of Apache.

When a request comes in, Apache checks for a static page. If no static page is found, the system will forward the request to the Rails application, just like a stand.

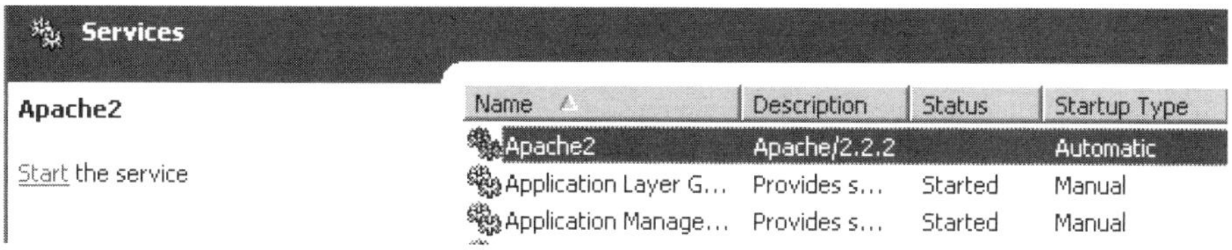

Figure 8.5: APACHE INSTALLED AS A WINDOWS SERVICE

Test Apache's Configuration

Open a command prompt, navigate to c:\apache\bin, and execute the following command:

```
httpd
```

If you receive no errors, Apache is running and listening on port 8080. If you have Mongrel instances listening on ports 4001 and 4002, then you can test the configuration by pointing your browser to http://localhost:8080/. You should see your Rails application.

This section showed you how to host a Rails application using Apache on port 8080. If you wanted to host the application using the standard port 80, you would simply need to change the virtual host definition.

Installing Apache as a Windows Service

Now that Apache has been correctly configured and tested, you can safely install the service.

Open a new command prompt, and enter the following command:

```
cd\apache\bin
httpd -k install
```

You should see the following output:

```
Installing the Apache2 service
The Apache2 service is successfully installed.
Testing httpd.conf....
Errors reported here must be corrected before the service can be started.
```

You should now see the service in your Services panel, as shown in Figure 8.5. Ensure that the start-up type is set to Automatic so it will restart when you restart your server. You might see a Windows Firewall prompt. In that case, you will need to unblock Apache or disable your Windows Firewall service for things to work properly. Apache is now configured to load balance between two back-end Mongrel processes. You can test this configuration by opening a browser and navigating to http://localhost:8080/. Your Rails application will appear.

Now you can go a step further and hide your Apache server behind IIS. Taking this step may seem strange to you, but read on.

8.5 IIS Integration

IIS is a popular web server in Windows-based organizations. Despite its reputation, it can be a very good static web server. In this section, I'll show you how to use IIS to forward requests to your Rails applications. This configuration will allow you to seamlessly integrate a Rails application into an existing IIS website.

Using IIS has a couple of benefits. First, you can use the same SSL certificate for all your Rails applications. Second, you have the flexibility to move the back-end applications to another server at any time. If you find that Windows isn't going to work for you as a deployment method, you can easily move your Rails applications to a Linux-based server and still have requests come through your main web server.

Before you can begin, you will need to get an additional piece of software. I am also going to assume that you will be performing all this on a server where IIS is running on the default port (80) and that your Rails applications reside on the same machine.

Install ISAPI Rewrite

ISAPI Rewrite is a URL-rewriting filter that provides some simple forward proxy support. Though it is not free, it is well worth the nominal fee its developers charge, and you have access to an unrestricted trial version, which will get you through this chapter.

Visit the ISAPI Rewrite site,[11] and download the trial version of ISAPI Rewrite 3.0. Launch the installation program, and accept all the default settings. The installation will restart your IIS service, because it needs to install an ISAPI filter on your server.

---

11. http://www.isapirewrite.com/

> ### What About Just Serving Rails Through IIS?
>
> Different groups of people have tried to serve Rails directly through IIS. Some tried to use the FastCGI ISAPI filter, but that configuration requires registry hacks and leads to instability. When I tried the FastCGI approach on three machines, I was able to make it work successfully only on one, and it wasn't very reliable. This option may become more viable soon, but for now, most Windows developers are going with the approaches outlined in this chapter.
>
> Microsoft has actually taken some great steps to make FastCGI better in IIS 7.0, but it has made no specific commitment to serving Rails applications with IIS at the time this book is being written. This stuff moves pretty fast though, so it's definitely something you should keep an eye on.
>
> Using a proxied approach does provide for better long-term scalability, because it is much easier to move your Rails application to one or more separate physical machines. If you plan to host several Rails applications from one server, FastCGI is probably not a good option for you at all.

If you experience trouble with the installation, you'll need to refer to the developers of this product. The support forum[12] is an excellent resource.

Forwarding Requests to Your Application

Say you want to forward all requests from http://localhost/mytest/ to your Rails application. You need to ensure that one of the following is true:

- You allow script execution from your site root.

- You allow script execution from the folder or virtual directory mytest.

Failing to allow script execution from one of those places will result in a 403.1 error message from IIS.

The file C:\Program Files\Helicon\ISAPI_Rewrite3\httpd.conf contains the rewrite rules that IIS uses to forward requests.

---

12. http://www.helicontech.com/forum/

Forwarding a requested URL to a back-end server is really easy. To forward requests to /mytest to a Mongrel instance on the same machine running on port 4001, you use this rule:

```
RewriteProxy /mytest(.*) http\://localhost:4001$1 [I,U]
```

If you're using Apache on port 8080, you just forward requests to that port instead:

```
RewriteProxy /mytest(.*) http\://localhost:8080$1 [I,U]
```

You can even go to a different server:

```
RewriteProxy /mytest(.*) http\://backend.mydomain.com:4001$1 [I,U]
```

On some systems, especially those that have tightened security, this file is marked as read-only. You'll need to remove the read-only attribute before you can change the file. Also, ensure that the SYSTEM user can read that file.

Testing It

Configure the filter to forward requests to your Mongrel instance on port 4001:

```
RewriteProxy /mytest(.*) http\://localhost:4001$1 [I,U]
```

You can now pull up your Rails application via IIS by navigating to http://localhost/mytest/. Unfortunately, it's not going to look very good. Read on to find out why.

8.6 Reverse Proxy and URLs

The big problem we're faced with now is that the URLs that Rails creates internally, such as style sheet links, url_for links, and other links, don't work as you might expect.

For example, if you pull up the URL http://localhost/mytest/ in your browser, you should see that the application comes up just fine, but without the style sheets. You will also notice that when you click a link, you're transferred to http://localhost/, and in some cases your proxy will be exposed. This situation could be especially bad for your users if your application server happens to be behind a firewall that can't be accessed from the Internet.

Neither IIS nor ISAPI_Rewrite has a method to handle reverse proxying. A reverse proxy rewrites the content served from the back end to mask the fact that the request was filtered through a proxy.

> ## A Note About relative_url_root
>
> At first glance, it looks like most problems with the URLs could be solved simply by applying the following code to the environment.rb file:
>
> ```
> ActionController::AbstractRequest.relative_url_root = '/mytest'
> ```
>
> That change fixes most of the issues, but it doesn't fix any links written using url_for :only_path => false. The reverse_proxy_fix plug-in that I wrote addresses these issues as well.

I developed a simple Rails plug-in that modifies the way Rails creates URLs in order to address this issue. The plug-in tells Rails to prepend your external URL to any URLs it creates through the system. This plug-in will force all user requests to come back through the IIS proxy. The URLs are altered only when you run the application in production mode, so you don't have to worry about changing routes or configuration files when you deploy your application. It's also safe to keep the plug-in with your application during development.

Installing the Proxy Plug-In

Execute the following command (but all on one line):

```
ruby script/plugin install http://svn.napcsweb.com/public/reverse_proxy_fix
```

from within your application's root folder. Once the plug-in is installed, it asks you for the base URL. Enter http://localhost/mytest, and press Enter. If all goes well, the plug-in will write the configuration file. If the configuration file can't be modified, you can configure it yourself by editing the file vendor/plugins/reverse_proxy_fix/lib/config.rb.

Using the Proxy Plug-In

Once you've installed the plug-in, you'll need to restart your Rails application. If you're using multiple instances of Mongrel, you'll need to restart all instances before the plug-in will work. Once the applications restart, any internal links in your application will now be automatically corrected, and your users will be routed back through the proxy.[13]

---

13. This assumes you used link_to and friends to generate your links and images. Hard-coded paths are not changed by this plug-in.

8.7 Strategies for Hosting Multiple Applications

You can use several strategies to host several applications, and the one you choose depends mostly on the number of users who will use your system. When you have many users and long HTTP requests such as file uploads, you will have to address scaling through adding more back-end processes. That was traditionally done by increasing the number of FastCGI processes, but now you can just add another instance of Mongrel to our cluster.

The next few sections will cover various strategies you can use to deploy several applications into production.

Serve Several Small Applications Using IIS and Mongrel

Serving many small applications is a simple approach. Each application is installed as a Windows service using Mongrel running on a different port. You can then use IIS with ISAPI_Rewrite and the reverse_proxy_fix plug-in to mount each application to its own URL within IIS as in Figure 8.6, on page 208:

http://www.yourdomain.com/app1 ⇒ http://localhost:4001

http://www.yourdomain.com/app2 ⇒ http://localhost:4002

http://www.yourdomain.com/app3 ⇒ http://localhost:4003

The ISAPI_Rewrite rules for this are simply as follows:

```
RewriteProxy /app1(.*) http\://localhost:4001$1 [I,U]
RewriteProxy /app2(.*) http\://localhost:4002$1 [I,U]
RewriteProxy /app3(.*) http\://localhost:4003$1 [I,U]
```

You would then need to apply the Reverse_Proxy_Fix plug-in to each of your applications, setting the BASE_URL parameter for each originating URL.

I don't recommend doing this for production. There's no support for page caching here, and there's just no way to scale up. However, this is a really great approach to demo a site to your stakeholders quickly without going through a lot of complex setup.

Applications, Users, and Requests

How do you measure the size of an application, and how do you choose the method of deployment? People tend to think about application size by thinking about how many users the app will have. There's a slight problem with that, though.

I could have an application with hundreds of models. The application could be very complex, but if there are only 100 people using the application, it's not going to be that problematic to just throw up one instance of Mongrel and let it do the work, provided that there aren't any simultaneous requests.

I could also have an application with five models and three controllers, and this application gets hit 100,000 times a day by students who are registering for a summer orientation session at a university. A single instance of Mongrel would probably work, but there would be a lot of waiting going on.

The number of users an application can support is really not a good measure, though. With Ajax becoming more and more popular and with Rails' support of REST, you may see more hits to your application than you expect, whether it be from a user's browser or another web service.

Requests per second is a much better measure for your site. How many requests does your app need to support per second? Three? Six? Twenty? A hundred? This is something you need to figure out by benchmarking existing applications and doing some forecasting. An application that supports five requests per second can serve 144,000 requests in an eight-hour period. That's not too bad. The problem is that a Rails application is single-threaded. A single instance of Mongrel can serve only one request at a time. So if you have an Ajax-based search on your site, the live updating that the search does can cause other requests to get stuck in a queue.

So, test your apps, and determine the requests per second. If you determine that your small internal application can run on a single instance of Mongrel, that makes life easier. You can easily scale up using the techniques in this book.

Keep in mind that on Windows, your app will typically perform much slower than on another platform, so you may require more balanced back ends to process the same number of requests.

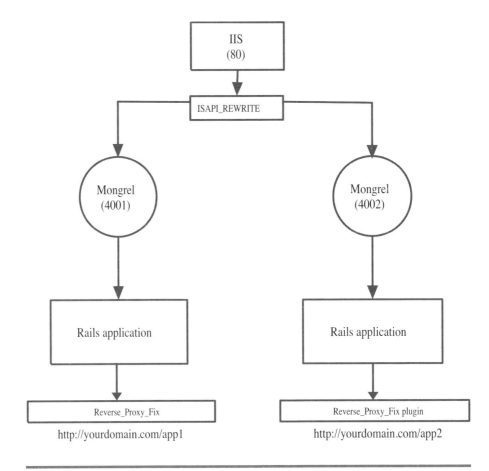

Figure 8.6: IIS FORWARDING REQUESTS TO MULTIPLE INSTANCES OF MONGREL

Serving Several Large Applications

You have several possibilities for serving large applications.

One method would be to use Pen to cluster several Mongrel instances and then use IIS to forward requests to Pen as shown in Figure 8.7, on the facing page.

This configuration is the same as if you were going directly to Mongrel. You would install multiple copies of Pen on different ports, each forwarding to their own group of Mongrel instances. You would then set up IIS to forward requests to each instance of Pen.

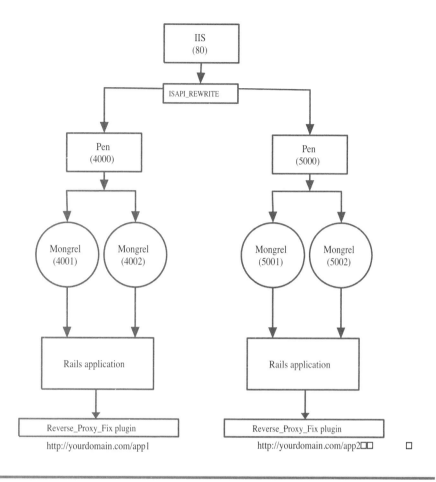

Figure 8.7: IIS FORWARDING REQUESTS TO MULTIPLE INSTANCES OF PEN

This is one of those solutions that works well for those cases where your organization has a "no Apache" policy.

This approach won't be the best approach if your application makes extensive use of page caching, but it is easy to implement and can work fine for systems where every user needs to be authenticated on every request, making page caching a nonissue.

The most performant method is to simply use Apache on port 80. Using the proxy_balancer method, Apache can be configured for multiple virtual hosts with each virtual host serving a separate cluster of Mongrel instances as shown in Figure 8.8, on the next page.

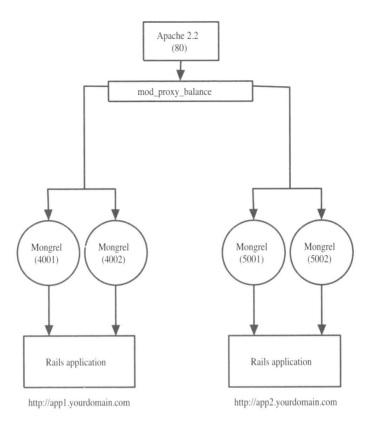

Figure 8.8: APACHE 2.2 WITH MOD_PROXY_BALANCER ON MULTIPLE VHOSTS

Implementing this approach is a matter of creating separate groups of Mongrel instances and then creating a virtual host entry for each of these groups in the httpd-proxy.conf file created earlier. Your DNS and local HOSTS file would then need to be configured for each virtual host.

This approach yields good performance, scales well, and allows page caching to work effectively. It's the fastest and most stable solution right now for Windows.

Finally, if you want transparent integration, you could make IIS send these requests to your various Apache virtual hosts. This is a more complicated approach with more points of failure, but it will allow you to use your IIS SSL certificates, will allow you to place your database and Rails applications behind a firewall, and will make your applications appear to be integrated. Remember to make use of the reverse_proxy_fix plug-in if you choose to use IIS to forward your requests.

Performance on Windows

Ruby does not perform as well on Windows as it does on Linux. Applications that routinely handle 60 requests per second on a Linux box with one instance of Mongrel can handle only six to nine requests per second on Windows. Any more than that, and your users start seeing delays as each request is processed.

If you have a really powerful server, like the fastest thing available with lots of RAM and very little running, then you might see around thirty-five requests per second with a single instance. Linux servers tend to provide much greater throughput with much less expensive hardware.

You can improve performance slightly by looking over the applications you plan to deploy and checking the following areas:

- Change how you use sessions. How are sessions managed in your application? The P-Store, or file-based store, can often be slow. Consider moving your session store into your database, or investigate other session-storing mechanisms.

- Go through your development logs, and make sure you're not making unnecessary calls to your database. Simply adding an :include to a finder can really help an application's performance, and it is often missed.

- Use fragment, action, and page caching as much as you can. Since Ruby is slow on Windows, you want to make as much use of page caching as you possibly can so that Rails is never invoked.

- Ensure that nothing is interfering with the process. Certain security auditing software, quota managers, and virus scanners can drastically reduce the amount of requests you can handle. Watch your performance monitor for any spikes when testing your application.

8.8 Load-Testing Your Applications

There are few good choices for load-testing your applications on Windows. If at all possible, get a Linux machine or a Mac, and use httperf to test your application.

If that's just not going to work for you, try one of these alternatives:

- *Microsoft Web Application Stress Tool*: This tool, available online,[14] is a free tool that lets you record your steps through a web application or website and then play them back and generate loads. It can be used to control remote clients as well so you can generate more realistic loads against your application. It has quite a few bugs, but it is still a very useful program. I have found its accuracy to be relatively good.
- *WAPT*: WAPT is a commercial tool that performs load and stress testing of web applications. Like the Microsoft offering, WAPT allows you to record your browsing session so it can be played back. Interpreting the reports can be trickier, but it's worth it because WAPT has the ability to connect to secure sites.

  Apache Benchmark (ab): Apache Benchmark is a command-line tool that can be used to hit a URL repeatedly, but it is known to produce extremely misleading results. I use this tool only to generate loads against an application.

8.9 Final Thoughts

I believe that Windows is a good platform for developing Rails applications and does an adequate job of serving Rails applications that have a moderate user base. However, as you begin to develop more applications and gain more users, your needs may change.

I also believe that Linux is the better choice right now. I have a 1GHz desktop machine running Ubuntu and serving a single Rails application from one instance of Mongrel that serves three times as many requests per second than a server with two Xeons at 2GHz.

In recent months, Windows machines are getting much faster, but they are not quite as performant. If your applications aren't performing at an acceptable level and you've done everything you can to optimize them, then you should consider deploying some applications to a Linux test server. The information and strategies I have shared with you can be used to help you migrate some or all of your Rails applications to Linux servers transparently. You could still use IIS or Apache on Windows and move only the Rails applications to Linux, which is a great transitional solution that I've employed a number of times with great success.

---

14. http://www.microsoft.com/downloads/details.aspx?FamilyID=E2C0585A-062A-439E-A67D-75A89AA36495

Testing Tips

- Run your tests from a different machine than the one hosting the application. Testing the throughput on the same machine can lead to unrealistic and inaccurate results.

- Run the stress test against a baseline such as your public home page. This will give you a good idea of how your application compares to your existing services.

- Run the tests from inside and outside of your network. If you can, try running the test from a cable or DSL connection to see what kind of an impact that has.

- Stress test your app on the production server. Some sysadmins may cringe at this, but you should test the application where you plan to deploy it wherever possible. Do some testing during some scheduled downtime or during off-peak times when your server use is low. If you can't do this, you should at least consider having a staging server that mirrors your production machine so you will be able to see accurate results and plan for the future.

- Use more than one tool and compare the results.

8.10 Developing on Windows and Deploying Somewhere Else

If you develop on Windows but plan to deploy on a Linux server such as a virtual private host, a shared host, or a new shiny Linux server that your wonderful bosses purchased especially for you, you should be aware of some issues.

Dispatch.fcgi Ruby Interpreter

When you deploy an application that you created on Windows to a Linux server, the very first line in your dispatch.fcgi file will be wrong.

On Windows, it usually reads as follows:

```
#!c:/ruby/bin/ruby
```

On Linux, it often reads as follows:

```
#!/usr/bin/ruby
```

You can figure out what path you should use by connecting to your remote host and typing which ruby.

This is a problem if your hosting platform is using FastCGI because the FastCGI server will be unable to locate the Ruby interpreter. If you're using Mongrel, then it's not really a concern.

Line Breaks

Linux uses different line breaks than Windows does. This can sometimes be a problem because the extra character that Windows uses can interfere with how scripts are processed. Many Linux distributions have a program called dos2unix that you can use to convert the line breaks in your files.

The best solution is to find yourself a good editor for Windows that allows you to specify what type of line breaks are used. Eclipse, NetBeans IDE, Notepad++, and Crimson Editor are just a few examples of editors that are known to work correctly. Windows Notepad should be avoided at all costs, as well as WordPad, because they are meant for Windows-formatted text files.

Permissions

When you deploy your application to a Linux server, you need to check permissions. If your server uses FastCGI, then you need to make sure that you allow the web server's user and group the right to execute public/dispatch.fcgi, or your application isn't going to work. If your application uses page caching, ensure that the public/ folder is writable by the web server's user, or Rails will be unable to write the static versions of the pages.

Preventing Problems When Deploying

Follow these tips to make deploying an application to production from Windows to Linux:

- Create the application on the Linux machine using the rails command. This will put all the files in the right locations and make sure that the paths are correct.

- If your production server or web host uses Apache and FastCGI for Rails application hosting, be sure to modify your copy of public/.htaccess on your server so that dispatch.fcgi is called instead of dispatch.cgi.

- Deploy your application files over the top of the ones you created, making sure to ignore overriding the dispatch.fcgi or .htaccess file. This can easily be scripted if you use Subversion.

- Edit your database configuration file on the production server, and then make sure you never overwrite it when you redeploy. I do not think it is a good idea to store your database passwords in a code repository, so I never check the database.yml file in to the repository.

- Run your migrations in production mode to ensure that your database is configured.

- Open the console in production mode (./script/console production), and attempt to retrieve some data. This will help test to see if you have any odd characters in your code that need to be converted.

- Test your application on the production server using WEBrick in production mode (./script/server -e production). If your host allows you to connect on port 3000, try pulling up your site using that port.

- Configure your production server to use your new application. Some providers like DreamHost have a control panel where you specify the public folder of your Rails app. Once your app is configured, try hitting it with the browser one more time to make sure it comes up.

- Check to see whether the production log is being used. If it's not, you'll need to modify your environment.rb file to force production mode. Some shared hosts have been known not to set the environment in their Apache configuration.

A better approach than this is to automate your deployment using Capistrano. You can safely make all these alterations to your files at any time and just check them in to your repository. You can then just deploy using a Capistrano recipe. Capistrano tasks can change permissions, alter files, and more. If you're going through all the trouble to write a program, take a little more time to learn how to automate the deployment. You're less likely to forget something later.

8.11 Wrapping Up

This chapter talked about various strategies you can use to deploy your application. You have a lot of choices to make now, because each method will yield different results. Some might be better than others, but you need to figure out which will work for you and your situation. I can't stress enough the importance of testing your stack. Run performance testing tools against your application before you deploy it, and keep a close eye on it when it's running. You want to make sure you are ready to move to a better deployment solution before you need it.

Don't be afraid to deploy on Windows, though—many people, including myself—have been very successful deploying applications with these methods. It's a great way to get Rails into a Windows-based environment. Once you prove you can be more efficient with Rails, you can push for a Linux deployment stack!

Chapter 9

Performance

In the old Chinese proverb, many people can look at the elephant from different perspectives and see different things. In very much the same way, a programmer can look at Rails and smile, experiencing near euphoria. When it's time to deploy that same application and make it scale, the system administrator who is charged with the daunting task of pumping users through it might run howling and shrieking from the room. Rails is very much a trade-off. The same high-level language that makes the beautiful domain-specific languages and allows the sweet dynamic programming enabling Active Record all takes time to execute. All that magic that goes on under the covers and makes things cushy for the application developers has a cost when it's time to push into deployment.

The good news is that you *can* make Rails scale. The framework is specifically designed with shared-nothing principles that will allow you to throw hardware at the problem, as you learned in Chapter 7, *Scaling Out*, on page 137. This has a tendency to make some developers procrastinate on the performance aspects of their applications. Though premature optimization is not always recommended either, you don't get a license to ignore optimization or scalability altogether. In this chapter, I'll walk you through some of the techniques you'll need to know to understand how much traffic a given deployment can handle, and then I'll show you the core techniques to dramatically improve what you have with a little hard work.

9.1 The Lay of the Land

Performance benchmarking is for two kinds of developers: those who take a structured and patient approach and those who love pain. So,

What Doesn't Work?

Before I walk you through the game plan for improving application performance, let me walk you through a few examples of approaches that we know don't often work:

- *Premature optimization*: Focusing on performance above all else may produce the fastest, slickest application whether you actually need the performance or not. However, you may find that this comes at the cost of code that is complex, hard to read, and even harder to maintain. Optimization also takes time, so you may also risk your project schedule and miss deadlines due to features taking too long to implement because of the additional performance enhancements. Instead, performance test your application often throughout the project. Ensure that it will meet an acceptable level of performance for your needs, and optimize only the critical bottlenecks as required.

- *Guessing*: When you find that your application is too slow, you may be tempted to guess about where the problem might be. You may hack through various performance optimizations in an attempt try fix it. You may guess right once or twice, but you'll eventually spend hours on the right solutions to the wrong problems. Instead, use profiling tools, load-testing, and monitoring tools to pinpoint the problem areas before implementing any performance patches.

- *Caching everything*: Rails makes caching fairly easy, so you might just think that caching will always save you at the last minute. But caching is almost always harder than it looks on the surface. This enigmatic performance enhancement creates opportunities for bugs to creep into production where they weren't seen in testing, because cached features can be hard to test. It's especially dangerous to simply enable caching at the last minute and hope that it will work. Instead, try to identify potential hot spots early, such as your home page or latest news feed. Then, design those features with caching in mind, and use a staging environment where caching is enabled so that you can test the application as it will be in production.

> ### What Doesn't Work? (cont.)
>
> - *Fighting the framework*: Rails is a convention-based framework that makes a lot of assumptions. This philosophy works best if you work within the framework. At times, you may feel like getting creative and breaking some of the known best practices and possibly even hacking on Rails to either modify it or work around it. However, you may find yourself using the framework in ways that the Rails designers never intended, so when it comes time to upgrade Rails to the next version or make use of a plug-in that assumes you're using Rails in the expected way, you'll feel the pain. Instead, do your best to work within the constraints of the framework you chose. Ask around and seek out experts in the Rails community, and ask them how they might solve performance problems similar to yours—without breaking the written and unwritten rules.

unless you're the one who loves pain, whenever you deploy a new application, you will want to make a deliberate plan and stay with it as best as you can. The basic steps are shown in Figure 9.1, on the next page.

1. *Be the best you can be: target baseline*: The first thing you want to do is set your expectations. You have to know when you're done. You need a best-case baseline to know your upper performance bound. To do this, take Rails out of the picture to see how many HTTP requests your production servers can handle—you cannot expect to go any faster than that. Then run the simplest possible Rails request to establish a target for Rails applications in general. If there's a large disparity already, you may want try tuning your proxy, FastCGI, or Mongrel. When you're done, this is your target baseline.

2. *Know where you are now: application baseline*: If you want to improve on any application, you have to know where you are so that you know how far you have to go. You'll want to run a simple performance test without optimization of any kind. This is your application baseline.

3. *Profile to find bottlenecks*: After you have a baseline, you should profile your system to locate your bottlenecks. A bottleneck, like the governor on an engine, limits how fast your application can

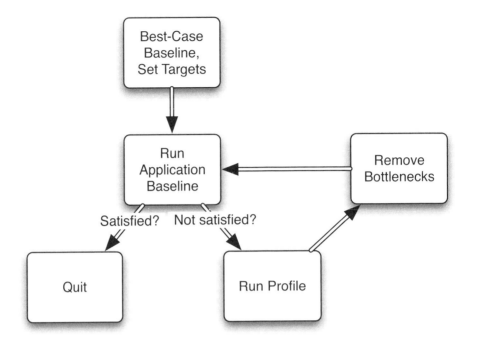

Figure 9.1: PERFORMANCE PROCESS

go, regardless of the rest of the system. You improve performance by systemically eliminating bottlenecks.

4. *Remove bottlenecks*: This is the proper place within your process for performance optimizations. Using profiling and benchmarking, you can understand exactly where your changes will make the biggest impact. You will concentrate on one specific inefficiency and eliminate it. Then, you can run your profile and repeat the process.

5. *Repeat*: Using a basic approach of profiling and benchmarking, making incremental changes to your code, and repeating the process will let you know for sure which code changes increased or decreased performance. You will change one parameter at a time and keep the process simple. Be sure to make a only single change at a time, and take a new measurement. This will save you time in the long run.

Now that I've walked you through the basic premise behind benchmarking, I'd like to walk you through selected pieces of the process and also through some basic bottlenecks and their solutions. First, you'll take a baseline with a benchmark.

9.2 Initial Benchmarks: How Many Mongrels?

When you are ready to benchmark your application, your initial benchmarks should give you the overall application performance. This means using HTTP load-testing tools to test your application over a network. If you are satisfied with these load-testing results, then you don't have to optimize anything, but many times you will find at least a few areas to tweak.

One question that pops up at this point is the classic "How many Mongrels do I need for my app?" In my experience, people tend to overestimate the number of Mongrels required for optimal performance. Of course, everyone wants to be the next Web 2.0 Google acquisition, but the reality is that most production Rails apps that get less than 100,000 page views per day can be served perfectly well with two or three Mongrels behind a proxy. The only way to know for sure is to benchmark.

I will be using Mongrel in my tests, but the same information applies to any other means of running Rails applications in multiple processes. To practice what I preach, the first thing to do is get a baseline, absolute best-case performance scenario for my current hardware. I will use ab (Apache bench) or httperf to measure the requests per second of the smallest request that invokes Rails. Create a fresh Rails app with one controller and one action that just does a render :text => "Hello!". This will measure the fastest baseline response time you can expect from a Rails app running on Mongrel on your current hardware.

```
ezra$ rails benchmark_app
ezra$ cd benchmark_app
ezra$ script/generate controller Bench hello
```

Now open the BenchController class (the file bench_controller.rb in the directory RAILS_ROOT/app/controllers), and edit it to look like this:

```
class BenchController < ApplicationController
  def hello
    render :text => "Hello!"
  end
end
```

This hello action is the absolute smallest and fastest request a Rails application can serve while still invoking the full stack including sessions. It doesn't call the database server or open and interpolate any templates. The application calls routing and instantiates the controller to serve the request. Rails has to go through the motions of setting up the session filter chain and all the other magic that happens during the service of one request. As you add code, templates, and database calls to your actions, the results will become slower, but at this point, I'm after a best-case target baseline.

Take a look at the output from the ab command. Here is the help banner:

```
ezra$ ab -h
Usage: ab [options] [http://]hostname[:port]/path
Options are:
    -n requests     Number of requests to perform
    -c concurrency  Number of multiple requests to make
    -t timelimit    Seconds to max. wait for responses
    -p postfile     File containing data to POST
    -T content-type Content-type header for POSTing
    -v verbosity    How much troubleshooting info to print
    -w              Print out results in HTML tables
    -i              Use HEAD instead of GET
    -x attributes   String to insert as table attributes
    -y attributes   String to insert as tr attributes
    -z attributes   String to insert as td or th attributes
    -C attribute    Add cookie, eg. 'Apache=1234' (repeatable)
    -H attribute    Add Arbitrary header line, eg. 'Accept-Encoding: zop'
                    Inserted after all normal header lines. (repeatable)
    -A attribute    Add Basic WWW Authentication, the attributes
                    are a colon separated username and password.
    -P attribute    Add Basic Proxy Authentication, the attributes
                    are a colon separated username and password.
    -X proxy:port   Proxyserver and port number to use
    -V              Print version number and exit
    -k              Use HTTP KeepAlive feature
    -d              Do not show percentiles served table.
    -S              Do not show confidence estimators and warnings.
    -g filename     Output collected data to gnuplot format file.
    -e filename     Output CSV file with percentages served
    -h              Display usage information (this message)
```

I'll start with a simple test against one Mongrel with one concurrent user and 1,000 requests.

```
ez rmerb $ ab -n 1000 http://localhost:3000/bench/hello
This is ApacheBench, Version 1.3d <$Revision: 1.73 $> apache-1.3
Copyright (c) 1996 Adam Twiss, Zeus Technology Ltd, http://www.zeustech.net/
Copyright (c) 1998-2002 The Apache Software Foundation, http://www.apache.org/

Benchmarking localhost (be patient)
Completed 100 requests
```

```
Completed 200 requests
   :       :      :
Completed 900 requests
Finished 1000 requests
Server Software:        Mongrel
Server Hostname:        localhost
Server Port:            3000

Document Path:          /bench/hello
Document Length:        5 bytes

Concurrency Level:      1
Time taken for tests:   9.196 seconds
Complete requests:      1000
Failed requests:        0
Broken pipe errors:     0
Total transferred:      255000 bytes
HTML transferred:       5000 bytes
Requests per second:    108.74 [#/sec] (mean)
Time per request:       9.20 [ms] (mean)
Time per request:       9.20 [ms] (mean, across all concurrent requests)
Transfer rate:          27.73 [KBytes/sec] received

Connnection Times (ms)
             min   mean[+/-sd] median    max
Connect:       0     0    0.0      0      0
Processing:    6     9    6.5      8     83
Waiting:       6     9    6.5      8     83
Total:         6     9    6.5      8     83

Percentage of the requests served within a certain time (ms)
  50%       8
  66%       8
  75%       8
  80%       9
  90%       9
  95%       9
  98%      10
  99%      32
 100%      83 (last request)
```

The main thing I want to see is Requests per second: 108.74 [#/sec] (mean).
I ran this benchmark on a 2GHz Intel Core Duo with 2GB of RAM.
A small fresh Rails application like this usually will use about 45MB
of RAM per Mongrel process. This first benchmark runs on the same
host as the Rails application. Remember that this test will provide an
absolute best-case performance baseline and does not simulate real-
world situations very well.

On modern hardware, you should expect to easily get more than 100 requests a second for this simple action. Your results will vary, but if you are getting more than 100 requests a second, then you are doing fine. You can improve this first baseline by turning off sessions for your action.

That tiny improvement actually increases the results to more than 400 requests a second! This just shows that if you don't need sessions, then be sure to use the session method of ActionController::Base to turn sessions off for any actions that don't use them. In the real world, most actions will require sessions, though, so assume a best-case baseline of 108 requests per second.

The next step is to use a cluster of Mongrels behind a load balancer proxy of some kind. This way I can test concurrent users and come up with our magic number of Mongrel processes that works best on the hardware at hand. Refer to Chapter 7, *Scaling Out*, on page 137 for information about installing and configuring a proxy load balancer.

Once you have your proxy set, then you should start testing with two Mongrels, and then three, and so on. For each battery of tests, you should increase the simulated concurrent users with the -c option. I like to test ten, thirty, and fifty levels of concurrency. Any more than that, and the stats become skewed because ab has trouble simulating that much load. I am establishing a best-case baseline. I'll do real load testing once I settle on a final configuration and my application is finished. I'll generate my load tests from another server or even multiple servers at once to more closely simulate real-world usage.

Another trick to more closely simulate real-world conditions is to use the -C options to set a cookie value. The results from the first benchmark will actually create and save a new session for all 1,000 requests! The real usage of your app will not create so many sessions because once someone logs in, they reuse the same session. Also, you will inevitably want to test protected areas of your site for performance, so you need to be able to maintain a session while benchmarking. To simulate a logged-in user, I will log into the site with a web browser and get the _session_id from the cookie. Check your browser's preferences for a cookie viewer of some sort.

Once you have copied the _session_id from your browser, then it's time to add it to the ab command.

Here is a sample of a sequence of benchmarks to run against your app:

```
ezra$ ab -n 5000 -c 10 -C _session_id=ee738c2fcc9e5ab953c35cc13f4fa82d ↩
        http://localhost/bench/hello
...
ezra$ ab -n 5000 -c 30 -C _session_id=ee738c2fcc9e5ab953c35cc13f4fa82d ↩
        http://localhost/bench/hello
...
ezra$ ab -n 5000 -c 50 -C _session_id=ee738c2fcc9e5ab953c35cc13f4fa82d ↩
        http://localhost/bench/hello
...
ezra$ ab -n 5000 -c 100 -C _session_id=ee738c2fcc9e5ab953c35cc13f4fa82d ↩
        http://localhost/bench/hello
```

Keep adding Mongrels until you don't gain any more requests per second by adding more. This step is especially important for software load balancers like Apache 2.2 or nginx. You might expect that by doubling the number of Mongrels you would double the throughput. You'd usually be wrong. Sometimes using more Mongrels than you need will actually slow down response times because the load balancer works harder to distribute the load. With expensive hardware load balancers, you can get pretty close to doubling throughput by doubling Mongrels, but these devices are out of reach for most application hosting budgets.

By testing in a methodical fashion, you can begin to get an overall view of the performance you can expect from your app. Without a good best-case baseline, it would be hard to know when to keep optimizing code and when to add more hardware. Rails applications tend to vary widely in the way they are coded and the way they utilize resources, so any generalizations about the performance of an app are very hard to make. Being scientific about your process and measuring heavily after every change to any part of the equation will let you know what has helped and what has hurt your performance.

9.3 Profiling and Bottlenecks

Now that I know the overall best-case performance characteristics of my system, I can move on to improving performance. If I've determined that performance is a problem, I can start to plan my attack. I usually work to find bottlenecks by using the Rails profiler, which highlights slower code. Armed with exact data that shows me how long each slice of code is taking, I can eliminate the slowest pieces under my control. Then, I'll benchmark again and repeat the process.

There are two profilers I'll use. The first will test performance of the full request—from the controller, all the way through to the database. The second will drill down a little deeper and focus strictly on the Active Record–based models.

ruby-prof

The Fast Ruby Profiler (ruby-prof) gem lets you profile Ruby in a fairly detailed way. It comes with a convenient Rails plug-in that will let you profile your application including the full stack of your application code. To get started, simply install the gem with gem install ruby-prof. Now navigate to the ruby-prof gem directory located under your Ruby installation's /lib directory.

Mine was located in <rubyhome>/lib/ruby/gems/1.8/gems/ruby-prof-0.5.2/ rails_plugin. In that directory, you'll find a subdirectory called ruby-prof. Copy that subdirectory to <your_rails_app>/vendor/plugins/. Make sure not to move it, because you will need a copy of it for any other Rails apps you want to profile. Finally, there's only one configuration change you need to make to your application.

In each of your environment configurations in /config/environments, including development.rb, test.rb, and production.rb, you'll see a line that reads something like config.cache_classes = [true|false]. In the test and production configurations, it is set to true. In development, it is set to false. This parameter needs to be set to true so that your profiling metrics aren't severely skewed by the unnecessary reloading of classes. Rather than using production for profiling or modifying development, you should create a new environment specifically for profiling.

Simply copy the development.rb file to profiling.rb, and set the line config.cache_classes = true. Don't forget to add a configuration to config/database.yml. You will use the production database instead of creating a new one. Feel free to create one if you want a fully independent environment for profiling. You can also tinker with other settings in the file as you profile. I tend to disable caching when profiling because I'm more interested in how I can improve my code than how it performs when my code isn't run at all. If you want, you can easily create two environments for profiling, one with caching and one without.

Now you're ready to profile your application. Simply start your server with script/server -e profiling, and then hit the home page of your application. The output of the profiler will appear in two places: in the console where you started the server and in log/profiling.log where profiling is the name of your profiling environment. Here's an example of what you should see:

```
Completed in 0.00400 (249 reqs/sec) | DB: 0.00200 (49%)
       | 302 Found [http://localhost/profiles/login]
 [http://localhost/profiles/login]

Thread ID: 82213740
Total: 0.005

 %self    ...  calls  name
 20.00    ...     18  IO#read
 20.00    ...      2  Mysql#read_rows
 20.00    ...     33  Hash#default
 20.00    ...      2  Kernel#respond_to_without_attributes?
 20.00    ...      1  ActionController::Benchmarking#perform_act...
```

This profile is an example of a login process that looks up a user's profile with a typical login and password. The first interesting line is a typical log line that Rails shows even without the profiler installed. The profile shows how the time was split between rendering in controllers and accessing the database through your models. A lot of the time, this output may tell you what you need to know, but your database access time will likely dwarf the rendering time. That's where the detailed profile numbers may help you out a bit. In the previous lines, you can see activity including network I/O to the database, the parsing of the MySQL row data, and a few calls to various libraries that probably don't concern you as much. If your application spends too much time in either IO#read or Mysql#read_rows, you could be returning too many rows, too many columns, or large amounts of data within the columns like large text fields. This profile is not everything you will ever need, but it does give you some place to start looking.

What about the rendering? It looks like Rails didn't render anything in the previous profile. The reason is that we're using a redirect-after-post pattern. Typically after submitting data, it's a good idea to redirect the user to a GET request–based view that is friendlier to page reloads and Back buttons. That's what this code did, so the rendering time was actually displayed as a separate request, and the profiler produced separate output for that.

Here's the output for the GET request:

```
Completed in 0.00700 (142 reqs/sec) | Rendering: 0.00300 (42%)
        | DB: 0.00100 (14%) | 200 OK [http://localhost/profiles/view]
  [http://localhost/profiles/view]


Thread ID: 81957820
Total: 0.007

%self   ...   calls  name
14.29   ...       6  ActionController::Base#response
14.29   ...      73  Hash#[]
14.29   ...      17  Array#each
14.29   ...      81  String#slice!
14.29   ...       4  Logger#add
14.29   ...       1  ActionController::Benchmarking#render
14.29   ...       1  <Class::ActiveRecord::Base>#method_missing
```

Here you can see where the controller is executed and various methods
are accessed inside the controller. Some of these might be your own
calls, while others might be internal to Rails. Again, any imbalance in
times should give you a place to start looking. This code deals with
a fairly simple and balanced request. Don't get too hung up on the
details of every single line. Look for the odd results and the long times,
and then start to drill down into why. The idea behind profiling is to
help pinpoint a place to start looking so that you can eliminate some of
the guesswork.

So, what do you do when you want more detail? Be careful what you
ask for, because you just might get it! If you need more detailed profiling
information to start your digging, ruby-prof can provide far more detail.
Luckily, it does so in the form of either HTML or even graphical format.
Open the Rails plug-in file found at <your_rails_app>/vendor/plugins/ruby-
prof/lib/profiling.rb. This clean little Ruby script has several configuration
options in it. The lines you'll want to look at are similar to the following.
I've numbered the comments to make it easier to reference here:

```
# #1 Create a flat printer
printer = RubyProf::FlatPrinter.new(result)
printer.print(output, {:min_percent => 2,
                       :print_file => false})
logger.info(output.string)


# #2 Example for Graph html printer
# printer = RubyProf::GraphHtmlPrinter.new(result)
# path = File.join(LOG_PATH, 'call_graph.html')
# File.open(path, 'w') do |file|
# printer.print(file, {:min_percent => 2,
#                      :print_file => true})
# end
```

```
# #3 Used for KCacheGrind visualizations
# printer = RubyProf::CallTreePrinter.new(result)
# path = File.join(LOG_PATH, 'callgrind.out')
# File.open(path, 'w') do |file|
#   printer.print(file, {:min_percent => 1,
#                         :print_file => true})
# end
```

By default the script has the Flat printer (#1) enabled. The result is what you've been looking at so far. As you've seen, the results are cryptic and informational at best. You can enable other printers by simply removing the comment characters from the appropriate lines for the printer.

The best one for tracking down specific lines of code is the Graph HTML printer (#2). That option will create an HTML file (and subsequently overwrite it) for each request. The amount of detail in this file is obscene, but here's a small sample, where I've removed many columns and left out most of the rows to make it readable:

...	...	...		...
	...	ActionView::Base#compile_and_render_template		325
	...	ActionController::Base#perform_action_without_filters		1101
66.67%	...	*Kernel#send*		*0*
	...	ProfilesController#view		1101
	...	ActionController::Base#template_class		1164
...	...	...		...

In each section of the report, you'll see a listing of methods, with one method in bold. The bold method is the subject of that particular section. The methods above it are the callers of the bold method. Methods below are methods the bold method called. The bold line also contains the total percentage of the execution time spent in that method. Where possible, the report also contains a line number, which links to the Ruby source on your local file system. Links to Rails code assumes Rails is frozen in your vendor directory. The report is very long, so make use of the text search facilities in your browser to find your own code or other items of interest.

The third printer, KCacheGrind visualization printer (#3), produces a graphical representation of the profile results. I won't go into detail here. If you want to see more examples and get more information about ruby-prof, please refer to the following links. The first is the ruby-prof home on RubyForge, which serves only to prove how poor Ruby docs are in general.

Therefore, I searched for a decent blog posting on the subject and found a very good one that goes into further detail:

- http://ruby-prof.rubyforge.org/

- http://cfis.savagexi.com/articles/2007/07/10/how-to-profile-your-rails-application

Standard Rails Model Profiler

Most of the time, your performance problems will center around your Active Record models. Either they're too slow or they're being overused by calling classes, such as a finder in a loop. Therefore, if you know that your performance issues are definitely within your Active Record models, you can use a built-in profiler script that comes with Rails.

This script works very much like ruby-prof but is probably already on your machine. Like ruby-prof, it produces an obscene amount of information. I won't exhaust the topic any further and instead just leave you with this example:

```
ezra$ script/performance/profiler 'Profile.find_by_id(1)' 10 graph
Loading Rails...
Using the standard Ruby profiler.
  %   cumulative   self              self     total
 time   seconds   seconds    calls  ms/call  ms/call  name
12.65     0.22      0.22       114    1.90     2.18   Array#select
10.90     0.40      0.19       498    0.38     0.87   Mysql#get_length
 9.09     0.56      0.16      1975    0.08     0.11   Kernel.===
 6.29     0.67      0.11       107    1.01     1.30   Mysql::Net#read
 4.60     0.75      0.08        72    1.10    31.40   Integer#times
 4.55     0.83      0.08      3724    0.02     0.03   Fixnum#==
 3.67     0.89      0.06        10    6.30    11.00   ActiveRecord::Base#co...
 3.67     0.95      0.06       109    0.58     0.58   Object#method_added
 3.55     1.01      0.06       137    0.45     5.58   Array#each
 2.74     1.06      0.05        12    3.92     5.17   MonitorMixin.mon_acquire
 2.74     1.11      0.05         8    5.87     5.87   Class#inherited
 2.68     1.15      0.05       963    0.05     0.05   String#slice!
 1.86     1.18      0.03        12    2.67    63.67   Mysql#read_query_result
 1.86     1.22      0.03        56    0.57     0.57   Mysql::Field#initialize
 1.81     1.25      0.03        98    0.32     0.32   Gem::GemPathSearcher#m...
 1.81     1.28      0.03      3445    0.01     0.01   Hash#key?
 1.81     1.31      0.03       736    0.04     0.04   Array#<<
 1.81     1.34      0.03        22    1.41    33.23   Mysql#read_rows
 1.81     1.37      0.03        93    0.33     7.53   Mysql#read_one_row
```

9.4 Common Bottlenecks

So far, all I've done is set up an ideal expectation for performance. The next step is to eliminate bottlenecks. Many experts have explored Rails performance. One of the best is Stefan Kaes. The noted Rails performance guru identified several common Rails bottlenecks in his often-quoted talk at RailsConf.[1] The items are still as relevant today as they were when the list was first released:

- *Slow helper methods.* Since views often call helper methods inside tight loops, it's easy to build helpers that take much too long to calculate. For such common helpers, make sure you keep them lean.

- *Complicated routes.* Each time the web server invokes Rails, the router calculates the routes in your routes.rb file. You don't want to have any complex calculations in there.

- *Associations.* Active Record makes it easy to build database-backed code—almost too easy. When associations get loaded too often, performance will suffer. I'll walk you through the most critical performance cases in the section that follows.

- *Retrieving too much from the database.* Active Record retrieves the whole database row by default, and sometimes, you just don't need all that data. If you're retrieving a row with a 4KB description field just to get a foreign key, you may want to trim down that query with :select.

- *Slow session storage.* Sessions across many users can add up. Since sessions represent shared memory that Rails holds for indefinite periods of time, you need to pay them special attention.

In the sections that follow, I'll walk you through a couple of the most common performance problems. I'll start with Active Record bottlenecks. Active Record is one of the most convenient persistence frameworks ever built. You can often find Rails developers mocking their Java counterparts with a few trivial lines of code that set up the database, process five relationships, process six custom validations, and even solve world peace—all with a dozen lines of code. Unfortunately, all that convenience and flexibility comes at a cost. A few months later,

---

1. http://Frailsexpress.de/blog/files/slides/railsconf2006.pdf

those same Java counterpoints are often the ones doing the mocking. Active Record, out of the box, is *slow*. Luckily, you have a few tools at your disposal to speed things up:

- *Includes*: When you have associations that you know you will use from the results of a find, you can use the :include option. With the include option, you'll generate one SQL query instead of many.

- *Piggybacked attributes*: Active Record dynamically builds objects from the objects in the result set for any given find. You can often add attributes to a result set with SQL. I'll show you more in a moment.

- *Custom SQL*: You can build custom SQL to return exactly what you need.

- *Selects*: If you don't need all of the columns of a database, you can eliminate the additional overhead by simply using the select option. Select specifies which columns you want to retrieve from the model's database table. By default, Active Record returns all of them.

:include and the N+1 Problem

By default, Active Record relationships are lazy. That means the framework will wait to access a relationship until you actually use it. Take, for example, a member with an address. You can open the console and type this command: member = Member.find 1. You'll see the following appended to your log, as follows:

```
Member Columns (0.006198) SHOW FIELDS FROM members
Member Load (0.002835) SELECT * FROM members WHERE (members.'id' = 1)
```

Member has a relationship to an address that was defined with the macro has_one :address, :as => :addressable, :dependent => :destroy. Notice that you don't see an address field in the log when Active Record loaded Member. But if you type member.address in the console, you'll see the following contents in development.log:

```
./vendor/plugins/paginating_find/lib/paginating_find.rb:98:in 'find'
Address Load (0.252084) SELECT * FROM addresses
 WHERE (addresses.addressable_id = 1
   AND addresses.addressable_type = 'Member') LIMIT 1
./vendor/plugins/paginating_find/lib/paginating_find.rb:98:in 'find'
```

So, Active Record does not execute the query for the address relationship until you actually access member.address. Normally, this lazy design works well, because the persistence framework does not need to move as much data to load a member. But assume you wanted to access a list of members and all of their addresses, like this:

```
Member.find([1,2,3]).each {|member| puts member.address.city}
```

Since you should see a query for each of the addresses, the results should not be pretty, in terms of performance:

```
Member Load (0.004063) SELECT * FROM members WHERE (members.`id` IN (1,2,3))
./vendor/plugins/paginating_find/lib/paginating_find.rb:98:in `find'
Address Load (0.000989) SELECT * FROM addresses
WHERE (addresses.addressable_id = 1
  AND addresses.addressable_type = 'Member') LIMIT 1
./vendor/plugins/paginating_find/lib/paginating_find.rb:98:in `find'
Address Columns (0.073840) SHOW FIELDS FROM addresses
Address Load (0.002012) SELECT * FROM addresses
WHERE (addresses.addressable_id = 2
  AND addresses.addressable_type = 'Member') LIMIT 1
./vendor/plugins/paginating_find/lib/paginating_find.rb:98:in `find'
Address Load (0.000792) SELECT * FROM addresses
WHERE (addresses.addressable_id = 3
  AND addresses.addressable_type = 'Member') LIMIT 1
./vendor/plugins/paginating_find/lib/paginating_find.rb:98:in `find'
```

Indeed, the results are not pretty. You get one query for all the members and another for each address. We retrieved three members, and you got four queries. N members; N+1 queries. This problem is the dreaded N+1 problem. Most persistence frameworks solve this problem with eager associations. Rails is no exception. If you know that you will need to access a relationship, you can opt to include it with your initial query. Active Record uses the :include option for this purpose. If you changed the query to Member.find([1,2,3], :include => :address).each {|member| puts member.address.city}, you'll see a much better picture:

```
Member Load Including Associations (0.004458)
    SELECT members.`id` AS t0_r0, members.`type` AS t0_r1,
    members.`about_me` AS t0_r2, members.`about_philanthropy'
    ...
    addresses.`id` AS t1_r0, addresses.`address1` AS t1_r1,
    addresses.`address2` AS t1_r2, addresses.`city` AS t1_r3,
    ...
    addresses.`addressable_id` AS t1_r8 FROM members
    LEFT OUTER JOIN addresses ON addresses.addressable_id
    = members.id AND addresses.addressable_type =
    'Member' WHERE (members.`id` IN (1,2,3))
    ./vendor/plugins/paginating_find/lib/paginating_find.rb:
  98:in `find'
```

That's much better. You see one query that retrieves all the members and addresses. That's how eager associations work.

With Active Record, you can also nest the :include option. For example, consider a Member that has many contacts and a Contact that has one address. If you wanted to show all the cities for a member's contacts, you could use the following code:

```
contacts</heading>
member = Member.find(1)
member.contacts.each {|contact| puts contact.address.city}
```

That code would work, but you'd have to query for the member, each contact, and each contact's address. You can improve the performance a little by eagerly including :contacts with :include => :contacts. You can do better by including both associations using a nested include option:

```
member = Member.find(1, :include => {:contacts => :address})
member.contacts.each {|contact| puts contact.address.city}
```

That nested include tells Rails to eagerly include both the contacts and address relationships. You can use the eager-loading technique whenever you know that you will use relationships in a given query. :include does have limitations. If you need to do reporting, you're almost always better off simply grabbing the database connection and bypassing Active Record all together with ActiveRecord::Base.execute("SELECT * FROM...") to save the overhead related to marshaling Active Record objects. Generally, eager associations will be more than enough.

Other Active Record Options

Controlling your associations with :include and defining exactly which columns you want with :select will give you most of the performance you need. Occasionally, you will need a few extra tricks to get you all the way home.

Nested sets: Rails provides a convenient tree for dealing with hierarchies of data. If you're not careful, you can easily build an application that does a query for each node in the tree. When you need to find all nodes in one section of the tree, such as with catalogs, you will be better off using a nested set. You can read more about it in the Rails documentation.

Smart inheritance: The Rails model of inheritance is single-table inheritance. That means that every Active Record model that participates in an inheritance hierarchy goes into the same table. If you try to build models that inherit too deeply, you will cram too much into a single table. You can often use polymorphic associations[2] instead of inheritance to represent key concepts such as an address or a common base class.

When that fails, you can take advantage of Ruby's duck typing instead of inheritance. Think of a website that uses little bits of content in many different forms across the whole application. Every piece of content may have a name and a description. If you tried to let every different type of class inherit from a class called Content, your whole application would be in one table. The Ruby way to solve this problem is to just add the name and description columns to each table that needs them. Ruby's duck typing will let you treat all kinds of content the same, referring to both the name and description columns.

Both polymorphic associations and duck typing can lead you to better performance but also to much cleaner model code.

Indexes and normalization: Though Active Record hides some of the concepts from you, underneath you're still dealing with a good, old relational databases. Your larger tables will still need indexes on the fields that you'll access often. The same database normalization[3] techniques still apply.

9.5 Caching

When you need to stretch Rails for high performance, your first impression will usually be to cache. Before you go down the caching path, take a deep breath. Caching is not a silver bullet. Even in the best of circumstances, caching is difficult to get right, nearly impossible to test well, and unpredictable. If you're not convinced, read the last sentence twice more and also the following list:

- *Caching is ugly.* You'll be polluting parts of your application with code that has nothing to do with the business problem you're trying to solve. Rails can protect you from some of the ugly syntax, but not all.
- *Caching is tough to debug.* You will add a whole new classification of bugs to your system, including stale data, inconsistent data, timing-based bugs, and many more. Keep in mind that it's not

---

2. http://wiki.rubyonrails.org/rails/pages/UnderstandingPolymorphicAssociations
3. http://en.wikipedia.org/wiki/Database_normalization

just the impact of a model on one page but the interaction between many cached pages that can give your user a strange experience.

- *Caching is complicated.* You'll need to consider all the pages and fragments that a given model can change, how to expire those pages across a cluster, the impacts of caching on security and roles, and how to manage the additional infrastructure.
- *Caching limits your user interface options.* You will have to answer many questions that should be independent of implementation. Can you show a flash message? Can you show a user's login and picture? Can you secure a page? Can you have dynamic content of any kind on a page or fragment? Your answers will often be "no" if caching is involved.

If I haven't scared you away from caching by now, I probably won't or shouldn't. You should also know that Rails has a broad spectrum of caching solutions. They are usually well designed and easy to understand. You can divide them all into two categories:

- *Page and fragment caches* let you save some part of a rendered web page. Page and page fragment caches are interesting because for any given page or fragment, you completely take the back end of the application out of the picture. For the cached page or fragment, there's no database access and no expensive computation.
- *Model caches* work exclusively in the realm of the model. Usually, you're trying to save a database access or other computation. By the time this book is published, you should be able to cache the results of an Active Record query. Other plug-ins allow you to explicitly cache any model that's frequently used or expensive to create.

In this section, I'll focus on the page and fragment caching techniques because the model caching techniques are in flux. Along the way, I'll walk you through the strengths and weaknesses of each caching tool and show you how to use them.

Out of the box, Rails provides three primary caching options, in order of performance: *page caching*, *action caching*, and *fragment caching*. You will see that page caching is the fastest because it creates static pages that your web server can serve. Action caching is not nearly as fast because the web server will invoke Rails for each request. Fragment caching is the slowest because Rails caches only a fragment of the page.

The solution you pick depends on the flexibility you will ultimately require. Fragment caching is the only caching solution that allows you to cache a partial page. If you absolutely need to use before filters in your controllers—to restrict a page to an authenticated user, for instance—you will need to use fragment caching or action caching.

Page Caching

Page caching is by far the simplest and most effective caching option if your pages and application are static enough. Getting the basics right is simple. Nailing down all the details can be unbearably difficult. I'll cover the basics first.

Say you have a controller with an index action. The index action creates a catalog page that is relatively complicated, but it rarely changes. Your current setup is not fast enough anymore, so after carefully considering your options, you decide to cache. Since your page is completely the same for each user and changes infrequently, you correctly decide that you should use page caching.

You will need to change your controller to cache the page. You'll also need some strategy for deleting the static page when you want Rails to generate an updated version of your page. You could easily cache the page like this:

```
class CatalogController
  caches_page :index

  def index
    # do something complicated
  end
end
```

When you run this application in development mode, you'll see no difference. Caching is turned off by default in development mode as you would expect. When you're developing, you want to immediately see code changes reflected in your web page. You can turn caching on by editing config/environments/development.rb and changing false to true in the following line:

```
config.action_controller.perform_caching = true
```

Now, when you point your browser to localhost:3000/catalog for the first time, Rails will create a static HTML page by the name of public/catalog/index.html. Page caching is very effective when you can use it because Rails *never even gets involved*. Your web server can just serve the static page, which can improve your throughput by a factor of 100 or more. Your web server will serve that static page until you physically delete it, which brings me to the next topic.

Sweeping a Page Cache

When you need to clear a cached page, you are actually deleting the HTML file. You can delete pages with file commands or with Rails directives. For simplicity, most people start with the Rails directives. Sooner or later, most complex applications will wind up moving to file-based commands.

I'll start simple. Say your catalog has gifts on the page. You want to expire the index page whenever you create, delete, or update a gift. First, I'll create a method to expire the pages I need to expire when my gift's controller changes a gift.

```
class ApplicationController < ActionController::Base
  def expire_all_gift_pages
    expire_page(:controller => 'catalog', :action => 'index')
  end
```

I'll typically keep this method in application.rb so any controller that changes the model can call the method, but if changes to gifts were isolated to my gifts controller, this method could easily be a private method on the gifts controller. Next, I can create a simple after filter for each action that changes gifts:

```
class GiftsController < ActionController::Base
  after_filter :expire_all_gift_pages, :only => [:create, :update, :destroy]
```

Keep in mind that the expire_all_gift_pages() method deletes only a single file on a single machine. If you cluster, you'll have to do something to synchronize your cache across all your nodes. Otherwise, users on different nodes could easily be seeing different versions of your catalogs! To keep things synchronized, you might consider a shared or clustered file system or building a simple web service that explicitly connects to each node in your cluster and expires the page.

The second way that you can expire a page is with a file-based command. Usually, you'll use a class structure called a *sweeper*. Often, you'll find that sweeping individual pages with Rails is a messy process because you don't know exactly which pages are cached. Many applications don't write very often, so it's a perfectly valid approach to sweep your entire cache when any model object changes significantly. A common approach[4] to sweeping an entire page cache is to observe a model object and delete a whole controller's cache when any model instance changes. I use a slightly different variation of the referenced algorithm because my page caches of my most active pages depend on a relatively narrow list of model objects:

```
class GiftSweeper < ActionController::Caching::Sweeper
  observe Gift

  def after_save(record)
    self.class::sweep
  end

  def after_destroy(record)
    self.class::sweep
  end

  def self.sweep
    FileUtils.rm_r(Dir.glob(RAILS_ROOT+"/catalog/*")) rescue Errno::ENOENT
  end
end
```

In your controller, you'll need to reference your sweeper:

```
  class GiftsController < ActionController::Base
cache_sweeper :gift_sweeper, :only => [:create, :update, :destroy]
```

You will notice that the sweeper is dead simple. Rather than worry about which pages are dirty, it simply deletes all the cached gift pages. That approach to sweeping may ultimately be too aggressive if you have model objects that change too frequently, but the simplicity of the approach makes it extremely attractive for many applications such as blogs or e-commerce sites where articles and catalogs are changed infrequently.

Page Caching Problems

In a book like this one, all these issues look simple to implement and simple to resolve. In practice, caching is incredibly hard to get right. The following list shows some things to watch:

- *Sweeping the right files*: Most caching complexity in Rails comes from knowing what to sweep. Whenever you change a model object, you must sweep every page that presents any data related to that model. Usually, the hardest part of caching is determining exactly which pages change when you make an update.

---

4. http://www.fngtps.com/2006/01/lazy-sweeping-the-rails-page-cache

- *Getting your URLs right*: The Rails page caching model depends on your URL names. If you need URL parameters to uniquely determine a page, you're out of luck. You will often need a more sophisticated routing rule such as :controller/:action/:id/:page_number for page caching to work. You must also beware of URL encoding. Special encoded characters in your URLs can defeat page caching.
- *Security*: If your content varies for each logged-in user, you will not want to use page caching. Even if you have special before filters to enforce security, Rails will happily show private content to all users because the router never invokes your controller for page caching.
- *Multiple paths*: If you have multiple routes for a given page, you will find page caching more difficult. You will need to make sure you clear the cache for every route that presents one piece of custom content.

A comprehensive page caching treatment of page caching is well beyond the scope of this book, but you should have enough to get started. It's time to move on to action caching.

Action Caching

Action caching works like page caching. You enable this kind of caching with a before filter, just as you do with page caching. Action caching has two major differences from page caching:

- *Controller execution*: When you use action caching, Rails will invoke the controller for each action, even if the action is in the cache.
- *Back end*: Page caching always uses the file system as the file store, but action caching uses a configurable back end.

Syntactically, action caching looks almost identical to page caching. To action cache the index and show actions on the catalog controller, you'd use the following code:

```
class CatalogController
caches_action :index

def index
  # do something complicated
end
end
```

The previous caching code will use the caching back end that you specify in your configuration, which is the file system by default. To expire them, you can use Rails directives like this:

```
expire_action(:controller => 'catalog', :action => 'index')
```

You can also use a regular-expression style of expiration, like this:

```
expire_action(%r{catalog/gifts/.*})
```

Of course, most complicated applications will use sweepers. The syntax of the sweeper remains the same regardless of the type of caching you use. Though the programming interface is similar, the strengths and weaknesses are much different. On the plus side, the action caching model allows greater flexibility. Since the Rails router invokes the controller even for cache hits, you have full access to before and after filters so you can enable features like security. Also, the back end is configurable, so you can use caching strategies that are friendlier to clustering. I'll talk more about the available caching back ends in Section 9.5, *Caching Back Ends*, on page 243.

You know by now that there's no such thing as a free lunch. The added flexibility of filters and a configurable back end comes at a price: performance. Page caching has a huge benefit. Each page service completely bypasses the Rails infrastructure and all of its overhead.

Fragment Caching

Fragment caching works exactly like action caching, but for partial pages instead of full pages. Fragment caching uses directives in the views to mark the content that you want to cache. You can use the out-of-the-box directives, or you can use some add-ons that support time-based expiration.

With out-of-the-box fragment caching, you use the cache helper within your view templates to cache content. Your cached code goes to a configurable back end (see Section 9.5, *Caching Back Ends*, on page 243) that you can later expire with expire_fragment directives. In your view, you'd have something like this:

```
<% cache do %>
<%= render partial => 'something_expensive' %>
<% end %>
```

Say you invoked an action called expensive/action for the first time, and that action rendered the view with the previous code fragment. The code helper would cache the code to the configured back end and name the cache fragment expensive/action. The second time you invoked the expensive/action action, Rails would retrieve that action from the cache.

The sweeper would be the same as the sweeper you'd use for either of the other caching strategies. Using a sweeper, you can expire cache fragments based on changes in the model.

Fragment caching has one critical weakness. The Rails programming model strongly suggests that you place any code that accesses your models in the controller. That means the controller will initiate most of your queries. But the fragment caching strategy does not help at all on the controller side. You can do only one of two things: you can run your queries in your views and suffer the consequences of poor application design, or you can extend the fragment caching model with a plug-in or custom code.

```
when_fragment_expired 'fragment_name', 20.minutes_from_now do
  @comments = Comment.find_favorite_comments
end
```

One such plug-in called timed_fragment_cache lets you expire fragments based on some time interval. Better still, the plug-in lets you bracket your *controller code* with caching directives. Say you wanted to expire a partial that presented the most popular blog comments every twenty minutes. In the controller, you would have this code:

```
<% cache 'blog_favorites', 20.minutes.from_now do %>
<%= render partial => 'favorite_comments' %>
<% end %>
```

And in the view, you'd use the cache directive with a name and an expiration time:

```
<% cache 'blog_favorites', 20.minutes.from_now do %>
  <%= render partial => 'something_expensive' %>
<% end %>
```

You can immediately see the benefits. Sure, you're saving the time Rails takes to render the view. More important, you're saving the time it takes to retrieve the favorite comments, possibly from a remote database server. The implementation is clean, convenient, and easy to cluster based on the configurable back end. The expiration is also dead simple. Every twenty minutes, Rails expires the fragment and computes a new one.

Caching Back Ends

Page caching always caches content as files in the public directory. This arrangement is easy to implement but harder to cluster. As you've seen, both action caching and fragment caching use the same configurable back ends. Out of the box, you have several back ends available. The most useful are these two:

- *File system.* The simplest and most convenient choice is the file system. This back-end choice works well with single-server deployments. The choice doesn't cluster as well because to do expiration, you would have to delete files across all nodes in a cluster.

- *Memcached*: The MemCachedStore option lets you use the memcached networked object cache.

Normally, you'll configure your caching options in one of your environments, typically config/environments/production.rb. Add the option line config.action_controller.perform_caching = true. You don't usually want to leave caching active within your development.rb file because you will often need to refresh your web pages, and deleting cached content is a pain. If you need to work with cached content in production temporarily, you can just set the appropriate cache option.

If you think you'll be spending much time working caching issues in development, you can add a new Rails environment. Typically what I do is copy my test.rb environment to a new one called staging.rb, in which I enable more production-like configurations such as caching. Keep in mind that a typical testing setup will not keep caching enabled!

When you set up the file system cache, you'll just need to make sure the root directory exists, and then you are off to the races. Memcached is a little more difficult. You'll typically need to set memcached up on every developer's local machine, on your production setup, and additionally on any staging machine you have. Testing will not usually use memcached at all.

To set up memcached locally on your development machine, you can use one of the following methods:

- On Windows, use the convenient installer found at http://jehiah.cz/projects/memcached-win32/.

- There are two ways for Mac OS X. First, you can try the script at http://topfunky.net/svn/shovel/memcached/install-memcached.sh.

- The second approach for OSX is more involved:

  - Download libevent from http://monkey.org/~provos/libevent/, configure, make, and make install it.

  - Get memcached from http://www.danga.com/memcached/, and uncompress it.

  - In the uncompressed memcached directory, locate memcached.c, and edit it.

  - Anywhere in the file before line 105, add #undef TCP_NOPUSH, and save.

  - Run the usual ./configure, and then make and sudo make install.

To set up memcached on your Linux server (or your Linux development box), you might want to find specific instructions for your Linux distribution. However, the following steps I found[5] worked for me:

```
# Install libevent
curl -O http://www.monkey.org/~provos/libevent-1.1a.tar.gz
tar zxf libevent-1.1a.tar.gz
cd libevent-1.1a
./configure
make
make install
cd ..


# Install memcached
curl -O http://www.danga.com/memcached/dist/memcached-1.1.12.tar.gz
tar zxf memcached-1.1.12.tar.gz
cd memcached-1.1.12
./configure
make
make install


# Then add /usr/local/lib to LD_LIBRARY_PATH in your .bash_profile
LD_LIBRARY_PATH=$LD_LIBRARY_PATH:/usr/local/lib
export LD_LIBRARY_PATH


# Then test:
memcached -m 512 -u nobody -vv
```

Memcached has a pretty limited command-line interface that is pretty much good only for starting memcached:

---

5. http://dotnot.org/blog/archives/2006/01/04/install-memcached-on-linux-centos-42/

```
ezra$ memcached -help
memcached 1.1.12
-p <num>        port number to listen on
-l <ip_addr>    interface to listen on, default is INDRR_ANY
-d              run as a daemon
-r              maximize core file limit
-u <username>   assume identity of <username> (only when run as root)
-m <num>        max memory to use for items in megabytes, default is 64 MB
-M              return error on memory exhausted (rather than removing items)
-c <num>        max simultaneous connections, default is 1024
-k              lock down all paged memory
-v              verbose (print errors/warnings while in event loop)
-vv             very verbose (also print client commands/responses)
-h              print this help and exit
-i              print memcached and libevent license
-P <file>       save PID in <file>, only used with -d option
```

To stop memcached, use killall memcached. Otherwise, flushing memcached can be done only via the API, which you can find more information for at http://www.danga.com/memcached/. You might want to stop
and start the memcached server with your Capistrano deploy scripts.
Similarly, you may want to create a couple of custom Rake tasks to
flush the cache when you need to in development and production.

9.6   Conclusion

There are good Rails projects and bad ones. Good projects benefit from
good planning and discipline. Getting good performance out of Rails
definitely takes discipline. In this chapter, I laid out a disciplined approach to get you the strongest possible performance quickly.

The first step in the process was to establish a baseline. I used Apache
bench or httperf to measure the smallest application that I could create with Rails. This best-case scenario for the application told me the
high-end expectation for my Rails application given the hardware and
resources. I could use the same technique to run an application baseline to show me the application performance, without optimizations.

If I detected a performance problem, I might decide to start making
arbitrary changes to improve performance, but I would probably guess
wrong. Instead, I profile to find out exactly which pieces of my code
base are breaking. Various Rails tools include the ruby-prof gem and the
basic profiling.rb script. Using these commands with various options, I
could find bottlenecks.

After locating a bottleneck, I could solve the bottleneck using several techniques in the chapter. Caching helped me sidestep a few lines of Ruby code or bypass Rails entirely, trading flexibility and power for speed. I also showed how to improve Active Record performance.

You learned that Rails is not going to squeeze every last cycle out of your hardware, but you can usually get a system that is fast enough and scalable enough, unless you're trying to put Google or eBay out of business. But getting the most out of Rails depends on your knowledge and your discipline.

Chapter 10

Frontiers

Both the Ruby programming language and Ruby on Rails are fairly well established, but the various Ruby deployment platforms are very much in their infancy. It is the hope of this team of authors that this book is the state of the art in Rails deployment for a very short time. For that to happen, a better deployment platform must emerge that radically changes the whole Ruby stack. There are already three good alternatives.

10.1 Yarv

The next version of Ruby, 1.9, will formally have a virtual machine at its core. The goal of Yarv is to build the fastest virtual machine for Ruby in the world. So far, they seem to have succeeded.[1] This implementation is much faster than the current implementation of Ruby. The bytecode support will lead to a more portable, faster code base. This implementation will be the first step in moving Ruby to a first-class virtual machine. But all eyes will be on Rubinius and Ruby 2.0.

10.2 Rubinius

Rubinius is a next-generation virtual machine written primarily in Ruby and loosely based on the Smalltalk-80 Blue Book. The current target version of Ruby is version 1.8.6, but once Rubinius is 1.8.6 compatible, work will begin on 1.9 and 2.0 compatibility. The virtual machine called *shotgun* is a tiny core written in C, with the rest of the runtime written almost entirely in Ruby. It uses newer techniques, such as a better

---

1. http://www.atdot.net/yarv/bench_20041002.txt

garbage collector, that were not available when Matz's Ruby Interpreter (MRI) was created. The team proclaims the goal that "anything that can be written in Ruby will be." The pure Ruby core makes it easier to extend. The compiler (also written in Ruby) generates bytecode, making the resulting programs more efficient than the current strategy MRI uses. The virtual machine will come with a packaging and deploying strategy for Ruby bytecode in the form of .rba files (Ruby Application Archive). This structure will allow you to package all of your bytecode for a project into one file for easy deployment.

Rubinius is creating a test suite using RSpec-like syntax. Since there is no official spec for Ruby, this suite of tests will serve as a specification of the language. This test suite is making it easier for platforms such as JRuby and Iron Ruby to prove compatibility with the core language implementation. Having all the new Ruby implementations share a common suite of specs will help keep Ruby the language from fragmenting as these alternate implementations evolve.

Rubinius is worth watching as a deployment platform for a number of reasons. For a good understanding of the impact of bytecode on a deployment platform, look no further than Java. The bytecode architecture for the Java virtual machine is an extremely successful deployment platform that will lead to the following advantages:

- Rubinius-compiled bytecode will be very efficient.

- Rubinius bytecode will be easier to package and deploy.

- The Rubinius virtual machines will insulate the programmer from the operating system, making Ruby code much more portable.

- Virtual machines can have configurable security policies, making Rubinius applications potentially more secure.

- The work on mod_rubinius aims to replace the multiple moving parts of a typical Mongrel deployment strategy with a simple-to-configure, true-Ruby application server that can sit behind Apache or nginx.

Rubinius is rapidly picking up momentum. Engine Yard has six full-time people working on the project with plans to make it the de facto Ruby VM. It already has improved libraries for concurrency and a better strategy for providing operating systems services without the need for a binding layer. Engine Yard's commercial support will lead to a stronger, supported project. For more information, visit the site at http://rubini.us/.

10.3 JRuby

JRuby is a Ruby implementation written entirely in Java. The implementation has many advantages associated with the Java virtual machine. While most Ruby applications run a separate process per instance, the JRuby implementation can use a separate native thread per instance. This implementation should eventually let a Rails application run with a fraction of the resources of a typical application running with a pack of Mongrels. Currently, though, most JRuby deployments still use a pack of Mongrels with mongrel_jcluster and thus consume more resources than a typical Mongrel deployment on MRI.

If you have significant investment in Java applications, you can access those Java classes directly from JRuby applications. Testing, scripting, Rails development, and user interface development are only a few places that developers are actively using JRuby today.

The key inroads of the JRuby platform in my opinion are political. The two core developers, Charles O. Nutter and Thomas Enebo, are now working for Sun Microsystems. This move has completely changed the JRuby project. Since Sun is committed to moving the technology forward, the team has better access to resources that will advance the platform. Most important, these two key developers have much more time to build and evangelize JRuby since they can work on it full-time.

10.4 IronRuby

IronRuby is a Ruby implementation on Microsoft's .NET platform. IronRuby, based on Ruby version 1.8.*x*, boasts seamless integration with .NET infrastructure and libraries. To date, most of the implementation is written in C#. The shared source project has been around since about April 2007. The project is released under the BSD-like Microsoft permissive license.

Unlike the Java virtual machine, .NET has some target features, called the Dynamic Language Runtime (DLR), that target dynamically typed languages like Ruby. This foundation provides a core set of services that permit fast and safe dynamic language code.

IronRuby has not been around as long as JRuby, but the parallels should be obvious. The managed .NET environment has important advantages for any team considering deploying a .NET application.

10.5 Wrapping Up

I hope you've enjoyed this pass through the Rails deployment scene. With the information in this book, you should be able to handle simple deployments on shared hosts, as well as complex deployments spanning several application and web servers. With the examples in the Capistrano chapter, you should have a good understanding of how to build custom deployment scripts. You can also take a reasonable shot at tuning your deployment for performance and managing the result.

I do urge you to listen closely to the state of the art. You've seen in this chapter that the Ruby deployment picture will move quickly. I've presented a few important frontiers in deployment. Others will emerge too. With any luck, the emergence of the new alternatives will be as exciting as the emergence of the current frontier—the Mongrel, Monit, and Capistrano foundations—that form the heart of the Rails deployment story today.

An Example nginx Configuration

In Chapter 7, *Scaling Out*, on page 137, I based Apache and nginx configurations on existing configurations. I used the base configurations that came with Apache as a foundation for that web server, but nginx has no consensus base configuration for Rails. The following configuration, complete with comments, serves as the foundation for the nginx configurations in this book:

nginx/nginx.conf

```
# user and group to run as
user  ezra ezra;

# Nginx uses a master -> worker configuration.
# number of nginx workers, 4 is a good minimum default
# when you have multiple CPU cores I have found 2-4 workers
# per core to be a sane default.
worker_processes  4;


# pid of nginx master process
pid /var/run/nginx.pid;

# Number of worker connections. 8192 is a good default
# Nginx can use epoll on linux or kqueue on bsd systems
events {
  worker_connections  8192;
  use epoll; # linux only!
}

# start the http module where we config http access.
http {
  # pull in mime-types. You can break out your config
  # into as many include's as you want to make it cleaner
  include /etc/nginx/mime.types;
```

```
    # set a default type for the rare situation that
    # nothing matches from the mimie-type include
    default_type  application/octet-stream;

    # This log format is compatible with any tool like awstats
    # that can parse standard apache logs.
    log_format main '$remote_addr - $remote_user [$time_local] '
                    '"$request" $status $body_bytes_sent "$http_referer" '
                    '"$http_user_agent" "$http_x_forwarded_for"';

    # main access log
    access_log  /var/log/nginx/access.log  main;

    # main error log - Do not comment out. If you do
    # not want the log file set this to /dev/null
    error_log  /var/log/nginx/error.log notice;

    # no sendfile on OSX
    sendfile on;

    # These are good default values.
    tcp_nopush         on;
    tcp_nodelay        on;

    # output compression saves bandwidth. If you have problems with
    # flash clients or other browsers not understanding the gzip format
    # them you may want to remove a specific content type that is affected.
    gzip              on;
    gzip_http_version 1.0;
    gzip_comp_level 2;
    gzip_proxied any;
    gzip_types        text/plain text/html text/css application/x-javascript
                      text/xml application/xml application/xml+rss text/javascript;

    # this will include any vhost files we place in /etc/nginx/vhosts as
    # long as the filename ends in .conf
    include /etc/nginx/vhosts/*.conf;
}
```

Appendix B

Bibliography

[Mas05]   Mike Mason. *Pragmatic Version Control Using Subversion.* The Pragmatic Programmers, LLC, Raleigh, NC, and Dallas, TX, 2005.

[PCSF04]   C. Michael Pilato, Ben Collins-Sussman, and Brian W. Fitzpatrick. *Version Control with Subversion.* O'Reilly & Associates, Inc, 2004.

Index

It All Starts Here

If you're programming in Ruby, you need the PickAxe Book: the definitive reference to the Ruby Programming language, now in the revised 3rd Edition for Ruby 1.9.

Programming Ruby (The Pickaxe)

The Pickaxe book, named for the tool on the cover, is the definitive reference to this highly-regarded language. • Up-to-date and expanded for Ruby version 1.9 • Complete documentation of all the built-in classes, modules, and methods • Complete descriptions of all standard libraries • Learn more about Ruby's web tools, unit testing, and programming philosophy

Programming Ruby: The Pragmatic Programmer's Guide, 3rd Edition
Dave Thomas with Chad Fowler and Andy Hunt
(900 pages) ISBN: 978-1-9343560-8-1. $49.95
http://pragprog.com/titles/ruby3

Agile Web Development with Rails

Rails is a full-stack, open-source web framework, with integrated support for unit, functional, and integration testing. It enforces good design principles, consistency of code across your team (and across your organization), and proper release management. This is the newly updated Second Edition, which goes beyond the Jolt-award winning first edition with new material on:

• Migrations • RJS templates • Respond_to
• Integration Tests • Additional ActiveRecord features • Another year's worth of Rails best practices

Agile Web Development with Rails: Second Edition
Dave Thomas, and David Heinemeier Hansson with Leon Breedt, Mike Clark, James Duncan Davidson, Justin Gehtland, and Andreas Schwarz
(750 pages) ISBN: 0-9776166-3-0. $39.95
http://pragprog.com/titles/rails2

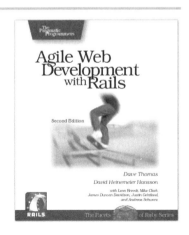

Web 2.0

Welcome to the Web, version 2.0. You need some help to tame the wild technologies out there. Start with *Prototype and script.aculo.us*, a book about two libraries that will make your JavaScript life much easier.

See how to reach the largest possible web audience with *The Accessible Web*.

Prototype and script.aculo.us

Tired of getting swamped in the nitty-gritty of cross-browser, Web 2.0–grade JavaScript? Get back in the game with Prototype and script.aculo.us, two extremely popular JavaScript libraries that make it a walk in the park. Be it Ajax, drag and drop, autocompletion, advanced visual effects, or many other great features, all you need is write one or two lines of script that look so good they could almost pass for Ruby code!

Prototype and script.aculo.us: You never knew JavaScript could do this!
Christophe Porteneuve
(330 pages) ISBN: 1-934356-01-8. $34.95
http://pragprog.com/titles/cppsu

The Accessible Web

The 2000 U.S. Census revealed that 12% of the population is severely disabled. Sometime in the next two decades, one in five Americans will be older than 65. Section 508 of the Americans with Disabilities Act requires your website to provide *equivalent access* to all potential users. But beyond the law, it is both good manners and good business to make your site accessible to everyone. This book shows you how to design sites that excel for all audiences.

The Accessible Web
Jeremy Sydik
(304 pages) ISBN: 1-934356-02-6. $34.95
http://pragprog.com/titles/jsaccess

Ruby Everywhere

From day-to-day chores to help you be more productive, to integrating enterprise technologies, Ruby can help.

Everyday Scripting with Ruby

Don't waste that computer on your desk. Offload your daily drudgery to where it belongs, and free yourself to do what you should be doing: thinking. All you need is a scripting language (free!), this book (cheap!), and the dedication to work through the examples and exercises. Learn the basics of the Ruby scripting language and see how to create scripts in a steady, controlled way using test-driven design.

Everyday Scripting with Ruby: For Teams, Testers, and You
Brian Marick
(320 pages) ISBN: 0-9776166-1-4. $29.95
http://pragprog.com/titles/bmsft

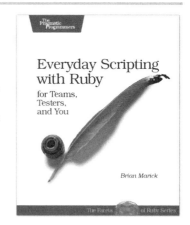

Enterprise Integration with Ruby

See how to use the power of Ruby to integrate all the applications in your environment. Learn how to
• use relational databases directly and via mapping layers such as ActiveRecord • harness the power of directory services • create, validate, and read XML documents for easy information interchange
• use both high- and low-level protocols to knit applications together

Enterprise Integration with Ruby
Maik Schmidt
(360 pages) ISBN: 0-9766940-6-9. $32.95
http://pragprog.com/titles/fr_eir

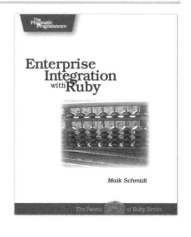

Where to Go Next

Take your Ruby on Rails application to the next level, or hone your Ruby skills.

Advanced Rails Recipes

A collection of practical recipes for spicing up your web application without a lot of prep and cleanup. You'll learn how the pros have solved the tough problems using the most up-to-date Rails techniques (including Rails 2.0 features)

Advanced Rails Recipes
Mike Clark
(300 pages) ISBN: 978-0-9787392-2-5. $32.95
http://pragprog.com/titles/fr_arr

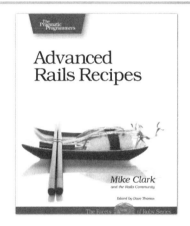

Best of Ruby Quiz

Sharpen your Ruby programming skills with twenty-five challenging problems from Ruby Quiz. Read the problems, work out a solution, and compare your solution with answers from others.

• Learn using the most effective method available: *practice* • Learn great Ruby idioms • Understand sticky problems and the insights that lead you past them • Gain familiarity with Ruby's standard library • Translate traditional algorithms to Ruby

Best of Ruby Quiz
James Edward Gray II
(304 pages) ISBN: 0-9766940-7-7. $29.95
http://pragprog.com/titles/fr_quiz

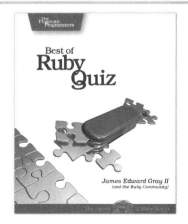

Real World Tools

Learn real-world design and architecture for your project, and a very pragmatic editor for Mac OS X.

Release It!

Whether it's in Java, .NET, or Ruby on Rails, getting your application ready to ship is only half the battle. Did you design your system to survive a sudden rush of visitors from Digg or Slashdot? Or an influx of real-world customers from 100 different countries? Are you ready for a world filled with flaky networks, tangled databases, and impatient users?

If you're a developer and don't want to be on call at 3 a.m. for the rest of your life, this book will help.

Design and Deploy Production-Ready Software
Michael T. Nygard
(368 pages) ISBN: 0-9787392-1-3. $34.95
http://pragprog.com/titles/mnee

TextMate

If you're coding Ruby or Rails on a Mac, then you owe it to yourself to get the TextMate editor. And, once you're using TextMate, you owe it to yourself to pick up this book. It's packed with information that will help you automate all your editing tasks, saving you time to concentrate on the important stuff. Use snippets to insert boilerplate code and refactorings to move stuff around. Learn how to write your own extensions to customize it to the way you work.

TextMate: Power Editing for the Mac
James Edward Gray II
(200 pages) ISBN: 0-9787392-3-X. $29.95
http://pragprog.com/titles/textmate

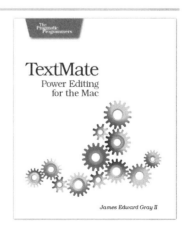

Leading Your Team

See how to be a pragmatic project manager and use agile, iterative project retrospectives on your project.

Manage It!

Manage It! is a risk-based guide to making good decisions about how to plan and guide your projects. Author Johanna Rothman shows you how to beg, borrow, and steal from the best methodologies to fit your particular project. You'll find what works best for *you*.

• Learn all about different project lifecycles • See how to organize a project • Compare sample project dashboards • See how to staff a project • Know when you're done—and what that means.

Your Guide to Modern, Pragmatic Project Management
Johanna Rothman
(360 pages) ISBN: 0-9787392-4-8. $34.95
http://pragprog.com/titles/jrpm

Agile Retrospectives

Mine the experience of your software development team continually throughout the life of the project. Rather than waiting until the end of the project—as with a traditional retrospective, when it's too late to help—agile retrospectives help you adjust to change *today.*

The tools and recipes in this book will help you uncover and solve hidden (and not-so-hidden) problems with your technology, your methodology, and those difficult "people issues" on your team.

Agile Retrospectives: Making Good Teams Great
Esther Derby and Diana Larsen
(170 pages) ISBN: 0-9776166-4-9. $29.95
http://pragprog.com/titles/dlret

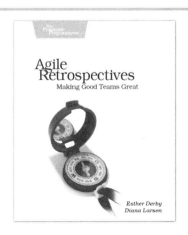

Getting It Done

Start with the habits of an agile developer and use the team practices of successful agile teams, and your project will fly over the finish line.

Practices of an Agile Developer

Agility is all about using feedback to respond to change. Learn how to apply the principles of agility throughout the software development process
• establish and maintain an agile working environment • deliver what users really want • use personal agile techniques for better coding and debugging • use effective collaborative techniques for better teamwork • move to an agile approach

Practices of an Agile Developer: Working in the Real World
Venkat Subramaniam and Andy Hunt
(189 pages) ISBN: 0-9745140-8-X. $29.95
http://pragprog.com/titles/pad

Ship It!

Page after page of solid advice, all tried and tested in the real world. This book offers a collection of tips that show you what tools a successful team has to use, and how to use them well. You'll get quick, easy-to-follow advice on modern techniques and when they should be applied. **You need this book if:** • You're frustrated at lack of progress on your project. • You want to make yourself and your team more valuable. • You've looked at methodologies such as Extreme Programming (XP) and felt they were too, well, extreme. • You've looked at the Rational Unified Process (RUP) or CMM/I methods and cringed at the learning curve and costs. • **You need to get software out the door without excuses**

Ship It! A Practical Guide to Successful Software Projects
Jared Richardson and Will Gwaltney
(200 pages) ISBN: 0-9745140-4-7. $29.95
http://pragprog.com/titles/prj

Get Groovy

Expand your horizons with Groovy, and tame the wild Java VM.

Programming Groovy

Programming Groovy will help you learn the necessary fundamentals of programming in Groovy. You'll see how to use Groovy to do advanced programming techniques, including meta programming, builders, unit testing with mock objects, processing XML, working with databases and creating your own domain-specific languages (DSLs).

Programming Groovy Dynamic Productivity for the Java Developer
Venkat Subramaniam
(320 pages) ISBN: 978-1-9343560-9-8. $34.95
http://pragprog.com/titles/vslg

Groovy Recipes

See how to speed up nearly every aspect of the development process using *Groovy Recipes*. Groovy makes mundane file management tasks like copying and renaming files trivial. Reading and writing XML has never been easier with XmlParsers and XmlBuilders. Breathe new life into arrays, maps, and lists with a number of convenience methods. Learn all about Grails, and go beyond HTML into the world of Web Services: REST, JSON, Atom, Podcasting, and much much more.

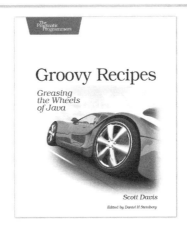

Groovy Recipes: Greasing the Wheels of Java
Scott Davis
(264 pages) ISBN: 978-0-9787392-9-4. $34.95
http://pragprog.com/titles/sdgrvr

The Pragmatic Bookshelf

The Pragmatic Bookshelf features books written by developers for developers. The titles continue the well-known Pragmatic Programmer style and continue to garner awards and rave reviews. As development gets more and more difficult, the Pragmatic Programmers will be there with more titles and products to help you stay on top of your game.

Visit Us Online

Deploying Rails Applications' Home Page
http://pragprog.com/titles/fr_deploy
Source code from this book, errata, and other resources. Come give us feedback, too!

Register for Updates
http://pragprog.com/updates
Be notified when updates and new books become available.

Join the Community
http://pragprog.com/community
Read our weblogs, join our online discussions, participate in our mailing list, interact with our wiki, and benefit from the experience of other Pragmatic Programmers.

New and Noteworthy
http://pragprog.com/news
Check out the latest pragmatic developments in the news.

Save on the PDF

Save on the PDF version of this book. Owning the paper version of this book entitles you to purchase the PDF version at a terrific discount. The PDF is great for carrying around on your laptop. It's hyperlinked, has color, and is fully searchable.

Buy it now at pragprog.com/coupon.

Contact Us

Phone Orders:	1-800-699-PROG (+1 919 847 3884)
Online Orders:	www.pragprog.com/catalog
Customer Service:	orders@pragprog.com
Non-English Versions:	translations@pragprog.com
Pragmatic Teaching:	academic@pragprog.com
Author Proposals:	proposals@pragprog.com

SOMETHING OF VALUE

SOMETHING

By

Drawings by DANIEL SCHWARTZ

OF VALUE

Robert Ruark

Safari Press

Books by Robert Ruark

HORN OF THE HUNTER

USE ENOUGH GUN

THE OLD MAN AND THE BOY

THE LOST CLASSICS OF ROBERT RUARK

The trademark Safari Press® is registered with the U.S. Patent and Trademark Office and in other countries.

Ruark, Robert C.

Safari Press Inc.

2008, Long Beach, California

ISBN 1-57157-280-5

Library of Congress Catalog Card Number: 55007158

10 9 8 7 6 5 4 3 2 1

Readers wishing to receive the Safari Press catalog, featuring many fine books on big-game hunting, wingshooting, and sporting firearms, should write to Safari Press Inc., P.O. Box 3095, Long Beach, CA 90803, USA. Tel: (714) 894-9080 or visit our Web site at www.safaripress.com

This is for
VIRGINIA WEBB RUARK,
with all my love.

If a man does away with his traditional way of living and throws away his good customs, he had better first make certain that he has something of value to replace them.

—*Basuto proverb.*

FOREWORD

This is not a true story. It is rankest nonsense to claim that any novel is purely the product of an imagination; it is only contact with people and places, with situations and conversations, that fertilizes the germ of any idea sufficiently to sprout the seed that finally grows into a book. But this is not a document—it is a work of fiction.

This is considerably more than a book about the Mau Mau terror which has claimed constant attention on the front pages of the world for the last two years. A great deal has been written about the Mau Mau. A great deal of foolishness has been committed in the failure of the British to recognize that what they saw happening to themselves in Kenya was not, as they first thought, a local brush fire but a symptomatic ulcer of the evil and unrest which currently afflict the world.

In order to understand Mau Mau it is first necessary to understand Africa, and the portion of Africa in which Mau Mau was allowed to flourish is only just fifty years old as we reckon civilization. To understand Africa you must understand a basic impulsive savagery that is greater than anything we "civilized" people have encountered in two centuries.

This might be possibly a true story of Kenya and of the events over the last fifty years which led to the present tragedy of the Mau Mau uprising, with all its sadistic murder and counter-murder. The book is completely true in reporting that its early skeletal structure rests on stony fact, which may be found in reference as fact. Some of these facts have been altered and condensed to comply with novel form, as is always customary. But they remain facts. The characters in this book are entirely fictitious.

There is much blood in the book. There is much killing. But the life of Africa was washed earlier by blood, and its ground was, and still is, fertilized by the blood of its people and its animals. This is not a pretty book, nor was it written for the pre-bedtime amusement of small children. And it certainly is not a political book.

Three years of intensive research, both personal and from collected works of acknowledged experts on Africa, went into the raw material from which this book was built. I am particularly grateful for, and drew heavily from, the works of such people as Elspeth Huxley and L. S. B. Leakey. I drew particularly from a book called *Facing Mount Kenya*, by the currently jailed Mau Mau leader, Jomo Kenyatta, which was important chiefly for its biased view of his own Kikuyu people. In this book, written sixteen years ago, the Kikuyu Kenyatta drew an explicit blueprint for the terror which now wracks his land.

Most especial thanks are hereby given to such personal friends as Harry Selby, Mickey Selby, Andrew Holmberg, Tony Dyer, Fred Poolman, Jack Carr-Hartley and Tubby Block, Jack Bonham, Lynn Temple-Borham, John Sutton, Brian Burrows, Eric Reed, Eric and Helen Jessop, Kitty Hesselberger, Dorothy Raynes-Simson, and all my other friends and their womenfolk in Nairobi. And of course to my godson, Mark Robert Selby.

Some attention might also gratefully be directed to the memory of the late Sir James Kirkpatrick, Bart., who shot himself in April 1954 in Nairobi, and who was always a kind friend in what I believe to be the best and most dedicated public service I know, the Kenya Game Department. And to Alan M. Ritchie, a good friend who helped me heavily in the preparation of this book.

I hope that by the time this work sees print some partial solution to the current horror of Kenya may have been reached, but the hope is doubtful.

Playa de Monestrí,
Palamós,
Prov. de Gerona,
Spain.

November 10, 1954.

HOME

Peter McKenzie stripped off his faded shorts and his green drill shirt and reached for a bowl of ocher mud which had been softened to a pliant paste with water. He smeared the mud over his face, neck, and shoulders, until his sunburned skin was dyed a deep coppery red. He picked up his trousers and took a small mirror out of his pocket. Holding the mirror in one hand, he painted circles of white lime around his eyes and made traverse scar marks across his cheeks. He pushed his black forelock down over his eyes and gummed the hair heavily with the ocher. He frowned fiercely at himself in the mirror and seemed satisfied. He tied iron rattles around his ankles and draped a goatskin from his shoulders like a toga. Then he put the mirror back in his pants pocket and hung the pants on a thornbush.

Peter McKenzie walked to the stream, where there was a small hut built of mud and dried cow dung over a frame of wattle. He crawled in and wriggled out, backward, with a short spear and a small buffalo-hide shield, an oval white shield carrying a red and black heraldic crest on it. He reached in again and took out a short stabbing sword in a red scabbard, a sword called simi. He stood erect, buckled on the simi, slipped the shield onto his left arm, and grasped his spear firmly. He spoke to the black boy who had been watching his preparations for war. Peter McKenzie and his campanion, Kimani, both were fifteen years old.

"Today, Kimani," he said, "I am a thousand Masai moran. I am an army of Masai, a thousand Masai from the Loita. I am on a cattle raid. You are *two* thousand Kikuyu, but one Masai is always worth ten Kikuyu, especially in an element of surprise."

Peter McKenzie was speaking in Kikuyu, and speaking it perfectly, since he had learned the tongue a little before he had learned English, he having been raised by Kimani's mother. When Caroline McKenzie died, Peter's father had not taken another wife but had given the care of his two children, Peter and Elisabeth, to the senior wife of his headman, Karanja. Kimani was Karanja's first son. He spoke now.

"I don't want to be two thousand Kikuyu, Brother," he said. "I was a Kikuyu war party the last time we played this. I am always a Kikuyu, while you are always a Nandi who kills me, or a Masai who kills me, or a Wakamba who kills me. I never get to kill you. It isn't fair. I want to be a thousand Masai."

"You *can't* be a thousand Masai," Peter said seriously. "You're too black. Also, I am already painted for the battle, and you don't have any Masai clothes. Anyhow, you *are* a Kikuyu, so you might as well be two thousand Kikuyu today. Go get your spear and your panga and your cattle."

"Well, all right," Kimani said in English, "but it still isn't fair."

"I tell you," Peter said. "I am chief of my thousand Masai, and you can of course be chief of your two thousand Kikuyu. We will both die gloriously in battle with each other, but my men will naturally win the fight and drive off all your cattle and steal your women."

Kimani walked away to collect his cattle, and Peter watched him go. Kimani was tall for his race, nearly as tall as Peter, who at fifteen was a big-boned, big-footed youth who already stood six feet tall. Kimani was shorter by two inches, but very powerfully built in the shoulders and chest, although his legs were and always would be spindly. Both boys were handsome. Kimani's face showed a possible Masai crossbreeding. His nose was thin, his features even, and his jaw and mouth were more of the Masai clean-cut than of the thick-lipped, jaw-retreating Kikuyu structure. His black skin shone glossy in the bright Kenya sunshine. Peter always felt sickly pale when he looked at Kimani, even though Peter sunburned as brown as an Arab from the coast. Peter had a short turned-up nose, a big mouth with square white teeth, and a sheaf of black hair that curved forward over his brow and generally fell into his eyes, which were a brilliant blue.

Bored, waiting for the battle to start, Peter balanced his spear delicately between thumb and forefinger and looked around him for a target. Farther down the twisting little stream, a herd of Thomson gazelles were grazing, small, golden, black-barred animals no larger than a pointer dog, their tails flicking as they fed. They fed out from the yellow-black mottled acacias about sixty yards away. Peter waited until the herd ram trailed out behind his flock, then rocked back on his heels and threw; threw with the quick, effeminate twist of the wrist that the Masai who made him his war shield had taught him. The spear whistled, singing like a bullet, rifling round and round in a low arc. It took the ram just behind the shoulders and spitted him to the ground, the short blade passing completely through him. Unconsciously Peter's body jerked in the spastic, head-bobbing leap of the excited African, the uncontrollable hysteric jump which forms the basis of all Central African dances. He drew his simi and dashed toward the ram, his war rattles clattering on his legs. He cut its throat with one slash, wiped his knife on the golden hide, and pulled the ram backward off the shaft of the spear. He jerked the blade from the ground and wiped the bloody haft carefully, but left the blood to clot on the blade. This would show Kimani that a thousand Masai warriors were not to be trifled with, even by ten thousand Kikuyu. Peter knelt by the dead Tommy and opened it with his simi, deftly turning out the stomach and hauling the guts clear with one jerk. He picked up the gazelle and took him down to the stream, where he rinsed him thoroughly inside and then hung him by his pierced hind legs to a sharp broken branch, as high up as he could reach. His father liked to eat Thomson gazelles. His father would be pleased.

The site of the impending battle was a gently rolling meadow behind the farm of Henry McKenzie, Peter's father. The rains had come and gone, and the downs were crisply green as an English deer park. They were deckled with white, blue, and yellow primrosy flowers. The sky was the faded blue of the Kenya highlands, freshly washed by rain and puffed with smugly contented clouds. It was possible today to see the snowy head of Mount Kenya, one jolly little black cloud passing just beneath its snaggled teeth. The comfortable chuckle-chuckle of sand grouse veering and sideslipping high in the sky lent a lazy and good-humored accompaniment to the bright day of battle. Somewhere out of sight a zebra barked, and along the edge of the stream a baboon cursed. It was a shining day for the young warrior.

The enemy hove into sight, driving his herd ahead of him. The herd consisted of three ridge-back hounds, a cocker spaniel, one goat named Mister Mac after a friend, and a tame buffalo calf. The herdsman was not truly got up for war, since this was a surprise raid, and the Kikuyu forces were supposed to be unprepared for the shattering surge of the Masai marauders. The Kikuyu forces were wearing only a battered pair of hand-me-down khaki shorts and a stubby spear to lean on.

"All right," Peter said. "You can sit down here by your hut. You are now dozing in the sun. This is the newest kind of surprise attack, because we do not come by dawn. We come when your bellies are full and you have had much pombe to drink and are sleeping it off in the sun. But you forgot your panga."

"We don't need it," Kimani said. "We can fight with the spears."

"No," Peter answered. "How are we going to have a duel if you haven't got your panga? If I threw a spear at you I would kill you as I just killed that Tommy."

"What Tommy?"

"The one whose blood stains this spear. He's hanging in a tree by the water. I hit him at a hundred meters at least."

"Nobody can hit anything with a spear at a hundred meters," Kimani said. "My father is as good as any Masai with a spear, and he couldn't hit a bull elephant at a hundred meters."

"Well, fifty meters, then," Peter said. "In any case, go and get your panga."

Kimani turned and went away again, heading for the cluster of thatched, mud-and-wattle huts where his father and his mother and his father's wives lived. He was looking for a big, curved, saw-backed bush knife, like a machete, with which he cut firewood for his sisters to carry, disemboweled sheep and goats, pared his nails, and occasionally picked his teeth. It was as heavy as an ax, but ground keen enough to shave with. As Kimani disappeared around a bend of the creek, Peter changed his strategy. He would ambush Kimani. He slipped into the brush alongside the creek and froze himself still, as he had been taught to do when hunting.

Kimani appeared five minutes later, carrying his spear in his right hand and his panga swinging loosely in the other. As he rounded the bend, one thousand Masai warriors leaped out of the ambush with a blood-clotting battle scream and hurled their thousand spears. It (the thousand spears) stabbed the earth two feet in front of Kimani's feet and quivered there. As a simple reflex, the two thousand Kikuyu hurled their two thousand spears at the Masai hordes, aiming straight at the Masai chieftain, who, leaping three feet into the air, charged with drawn simi. The Masai chief took the two thousand Kikuyu spears square in the center of his buffalo-hide buckler. It (the two thousand Kikuyu spears) penetrated only a portion of the iron-hard buffalo hide, clung for a moment, and then fell out as the Masai hordes shook the shield irritably. The battle was joined.

Leaping, screeching, the two forces collided. Peter's simi swished viciously at Kimani's head, and Kimani blocked the slash with the panga so sharply and effectively that the arms of both boys stung to the pits with the impact. Kimani feinted at Peter's legs, and when Peter dropped his simi to parry, Kimani upswung a cut with the panga that would have ripped Peter open from belly to chin if he had not fallen back. Then, rolling completely over, he aimed a stab at Kimani's face that went past his ear and carried Peter off balance again into another somersault. With the edge of the battle changing into Kikuyu favor, Kimani uttered a ululating scream and charged his temporarily unprotected enemy. The enemy rolled away on the ground, and the panga hacked a great gash into the turf. Peter kicked Kimani's legs from under him, and they grappled. Each warrior now had his enemy's knife hand locked, and the combat froze into a surge of individual strength. Peter, the larger, the stronger, slowly forced Kimani's panga away from, and to one side of, his chest, and the needle point of Peter's simi moved slowly, by quarter inches, toward Kimani's throat. It finally touched his Adam's apple, and a slow trickle of blood appeared. Peter then rolled over, stuck his knife into the ground, and hauled his conquered enemy to his feet.

"You are dead," he said. "Killed honorably in single combat. Now you got to think up a way to kill me. I am going to disappear into the bush for about five minutes and let you work out your own plan of counterattack."

He walked away, and when he disappeared, Kimani drifted into the scrub. He went directly to the bole of a fallen tree and reached into a rotted hollow. He took out a short bow and a sheaf of arrows. He selected a knob-pointed arrow, which he used for shooting francolin and sand grouse. He crouched, hidden in the tall grasses, and when Peter appeared, walking cautiously in a half crouch, Kimani let him pass. Then he notched his arrow and winged it at the unprotected behind of his friend. It struck with a thump, and Peter let out a howl of anguish and fell flat, flopping like a headless chicken. Kimani, making great leaps like a frightened impala, screaming horribly, rushed to his fallen enemy and cut off his head with a single mighty sweep of the panga. The fact that the panga shaved Peter's ear and touched only earth did not cheapen the spiritual implication that the Masai chieftain had just been decapitated in war. The decapitated Masai chieftain got up and rubbed his tingling tail.

"That *hurt*," he said. "I didn't know you had a bow here. I reckoned we'd fight again with swords. I don't think that's quite fair."

"All's fair in your kind of war." Kimani grinned. "Maybe the Masai are braver than the Kikuyu, but we are craftier. Anyhow, the arrow couldn't have hurt, because it is well known that the Masai moran feels no pain, even when he is mauled by a lion. What do we do now?"

"I will drive off your cattle," Peter said, "to my manyatta on the Loita, by the Telek."

He picked up a rock and hurled it at the three hounds, the cocker spaniel, the baby buffalo, and at Mister Mac, the goat. The rock hit Mister Mac in the brisket. He bleated and departed, the other cattle barking happily at his heels, save the buffalo, who bellowed.

"There go your herds, to fatten my flocks," Peter said. "There will be famine in Kikuyu this year, amongst the old men and the old women who remain when my men have finished with the spear. The only thing now is to carry off all your young maidens."

"What will we do for young maidens?" Kimani asked. "I don't see any young maidens around here."

"Ah," Peter replied, "I have taken care of that. You know that little girl, Holly, who's staying at our house whilst her mother goes to Nairobi to have her baby? I have had my scouts out all day. I'm told that at this moment young maidens are easily available in the rose garden behind my house. We will make a raid."

"All right," Kimani said, "but it seems to me that one little white girl is not enough maidens to satisfy what's left of a thousand Masai. And what about me? I'm dead, and you're dead, each slain honorably by each other, so *who* is what's left of the thousand Masai warriors?"

"*Both* of us," Peter replied generously. "We are the young Masai, both of us now, who have risen in battle to replace the slain chiefs, and we will win honor in our clan when we drive our cattle and the maidens home before us. Also, my scouts have told me that in the garden by my house, playing at dolls with Holly, is a girl named Kabui, daughter of Kamau. Here, Kimani. You may wear my war rattles, and I'd best put on my shorts again. Father'll wallop me if we go and kidnap the girls wearing only a goatskin over my naked hide."

The Masai war party proceeded cautiously toward the big house of the property called Bushbuck Farm. The young Masai moran wore his shorts now for propriety's sake, and his lieutenant had never relinquished his pants. It was a very decently clad war party, even if it had the rape and capture of five hundred maidens in mind.

The house crouched comfortably against a green hill. A low damp-mottled plaster wall overgrown with bougainvillaea, great white-red-and-purple flagrant blooms, surrounded a square, one-story building of fieldstone. Its roof was heavy papyrus thatch, hammered by the rain of years into a solid mass almost like concrete. It rested calmly under immense wild figs, under cedars and yellow thorn acacias with tall umbrella tops and trunks mottled like leopards. A few brilliant trees of Nandi-flame and the showering blue blooms of jacaranda produced a forest of color and a cathedral-like atmosphere of coolness without oppressive damp. Henry McKenzie liked his house, since he had built it all himself, starting first with a mud-wattle hut like a native's and later progressing from a slatternly cottage to a proper house to an opulent estate, all done or directed with broad callused hands on which the thumb curve of the palm was geometrically square and as heavily horned as the foot of an African.

Where once there had been nothing but scraggled bush, the lawn was clean and closely clipped as any tennis court to be found in Surrey. Ordered rows of flowers made a prim mosaic against the green of the lawn. Caroline McKenzie had loved her flowers and had managed to produce a formal rose garden in back of the house. Henry McKenzie kept the flowers flourishing with even a little more concentrated effort than he gave to his acres of tea and pyrethrum, his coffee slopes and his wheat fields. He looked after the roses with more passion than he spent on his Frisian dairy herd and his upgraded Boran cattle, which he had lifted from scrub to magnificence by nearly twenty years of meticulous breeding. It was in the rose garden that the wild warriors of the Masai found their five hundred maidens.

One half, or two hundred and fifty, of the about-to-be-ravished maidens was just twelve years old, with pink pigtails, keen green eyes, and a starched skirt that stood out like a ruff around her long knobby-kneed legs. She wore pants to match the skirt, which was green. She had freckles scattered aimlessly across a rather long nose, but a nose whose length was positive by its straightness and the heavy-lipped accent of her mouth. The hair was light red now. It would grow darker and would not be unduly annoyed by the black lashes and clearly marked brows.

The other half of the hapless maidens was as shiny as an ebony idol, with great sugar loaves of teeth, a shaven skull, pierced ear lobes, huge round reddish-brown eyes, and the beginnings, under her single shift of cotton, of definite breasts. She too was twelve. Kabui, daughter of

Kamau, head herdsman for Henry McKenzie, was ripening fast and would soon be ready for circumcision, the second apron, and marriage.

The little girls were playing an involved game with dolls when the Masai warriors crept slowly upon them, threading their way quietly, duck-walking to keep low, through the peonies and lilac that formed the fringe of the rose garden. The dolls were expensive. They had stupid blue eyes and stringy flaxen hair, and one of them wept when upended and wet her pants. The other neither wept nor wet, but was gorgeously attired in checked gingham and seemed the more emotionally stable of the two. Both belonged to Holly Keith, whose mama was in Nairobi to allow God to bring her a baby. Kabui owned no dolls. She was happy to adopt whichever of the pair Holly decided to lend her for the ancient female game of house. Kabui had a goat of her own and a sheep of her own and some bracelets of her own and some beads of her own and some coils of copper wire of her own, which made her a pretty rich little Kikuyu girl, and she was willing to humor the English little girl in this silly game of dolls and house because the little English girl owned no goats.

Somewhere between the mama doll's being angry at the daughter doll and an involved conversation about the duties of daughters to their mummas, the blood-mad Masai swept down, laying waste the rose garden, trampling the phlox, bent on sweeping the maidens off to cruel bondage.

Both little girls shrieked, largely from delight, when the fierce moran seized them after murdering their dolls with butt of spear and handle of panga. Peter tossed Holly over his shoulder and whipped into the laurel bushes, careened round a corner, attempted to hurdle the wall, stumbled, and dropped Holly on the seat of her trousers in a decorative cactus bed. Holly shrieked again, this time from pain. Kabui, slung over Kimani's shoulder, turned her head and bit him viciously on the ear. Kimani uttered a most unwarrior-like squawk and dropped his fifty per cent of the about-to-be-ravished maidens. As she hit the ground, Kabui kicked Kimani in the shins at precisely the same time that Holly Keith seized Peter's newly ochered hair and removed a good portion of his clayey bangs.

Something had gone very wrong with the raid. It appeared that the blood-hungry warriors had been temporarily repulsed, and a most delicate problem was posed. One did not, definitely, bite, kick, or pull the hair of five hundred Kikuyu maidens, because five hundred Kikuyu maidens would weep and tell certain fathers, such as Henry McKenzie and Kamau or Karanja, or certain sisters such as Elisabeth, or certain mothers such as Wangu or Wanjira, and then certain Masai bottoms would be smacked. If there was anything a marauding Masai moran hated, it was to have his bottom smacked, especially by manamouki, such as Elisabeth or Wangu or Wanjira.

Providence, a shauri a Mungu, saved everyone's face.

"Time, gentlemen," said a soft female voice. "Chakula is served. I expect that at least one warrior had best go and wash his face, or I'll tell Papa who's been at his tobacco lately. The other warrior had best nip off to his own thingira, or there are some other dreadful things I can tell Karanja as well. As for the captive slave girls, I think they have served their purpose this morning. One at least may come with me and I will pluck the cactus spines out of her pants. The other might report to Wanjira, who has some chores that need little slave girls to help with. Kwenda!"

This was Elisabeth. This was the Elisabeth who was to be married soon to Geoffrey Newton. This was all that was left that was female of Caroline McKenzie, who had died in the birth of Catherine, who dwelt with young Donal and young Robin in the boma on the hill, the four white stones accenting some of the investment Henry McKenzie had made in Kenya. There were times when Henry McKenzie could not bear to look at Elisabeth.

She had her mother's blue-black hair, and her mother's great violet eyes, and her mother's tremulous smile, and her mother's translucent skin that never tanned, and her mother's delicate bones, and her mother's fine jaw, and her mother's unbending will, and some quality of sweetness that Henry McKenzie had never quite understood, some mocking sweetness that made small and gawky boys of men. Lisa McKenzie was eighteen and a bit. Next week she would marry Jeff Newton, and Henry McKenzie silently said thank God. The Newton farm adjoined Bushbuck Farm. On the other side was the Keith farm. Henry McKenzie had a sound idea that someday young Peter, if the buffalo didn't stomp him, would be marrying Holly Keith. The three properties would then join, and the seed of Henry McKenzie would take permanent root in the land he had cuffed into unwilling obedience with his heavy, hooked hands. The Lord God knew that Jeff Newton was a good man. He was a big, shambling, friendly fellow with a Newfoundland's eyes and a Newfoundland's manner, but he was basically as hard as the shale of the land from which his dead father had forced a life. Henry remembered that Jeff had never angered publicly but once, and that in Nakuru, but they mended heads for a month after. Jeff was a farmer, and a good farmer, and all he wanted to be was a better farmer. Henry wondered sometimes what his lovely Lisa saw in Jeff but, without knowing, was bloody grateful for whatever it was.

The bride-to-be smacked the one-thousand-Masai war party gently on the backside. "Off with you, my lad," she said. "Pa'll be cross if we're late for dinner. And that ocher'll take some washing out. Dinner in ten minutes. Jeff's here already, having a beer with Pa. Wants to see you over some silly matter or other."

The renegade Masai scampered off to his room, stripped his clothes —which he left on the floor and kicked carefully under the bed—and scrubbed himself under the shower. He had his own room now, with a bath of his own.

He scrubbed himself gleamy-shiny, leaving red ocher marks on the towel, which he hid carefully in a closet against the day he might find time to rub out the clay marks, and put on fresh khaki shorts and a shirt. He went barefoot in the house. He wet and combed his black sheaf of hair carefully and knew very well that the first time he tossed his head it would all be right back in his eyes again. He leaned his Masai shield against the wall of his room and placed the spear in a rack. Then he remembered something. He remembered the dead Tommy hanging in a tree by the creek, and he knew that Jeff Newton would be impressed by the Tommy and the spear mark through its shoulder. He raced out of the house and clapped his hands. He called to Kimani. Now he spoke Swahili.

"Kwenda tasama Tommy na letti hi pese pese bloody nugu [Go and look for the Tommy and fetch it here in a hurry]!" knowing as he said it that Kimani hated to be spoken to in Swahili, the trade language, the common baby talk of all the tribes who could not speak more than one dialect, and wondering as he said it why he hadn't spoken in Kikuyu, which he spoke perfectly, or in English, which Kimani spoke as perfectly as he spoke Kikuyu. And Peter wondered why he added the "bloody nugu"—"bloody *baboon*"—for emphasis, to his friend and brother and fellow Masai warrior and leader of two thousand dead Kikuyu; rapist, robber, and companion-at-arms.

"Ndio, Bwana Mkubwa," Kimani yelled back sarcastically. "Suria." The sarcasm was heavy. Kimani was saying "Yes, Great White Lord," and in such a hurry that the translation is unprintable. Peter didn't really appreciate the edge in Kimani's voice. He turned and re-entered the house to see his god, the man who next week would be his brother and who would live close to him always. Jeff Newton was Peter's idea of St. George, with dragons complete, or of Philip Percival, the white hunter, or of Karamoja Bell, the old elephant killer, or of Livingstone or Selous, all folded into the same sandwich. Jeff Newton was the man that, if Peter had been buying a brother-in-law, he would have bought at any asking price.

The giant was sitting on the veranda with his veldschoen of raw buckskin propped on a wicker chair. He was drinking beer straight from a bottle, the foam clinging to a magnificent hedge of guardee mustaches, roan in color, which rose nearly to his eyes. (Peter had asked him once, out of purest curiosity: "How do you manage to kiss my sister through that bush?" and had got a lascivious grin from Jeff and a tweaked ear from Lisa. "I *manage*, old boy," Jeff had said. "I *manage*.")

"Well," the giant said. "Look at young Wild West here, as neat and clean as if he hadn't been a thousand Masai ten minutes before. How fares the carnage? All the men put to the spear, the cattle driven off, the women raped and transported to a life of shame?"

"We had a little trouble with the women," Peter admitted.

"What's all this about Masai?" Henry McKenzie asked. Henry McKenzie was also drinking beer, but he was drinking it out of a glass. He was dressed in a khaki bush jacket, in khaki slacks, wearing raw-calf jodhpur boots, and a scarf knotted round his throat. Like many African farmers, he wore his hat on the shady porch. It was a double-brimmed terai slouch hat that formed an awning over his shoulders. The shoulders were stooped, but the muscles in the shoulders were ropy and seized fast, close-bound by toil.

As he sat in the wicker chair on the veranda of his home, with a clear view of Mount Kenya to soothe his soul, Henry McKenzie was easily worth, potentially, a quarter million pounds sterling, or as easily could be bankrupt again if the locusts came or the drought persisted or the rinderpest crept into the flocks or the market dropped or the dockwallopers struck or the dairy herd became tubercular. His eyes were pale blue, washed light as an old denim shirt by brilliant sunshine. His skin was scored by wrinkles, horizontal and vertical, that bisected each other. His teeth were false and fit him badly. His mustache was scrubby and short-clipped, bleached yellowish by nicotine. His ears were big and hairy and his hands and feet matched his ears. What hair he showed under the hat was white. When he tipped back his hat he revealed a shocking, almost indecent, space of white forehead, contrasting violently with the baked clay of his face. Henry McKenzie had lived in his hat. He also smoked a pipe.

"What's this Masai business?" he asked again.

"A joke," Jeff Newton said easily. "Man-joke between me and the Bwana Kidogo here. And speaking of the Bwana Kidogo here, Henry, would it be all right if I took him off the reserve for a few days? There's some men's work to be done. . . ."

"What sort of men's work?" Henry McKenzie asked.

"Well, it's *young men's* work," Jeff said, "and I'll have another beer, please, unless you'd rather make it a gin."

McKenzie clapped his hands. "Letti ginni kwa Bwana pese pese," he said when a black face under a red fez peered onto the porch from the living room. "What sort of men's work?"

"Well," Jeff said, "there's a mangy old lion been sneaking in and clobbering the cows. There's a rude mob of hyenas been annoying my calves. There's an insufferable type of rhino that just walked all over one of my Wogs. There's an old elephant with a toothache, frightful temper he's got, and a herd of buffalo that keeps tramping down my young maize. I thought maybe, if I could find a man to help me I might go on a short safari so that the old homestead might be rendered fit for the bride. I'd be embarrassed any amount if my new spouse got trod on, specially on her wedding day. So I thought I'd borrow your son for three or four days, if you don't need him, and take a few boys and go and tidy up the dismal details. Probably be boring for the boy, but . . ."

Henry McKenzie smiled carefully around his false teeth.

"I'll have to inspect his table manners at dinner first," he said. "They've been shocking lately."

Kimani appeared around the corner of the house with the dead Tommy ram, held by the stiff forelegs, curled limply over his neck. He was still speaking Swahili.

"Here is the trophy of your spear, Bwana Mkubwa," he said. "Where'll I put it?"

"What's that?" Henry McKenzie asked. "I didn't hear any gunshot today."

Kimani slung the Tommy ram onto the steps.

"The Bwana Mkubwa Kidogo," he said. "The Little Great White Lord slew it with his Masai spear. That," he added, "was when he was one thousand Masai moran only this morning. Kwaheri, O Great White Little Lord," he said. "I bid you good-by."

"Cheeky little bugger," Jeff commented. "Karanja's brat?"

"Karanja's eldest son," Henry McKenzie answered. "As close as damn to swearing to being a son of mine. That's to say his mother raised my mtotos. He sort of grew up in the house. Decent little bloke, but full of the imp."

"I think," Jeff Newton said, "we'll take him along on the walkabout. Time Peter trained himself a major-domo. Old Karanja isn't going to live forever, and we might as well keep the family in the family."

The men finished their drinks as the houseboy announced dinner. The kitchen mtoto, the chef's apprentice, came out to take the dead Tommy to the kitchen for butchering. They would eat his chops, liver, and heart for the evening meal. They would have his hams for the morrow, and they would finish up what was left as a cold meat with relish on the following day. Even bled, gutted, and hung in the shade, a carcass kept only three days.

Herded along by Elisabeth, the two men, the little girl, and the boy walked to the dining room. The dining room was an extension of the living room. The two rooms formed an exact half of the house. The veranda was nearly as deep and fully as long as both rooms. The walls were paneled in unvarnished cedar, with the wormholes and deeply bitten grain showing through. At the right end of the living room a red-black stone fireplace was big enough for a tall man to walk into without stooping. Over it was the head of a Cape buffalo, a big one, forty-eight inches and a bit on the inside curve. A recessed glass-fronted gun cabinet, locked, hugged the corner between the fireplace and the wall. It was framed by the tusks of a big bull elephant. Each tusk weighed a touch better than one hundred and thirty pounds. The butt ends were deeply inset in hammered, oxidized copper. They formed a gleaming parenthesis around the glass which housed the arsenal. The arsenal consisted of a matched pair of Rigby .416s, a matched pair of Jeffery .500s, and a matched pair of Westley-Richards .470s. There had been a time when Henry McKenzie shot elephant on control, for money to keep his farm alive. There had been a time when Henry McKenzie had poached elephants along the Tana River, and over in the Belgian territory, and in the Karamoja country of Uganda, to keep both the bankers and the locusts suitably fed. In the gun rack there was also a pair of Purdey 10-gauge shotguns, a Westley-Richards .318 rifle, a Czechoslovakian .22 long rifle, a Browning 16-gauge automatic, a Remington .30-'06, a 9-millimeter Mannlicher-Schoenauer, a Sauer 20-gauge shotgun, two .38 pistols, and a mammoth .45 American frontier-style revolver. Henry McKenzie had never allowed himself many personal luxuries, but he did not consider expensive guns as luxuries. None of his double rifles had a safety catch or an automatic ejector. Henry McKenzie did not believe in overcomplication of weapons, nor did he believe that any man fit to carry arms was milksop enough to need contrived protection against himself. The purpose of a gun, Henry McKenzie thought, was to shoot as fast and as accurately as possible, with a minority of potential mechanical breakdown. Holding two extra-heavy express bullets in his left hand, he was able to fork them into a double rifle, after shaking out the expended shells, so swiftly that he could fire four bullets out of his doubles more rapidly than most men could shoot half a magazine from a rifle with a bolt action. Each of these guns had been fired many times, and as many times cleaned, by Peter McKenzie, even when he was so small that the huge .500 left a purple-tan bruise on his skinny shoulder.

It was a comfortable, happy-shabby room. The deep rump-sprung chairs and the two sofas were of shiny-worn brown cowhide, and the smaller chairs were of mottled black-white-and-red calfskin. A very large and very dark leopard skin sprawled along the length of each divan's back rest. The floor, of well-shined cedar, was covered in pelt: zebra, lion, and greater kudu. Only a few heads were hung on the wall—a kudu, a roan from Tabora, a sable antelope, one waterbuck, a very large eland, and the bleached skull and tusks of a huge wart hog. There were Masai shields of white buffalo hide and a couple of ancient hand-hammered Masai spears, their blades of the extravagant length of senior moran, which meant that the haft was only a handle and all the rest was crudely forged iron cutting edge. A couple of ebony idols rested in niches. There were also iron war rattles, colobus-monkey-skin and marabou-stork war dresses hanging from the walls, with a few simis in carved red leather scabbards. There was one magnificent black-maned lion headdress from Ikoma in Tanganyika and an ostrich-plume bonnet from the Loita Masai. The pictures on the wall were blurry reproductions of Gainsborough's Blue Boy, of etchings of Devon ducks, of a lithograph of a Scottish stag, and there was one very bad hand-painted portrait of Caroline McKenzie. The obvious ineptitude of the artist still was unable to distort a certain blissful tranquillity of smile and level gaze.

There was a big, battery-driven wireless in the room and an obsolescent hand-crank phonograph. The books were comfortably recessed in the cedar panels. A great many of them were mildewed old Africa stuff, the books of Speke and Bell, the technical volumes on game and guns and shooting, and one volume by a Kikuyu college graduate called Jomo Kenyatta. It was titled *Facing Mount Kenya.*

If the room had been fully decorated it might have contained the stuffed figure of a rinderpest-wasted bullock, a rusted plowshare, a locust hovering over a field of destroyed maize, a sheep starved of drought, and the mounted head and shoulders of a Nairobi banker. It might also have contained the name plates from the coffins of Caroline McKenzie, Robin McKenzie, Donal McKenzie, and Catherine McKenzie, all dead now and portion to the greasy red earth which blew away in red dust in the droughts and which held the fortune of Henry McKenzie to its breast. The room did not contain these extra trophies. Henry McKenzie carried them constantly in his head and did not need to see them on his walls.

The dining room was merely an expansion of the living room, but it contained its own, smaller fireplace. The heads which accented the walls were smaller and more delicate—Thomson gazelle, Grant, impala, duiker, steinbok. A dik-dik, dearly dainty, was mounted whole and stood alertly on a side table. It was no larger than a hare.

The table was of a heavy mahogany, very long and narrow, and built for a larger family. It was spread, for this midday meal, with a blue-and-white-checkered linen tablecloth. A flat silver bowl held some casual flowers. The service was heavy, soft, clumsy Edwardian silver, which Caroline McKenzie had brought as a dower. Henry McKenzie sat at the head of the table, with Elisabeth to his right, Jeff Newton on his left, and Peter sitting next to Jeff. Holly Keith sat by Elisabeth. Three Africans served the meal—Juma, the Swahili major-domo, and two Kikuyu assistants, Waiwaro and Kariuki. Juma wore a red, flat-topped fez, a white kanzu like a nightgown, and a red-and-gold-embroidered bolero jacket. The two Kikuyu servants wore green jackets over the white kanzus. They wore no fezzes. Juma owned tan tennis shoes with holes cut to ease his bunions. The two assistants went barefoot.

There was little conversation during the meal. Juma first brought smoking bowls of mulligatawny soup richened and thickened by stock from eland bones, and the assistants placed green plastic bowls of fresh butter alongside a platter of golden, fresh-baked bread. A cluster of condiments—House of Parliament sauce, ketchup, Worcestershire, mustard, salt and pepper, and Major Grey's chutney—stood next to the flowers and were not passed, but individually seized. The soup was followed by fish curry and after with cold francolin, a pheasanty sort of bird cursed, unfortunately, with white meat all the way down to his feet, while being stupid as well. They ate the cold francolin with mustard mayonnaise and chocked the corners with canned baked beans, cold potatoes, and canned spaghetti. There was a salad of fresh green tomatoes, a cherry tart for a sweet, and a rich array of homemade cheeses. Henry McKenzie, Peter McKenzie, and Jeff Newton ate tremendously, since Peter was eating for one thousand Masai warriors and Jeff had had a long morning on his horse, looking to his crops. Lisa McKenzie had an appetite most unbecoming to a nearly, almost bride, since she had been roused before dawn to start the household moving and to supervise the completion of her wedding plans. Henry McKenzie ate ravenously because he always ate ravenously, being simply hungry.

These rooms were the private territory of the farm. These were the special rooms which the Asian—Indian—clerk never entered. He worked in a small stone house which combined office with living quarters and in which he and his small, blue-caste-marked wife and ever-increasing litter of small brown children ate and slept and toiled. These private rooms were entered only by family and friends and the three personal servants. The kitchen was separated from the house by a covered archway, because Africans are noisy at work and the cook was a Wakamba, given to singing a heathen variation on the theme of "Jesus Wants Me for a Sunbeam," which he had once learned by osmosis from living near a mission school.

Off the hall leading out of the dining room were five bedrooms, three of which owned complete and expensive baths. Lisa McKenzie now lived in her mother's room, which adjoined her father's room on one side and her brother Peter's room on the other. The rooms leading off Peter's room were for visitors. These rooms shared a bath between them. The water came from several bores, one of which almost always managed to function even in a drought. The water was motivated by a windmill.

Outside the small compound provided by the low, scabrous rock-and-plaster wall, a separate village existed on its own. Two hundred Kikuyu lived on Bushbuck Farm as squatters, under the direction of Karanja, Kimani's father and the informal elder of the village. Each man had seven acres on which to graze his controlled flocks of sheep and cattle. Supposedly, no goats were allowed because of their habit of ruining the earth by snatching out the grass, but certain herds were grazed clandestinely, with Henry McKenzie's tacit consent. Each man owned his private hut, or thingira, for contemplation, and a hut apiece for each wife. No man on Bushbuck Farm owned more than three wives. Each man owned, as well, five acres for planting; for personal planting of maize and millet and sweet potatoes and arum-lily root. Each man received a daily ration of posho meal, a once-weekly meat ration, a weekly ration of salt and sugar and tea. In money the wages ranged from twenty shillings a month to seven pounds, Kenya-fashion. Their huts were built of mud and wattle, papyrus-thatched. Next to each major hut stood a granary of wattle and thatch. There was plenty of water in the stream for washing.

Henry McKenzie was what is called a "mixed" farmer. He concentrated on beef and dairy cattle, but he also raised a bit of tea and a bit of wheat and a bit of maize, all of which occasionally flourished on Kenya's slopes. He kept rather an extravagant orchard, and he had five acres in vegetables for the personal use of the main house. His dairy herd was milked at various stations on the property, according to how the grass grew and where; milked by Kikuyu youngsters who fed the cows linseed cake and who washed their hands constantly in steaming water which was kept bubbling in iron caldrons fed by nearly naked black mtotos whose sole duty was to fetch firewood and keep the blaze crackling. There was a stone barn in which Henry McKenzie housed his stud bulls, and a stone-fenced piggery. There was a stone dairy house for the sterilization of the foamy, cream-yellowed milk he sent daily to Nairobi by van. There was a huge garage which housed the two utility jeeps and a brace of five-ton Chevrolet trucks. The agricultural arsenal of the farm contained one small bulldozer, three tractors, and assorted disk harrows, seeders, and plow attachments. Henry McKenzie collected his major fertilizer from the excrement of his own stock, but one entire building was devoted to imported phosphates.

Henry McKenzie hired no bright young English manager. He ran his farm himself and intended to deliver it, intact, to Peter when Peter finished his schooling. Henry McKenzie bought his whisky and tobacco, his beer and his condiments, his flour and his sweets from old Patel, the Indian ducca-keeper in Nanyuki. For the rest, save shotgun shells and the rifle bullets he ordered from England, and the periodicals which came by boat, and the clothes made by Ahamed in Nairobi, he was self-contained. If Caroline McKenzie had lived through the birth of her last child, Henry McKenzie would have been a man whose happiness was sweetly solid and backed by a sense of complete adequacy.

As it was, he had Peter, his son, and Elisabeth, his first-born, to write a plus on the ledger sheet of negatives in his Kenya investment— an investment which had started with a lick and a promise and a faint hope when the Government was madly parceling out land after the first war and screaming for settlers. He had never been free of overdrafts at the banks until the second war brought a meat-hunger that chiseled off his financial shackles, veering him suddenly from a work-worn, mortgage-harassed farmer into what might be called a rich man. He had served several terms, since, on the Legislative Council as the member from the Mwega area. In his late forties, Henry McKenzie, now about to take coffee with a nip of French brandy in it on his breezy veranda with a clear view of Mount Kenya, was a sound success at a task that had made drunks of some men and suicides of others.

2

Henry McKenzie never went to bed without remembering the sum of it, starkly and with some horror and with occasional great gratitude. He remembered when he and Caroline, coming slowly and painfully by bullock cart from Nairobi, owned only a mattress and some pots and pans and one bottle of medicinal whisky and a rifle and a shotgun and two changes of clothes. What the Government had given him then was the hut of suicide, with one whole wall collapsed and the weeds and grass high-grown in the yard, with holes in the roof big enough for a baboon to jump through. He owned just over two hundred pounds sterling to buy plows and axes and stock and seed and fertilizer. When the two hundred pounds were all gone he had arranged an overdraft at the bank. It was the first of several overdrafts at the bank, more than he liked to remember, now, as a momentarily paid-up governor of the Muthaiga Club in Nairobi, the Rift Club in Nakuru, and of the country club at Limuru.

When Henry McKenzie reviewed his life he did not mark the years and months by the formal dates of Christmas and birthdays and ordinary calendar red lines. He remembered that in 1921 he had his first five hundred acres, and that in 1924 he bought another five thousand for a pound an acre, and he did it all with the help of the bank. He remembered that when the slump came in 1928 he went to Nairobi and told the bank to take the whole bloody lot and they knew where they could bloody well shove it. The bank was pretty decent, for banks, but they were starving too. They threw some good money after bad, and he was by way of being damned well clear when the locusts came in 1932 and wiped him clean. He almost quit then, because locusts in mass are bigger than anything a man can do to fight them. They ravished what they passed, and they filled the air with hurtling bodies in such quantity that once they even stopped a train. But what he remembered mostly about 1932 was not locusts.

He was off, up to the Northern Frontier, on an elephant safari, hoping to shoot enough ivory at least to tide him past the locusts and that year's bank note, and to feed his Africans and to buy new seed and fertilizer. He remembered the big bull he had shot the day the Somali came out from Isiolo, the messenger from the D.C., all the way up past Archer's Post to the Seralippe lugger on which he was camped. He had shot that day the bull whose tusks surrounded his gun cabinet. He wouldn't sell the tusks then, although he needed the money badly and the Indians were ivory-mad, because it was all the good he had of that day to remember. The bull was very big and very old, his tusks outstanding like dirty great logs. The wind swirled and gave the bull his scent and the bull charged, his ears flattened, trunk curled around his chest, and Henry had to stand firm and wait for him. Suddenly the trunk snaked out, its gaping red end as big as the mouth of a cannon on Government House lawn, reaching and writhing, and then the bull stubbed his sore, age-cracked foot on a sharp rock and showed Henry McKenzie just enough of the corner of a shoulder to shoot at. He shot at it twice with the big .500 (wasting one shell, a four-shilling cartridge), and the bull screeched and swerved and ran off some sixty yards to moan and rumble in his belly and die, with one tusk, the left one, dug deep into the rock-strewn red-sandy soil of the N.F.D. Henry McKenzie remembered that he reloaded the big .500 and went carefully up to give the elephant the finisher in the back of the skull and that the trigger sear fouled and both barrels went off, knocking him arse over tip into a thornbush and wasting another expensive bullet. He remembered his two Wakamba boys hewing and chopping at the tusks, cutting them loose from the spongy coral-like bone of the big bull's skull, and the

Turkana tribesmen impatiently standing by, waiting for the orgy of feasting when the Bwana was finished with the teeth, because the old Turks were hungry too, just like the bankers. He remembered one little Turkana making a great incision in the elephant's anus and crawling inside the beast, and the riot of slicing with spears to cut off coarse-grained, juicy hunks of the elephant, and the one dead man they had to haul out of the elephant's belly, he having been stabbed to death accidentally by a near relative whose only interest was in cutting off as much meat as he could slash with his spear to fill his growling belly. He also remembered that he was hunting that year with the two unpaid Wakamba boys, his unpaid headman, Karanja, a couple of cans of beans, and one slick-worn blanket. He remembered that he and Karanja and the 'Kambas sweated each tusk five miles back to what he called a camp and which consisted only of the canned beans and the slick-worn, greasy blanket and three or four rude rocks to make a fireplace. There was a sad-looking Somali waiting for him at the burned-out, ash-swirling cook fire when he stumbled in, sick with fatigue, and dropped the tusks. The Somali started to say something. Henry McKenzie shut him up and told the 'Kambas to draw out the nerves, and clean the tusks, and stuff them full of grass to keep out the termites. Then he turned to the Somali and said in Swahili: "Jambo. Nini?"

The Somali said briefly: "Memsaab. Kufa. Mtoto. Villi-villi."

Thus in one sentence in baby-talk trade language Henry McKenzie learned that Caroline, his wife, had died bearing his last child, and that there would be no more seeing either Caroline or the child because burial is speedy and mandatory in that country since there are no embalmers and the hyenas wait eagerly for death, and that it would take at least a week to get from the Seralippe to Isiolo to Nanyuki to Mwega. And that was how he remembered the elephant. He also remembered that Caroline was barely six months pregnant when he had left on safari and that he reckoned to be home in plenty of time to take her into the hospital at Nyeri for her lying-in, and he wondered what she had done foolishly to hasten the birth and why nobody had been able to do anything about saving her. But it was a hell of an elephant that the Indians were never going to be able to chop up into chessmen.

There was nothing that Henry McKenzie could do about Caroline and the child they were to name Catherine if she were a girl, or the child they were going to name Hugh if he were a boy. So Henry McKenzie hoisted his tusks high in a tree to dry and went out the next day and the next and the next and he shot many more elephants for the bank, only for the bank, this time. None was as good as he shot the day he got the news that his wife and his son, or daughter, were dead in his absence.

When Henry McKenzie was remembering well he remembered the night the leopard came into the house and bounded off with Caroline's pet dog, a big springer spaniel named Robin. He also remembered that Caroline named one of the dead babies Robin as well, and he never knew why she named the dog she loved and the baby she loved, that died, Robin, unless there was somebody else she had loved away back in her life whose name was Robin and about whom, in shyness, he had never asked. Maybe it was a childhood lover in her home town in Sussex, before he met her and courted her and married her and rushed her off to Africa to die before she had ever experienced the joy of a decently regulated life and her family growing tall around her.

What Henry McKenzie remembered of the leopard was thinking at the time that the leopard had a taste for dogs, and of buying a *pie* cur from a native for a shilling and killing it and hanging it in a tree alongside the stream, where the leopard's pug marks dented the soft white sand and where his claws had scratched the tall wild fig. And of sitting in a thorn blind for three straight nights until the leopard, hungry once more, came to the stinking dead dog hung high in the tree. He came in a bound, a yellow blur too swift for the eye to follow, and stood arrogantly in the first fork, turning his head slowly as he stared through cold beryl eyes, and then melted into another yellow blur as he leaped to the second fork, where the dead dog was lashed to the tree. And then the profile, the elegant dip of the head as he fastened his face in the dead dog's viscera, and then the gun going off and the leopard coming down with a soggy thump, and that was the biggest leopard, the best leopard, on the back of the biggest and best divan. When Henry McKenzie sat on the soft sofa, the word Robin came into his brain.

They went out on the veranda to take coffee, after which they would sleep briefly through the heat. There had been many years when Henry McKenzie had not had time to sleep through the heat, or even to come in from the fields for lunch. A cold meat sandwich and a warm bottle of beer, when he could afford it, had been his lunch in those days, and on other days he had merely shot a Tommy or a reedbuck and half cooked the quivering flesh, eating it with his hands and spitting out the hairs that clung to the rank fresh meat.

When Henry McKenzie thought of passed time he thought in terms of stumps achingly grubbed from the ground, and rocks painstakingly hauled away by teams of oxen. He thought in terms of dams built, and water rechanneled, and bore holes dug, and cows down with the bloats, and mules and horses dead of tsetse-fly sickness. When he looked at his hands he could feel the smooth curved handles of a plow still imprinted on the horn of his palm. The big square hands, with the broken, opaquely thick nails, had been trained by the plow, but they had been tender hands on occasion. They had hastened calves that were slow in coming, and splinted broken bones, and they had delivered his eldest child, Elisabeth, on a wild wet night he would never quite manage to forget. It was the only time in his life that he could clearly remember cold fear and controlled panic.

He had not known fear the day in the bush when he had killed the mad Kikuyu with the same hands that gripped the plow and held the gun and drew forth the calves and lambs and his own babies into life. This was in the very early days, when the Kikuyu were wilder and more angrily direct in their actions and the white men were more basic in their administration. Henry McKenzie couldn't remember now what the fuss was about, but some Kikuyu—Njuguna or Njogu or Wainana —Henry McKenzie couldn't even remember the man's name—had stolen or illegally housed his goats in a pasture or something, and Henry McKenzie had flogged him. He had flogged many Africans in his time, believing that it hurt them less than the legal fines and was more in keeping with their understanding of sins committed and punishment rendered. The native had gotten monumentally and broodingly drunk, and he had trailed Henry McKenzie into the bush when Henry McKenzie was searching, on foot, for a mob of strayed steers.

Henry McKenzie never really knew what made him stoop suddenly, possibly to look at a track or to tie his shoe or to examine a specimen of rock. As he paused, a long-bladed spear whistled past him, where his back had been, and passed on to embed itself in a tree. He turned to meet the screaming charge of the Kikuyu, who had drawn a simi and was coming like a cheetah from the thicket in which he had waited.

Henry McKenzie took the first cut of the simi on his arm, flung up to guard his face. It was a glancing blow, but it sliced into bone. Then he grappled the African, taking the knife hand by the wrist. He fell backward to the ground, with the African on top of him, biting at his neck and trying to force the simi hand downward to Henry Mc-

Kenzie's belly. Henry McKenzie still remembered the stench of the Kikuyu's beery breath, the smell of the sweat and of the rancid fat with which the naked body was rubbed, and the slippery feel of the snaky, muscular body as it clawed and bit and thrashed at him.

Henry McKenzie's left hand, unwounded, held the knife away from his stomach, and his right hand, covered with blood from the simi slash, had crept up and fastened in the Kikuyu's neck. The crooked thumb bit into the African's Adam's apple. The gnarled fingers sank into his neck, almost absent-mindedly, because Henry McKenzie's attention was centered on the bright, two-bladed stabbing knife that was poised over him.

It was almost a surprise when the African's knife hand opened and the simi fell out of suddenly relaxed fingers. Then Henry McKenzie looked at his other hand and saw that it was sunk to the knuckles in a neck, and that the African's mouth was open and the tongue bulged out, that the eyes were popped and bloodshot, and that the African was dead. Bleeding from tooth wounds on the neck and the simi slash on the arm, Henry McKenzie rolled the Kikuyu's body to one side and lurched to his feet, like an old buffalo bull coming crook-kneed up from a wallow. He took his own knife and hacked off a shirttail to bind his wound and twisted his belt into a tourniquet above the slash. Henry McKenzie picked up the gun he had dropped when the African charged him, stuck the bloody simi into its scabbard, took the scabbard with its thongs from the dead African's girdle, and headed home. There he washed his wounds with permanganate and then mounted a horse to ride to Nyeri. He called on the Provincial Commissioner and reported briefly that he had killed a Kikuyu, and described the circumstances. Then he got back on his horse and rode home again and poured himself a stiff drink of whisky. Then he called his wife, Caroline, and asked her to come and dress the wound.

"One of the Wogs had a go at me," he said briefly. "He got a bit damaged in the process, I'm afraid. I've sent some men to go and fetch the body." And that was all there was of that.

After Caroline had died, Henry McKenzie could not stand the sight or the sound of the house. He left Elisabeth and the baby Peter in the care of Wangu, Karanja's wife, and went off to the Wakamba country on an elephant-control assignment for the Game Department. That was the time when he first became bewitched. The Wakamba were hungry, and they had a fierce love of elephant meat. Henry McKenzie attempted to assign the carcasses of the beasts he slew to various clans. When he found some clans poaching on other clans' carcasses, he laid his stick on the backs of the poachers and incurred an enmity. Thereafter he shot no elephants. He spoored them and got up to them, but always something happened; the wind would veer and carry his scent to the herds, or they would mysteriously move off. There was much whispering among his Wakamba trackers, around the cooking fires at night, and one day Metheke, a local tracker, came to him and informed him that he was bewitched. A curse had been laid on him by the mundumugu, the witch doctor, of the clan whose men he had beaten. A penalty must be paid, Metheke said, or the curse would stay in force and he would never shoot another elephant. Henry McKenzie laughed and continued to hunt. He hunted for two more weeks, and he did not fire a rifle. He saw elephants and tracked up to elephants, but always something happened and he shot no elephants. He sent for the sorcerer.

"I want you to lift the curse," he said to the grizzled, white-haired old man, who was dressed simply in a monkey-skin cloak and whose front teeth had been knocked out and replaced by carved ivory fangs and whose pierced ear lobes were neatly folded over the tops of his ears. He wore a necklace of bushbuck horns depending from a fine iron chain, and he carried a dik-dik-skin pouch in which his medicine lay. He wore no weapons and limped painfully along with the aid of a gnarled staff, its pommel carved into the likeness of an elephant's head.

"How much to lift the curse?" Henry McKenzie asked.

"Fifty shillings," the old man said.

"Too much," Henry McKenzie replied. "Thirty shillings."

The old man got up from his high-kneed squat by the campfire. He limped off.

"All right," Henry McKenzie said hurriedly. "Fifty shillings it is. Lift the curse."

The old man came back and hunkered down again by the fire. He dipped into his pouch and brought forth bottles of red and black beans, some cowrie shells, the horns of a goat, and various relics of animal anatomy. He spilled the beans and counted them over, arranging them in piles and pouring the leftovers back into the bottles. He did certain things to the horns, the cowrie shells, and the relics of anatomy. He took a length of dirty string and tied seven knots in it and draped it round Henry McKenzie's neck. He spat seven times in Henry McKenzie's face. He built a fire one hundred yards away and commanded Henry Mc-Kenzie to move his equipment through it.

Then he said:

"The curse is now lifted. Go to bed tonight and sleep late in your tent tomorrow. Shout for your cook boy to bring you your breakfast in the tent. Take your time in dressing; there will be no hurry. Remain in your tent until Metheke comes to tell you that three big bull elephants with heavy ivory await outside, no more than a thousand yards from your camp. You will shoot these elephants. Then you will move your camp to Mbeyu, where you will shoot seven more big elephants in one day, and then you will shoot no more elephants this year. Kwaheri, Bwana Mkubwa." And the old man picked up his magic pouch and limped away.

Henry McKenzie always grinned sheepishly when he recalled the purification that lifted the curse. But he also remembered, as he said, that he was in for a penny, in for a pound, and he might as well give the old devil's magic a chance to work. He followed the doctor's orders.

He had breakfasted and shaved and dressed when Metheke came running the next morning.

"Oh, Bwana, Bwana," he said. "There are three big bull elephants feeding down by the river, in a grass patch in a grove of acacia trees. The wind is right for a stalk, and the elephants are no more than a thousand yards from here."

Henry McKenzie finished pulling on his boots and told the tracker to fetch his two .500s. They made a short and easy stalk, with the stiff morning breeze holding in the right direction. The three bulls, one outcaste with two mature askaris, had worked closer to the thickly wooded edge of the river. It was a piece of cake. Henry McKenzie didn't even have to crouch as he walked up to the elephants. He got to within thirty feet before he raised his rifle. He took the old bull first, broad on, shooting for the earhole, and the old outcaste slumped where he stood. Henry McKenzie whirled and shot the second largest bull, who also had not moved, between the ear and the eye, on the line that marks the entry to the brain. He also toppled and sank on his side. The third bull, who by now should have been in Tanganyika, merely swayed irritably from side to side. Henry McKenzie had ample chance to reload, using the big bullets he carried in his left hand, like cigars, between the fingers. He fired the double twice at the last bull's heart, aiming just behind the edge of the ear as the bull stood quarter-on, heard his bullets whunk behind the shoulder corner, and watched the last bull thunder off in the mad death gallop. When the bull died in mid-stride a hundred yards away, the noise he made as he struck the earth sounded like the end of an avalanche. Henry McKenzie could hear his belly rumble briefly, and then he was finished. They were all good bulls. The big one would weigh out at one hundred twenty pounds per tusk. The first askari would touch eighty, the second seventy pounds at least.

Firmly gripped now by the old 'Kamba sorcerer's imagination, Henry McKenzie struck his camp and moved on, according to the instructions, to Mbeyu. He repitched the camp and went to bed convinced that he would see and shoot seven elephants the next day. He saw, and approached, and shot seven elephants, all bulls, the next day. One was like the other day, accompanied by two askaris. The others were lone wanderers. It was necessary to use only one bullet each on all seven, since he crept to within poking distance of each. Then he hunted on another two weeks and saw no single elephant. He went back then to the farm, considerably shaken by the power of some reedbuck horns, a goat's guts, and seven salvos of spittle in the face.

This was, really, Henry McKenzie's first full realization of Africa and the difference between himself and its people. He thereupon made some effort to study the business of witchcraft and its workings. On subsequent safaris he went back to see the old Wakamba doctor, and for a fee learned some of the inner operations of the power of suggestion. Not so long after his final examination in the old man's tricks he had occasion to use them.

Prior to this time Henry McKenzie had employed an old device to determine theft. He would line up his suspects and, heating a smoothing iron rosy-hot in its nest of coals, would pass the iron lightly over the tips of the suspects' tongues. The innocent suffered no scorch. The inner knowledge of guilt dried up the thief's mouth and tongue, and thus the iron burned. The man with the burned tongue usually confessed to the theft.

Once, in an epidemic of thievery, when skinning knives and axes and sugar and salt were disappearing in mass lots, Henry McKenzie decided to practice his new knowledge of darkness. The word, naturally, had spread among his Kikuyu squatters that the Bwana Mkubwa was possessed of the correct devils. He merely summoned his laborers and announced that he was going to curse the lot and that the guilty men would die in their tracks. He got out his beads and his beans and his bones and his symbols of seven, and he slaughtered a goat slowly, and he made some passes and muttered much, and all of a sudden two of the assembly tottered and fell forward in a cataleptic faint. Henry McKenzie revived them with Anglo-Saxon curses, a basin of soapy dishwater, and some more symbolic hand passes. When they recovered consciousness they led him to where they had cached the loot, after which he beat them soundly with a rhino-hide kiboko and fined them a month's wages. He never really had any trouble with his people afterward, since he had killed one with his hands and was able, soundly, to curse the others.

The practice of local voodoo had not ended with the natives. When Henry McKenzie went to Nairobi to arrange for his last, decisive overdraft, his powers of persuasion were such that he got it, and the bank manager was a Scot. He told his wife later that he seemed powerless in Henry McKenzie's presence, as if he had been drugged. But Henry McKenzie got the final, most-needed loan, after the locusts had ruined him, and from that loan came the necessary force which had made the farm a millionaire's dream of working perfection. Henry McKenzie would have struck the man who dared accuse him of communion with his magic bag the night before he went to Nairobi.

3

The war was not yet over, the Second World War, and only a certain amount of structural steel in one leg, plus some shiny pink scar tissue from third-degree burns from a shattered, magazine-exploding Royal Navy destroyer, now allowed Jeff Newton to work his farm. He had cut off his mustache and joined up early; his ship had been hit nearly a year later in the gray waters of the Western Approaches; his Kenya farmer's vitality had kept him alive on a life raft in the freezing sea, and he had been mustered out early, to return to Kenya and the job of producing meat for the forces. First he grew back the bushy guardee mustache. Like most of the other Kenya settlers, Jeff Newton had become free of his overdrafts only because of the screaming need for meat and produce in a war that was being fought with food. If it held a little longer and the postwar demand kept up to the promises of Mr. Roosevelt and Mr. Churchill for bountiful production to feed the world, men who had been balancing on the edge of bankruptcy would be rich and would found dynasties. Jeff Newton was going to begin his dynasty, just for a start, with Elisabeth McKenzie, who sat chattering by his side on the shaded veranda of her father's home, while the old man chewed his pipestem and young Peter McKenzie waited impatiently for amplification of the proposed safari that Jeff had mentioned to him earlier.

"It's mostly that property around Naivasha, Peter," he said. "The wild stuff has been overflowing out of the Masai, and I seem to be running a farm for the benefit of everything that can eat, trample, or knock down. I thought we'd do for the hyenas that've been at the stock, and maybe thin out the buffalo a little bit and wallop a couple of the elephant. Then we can hop in the lorry and buzz off down to Naivasha and reduce the lion population a touch. They've got so cheeky they come and sit by the herdsmen like dogs. The whole job shouldn't take us more than a long week end. Merely a matter of shooting it, not hunting it. I've got some special permits from the Game Department. You can sort out the country a little better than you know it now, and kind of take over the control end of this business. I expect that between farming and learning how to be a husband, and having babies all the time, I'll be a mite too busy for the bush. And you're nigh enough to a man now to quit playing red Indians and do some man's work."

"When do we start?" Peter asked. "And what about Pa? Did he say I could go?"

"Sure," Jeff said. "I asked him before lunch. He was just chaffing you. You'll need to fetch a couple of big doubles and the .318. We'll take a can of coffee and a pot and a blanket and a little biltong and live off the shot meat. What I mainly want to do is get off the premises whilst the old girl tidies up her fluffy ruffles and things. Supposed to be bad luck to see too much of the bride before the happy event. Also makes *me* damned well nervous. I'm going to have this woman on my hands for a long time, anyhow, and I'd like to go and get meself fit for the ordeal."

"Go and stay until the day before the wedding, if you like," Elisabeth said. "Or the day after, as well. I'm not exactly desperate, my good fellow. I've not been entirely idle with my time when you were spending all your substance telling lies about the war and trying to drink all the beer from here to Nairobi with those disgusting hairy friends of yours."

"Precious few disgusting hairy friends I've got," Jeff said cheerfully. "My friends are all off in Abyssinia chasing Eyties, or swimming round in cold water without sharks, or warm water *with* sharks. I'm deposited in a wilderness of women, children, and old crocks. That's how you snared me so easily. I was sick, wounded, and totally defenseless."

"Well, in any case, off with you, and take the child out from under my feet. I've enough to do looking after Pa and Holly without having you and Peter underfoot as well, and a thousand warriors on the rampage in the rose garden every morning. Try to keep the infant from being consumed by one of those wild beasts, will you?"

"That I shall, old lady, that I shall," said Jeff, casually swinging her round his head like a lasso and kissing her solidly as he set her on the floor with a thump. "Peter, go whistle up young Kimani, or whatever his name is. He'll be your gunbearer. Then come back and collect your guns and we'll be cracking."

As he raced toward Kimani's compound, Peter was thinking what a wonderful thing it was to have a sister like Elisabeth, who had sense enough to choose up a bloke like Jeff Newton for a husband instead of some city sissy who only talked about books and music and who always shaved and looked neat in his clothes. Peter was very fond of Elisabeth. There were only three years and a bit between them, but she had controlled him like a mother ever since he could remember, without ever patronizing him or making fun of him. She had allowed herself to be killed and captured many times in his baby games, and she never purposefully trod on his dignity. She always seemed interested in the birds and animals he brought in, dead or alive, and she used to read stuff to him that she couldn't possibly, as a girl, be really infatuated by, things like *Karamoja Safari* and others of his father's library. She had a gentle, half-sarcastic way of teasing him that was never embarrassing, and when she had warmed his pants when he was younger, she did it with foreseen justice, immediate force, and no later recriminations. She was one damned fine girl to have for a sister, Peter thought, and she must have more sense than most or she wouldn't have picked Jeff to marry. He ran into the native compound and yelled for Kimani.

Kimani's compound was standard. There were sheep penned, and sheep loose—black-and-white, black-and-red, white-and-brown, all woolless and looking more like goats than sheep. There were bananas hanging, yellow, heavy, from the shade of thick, fleshy fronds. Several monstrous figs cast a shade over the courtyard of the shamba of Kimani's father, and the creepers from yam vines crawled round and round the trees called mukongogo. Some of Kimani's sisters were pounding maize in a stone mortar. One of Kimani's father's younger wives was toiling down the hill from the forest with an immense pile of firewood clewed to her sweating black back by eland straps which bit deeply into the flesh of

her streaming forehead. Naked, shining, potbellied children played aimlessly with emaciated dogs inside the euphorbia-thorn boma which surrounded the cluster of beehive-shaped wattle-and-mud houses which
contained Kimani's father's family—each of his three wives with a separate hut of her own, a separate patch of maize or millet or potatoes to till,
separate sheep to tend, and separate children first to bear and then to
breast-feed and then to raise. There were no obvious goats, goats being
formally banned by Henry McKenzie to all the Kikuyu who worked his
farm. The goats were hidden outside in the woods.

Kimani was sitting on the ground, listening to his father, in front of
his father's thingira, or bachelor hut, in which no wife was welcome.
Both Kimani and Karanja were squatting on their heels, the old man
drawing a picture of something in the smooth trampled dirt with a
pointed stick.

4

Karanja, Kimani's father, was lean and wiry. His ears were hugely
pierced and hung limply flapping nearly to his shoulders, the lobes having been distended by the circular wooden disks of his early adornment
as a young warrior. His face was keen and thin-nosed, from the Masai
forebear who had also fined the features of his son. The old man was
wearing only a pair of shorts. The muscles across his chest were fallen
in ropy ridges and his sharp breastbone glistened with sweat and oil.
He was headman for Henry McKenzie. He was the implicit chief of the
two hundred Kikuyu who squatted on Henry McKenzie's acres, and who
farmed, for each family, personal shambas such as Karanja's, and who
lived in smooth-swept compounds exactly like Karanja's, hard-packed
earthern islands on which stood the same mud-wattle houses and the
same beautifully woven cane granaries on stilts. Peter was very fond of
Karanja, who had made him carefully carven toys of animals and birds;
who had made him a little bow and arrow when he was a baby of six
and who taught him to shoot it; who had made him a spear and taught
him to throw it, and who had told him all the classic legends which are
handed down from father to son. At Karanja's knee, and at the side of
Karanja's senior wife, Wangu, Peter had learned to speak faultless

Kikuyu while he played with Kimani since the creeper stage. The old man looked up and smiled, saying him welcome in Kikuyu.

"What brings you to my ridge?" he asked.

"I am going off on safari with the Bwana Jeff," Peter said excitedly. "He wants me to bring Kimani with me, to learn to hunt lions and elephants and——"

"To hunt animals like a 'Ndrobo, like one of the wild men who live in the forests and eat elephants?" the old man asked gently, smilingly. "To be an outcaste Kikuyu like his father?"

"You hunted all your life with *my* father," Peter said.

"Ah, but I was a wild and footless young man, a beer drinker and womanizer at a very early age," Karanja said. "I am trying to make a gentleman out of my son, since I can no longer make of him a warrior, warriors being disallowed by the Crown these days, these peaceful days, in which it is even illegal to steal from the Masai except in a child's game. How many men did you lose in the raid this morning, my chief from the Loita Plains?"

"That was a game," Peter said irritably. "This is real. Go and get your panga, Kimani. Jeff wants us to hurry."

Kimani looked inquiringly at his father. The old man nodded.

"Go, son," Karanja said. "Go and learn to hunt like the shenzis who live with the baboons. Like the Athi who was my uncle. It may possibly keep you out of the cafés and joy-houses of the bazaars in Nairobi. Hurry. Do not keep the Bwana Jeff waiting."

Peter remembered his manners and bowed a thanks to the old man, who remained squatted dreamily on his heels, looking at nothing. He had been telling his son again the story of how the world began. It was a story not unsimilar to the one found in the Old Testament, in the chapter of Genesis.

In the beginning God made the world, mixing it carefully with His hands from red clay and water, and then He built the mountain called Kerinyagga, which today men call Mount Kenya, and then He shaped the whole world around it. Then God made the first man, whom He called Gikuyu, and sent him to dwell on the earth. Gikuyu conquered a great snake in battle, and as a reward God sent him a wife, called Mumbi. Mumbi bore nine daughters but no sons, and Gikuyu's heart was heavy. He prayed to God, and God answered his prayers. He sent the nine young daughters to rest under the sacred fig tree at the foot of the mighty mountain, and lo, there were nine fine young men awaiting them. Each man chose his mate, and from the union all the important people of the world were sprung, and all the important part of the world belonged to the men of Gikuyu. God gave the issue of Gikuyu sheep and goats and cattle to stay their hunger, and so naturally all the sheep and goats and cattle of the world belonged to the Gikuyu. God made one slight exception when He created the Masai, for He gave them some special plains and special cattle and a river of their own, but all the other land on the fertile side of the mountain God nominated expressly for the Gikuyu. There was a very slight misunderstanding between the Gikuyu God and the Masai God, as among cousins, because the other Ngai, the Masai Ngai, gave the Masai to understand that they too owned all the cattle in the world. And as contrast to the nobility of the Gikuyu, God created a race of poor hunters, who lived in holes and were called Agumbu, who fed off wild honey and the flesh of savage beasts. God then told the Gikuyu never to eat wild flesh, at the risk of becoming unclean. The orthodox clan-generations of the Gikuyu flowed from the nine maidens and the nine young men, making all the Gikuyu blood brothers, since they were all forced from a common womb. The clans were called Agachiku, Mwesaga, Eithaga, Mandoti, Mathathi, Chiera, Ndemi, Iregi, Maina, Mwangi, and Muriungu. The man, of course, was not allowed to marry inside his own clan. Since the true God had no children or cattle, the Gikuyu became His children and their stock His herds. So when a Gikuyu increased his cattle God was very pleased, because then new sacrifices were made to Him at the foot of the sacred fig trees. This did not, of course, apply to the Masai God, who was displeased by Kikuyu prosperity.

Kimani and Peter had heard this story many times. As Kimani was being prepared for circumcision, Peter unofficially prepared with him. There would be no real circumcision bond of brotherhood for Peter, that operation having been performed with less mysticism and considerably more sanitation when Peter was a child of six months and was colicky and irritable from a constricted foreskin. A white doctor in Nyeri had circumcised him with a casual scalpel, with a minimum of ceremony.

5

The boys raced off toward the big house.

"Will I be able to shoot a gun?" Kimani asked as they bounded along, leaping like impala.

"Of course not," Peter said scornfully. "You know that the Kikuyu are not allowed weapons in Kenya, except when they are members of the Kenya police or of the King's African Rifles, or are special askaris. You will be my gunbearer. You will carry the guns and load them and clean them and be ever close to my shoulder with a loaded gun and fresh ammunition."

"I want to learn to shoot a gun and kill a lion with a gun," Kimani said. "It seems to me that you have all the fun and I do all the work. Suppose you are trodden by a buffalo or a leopard has you down and I do not understand how to point a rifle. What then? You will die, and all because you did not teach me how to shoot a gun."

"I will never be in danger if you perform your duties properly and hand me the loaded gun without being afraid and running off and leaving me," Peter said haughtily. "But we will ask Jeff if maybe you can shoot a gun a little, at some harmless target like a zebra or a wildebeest, just for practice. Shooting it will teach you to care for it properly."

"I don't want to shoot a wildebeest or a zebra," Kimani said. "I want to shoot a lion and stretch his hide in my hut."

"Everyone knows the Kikuyu are not hunters," Peter answered. "They tend herds and raise crops. They never even used to be allowed to eat wild animals' meat, your father says. The Masai, they kill lions. The Wakamba and the Turkana kill elephants. Kikuyu kill goats and slaughter sheep and drink cow's blood to make them think they are as fierce as the Masai."

"Well, if I can't shoot a lion, I'm not going," Kimani said.

"Yes, you are going, or I will tell my father and he will beat you. Or I will ask him to let me beat you."

"It is against the law for a white man to beat a Kikuyu."

"On my father's farm he is the law," Peter said. "And I am the law after my father."

"But," Kimani was saying, "I——"

"See here," Jeff Newton said, coming suddenly up behind them. "I didn't ask you kids to hold a palaver or to arrange a special ngoma. I want to go and shoot some hyenas. Are you coming or not?"

"Yes, sir," both boys said. "We'll just nip off and collect the guns."

"The arsenal is already in the lorry," Jeff said. "Go and say good-by to your sister and father, Peter, and you, Kimani, come along with me and help me load a few bits and pieces into the Chev."

The lorry roared down the lane in a puff of dust, and Henry McKenzie turned smiling to his daughter Elisabeth, who was waving from the yard.

"He's very good with the boy," he said. "He's really a very nice chap, Elisabeth. I'm very happy about it all."

"He's a nice chap, and he's also very good with the girl," Elisabeth replied. "And *I'm* very happy. I think he'll make you a good son-in-law, Pa. I think Mum might have liked him too."

"I'm sure of it," Henry McKenzie said shortly. "I think I'll go now and have a little lie-down. Wish, though, that Jeff'd asked me to go along. Could do with a bit o' bush. Been donkey's years since I tackled a real safari."

"You know as well as I that this was a special present from Jeff to Peter, to sort of make up for my leaving the farm. Going off as man-to-man's one thing. If you went along you'd cramp the kid's style a bit, Pa, because he'd always be conscious of your being there. This is Peter's special shauri, and you'd just spoil it. Go and take your nap. I've work to do."

The old man walked heavily off to his bedroom. Elisabeth looked around for Holly Keith. The child was curled in a corner of the sofa. She was painfully reading a book called *African Rifles and Cartridges*, by John Taylor.

"Time you went and had your nap," Elisabeth said. "What's that book you've got there?"

"It's a frightfully dull thing about guns," Holly said. "But I thought that maybe, if I sort of swotted up, next time they might take *me*."

"Ruddy small chance of it, I should imagine," Elisabeth said. "But you never can tell. Just what would you use on a wounded elephant, poppet?"

"It says here that nothing's any good under the caliber of .450," the child said seriously. "What does that mean?"

"Blowed if I know," Elisabeth said cheerfully, "but I suppose it's important. Leave it to the menfolks, love, and whistle off for your nap now. Your old auntie Lisa has work to do. Such as something called trousseau trouble."

"What's trousseau trouble, Lisa?"

"That you'll know about later, Holly. When you're a lady."

"I don't *want* to be a lady," Holly said. "I want to go on safari with Peter and Jeff."

6

The men stopped at Jeff's house to collect his Number One, a Masai-'Ndrobo named Lathela, who called himself a Samburu and was actually Rendille, which is to say that he didn't know what the hell he was except an exceptional tracker, walker-up of trees, spear thrower, game knower, honey hunter, gun carrier, and slave to Jeff Newton, whom Lathela regarded with some of the same idolatry with which Peter viewed his new, about-to-be-brother. Lathela was obsidian black and unadorned by the Masai folderol. He looked uneasy in khaki pants and a tattered old shooting coat and usually shed them when they left the farm and went into the bush. Tonight they would hunt over the farm, so Lathela left his pants on. He was waiting when they got there, waiting with a heavy tin safari box which held such necessities as coffee and tea and sugar and tins of cigarettes and a bottle of whisky and an anti-venom snakebite kit, extra ammunition, and blankets. He had the weapons stacked in cases on top of the safari box. He was wearing a simi in a plain cowhide sheath and carried the spear of a full moran. When Lathela went to hunt with his master he balanced the spare gun over his left shoulder. He carried the spear in his right hand because he did not fully trust guns.

Jeff leaped down from the lorry's front seat and helped Lathela heft the heavy safari box into the back of the truck. He motioned to Peter to stay in the front seat and then told Kimani to ride in the back with Lathela. They drove off, heading toward a corral some five miles away where the hyenas had been especially persistent in harassing the calving herd, seizing the babies as they were dropped, ripping the udders off birth-weakened cows, hamstringing the heifers. Actually Jeff loved hyenas—when he was in the bush and they came to ring the campfire, drawn by the smell of fresh-killed meat and human habitation. But Jeff loved his cows and calves better than he loved the night symphony of the hyenas, since the sight of a cow with her teats bitten off is not amusing, and a calf consumed alive as it drops from its mother's womb is not the subject for a joke, not with the price of beef at a fool's pinnacle.

They stopped just at dusk under a tiny island of umbrella-topped thorn trees. The sun had set blood-clear somewhere over Longonot, the crater at Naivasha. Kerinyagga had dispersed its clouds in the late afternoon and was white-headed and austere. It was getting nippy-cold. Just at sundown they came on a herd of zebras, standing, ears flanged forward, stupidly gazing, unfrightened.

Jeff jammed his brakes and spoke sharply to Peter. "Get out," he said, "and wallop me that big stallion. Use one of the big guns so's we don't have to chase him half the night. Lathela! Toa bundouki mkubwa kwa Bwana Kidogo pese pese na tia risase!"

He turned his jaw toward Peter. "Might's well get used to doing your gunbearer business in Swahili. It's a good habit to form, because whilst you speak Kikuyu and I know a lot of Masai, one day you'll wind up with a 'Kamba or a 'Drobo or a Nandi or a Turkana for a bearer and you'll want something in a hurry and you'll say it in Meru or English or some silly such and get yourself stamped on before you remember that the bloke behind you doesn't know his bum from his breakfast about whatever you're speaking in. Not so stupid, the old Arab slavers. They built a pretty good utility language when they invented Swahili. Hop, now, and piga me this punda."

Lathela reached down one of Henry McKenzie's .500s, loaded, and Peter slipped away from the protective shield of the lorry, creeping in the growing dark from clump of thorn to clump of thorn until he came onto a low-forked bush next an anthill which gave him cover and a place to rest his rifle. The big stallion had turned, warily looking, offering no shoulder and only a little neck, so Peter held the big double on his behind, sucked in his breath, waited for the limber twig to ride the gun to where he wished the gun to be, and then squeezed off before he exhaled. There was a soggy, clumping sound like the smack of a rug beater on a thick carpet; the zebra flinched and went away with desperate speed. He ran four or five hundred yards and folded, in mid-flight, dropped flat and dead before Peter could walk back to the truck and Jeff could drive the truck up to where the stallion lay.

"I'd imagine that, from the way he was standing, you shot him up the arse and hoped it would hit the heart," Jeff said. "You had enough gun there to move a small mountain."

"That's what I did," Peter said. "Who was it, you or Pa, that always said to aim for where it was biggest?"

"In all honesty it wasn't either one of us said it originally," Jeff answered. "It was some old rogue that made a living poaching elephants. But we need this boy tonight. Let's go drag him over close to the camp."

Lathela, the Masai-Wandrobo-Rendille-Samburu, leaped out of the lorry and hitched a rope to the dead zebra's head, and Jeff let in the low gear without waiting for Lathela to get back aboard. They went off and away to the clump of trees, the zebra bumping slack-jawed and tongue swollen-distended behind the car, the gunbearer running easily, barefoot, alongside the animal. Jeff stopped the car and spoke again.

"Tell Kimani to let out his guts," he said. "He can use that panga he carries. We don't want to bugger about with the hide or the fat or anything tonight. Just open him up and leave him lay."

Peter addressed Kimani in Kikuyu.

"No, not Kikuyu, nor English," Jeff said. "*Swahili.* Form the habit when you're talking to blacks. Kata hi ya tumbo."

Kimani, looking surly, walked up to the dead zebra and ripped him from anus to breastbone with one sweep of the big curved knife. "Lad keeps that panga honed. Good show." Jeff nodded, satisfied.

Jeff went over to Lathela and told him to take down the safari box. Then he spoke again to Peter. "I want the box unpacked and one tent set up and a fire lit and the guns taken down and cleaned and the ammo sorted and some tea on the hob and a tin of bully opened and a bottle of whisky broken out and some fresh water in the karibu by the time we get back," he said. "Your man is in charge of fire and water and gun cleaning. Tell him. *And* in Swahili. I'll tell my man about the rest. Then we will go and circulate this dead zebra a bit to sort of send an invitation to our friend Fisi. No need to cause the hyena a lot of extra trouble when we can make it easy for him to commit suicide."

Jeff briefly addressed Lathela. Peter as curtly instructed Kimani. Kimani started to argue.

"Hit him," Jeff said. "With your fist." Peter looked puzzled and a little frightened. "*Hit him!*" Jeff said. "Hit him hard!"

"No," Peter said. *"No. I won't."*

Jeff walked over to Kimani and cuffed him across the face with the flat of his hand. "Do what the Bwana says, suria!" he said in Swahili. "Now and in a hurry or I will thrash you with a kiboko. And when the Bwana tells you something in the future, do what he says or maybe the Bwana will have to kill you to teach you obedience. Now, jump!"

He turned to Peter. "Go and fix that rope to the zebra's hind legs and tie it to the stanchion in the back of the lorry and then get in the front seat with me. Hurry."

Peter took the rope, unsheathed his knife, and slit the skin between the bone and tendon of the crook of the zebra's hind legs. He ran the rope through the slits in both legs and then made a half hitch to secure the rope, and then took the other end and tied it with a double hitch to a stanchion in the back of the lorry and jumped into the front seat and looked at Jeff, really for the first time. What he saw was a long, down-turned nose and knotted black brows over squinted eyes and a lump of muscle white against the dark tan. The mustache, bushy and oddly red, wasn't funny any more. The black hair was tangled and curly and wild enough to hide a covey of sand grouse in. Jeff was angry, angry at Peter and angry at Kimani and a little angry at himself.

"Now, see here, young man," Jeff said as he eased in the clutch and the lorry started to move. "If you're going to use that Wog of yours, you'll have to cease some of this brother-playmate business. I know you were brought up together and all that, but you're coming on now for being a man, and I presume you'll be running your farm when your pa pegs out someday, and what you have to know about blacks is that blacks are blacks, and one thing you don't do is argue with them. You *tell* them. There are times you can joke 'em. Boot 'em in the tail on occasion, forgive 'em when they're bad, look after 'em when they're sick, but never, never argue. I really should have given *you* that wallop except for your losing some face in front of the Wogs. I'm sorry, but I think it did that cheeky little bugger a bit of good."

"But mostly I don't think of Kimani as a 'local,'" Peter answered, still uncertain. "We sort of grew up together."

"In your life, son," Jeff said seriously, "you aren't going to see the white man and the African on even footing out here. There's no place in the scheme for it for a long time. These people just aren't out of the tree long enough. They were eating each other and selling each other just yesterday. Best we make a decent gunbearer and eventual Number One out of Kimani than to turn him into a Nairobi spiv."

"His father said something like that this afternoon when I went along to collect Kimani. He said something about so long as Kimani wasn't allowed to be a warrior any more he might's well be a good hunter and stick to the bush."

"The old man's right," Jeff said. "Now let's kill some of the conversation and spread this carcass around the real estate a bit. I want to make enough trails to entrance every hyena in the area."

He drove the lorry in sweeping circles, trailing the dead zebra behind him, it bumping and scuffing along over the ground, losing hair and leaving a trail of yellow-fatted grease and old dark blood. Jeff completed a grand circle finally and then drove straight for camp. Three hundred yards away he stopped the car and unhitched the rope from the zebra's hind legs. The zebra, yellow teeth bared and tongue fatly protruding, looked a bit scraggy from his trip. He was ripped and torn by rocks and worn hairless on his underside from friction, and he was already beginning to smell. The moon was rising low when they got back in the lorry and drove up to the camp. A fire was lit, dancing gaily upward from its dry thorn logs, a small tent was pitched, and the safari box was gaped open and unpacked. There was a bottle of whisky and a pair of plastic cups standing on the top of the safari box. A canvas water bag, its pores oozing bright droplets of moisture, swung from a branch of one of the acacias. A kettle chuckled on the fire, and a can of cold corned beef was sitting atop the safari box, between the whisky and a can of baked beans. Black licorice-stick strings of biltong, the dried jerked meat, were hanging from another branch. Kimani and Lathela were squatted on a blanket next the raised knee-like roots of a towering tree, with broken-down sections of rifles scattered on the blanket. Kimani was wiping each section with a greasy rag. Lathela was squinting through the barrels of the fired double, with a ramrod across his knees.

"You see?" Jeff said. "Only one thing missing. They forgot to build their own fire. Lathela! Take the shovel from the lorry and make a fire of your own, over there," pointing to another tree a hundred yards away.

Lathela got up, found the shovel in the back of the lorry, robbed the blaze of a heap of glowing coals, collected a couple of small logs and a handful of twigs, and went over to the other tree. He made a pyramid of the twigs over the coals, laid the little logs across the twigs, and disappeared into the bush. He returned with a big, sharp-twigged thorn log in each fist. He dragged both logs across his small fire. The logs caught immediately, and the sparks sprang up and died suspended in the night air.

Kimani now was snapping the barrels back onto the rifles and re-placing the guns in their cases.

"Leave the .318 and my Mannlicher out of the cases," Jeff said. "Then go and fetch me two torches from the toolbox of the truck. And a roll of bicycle tape as well. Then take half of that biltong and that other kettle down to your own fire. There's some tea and sugar in the chop box, also a couple of drinking cans. Fetch me the tea and sugar first."

Kimani got up and started to walk away.

"I didn't hear you say you understood me," Jeff said sharply.

"Yes, sir, I understood you," Kimani said.

"Well, say it then, and say it in Swahili," Jeff said.

"Ndio, Bwana," Kimani replied. "I will do as you say." He walked off toward the lorry.

"Little bugger dies hard," Jeff said. "He's a proud one, and spoilt, as well. We'll fix that."

Jeff walked over to the safari box and poured a large dollop of whisky into one glass, a tiny spoonful into the other. He took both glasses over to the goatskin-shaped canvas water bag, tipped it with the crook of his arm, and spilled half a glass of water into each whisky glass. He handed the glass with the minute quantity of whisky to Peter.

"You'll start to drink this stuff one day," Jeff said. "I'd rather you had your first official one in the bush with me. Here's cheers. And you might remember that there's nothing as nice as a drink at the end of the day, with the work done and the fire going, and nothing quite as foolish as one in the middle of the day, with the sun hot and the work undone. I've done both, and will again."

Peter sipped his drink appreciatively. It was not his first. Liquor was freely used in Henry McKenzie's house, and as a small boy Peter once had become violently ill from the dregs of his father's sundowners. He had pinched a beer from the water bag occasionally and had sampled his father's stock of wines and liquors on other occasions. He sipped his drink.

"Bitter," he said. "Tastes dreadful."

"You don't come that innocent stuff on me, my lad," Jeff said. "It's not the first time you've dipped your snout in a whisky, if I know boys. Cigarette?"

"Thanks," Peter said. "I'd love one. I've been smoking about a year now, but not in front of Pa. He doesn't like it, but he said I could when I was fourteen, and I edged up a little on him."

"Dreadful habit," Jeff sighed. "I love 'em. Must say, though, that it interferes with your sense of smell. Here's Kimani back with the flash-lamps and the tape. Weka hi, Kimani, then go and help Lathela with your supper."

"Ndio, Bwana," Kimani said. "How much sugar and tea do I take?"

"A pound of each. It'll have to do you for the trip. Tell Lathela I said so. Oh, and here's a bag of posho and a skillet. Off with you now."

"Ndio, Bwana," Kimani said, and went away.

"He's learning," Jeff said. "That smack in the chops helped. Now let's fix these guns."

He took Peter's .318 and one flashlamp, taping the torch firmly to the barrel's underside as it emerged from the wood of the stock. He drew back the bolt, clicked his tongue, and yelled.

"Kimani! Come here!"

The young Kikuyu came running from his fire.

"Where are the bullets?" Jeff asked. "Why are there no bullets in the magazine?"

"I don't know," Kimani said. "You didn't tell me to load the guns."

"I'm not supposed to *have* to tell you to load the bloody guns," Jeff said. "An unloaded gun is no damned good to anybody."

"Ndio, Bwana," Kimani said. He broke open a yellow flat case of Kynoch soft-points and turned to Jeff again. "Are these all right for to-night?"

"Yes," Jeff said. "Load the gun and leave the rest by it. And *don't* lean the gun against the tree. Either wedge it in a crotch or lay it on the blanket or stick my hat under the trigger guard and let it rest on that, with the barrel out of the dirt."

"Ndio, Bwana." Kimani laid the .318 gently on the blanket and went back to his fire. Jeff looked at his own weapon, the Mannlicher. The dull gray snub noses of the bullets were in the magazine, the cham-ber lever depressed over them so that the gun could not fire until the bolt had been turned and back-drawn to shift a cartridge from magazine to chamber. Lathela had learned long ago.

"We'll eat, chum," Jeff said to Peter, who had listened with rounded eyes to the lecture. "Not much for tonight. A bite o' biltong and a slice of bully and some beans. You can heat yours if you want, but I'm going to eat mine cold and save some time and trouble. Our guests will be coming along shortly, roaring for the feast. Hey! There's one now."

Against the backdrop of bush, against the cold flicker of the stars in the moon-silvered sky, a lunatic giggle sounded, answered by another scream on the other side of the camp. The giggle and the scream were followed by a series of boisterous whoops, like the howler system on a destroyer. *OOP, OOP, OOP*, it went, and was followed by the thin *heeheeheeheeh whoop* of the hyena laughter.

"Friend Fisi, come to call," Jeff said. "Let's eat now, because shortly we will be in business."

Peter took a tinni-kata and opened the beans and the bully beef, while Jeff made the tea and chewed on the tough black jerked meat of the biltong. Biltong, cured by drying thin sheets of fresh meat spread like laundry in the sun on bushes, has the consistency of buckskin but conveys a great sense of satisfaction to the chewer, since he almost never gets it ground down to where it is swallowable. Squatting by the fire, Jeff and Peter cut white-fatted chunks of the pink crumbly corned beef with their knives, eating it with their fingers, and digging into the can of beans with spoons. They drank their tea, three cups each, and waited. Suddenly a madman's symphony of hyena voices struck an overture near the carcass of the dead zebra, like woodwinds, with answering calls coming stronger and stronger as other hyenas coursed the trail made by dragging the dead zebra. From around the body now came roars like lions, growls like leopards, shrill shrieks and hysterical gibberings as the flocking hyenas expanded the full force of their fantastic library of noises. On the thin night air the sound of the hyenas' powerful jaws chopping through bone came as loud as a man felling a hardwood tree with a dull ax.

"Time to go," Jeff said. "Take your rifle. Take plenty of ammo in your pockets. We won't have the boys with us to carry it. Two men are just enough to see after each other in the dark. When we get up to them flash your torch around the kill, and when you pick up a pair of eyes fire under them and you'll see the eyes go out, like you'd blown out a lamp. We won't bother finishing any of them off; the relatives will eat the wounded ones."

They strode out toward the growling, yapping, screaming ring of hyenas, Peter to the left, Jeff to the right, and suddenly drew up close to where the zebra lay, his body infested with hyenas, as thickly as by ticks. Jeff threw up his gun. The yellow tongue of torch licked out and picked up a pair of luminous eyes. Jeff fired and the little lanterns disappeared. He swung and fired again. Peter stopped watching Jeff and held a pair of eyes steady in his own torchlight. He squeezed the trigger of the .318 and the lights went out. He chose another pair and fired. The lights doused. The night was filled now with the steady splitting crack of the two rifles, with the sodden smack of bullet on bone, with the shrieking of the hyenas, and with the gurgling grunts of the wounded animals ripping and tearing madly at their own guts and at the dragging guts of their wounded brothers. The shooters shot their rifles hot, until no more eyes reflected in the searching beams of the torches, and the few survivors had gallumped, high-shouldered, slope-spined, and shuffling, off across the plain.

"That'll be enough to hold them for a while," Jeff said. "There'll be another batch back later on when the blood smell spreads, and we'll go out after them again. Ought to pretty well clean out the lot. Let's go back and have another cup of tea with a little of that fine whisky in it."

They walked back to the little camp, where the two fires had shaken down into steadily glowing coals and where the bodies of the two Africans were sharply profiled against the fire as they squatted on their hams and talked. Jeff poured some more of the cooling tea and tipped a little whisky into each cup. Then he and Peter rested on their heels to wait for the next consignment of hyenas.

"I suppose you'll carry on farming when you've got a bit older?" Jeff asked, filling in the boredom of waiting. "You really ought to go to one of those agricultural schools and learn something about all the new techniques and things. Someday you'll have to take over for your old gentleman, you know."

"I don't want to be a farmer," Peter said. "I'd rather be a hunter, like Pat Ayre or Philip Percival, and take out safaris. I shouldn't mind farming when I'm a lot older, but from all I remember of our farm it's just work and work and hope the drought doesn't last or the locusts don't come or the prices hold. White hunters make a lot of money and have a lot of fun as well, and they get to see all of the country. I haven't seen near enough of it yet to do me."

"I suppose it looks very glamorous to a young'un," Jeff said. "But there's not a lot of future in it. The game's gradually going. The country's filling up with people, and the farms will be crowding out the animals. You can't mix habitation *and* game. You can't raise cattle and have tsetse flies, and tsetse flies *do* live in bush, and animals *do* need bush.

"You remember how many rhinos they shot out of the 'Kamba country when they were cleaning out Makueni, to kill off the tsetses and let the 'Kambas spread out their shambas? That's been happening and will keep on happening as the country fills up when the war's over—and mind you, every third man who's discharged from the forces will be wanting to come out here to try his hand at tea or sisal or coffee. They've some sort of idea in England that all we do in Kenya is drink whisky, play polo, and chase each other's women, whilst the Wogs do all the work."

"But there's plenty of game now," Peter said. "There's more than you could possibly kill off. That's why we're out now. . . ."

"Only proving my point. With the war going and not much hunting, game's been breeding up again, but it was on the fade before the war. And we're thinning it out because it's a threat to the cultivated land. We'll always kill it off and drive it off if it threatens the farms.

"The game has got to go if the country's settled. Game just won't breed around habitation when it gets real thick. You can have bush *and* animals or farms and *no* animals. Before you're a lot older all the wild animals will be on reserves."

"All the same, I'd like a whack at it when I'm a little older and Pa's still running the farm," Peter said. "I can help out enough when I'm not actually on safari, and if the game runs out, I can always farm."

"Safari's no life for a man," Jeff replied. "You're out in the bush nine months a year, wet-nursing some rich Yankee or scared maharajah as a glorified guide, risking your life a couple times a week going after the stuff they wound, burning out your lungs with alkali dust, drinking too much whisky, and trying to live up to their standards when you're in Nairobi between trips."

"Sounds rather fun," Peter said.

"It's fun when you're young, all right, and glamorous, too. There used to be some money in it as well, when you could shoot enough ivory to make elephant safaris worth while, but that's all over now and the Game Department hang you for poaching."

"I don't want to get rich. I just want to see some wild country and have some fun, and not break my back on a farm. Look at Pa. He's not fifty yet and he's an old man. He's been broke most of his life, trying to keep the farm away from the bankers. My mother died when he was off trying to collect enough ivory to keep the farm running. Not for me if I can help it, Jeff."

"You're just a kid. You don't know what you want yet. One of these days that little Holly girl or some other little Holly girl will wall an eye at you, and you'll be mad keen to get married. And there never was a woman who would put up with being married to some bloke who's out of the house nine months a year, tying knots in leopards' tails and explaining to New York society ladies the difference between a giraffe and a gerenuk."

"It seems to me you're mighty young to be content to settle down, after the war and all, to the same old dull do on a farm. And my sister. Don't you s'pose she wants a little something different from what she's always had?"

"Elisabeth wants *me*," Jeff said, grinning. "*I'm* the difference. And she likes the life. I have a keen hunch that p'aps Lisa has some idea of making up for herself what her mother missed, which is all the wonderful life that can come out of your own land after the first backbreaking is kuisha-ed and done with. Your mum missed all the pleasure and absorbed all the pain."

"I hear the hyenas again," Peter said, turning his ear toward the plain. "Time we went back to clobber the rest?"

"You're a bloody murderous little bugger," Jeff said. "You'll find that also wears off in time. But I reckon you're right. Let's go and do for the survivors."

The plain, when the sun first rubbed it glossy in the cold, new air of early-morning Kenya, seemed to be the site of an old-fashioned Masai massacre. Vultures circled and skidded down from the sky, to land stiff-legged and awkward with an undercarriage bump. The obscene marabou storks prowled among the corpses like dirty old deacons, their heavy beaks probing into the dead hyenas with the detached air of an elder passing the plate. The vultures hopped and flapped and quarreled among themselves. A few wounded hyenas still moved. Humping belly-distended among their dead relatives, a handful of survivors had gorged themselves to bursting. Jeff finished these with his Mannlicher before he walked up to the bloody mess to make a tally. The sight made Peter sick. All the excitement of the night shooting was gone, all the magic of the evening spent, in a stinking pattern of blood and tattered fur and scattered viscera, with the scavengers bloated and daubed with the bloody afterbirth of death. By rough count they had killed forty-three hyenas.

They struck the camp and rode along, heading for the densely forested slopes of Mount Kenya. They had finished a meager breakfast of tea and what was left of the biltong. Jeff was feeling talkative. He had lit a pipe and they were driving along in the fresh loveliness of the morning, the grasses still gallantly stiff with dew, and the lorry bumping leisurely on no particular track, jarring teeth as it hit an occasional pig hole.

"I always feel bad when I have to kill hyenas," Jeff said. "They have such a wonderful part in the scheme out here. They are the sanitation corps, of course, and they neat up the mess that man and beast leave behind them. They're a dreadful brute, but I reckon they're necessary. First they come, and then the vultures and the storks, and finally the ants—all part of the same plot. The hyena can't catch and kill his own meat unless it's weak or sick, so it eats the bodies of the dead niggers and it eats what the lion leaves. Then comes man and the farms and the poor old fisi sees a cow calving and he eats the calf or he sneaks in amongst the herds and rips off the udders or hamstrings a heifer and throws her down and has her half digested before she's dead. That's what we were talking about last night, y'know, about the fight of farm against bush, and cattle against game. The hyena's business is consuming carrion, but the balance gets out of hand and so you have to make carrion out of the hyena for something else to eat. There doesn't seem to be any way to avoid it. But I hate to kill them, all the same."

"I don't," Peter said. "They're a dirty, stinking, ugly beast, and next the wild dogs, I hate them the most. I'll kill all I can."

"You're a savage, a bloody-handed savage, that's what you are," Jeff said. "You're like these damned Boers. They'll shoot an animal across a river just to see it die, even if they can't use the meat. Killing is no good unless it has some point to it. It's a plain waste."

"What about the war?" Peter asked him.

"That's about the most pointless waste of it all," Jeff said. "War is like a hyena eating itself when it's wounded. Nobody wins, except, occasionally, the losers."

"I wish I was old enough to get in the war. The R.A.F., maybe, and fly a Spitfire. But I suppose it'll all be over before I'm old enough," Peter said sadly.

"What a tragedy. Maybe I can get you killed by a buffalo instead, or at least gored by a rhino," Jeff said. "In the meantime, imagine those impalas over there are some Germans or Japs, and get out and wallop one for me. We need some fresh meat to eat."

The impalas trooped, heads down, into a thick patch of green wet wood. The horns on the rams seemed too heavy for their skulls, and they stepped delicately, as if the heaviness of the horns made their tiny feet hurt. Their hides glistened bright as new pennies in the morning sun.

"Don't wallop the old boy," Jeff called softly as Peter took the .318 from Kimani's outstretching hand and walked stoopingly away from the lorry, heading for the point of bush, down-wind, from which the impalas must certainly emerge. "Choose one of the young rams. The old 'un isn't good enough to hang on the wall, and he'll be tougher than cow chips, with about as much taste."

Peter faded into the bush, found a likely clump of thorn in a likely place, and paused for the herd to pass. The ewes came first, the lambs frisking at their heels, and then came the young rams, with short, curved horns, not yet broadly backspread in the brandy-snifter shape of the old gentlemen. Peter sat flat on his heels now, his knees up nearly to his nose, the elbows planted and anchored to the knees, the gun firmly held by the knee-braced elbows. He waited for the ewes and the lambs to cross, and held on the shoulder of a young ram as it minced along a few feet at a time, stopping occasionally to look around or test the breeze. When the young ram stopped, Peter stroked the trigger gently and the ram leaped high, almost ten feet, into the air. Peter could not hear the bullet whunk, but Jeff could hear it, being farther away from the gun's explosion, and he started the lorry and began to steer it round the point of green wet bush. The ram came down in a spraddle-legged sprawl. He was not quite dead when Peter walked up to cut his throat, but the great opalescent green eyes were already turning cloudy blue. The bullet had taken both foreshoulders and the heart.

"You shoot very well, chum," Jeff said, and Peter's ego leaped. "This un'll make nice eating. Lathela! Skin him out."

The Wandrobo-Masai-Rendille-Samburu sprang out the back of the lorry, and Kimani leaped with him. Kimani held the young ram by the horns while Lathela zipped open his belly and clawed the paunch and intestines free with a bloody hand. Holding firmly to a foot, he slid his simi up inside each hind leg, from the knee joint to the stomach slash, and continued the stomach slash up to the top of the breastbone. He slit the forelegs in the same manner, and then, with Kimani still holding the head, neatly peeled the skin from the body. He cut off the head and neck, amputated each of the legs, removed the rib section, detached the liver from the stomach mass, and wrapped the lot in the wet dripping skin. He wiped his hands and knife then in the green-grassy contents of the stomach and dried the moisture of hand and knife on the grass. He picked up the bloody bundle and threw it into the back of the truck. The operation took less than ten minutes. That night they would eat well. The ram would be tender, even so freshly killed, and they would eat the rest of him tomorrow, when he would be especially tasty from twenty-four hours' hanging in the heat.

Hunting the hills that day, the low green hills that drifted into the side of Mount Kenya, they shot twenty buffalo out of a troublous herd. They were not after sport, and the shooting was ridiculously simple. Jeff spotted the herd through his glasses, the buffalo looking like big flat beetles against the pale green glades, and they stalked up to a high piece of ground with several large thorn trees for protection. They had replaced the magazine rifles with two sets of doubles, Henry McKenzie's .500s and Jeff's .470s. Bulwarked from stampede behind the trees, Jeff sent Lathela round to circle the herd and let his scent drift down-wind. The buffalo moved uneasily from the man-smell, walking toward Jeff and Peter through a small misty green avenue of grass. As the buffalo passed the trees the men began to shoot, aiming for the shoulder and bone and the heart inside the ropy network of muscle and the inch-thick hide. They reloaded rapidly from the clumps of bullets, as big as asparagus stalks, that they stuck in their gun-holding fingers. The bullets struck with solid slaps, the hit beast startled into a lumbering death gallop, the others pausing shocked and puzzled at the rifles' reports, then finally moving off in an uncertain halfhearted stampede away from the noise and the panic of their wallowing, bellowing cousins and uncles and mothers and fathers. They galloped a thousand yards and then picked up the down-drifting scent of Peter and Jeff. They turned again, stupidly, and galloped back to the scentless safety of their killers, the safety where there was no scent but only noise. Peter and Jeff turned, and as the gallop jounced down to a shuffling walk, now the man-scent was gone, they began to fire again. The buffalo raced upwind, away from the noise, only to strike Lathela's body-scent, and then they turned again and ran back to the guns. This time, when they had passed the slaughter point, they did not return in panic from the man-scent. They burst into a full-gallop stampede and went away high into the green bush, up the mountainside.

The exterminators had shot very well. There were no wounded, since they were shooting at an average of twenty yards, and a buffalo at twenty yards is a long ton of target. The twenty buffalo, mostly bulls, were down and dead within a thousand-yard radius. All four double rifles were scalding hot to the hands, and Peter's shoulder felt as if it had been pounded to pieces by a hammer. Jeff sent Lathela and Kimani off to cut the tongues out of the buffalo. There were no horns worth saving, and the meat was left for the vultures who now were beginning to dot the sky by hundreds. The birds skidded in before the men had finished slicing out the tongues, which, properly cooked, would be tastier than beef tongue. When they drove off in the lorry, a thousand birds were hopping and fighting over the carcasses. Tiny bat-eared foxes and little silver-gray jackals and a few hyenas had come out of the bush and were beginning to dispute the right of ownership with the birds. It was just on noon when Jeff stopped the lorry under a giant mimosa and announced lunch. Lunch was a can of beans and two bottles of Tusker beer which Jeff had stuck into the water bag. The beer was chilled and beaded from evaporation of the water in the karibu. The Africans, according to custom, ate nothing at midday. They lay in the shade and went promptly to sleep, unaware of the tiny, persistent little hold-me-close flies which crawled over their faces, around their lips, and into their ears and eyes.

Peter, drowsy after his beer and resting with his head on one of the cushions from the front seat of the lorry, thought about the buffalo. He had shot his first one when he was ten. He was no longer very impressed with the buffalo, which was supposed to be so huge and unkillable and so viciously dangerous when wounded. Not that he underrated them. A man would be a fool to underrate a Cape buffalo. It was just a matter of knowing them and knowing their habits and their reactions, and when you knew that, they were simple as cattle to handle. Peter knew about the insatiable curiosity they had, that fatal curiosity which made them hold for the ten or twenty or even thirty seconds after being startled, staring stupidly, before they made up their minds to run one way or the other. He knew that they were sensitive only to scent and noise and movement, that if you held yourself frozen in the midst of a herd they would graze round you so close you could see the tickbirds upended and pecking at the vermin in their nostrils. He knew that they always traveled under a fighter cover of tickbirds or snowy egrets or both, and that when the birds jumped, the herd was alarmed, just as the tickbirds were always what you watched when you were creeping up to a rhino. When the tickbirds jumped, the old faro would be bursting into a frenzied, foolish charge, his tail sharply down. It wasn't until the tail went down that you knew the rhino wasn't going to stop.

He thought idly of the curious relationship between all the animals and birds he knew. The leopard, say. Any leopard would drive another leopard, even his mate, from a kill hung high in the crotch of an acacia. But the leopard was in firm partnership with the battler eagle, who perched in the summit of the kill-tree all day long, ready to warn his friend, the leopard, if something came along to poach his meat. The buffalo had his tickbirds and his egrets, who warned him in return for the feast of ticks and other insects which infested the buffalo. The rhino, stupid, nearly blind, had his affinity with tickbirds instead of eyesight. And take the lion. He couldn't abide a vulture or a hyena, and would come rushing out of the bush at the first sign of a bird or a hyena. This was what got lions killed so easily. All you had to do was shoot a zebra or a wildebeest or a kongoni and leave it out in the open and wait for the ndege or the fisi to come. The oldest, smartest lion in the world couldn't stand the sight of a buzzard or a hyena eating freely from his kill. Peter once had seen a big male lion standing on his hind legs, swatting angrily at vultures with his forefeet, like a boxer punching a bag. Yet the lion was perfectly happy to share his dinner with the little foxes and the jackals. It was not unusual to see the tiny scavengers eating serenely alongside the king, while the old boy might even refuse to share his food, momentarily, with his bride.

Lions were funny, Peter thought. Neither he nor Jeff nor his father had ever known a male lion to make a kill when the male lion was a member of a pride. He made the lionesses do all the work. The old boy might stand on a hillside and sort of let his scent float down to a herd of zebra, and maybe growl once in a while, but it was Mum who crept silently through the long grasses, ear tips barely showing, feet placed gently, claw-end first, on the ground, soft pad to follow, tail whipping gently and sinuously, until she reached the point of charge, when the tail sprang out as stiff and strong as an iron bar, and she inaugurated the first of a series of twenty-foot bounds that nobody, nothing, not even a cheetah, could match for speed inside a hundred yards. And then the last leap, onto the zebra's back, fangs buried in his neck—not to kill, but just to hold—hind claws sunk into the zebra's back and hips, and then the long, strong arm, with its dewclaw like a ripping hook, shooting out and grabbing the zebra by its nose and bending back the neck until it broke with a crack like an Australian cattle whip. Then like as not the old man would saunter up and drive her off the kill, not even allowing her near until his meat-swollen belly touched the grass. Yet he had seen a whole pride of lions, the papa, the lionesses, and the half-grown cubs and baby cubs, all feeding off the same topi. Curious.

Peter loved to think about animals and how they lived. There was grass, for instance. Rain made grass and grass determined where the animals were or mightn't be. Well after the rains, when the tall grasses towered over a man's head and were heavy-tipped with seed, you'd find a lot of the hoofed animals still in the hills, where the plentiful water gathered in pockets and they were mostly free of the threat of the carnivores. The zebra and topi and wildebeest and kongoni herds hated the high grasses, because the high grasses provided protection for the hunting cats. When the grass was high they stuck to the hills and to whatever fairly barren plains they could find, so that a man who was hunting automatically looked for places where the grass was low, and there he would find the vast herds of common game moving in, with the cats just behind them. Peter thought it wonderful that the animals dropped their young just before the rains, when the grass was sere and afforded no ambush for the cats. And then the rains would come, making it difficult for anybody or anything to move very much, and when the short, tender, young sprouting grass appeared on the fire-and-sun-blackened ground, the youngsters would be old enough to graze the juicy green shoots and grow strong. By the time the grass was high again, the kids were adolescent and smart enough to look after themselves. The baby animals fascinated Peter. He had seen a kongoni cow drop her twin foals, lick them into shape, browse at the bloody spot of afterbirth, and carefully muzzle her young as they tottered on ridiculous, knob-kneed legs for a couple of hours. In two hours they tottered less aimlessly. In three hours they did not totter very much. In four hours they didn't totter at all. Given a draft of milk and a night's rest, they were galloping at their mother's heels the next day. You could, by lying quietly, watch a baby antelope grow before your eyes from a rumpled clot of bloody matter, fresh from the mother's womb, into a functional, self-sufficient creature in just a few hours' time.

That, of course, and then there was the communication. They say the wildebeest is the stupidest of all the animals, and certainly he looks stupid and grotesque, ugly-faced, ridiculously bearded, high-humped like an American bison, tail twisting, damn-fooling this way and that, snorting and nonsensical and fit only for crossword puzzles under the three-letter word "gnu." His horns are too small to fight with and his meat is no good to eat and his long, tufted tail is the only valuable part of him. The natives slew him by thousands to make fly whisks of his tail, which sold for a shilling in Nairobi or Nyeri or Nanyuki, fitting the skinned-out tail over a haft of whittled wood or, more expensively, over a handle of ivory or an expended cartridge. But Peter had seen communication work even with the idiotic wildebeest. He had seen a madly galloping column of a thousand wildebeests, stretching by twos and threes for better than a thousand yards in a straight line, suddenly wheel into a precise cavalry maneuver at a right-flank turn of ninety degrees, each calf turning by the number at its mother's heels, and the animals at the head of the column turning precisely at the exact moment that the animals at the end of the column wheeled. How, Peter wondered, did the one at each end know when to turn when there was no obstacle in the path and they were a thousand yards apart?

Everyone knew that elephants talked, of course. They talked as people talked, but with belly rumbles and the sensitive, gentle prodding and grasping of each other with their trunks, as men will seize each other to impress a point. He had seen old cows surround a stricken bull, trying to lift him and lead him and take him away, and then standing as fearlessly and as lovingly stupid as the harem of a shot zebra stallion, refusing to leave until driven off. Peter had read all there was to read of elephants, and he knew that there was nothing to the old fable of the communal elephants' graveyard. An elephant died where he was when he was sick, and he died at about the same age a man could expect to die, somewhere in his seventies or eighties. Of course there were exceptions. You could compute ivory roughly at a year for each pound, in a big bull, and the monster bulls of over a hundred were probably the exceptions that lived past the hundred span. But diet and water and surroundings had a lot to do with it too. The biggest ivory came out of the Northern Frontier, up around the Tana River, past Isiolo and all the way up past Marsabit, or from the almost impossible jungle country around the Great Ruaha River in Tanganyika, where you couldn't get at them to hunt them and that was why they lived so long and grew such huge teeth. But up in the Masai, for instance, where the best and biggest buffalo herds grew the best and biggest horns, and the best black-maned lions and the biggest leopards were, there were herds on herds of the surliest elephants in Africa and nobody bothered to shoot them because the ivory was so poor. So it had to be diet, didn't it? Or minerals, or something, because foraging was nowhere so good in the N.F.D. as it was in the Masai, the N.F.D. being nothing but a waste-land of baked clay and scrubby thorn and myrrh and sansevieria bushes, with no water worth mentioning and nothing but dwarfed bamboo for cover. Maybe, then, there was some sort of strange herb along the Great Ruaha, a bush that dragged the bachelor bands of big, spooky bull kudus down from the safety of the high hills to browse as dully tame as topi along the riverbanks.

All the mystery about elephants was a lot of bumf, Peter thought. An elephant cut his life into three parts just as a man divided his life. He had about twenty-one years to grow up in, and about thirty years to be a prime breeding male in, and another twenty to twenty-five years to grow old and grumpy and die in. He kept his own counsel and watched his elders for the first quarter century and minded his manners, and then if he were lucky he went out of the herd with the old, deposed bull as an askari, and, in return for running errands for a few years, he learned all the things there were to know from the old gentleman. When his knowledge was complete and he was about forty or fifty years old he went back and challenged the herd bull and they had a hell of a fight and the askari usually won. The newly deposed bull went off with two more neophytes and lived alone, as a bachelor, while the new chief mounted all the cows and left his issue behind him. Then there would come a day when another bull would challenge him and defeat him and drive him off from the herd, and he would then roam about with his own acolytes, growing older and sourer and fuller of malice toward everything. His feet would hurt and his teeth would ache from decay in the mammoth nerve, and ants would crawl up his trunk and drive him mad. He would run amok and trample native shambas and crush in the water holes, and finally somebody from the Game Department would come along and shoot him and take his tusks back to the D.C. in Isiolo. That's why you didn't find many of them dead. If they died of disease they died away up the mountain in some cul-de-sac or they died in thick bush away back from the rivers, but mostly they got shot by sportsmen and Wakamba and Turkana ivory poachers, or by white poachers who shot everything they could find if they could see a speck of white sticking out of his mouth, or if he came down off the Thomson Range and started to raise hell with the natives the Game Department blokes would search him out and kill him. There wasn't really much future to being an elephant, Peter thought, because Jeff and I are going to wallop a good portion of that maverick herd here, with no respect to ivory, just because they're trampling down the maize and uprooting the Kikuyu shambas. I never shot an elephant yet, Peter thought, but I know how to. You shoot him in the ear if he's standing still, or just between the ear and the eye. If you're uncertain you shoot him in the heart and he will run a hundred yards and then drop dead.

I wonder why it is that leopards love the wart hogs so well, Peter thought, and why they never think it is strange to find one, or even two, or sometimes one pig and one Grant gazelle, neatly tied into the right fork in the right tree by the right river bed? Do they think it's a shauri a Mungu and God just left the pigs there for leopards to find in trees, when leopards are so smart? How can they be so smart and still be so stupid? Then Peter quit thinking about animals and grass and went to sleep, because the sun was high and the breeze had stilled and the shade was drowsy-cool under the big mimosa and he was very tired from all the buffalo and the beer.

Jeff was dozing, too, and a herd of oddly assorted thoughts skipped lightly through his brain. One thought was that my God, I hate this killing things, not so much the killing when it's a game, but this going out and assassinating it when maybe it's as much the animals' land as mine, and maybe they were here first, and what right have I got to shoot it? A hyena is important to another hyena, Jeff thought, and I suppose even beautiful. And the buffalo. I love the mbogo. He's so damned ugly and stupid and congenial unless you hurt him, and then he is smarter and meaner and craftier than any of the others, even the elephant.

I remember that one Wog I found dead in the thorn tree, with the dead buffalo under it. Some visiting sportsman had wounded the old buff and let him go off to die without finishing him. Then some poor ignorant local comes blundering along, and here is this sick mbogo, doubled back on his own trail and just waiting for whoever hurt him to come by, and it isn't the person who hurt him at all but some poor Wog with a tin spear and a heart full of hope for a square meal next week. And the sick buff jumps him and the Wog takes off for a thorn tree and can't climb high enough. He tries to pull his feet out of the way, but the old mbogo stretches his neck and starts to lick at the Wog's feet with a tongue like a wood rasp—the same sort of tongue I will eat boiled to-night, and goddammit, I forgot the mustard—and licks the poor Wog's feet right down to the bone, like a kid tackles a lollipop. He licks off the skin and the meat of the feet and when he's finished with the feet he licks the meat off the legs as high as he can reach, and the poor Wog can't get down, even if he's got something to walk on, which he hasn't, so he sits up there with his arse full of thorns and all sorts of ideas about somebody cursing him and he bleeds to death, and so does the old buffalo, and there they are for the flies and vultures to play with and for what? The buff wasn't mad at the Wog and certainly the Wog wasn't mad at the buff. Yet the kid and I shot twenty of them a few hours ago and never even bothered to take the hides for shields or the meat for any amount of people who need the meat, because there isn't any sense to either. We haven't got the time or the refrigeration to keep the meat fresh and they don't let the locals carry shields any more, so the hides are no good. But the herd's dispersed and gone to the hills and will maybe stay the hell out of my crops until next year, when they will come down again and I will have to shoot some more of them the same way. And one day I will wound one and maybe not go after him, because by that time Elisabeth will be pregnant and some other poor dumb local will stumble on him and the buff will jump up and down all over the local or maybe lick his feet off and in the end there will be some more tatters of meat on the ground and more birds coming down out of the sky.

It never seems to end, Jeff thought. I remember the one time I found the dead cow giraffe with the dead lioness crushed under her body. I don't know how it got started, but I surmise a hungry pride of lions jumped a yearling giraffe and the old lady came along and objected. It must have been a hell of a fight because nothing, not even the hyenas, stayed around to feed off the remains and even the vultures wouldn't touch it. Peculiar about vultures too. You can leave anything, just any-thing, like a handkerchief or the door off a hunting car, on a carcass, and the birds won't come close to it. They're moody, the ndege. Some-times they'll fair smother you coming down and run you off your own kill, and another time they won't even land at a distance. They'll slip down out of the sky and sit in the thorn tree and wait, but they won't come to the kill, and nobody knows why they didn't come that day when they'll come tomorrow as happy as a kid to candy. And nobody ever told

me exactly what it was they responded to when something died. It can't
be smell and it can't be eyesight, because when nothing's dead you can
sweep the sky with the strongest glasses and there's nothing there. Shoot
it and in five minutes the world is full of birds. They can't smell it up
there in the stratosphere, it's not possible, and they can't see it, but where
the devil do they come from if they can't smell it and can't see it?

I would much rather think about Elisabeth than about vultures,
Jeff thought, drifting lazily off into siesta. I would rather think about
Elisabeth, who has the eyes to go with the hair and the body which I
have, rather originally, not explored very far, because I have explored
enough of them over a period of time to know that they are basically
pretty much alike unless you have got something special to make them
worth waiting just a little bit for, and sort of solemnize the whole business if you want it off to a good start and an early foot at the barrier.
I remember a lot of them, Jeff thought, and they were all pretty fine at
the time, but somehow you can't really recall whether the Peggies were
the blondes or the Sheilas were the brunettes or just which one was the
redhead who left you that little gift in London on sick leave, and God
bless Alexander Fleming, who invented penicillin.

It was funny about Elisabeth. You knew a girl from the time she
was just a bloody nuisance with an uncle fixation about the older bloke
on the next farm, and then you sort of whipped off to the wars and
when you got back the bloody nuisance was a smasher, a stunner, with
the right knobs and bolts and all the necessary things, and you met it
at a dance at the Outspan in Nyeri one Saturday night and you said,
like a great noble hero: "Is this the child I used to wallop for being
such a *bloody* nuisance?" And she said as glibly: "I'll warrant you
couldn't do it now," and you said: "Well, come on outside and we'll see,"
and there was some scrap of moon and some jacaranda dropping the
great lavender blooms all over the place, and some hibiscus and a scent
of tuberose on the breeze. Once you were clear of the people and strolling down toward the garage, she just tucked the one hand under the
one arm that wasn't quite healed yet and sort of pulled you around and
said: "Oh, Jeff, it's *so* nice to have you back again," and you kissed all
of her, starting at the forehead and feeling it tingle clean down to the
toes, like a big belt of issue rum on an empty stomach, and her hands
came up and touched your face very gently with the fingertips, and then
she took you by the ears and looked up at you with the moon making
Lake Victoria out of her eyes and then she said: "I'll have this, please,"

and you didn't even kiss her again for fear of mangling up the moment. What you did was pick her up in your arms, all full of pride and certain ownership, and walk bang back into the party and say in a very loud voice, which carried over the fuss the band was making and the gabble of conversation the drunks were making, "I wish to announce an engagement without permission of the parent I have not consulted but whom I will kill if necessary if he objects." The parent being a nice bloke, and leaning on the bar, said: "Don't kill me, Jeff. Shout me a gin instead." Everybody laughed, and that is how a man got engaged. It was funny since then how he had really run away from Elisabeth when they were alone. Somehow he didn't want to spoil it in advance. He would kiss her boisterously in front of her father and her brother and anybody else handy, and pick up her unbelievable lightness and swing it around, but he didn't want to—what did they use to call it?— go all the way. What a moral bastard I turned out, Jeff thought, the old slap-and-tickle kid, the scourge of WREN and the WAAF and any odd bod that was gathered round the drinking circles in London and Liverpool and Dover. Go to bed blind and wake up with a countess— or a waitress, it didn't matter—but you weren't marrying the countess or the waitress, and you weren't going to have to spend your life looking at them in the morning, because the good Lord God Ngai had invented a very handy war which got you out of the house early and off to look after the hog-fat merchant ships that the Jerry subs were so fond of. Funny, like the dead lioness was funny, Jeff thought. I knew I wouldn't cop it out there in the cold. I'd be left to come back here. Funny how I knew it and knew at the same time that some of the ruddy great noisy ones wouldn't make it to the raft. Peculiar. Never knew a man to cop it that really believed he wouldn't cop it.

Then he thought: Elisabeth is five feet three inches tall and weighs about as much as a ewe impala and has blue-purple eyes and curly black hair and smells like an early morning in the spring in the Masai when all the acacias and mimosas are freckled out in their white flowers, like the May hedges in England, and the spicy air smell from the fresh burning of the high grass with the rain nice and wet atop it. She is going to come to my house to live and run my house and her father is a nice old coot and her brother a wonderful little idiot and we are going to have at least ten children and the first boy will be named Jeff and the first girl after her mother and then we will start on the male grandparents and the uncles for names and then probably wind up finally calling the latecomers after the best niggers in the squatter settlements. But the first boy—and the first child is bound to be a boy—will be named Jeff. Whereupon Jeff went to sleep, snoring slightly with his mouth parted in a smile, an opportunity which was not overlooked by one of the persevering little flies.

A good distance away, under another thorn, Kimani and Lathela lay dozing. The 'Ndrobo was snoring with his mouth gaped. Kimani was barely asleep. He was too angry to be all the way asleep. He kept thinking about the slap Jeff Newton had given him. His father had never cuffed him. No one had ever hit him in anger. A father who struck a son would be guilty of a grievous sin, because he would be, in Kikuyu family structure, guilty of striking his own father, since eldest sons are always named after their father's father and are formally addressed as "father."

Someday, Kimani said in his brain, I'll kill him for that. When I am bigger, a man full-grown. In the meantime I will learn all I can from the white bwanas, because they have many things we can use. And someday I too will have a Chevrolet and a wireless and perhaps a white man to come when I call "Boy!"

There is no difference between Peter and me, Kimani said to himself. Peter speaks Kikuyu and I speak English. Peter has been to school and I have been to school. My father is the friend of his father. We are the same age and would be circumcision brothers if he and I were of the same color and tribe. But Peter is white and I am black, so already he is the master and I am the servant. He is rich and lives in a big stone house and has a bicycle. I am poor and live in a mud-wattle hut and have no bicycle. Yet the land he lives on belongs to my people. So my father has told me of the old days, when the Kikuyu owned all the world on this side of the mountain, until the English came with guns and took the land, driving the Kikuyu ahead of them like stolen sheep.

Someday we will take the land back, Kimani thought, and I shall be a big chief and kill many of the white bwanas, and I will kill Jeff Newton first, for hitting me in the face. I won't kill Peter, though. I will let him be my overseer on my land and treat him very kindly, as his father has treated my father. But I will kill all the D.C.s and P.C.s. I will kill the whole Serkali. And I will have a motorcar to drive and wear a pith helmet and carry a rhino-hide kiboko in my hand. I will have guns and shoot elephants and lions, and maybe if Peter is obedient and serves me well I will let him shoot the guns once in a while. . . .

Kimani's wrath disappeared in the final fancy. He joined Lathela in dreams, although the dreams were dissimilar. Lathela was grinning broadly in his sleep. He dreamed that he had just discovered a beehive as big as the huge iron karibus on legs that lined the railroad tracks for the iron buffalo, the locomotives, to drink from when the train stopped. It was full of the finest honey, and there were no bees in it to sting him when he took it.

7

Back on Bushbuck Farm, old Karanja, Kimani's father, squatted on his heels in front of his thingira, the bachelor's hut into which no wife might enter. He was scratching with a stick at the hard-baked clay, and to his mild astonishment he saw that he drew a spear. He had not thought about spears for a long, long time. For many a year he had carried only a hand-polished stick, as badge of his informal office and also to lean on when he sometimes stood stork-like on one foot, his other foot braced comfortably in the hollow behind his knee.

How different it all is now, he thought. I do not understand much about it, but it cannot be very good. The children have no respect for elders. The young men hang about Nairobi, drinking and gambling. They have forgotten all the old ways, all the old good ways, and will not listen long enough to be taught. They know nothing of their people or of their people's law. They heed only the fool's talk of that Jomo Kenyatta, who has been across the seas to England. They join secret societies. They dance openly with young women, holding them obscenely as white men do. They wear white man's clothes and lie with whores. They will not work their land. Only the old men and women work the land. The young people go to Nairobi to loaf and plot and get drunk in the bazaars. Only the old men should be allowed the right to a beer drink. . . .

The thought of beer made Karanja thirsty. He clapped his hands, and his senior wife, Wangu, crawled backward out of her hut. Wangu was getting old, Karanja thought, as we all are getting old. It was only yesterday she was fat and young. Her breasts now were withered and hung like pouches on her chest, badly concealed by a cheap dress of shoddy cotton. The scar mark of carrying-thongs deeply dented her fore-head. Her back was bowed permanently from toting immense loads of potato tops, firewood, or thatching grass up the steep, winding trails of the high Kikuyu-land. She was of course well past breeding and no longer good to look at, but she was his first wife, she had been a good wife, and Karanja was fond of her. Because Karanja now was rich she wore thick necklaces of blue and red and white beads and many wristlets of copper wire bartered from the Masai. She no longer had to work very hard. The other wives carried the firewood and broke the ground for the maize and millet and yams. Karanja liked Wangu's beer, made of sugar cane or maize or honey. It was better than the beer of any of his other wives, but he was careful not to show too much preference lest he offend the others. At his age he could not afford to offend his other wives too often, else they might run away to lie with the younger men, and neglect their other, more important duties. Nor did he wish to pun-ish them for repeated runnings away. It was his pride that no wife of his had ever limped. He had never found it necessary to bind a hot stone behind their kneecaps to cripple the tendons and serve as a permanent reminder that a flighty wife was as useless as a cracked water jug.

"Bring me beer," he said. Wangu turned back to the hut and emerged with a calabash of beer. As she came toward him she glanced at the ground and shrieked. She stumbled and dropped the calabash, which burst on a stone.

"What is it?" Karanja asked in great fear. She pointed speechlessly. A hyena, doubtless drawn by the smell of food, had violated the com-pound the night before and had left his droppings near the hut. Wangu began to wail.

"Be quiet," Karanja said, although he too was trembling. "I will go and talk to the mundumugu. There is a thahu on this house. Perhaps some enemy has cursed us."

It was an accomplished tragedy. To break a household vessel was an omen of the most dreadful sort. To find the dung of a hyena near a dwelling was doubly bad. To have one occur as the result of the other constituted a thahu of the worst order and could only result from a curse. Unless the curse were removed by purging, some awful thing would swiftly occur, such as an epidemic of rinderpest to the cattle, or foot rot to the sheep, or a plague of locusts, or at least a death to some member of the family. The removal of the curse could be effected only by sacrifices of many fat rams and a purification ceremony by the mundu-mugu, or witch doctor. That was very expensive.

"I will go to see Waruhiu, the mundumugu," Karanja said again. "Calm yourself, woman. If there is a curse Waruhiu will remove it. We are rich in cattle and sheep and shillingi. I will go now to see the mundumugu."

Karanja grasped his stick and lurched to his feet from the squatting position from which he had not risen even at the scream of his wife. He reached into his thingira for an old goat-hide cape and placed a shape-less felt hat on his head. He walked a few hundred yards to the back of the compound and paused before a very old man squatted on the ground in front of his hut. The day was glowing warm, but the old man's bones were stiff and clammy. He wore a heavy monkey-hide cloak wrapped tightly round him. He looked like a cold and miserable baboon as he sat there, his skull covered with gray wool, and a few long white hairs, unplucked recently by tweezers, drooping from his chin. His pierced, vastly stretched ear lobes contained carven cylinders of wood, and a long fine-linked iron chain hung from his neck. Near at hand rested his medicine bag. Karanja jammed his staff into the ground, butt first, un-consciously. When the stick had been a spear, the sign meant he came peacefully, and the spear's point would have been capped with a puff of ostrich feathers. He joined the old man hunkered on the ground, and they spoke awhile of crops and weather.

Presently Karanja mentioned the evil omens of the day.

"When my wife went to fetch me beer," he said, "she saw the dung of a hyena upon the ground, whereupon she cried out in fright and dropped the beer gourd, which broke. Yesterday a vulture dipped low over my shamba and cast his shadow across the huts. I am fearful that some enemy may have cursed me and evil will come to my family or to my herds."

"Have you affronted anyone?" the old man asked. "Have you be-come unclean by contact with any person who may have transferred the thahu to you or to a member of your family?"

"How can I say?" Karanja spoke bitterly. "In these days, when one is forced to rub shoulders with 'Ndrobo and Kavirondo and white people and other men of evil, when the young people go to the bazaars to learn to drive cars and laugh at their elders, who can say whether one has become unclean? It may be that my eldest son, Kimani, has found a thahu in the mission school, where they teach against the old ways and give the young men Christian names."

"Where is Kimani now?" Waruhiu asked. "Is he here in the village?"

"No. He has gone on safari with the Bwana Kidogo Peter and the Bwana Mkubwa Jeff. They left yesterday in the Chevrolet."

The old mundumugu reached into his cloak and brought out a long, cow-tail-stoppered, glazed-clay flask. He spilled the shiny black mubagé beans into his palm and began to arrange them into heaps of twenty. The leftover beans he placed in little piles and then reshuffled them. He sat, wordless, for ten minutes. Then he spoke again.

"In the old days," he said, "any contact your eldest son might have with various people and things would be enough to cast a curse upon your house. But since the white man came things have changed. Old magic has thinned out its strength, as men become salted from the pox once they have recovered, and the pus from their sores is rubbed onto the healthy to prevent them from becoming sick. Familiarity breeds immunity from many things, and magic likewise replaces itself. The white man has a greater magic than I, in many respects, because he can drive an iron bird through the skies and he can heal in his white huts the ills that used to destroy our people like the Masai once killed our old people and children. It would take a very serious contact with uncleanliness to place a thahu in the body of a Kikuyu today. It would take a very great curse; a very great affront to the old laws. The curse is in your son, Kimani. I cannot say how it came to be, but it happened yesterday, after Kimani left to go on safari. Perhaps a snake crawled into his bed. Perhaps another man struck him and he did not return the blow. I do not know. I do not know even if I can remove the curse. New thahus have grown strong; old purification has grown weak. We shall have to wait until Kimani returns, and watch to see what evil befalls between now and his return."

"Is there nothing to be done to forestall the curse? Nothing that we can do to prevent a tragedy?"

"Something? In the old days, yes. Certain charms might ward off evil magic. Today, no. If the thahu is in a man, it must be driven out of that man with suitable ceremonies adapted to the present. In the meantime I might slay a goat and surround your huts with a magic line to ward off harm, but," the old man said, "personally I think it is a waste of a good goat. We will have to wait and see."

Karanja went away, but his heart was troubled. It would be a week or more before Kimani returned, and there was no way to find him or send him a message, even if the Bwana Mkubwa McKenzie would consent to go and look for him. Kimani might be anywhere, and lorries left no footprints on beaten paths. In the meanwhile he would have to wait and see. He was very much afraid. His stomach felt full of ants. His youngest wife, Mwange, was nearly due her time for a first child. What if she saw a snake before she came to bed in labor? What if a cook stone cracked? Piled atop the accidents of the vulture, the hyena, and the broken calabash of beer, anything might happen. Suppose she was delivered of twins? Suppose the baby came feet first?

Karanja rocked back down on his heels outside his bachelor hut, cast off his cloak, and reached for his snuff bottle. He tucked a fingerful of snuff under his lip and began to brood on the sad estate that had fallen on professional magic. From his earliest infancy the air around him, and especially the night air, had been populous with ghosts, both benign spirits and malicious imps, and his daily living full of omen and portent, good and bad. No morning sun shone, no moon shimmered over the hills but that some manifestation of the great God Ngai, and of the long-perished ancestors, and of evil spells cast by enemies, and of tokens calling for plague or famine, sickness or death, had not ridden on the wings of morning or clung to the cloak of night, to bewilder or frighten or to inspire joy or despair.

As a tiny boy Karanja had first scarecrowed the birds from the grain fields and later chased the wild pigs off the sweet potatoes and the arum-lily roots, and then he had graduated to tending flocks. Of all the things in his life, he remembered most keenly his circumcision ceremony; the first man—a Masai—he ever killed with the spear; his marriage; the death of his father, and finally, the coming of the white man. Each of these events had been foreseen and prescribed for suitably in terms of magic. He remembered the liar's ceremony in the lawsuit, and the scourging of the plague, and the preparation for war, and the preparation for childbirth, and the disposal of death. All had been accompanied by magic. There was no other way to live, except by magic, for the ghosts of the ancestors were everywhere, and a well-bought curse, especially if laid by the brotherhood of ironworkers, the smiths, could make a woman barren, or cause illness and death in a man, or kill a crop or ravage a herd with disease.

Two ceremonies Karanja recalled with the vividness of lightning before the rains. One was the test for lying, when two men, each accusing the other of spell-casting, had been subjected to the ultimate proof. They had already undergone the ordeal of the licking of the hot knife, so that he whose guilt was most apparent would scorch his tongue when the saliva dried up from the knowledge of fear. Neither man had burned his tongue, yet one man must be a liar, since two men cannot tell differing truths. There is only one truth, as there is only one God, Ngai.

The next test had been the trial of the gituyu, a sharp-toothed forest rodent whose tenacity in biting was famous. Each man had been subjected to the bite of the gituyu, its fangs fastening in the nostrils. It had bitten both men, one slightly, so that blood had merely trickled from his nostrils, and the gituyu had detached itself of its own accord. It had seized fiercely onto the second man and had to be forcibly removed. A certain guilt had been indicated on both sides; the council of elders could not arrive at a verdict, since it was clear that both men were lying, one telling a bigger lie than the other.

The next test was the ordeal of the goat. In this test a goat was beaten. Both parties were allowed a final chance to confess before beating the goat with clubs. After the goat was beaten, it was too late, and the liar would fall sick and surely die within six months. Two he-goats were led in, and the mundumugu bound their legs and smeared medicine into ears, nose, and eyes. Then each man took a club and beat his goat slowly to death. When the goat was crushed, bone by bone, it was thrown into the bush. Two months later one of the men was bitten by a black mamba and died. The elders found in favor of the other man and ordered penalties of fat sheep and cattle paid. Now the disputes were settled before the District Commissioners or in the court trials in the cities.

There is no more importance to a man's word, Karanja thought; it has no position in the law of the land. The white men swear on a thick black book of wisdom compiled by their elders, when they enter a court of law, but it cannot compete with the beating to death of a goat, when every crunching bone is the sound of a man's crunching bones, as he repeats with each blow, "As this goat dies, may I be broken in pieces as this goat is broken in pieces, if I be telling a lie."

"Nor," Karanja muttered half aloud, "can it compare with the githathi, the third oath for murder or stealing. No thick black book can extract the truth from a man like githathi."

Karanja, as a child, had eavesdropped a githathi trial, of one Kungo, accused of poisoning. He had peered horrified through the bushes of an out-of-the-way strip of land, because the ceremony was so awful in implication that it could not be conducted near land which was used in the cultivation of crops, for the evil of the oath symbol might spread to the crops and destroy them.

A small black, shiny stone with seven holes, each representing the orifices of the human body, had been placed on the ground. The witnesses were asked to pass grass stalks seven times through the holes, each time swearing: "If I tell a lie, let the symbol of truth kill me." While this took place, each of the tribal elders stuffed a piece of mokengeria creeper in his ears to protect himself against the evil of the symbol of the oath. Women were not allowed to take these oaths, women being fit neither mentally nor bodily to withstand an ordeal so potentially destructive that it affected not only the whole family but the clan as well. No man was ever known to tell a lie and live through this ordeal. Kungo had evidently lied, because he was trampled by a sick buffalo before the moon waned. The buffalo had stamped him into bleeding tatters.

Karanja also remembered the great epidemic that had nearly wiped out his village many, many years ago. Men's hair had fallen out. Pusy sores formed on their faces. They had run tremendous fevers, as hot to the touch as a stone long left in the sun. Then they had turned on their faces and died.

A very famous mundumugu had been summoned, and he had studied the situation. Then he had ordered runners to go to all the outlying villages and to tell every man, woman, and toddling child to capture one fly and bring it to the mundumugu beneath the ceremonial fig tree that grew near Karanja's village. They came in hordes from a hundred miles around, flies hived in their fists.

The mundumugu was waiting inside a circle of reverent elders under the sacred fig. A small boy held a young goat. The witch doctor slit open the goat's stomach and rubbed ointments into the hole. Each person approached in his turn and stuffed his fly into the goat's belly. When every person had placed his fly, the mundumugu sewed up the flap in the belly, and they took the living animal away, bulging and internally buzzing with flies. When they came to a suitable spot, near a spring, they buried the goat alive. Whatever disease had ravaged the land was thus imprisoned in the goat, cleansed by the flowing water above, and of course sickness departed the country.

Now, Karanja thought wryly, *the white mundumugus tell us to kill flies to avoid spreading pestilence,* as if it were something new.

It had been quite a long time since Karanja had thought about the very old days of careful prevention of evil. The more he thought of it, the more he regretted the sophistication that had come with the late years, as heat lightning comes with the false rain squalls. If tragedy comes, he thought, it may well appear in the hut of my youngest wife, Mwange, who is about to bear a child, her first child, and is hence very susceptible to thahu. Mwange, young, plump, jolly, and very, very expensive. She had cost him forty goats, a fat cow, two fat rams, two Indian-trade-store blankets, and one hundred and twenty shillings. He could not afford to lose her at those prices, even though he had more money hidden in the post office. Karanja got up again and went to where his sheep flock fed. He selected a young ram and took it to Mwange's hut, where he slew it with his panga. Then he dribbled its blood in a circle around the house. Holding the goat high, he dripped its blood on the roof, in case the evil should strike from the sky where the vultures soared, hidden from human sight until death brought them sliding down. Then he took some thongs of eland hide and bound them round the hut in order to contain the good and keep out the evil. Then he went back to his own hut and clapped his hands for beer. Wangu was not there to bring it. Mwange answered his call for brew, and when she came with a gourd, he noticed her belly swollen very big. This frightened him again. Everything was wrong. Suppose it was twins. By ancient law, first-born twins must be immediately killed. Karanja decided to get drunk. He had done his best to appease the spirits, and he could only wait until his eldest son, Kimani, came home again, to see where and how the disaster would strike, and try to compensate for it if he could. In the meanwhile, beer was good, and the evening was getting cold. He dragged a log onto his small, slumbrous fire and put on his cloak again. He took a long drink of the pombe and idly began to scratch in the soil with a pointed stick. Again, he drew a spear. . . .

8

The first spear was not to be forgotten, never to be forgotten. This first spear came after his circumcision ceremony, of course. That was what? Seventy seasons, seventy-five seasons ago? He couldn't remember, but it was more than thirty-five years as the white people estimated the time. What a silly way to mark it, because rains came twice a year and each rainy season counted a full span of life of its own. The crops were sowed and tilled and harvested, and the animals dropped their young to coincide with the rains, which came at such-and-such a time except when they were unseasonably late or very occasionally did not come at all.

The rains had just come to fuzz the soil with delicate green when they started to practice for the man-making ceremony. Karanja's blood was hot as pepper and raged in his veins like the waters in the lugas of the Boran country after the spring torrents. He had been dancing for months before, informal dances, but dances which invariably ended with the creeping into a hut with one of the young girls. It was all right to lie with a young girl so long as her second apron was not removed. But it was not enough; it did not fully satisfy a young man whose blood seethed and bubbled inside him, a young man greedy for a long-bladed spear and status as warrior. And for the women from whom the second apron could be torn and who could be easily bought for goats and cattle, won in combat with the Masai to the south.

Karanja was bravely attired to practice the steps of the kahura. He had painted himself all over, in the classic lightning pattern, with lime and ocher. His father had bought him iron rattles for his legs. His head was shaven smooth as a stone and painted as well. He had leggings of marabou-stork feathers, and he wore a black-and-white colobus-monkey-skin cloak, the gift of his circumcision sponsor. His father had given him a kilt of leopard skin, with the tail binding round his narrow waist as a belt. The kilt flapped dramatically when he danced, leaping high as a shot impala.

All the boys of his circumcision group were similarly dressed. After they had perfected the steps of the kahura they traveled as a band all over the country, dancing day and night, and wherever they went they were warmly greeted and given food, because Karanja and his brothers were the warriors of tomorrow and must be treated with eager hospitality and calculated respect.

During the final weeks prior to circumcision the boys came home to receive minute instructions from the mathanjuki, the circumcision master. The mathanjuki was, inevitably, the witch doctor. He built a magic arch of sugar-cane poles and banana leaves at the entrance to his house, through which no evil could pass. His home was then the scene of much feasting by the parents of the candidates, and the sponsors. The boys lived in a specially built hut in the bush, the girls in another. They called daily on the mathanjuki and his wife for instructions.

In these days the complete outline of living was taught the young men and women by the mathanjuki and his wife. *It was very good advice*, Karanja thought, *and I still remember it*. All the things that might bring thahu were listed: the curse of an enemy; the careless praising of crops or cattle; the enmity of a smith; eating the flesh of wild animals; accidentally allowing the milk from the breasts of a woman not his own mother to fall on a child; contact with death; the sight of a snake; a hyena's droppings within the compound; breaking a household vessel; cracking a cooking stone; sexual intimacy with a member of your own clan—on and on and on the list went, differing for men and women in particulars.

All the history of the Kikuyu tribe was recited; all the legends recounted. Industry was especially preached, because without industry a man could not have flocks and wives. If a man had no flocks, he could not sacrifice goats and sheep to propitiate his ancestors and through them the great God Ngai. Since each contamination by thahu called for the killing of an animal, and each planting, housebuilding, marriage, death, harvest, business transaction, or legal discussion demanded the slaughter of a sheep or goat or fat ram, a man must be constantly industrious in order that his flocks might swell.

A man's two salient duties were war and breeding. The warrior must at all times be prepared to give his life for the safety of his clan. He must marry early and he must accumulate as many wives as he can afford, otherwise his clan would soon perish. Wives were expensive, costing many goats and much beer and many cattle. A man must not lie with his wife for twenty-four months after the birth of a child, lest her milk fall on him and cause a thahu. Hence it was necessary to have many wives, since for more than twenty-eight months a man could not cohabit with his wife. Nor must he ever lie with his wife when a cow was about to calve, lest his wife give birth to a calf instead of a baby. Nor might they cohabit while meals were cooking, nor soon after a death in the family. The girls were especially warned about childbirth. Abortion and the necessary herbs for it were explained; if a pregnant woman see a snake, she must immediately take the brew of herbs or ergot from the maize and lose the child. If her first birth be twins, the children must be smothered or strangled. Similarly, if a child be born feet first, in breech presentation, it must be swiftly killed.

A woman, once married, was free to lie with any friend of her husband's, in her own private hut, but she must not run away for carnal love nor deny her body to her husband within the correct times for cohabitation. Any circumcision brother might demand the right to lie with his brother's wife, and the wife must submit, because the bonds of circumcision made a man one with his companions of the age group, just as the girls were as one in their age group.

A woman must obey her husband; must cook and carry for him; must brew his beer and tend his goats, keeping them in her hut for safety and warmth. But the husband must not abuse the wife and never beat her except for cause, such as laziness, nor must he force her to do heavy labor, such as felling trees, breaking ground for cultivation, or building huts. If a woman ran away from her husband once, her father must beat her and send her back, or the bride price would be forfeit. If she ran off twice and got clear away, then all the goats and sheep, plus their yield, must be returned to the husband. But if she were caught, she was beaten again and given one more chance. If she defected a third time, she was caught and thrown down. A small round stone was heated red-hot. It was tucked behind her knee, and her leg was drawn up over it and was bound to the thigh. When the seared tendons finally healed, she walked forever with a limp, but she did not run away again, because contact with her would bring thahu, and the mark of shame was deeply graven on her.

Both boys and girls were taught the tricks of clever manipulation of each other's sexual organs, because in this way they might bed before marriage without causing pregnancy. To become pregnant before marriage was a disgrace; a thahu entered both mother and child, and contact with either was pollution. Also, a fine of ten goats must be paid. Hence the girls must be given a second apron to bind tightly under the first, loose kirtle to protect the precious parts, and any man who attempted to remove the second apron was a wicked man, to be avoided. He was no better than a thief, because by seducing the girl and getting her with child he was attempting to cheat the father of the bride price, and the bride price constituted the social security which made an old man snug in his hut when he was far past his prime and could no longer fight. The wife of the mathanjuki pointed out to the girls that it was necessary to bed with many young men and to have much sexual relationship short of actual intercourse, for how else might a girl determine the man she wanted most to marry, and how else could the man decide on whom to spend his carefully schemed-for bride price?

The mathanjuki ended his long course of instructions with a stern lecture. No single thing was free in this life, he said, but must be worked for. If a man enjoyed privilege, he must be prepared to fulfill his obligations. He must obey the law. He must act always with dignity. He must not lie or steal, except to or from an enemy. He must remember always that the world on this side of the mountain belonged to the Kikuyu. He must pay strict attention to the council of elders. He must respect all his relatives and the relatives of his wife. He must at all times give aid to any member of his circumcision group. He must properly worship his ancestors and remember that in truth he is the father of his father. He must always remember that only by implicit trust and close co-operation with his clan and his tribe could he fend off the threat of hostile Masai and Nandi, of lion and drought, of evil spirit and famine.

Karanja remembered very well how all the grownups got roaring drunk the night before the circumcision ceremony. There was a big ngoma at the mathanjuki's lodge, with roasted sheep and a special maize beer that fermented in the stomach and maintained a constant, even drunkenness for days. The young candidates, however, did not drink or feast. They danced separately, the boys and girls, in front of their temporary huts in the bush, but they could hear the adult merriment going on in the village. When their parents and sponsors staggered out to collect them in the early dawn, the boys and girls were all whetted to a nervous knife edge.

The procession marched off to the icy river, and their ornaments and clothes were torn from their bodies, and they rushed naked to the stream. They sang the circumcision song and splashed each other, partly as ritual, but mostly so that their sexual organs would be numbed by the cold waters, in order that they would experience less pain from the circumciser's razor. As the sun broke they stepped from the river and marched up the hill to where a tremendous fire had been lit. The ceremonies started. The boys, each with a sponsor, were seated on the ground with their legs stretched out in front. The circumciser, a consecrated specialist with the round-edged razor, appeared for the first time. He was an old filthy man, wrinkled and bent, and so loaded with bangles and rattles and flapping with plumes that you could scarcely see the old man at all. He stopped in front of Karanja and with a swipe of the knife freed the foreskin, pinning it back with a sharp sliver of hardwood. Of course Karanja did not wince, moan, or even quiver. None of the boys perceptibly reacted to the pain. As each boy was circumcised, the circumciser threw the boy's cloak over his head and passed on to the next.

In a group a little apart, a woman circumciser was operating swiftly on the girls. Each girl sat flat on the ground, braced against the breast and bulwarked by the outstretched legs of her sponsor. The old woman was slower, in a much more painful operation, since it was necessary to remove the clitoris and also the two major lips. To stanch the blood, a small roll of soft, greased leather was pushed into the vagina. No girl screamed, flinched, or wept, for now they were women, rendered respectable and eligible for courtship and marriage. They were now wildly happy, even if it hurt, because no decent man would marry or even lie with uncircumcised girls, who were regarded as unclean and the source of a thahu. The removal of the clitoris destroyed the seat of preliminary sexual satisfaction; only the deeper, more profound act of marriage would satisfy the woman's urges, and surely she would not be harassed by purely sexual cravings when her husband was off in a war. Now she might bear children safely and more easily, with less chance of infection, less danger to the child. Truly, it was a great day for the boys and girls.

Now came the period of feasting and the ceremonial shaving. The boys had their heads scraped clean again. It was the last head-shaving they would have until they retired as warriors and became elders, fifteen or sixteen years later, when their sons and daughters also were circumcised. Now the boys would let their hair grow long, plaiting it into pigtails like the Masai, anointing it with fat and red ocher, the sign of the warrior. Now the boys would go to the smith with gifts and goats, to have their fighting spears forged and their short swords—simis—pounded thin in the fire and razor-honed on both cutting edges.

But first they would feast and dance and drink beer. The temporary initiation hut was burned down, and so was the sacred arch of leaves leading to the mathanjuki's hut. Many days later, when Karanja was taken back to his father's hut by his sponsor, his father smeared him with oil and touched his nose, feet, and chest with lime. A small goat was given him in apology for any reprimand his father might have bestowed on him as a boy. Then he went off to snore in the thingira—the bachelor hut—because he had become a warrior and a man and no longer was allowed to sleep in a woman's hut with girls and goats.

Karanja's spear and sword had cost his father many fat goats and much honey beer, because iron was dear and must be bought in the market at Karatina; charcoal had to be furnished and the smith over-well paid for his work, lest he curse you. But it was a fine spear, and Karanja seemed to have been created especially to throw it. He had practiced all his life with throwing sticks. The heavy iron spearhead now gave potency to the act and swift meaning to the wood. He practiced for hours daily, throwing with a quick, petulant flip of the wrist. The spear would spin and whistle like a sand grouse as it flew through the air, darting to earth on a slant, to bury itself in the target. He practiced also with the bow and arrow, for the Kikuyu had learned the trick of poisoned arrows from their outcaste cousins, the Athi, the wild men who hunted in the forests and who ate the meat of wild animals without suffering thahu. Karanja also practiced fighting with the simi, the short stabbing sword, pretending such ferocity against his circumcision brothers that one of the duelists was nearly always cut, and the wound had to be treated with herbs and stuffed with spider webs and bound with bark.

Karanja had been a young warrior for a year when he met his first battle, a cattle raid against the Masai on the Laikipia Plain. A small band of Masai warriors was escorting flocks and families to a new reserve on the Loita Plains to the south, and the Kikuyu were brave and strong that year. Scouts brought word of the emigration; the Kikuyu prepared an ambush. Muffling their war rattles with grass, they lay in wait for the Masai and fell upon them with the stealthy ferocity of leopards. These Masai were the first Karanja had ever seen. They were tall, thin-nosed, handsome men, the same sort of people from whom Karanja had inherited his delicate features and lighter color. They were slim brown men, painted fancifully in red ocher and blue and white clay, their faces daubed scarlet. They wore their ochered and fat-greased hair long, some in ancient page-boy bobs, others in short pigtails, still others with the hair clubbed and tied at the back of the neck. They wore lion-mane and ostrich-feather headdresses, for each Masai moran must kill his lion before he is accounted a man. Karanja had heard of how the Masai hunted lions, the beast surrounded and driven toward a lone youth, who accepted the full, roaring charge on his shield, falling under the goaded lion, while others seized the lion's tail and stabbed at him with spears and simis. A man must be very brave to fight a lion thus, Karanja thought as the Kikuyu ambush party crept through the green fleshy leaves and tangled, ropy lianas of the thick forest.

The ambush was spectacularly successful. The Masai were outnumbered five to one, and the element of surprise was with the Kikuyu, who had been extensively purified and treated with a magic to make them invincible in war. They had drunk blood and honey and various medicines which caused enemy spears to splinter into matchwood and sharp knives to blunt harmlessly on bodies. They had passed beneath the secret war charm which none but warriors ever saw and they had trodden on the sacred anthill, and each warrior had been personally spat upon by the mundumugu. They were invincible, immune from harm.

The Masai were sleeping when the Kikuyu crept upon the encampment just before dawn, and when the sun's first pale light struck upon the buffalo-hide war shields, the Kikuyu unstuffed their war rattles and surged upon the camp like a visitation of locusts. They screamed and leaped high in the air, killing the sentries, filling the manyatta with a thundercloud of noise, a slashing torrent of arrows and spears. The Masai moran fought back valiantly, seizing their spears and shields, knives and knobkerries, but the Kikuyu magic was too strong. They smothered the manyatta as maggots cover a carcass.

Karanja killed two senior moran that day. One he slew by hurling his spear at the Masai's tawny back as the man faced about to meet another of the Kikuyu njamas. The spear took the Masai under the shoulder blade, passing through him and embedding its point in the underside of the white shield he held before his breast for protection. The other Karanja stabbed with his simi, grappling the lean, greased Masai warrior, falling to the ground and forcing the Masai's knife away from his own breast, while pressing the point of his own blade steadily against the Masai's pulsing throat. Ever so slowly the tensile strength of the Masai's hand on his own wrist quivered and receded before his superior weight and thews, because the Masai, while brave as outcaste bull elephants, were as fragilely slim as women, as frail as impala ewes. Only when they attacked in massed battle array, with shields and spears, were they invincible. The point of Karanja's simi pressed against the Masai's throat, denting without piercing. Karanja summoned all his strength in one mighty surge, and the simi's point emerged in a spout of blood from the back of the Masai's neck. Karanja twisted the blade, right and left, and severed the Masai's head from his shoulders.

When the warriors were all down, the Kikuyu njamas went from man to man, killing the wounded with clubs or severing heads with a slash of simi or spear. No Masai cried out or asked for mercy. Most of the wounded men managed to gather a mouthful of saliva in order to spit into the faces of the Kikuyu who poised a spear or sword over their lives. There was no real enmity, only admiration, among the warriors. Under similar circumstances the Masai always did the same. A warrior's business was to kill other warriors, and the weaker warrior died.

After the fighting men were finished off, the Kikuyu war party turned its attention to the older men, the women, and the children. One group of warriors stayed to round up the cattle and goats and sheep. Other bands split off to sniff the forest for the Masai who had fled when the battle began. The search was easy, for only the very young, the very old, and the women had run away. Each was methodically hunted out. The male children were struck down with clubs and the male babies killed by seizing them by the heels and bashing their heads against a tree or rock. The female children were brought back, trussed with creepers. The old men and the old women were killed where they were found. The younger women were also tied up and returned to camp. They would be absorbed into the tribe as slaves. The young girl children would be reared as true Kikuyu, and their eventual bride price would go by strict apportionment to the men who had made the cattle raid, just as the loot of sheep and goats and cows would be rationed according to seniority, rank, and battle performance.

Karanja ran down and caught one young girl of about fourteen years old. She was very comely, he thought as he seized her and threw her to the ground. Her breasts were small and firm, her legs long and shapely—not like the thick, crooked legs of the Kikuyu women—and her eyes were huge and frightened, like a wounded animal's eyes. Karanja, heated to unbearable excitement by the blooding of his spear, leaped upon her, cuffed her half unconscious, struck down her clawing hands, and dragged her legs apart. Bloody, exalted with blood, he mounted her body and took her brutally. It was his first complete penetration of a woman, totally different from his frustrating experiences with the Kikuyu girls as they bedded together after a dance. As he lay panting on her body, spent and quivering, he determined to have this woman for his own, as his spoil of war. The Masai girl saved him further trouble. She pretended unconsciousness and then suddenly snatched his simi from its scabbard. She aimed a mighty stroke at his back as he lay atop her, and just as the sword descended, by accident he moved slightly to the right. The sword just grazed his side, but the force of the blow carried the simi half its length into the girl's breast. She quivered. Her mouth opened, gasped, blood came, and then she died. Karanja rolled completely off her, slipped the simi from the wound, wiped it on the girl's thigh, and walked away. The dead Masai girl lay almost invisible in the grasses. The hyenas would have her later, with Karanja's seed still swimming inside her. He would need a special purification from the mundumugu when they returned to the village with the cattle and the captives.

Ah, Karanja thought, *how an old man remembers.* He is no longer hot in the loins. He is no longer mad for blood. He sits in the sun, or before the fire, and thinks only about the past. It is strange how one remembers little things like the Masai girl and forgets the big things, except for a few. He had not thought about the Masai girl for years. He had not thought about the Masai men for years, either, because it had been a long time now since the Masai and the Kikuyu fought each other . . . fought each other happily, almost, in those days, creeping up on each other's villages, stealing each other's cattle, killing each other. None of this was *allowed* any more. The white man disapproved of killing, although the white man had engaged in two big wars across the seas within Karanja's memory and had taken Kikuyu men to work in the labor battalions in both of the wars. Karanja smiled a little. He remembered how, in this new war that was still going on, the young men of Kikuyu had heeded the war horn of the Crown and had eagerly swarmed into Nairobi to enlist. Not so the Masai. Not since their treaty of peace had been signed with the white men and the broad grazing lands to the south had been given them. The white lords had harangued the Masai when the war came with the Germans and the Italians, bidding them to fetch their spears and lion manes and their buffalo shields to fight for the white men.

"Oh no," the Masai chiefs had said. "We must not fight. Fighting is very wicked. *You* have told us so. Our laibons have signed treaties to say that we will fight no more. Also, we have no buffalo-hide shields. Shields are not permitted any more to the Masai, lest they invoke unpleasant memories of the warring past. We are men of peace, made so by Crown law. We do not fight. We bear no grudges. We wish only to tend our herds and live in peace."

There had not really been much that the English could say to that. The Kikuyu went away to fight, and the Nandi fought, and the Kavirondo and the Wakamba fought, but the Masai did not fight. They were men of peace—the Masai, fiercest of all the warriors, drinkers of blood and milk, curdled in wood ash and urine; men of the long-bladed spears; men who used to scourge the land for hundreds of miles around, killing all and burning everything as they passed. The Masai now were men of peace, by Government order.

How strange it all is, Karanja sighed, reaching out for his beer. The fighters no longer fight. The tillers of the soil go away on big boats from Mombasa to fight strange red people all the way across the sea, but the Serkali does not allow us to fight with each other. The Serkali does not wish us to dance. The Serkali says that it is wicked to circumcise our women. And the Serkali makes us carry a kipandi, a working card, with our fingerprints stamped on it, or we are put in jail for the sin of not smudging the card. What a strange people they are, the white bwanas, to go so far to fight people they do not know, and never to bring back a single goat or sheep as a prize of conquest.

9

But there was one who was different. The Bwana Mkubwa, Henry McKenzie, the Bwana Mbogo, he used to be called, because he was as big and burly and as strong as the buffalo, and as dangerous. For most of his manhood the Bwana had been Karanja's friend.

He remembered when the Bwana Mbogo first came to Kikuyu. He had come like a nomad from the North, like a Samburu, bearing his few possessions in an oxcart. He had a gun and one wife who was small and weak and for whom the Bwana constantly fetched and carried. Karanja had not understood it then. Now, of course, he knew that the white women owned a very potent magic which enabled them to rule their men; which made their men as weak as women and as meekly tractable as slaves. This magic came from a hidden water source inside the white women. Through some magic the white women could screw up their faces and bring forth great freshets of water from their eyes, while they made mournful sounds with their mouths, like the doves calling to each other at nightfall in the forests. This magic water had the power of placing panic in the white men and made them as docile as ewe lambs for days. He, Karanja, had hunted elephants and lions and buffalo with the Big Bwana. He knew once that the Big Bwana had killed a Kikuyu with his hands. The Big Bwana had a fist that could stun a steer.

But he had seen his Big Bwana become panic-stricken at the slightest sign of distress or disapproval from the Memsaab.

They are all so very rich, Karanja thought. At first I never understood it, why they didn't take more women, so that they could breed more children and so that the women could work for them. But now I know that they do not know how to make women work, and so if a man had five wives he would have to work five times as hard as a man with one wife in order to please the five wives. Yet they lie always with each other's women and occasionally shoot each other or the women when the fact of lying with another's woman is discovered. It makes no sense. A woman is valuable, and to shoot her for sleeping with another man is as foolish as killing a cow because her calf is sired by another bull than your own. You still own the calf. A woman is made to lie with; women are tireless creatures who can accommodate many men, while a man can barely satisfy one woman with any frequency. But now they tell us it is wicked to own more than one woman. You cannot be married in the Christian Church, they say, if you have a wife already. What are we to do with those other wives if we wish to follow the teachings of the Bwana Jesus? Turn them out to starve, perhaps? Is this the teaching of the Bwana Jesus Christ?

Karanja had to admit that life with the Big Bwana had been good. Good from the very day the Big Bwana had come to his village. Karanja had been very sad. An epidemic of the pox had nearly finished the tribe. Karanja had just taken a wife, who had died, together with the child with whom she was pregnant. There was much change and trouble in the land. The red-faced foreigners had come to claim the country. The city of Nairobi was growing swiftly, and very ugly, as they ran the iron game trails through the country, from Mombasa to Lake Victoria. Many strange little plump dark men called Indians had come on the ships from another far country and were setting up shops called "duccas," where most of the trading now was done instead of in the market places, where a woman might spread her skins and tobacco and beans and maize on the ground, so that all could see their excellence, where she could sell her pots and other handiwork directly to some other clan in return for whatever specialties that other clan had to offer. Little bright bits of metal called "rupees" first, and later "shillingi," had come to use, and trading was no more direct. At first, when the red-faced white bwanas had come to get men to work on the roads and in the fields of big shambas, they had paid in these bright bits of metal. One man, Karanja remembered, had saved the bits until he had hoarded enough to take to the smith to make a sword. But when the smith made it, it was beautiful and gleaming as the full moon on water, but it was so soft it would not cut, and it crumpled, the blade bending on the tenderest piece of wood. Some people buried the bright bits of metal, and others merely threw them away. It was a long time before everybody understood that these bits could be exchanged for blankets and even sheep and goats, and that also they bred like sheep and goats. If you trusted the man at the post office, he would take the metal from you and put it in a cave. After a while it would breed, and when you went back next year there was more metal than before. But it did not increase as swiftly as sheep or goats, and besides, there was no pleasure in thinking about little bits of metal in another man's cave. You could count goats and sheep and watch them increase, and you could take them with you into the hut at night, to be safe from the leopards and hyenas. You could hear them stirring in the warm, smoky dark of the hut, and smell how clean and beautiful they were. Also, there was no way to kill a shillingi in order to appease the spirits.

How young I was, how untaught in the new way of living, when the Big Bwana came that first day to the village, when I had burned down the hut of my dead wife, and had taken her to the fields for the hyenas, and had slain my last skinny ram as a sacrifice to exorcise the thahu of death. I was what the white bwanas call a savage, a young njama with plaited, ochered pigtails, a blooded spear, but no wife, no herds, and nobody to fight, either.

I remember the Big Bwana was wearing funny clothes, little short pants above his knees, big stout sandals, and a yellow-colored cloak with bright shiny metal things stuck into loops on his chest. He took off his hat to fan himself, and the top half of his head was as white as the belly of a fish, while the bottom half was as red as an ocher pit where the women go to dig clay for paint. He had a shiny metal thing with a wooden handle in the crook of his arm, a thing with two hollow metal canes growing out of the wood. It was too short to serve as a staff and too heavy to throw. I wondered why he bothered with it at all.

How young, how very stupid I was. That day a leopard came in the dusk and slew a young bullock. The Bwana would not let it be butchered, although the flesh was sure to rot. He said, as best he could, with many signs, that we must hoist the bullock into a tree and build a boma beneath the tree and off to one side. He had a man from Mombasa, a light-colored man called a Swahili, with him, and the Swahili explained that the Bwana thought it was better to expend one young bull and kill the leopard than to butcher the bull to eat and allow the leopard to come and kill and kill again, further depleting the herds that were already ravaged by sickness. The Swahili said that the Bwana wanted some young man to go and sit with him in the thorn boma, to wait for the leopard to come again, some man who was good with a spear, and he looked directly at me. I did not know what I was doing, but I stepped forward. The Big Bwana touched me on the shoulder and nodded his head. We hung the bullock in the tree, and when the sun began to sink we went and crouched inside the thorns. Just before the sun disappeared over the crater, we heard the monkeys scream and the baboons bark, and we heard the leopard growl. He bounded into the tree and stood on a branch near the dead bullock. The Bwana pointed the metal canes at the leopard, and fire and thunder came out of the end of the canes, and the leopard tumbled down. I was too paralyzed to move. I had never imagined magic like this, although I had been told that the white men had a way of killing by calling up thunder and lightning. I sat there and shook and shivered. The Bwana patted my shoulder and beckoned to me to go to the leopard. It was lying on the ground, and I could not see if it was dead, so I threw my spear and pinned it through the shoulders, but it was already dead. There was a little hole in its shoulder, no bigger than the hole in a whistling thorn, an inch away from my spear, and much blood on the ground. I did not really have to throw my spear, because the Bwana's magic could kill without the aid of a spear. The Bwana told me to climb the tree and cut down the bullock. That night we feasted off the dead bullock and were very happy, because the leopard would never come again, and if a member of his clan came again, the Bwana could point the metal canes at him and we would have another feast. I was a very simple young man, Karanja thought, not to know that the metal canes were the barrels of a gun, and that it was not actually the magic that killed but the big *noise* of the gun.

The Bwana came often to my ridge, and always I waited anxiously to see him come. He would come to get men to work on a shamba he was clearing. He would come to bargain for food. One day he came and he said to me: "Karanja, I need a man to be a njama on my shamba, to guard my wife from harm, to go with me into the forests to hunt elephant, and to serve as chief of the people on my shamba. You have no wife to tend your flocks. You have no flocks, even if you had a wife to tend them. Come with me, and I will give you many shillingi, and someday you can buy a new wife and new flocks and be the chief of your own shamba, on my shamba."

I did not know what to say. The Athi, our cousins, hunted in the forests and ate the flesh of wild animals, but they were outcaste Kikuyu and had their own special gods. It was very dangerous to incur the wrath of the Athi, because next the smiths theirs was the most powerful magic of all, and besides, they were cunning in the forests and made poison from gum trees. Nor did I know what thahu would enter my body if I went away to work for the Bwana. I was a warrior, but I had nobody to fight, and no flocks to protect, and my wife was dead. A warrior with nobody to fight is less than a woman. I went to see the mundumugu to ask his advice.

We have come a long, long way, the Bwana and I, since that day the mundumugu told me to go with the Bwana, that the times were changing and the white masters would rule the country for a long time and that they would no longer tolerate war and cattle raids; that they disapproved of night-long dancing, because it filled the men with unrest; that to marry many women was wicked if a man was to become a Christian, and a man must become a Christian because by order of the Serkali the Christian God now sat on the mountain Kerinyagga and ruled the world. The Christian God's magic was much stronger than the magic of Ngai, and the Christian God had doubtless vanquished Ngai in battle, as the first man, Gikuyu, once vanquished the great rainbow who was also a snake and who still lived in the water that white men now call Thomson's Falls.

We were very poor, the Bwana and I, when we first started to work on our land. The Bwana worked like a woman at the crops. He made me do things that no warrior should do without disgrace, such as plowing and pulling up stumps and tending cattle. When we went into the forests and up on the great hot plains past Isiolo to hunt elephants for the ivory and the shillingi the ivory brought, I ate the flesh of wild animals and was greatly afraid of the thahu that the eating of wild flesh might bring: it brought nothing, except to make me stouter and stronger. Very slowly we gained an advantage over our land, the Bwana and I, and soon I was able to go back to my village and buy a wife, Wangu, who was strong and fat and comely. But there was a thahu on Wangu, and for years she did not conceive, although she lay with my circumcision brothers, and hence the fault of sterility could not be attached to me. The thahu was in her womb, because one day she became very sick with great sharp pains like thorns in her stomach, and although we slew sheep and bought many charms, she wasted and weakened until she was thin as a rinderpested cow, and so ill that she could barely bring firewood and potato tops. That was when the white Memsaab came to look at her and insisted that she be taken to Nyeri for the white mundumugu who lived in a bad-smelling white hut to purify her with a knife. I gave Wangu up for dead when they took her from me and put her in a room where young girls, both Kikuyu and white, rushed back and forth. They were dressed in white kanzus and they stuck a little stick in Wangu's mouth, took away her clothes, and put her on a couch that rose and fell like the ocean when somebody turned a handle round and round. Then the white mundumugu came and defiled my wife by placing his hand inside her body, shaking his head and saying incantations. Finally they took her to another room where no one but the witch doctor and two of the witch doctor's assistants were allowed to enter. Wangu told me later that they placed a charm over her face and a horrible odor came from it; that soon she fell asleep and dreamed fearfully of sorcery unknown to our people. She dreamed that the white witch doctor took a panga and cut her stomach open, and that he slew the various devils which lived in her belly, and took them out, and threw them away, and then he took a big iron needle and sewed her up again as a woman stitches a garment. When she awakened she was very sick for a long time, and her stomach pained her greatly, for the doctor had wrestled mightily with the demon who lived in Wangu's belly, and his dwelling place had been torn down, as men tear down a hut in which an evil sorcerer lived. There could be no doubt of the power of the witch doctor's magic, because Wangu got fat again, and the scars on her belly were marveled at by all the people in her clan as proof that the white witch doctor's magic was so strong that he could cut open a woman to let the demon out, and the woman still might live.

Soon after Wangu came out of the hospital, fat and well enough to tend the fields and mind the goats and make beer again, her menses stopped flowing and she gave me Kimani, my first child, a fine strong boy, and many other sons and daughters.

But the white witch doctor's power was not enough to fight against the devils that beset the white Memsaab. Perhaps the thahu that he drew out of Wangu's belly entered into the white Memsaab, for her babies died and finally she died as well, when the Bwana and I were off in the desert country hunting elephants. Perhaps if the Bwana and I had been here we might have slain the thahu with the Bwana's gun, as we slew the big elephants for their teeth. But that is how Wangu became the foster mother of the little Bwana Peter, and that is why my son, Kimani, and the little Bwana Peter are brothers. That is why they are off on safari with the Bwana Jeff today, and I wish they would return so that the mundumugu might purify Kimani of the thahu which has fallen on him and which threatens the safety of our family and herds.

It would be terrible, Karanja thought, if the thahu were so powerful that it might bring back the days as they were after the first war, when the Great Famine swept the entire world, even beyond Mombasa, and the Bwana could not make the payments on his shamba, and the cattle sickened, and there were the droughts, and the locusts came like low clouds to eat the crops, and the cattle sicknesses crept in from the Masai country and killed all the fat oxen and the milch cows. Perhaps we may have no home and no wives once more, and we must rove the parched land like the Samburu and the Rendille in the North. *I did not like those days,* Karanja thought, when we lived by the Bwana's gun and my spear, and there was no maize for the posho pot, and the Bwana Shillingi Mingi, the man with the shamba in Nairobi where the money harvest flourishes, came and told the Big Bwana that he must take the farm away because the Bwana could not make any more payments. But the Bwana's magic was more powerful than the Bwana Shillingi Mingi's magic. The Bwana placed a curse on the money shamba in Nairobi, and soon he was able to pay off the debt and remove the curse. That is when we began to get rich, and I bought more wives, more sheep, more cattle, and began to hide shillingi in the post office cave to breed for me. We have had a good life, the Big Bwana and I, although it certainly was not a warrior's life, and many of the old good things have passed. There are some other good things to replace them, perhaps, because my son, Kimani, has been reared as an English gentleman is reared, and he speaks English and may someday be a powerful chief among our people. Perhaps if the Big Bwana will argue in his behalf he may even become clerk to the Provincial Commissioner in Nairobi. In any case, the Big Bwana considers Kimani a son, as he considers the little Bwana Peter a son. It is a fine thing to be considered as the Big Bwana's son in times like these, when the young men have become like the 'Ndrobo, the wild men who live in the hills and rob bee trees and steal, except that now they rob strangers of money in Nairobi and are constantly drunk among the harlots in the bazaars.

I *wish* Kimani would come home, the old man said, and went into his thingira to sleep.

10

Mwange's baby came before Kimani returned from the safari. She lay on her low cot of skins in the maternity hut only a week after the men had gone away to hunt. The pains surged regularly. Two withered old women of her clan sat with her. The child, a boy, came easily, for Mwange was young and healthy and well circumcised. But the thahu was there. The child was born feet first, as Karanja had feared. The two midwives took one horrified look at the baby's feet, withdrew the child hurriedly, and cut the umbilicus. Then one of them smothered the child with a goatskin. The thahu was fulfilled. Neither the slain sheep nor the eland thongs drawn tightly round the hut had been able to ward off the curse which came through Kimani, the eldest child of Karanja. The hyena's droppings and the broken beer gourd had correctly heralded the disaster.

Henry McKenzie walked into Karanja's compound as Karanja was tearing down the mud walls of his wife's hut, pounding the plaster into bits with a mattock. The thatch, the ridgepoles already were crumbling into ash and ember.

He placed his hand on Karanja's shoulder, grasping it gently.

"The baby?"

"It came feet first," Karanja said. "It is dead. We placed it in the field for the hyenas last night. A thahu was transferred to my wife, Mwange, and the baby came feet first. Mwange's hut is contaminated." He inclined his head, and Henry McKenzie's hand dropped from his shoulder.

"God damn it, Karanja," Henry McKenzie said. "You cannot kill your children any more just because they are born wrong-end-to. The Serkali doesn't permit it. I am not going to permit it. I'm not going to turn you in to the P.C. for murder, but you know the word will get to

Nyeri, and there will be policemen here. What can I do? You put me in a hellish position."

"The baby was cursed with a thahu," Karanja said. "The thahu came through Kimani. Kimani was not here to be purified. The baby was born wrong. It died. The curse must be removed, or other things will happen. What would you have me do, else?"

He struck his own chin with his palm.

Henry McKenzie shook his head.

"When the P.C. has you into court in Nyeri to run you for murder, there will be some more thahu, some big thahu. If they don't hang you and the old women, you'll certainly go to jail for a long time. There's your *real* thahu. I just hope to God that the people around here keep their mouths shut, which they certainly won't. In any case, I'm dreadfully sorry. How's Mwange?"

"Her heart is sick. Her body will recover. But there is a curse upon her as well, and I shall not lie with her until it can be removed. I shall not lie with her, nor eat of her cooking, nor drink of her beer, because she is accursed, and the thahu comes indirectly to her through my son, Kimani. This has been told to me by Waruhiu, the mundumugu."

"Christ," Henry McKenzie said to himself, aloud, in English. "In England they have television, but here they still strangle the babies." In Kikuyu he said, "I shall help you all I can when the police come. And the police will surely come."

The law was not over-long in coming. The Bwana P.C. drove up to Bushbuck Farm one day and climbed out of his car. Henry McKenzie was sitting on the veranda, smoking his pipe.

"Well, Henry," the Bwana P.C. said. "Could you give a bloke a cool beer?" He stood hesitantly on the steps.

"Sure," said Henry McKenzie. "Nice to see you, Noel. I imagine I know what you've come about. Come and sit. Boy! Letti beer-i kwa Bwana!"

The Bwana P.C. was a long, lean, gray, sad man who wore his pipe welded to his mouth. He suffered from recurrent malaria and also from a chronic inability to convince anybody in Government that civilization of the Kikuyu was not merely a matter of giving a man a pair of khaki pants, pointing out a school and a church, and calling the civilization process closed. He sat down in a low rocker and accepted his cool beer from the servant, and looked at the misty blue hills for a bit before he spoke.

"I'm here about the dead-baby business," he said. "It only took a day for my boys to have all the gen in their quarters. There's a curse on Karanja's house, they say; the baby was born upside down, and the baby was killed. No—don't interrupt.

"Some of these things the Kyukes do must stop. Baby-murder is one of them. You're the biggest Bwana in these parts, Henry. Your man Karanja is the biggest Wog in these parts. The others look to him. If we're ever going to get these damned people all the way down out of the trees we've got to take some steps where they'll count. You're too cozy with your blacks, Henry. Sometimes I reckon you think like they do."

Henry McKenzie sucked at his pipestem and said nothing. There was really nothing to say. The Bwana P.C. seemed ill at ease.

"I came in person before the police officially arrived because I wanted to talk to you about this thing," the Bwana P.C. said. "I'm going to run Karanja and the two old midwives and I'm going to try the whole bleeding lot for murder. This business has got to stop if we're ever going to get anywhere. The next you know they'll be dancing the old dances again and off we go."

"You can't try Karanja for murder," Henry McKenzie said. "He'd nothing to do with it. He wasn't in the hut when the baby was born. For all I know, the brat was born dead."

"Look here, my dear good man," the P.C. said. "I've lived hereabouts as long as you. The child was born feet first. There was a thahu on the house. The old women either strangled or smothered the child and chucked it out for the hyenas. This makes your Number One at least an accessory in a murder, and it makes murderesses out of the midwives."

"I suppose you intend to try the mother, too, for the crime of having borne the baby upside down?" Henry McKenzie sounded bitter. "What in the name of God Almighty are you trying to do with these people? You tell them to quit killing the Masai and not to dance the big dances and don't circumcise the women. You teach 'em to read and write and don't give 'em anything to use it on. The men who used to be warriors are spivs in Nairobi. The wenches want lipstick and jazz-dance halls. On the very few shambas that try to operate in the old way, there's a Government howl every time they slaughter a goat for a powwow. You take away all the old stuff and you don't give them anything to replace it with. They've always killed upside-down babies and first-born twins. You're going to call this murder? You're going to correct it by putting

Karanja in jail, p'aps, and maybe hanging the two old hags that only did what a thousand generations of old hags have always done?"

"Precisely. Things have changed since we came here, Henry. Like it or not, the Kyukes at least are going to have to live in a white man's world. This is white man's country, the Highlands. A little white island in a bloody great black sea. It's all right for the Masai to run around naked and drink blood, on their own ground, with their own tsetse flies, and we will leave the old Turkana and the Samburu alone up in the N.F.D., because nobody else wants it. One of these days the Kikuyu, the Nandi, and the Wakamba will get civilized and want to kick us out and run this country."

"God forbid." Henry McKenzie gazed upward in mock reverence.

"God forbid or God not forbid, it's going to happen. I don't suppose you ever heard of evolution, but it's a process that has been happening for some time, and in my district, man, in the interests of evolution, there is going to be an end to those big circumcision dos that're always going on, and an end to baby-killing, and an end to blood prices when some wild-eyed Wog gets himself full of pombe and scrags his chum, and an end to as much of this witch-doctor mumbo-jumbo as I can tread on. And I am starting to tread on some of it with your boy, Karanja." The Bwana P.C. smacked his fist in his palm.

"It'll kick up a bloody great row with the Wogs—the bush Wogs, I mean, and also the political ones. That fellow Kariuki and that Pommie-fied ass, Kenyatta, just want something like this to set their teeth in. And it'll do me out of my best man, as well, for as long as you can keep him in clink."

"Can't be helped, old boy. There's been enough town talk about the way you run your shamba, and this business'll practically make you a Kikuyu. 'Come to Henry McKenzie's farm and be a noble savage in the best old Rousseau fashion,'" the P.C. said, raising his voice to a sarcastic falsetto. "'Come and live with Henry McKenzie, the white Kikuyu. Come and watch the lovely, interesting circumcisions of the young maidens, and get drunk at the illegal dances, and step lively this way for the baby-smothering.'"

"I'd watch my mouth if I were you, Noel," Henry McKenzie said. "We've been much too good friends for much too long for me to have to chuck you off my front porch. Why don't you have another beer?"

"I'm sorry, Henry. Truly. I didn't really mean it that way. But God damn it, man, they're always at me about this thing, and it makes one nervy. Beg pardon. And I'll have the other half before the police come."

"You're really serious? You're going to arrest Karanja and the old women, haul 'em into a pukka court, swear 'em on the Bible, and chuck a proper murder thing at 'em?"

"I am, Henry, so help me, that I am. This voodoo business has got to stop. Asante sana, Juma." The Bwana P.C. smiled at the servant, taking the fresh beer bottle. "These people are sliding back into a way of doing that we've spent forty years trying to change, and I don't like it. I don't like it a bloody bit. And you don't help me any here."

"Pity we came at all, you know," Henry McKenzie said. "They had it pretty well sorted out before we got here. The Masai killed the Kyukes, and the Kyukes killed the Masai, and the lions ate both, and smallpox and famine and drought kept 'em pretty well tamped down. There was plenty of room for everybody then. To my mind, a monkey's a monkey, and whilst you can teach him some tricks, he's still a monkey when all's said and done. I say let 'em alone, within reason."

"What's 'within reason,' for Christ sake? I've ulcers from trying to define '*within reason*.' You must start somewhere. The noble savage is finished. And one of the first steps in converting the heathen is to teach him that he can't go around coshing his own kids. Selling his daughters is bad enough, even if it's logical, and clobbering a goat every ten minutes in the dark of the moon, but God Almighty, man, murder is murder. Murder means killing people. There are laws against it, and I'm paid to enforce the laws. Not that I like it, in the strictest letter of it."

"Enforce away then, chum," Henry McKenzie replied. "Put everybody in jail. But put Kenyatta and all the trade-union boys in as well. At the same time I suggest that you put the Norfolk bar and the New Stanley Grill on limits for niggers and start calling them all 'mister.' Because when you do one you've got to do the other, and I can see my old skinner, Gathiru, sitting in the Legislative Assembly next year as the new member from Rumuruti. But you'll have to buy him some pants first. And possibly shoot three or four of his wives so's he won't be a bigamist."

An official station wagon drove up, raising a long plume of dust. Two Australian-hatted Negro members of the Kenya police and one bereted white policeman were in the car. The white policeman got out, walked to the veranda, and saluted.

"I believe you know young Les Darcy," the Bwana P.C. said to Henry McKenzie. "Charlie Darcy's boy."

"How do you do," Henry McKenzie said. "Come and have a beer. Send your boys back to the shambas and ask for two old women named Nduta and Gachere. I'll collect Karanja myself when you're ready to barge off."

"Thank you very much, sir," the young policeman said, and dropped into a chair. The fez-wearing servant fetched him a beer. The men talked of crops and weather and the acute shortage of decent scotch whisky since the bloody Americans were getting all the imports owing to the dollar restrictions and the sterling bloc.

11

When Peter, Jeff, and Kimani returned from safari, Karanja and the two old women were in jail awaiting trial. Henry McKenzie told Kimani what had happened. Then he went to speak with his mother and his father's other wives.

"Your father is in jail because of a thahu on this house. Because of it, a hyena's droppings were found in front of the hut, and a vulture cast his shadow on the ridgepole. On the day of the hyena dung, I dropped a calabash of beer, which smashed on a stone. Your father went to see the mundumugu, who told him of the thahu," Wangu said. "He said that the thahu came to the household through you. But you were not here to be purified, so Mwange's baby was born feet first. Naturally the midwives smothered it and took it into the fields for the hyenas. But the Bwana P.C. came with police and took your father and the two old women off to the big hut in Nyeri where men are kept in cages like wild animals and where the askaris carry guns."

"How long will they keep my father in the big hut with the iron boma?"

"I do not know. Soon a council of white elders will sit in judgment. They say that to kill a child, even if it is born wrong, is to take a life unlawfully, although this is very strange when it is actually more unlawful to allow such a child to live. Perhaps it is not too late to save your father from prison. Perhaps if you will visit the mundumugu he will purify you of the thahu and your father may yet be saved."

"I will go immediately," Kimani said. "If the evil is in me, it must be vomited out."

The old witch doctor looked up from his old man's drowse in the sun when Kimani approached. Kimani squatted and waited for the mundumugu to speak.

"There is a powerful thahu which dwells within your body," he said. "Because of it, tragedy has come to live in your father's shamba. You have been defiled in some way. Did any man not of your clan strike you?"

"Yes, mzee. I disobeyed the Bwana Jeff whilst we were on safari, and he struck me across the face with his hand, and my head was filled with the buzzing of bees."

"Thence came the thahu. It must be driven out. Fetch me beer and a goat, and I shall purify you. It may not be too late to save your father."

Kimani went to his circumcision sponsor, who in his father's absence was Kimani's father, and told him what the mundumugu had said. The circumcision sponsor went to talk to the witch doctor, and the witch doctor fixed an hour for the ceremony.

"We will drive out the thahu by the water, there by the big hill," he said. "Come just after sunrise tomorrow. Now have the boy bring me beer of honey, because I must meditate, and a man may not meditate without beer."

Kimani brought him beer and then went to sleep outside the compound, for a strong curse was on him and he did not wish to contaminate the shamba further. The next morning Kimani met his circumcision uncle outside the compound, and they chose a red-black-and-white-spotted he-goat from the flock.

Kimani's circumcision sponsor took the boy to an appointed place, an open space outside the shamba, and drove the he-goat before him. The witch doctor dug a hole in the ground with his simi and spread it with banana fronds. He filled the hole with water from a gourd and then sprinkled it with powders he took from three flasks. He chanted:

"Thahu, go away, go away and grow thin, as this powder I have sprinkled in the water grows thin and disappears. Grow thinner and thinner and dissolve like clouds before the wind."

The circumcision uncle brought the goat forward, and the mundumugu took a knife and split its nose, rubbing powdered lime into the cut. He grabbed the goat by the hind legs and walked it around the leaf-lined pit, once in each direction, so that it left a trail of blood on the ground. He chanted loudly, commanding the thahu to leave the boy's body.

He then took the goat's right forehoof and dipped it into the water in the hole. He held it to the boy's mouth and commanded him to suck it. Kimani sucked the hoof and spat to the right. Then he sucked the left hoof and spat to the left. The witch doctor chanted: "Vomit, vomit, vomit out the thahu."

He dragged the goat behind Kimani's back and pushed its bleeding nose beneath each of the boy's armpits. Then he saddled the goat on Kimani's back and cried: "Let the thahu be like a load on the back that is cast off as I cast off this goat."

He then stretched the goat with its legs spraddled in the air and slit its belly. Opening the stomach with the point of his knife, he scooped a palmful of the half-digested contents and threw the yellowish mess into the basin. With a small sharp stick he pinned the edges of the stomach together. Then he tucked the bulging stomach back into the goat's belly.

The mundumugu took two bushbuck horns from his medicine bag and dipped them into the dark, bitter waters in the leaf-lined hole. He pushed them into Kimani's mouth, commanding him to spit out the liquid. Each time the boy spat, the mundumugu chanted, "Vomit out, vomit out, let the thahu be vomited out!

"If the thahu came from the arms, from the feet, through the navel, through the mouth, through the nostrils, through the eyes, through the anus, through the penis, let the thahu be vomited out. If it came through the roof, if it came from the milk of the breasts of a woman, let the thahu be vomited out. If it came from the hut, from the shamba, from the earth, or from the sky, let it be vomited out. If it came from the dung of a hyena, if it came from a curse, if it came from a snake, let it be vomited out. If it came from a blow, let it go away and be dissolved in the mists."

Then the mundumugu choked the goat until it was nearly dead, and skinned it while still slightly alive. Then he broke each of its legs. He opened it again, taking care to preserve a little life, and cut strips from the stomach, cut off the testicles, cut out the eyes, and finally cut out the heart. He made little circles of stomach skin and slipped them over the reedbuck horns. He hung a strip of gut over Kimani's shoulders like a wreath, and cast the goat's eyes into the basin, together with the testicles and heart. Once again he dipped the horns into the mixture and commanded Kimani to spit. Then he cut the strips of intestine from Kimani's shoulders and buried them at the foot of a tree. Thus the thahu had passed into the intestine of the goat. He buried the eyes separately under another bush. Then he prayed, his eyes cast upward toward Ngai in his home on Kerinyagga. He stirred three fresh mixtures of white chalk, black ash, and red powder, and smeared them onto Kimani's nose, in between his toes, and on his neck and navel. Then they roasted the flesh of the goat and ate it. After which the thahu was dismissed. Surely, now, Karanja would be released from jail.

As usual, Henry McKenzie knew most details of the backstairs doings before they happened. When the purification ceremony was finished, he watched the Kikuyu disperse. Then he got in his jeep and drove over to Jeff Newton's farm. Jeff was back in the stables, smearing tar on the cut hoof of a riding horse. He released the horse's fetlock and walked out into the open to meet Henry McKenzie.

"I don't mind saying, young feller-me-lad, you've stirred up hell's own amount of trouble," Henry McKenzie said.

"Me? Don't tell me that I've been jilted, or that my bride has decided to join the FANNIES or WRENS or some equally horrible penance for knowing me?"

"No, dammit, I'm serious. All this trouble on the farm seems to have come through Kimani, because you smacked him whilst you and Peter were in the bush. That was very damned silly of you."

"Cheeky little bugger had it coming. Anyhow, I didn't hurt him, any more than you've ever hurt Peter when you've warmed his pants. Kimani wanted a wallop, and I gave him one. You'd have done the same."

"Yes, but coming from me, there wouldn't have been any thahu attached, because I am Kimani's white father, more or less blood brother to Karanja. You're not of his clan."

"Honest to God, Henry McKenzie," Jeff said, "sometimes I have mingi sana trouble remembering that you're a Scot and the father of the woman I am going to marry. You talk like a bloody witch doctor. Come and have a beer and pretend that there aren't any ghosts."

The men walked up to the broad fieldstone porch of Jeff's house, which was a smaller replica of Henry McKenzie's home. Jeff clapped his hands, and the headboy brought two bottles of beer, beaded coldly from the water bag. Henry McKenzie took a long pull at his bottle and wiped his mustache with the back of his hand. He filled his pipe and puffed it strongly alight before he spoke again.

"My dear boy, *you* know it's a lot of bloody nonsense and *I* know it's a lot of bloody nonsense, but the facts are these: You smacked Kimani. The hyena dropped dung inside the compound. A vulture flew over the hut. Wangu dropped a beer gourd and broke it. A baby was born feet first, and the old hags smothered it and chucked it out for the fisis to eat. This is all normal procedure for the old times, but the P.C.'s been told to start making examples of some of the more flagrant native violations of the raj. This comes, possibly, as a result of that Masai herdsman running a spear into the Game Department bloke last year in that dispute over the white cow.

"So old Noel nips down from his ivory tower in Nyeri with a carful of askaris, and now my oldest friend and headman is in jail as an accessory to a murder, and the two crones are nearly certain to swing. This morning old Waruhiu, the bone pointer, did a lot of fancy things to a goat in order to drive the devils out of Kimani, and so now all's sweetness and light again. To their way of thinking, that is. This hocus-pocus on the hill makes everything all right.

"I'm going to make one last effort to talk Noel out of running my Wogs, but I doubt it'll do any good. Bloody Whitehall's been eying us from afar for a long time. When the Socialists get in—and they will get in, soon's the war pressure's off and Winston can't use the Huns any longer as an excuse to stay in power—there's going to be any amount of hue and cry to make the niggers magically white gentlemen. The pressure has been getting stronger for a long time. Colonies, my dear boy, just ain't fashionable any more. We are entering the age of the glorified Wog, black, brown, yellow, or whatever. You can see it in the East, and down South, and already in Uganda and Tanganyika, and now here. But I didn't come here to give you a learned lecture on world politics.

"What I came for was to tell you that if they put Karanja in jail he'll die for sure. And if he dies, the thahu is back again. And if the thahu is back, the only way to be rid of it is to be rid of the man who caused it, and that man is you. Kimani'll have a damned good go at you, and if he doesn't kill you, you may have to kill him, and then there'll be any amount of flap in Nairobi and in London as well, and unrest all over the Highlands, and the Socialists and the Communists setting up a dirty great screech in the press. And my girl will be a widow, or at least husbandless, because if you go about killing Wogs today, even in self-defense, the happy Home Office is going to look for an example and you, my beamish boy, are a bloody beaut bet to be *it*."

"What a cheerful father-in-law I picked out," Jeff said. "If that cheeky little thug comes buggering about these premises, I'll give him more than the back of me hand. I'll give him a real thahu with a charge of buckshot in the seat of the pants."

"I'm telling you again," Henry McKenzie said. "I don't want a widow for a daughter. Kimani's whole circumcision group is your enemy if the old man dies in jail. Whitehall and a lot of white people out of here still don't understand that a mission school don't make a man out of a savage in less'n half a century. You remember the missionary woman?"

"No, Papa McKenzie. I've been away to the wars. What missionary woman?"

"Jolly wonderful old duck, mad on the Wogs. Thought their habits barbarous and shameful. Went about tending the worthy sick and preaching the gospel and reforming the world. Started a Kikuyu girls' school and told the girls they didn't really have to go with their fathers to be circumcised. Thought female circumcision was a dreadful, horrible, outdated thing and set out to abolish it."

"I'm sure something frightful happened. What?"

"Well, the Kyukes felt very sad for her. Thought she had a thahu that had driven her mad. Thought the thahu came from the fact that she hadn't been circumcised, like all decent women should be, and that was the seat of the trouble. So a flock of 'em collected her one night, she screeching a bit, with the aid of the cook boy and the household Number One, and took her up on the hill and circumcised her, as a favor. Only trouble was she was just a touch old for it. She bled to death."

"I remember reading something about it in England. They stretched the cook and the Number One, didn't they?"

"Yes. The cook and the Number One sat serenely in the dock and swore they never saw any one of the types that the Crown pushed past 'em as suspects. Swung cheerfully, wondering mildly all the while at the complete idiocy of the white man, as all they'd done was to try to do the old trout a favor."

"Well, Henry, what do you want me to do? Move? Sell the farm? Go to England? Because some local's got a curse?"

"Don't be so damned sure you won't have to one day," Henry Mc-

Kenzie said. "In the meantime I'll try to do what I can to cool this thing off. But for Christ's sake, man, be careful. I've grown fairly fond of you, and I'm certainly fond of my gel. I'd hate to see the wedding wrecked. See you for supper tonight?"

"Sure. How's the bride? Fluttery?"

"Elisabeth? Fluttery? Not bloody likely. Mother's daughter. Got the whole house organized, everybody creeping about, scared to bits. See you for sundowners, eh?"

"Right. And *not* to worry about the little blackamoor. I'll keep an eye skinned."

"See you do. Kwaheri."

"So long."

Jeff Newton went back to finish fixing the horse's hoof. He hummed as he pared at it, daubing it well with tar. He thought to himself that a man like Henry, for all his established virtues, could get too close to the Wog way of thinking. That's the trouble with the old-timers, he thought. They don't own the locals. The bloody locals wind up owning *them.*

"Be a damned strange day when those savages of mine tell *me* what to do," he said to the horse, who seemed to nod agreement.

Henry McKenzie drove into Nyeri. He met the Bwana P.C. for a drink at the bar in the Outspan Hotel. Then they went to the P.C.'s cottage for lunch. Henry McKenzie plodded through the soup and the fish and the fowl and the sweet. When they went out on the porch for coffee, he spoke again of the troubles on his farm. He looked intently at his coffee cup and stirred it with deep concentration.

"Noel, you just *can't* try these people. There's nothing to be found but murder and complicity in murder. You'll have to hang at least one and put the others away. You shove Karanja in jail and he'll die, like a penned-up animal. This business has got too deep into thahu. The old sorcerer on the farm has already purified Kimani in the oldest, most effective orthodox ceremony. You and I know it's all a lot of nonsense, but if Karanja goes to jail you are going to have trouble untold with the whole district. You just can't go through with this thing."

"Henry, I'm sorry, I really am, it's no use. It's out of my hands. I just had a letter this morning from H.E. in Nairobi. The Governor says that we must, by all and any means, put a stop to some of these old-fashioned barbarities, and that the place to start is with your man. He has given me a direct order to go through with the trial. Every Wog in the bazaars is watching and waiting to see what happens on this one. If we don't stop it, there'll be a general reversion to the old practices, and we just can't have it. We don't need a few Kikuyu wars with the Masai, actually, and an outbreak of spell-casting and poisoning and cattle raiding and old grudge-paying right now. It may sound trite, but we've got a bigger war on, and most of the white men are away, and there are seven million savages in Kenya alone. Nothing you say can change my mind, although I'm heartily in sympathy with you. I couldn't change it if I wanted to now."

"Very well. You'll regret it, mark you. In the meantime I must be going. Thanks for the nice lunch. See you at the wedding, right?"

"Of course. My love to Elisabeth, and best to Jeff. Sorry, dreadfully sorry, Henry. Bye-bye."

"Good-by," said Henry McKenzie, and climbed into his car. He cursed violently to himself as he went to the jail to see what was going with Karanja. The warder, a pock-marked Meru whom Henry McKenzie had known all the Meru's life, opened the door to the cell in which Karanja sat cross-legged on the floor, and handed Henry McKenzie the key. Karanja's face lit up when Henry McKenzie entered the cell.

"Jambo, Bwana," he said. "You have come to take me home?"

"Not yet, old friend. You must stay here until the council of elders decides your guilt. That will be a month or more. Are they treating you well?"

"Yes, Bwana. The food is of course not so good as my wives make it, but that ugly Meru brings me a little beer each day, and it is warm here, with no work to do. Has Kimani returned?"

"Yes. He came back two days ago and was today purified of his thahu by the mundumugu. A he-goat was slain this morning and suitable things were performed."

"Whence came the thahu? Did some enemy curse him?"

"No, it was an unfortunate accident. He was struck in the face by the Bwana Jeff, who meant no harm. Kimani acted unseemly and the Bwana Jeff struck him mildly in reproof."

"Oh, I am sorry it was the Bwana Jeff. He is a good man and soon will be your son. Kimani must have acted very badly to have forced the Bwana Jeff to strike him. It is a pity the thahu came from a friend instead of an enemy, because enemies may be killed if one wishes to cast a spell or hire a poisoner."

"We'll have none of that talk now, Karanja. I'll come and see you often, and I shall bring your son, Kimani. You must tell him for me that under no circumstances is he to do anything about this affair without my permission. It is very important to you and to me and to the Memsaab Elisabeth and to all the Kikuyu who work on my shamba. Do you understand?"

"Yes, Bwana. Thank you for coming. When you bring Kimani I shall do as you say. Kwaheri."

"Kwaheri, Karanja," Henry McKenzie said, and went out into the blinding afternoon sunlight, shaking his head. There was a polo game going, later, at the Polo Club, when the day cooled, and ordinarily he would have stopped on to watch at least a couple of chukkers. But tonight he wanted to get home.

12

There was no such thing as a bad day at that time of the year, but a little extra effort by the great God Ngai seemed to have been laid on for Elisabeth's wedding. The air sparkled like bubbles in a fresh siphon. The jacarandas wept purple blooms, dripping to the ground, and the Nandi-flame trees blazed and crackled like a bush fire in the golden sunshine. A determined light breeze stirred in the bougainvillaea, rustling it gently, and caused the heavy blood-red coxcomb blooms in the garden to nod lazily. The surrounding plains were dotted like a Swiss curtain with the blue and white primroses, and the heavy-podded long grasses swayed as softly rippling yellow as wheat. Juma, the headboy, had been busy all day arranging flowers in the house, where the wedding was to be held. Henry McKenzie wanted to give away his daughter from his own home. He felt that somehow his dead wife might thus be a little closer to the ceremonies. The preacher would drive over from Nyeri, and there would be a big reception on the rolling lawn. The boys from the compound had pitched the big safari tents, with their sides lifted to form canopies, and Henry McKenzie had dug suicidally into his grog hoard, setting out enough whisky, gin, and beer to get the entire population of the White Highlands completely shikkered. Guests had been trickling in for two days and were either dossed down at Jeff's house or had brought their own small shooting tents and were encamped all along the stream on Bushbuck Farm. They had started the celebration the night before, in Rumuruti, in Nyeri, in Nairobi, Nanyuki, and Nakuru. Most of the men and a few of the women were puff-faced and bleary as they plunged their heads into the cool waters of the stream.

Having nothing much better to do for a couple of days, Jeff had taken Peter and gone out on the plains to find some fresh meat for the feasters. They returned with a couple dozen Tommy rams, and the haunches and filets of two eland, those massive antelope which weigh out at a ton or more. They had shot their guns hot at a water hole in the early mornings, waiting until the sky-dotting clouds of speckled, chuckling sand grouse swirled like a tornado and spiraled down to drink in a solid ball of hundreds, just hovering over the water, the men dropping twenty to forty birds with each barrel. They shot the lorry full of birds, for the boys to pick and clean, and while the boys were preparing the succulent plump grouse they took .22 rifles and filled another lorry with guinea fowl and francolin, the stupid little pheasant with his burden of tender white meat. In the evening they went down to Lake Naivasha and blinded themselves in a roosting place that Jeff knew, and filled the boat twice over with mallard and teal. There would be salted buffalo tongues in the smokehouse, and smoked fowl from the farm, but Kenya people liked their game and they liked it fresh. The beeves that had been butchered for the barbecues would be amply flanked with fat lambs and game.

This would be a proper beano. Henry McKenzie was having fifty bushels of the delicate, plump, coppery-greenish oysters shipped in ice from Mombasa. He had gone into the locked doors of his cellar for champagne for the bride-toasting, but mostly the men would drink gin or beer, leaving the bubbly to the ladies. The men would be drunk for as long as the women would allow, a day or a week, according to the temper of their females, and then they would go, red-eyed and shaky, back to their farms.

They came in singles and in groups, according to distance and inclination. Most rode horses, since petrol was in short supply, but a few clubbed their rations together to make the more distant journeys from Nairobi and Mount Elgon. Old Lord Waterholme from Eldoret came in an ancient Rolls-Royce filled with celebrants, mostly drunk and waving bottles. Young Sir James Fitzroyce, who had lost a leg in a motor accident before the war and hence had missed the fun of this one, came on a blooded Arab stallion, his wooden leg screwed into the iron of his stirrup. Some jounced in dogcarts, others bumped on bicycles. It seemed to Elisabeth, looking out from her room at the blackening plains, that the yard resembled a wildebeest migration on the Serengeti. It was equally dusty and twice as noisy.

"We'll have the wedding in the morning, about eleven, Papa," Elisabeth had said. "That'll be when they're still hung over from last night and before they've had a real chance to get at the grog. We'll have the meal at one, and after that Jeff and I will just nip off to the Outspan and let the carnage continue. Please lock up anything that's breakable *inside* the house, and try to keep the guests from trampling *all* the flowers."

"Bloody small chance of salvaging anything from this mob," her father said. "Just lucky that most of the young bucks are off to the war. I would rather go through a Zulu war than try to control the likes of David Morrow and Ron MacDonald and Gerald Fitzwilliam and those other ruffians that your bridegroom chums about with. I have never really understood why they always *have* to fight each other just because they are such dear friends. The last wedding I remember from before the war, when Pam and Andrew Newby got hitched, they beat up the bridegroom and nearly tore the wedding dress off the bride. The bridegroom, the best man, and the bridegroom's father were all in hospital for a week. Poor bloody bride went back home with her mum and patted her foot until they'd patched up the husband sufficiently to start him on his honeymoon. Even then Pam had to help him in and out of the marriage bed with his crutch."

"Don't be coarse," said Elisabeth, laying out the newest batch of wedding presents, which had been drifting in for weeks. There were very few presents that could be contained in the house.

Outside, in the paddock, a young bay stallion nickered and fought the fences. This was a gift from Sir James Fitzroyce, who bred horses successfully since he had been sent out to the colonies as a result of general debt and disgrace. A fine Frisian stud bull, gift of Lord Waterholme, snorted in his stall. A rich Argentine stock saddle, silver-mounted and hand-carven, squatted on the veranda, and a leather case of matched Purdey shotguns rested on its end against the veranda wall.

A herd of sheep, fat-wooled Merinos imported from Australia, was a gift from Count Olaf Holmberg. There was a blue-ribbon Poland-China boar and a brood sow from Mark Malone, who lived close by

Thomson's Falls. There was an English two-handed crosscut saw, and a cask of Spanish sherry, and two pairs of Texas riding boots sent by somebody's cousin in Dallas in Texas in America. Carr Hartley, who had the game farm, had sent over a semi-tame female hunting cheetah, who paced restlessly at the end of her tether under the big thorn tree, which tilted its umbrella of cool shade over the porch.

What price the poor bride, Elisabeth thought as she surveyed the loot. What I really want is something bridy, like a portable sawmill or a tame bull buffalo. I'm surprised nobody thought of it. Some of the things *are* nice, though.

Some of the things *were* nice, such as the six perfectly matched leopard skins, sent by one of Jeff's professional hunting pals, and representing a young fortune and the cream of possibly five hundred pelts, since each inky rosette and the dark gold coloration of each hide was identical. Such as a really smashing evening cape made of black-and-white colobus-monkey fur. Such as two hundred-pound elephant tusks, hand-polished to creamy white and mounted in oiled teak. Such as a complete carving set of Sheffield and another of Danish steel, the one inset into ebony handles, the other into ivory. Such as a dozen pewter Pimm's mugs mounted on brilliantly polished ivory of wart-hog tusks, and an elaborate ebony serving table from the Congo. There were two Irish setter puppies, a boar hound, and a tame monkey.

There was also a trunk of linens and lace that had belonged to her mother, because when Lisa was finally out of the house Henry McKenzie wished to be quit of the more painful mementos of Caroline McKenzie.

"A fair haul, old lady," Jeff said the day before the wedding. "A fair haul. But I fail to see any encouraging signs of bassinets or christening mugs."

"They're supposed to come after a decent interval, you hairy nugu," Elisabeth replied. "Go and play with the other children. The bride's busy."

"By God," Jeff said, scuttling away, "I hope you won't be too tired out tomorrow night for the main business. . . ." Then he ducked as she hurled a coil of heavy copper wire, gift of one of the nearby Masai herdsmen, at the back of his neck.

The surrounding natives, Kikuyu and Masai, had also brought many gifts. There were easily a dozen beautifully wrought, bleached and decorated shields, made illegally in the dark of the moon. There were heaps of the blue, red, and white beads, coils of copper wire, for the bride's adornment. There were literally faggots of ostrich plume. There were several lion-mane headdresses—illegally killed, of course— and a cloak of white marabou feathers that brought a gasp from Elisabeth and even fetched a whistle from Jeff. There were several live goats, and clumps of chickens tied together by their legs. There were oddly constructed drinking gourds, and calabashes for beer, and delicately wrought iron bracelets and bangles. There was even one naked girl of eleven or twelve years, a fancifully painted little thing who dug her toe into the grass and sucked dedicatedly on her finger.

"What'n the name of God's this?" Jeff asked. "Not one of *mine,* I hope, although she might well be, as she's very light under the grease."

"I should hope not," said Elisabeth. "We'll have to return this present. One of Papa's old Wakamba cronies has sent us a *slave.*"

"Jolly good idea, a slave," Jeff replied. "I can call it the nucleus of what I hope will be a large and multicolored harem. Come here, little girl, and let your new master inspect your teeth."

"A proper beast, you are. Take her down to the shambas and give her over to Wangu to look after until we can ship her back to her family. We'll leave the concubine business to that peculiar Englishman you know in Uganda, the one with all the muddy-colored children."

"Shame," Jeff said. "Here I am, about to yield up my virtue without ever having tried out the local product. Damned close to it once, though. It was donkey's years ago, up in the Masai, when we saw this bibi taking a bath. Very pretty, too, she was, and as naked as dammit. Been out such a long time that I thought of boiling her for a few days in a petrol tin to rid her of the lice and the topsoil, but she read my mind, evidently, and buggered off. This marrying a white girl seems an anticlimax after those possibilities, doesn't it?"

"You *are* a beast, darling. If I see you make one move toward me I shall scream the house down."

"Do you object to bathing that much?" Jeff asked politely. "I don't *really* insist on a clean bride. Give us a kiss and I'm off."

It seemed to Jeff that he had never smelled anything quite like Elisabeth. He had known such a lot of women in England, the odd Waaf or Wren and a viscountess or so, but none he ever remembered seemed to smell simultaneously of soap, violets, May haw, moonbeams, and clean, sunburned, healthy girl, like any lovely girl smells on the silver beaches of Mombasa after a dip in the clear green salt water while you sit close on the beach to towel off and smoke a cigarette and sweat a little, cleanly, in the sun. He stopped kissing her long enough to say:

"You'll bloody well smell right in Mombasa or the marriage is off," and fell to kissing her again. He could feel her body quiver and press against him, and the slight change, the change of smell, the change of taste on her mouth, which first was fresh and sweet as a cow's breath in a clover field, suddenly growing hot and slightly, ever so pleasantly, acridly musky with want. She pushed him away.

"No hanky-panky out of you, my good fellow," she said, breathing heavily. "Wait'll tomorrow, when you've got me penned up," and grinned a delightfully salacious grin, accompanied by a lewd wink.

"This is the goddamnedest woman I ever encountered," Jeff muttered, herding the little slave-girl-cum-wedding-gift back to Wangu's hut in the native compound. "Good thing I've been out in the bush for the last couple of weeks. Somehow I don't think that my bride is the shyest bride I ever knew, considering she practically raped me that night in the Outspan and I wound up engaged before you could say knife."

Peter had been pleased enormously when Jeff asked him to be his best man. He knew, of course, that one of Jeff's contemporaries, like Alan or Terry or Peter Voorhees would normally have been asked, but they were all off to Abyssinia or Libya or Burma or someplace, and it tickled him that he had been chosen over the few remaining fellows who had gone to school with Jeff. It pleased him, too, that he and Jeff had been able to go out the last couple of days before the wedding, to shoot the game for the feasting.

They had chatted a little, between the sand grouse and the francolin and the ducks, sitting in the shade of an acacia and drinking a lukewarm beer.

"What do you suppose it's like, being married?" Peter asked idly. "Make a whole lot of difference in a man's life, or what?"

"Should think so," Jeff said, chewing on a grass stem and fumbling for his tobacco. "Slows a chap down a bit, I shouldn't wonder. I've known a lot of blokes to change completely. One week they're doing over all the girls and sloshing down grog madly till all hours, the next they're dull's dirt and scared pissless of the first frown out of the old lady. I imagine you worry a lot more, specially when the brats start to come and the problems increase. I certainly will have to spend a lot more time tending to the farm and a lot less in the bush. Chap can't just whiz off every time he gets a hankering for space, and leave the good woman to tend the pigs for six months. One of two things happens: Eventually he finds somebody else in his bed, or he makes the woman into a bloody shrew who's cheesed off at him all the time he *is* home, and that's no fun either."

"I expect I know who'll be boss in your house, chum." Peter grinned. "*I've* been brought up under the iron hand of this particular girl. She'll wallop you as soon as kiss you, or more so, and she's tough as a rhino kiboko."

"Glad of it, couldn't be more pleased. No place, Kenya, for one of those sweetie-nicy, scream-at-a-mouse sort of Englishy girls that the boys all seem to fall for. The first time they find a hyena in the cookhouse or a leopard in the hen coop, it's bung off to Merrie England again and back to Mother. Not for me. Your sister is Kenya-born and Kenya-raised. She's seen a cow drop a calf and a hyena eat the calf, and me shoot the hyena. She has caught a cobra in the kitchen and found a scorpion in her shoe. She knows about drought and locust and grasshoppers and screwworm. At least I won't have to go through all that nuisance about trying to convert some Mayfair debutante into a farmeress."

"I think you're very lucky," Peter said seriously. "She's quite the nicest girl I know."

"I reckon that to be high praise from any brother. And I know damned well I'm lucky. Let's go see about those ducks."

On the morning of the wedding the best man bathed very carefully and gave minute inspection to his fingernails. Finding them a bit grimy, he took his hunting knife and pared them closely, digging out as much of the entrenched soil as he could. He got out his best suit—his only proper suit—and hung it up in the back yard for a bit, to let the sweet early-morning breezes blow away some of the scent of moth balls. It was a blue double-breasted serge suit, and it fit him very badly. He had shot up like grass after the rains, and his knobby brown wrists stuck too far out of the sleeves. The coat was too short behind and stretched too tight across. Even dropping his pants as low as possible on his hips, they were still too short and showed considerable sock.

None of his shirts fit well enough to be buttoned, for Peter's neck had swelled, and he never wore a tie, anyhow. Walking carefully down the hall, he knocked on his father's bedroom door. There was no answer, so he entered the room and went over to the old-fashioned walnut highboy where his father kept his town clothes. He pinched a clean white shirt off the top of a heap of freshly laundered shirts and went back to his room to finish dressing. The shirt, he found, fit him perfectly, causing him a moment of amazement over the realization that he was big as his father. Jeff had bought him a necktie in Nairobi, and he looked at it with distaste. It was a pearl-gray cravat, slashed diagonally with black stripes. Peter thought that something in red or bright blue would be more fitting to a wedding, but Jeff had said to wear it or he'd wallop him. He put it on, having a great deal of difficulty with the knot. Peter put a tie on about once a year, on average, and felt he was being garroted, like a giraffe caught in a fence, until he could rip it off again.

"Christ," Peter said half aloud as he jammed his feet into black calf shoes. "I would much rather be going on safari. When I marry I think I shall just grab the girl and run away to some registry office and do it without all this fuss."

Peter snapped open his lips, to inspect his teeth in the mirror, and daubed his downcurving bang of black hair with some pomade, slicking it back. It was a funny face now, a small bit boy, more of it man. The teeth were white against the baked brown, and the eyes very blue. His brown, muscular neck looked odd, swelling out of the starched white collar.

"I look like a young wart hog trying to get out of a hole," Peter said unjustly. "Me for khaki drill as soon's the bride's kissed and the happy couple away. Can't see why people wear these things for fun. My feet are starting to hurt already in these damned spiv shoes. I think perhaps, if nobody's about, I shall just whip down and borrow a beer. Make myself absent until Jeff shows up. Where's the bloody ring? Oh, good. Safe and sound."

He could hear all sorts of rustly, bustly sounds coming from Elisabeth's room, and skirted it swiftly. There was a staccato chatter of Swahili as she directed the maids in some female doings or other. Peter went down to the living room and saw his father pouring a gin for himself from the sideboard. On the lawn, people were milling. Horses were tethered, cars drawn up, teams outspanned, and carts standing forlorn, their shafts slanted to earth. There was a gabble of conversation from the visitors. It sounded to Peter like a flight of knob-billed geese flying low over the marshes at sundown. Henry McKenzie smiled a trifle guiltily as he sloshed his gin into a glass. He too was gallantly arrayed in his rusty best, another blue suit which, while it fit him more precisely than

Peter's suit fit Peter, seemed equally uneasy on his body. His big out-flanged ears and bushy mustache conformed oddly to a stiff white collar that left a red mark on the brown of his neck. The unbaked white of his balding head exactly matched his collar. Peter had to laugh.

"We both look like a couple of tame animals dressed up for a variety turn," he said. "I feel like a performing bear in these clothes."

"Me too," his father said. "I am not much of a man for gin in the morning, but I felt I couldn't face that stampede out there without a peg. Would you care to join me, son, in honor of this great day? Not that I approve of it as a habit."

"Yes, thanks," Peter said, feeling very grown up now, and happy that his father recognized it.

"What'll it be?"

"Gin, please, with a little pink."

His father's eyebrows shot up, but he poured a good-sized dollop of gin into a small glass and seasoned it with bitters. Peter watched the pink swirl through the clearness of the gin and raised his glass to his father.

"Cheers," he said. "To the blushing bride."

"Cheers," the old man said. "To the lucky groom. And he *is* a lucky groom, by God, at that. If he uses her badly I'll kill him happily."

"I doubt you'll have to," Peter replied. "Judging from our experience, it's more likely she'll beat *him*."

"I think perhaps you may be right. Let's go and welcome the guests and try to keep 'em just a touch sober until after the ceremony."

"That," Peter said, "would call for a territorial army *and* magic, laid on."

Holly Keith, who was going to be the bride's attendant, ran a bath and dumped some of her mother's bath salts, which she had stolen, into it. Holly's head was full of bridal thoughts as she stretched in the big tub, solemnly regarding the pink mosquito bites which represented her nipples, and wondering how long it would be before she pooched out in front like Elisabeth. In Holly's mind there was something mysterious connected between matrimony and breasts that pooched out the front of a frock.

Holly knew very well that babies were born because of something men and women did to each other, but she was a trifle confused about the process. She knew that babies were built in their mumma's tummy, and the husband did something peculiar to put them there, and that it had to be the odd machinery which distinguished boys from girls. But she didn't think it would be much fun. It would probably be painful. If *she* were getting married, there wouldn't be any of that monkey business until after they'd had a glorious holiday, maybe in France or England, and then if the husband were very good, she might consent to let him make a baby. Her mumma had just produced one, a wrinkled, nasty little red boy, named Jerry, and she was still feeling dreadful. Holly remembered that her mumma threw up every morning for months and that Elisabeth had told her it had something to do with the baby in her mumma's tummy. Holly looked at her flat tummy and wondered if there would ever be a baby in it. Then she wondered whose baby it would be, and settled then and there on Peter.

Holly got out of the tub and put on a pair of pink rayon pants and a bathrobe. She dug her toes into zebra-hide slippers and slopped down to the living room for her brekkers. She had had tea and toast, of course, brought to her on waking by Kamia, the Kikuyu headboy, but the day had made her excited and the bath had spurred her appetite. She was hungry as a vulture.

"Morning, ducks," her mother said. "I waited to have my coffee with you. Daddy's off somewhere on his horse. All ready for the wedding?"

"I had a bath," Holly said.

"You smell like it. My bath salts, doubtless?"

"Yes, Mum. I didn't think you'd mind this once. They make you feel just lovely all over, don't they?"

"That's the general idea, love," her mother said. "Hungry?"

"Ravenous. I've heard brides don't eat; is that so?"

"I was starved on my wedding day. I ate like a horse. Then I got so excited I threw up."

"That won't happen to me," Holly said, starting on the cold seed-specked yellow papaya that Kamia set before her. She followed the papaya with scrambled eggs and ham and hot bread and marmalade and drank three cups of strong tea. Then she ate an apple.

"Is my dress ready? I expect I'd best try it on now."

"It's a lovely dress, darling. Let's go and see it, shall we?"

It *was* a lovely dress, of starchy white embroidered organdy. Holly slipped into a stiff cotton petticoat to make the frock flare, and it stood off from her long legs like a ruff. Her mother tied a blue velvet sash round her waist. She whirled, still in her slippers, admiring herself in the mirror.

"You look a treat, sweetie," her mother said. "Now take it off, because we don't want to muss it."

"I'd rather have a *long* dress," Holly said. "I look such a *child* in this, and I'm not a child any more."

"I'm afraid you're still classifiable as a mtoto," her mother said. "But it'll be all too soon when you're dressing for your own wedding."

"With Peter," Holly said complacently, looking at her red hair in the mirror and thinking that it looked *carroty*. "I expect he'll make a very nice husband for me. And he lives so close it'll be very convenient for everybody. What a horrible boy he is; he probably will make an elegant man. But now he smells sort of bad from all those animals he's always doing about."

"Peter's a very nice boy, and I'm sure he will make a wonderful husband. Now take off the dress and go and choose some roses for your tiara. All the better bridesmaids wear tiaras this year, I'm told. Get some of those little pinky ones. They'll be sweet with the dress."

"Is being married fun, Mum? Always having a man about, I mean?"

"Perhaps you couldn't call it fun," her mother said. "But it's sort of necessary to a girl's peace of mind, unless she really wants to be an old maid, and I'm sure you don't. Nip off, now, and do your flowers. I must dress myself and feed the baby and we mustn't be late."

"What do husbands and wives actually *do*, Mum? I mean, what do they do that makes them different from just being engaged? I don't mean kissing and all that nonsense."

"Someday I'll tell you," her mother replied. "But now I'm busy. Off you go."

Holly put on a pair of khaki shorts and a jumper and stuck her feet into jodhpur boots. She turned an exuberant cartwheel as she entered the flower garden. Her breakfast felt fine and warm inside her, and the sun added an extra freckle to her nose, and she thought it was just simply a marvelous day for anything, but she wished she were going hunting with Peter instead of wearing that silly little girl's dress and a dumb old tiara of roses on her head. But the roses, heavy with big fat tears of dew, were lovely, and the garden smelled like heaven. Holly took the shears and warily stalked one of the rosebushes, as she had seen Peter do with animals. She didn't want to be gored by the thorns, not if she could help it.

Jeff Newton dressed very carefully in his naval uniform, which for some peculiar reason his bride had insisted he wear. It was heavy doeskin No. 1's and was a bit musty despite its airing. The stiff white collar looked very strange with its neat black tie, although it hadn't been so long ago when this tie had hung over the backs of some very strange chairs, hastily torn off and tossed back-handed while he unmoored his trousers and kicked off his shoes.

"Well," he said to himself. "There's the end of that. No more fun and games for the lieutenant. Geoffrey Newton, husband. Geoffrey Newton, father. Crikey. Never thought I would face this day, not so soon, anyhow. If the bloody destroyer hadn't pranged me I'd still be tumbling into bed with the world and his wife—that's if I wasn't dead, which is fairly likely.

"It was a lot of fun, though, and I'm glad I had it. Think it's bloody foolish for a man to come into the marriage cot not knowing much, and God knows the opportunities out here are pretty seldom. One thing I can thank old Adolf for—he got me out of Kenya and into a lot of wonderful beds. What *was* the name of that one in Surrey on that long week end? Peggy? No. Sheila? No. Ah, yes, Leslie. Lovely little thing, and a dirty shame she got blown up in the blitz. What's this on the chin? A pimple? No. Only a tsetse bite.

"Hope that little bugger Peter hasn't gone and lost the ring. And thank God those ruffians I used to run with are all off protecting us from the Hun. No telling what they'd have thought up in the way of wit, once they'd got a few grogs aboard. Probably kidnaped me and held me prisoner for a week or something, laughing madly all the while. The old boys'll be drunk, but not so exuberant.

"I say," Jeff said to the lavender-water bottle, dousing himself with the lotion, "I *shall* have a bloody good try at making her happy. She is *such* a bloody *wonderful* girl. And now I shall have a drink to the bride."

He walked over to the sideboard in his bedroom and seized a partially empty bottle of John Haig. He toasted the morning and said: "Here's to you, old lady, and long may we last, because I love you very much and want at least ten kids."

He took a heavy swig from the bottle, shuddered, and smiled at himself in the mirror as he began to brush his mustache. "What the hell she ever saw in me, *I* don't know, unless it was the pure gold that shines from me soul," he said. "I think I will have another drink." And did.

The bride shooed the Kikuyu maids from her room and did a most unbridal thing. She took off her clothes, lit a cigarette, lay full length on the bed as naked as a Turkana girl, and sipped slowly from a bottle of beer. The beer tasted just fine, even if it was unmaidenly.

I wonder, Elisabeth thought, if I will be any good in bed. I hope I shall be, because I'm told it's quite important. This monster I'm marrying, and how sweet he is, with that ridiculous mustache, must have been in and out of half the beds in England. He never talks about it, but he's got a way with him that must have led him straight to all the bitches on the loose in London. He could have had me for a farthing any time since he got back, but I think it's rather dear of him that he didn't. Means I'm a little specialler than the others, anyhow, and he's saved me up for a treat.

I suppose I'd best be all dewy and virginal and frightfully bridy whilst everyone's looking on, but I can barely wait to get the man in that big suite in the Outspan. I'll *show* him a couple things he never learned from that nasty Lady Something that used to write him all the time.

But not to get preggie too early. There's nothing I can think of less appetizing than a woman who's always sick in the morning, with her skin all blotches and her tummy pushed out in front of her like a wheelbarrow. I'll not have *this* lad looking round about him too soon because I'm so horrible. My, this beer is good. I suppose poor old Mum is shuddering right now at the idea of her daughter drinking beer and thinking about sex. Odd there's not a decent name for the actual act. Fornication's nasty. So's intercourse. So's "sexual congress." Come and have sexual congress with me, my pretty maid. Horrors. The coarser ones are funnier, but none of it describes a thing that's supposed to be so important. I've heard 'em all, one time or another, and to me that most dreadful word is very funny, even if nobody's supposed to say it, and "poking" reminds me of a bad little boy doing something horrible with a stick. This beer *is* good. But I wonder what this wonderful man of mine would say if, after we've left the party and go to the Outspan, I looked demurely at him and said: "Well, come on, my good fellow, don't hang about. Let's nip upstairs and get on with the poking." He'd drop dead, and I'd be the only virginal widow in history.

The idea amused Elisabeth very much. Having been raised among and entirely with men and animals in their most basic relationship with each other, and having kept her eyes pinned on the doings in the fancy set in Eldoret and Muthaiga and Limuru, she was completely lacking naïveté. She had heard all the words used naturally. She had read most of the books and knew about the things her young male friends did in town when taken a little in drink. She had stumbled over more than one good girl friend, frock tumbled in the azaleas, after a wet party at the club in Limuru; she knew all about why young John Masters shot young Arch Williams, and why Polly Stanton had such an early baby, and by the wrong husband, because she had to marry that awful old Tom Desmond in a hurry.

"I doubt very much if it's as much fun when you're married as it is when you grab it under a bush," she said coarsely, looking downward over her body, which lay pink and spraddle-legged on the bed. "But I'm not an entirely nasty bit of work, and I intend to get as much fun as possible out of this baby-making business, even if there isn't a lovely word for it. Ah, well, these unbridal thoughts must stop, and I must get on with my frills and ruffles, including the lacy pants. I *wonder* if it'll hurt much."

Elisabeth finished her beer, smacked her lips, and yelled for Wamboye to come and fix her bath. She grinned. "Guess my lad's a stickler for cleanliness, if that story about the Masai girl is in point. At least I'll come to him without any odious diseases I can think of. He *is* a dear, Jeff, and I am certainly the luckiest woman in Kenya to have snaffled him. I expect he'll want at least twelve children, all of them at once, so he can buy elephant guns for the boys and teach them to hunt before they walk. Well, bride. It certainly is a nice day for it, whatever they call it, and I shall now anoint the fair white body with spices and crawl into my bride clothes. It would have been very nice if poor Mum could have stuck around a bit longer for this event, because she adored Jeff as a little boy."

Elisabeth plunged into her bath, where she happily snorted and kicked, her hair safely done up in a towel, for half an hour. Then she got out of the tub, dried, slipped into a robe, and had another beer. It tasted better, if anything, than the other.

She was half asleep on the bed when Wamboye knocked on the door.

"Please excuse me, Memsaab," the maid said. "But you're wanted down at the compound of Ngatia. His wife is very ill and is asking for you. She has a great pain in the stomach."

"Oh, for God's sake," Elisabeth said, rolling out of bed. "Hand me some trousers and a sweater, and go to the medicine chest for some salts and paregoric. You would think that on a wedding day the bride would have at least one free hour from some Wog's stomach-ache. Here, not those shoes. The slippers'll do."

Elisabeth got into her pants and pulled on a high-necked sweater and went down to the native shambas. She thought as she walked with the medicines in her hand that she would need another bath when she came back to dress for her wedding.

The bride was unbelievably lovely in her grandmother's Empire wedding gown. Elisabeth had diminished the bustle to a mere suggestion and had eliminated the train. The dress was of white lace over a satin slip, with long, close-fitting sleeves that came to points on her hands. She had snipped the yards and yards of veil to where it barely reached her hips. The neck was high and square, and she wore the pearls of Jeff's mother. When she looked at Jeff as she came in on the arm of her father, and gave him a not entirely demure smile, Jeff's stomach turned as it had turned when a buffalo came snorting, wounded, from the bush. It felt like being so drunk that the bed spun and you had to put a hand on the floor to steady it.

Jeff looked exactly like any other sunburned young naval officer, bar the mustache, with three small ribbons pinned high on his chest, and with his hands too big. But there was an extra bristle to his unnaval mustache, which seemed to be a thorn bush set afire.

Peter had the ring squeezed around the tip of his littlest finger. As young Holly Keith came in, a crown of pink roses on her head and her organdy dress saucy over her white socks and flat-heeled patent-leather shoes, Peter thought, *My, what a pretty little girl,* and really not such a dreadful nuisance. Mightn't be bad-looking with that red hair and green eyes when she gets a little older.

Everyone said there had never been a prettier bride, and that hound, Jeff, was a bloody lucky dog to get such a pretty one, and wasn't it nice that the two farms were so close, no trouble over boundaries, and that young devil, Peter, was getting on for being quite a man, big or bigger than his father, and what a pity poor Caroline wasn't here to see it, but lucky for Henry, he wasn't actually losing a daughter so much as gaining another son, for everybody knew that young Peter worshiped Jeff's shadow, and there was no need for anybody to be lonesome, especially after the grandchildren start to come and young Peter takes over on the farm. And now, now that the rector has tied up everything nice and neat, let us go and kiss the bride and shake the bridegroom's hand, and then let us have a bit of a look at the grog. My bloody oath, old Henry's done himself well. Haven't seen so much champagne since the Prince of Wales was here. And those beautiful oysters, darling; it must have cost a fortune. Well, young Elisabeth. All the very best, and you're a lucky dog, Jeff. Mind you treat her well and give her lots of babies. You know the old say; one in the lap and another on the way. . . .

13

The men clustered on the rolling lawn, after the brief congratulations, and dived into the drink. The women flowed to each other in smaller pools, mostly according to age. The older ones inspected the presents, and the younger, prettier ones slid quietly over to what few young men were available. But it was not the young, freshly pretty faces and the slim young legs and proudly carried bodies that really explained the group.

The older women, fat and skinny, were cut in the same pattern. They wore their dresses as if they had been borrowed or shaken out of moth balls for the occasion. Most of the oatmeal-tweed skirts bagged at the seat. The corseting was all wrong, leaving odd bumps and points under the clothes. Most of the older women wore stout shoes and common-sense stockings. Quite a few wore men's broad-brimmed slouch hats, slanted over one eye, hats from which wisps of hair straggled loosely.

Nearly all had false teeth which fitted badly. Without exception, they were baked sallow-brown by years of sun, and their eyes, mostly blue, seemed diluted in the harsh morning sunlight. They were spare women, some tiny, some big of bone, but all close-honed, nearly all prematurely gray, many stooped. No amount of cream lotion could freshen once-delicate English complexions which had been dried by wind, coarsened and roughened by alkali dust, and broiled by sun. All the women had white creases of wrinkles around their eyes, caused by squinting. Their hands were either heavy and callused or worn fine, as a cake of soap maintains original shape but erodes with use. On many, the wrists were as ropy as men's wrists, thickened from riding and lifting, and under the frocks, some thighs were as heavily muscled as men's, from years on horseback.

Most of them now were medium rich or well to do, in the new prosperity of the war, with their farms secure and money in the bank. But at one time or another most had trod fearfully, gently, on the delicate crust of desperate failure and had known tremendous toil and hardship. Some had borne their children with only an old hag from the shamba to help. Some had borne their babies alone. All had washed and scrubbed and planted and cooked and plowed and fought fire in the dry season, had squelched through the impossible red muck of the rains, had battled to save the lives of their beasts, knew wind and dust and the necessary earth that washed and blew away, and had lived at altitudes which turned women old at thirty. They had their security now, and some even riches, but they had bought it dearly, hewing an approximation of English life out of virgin African bush and stone. Few of the old ones had been born in Africa. They had come out as young marrieds and as children, fresh from the misty green trees, clipped yew-hedged cool lawns and perennial flower-bright gardens of England, to confront a land in which harsh climate, animal, and man offered a constant, daily challenge. Women who once screamed at a mouse had driven lions from the cattle pastures. Women who had been reared gently by Scotch nannies now had filed-toothed savages as nursemaids for their babies. Women who had once been afraid to spend a night alone in a city house now spent months alone, but for a savage or two, on desolate farms while the men were on safari or off to the wars. Women who used to be desperate when a stoat got at the chickens now found leopards and civet cats in the hen coop, with elephants and buffalo trampling down the flower beds and wart hogs rooting up the potatoes and hyenas waiting expectantly for anything, human or animal, that might be weak, small, or sick. There was no woman there who could not remember running onto a rhino in the footpath, or an elephant bulking huge and blocking the road. One woman's baby had been taken by a hyena. Their wrists and faces were permanently scarred with the bites of mosquitoes and tsetse flies, and when they took up a gun they handled it as swiftly and as competently as a man. They inspected their shoes each morning to see if there might be a scorpion inside, and the killing of a cobra or a mamba or a boomslag in the front yard was routine. Their contact with the out-side world was mainly a battery-driven radio which received the BBC broadcast relayed through Nairobi or Dar-es-Salaam and which usually failed at a crucial moment in the news. Their music came from hand-cranked phonographs and consisted of selections from such modern operettas as *Chu Chin Chow*, *The Chocolate Soldier*, *Blossom Time*, and *The Merry Widow*. They were used to solitude. Save for the ones who lived on the fringes of towns like Fort Hall, Nakuru, Nyeri, Nan-yuki, Thika, Eldoret, Nairobi, and Kusumu, going to town was a three- or four-times-yearly occasion, especially since petrol was short owing to the war, and a near neighbor might be fifty or sixty miles away. They were used to loneliness, and were happy in it, now they had cookboys and Number One boys and kitchen mtotos and many black hands to feed and tend the flocks and turn the soil for wheat and coffee and tea and pyrethrum and pineapples. But they still drove the trucks to town and pitched in at whatever daily crisis called them.

Sally Henderson was such a woman, and so was the woman with whom she lived at Mwega, on a huge farm at the edge of the Aberdares. Sally Henderson's husband had died of blackwater fever four years ago. Marian Sorrell had divorced her husband in a nasty affair which in-volved a non-fatal shooting. Now Marian and Sally—Marian lean, horse-faced, and sinewy, and Sally big, broad, blowzy-blond, with a deep bosom and a man's booming voice—lived together and worked the farm, running a labor force of more than one hundred Kikuyu. The farm spread downward on the slopes of a mountain. The farmhouse was perched high atop the mountain. Dressed today in light summer frocks and floppy picture hats, Sally and Marian looked like two tough old men masquerading in women's clothes, because for three hundred and fifty days a year they wore blue jeans, flannel shirts, and ankle boots. Either could hit a running dik-dik, no bigger than a hare, with a pistol at fifty yards. Either could break a fractious colt, doctor a steer, deliver a calf, or kill an elephant. Either could mend harness, fix the Delco light machine, rip the guts out of an auto, or repair a tractor. Neither could cook worth a damn, as Sally was then saying in her deep, rough voice.

"I couldn't be happier," she said. "We've finally found the most wonderful cook. He used to cook for John Martin's safari outfit, but he got hurt when they turtled a lorry somewhere in Tanganyika and he can't do safaris any more. But he learnt to cook for American millionaires and Spanish grandees and dago counts, and he is simply divine. Makes the finest lemon tart I ever laid mouth to. For a while I thought I'd have to kill Marian. She hasn't a clue in the kitchen."

"No more have you, sweetie. Everything that Sally makes tastes like either boot or glue. After she sacked that last cook we bloody near starved. I can't cook, which is maybe why I had that trouble with Sorrell, damn his lying deceitful soul, wherever he may be. I'm all thumbs and I never know how big a pinch of this or a touch of that is supposed to be. Gimme a cigarette, Sally." She accepted the cigarette, took a kitchen match out of her pocket, and automatically started to strike it on the seat of her pants. Remembering swiftly that she was wearing a dress, she cracked the match head expertly with her thumbnail and took a deep drag, exhaling two thin streams through her nose.

"What happened to the other cook?" somebody asked. "I thought you had a wizard in that last Kyuke."

"Cheeky blighter, he was, and a thief as well," Sally said. "I had to sack him a month ago. He pinched everything—cigarettes, sugar, salt, tea, grog. But when he pinched a box of Marian's Kotex—God knows what he wanted with it—he went too far, and I laid my sjambok on him smartly, I can tell you. He came back drunk and ugly a week later, and I powdered his pants with a charge of No. 8 shot. He's not been back since, and if he does return I'll use a larger charge on his black backside."

"We never seem to have any trouble up there except with the kitchen, otherwise we'd be happy as sandboys," Marian said. "Cattle all fine, and a ripping crop this year. I've had a lot of books sent out, and the wireless works beautifully. Some admirer of Sally's—blighter's probably got his eye on the farm—just gave her the two most adorable Doberman puppies you ever saw. We've got enough grog to last out the war—thank God Henderson was a toper, his cellar's still fantastic—and enough near neighbors in Nanyuki and Nyeri to drop in on for a drink when the horses need exercising. Now this new Kikuyu cook, bless him. He can even make lamb stew without your tasting the collie in it."

"Well, I shall have to come up and try him out," another woman said. "Maybe Saturday, if you'll be home."

"We're always at home," Sally Henderson said. "Do come for lunch and bring somebody else, and we'll get a little tiddly and play some poker. It's no good our always winning each other's money."

The women drifted over to inspect the new young bay stallion that had come as a wedding gift from Sir James, he of the wooden leg.

"Did you get the gen on what actually happened last week in

Nakuru?" one slight, withered little woman asked another slight, withered little woman, who might have been a twin.

"The details are a bit foggy, but I believe Charles came back a bit early from some safari or other to Mombasa and found Leslie caught out, finally. Seems Piers was just leaving, more or less adjusting his clothes, at 4 A.M. It was too late to be legitimately late and much too early to be decently early. I'm sure Charles has known about it for a long time, but he was by way of being in no shape to take notice of it, not with that little bit he's been sneaking off with in Thomson's Falls."

"I'm surprised he didn't shoot Piers; he's got a devilishly hot head, Charles."

"No, actually he was sober at the time, and Charles is a dear when he's not tiddly. And after all, he is Piers's best friend. Piers got clean away, with his shoes in hand, more or less, and then Charles went in and gave Leslie a hell of a hiding. Not that she didn't deserve it. I'm told there'll be a divorce now, and Piers'll *have* to marry her. Pity, because he's clung onto being a bachelor and poaching other men's women for so long now. . . ."

"Shush. Here comes Leslie." A slim, blond, pretty young woman, rather more modishly dressed than most, strode up. She was wearing a short printed silk frock and had elegant long legs in high-heeled shoes. She also had a lovely black eye under her sunglasses.

"Hullo," she said. "Doing me over? Need me to fill in any dirty details, girls?"

"Of course *not*, darling. Where's Charles?"

"Stopped on home. Only decent thing he could do after giving me *this*," and she flicked the glasses off her purpled eye. "Not that I hadn't it coming, in one way, but you'd think his conscience, if so he has one, might've argued a little restraint. You see, I've known for ages about what he does in Thomson's Falls, and with whom. Whoa, there, now I *must* be going. *She* didn't have the decency to stop on home." And the slim, pretty, blond lady with the good legs and the bad eye walked off to join another group. Male.

The menfolk were mostly past forty or well under eighteen. The few young adults, nearly without exception, all had some physical defect, such as young Sir James's lost leg; a chronic eye weakness masked behind inch-thick lenses, such as young Robin Masters, who was blinking owlishly in the bright sunlight. The rest were at war. There was not one sound unmarried man of Jeff Newton's age at the reception. A few men of thirty or more already had become so burdened with family and work that they had been passed over in the call-up, in the interests of food production, and they too seemed as old as their fathers. The print of Kenya was already on them, and they looked, all of them, like brothers and cousins and uncles of one family, from old Major Jarrabee, the retired India hand, to Commander Whitehead, R.N. (Ret.), to Henry McKenzie.

Mostly, they stooped a little, from long hours in the saddle, from long hours behind plows, from long hours of looking speculatively at crops and soil. Their eyes, as with the women, were washed by many suns, and the wrinkles crisscrossed their leathern faces. With the possible exception of Sir James and old Lord Waterholme, there was not a well-kept pair of hands among them. Their nails were thickened and broken, with an accumulation of dirt and grease that simply would not come clean under a file. Most wore hats, and when they took off the broad-brimmed, floppy terais, the upper half of their skulls was the same fish-belly white as Henry McKenzie's. In most of their faces tiny purplish broken veins were visible, even in the young men, because Kenya was known for its drinking, and there were few men who passed a day without the long cool ones before lunch, the frequent beers, and the short hard gins at night.

They were drinking now, mostly gin and whisky, their faces flushed by the heat and the alcohol. They were talking of the war, mostly, and crops, mostly, and shooting, some, and polo, a little, and weather, always weather. The blur of conversation made a queer but regular pattern, like a fancifully thatched roof.

"My boy Tom, the R.A.F. one, says the old Hun's had it, and he wouldn't wonder if he packed in before long. All we've got then's the bloody Japs, dirty little yellow monkeys. . . ."

"I say, did you see that photo Will Forrest took of the old bull on the Thomson Range. Dirty great tusks swung down, hid themselves in the grass, and then swooped up again, like the runners on a sleigh . . ."

"No water in the Masai yet, and away overdue. Damme if I know what's come over the weather. Chum up past Isiolo the other day dropped me a note and said it's raining buckets in Marsabit, and all the luggers are in flood, a month early. Bloody weather gone bloody well mad . . ."

"Don't know what happened to that Hereford bull of mine. Right as rain on Monday, started to stagger and cough on Tuesday, swelled up like a ruddy great balloon, and deader than herring by Thursday night. Vet said he hadn't a clue. Hope to Christ it isn't catching, a good epidemic of anything would ruin me, I've only just got clear of the banks, and with the price of meat where it is, any cow that dies of any disease is a catastrophe . . ."

"I don't care what these fancy small-bore boys say, I say give me enough gun with enough bullet weight and there won't be *any* wounded animals. Perhaps old Karamoja Bell did shoot elephants with a .318, but I choose anything over the caliber .470. Suppose it does weigh a ton, you can always get a Wog to carry it . . ."

"The last kid's not been at all well lately. Can't imagine what's gone crook with the boy. Can't hold anything on his stomach. The doctor's been out ten times at least, and nobody seems to know what's wrong. *I* say he's got worms . . ."

"I've said Montgomery's been right all along. There's no point in attack until you hold the best cards. So let the Yankees laugh at him. *I* was at Mons . . ."

"You must say, though, these Yanks know about equipment. Bloody marvelous stuff they've got, amphibious lorries and all. The production must be fantastic, but it's always England gives the men. I'm glad I've not been living in London with Jerry over every hour on the hour. Eric writes it's a frightful shambles . . ."

"You know, when Helen first got the news about Teddy, I thought she'd crumble to bits and go moping about like a glandered ewe. Not a sign of it. She cried a little, only just, and then she dried her eyes, and now she speaks of him as normally as if he weren't dead. *I* was the one who fell sick, because I keep thinking of him as the kid he was, full of hell and the devil to fuel it, always into mischief, and not as a pilot officer, deceased, with a posthumous D.F.C. . . ."

"Doris says the WRENS are great fun, except the black stockings make her legs look like burnt stumps, but she's got herself engaged to some American N.C.O and reports the Yanks aren't half bad. Never thought I'd have a Yankee for a son-in-law . . ."

"Say what you want to about the old Eytie, but the first decent roads we've had in Kenya these P.O.W.s built. It's a pleasure to drive to Nairobi now. I'd like to see some of these dagos come out and settle after all the fuss is over. Make bloody good citizens . . ."

"I don't see what the Game Department's got to be so shirty about. It's not the settlers kill off the game. It's the Wogs, loosing off their poisoned arrows into every wildebeest they see, just so they can cut off the tail and sell it for a shilling as a fly whisk. And the Wakamba poaching elephant. *And*, of course, every bloody Boer and his brother taking out a full license and shooting up the countryside for biltong to feed the blacks on. I swear, I know one family where even the old grandmother has a full license, and she's eighty if she's a minute . . ."

"They're killers, the Boers, crazy blood-mad slaughterers. I saw one old boy with a square Dutch beard cut loose at a springbok one day, the buck across the river, and the bloke with no boat. Shot him anyhow, just because he was there . . ."

"I say, did you hear about the Boer who was sitting up at a salt lick, hoping to shoot himself a piece of meat? All he had was a 12-bore shot-gun with slugs in it. Whole band of beasts came down and the old boy loosed off his cannon and missed with the first barrel but pulled down something with horns on the next salvo. He went over and cut the head off the thing, butchered it, and went home. Next day one of the Game Department lads came on the head, and all the old Boer had shot was the world's record bongo. Considering that you can't even see 'em except every seven years, when the wild grape dies . . . and this old bastard doesn't even know what he's shot. Probably thought it was a bushbuck, and I've been hunting bongo for twenty years and haven't even looked like seeing one, much less shooting one . . ."

"Say what you will about the Hun, he's a bloody good engineer. Those bridges he built in Tanganyika in the 1914 war are still as true and plumb as the day some square-headed, red-necked old slave driver laid a lash on his Wogs and built 'em. I was 'cross the Ruaha the other day, and that bridge hasn't sagged a quarter inch, not even with all the traffic to Iringa . . ."

"My Wogs will be the death of me yet. The other day old Thuo pranged the tractor on a dirty great stump and came along to inform me that it was bewitched, it had a thahu in it. The next day Karinga tells me that the lorry's bewitched, as well, it won't run, because of the devils, you see, and he was dripping a dead goat around it in a circle. I pointed out with the toe of me boot that *syrup*, for Christ's sake, was an un-likely substitute for Lubeoil, even if they did look alike and have the same consistency . . ."

"You know the new thing, give them the work, and they'll finish the tools . . ."

"You can't say that Winston didn't really rally the people . . ."

"I *like* hogs. They've got a natural resistance to a lot of these diseases that ruin cattle and sheep . . ."

"I say, what a lovely piece of work is that Elisabeth. Twenty years younger, I'd have given Jeff a bit o' trouble over that one . . ."

"Old Henry doesn't change much with the times. I remember him when he hadn't a shilling to bless himself with, and he didn't look any glummer then than now. He must be richer than Sir Basil Zaharoff. Worked hard for it, though, and been a little queer since Caroline died . . ."

"Too close to his Wogs. Man must keep a distance. I'm told Henry spends an awful lot of time with that man of his, Karanja, and that he isn't above scragging a sheep himself and playing with his cowrie shells and goats' horns if he thinks he needs a little help from on high from time to time. Must be something in it, though, because they worship him, and nobody runs a better show than here at Bushbuck. You've only just got to look at it to appreciate the fact that he does get work out of his blacks . . ."

". . . and then the flying type said: 'I know, I know, Eric old boy, but what with the fog and the grog, I seem to have got hold of an old aunt of mine . . .' "

"No, but have you heard this one . . ."

"And then the Queen said: 'In that case, bugger him, Bertie, don't give him his bloody gong . . .' "

"I don't give a good goddamn what the vet says, you can do more with burnt sump oil and sulphur than you can with a hundred prescriptions . . ."

"Well, dry again. What about another, seeing as old Henry's paying . . ."

The men strolled back and forth across the lawns, not yet ready for food, full of personal news and gossip to swap, because only once in donkey's years did they get a chance to congregate. There were brothers who had not seen each other in two years, sisters separated by corrugated clay roads as thoroughly as by an ocean. Mostly the men had not dressed up for the wedding. Sir James had on a polka-dotted blue muffler inside his clean white polo shirt and was wearing an old tweed coat with flannels. Lord Waterholme had, for some reason or other, resuscitated a dove-gray morning suit, with gray topper, from its nest of moth balls and was resplendent with a bright buttonhole. But mostly the men wore drill or corduroy bush coats, with short sleeves and bullet loops. A few wore shorts; most had their trousers tucked into the tops of jodhpur boots. Kenya dust made any uniform indistinguishable after a few miles over the lava-drifting tracks. By one o'clock, most were in various stages of drunkenness and were sweating freely.

Peter was drunk, as well. As the brother of the bride and the groom's best man, he had been heartily accepted into the male society as a man grown, and he had made the grievous error of matching gins with old soakers whose stomachs were lined with zinc and whose hobnailed livers had long since ceased trying to fight back. Peter had drifted over to a group of professional hunters turned farmer since the war had stopped hunting, and was lost in a ginny fog of admiration as the men swapped stories, some of which contained a grain or so of truth, about the old days, when the Game Department was more reasonable and a man could get rich in one good year poaching ivory in the Lado Enclave.

Late in the afternoon the lawn started to spin for Peter, and he made his way to the stream, where he was violently sick. He went, pale and shaken, back to his bedroom, and for the first time in his life he passed out. When he awoke it was dark, and the guests—those who could still stand—were dancing on the lawn to the noise of the creaky phonograph. They looked exactly like a bunch of Masai warriors warming themselves up for a big ngoma. Portions of the party lasted three days, during which time Derek Johns found his wife, Emily, kissing Tom Dawson, and a splendid fist fight followed. Emily Armstrong drifted down to the stream in the moonlight with her fiancé, Cedric Holmes, who was back on a short leave from Addis Ababa, and Emily became pregnant, thereby hastening her marriage. There was a big, though separate, feasting in the blacks' compound, and much beer was drunk in honor of the wedding. Lady Waterholme had too much champagne, became ill, and had to have her stays removed.

Sir James Fitzroyce fell off his Arab horse and broke his remaining leg, and Donald Considine pranged his jeep going home when he ran full-tilt into a herd of zebras crossing the road. He suffered only a mild concussion, but the jeep was a total loss, as was one zebra. The party splintered and broke up. Some several sections invaded the Equator Club, others wound up in the Norfolk Hotel in Nairobi. Some progressed to Limuru and horrified the stewards of the golf club. Everyone agreed that it couldn't have been a nicer wedding. The blacks were a bit puzzled, since they had been forbidden to dance certain dances by the Crown and too much beer drinking was frowned on.

Henry McKenzie decided not to notice that his young son, Peter, had been disastrously drunk off a mixture of wine, gin, beer, and whisky on the afternoon of the wedding. Peter had disappeared with his horse and gun the following day and returned only as the last guests were leaving.

"Thank God that's over, son," Henry McKenzie said. "Care for a spot?"

"No, thank you, sir," Peter said. "I'm going to bed."

"So am I," said Henry McKenzie, downing a neat whisky and shuddering as it hit bottom. "I'm glad I haven't got any more daughters to marry off any time soon. One's a-plenty." He stumped up the steps and headed for his room. Already Juma, the headboy, and his assistants were beginning to clear up the wreckage. It had been a very good wedding.

14

In jail, Karanja got drunk off beer which Henry McKenzie had commanded the Meru jailer to fetch his old friend. Karanja was very sorry he had missed seeing the little Memsaab marry the Bwana Jeff. It was all part of the thahu, and he hoped that none of the thahu would affect the lives of the Bwana Jeff and the Memsaab Elisabeth. There had been too much trouble already. Karanja took another gulp of beer and smiled as he remembered his first wedding. *What* a wedding that had been!

The crops had been good that year, and the flocks had thrived. Karanja was a full-fledged njama now, and he wanted a wife. He had been dancing for two years since he became a warrior, and he had lain in the huts after the dances with many maidens. But he had scrupulously observed the mathanjuki's teachings about sex, and he had not impregnated any girl, although the experiences were frustrating in light of his memories of the Masai maid. Finally he settled on Kamore, daughter of Koinange, a respected elder, although poor. Kamore was beautiful, fat and shining like a zebra filly, with strong legs and big breasts. He had lain with her often in her mother's hut, and he knew she loved him. Also, he had noted that she worked very hard, helping her mother cultivate her father's fields. Her broad pelvis would yield him many sons, and her strong back would never tire beneath its load of firewood, of bananas, of wattle saplings and potato tops.

Karanja consulted his father, who agreed that the choice was good. Karanja then asked his mother to make him some cane beer, and then he went to the wife of his circumcision sponsor, to ask her to go with him to call on Koinange, the father of the woman he wished to marry.

Koinange was sitting on his heels in the shade of a big cedar tree, talking with his relatives, when Karanja came with Wairimu, the wife of his circumcision sponsor. Wairimu was carrying two gourds of beer suspended from a limber stick across her shoulders.

Karanja offered a polite formal greeting and squatted on his heels. Wairimu set down the beer gourds in the shade and joined the wives of Koinange underneath a nearby fig. The women chattered excitedly, like squirrels, but the men talked sensibly of crops and rains for a long time. Then Karanja said gravely:

"For some time I have partnered your daughter at the dances and I have lain with her in her mother's hut. I have not removed the second apron from her, and so I come to you in honor, with my father's permission to speak. I have also watched your daughter labor in the fields of your shamba, and I have noted that she is a steady and diligent worker."

"She is a good girl," Koinange said. "She is obedient and healthy and fat, and she works hard in the fields with her mother."

"I want her to come and cultivate the fields of my shamba, for now I am a warrior and a man and I need a woman to tend my shamba and dig deep around the roots of my plantings, so that they may grow well and bring prosperity to my house."

Koinange clapped his hands and jerked his head at the women. They joined the group of men, with Wairimu bringing along the beer.

"Do you consent to till the shamba of Karanja, son of Kimani?" he asked his daughter, whose eyes glistened wide.

"Yes," Kamore said. "I consent." She bowed her head.

Kamore's mother took the beer gourds from Wairimu and poured out a hornful. She handed the horn to Koinange. He turned to face his daughter again. "If this man does not please you, I shall spill this beer upon the ground," he said. "Do not spill the beer," replied Kamore. "Drink." Koinange drained the horn and refilled it. In turn, he filled it and handed it to each of his wives and to his assembled kinsmen. They drank. Then the wife of Karanja's circumcision sponsor went off to fetch Kimani, the father of Karanja. The men thereafter haggled all day in the shade of the big cedar tree, drinking beer and discussing the bride price. Koinange said that his daughter, being so fat, so comely, and so industrious, was worth more than the usual thirty goats. This fact was admitted. The price was finally settled on thirty goats, six fat rams, twenty gourds of beer, and a long-term payment of ten goats for the first child and five goats for each successive child, up to five. It was a very dear price to pay for a woman.

There was a great to-do about choosing the goats from the herd of Karanja's father. There must be some fat ones, of course, and some medium-grade ones, and an equal number of thin ones, to strike a balance. Only twenty goats were selected, and Karanja's father, together with two friends of his own age grade, drove the goats to the shamba of Koinange. The father of the bride carefully looked at the teeth, hoofs, and bellies of each, lifting them to test their weight, and a very long argument followed. Then Koinange accepted the goats. The next day ten more goats and three of the six fat-tailed rams were driven over, and Koinange accepted these, as well, after protesting that he was being robbed.

The next day was the day of the first big beer drink, and all the womenfolk of Karanja's household went over to Koinange's shamba, bearing gourds frothy-full. One of the fat rams was slaughtered, and all day long the two families drank, danced, and feasted. The bridegroom's mother poured gruel over her head as a sign of happiness, and the empty gourds were stuffed with grass, signifying friendship between the two clans, and the bridegroom and his family staggered home, drunk and bloated with the roasted ram. When he had slept a little, Karanja went in the cool of the evening to beseech land from the chief of his clan and was given an unclaimed plot adjoining the shamba of his father.

While Karanja and his entire circumcision group busied themselves in breaking the ground and clearing the brush from the new shamba, the womenfolk of his clan massed to grind cane for more beer, because the ceremonial drinking had just begun. There were three momumental drunks in the shamba of the bridegroom's father, the drunk of the building of the new home, the drunk for its furnishing, and finally the drunk for the taking of the bride. More fat rams were killed and roasted.

Karanja remembered that every morning he had a colossal hangover as he and his age companions went out to uproot stumps and dig ground; that his skull felt constricted by a tight cord, faery specks danced before his eyes, and there were ominous upsurgings in his throat. But on the final day, the day of the bride-taking, he and his friends built a mud foundation and erected a mud-and-wattle hut. The women of his clan were busy all day long, weaving thatch for its roof and for the roof of the beehive-like granary which stood to one side.

When evening came a group of Karanja's circumcision brothers dressed magnificently in ostrich-feather headdresses and paint of lime and ocher, wearing rattles on their legs and bracelets on their arms. As Kamore came out of her mother's hut, they ambushed her and carried her, screeching and kicking, to the new hut. They shoved her through the doorway and then left her alone. She remained in the hut for four days, loudly weeping, and singing sad songs—songs which had been taught her as part of her circumcision instruction and which were shaped to extol her clan and appease its members for her decision to desert it for the clan of another. All this time Karanja feasted with the bachelors, sleeping in the thingira, and not once daring to see his bride. Food was brought to the bride by the groom's mother, and her only other visitors were girls of her own age grade.

At the end of the fourth day she paid a formal call on her family, returning at nightfall to what was now her own hut. That night Karanja crawled through the door and settled down beside her on the goatskin bed. He could not see her in the dark, but he could smell the fragrance of the fat with which she had been smeared by his mother. Karanja's hands groped for her big breasts and then swiftly tore off the second apron. He entered her greased body, snorting and snuffling heavily, like a bull, and she moved her loins upward eagerly to meet him. This time he did not have to leave the body of a dead girl. After he had spent himself, she caressed him until soon he was ready to enter her again, and now he knew fulfillment. The next morning he got up from Kamore's bed and took the last offering of beer to her father, and the final three fat rams, as payment for the theft and rapine of his daughter.

For one month they enjoyed a lazy honeymoon. Food was prepared and brought to the bridal hut by Karanja's mother, and the bride did no work whatsoever. At the end of thirty days Kamore's head was shaved and she went to pay a final visit to her family. This was the last chance to annul the marriage. By a sign she could say that she was not happy with this man, her husband, and the bride price would be grudgingly repaid. No one's honor would be damaged, and even though she might be pregnant, no stain would attach to her character, and she would again be eligible for marriage, although there would be less hesitancy about observing the formalities of the second apron, because a cow heavy with calf could not be damaged by the seed of another bull.

But Karanja had been a faithful and sturdy mate to her, mounting her daily several times, and her menses did not flow at the appointed time. She judged herself to be happily pregnant and placed a bunch of flowers before her face to signify that she was satisfied. She was given a young goat as a final present from her family, and her mother poured sheep's fat over her head and neck. She was given also a gourd of gruel to take back to her husband, and she returned at nightfall to her own hut as wife, no longer bride.

Her wifely duties began the next day. She went to the forest to gather firewood and returned home behind Karanja, bearing an enormous load of dry wattle, thorn twigs, and small logs of punk, which, held by a strap round her forehead, she carried on her back. Then Karanja took her to the river to choose the three stones which would form her cooking hearth. These stones were the most sacred symbol of marriage and would be so closely tied to her new life that they might never be left behind without extra-special purification against an emergency of the most violent nature. Karanja also gave her digging implements, cooking pots, and gourds. His mother brought the beans for the first meal. The honeymoon was over. . . .

Karanja, now in his jail cell, rattled the bars, and the pocked Meru came again. Karanja thrust his beer pannikin at the turnkey, who returned with another gourd. The Big Bwana had bribed him well. Karanja drank deep again and sighed as he remembered.

Because in six months, as the fields waved plumy-green and the birds sang in the high trees, the big sickness came. In a few days Kamore and the baby she carried in her belly were dead. It was after that he met the Big Bwana, and a long time after that before he was able to afford to marry his second wife, Wangu, mother of his son, Kimani, and his second son, Kibarara. Kimani, who bore the name of Karanja's father and who now possessed a thahu which had put Karanja in the white man's jail hut. Karanja sighed again and reached for the beer. As long as that son of a Meru hyena kept bringing it on the Bwana's orders, things might be worse, although he was very sorry he had missed the fun when the circumcision brothers of Jeff Newton snatched the bride away and threw her in the automobile.

15

Jeff and Elisabeth Newton went into the house to dress after the mammoth meal of oysters and game and barbecued beef, none of which they had touched. They had cut the cake—with a panga, appropriately, instead of a sword, which Jeff did not own, he being of the wartime Navy. They had drunk quite a lot of champagne, and both were feeling pleasantly tight. They had had no private time together, since all the women had to kiss Jeff (to see how those mustaches actually feel, my dear) and all the men had had to kiss Elisabeth (to see what the lad's letting himself in for, old chap) and everyone had shaken hands and slapped the groom's back, the men winking and leering and making the crude, good-humored jokes that have ever been the unfortunate penance of all bridegrooms. Jeff slipped into Peter's room and shucked his uniform, throwing it carelessly on Peter's bed, and re-dressed in an old gray flannel suit and a soft shirt. Elisabeth ducked away at the same time and went to her room, with Holly Keith's mother, to change to a white gabardine suit and a blouse which almost but not quite matched her eyes. Peter, by then pleasantly tiddled but still not yet drunk, came with Juma and took Elisabeth's bags, Peter remaining by the Chev to ward off the last-minute violent humor and to superintend the attachment of shoes, gin bottles, biscuit tins, and one dead wart hog, which some wag had shot and tied to the bumper, just under the "Just Married" scrawl. Jeff called a servant and had his own bags sent out and then went back to the lawn party to have a final peg with the gentlemen while the bride dressed. The bride appeared swiftly, pitched her bouquet at young Holly Keith, and fled like a cheetah for the truck, with Jeff just behind her, and the crowd baying at their heels, screaming like foxhounds before a kill, and pelting the pair with rice and chunks of bread and pieces of the wedding cake. Jeff popped Elisabeth into the seat, locked the door, and jumped into the car. He trod on the starter, which exploded with a dreadful blast and removed a good bit of his mustache and most of his eyebrows, since one of the merrie gentlemen had thoughtfully affixed a small powder charge to the treadle. But the engine caught and the lorry lurched away, while several enthusiastic friends fired at it with weapons ranging from elephant rifles to pistols. It was typical of the gentle send-off that only one slug actually hit the truck, glancing off the roof, because no Kenya gentleman would ever seriously endanger a lady on her wedding day.

"Light me a cigarette, will you, bride?" Jeff said, steering the Chev around a pig hole and hitting another with a rattling thump as he turned to look at his wife. She lit the cigarette and placed it in his mouth.

"Thanks awfully, darling. We'll be onto the road in a jiffy, and I'll stop this catamaran and cut loose most of the bits and bangles. I wonder what bloody idiot booby-trapped the starter? Damn near marred me beauty for life."

"It was a *sweet* wedding," Elisabeth said. "So well behaved, for that crowd. Only signs of sparks I noticed was when Leslie Simmons and her husband's girl friend came to face, and I must say both were very good about it. Leslie looked charming with her black eye."

Jeff swerved the car off the plain and onto the track. He turned and looked at his wife. Her eyes were as big and blue as cornflowers, her mouth very soft and very red. He jammed his foot on the brake and the lorry ground to a stop, stalling. He took Elisabeth in his arms and kissed her hard, knocking her hat askew. Then he took her very lightly by the elbows and pushed her away, a little.

"There'll be none of that bloody nonsense in this family, on either side," he said quietly. "I've watched it out here ever since I was a boy, and I shall beat you half to death if there's any hanky-panky with anybody, I don't care how bored you get. And you're at liberty to shoot me, or have Peter do it."

"I love you very much, you great oaf," Elisabeth said, straightening her hat. "Now come and kiss Mama very sweet, and let us drive on to Nyeri so we can get on with the more serious business."

"Nothing better than a basic woman," Jeff said, kissing her on the end of the nose. "Now I'll just chop off these tins and things and we'll whiz off to the Outspan." He climbed out of the car and walked round to the rear.

"Well, for Christ's sake, see who's here."

Elisabeth turned her head and looked backward through the rear window. Perched on the mound of baggage was Lathela, the Wandrobo-

Masai-Rendille-Samburu gunbearer. He was wearing his best—an old pith helmet with ostrich feathers pinned to one side and a sheaf of brilliant blue guinea-fowl wing feathers on the other. Instead of his usual khaki shorts, he was wearing a pair of lady's bright pink bloomers. He had found some old tan tennis shoes somewhere and had cut holes in them for his toes to stick out of. He smiled a sunburst of a grin and waved a hand. The other hand still contained his spear.

"Jambo, Bwana, Jambo, Memsaab. Mimi na kuja kwa wewe. Iko hapa bundouki na lisase." He pointed at a leather case and an iron box.

"Bugger's asked himself along on the honeymoon," Jeff said. "And he's certainly got up grand for it. I wonder where he found those drawers. They look about the right size for Sally Henderson. And he's brought a bloody great gun case and a mound of cartridges, as well. I wonder what he thinks I intend to shoot on this safari."

"Whatever it is, you won't need a gun for it," Elisabeth said, and turned scarlet. "I mean . . ."

"I know what you mean, you shameless hussy," Jeff said, climbing back into the car. "We might's well take him. He can look after the luggage and things, and you never know when you'll need a gun. Lathela! Take your panga and cut off those tins!"

They drove quietly, talking little, on the road to Nyeri, and when they entered the courtyard of the Outspan Hotel, Jeff killed the car in front of one of the annexes. "That's us, up there," he said, pointing to a big corner room. "Everything's fixed. We don't have to go in through the hotel and listen to a lot of rude jokes and have everybody standing us a drink and flicking rice off us. I'm glad it's over now, aren't you?"

"Mmmm. Such a nice wedding. Such a nice hotel. Such a nice husband."

"Such a pretty, beautiful, wonderful, gorgeous, amazing bride. Oversexed, maybe, but useful. We'll just nip up to the rooms. Lathela! Letti sandouki na bundouki na lisase, na kwenda tasama chakula. Na taka lala lorry. It's just as well he hitched on, sweetie. He can fetch us the boxes and then go scrounge some food for himself, alert the reception that we're here, and sleep in the lorry. Glad he came."

"So'm I. I shouldn't like to face that group in the bar tonight. It'll be bad enough tomorrow. Up we go, shall us?"

"Up we go, Mrs. Newton. Sounds strange. Mistress Newton. Memsaab Newton. A matron."

"Not yet I'm not. I'm still a bride, and don't you forget it, my lad, and I'm still subject to all the odd whims that are the right of brides. Are you going to carry me over the threshold, for instance, or do I have to walk on my poor sore feet in these new shoes?"

"Not only over, but up two flights," said Jeff, and swept her up in his arms. "Here we go. Come on, Lathela, fetch the bags!"

The room Jeff carried Elisabeth into was not *a* room, but a vast beamed structure of white plaster, with a huge double bed and mirrored table, an armoire large enough to hide an elephant in, and two chintzy chairs. It let off into a large dressing room, which opened again on a grand bath, striped marble and regal. When you opened a door of the bedroom, you went down into the lounge, whose white wool rugs stretched before a fireplace large enough for a man to step into without stooping. Through the broad windows running the whole length of the room, one could see Mount Kenya—Kerinyagga—wreathed now in white clouds below the snaggled peak, backdropped by blue. There were bright pictures of Kikuyu men and women, of animals and flowers, on the plaster walls, and an enormous divan of blue, flanked by two white easy chairs. The room was banked with flowers, great sheaves of gladioli, roses, carnations, fern, and lilies of the valley. Jeff punched a buzzer button, still without dropping Elisabeth, then kissed her gently and set her on her feet. Lathela came in behind them with the first of the bags, and Jeff waved him to the dressing room. Behind Lathela came three room servants, barefoot black boys in white kanzus with red fezzes. They stowed the luggage, and one came to ask the Bwana which cases he would like opened.

"This," Jeff said, indicating his own bag, and then turned to Elisabeth. "I'll open mine myself," she said. "Right now I'm cold. Let's have a fire." She hugged herself, grasping herself by the elbows. "I don't know whether I'm just nervous or if it's the temperature drop."

"Fire," Jeff said. "Light it meself. First fire-lighting of what I hope'll be a long and happy life, with maybe twenty kids. Presto! Flame. What a wonderful thing a fire is."

The match licked out to the paper, and the paper caught the conifers and dry sticks which formed the tinder, and the tinder flared, and the great resiny logs responded eagerly to the flame. The fire crackled and then began to roar, and the white walls of the lounge were pinkened, then black-shadowed by the flames. The manager, frock-coated, striped-trousered, arrived bowing. The flowers had been his. So was the sideboard stocked with precious whisky, and the bottles of champagne that beaded in a silver bucket.

"Hearty congratulations to you both, I'm sure," he said. "I've taken the liberty of ordering you a little snack for later on. Ring when you want it. And anything I can do for the bride or groom . . ."

"Nothing, nothing, thanks very much, and thank you for the flowers. They are beautiful, and so is the grog. I don't know about you, Elisabeth, but I'm hungry. Didn't eat anything at lunch. What do you say to half an hour?"

"Lovely, I'm starved too. I'd like to get some of this dust off first. Thank you very much for the flowers, Mr. Manson. They are divine, and the champagne too. I'm feeling dry after the trip in. Jeff, will you open a bottle and let's all have a drink with Mr. Manson, and then I'll just nip out and bathe."

"Allow me," the manager said, and expertly thumbed the top off a bottle of Heidsick which had survived the war until now. He filled the glasses and raised his in a sweeping toast.

"The beautiful bride, the lucky groom," he said. "Here's cheers, and the very best wishes for a long and happy. Cheers," and bowed.

"Thanks very much."

"And now, if you'll excuse me, I must just whiz off and see to your supper. Ring when you want it, and the boys'll bring it. I'll see you shan't be disturbed. Good night, and again, congratulations. Good night," and the manager bowed out backward, as only hotel managers know how.

"Nice chap, Manson, you know," Jeff said. "Jolly thoughtful of him. He knew we were coming, of course, and would have had everything laid on, per my instructions, but he didn't have to go and do it all on his own."

"Jolly decent. I say, I *am* a wreck, darling. I think I'll just take my lovely bubbly giggly water and carry it into the bath and make myself all nice and clean and bridy. I can still taste the grit from that ride. You want to drop down to the bar, or what?"

"No, sweetie, I'll sit here and have a whisky—I *hate* champagne— and stare into the fire and plot the future. I haven't decided yet on whether it's to be a boy first or a girl first. Gallop off and get all ruffly like they do in the books. I'll ring for the supper when you're sweet and clean."

"Right. 'By." Elisabeth blew him a kiss and went into the bedroom, closing the door. Jeff walked over to the sideboard, put down his champagne glass, and poured himself a stiff scotch. He squirted in a little fizz, shucked his coat, loosened his tie, and sat down in front of the fire.

Funny, he thought, now it's here, and we're both scared stiff and want to keep putting it off, like some goody the kids save as best for last. In the morning she'll wake up in the crook of my arm and grin at me, but right now I'm as scared as I was when I stalked my first elephant. I'm as scared as I was the day the ship blew. I'm scared, and yet I ain't.

What I am is lucky, he said, nibbling at the edge of his glass and watching the dancing shadows from the fire. Oh Christ, what a lucky chap I am. The prettiest and smartest girl in Kenya. I lived through the war. I have a farm as fine as any in the country, with no debts. *I* haven't got any close people at all to mess up the marriage, and her people are all fine. If I were a praying man I'd pray a little bit here, because no one man deserves all this luck. Heigh-ho, Newton. I'm not a praying man, so I will just say thanks to whoever runs it and let it go at that. Hmmm, I hear splashings. I think I shall just whip into the lav and wash my face and then get out of these clothes and into something lascivious, like pajamas, slippers, and me best brocade gown. Me *only* dressing gown, as a matter of fact, and it's a crying shame it's only flannel, fresh off the nail at Ahamed's.

Jeff walked into the bedroom to unpack his pajamas, and through the bathroom door he could hear splashings and singing. The bride, for some peculiar reason, was singing, "Lay that pistol down, babe, lay that pistol down, pistol-packin' mama, lay that pistol down," a most unbridified song made recently popular by the Americans. Jeff grinned at the song. "'D say that the old girl doesn't sound unhappy," he said, and took off his pants. This time, he noticed, he took them to the clothespress and hung them neatly over a hanger. He washed his hands and face and got into his pajamas, slippers, and robe. He got out his toothbrush and cleaned his teeth, dampened his hair, and ran a comb through it. As he started back to the lounge, Lisa called through the door: "I'm coming out. You can ring for the food now if you'd like, darling."

Jeff picked up his glass, had a drink out of it, and then punched the button. He heard a door open, a door close, and then the sound of another door.

Elisabeth had paused at the bedroom door. Her hair was brushed up and stood in ringlets, springing softly about her luminous face. Her eyes were wide in the special way she had, except now they were twice as wide and twice as large as any other eyes in the world, and twice as blue, twice as violet. There was a stiff sort of frilly stand-up collar that framed her face above the fine thin robe she wore, and with the light behind her he could see the soft rounded outline of her body through robe and the gown underneath. Her face seemed tiny, her eyes grew more enormous, her mouth was tremulous and slightly parted.

"Here I am," she said. "Jeff. Oh, Jeff." And held out her arms.

The supper so carefully planned by Mr. Manson, the manager, was beautiful, but it had been slightly nibbled at by cats. Jeff stepped in the beautiful oysters, the lovely thin-sliced salmon, the delicate aspic, the fine cold fowl, and the wonderful cheese. He stepped in the miraculous supper the next morning as it rested outside the door, as they left on their way for a month's honeymoon at Malindi on the coast. The servants had tired of ringing the doorbell and had left the tray on the floor, and the house cats had come and had a fine time with the wedding supper.

"I'm hungry," Elisabeth said when she woke the next morning. She stretched, and kicked her feet under the covers. Her hair tickled Jeff's neck as she made herself small and snuggled into his shoulder.

"I'm hungry, and I love my new husband so very, very much."

The last statement removed any remote possibility of breakfast, and so they were forced to stop off to have sausage rolls and beer with the little Indian in the ducca at Fort Hall, on the way down to the coast. The sausage rolls were wonderful, just what they wanted, and the beer was simply divine.

16

They laughed and swam in the opalescent waters at Malindi, and they went spearfishing and sat on the shining sands in the sun and listened to the breezes rattle the palm fronds. They played sand-crab poker and they ate a great deal and took long naps after lunch. They went over to Mombasa, where Jeff knew an Arab dhow captain, and they sailed with him to Zanzibar, sleeping on the carven poop under the brilliant stars, resting on soft high-piled Afghan rugs and listening to the plaintive minor-keyed crooning of the fierce-mustached Arab sailors who lay in the waist of the big dhow, smoking kif and picking idly at queer mandolins or blowing softly into flutes. They walked slowly round the bazaars and inspected the rosy stone buildings of a civilization that went back to A.D. 950 and of which the poets sang. They hooked a ride back from Zanzibar with an old friend who owned a little airplane, and went on the tiles in Nairobi for a week. Then they got into the Chev and drove back to Jeff's farm. He had a surprise waiting for Elisabeth. It was a complete new wing on the old stone house, melded so carefully into the old structure by Italian prisoners of war that it even seemed aged.

It was masoned of yellowstone chopped crumbly from the nearby hills, and formed a careful L away from the old dwelling, with a broad, flagged patio in the hollow space between the old and the new house. The living room was huge, its ceiling sixteen feet, its floor space forty feet by thirty-five. One wall was natural black-and-red stone, and into it was carven a fireplace so large it had stone seats inside. There was a deep bay overlooking the patio, from which already were springing annual and perennial flowers. Great showy blooms of bougainvillaea had been enticed from the old house and were crawling up the walls.

Sliding panels, stained gray-green, hid a bar, an icebox, and a small kitchenette-pantry at the far end. At the other end, vast french doors let in the sunlight and opened onto a cool green terrace which was rimmed with herbaceous borders and shaded by a towering cedar.

The short end of the L consisted of two one-storied bedrooms divided by an immense bathroom containing tub and shower. The first room held only a tremendous double bed and a chest of drawers flanked by leather chairs. The other room, green-paneled on three sides and white-stoned on one, owned a small fireplace pierced halfway up the wall, a single bed, a big chintzed easy chair, a blond-wood vanity table with triple mirrors, bookshelves, and a yellow Indian chenille carpet. Jeff had stretched a magnificent leopard skin along the wall over the fireplace, its mounted head held in a bracket. On the day they arrived there were yellow roses in a silver bowl, a special assignment Jeff had assigned to Peter before they left on their honeymoon.

The big living room contained an old but newly varnished and tuned grand piano, once the delight of Jeff's mother, which had sat in storage for years in Nairobi. One whole wall was bookshelves. The floor was polished African ebony, actually the black heart of a certain thorn tree. Over the mantel Jeff had hung his best buffalo, a huge beast with an enormous boss, mounted so that he looked downward into the room. There was a lion-skin rug on the floor in front of the hearth, and on the two matching cowhide sofas leopard skins sprawled along the backs. There was a huge writing desk in one corner and several deep leather easy chairs scattered around. Jeff's gun cabinet, as always parenthesized by elephant tusks, stood next the bar, and the oiled guns gleamed through the glass front.

Jeff picked up Elisabeth and carried her once again across the threshold.

"This is your new home, sweetie," he said, setting her down with a thump and a misdirected kiss which nearly removed her nose. "I hope you like it. These Italians are bloody marvelous workers. They've had exactly six weeks to get this finished, and it already looks like we've been living in it."

"I think it is just the most wonderful wedding present anybody ever had," Elisabeth said. "And you are *the* most thoughtful man. Because this is *my* house, not my mother's or your father's, and it takes a very clever fellow to understand what that means. To come to a place nobody else ever lived in, I mean, her very own place."

"I'm a bloody genius as well as being a fantastic lover," Jeff said. "Come on. I'll show you around, and then we'll see what the bed's like."

"I hope this healthy boyish enthusiasm continues to continue," Elisabeth said. "What's this other bedroom?"

"That's your boudoir, silly. Secret female country for when you're mad at me or want to read old love letters from other men. Also a place to retire to when the boys come home and it gets a little wet out in the big room. Now, about this bed . . ."

"Last one in is a nigger baby," Elisabeth said, unzipping her skirt.

Some mornings later Elisabeth poured herself a second cup of coffee at breakfast and announced:

"I'm glad you built us the new house, Jeff."

"Mmmm? What?" Jeff turned the pages of a week-old *East African Standard.* "Long as you're bent over, pour me another cup as well. What is all this about the new house?"

"It looks very much as if the old one's going to come in very handy. Unless the signs are all wrong, I think I'm pregnant, despite my fine precautions. Do you mind dreadfully?"

"Mind? His name's Geoffrey, of course." Jeff lit a cigarette and buffed his nails smugly on his sleeve. "Unless it's twins, in which case we'll call the other boy Harry, after your old man."

"I had more or less settled on a girl. Little boys are so *smelly*."

"We'll drown it if it's a girl," Jeff said. "Can't get a decent bride price for manamouki any more. Nope. Got to be a boy. I went and had a chat with the witch doctor. Boy guaranteed. Boy named Jeff. And why else, my good brood mare, do you think I built this new wing? I'd planned on filling up the other one with kids. I'm pleased to find you so co-operative. Try not to be one of those throwing-up pregnant types, will you?"

Elisabeth turned up the corners of her eyes at him.

"Aren't you supposed to do something frightfully tender, like kissing the young mother and falling on your knees at her feet when she announces a thing of this sort?"

"Kiss 'em? Not me. If they'll do it with you, they'll do it with anybody," Jeff said coarsely. "None of that silly kissing stuff for me," he said, pulling her to her feet in order to make himself a liar. "As a matter of fact," he whispered against her mouth, "I didn't really want to do any work this morning, anyhow."

17

Two months after the marriage of Jeff Newton and Elisabeth McKenzie the trial of Karanja and the two midwives was convened in Nyeri. Karanja was charged with being accessory to murder. The two old women were charged with murder. The trial was pathetically brief. The two old women gave testimony. Yes, they said. A baby, born feet first, was taken from the womb of Mwange, wife of Karanja. Was it a healthy baby? Yes, Bwana, it was a very healthy baby, a fine big boy.

"Then what did you do with the baby?" the Crown asked.

"I bit its navel cord and handed it to Gachere," Nduta said. "Then I saw to the baby's mother."

"What did you do with the baby?" the Crown asked.

"I smothered it with a goatskin," Gachere said. "Then I wrapped it in the skin and laid it to one side."

"What did you do then?"

"I assisted Nduta in seeing to the welfare of the mother."

"Did anyone tell you to kill the baby?"

"Oh no, Bwana. We always kill babies born feet first, because they are cursed with a thahu."

"Do you kill other babies?"

"Ndio, Bwana. We kill first-born twins, always, because they too have thahu."

"What did you do with the baby after the mother was seen to?"

"We took it to the fields for the hyenas, as is the custom, Bwana."

"Was the baby quite dead? When you took it to the hyenas?"

"I think so, Bwana," Nduta said. "It did not breathe."

"When you take your dead, old and young, to the hyenas, are they always dead?"

"Not always, Bwana. Sometimes, when an old person is very sick and near death, it is better to take them to the fields before they die. In this way the hut is not contaminated, and so it is not necessary to burn the hut and leave the shamba."

"Do you recognize the fact that killing is against the law?"

"Oh yes, Bwana. Everyone knows that to kill is very bad, except in war, or when a poisoner is discovered, or when an enemy has cursed you. And a blood price must be paid to the relatives of the dead one, which is very expensive, needing many sheep, goats, and cows. Killing is very bad, especially if the slain one be of your own clan."

"Is killing children against the law?"

"Oh yes, Bwana. Nobody would kill a child. Killing a child is much worse than killing an adult, because women children are the riches of their fathers, and men children are the warriors who fight to save the tribe from harm."

"But killing a baby, a newborn baby? Is not that killing a child?"

"Oh *no*, Bwana," both old women said, horrified. "A child is never officially born until the second year, when it celebrates its birthday. This was no child of whom you speak. This was a demon which had taken the body of the child and, thanks to God, made its presence known by being born upside down. A true child is not a child until it has passed one year. We merely took this demon from the woman and cleansed her of thahu by destroying it. After which we gave it to the hyenas, as is customary."

"Which of you, once more, actually smothered the child?"

"I did," Gachere said. "Because Nduta was very busy with the mother. But do not call it a child. It was a monster."

"If I had not been busy with the mother, I would have smothered the monster," Nduta said. "It is nothing, really, to destroy that kind of thahu. But there was the cord to be cleaned and tucked back and the matter of the afterbirth, and so Gachere smothered the monster."

"Will you smother other children when you return to the shamba?"

"Oh yes, certainly, Bwana. It is our duty to smother children who are born wrong-end-to, or who are first-born twins. It is very bad to let them live, because they become monsters in human flesh and give thahu to all with whom they come in touch."

"Holy God," the Crown said to himself. "And these are the people who will someday govern themselves."

The Crown then summoned Karanja to the stand. Karanja scratched himself. There were lice in the jail.

"Did you order the killing of the child?" the Crown asked.

"No, Bwana. The birthing of children is work for women, and the man is not allowed in the hut. Only when the news comes of whether the child is a boy or a girl and signals are made by cutting the sugar canes, five for a boy, four for a girl, does the father celebrate the birth. There was a thahu on my house, and so when the child was born feet first, in the sign of the demon, the old women naturally smothered the child. It has always been so."

"But you approved of the killing of the child?"

"Of course, Bwana. What else would one do with a demon?"

"All right. Stand down. This honorable court is adjourned."

The black askaris came and took Karanja and the two old women away to the jailhouse. The Crown pulled off his wig and shucked his elder's robes. He went home and mixed himself a gin in which there was practically no pink at all. Then he mixed another.

"Helen," the Crown said to his wife, "perhaps you can tell me what I do now."

"You poor, poor man," his wife said.

The woman Gachere was sentenced to be hanged. The woman Nduta was given life imprisonment as an accomplice. Karanja was sentenced to five years in jail as an accessory before the fact. When the sentence had been pronounced the Crown went home and got hopelessly drunk off brandy and wept.

18

When Kimani heard the sentence of death for the woman Gachere and the prison terms for Nduta and his father, he could not understand how it could be so. Had he not been purified of the thahu that had entered him as a result of having been struck by the Bwana Jeff? Had not the mundumugu slain a goat, and had he not worn its entrails and vomited out the curse? If this were so, then why was his father in jail? He didn't care about the old women, they were old and would die soon, anyhow, but his father was innocent and it was all his, Kimani's, fault, and the fault of the Bwana Jeff, who had struck him.

He went to the old witch doctor and asked him where the purification had failed.

"Why is my father not freed?" he asked. "I am cleansed of the thahu, yet my father is in jail. Is your magic no longer strong?"

"My magic is strong enough," the old man replied. "But the damage had been done before I cleansed you. The white man's magic is also strong, and he has might on his side, askaris and white officers of Kingi Georgi, soldiers and elders who wear wigs and pass down sentences in the council. I cannot help your father more, for the thahu must be yet in your body."

"What can I do further to purify myself, old man?"

"There is nothing further to be done. Unless . . ."

"Unless what?"

"Nothing. There is nothing more to be done." The old man took his bean gourd and spilled the beans idly on the ground, piling them in little heaps. He counted the extras and looked up like a wise old monkey at Kimani. "No. There is nothing more to be done. What is finished is past. Kwaheri."

Kimani went away in search of Peter McKenzie, his friend. He found Peter lounging on the lawn, resting his elbows on the grass as he talked to his father, who was smoking on the porch.

"Excuse me, Bwana," Kimani said, looking from the boy to the man. "But I am very sad that my father is in jail and that it is my fault that he is in jail, because of a thahu that I brought to his shamba. I did not seek the thahu. It was the fault of the Bwana Jeff, who struck me."

"Enough of that talk, Kimani." Henry McKenzie spoke sharply. "It wasn't your fault, and it wasn't the Bwana Jeff's fault, either, and this thahu nonsense is just that. You've been to school and you are a Christian, and you should know better. It was just damned bad luck all round. I'm trying to get the sentence suspended, or at least lightened, after things quiet down. Be patient, and remember that you are now the head of your father's house while he is gone. You must be a man, and leave this to me. Do you understand?"

"I understand, Bwana. May I go occasionally to visit my father in the jail? To take him beer and snuff and see that he is not treated badly?"

"Of course, boy. You may go when I go, which will be once a week. Your father will be treated well. But you must undertake his duties until his return. There is a sick heifer in pasture, and I wish her to be brought to the barn. She is the big white one with red spots. Go and fetch her now.

"Poor little bugger," Henry McKenzie said as Kimani went away, holding himself stiffly and proudly. "Poor little bugger. Caught halfway between yesterday and tomorrow, and not quite sure of either. Confidentially, when the hubbub dies down I think I can get Karanja paroled to me and at least lighten the sentence on the two old women. Not that they'll mind being in clink for a bit. The food's fair and there's not much work for them to do. Now, back to what you were saying, Peter. . . ."

"It's just that I don't want to be a farmer for a while, Pa. You don't need me on the farm, not with Jeff next door. The war'll be over one of these days and people will be coming back to Kenya, and I want to be a white hunter. Anyhow, for a few years. It's not that I don't like the farm. But it's your farm, and you'll run it for a long time. Someday I'll have to give it all my time, just as you have, but I want to have some fun first. There's so much I haven't seen. I haven't seen the Congo, and I haven't seen truly into the N.F.D., and I don't know anything about Tanganyika or Uganda. I want to see the Sudan and Portuguese East. I was talking to old Dan the other day, at the wedding . . ."

"Before you got disgracefully drunk and passed out, after being sick in the stream?" Henry McKenzie grinned. "Or after? Because if it was after, I doubt you'll quote him accurately."

"I told you I was sorry about that," Peter said sheepishly. "No, sir, Dan said that when he started hunting again he'd take me along as his apprentice for a couple of years, and then when he retired I could have his string and strike off on my own."

"Said that, did he? Must have a fair opinion of you, as he's the best there is. So you want to be a vagabond, eh? Can't say as I blame you too much, but it's a lousy life, Peter. If you get caught up in it, it's likely to spoil you for settling down ever. I've seen it happen too often. It's a false life, full of liquor and awful rich people who see you as a freak and a thrill, like a two-headed lion or something."

"Well, I don't mean it to be forever, Pa," Peter said, pulling a blade of grass out of the lawn and chewing on it, kicking his feet slowly up and down. "I'll probably have to go into the forces for a year or so at least, and when I'm demobbed I'd like a few years o' fun. You never had much fun yourself, not from what you've told me, and I'll be a bloody sight better farmer if I get a little curiosity out of my system. I promise, Pa, if you'll let me run loose for a few years, I'll come back and settle down the very second you can honestly say you need me. Isn't that fair?"

Henry McKenzie stuffed his pipe carefully with tobacco and looked down at his blunt, square-ended fingers with the thick raised ridges of nails.

"I suppose I'll say yes in the end. If I tell you no, then you'll probably run off and do what you want anyhow. I know I would. But it's not tomorrow and not next week and not even next year. The war isn't over and you haven't done your service yet and a lot of things can happen. Suppose we say that if everything turns out pretty much on schedule, and I don't get kicked in the head by a horse or something, we'll give you a shot at what you want if Dan will take you on. That's for a lot later, of course. Meanwhile you've not finished school and there's any amount you don't know about running a farm. You're going to be *my* apprentice until the Army get you. Understand?"

"Yes, sir. Thank you, sir. If it's all right with you, I think I'll saddle a horse and nip over to Jeff's and talk to him a little. He tried to talk me off this before, you know."

"No, I didn't." Henry McKenzie took off his hat and fanned himself with it. "But I'm not surprised. Solid type, Jeff. No moonbeams in his head. He tells me, by the by, that he's going to make a grandfather of me and an uncle of you. They didn't waste any time starting a family, did they? And I'm damned glad. It'll be nice to have some young'uns running around, now you're near grown and wanting to be off on safari with a lot of French counts and American millionaires."

"Well, I'll see you later, Pa, unless you want to ride over with me?" Peter got up and brushed the ants off his knees.

"No, boy. I want to have a look at that heifer I sent Kimani after. I hope to Christ whatever's she's got isn't catching. See you at suppertime, eh?"

"Yes, Pa. Good-by."

Peter was very happy as he rode his horse over to see Jeff and Elisabeth. Things were working out just dandy, now that Lisa was married off and Pa had a son-in-law to talk farming with and plenty of company in the shape of relatives. He wouldn't be lonesome living alone, not with the yard full of grandchildren and Jeff and Lisa to ride over for dinner. The old man didn't need any real help on the farm, because it ran like a watch, anyhow, but if there were any emergencies, emergencies that called for a white man's assistance, why there was Jeff, no distance at all away.

"This works out just fine for me," Peter said to his horse. "Now I can whiz off with old Dan and have some fun hunting. Then, when Pa gets too old to run the shauri, I'll be fed up on hunting, anyhow, and glad of a chance to come back and get married and do the farm. Then I'll move my wife into the house and become a gentleman and raise hogs and kids. It couldn't be better, old boy. Whoa!"

The horse, shying at a fox, danced sideways, snorting in alarm. The horse stepped into a pig hole and lurched nearly to the ground, throwing Peter over his head. Peter got up, swearing but unhurt. The horse was limping badly in his left front foot. Peter looked at the leg. It was already beginning to puff around the pastern.

"Damn," Peter said. "I'll have to walk him home and do for that leg. Come on, old boy. You're just bruised a bit."

When Peter returned with the lame horse, his father looked up from a book. "What happened to the horse?"

"Pig hole. Nothing serious. Bit o' liniment and rest'll fix it. I'll take him back to the barn and swap saddles and see to the horse. Kimani come back with the cow yet?"

"No, he hasn't. If you see him, tell him I meant today, not next week."

"Yes, sir."

Peter walked the horse to the barn, unsaddled him, and led him into a loose-box. He took the leg between his knees and looked at it again. Nothing serious. He smeared it with liniment and wrapped it in a clean white cloth. Then he saddled another horse and rode to the front of the house.

"No sign of Kimani and the cow," he told his father. "Maybe he couldn't find her and is still looking. Well, the horse is right. I'm off. See you later."

He swung the fresh horse into a canter and headed for Jeff's.

Kimani took a spear in case of snakes and went off to look for the spotted heifer. As he walked he brooded. Now his father was in jail and he had brought dishonor to his father and it was his fault. The thahu was still working or his father would not be in jail, and so it was still his fault. If his father died in jail, then he, Kimani, would have killed his father. But it wasn't his fault, really. The real fault lay with the Bwana Jeff, who had hit him and brought the thahu. If the Bwana Jeff had brought the thahu, then the thahu could be lifted only through the Bwana Jeff. The Bwana Jeff had struck him, and he had not struck back, as a man should. He had been insulted, and because of the insult the thahu had come and the baby was born feet first, and even though the baby was killed to remove the thahu, his father was in jail. If there were some way to atone for the insult, some way to retaliate for the slap, then the curse would be gone and his father released from jail.

Kimani stopped dead still. He felt the spear, clean and smoothly balanced in his hand. Suddenly he began to run, leaping high in the grasses, springing like an impala. The spotted cow was forgotten.

When Peter walked his horse into Jeff Newton's yard, he heard a great hubbub of shouted orders from within the house. He threw the reins over the horse's head and ran into the house. Jeff Newton was lying stretched on the divan. He had his shirt off and held a glass of whisky in his hand. He was very pale. Elisabeth and one of the houseboys were just tightening the bandages that circled his right shoulder. A basin of water, purpled with permanganate, stood on the table.

"Oh, it's Peter," Jeff said, and grinned. "Fine friends you've got, my lad. Damned near cost you a brother-in-law."

"What happened, for Christ's sake?"

"I was ambushed. Went back to the barn a few minutes ago to doctor a colt, and as I walked past that low hedge next the paddock, there was a hell of a yell and this dirty great spear came whistling and went all the way through my shoulder. A little more center and I'm dead as bones. As it is, I'll not be able to use an arm for a month."

"Did you see who it was?"

"No. Catching a spear in your own back yard happens so seldom these days. All I heard was a yelp, and then the spear flew and knocked me down and I heard feet running off into the woods. By the time Elisabeth and the boys heard me yell and came and untransfixed me from the bloody thing, whoever did it would've been a mile away."

"Where is the spear?"

"I don't know. Lisa, where's the spear?"

"On the back porch. It's still bloody, and I don't want to see it."

"*I* do," Jeff said. "Kaluku! Go and fetch the spear."

The boy returned with the weapon. Its long, thin blade was blooded nearly to the haft. It had passed all the way through Jeff's shoulder but had missed bone. Peter took the spear in his hands and balanced it. He looked at Jeff. Jeff nodded.

They both knew that when Peter returned home for supper Kimani would not be there, and neither would the spotted cow he had been sent to find.

"Police business?" Peter asked Jeff.

"No. Pour me another drink, will you, and one for Elisabeth and yourself. No. There's been trouble enough. Poor little bastard. I guess he thought that if he killed me the curse would be wiped out and his old man would get out of jail and all would be serene. Thanks for the drink. This shoulder hurts like hell. No. Best just to let him go. He'll have trouble enough without any more from me. Take the Chev now, will you, Peter, and go and collect the doctor. This thing's going to need some extra cleaning and stitches."

As Peter drove off to fetch the doctor, he thought: What a pity. Now Kimani will never get to be my gunbearer. And I *would* have let him shoot the guns once in a while. Maybe even at a lion. I wonder where he'll go and what he'll do.

Several times he saw movement in the bush close to the track, but it was only buck and once a monkey. One thing only lightened his gloom. His pa had said that he could go with old Dan one day and learn to be a white hunter. He would find another gunbearer meanwhile. Maybe someday Kimani would come home.

BOOK TWO

THE
YOUNG
WARRIORS

Peter McKenzie stood leaning against the bar in the dim cool malty-smelling taproom of the Norfolk Hotel in Nairobi and flicked his thumbnail twice against his glass. "I'll have a martini this time, please," he said to the steward. He turned toward his companion. "Pimm's is fine to cut the dust, but I need something a little sturdier after this last business. The same for you, Little John?"

"No, thanks, I'll have a martini too, please. Just what is it you call them?"

"Martini a maui mbile. American chap I had out last year thought it up. Seems they have some sort of drink called 'on the rocks' in the States, when it's just ice and double booze with no mixing. 'Martini twice on the mountain' was as close as we could come to it for Moussa's benefit. Right, Moussa?"

"Yas, Bwana. That other Bwana, he drinking very much. We call him the Bwana Ginni-Bottle here in the hotel."

Peter McKenzie was standing with John Thompson, another professional hunter, who had been second hunter with Peter on the safari from which they had just returned. John Thompson was a short, wiry, muscular blond man with bright monkey's brown eyes and a broken nose. He was Peter's best friend, and each was happy to defer to the other as second hunter on a big safari, although neither would serve as Number Two to any other hunter.

Peter was just twenty-five. He was a big man now, topping six feet. His black hair still curved down over his forehead, and a damp, white-dusty lock was visible under his tipped-back hat. His skin was burned so dark from the hot sun of the Northern Frontier that his teeth looked almost grotesque against his face. He had the strong sloping shoulders of a boxer, running smoothly into a corded column of neck. He was wearing a green short-sleeved bush jacket, faded nearly white, and green shorts. His legs, burned black as his face, were abnormally sturdy, enormously thewed, with the broad thick bands of the hard walker. Peter

McKenzie could trot thirty miles a day in the smiting sun after elephants and still have enough gas left to run over a mountain at the end of it. His wrists were nearly as thick as his ankles, and his hands, callused and scarred, were as heavy as flatirons. The black hair of his naked legs and forearms was furry with dust, and the hair of his head was stiffly gray with dust and sweat. He and John Thompson had just driven their Land Rovers down from Isiolo, north of Nanyuki and near the Abyssinian border, that day. The clients had stopped on at the Mawingo Hotel in Nanyuki for a few days of relaxation after the hot, dirty hunt. They would come on to Nairobi by car, for the roads were good now and you didn't tear a saloon car to pieces any more.

Peter was something of a legend in Nairobi, young as he was. The natives called him Bwana Nyeusi, the Black One. He had been hunting professionally for seven years. He was in the Army only one year before the war ended and he was demobilized. He was just eighteen when he came back to Kenya, having been no farther away from it than Addis Ababa. He had seen no fighting and had gone no higher than lance corporal. He had fussed about the farm and prowled the towns aimlessly for six months but found that the farm bored him badly and the towns bored him worse.

It was fine seeing the old man again, of course, and wonderful to catch up with Jeff and Elisabeth and the kids, three of them now, two boys and a girl. Jeffy was quite a big boy, must be nine or thereabouts, little Harry fivish, and the baby, Caroline, two and a bit. Quite a family old Jeff had started. Still the best, old Jeff. Quieter and heavier and more serious generally, but still his own man. Marriage hadn't tamed him completely, the way it did a lot of people. He still joked Elisabeth, and he teased the kids, and latterly was quite rude about Peter's Nairobi doings with the girls. One thing about Jeff, though; he wasn't one of these blokes that go whipping off after every skirt they see soon's the first brat's toddling and there's another on the way. He and Elisabeth had a wonderful, quiet, sort of shining happiness with each other. Lisa had heavied up a little, but not much, and the extra stone was awfully becoming. She was a strikingly beautiful woman now, where she'd been all blue eyes and tender smile as a filly. The old man was about the same, a little grayer, a little gruffer, except when he was playing with the grandchildren. He spoiled them rotten, naturally, and they could get round him on anything. But it was marvelous for the old man, with the kids and all. It made it so easy when Peter told his father one day, six months after the war finished, that he thought he'd be pushing off. The old man grunted.

"Going to hold me to that thing about apprenticing to Dan, eh?" Henry McKenzie said. The old boy had grown stouter and much whiter in the hair; no doubt of it.

"I thought I might. The safaris have started again, now the war's done. I saw Dan in town the other day and he said he's starting to operate and he's already booked up for the next couple of years. Masses of people who shot out here before the war with Dan want to come back again. Cinema companies making flicks too. He reckons the next few years'll be bumper in the shootin' business. Wants me to come along as his mtoto. He says he thinks he'll quit after two or three years, and then I can have his boys. It's a good string."

"What's he paying you?"

"Bloody nothing. Twenty quid a month and my chakula. I'm to furnish my own guns, of course. He wants me to drive the lorry and look after the camp and do the mechanics and sort of flunky about for a while, and he'll teach me most of the tricks. Then I can go as his second hunter for a year or so, and then he reckons to quit and turn the whole show over to me. I want to do it, Pa, really. You won't need me actually around here for donkey's years. All right if I go?"

"I suppose so, you're mad keen to do it, and always were, ever since you were a nipper. You'll need guns. I never use mine on anything any more, bar the odd buck for the pot. You can have the .470s and the .416s. Leave me the old .500s; I'm sentimental about them. Leave me the Mannlicher, as well, and one set of shotguns. Take the Remington. It's a useful little gun, and you might's well have the .318. You can damned well buy your own .22. I consider I've given you a hell of a good start. That's about two thousand quids' worth of artillery I'm dowering you with. Go on now and be a Nairobi attraction for all the tourists to point at in the bars. Grow a beard and maybe you can go on the films. I should listen carefully to Dan if I were you. He knows more about it than most anybody else, and there's no point to getting yourself killed. You don't build good hunters in a day or a year. I used to do the elephants myself, and I know."

Peter took the oily-gleaming guns out of the cabinet and Jeff drove him to town to pick up old Dan, and that was the start of it. Dan was the opposite of the cinema idea of the white hunter. He was fat and stubby-legged. He had a round, pink cherub's face, a tiny button nose, white hair, and a clipped white mustache. He was a great believer in the therapeutic qualities of gin, and he hated hard work. He was custodian of a thousand changeable stories, some hair-raising, some rude, some self-deprecating. He also had a reputation, forged between the two last wars, for being a dashing man with the ladies. There was at least one loud divorce in Europe which resulted from his presence in the bed of a viscountess while the viscount was out after waterbuck with the second hunter. The viscount had found his horns that day, but he had sprouted them on his own head when he returned a mite early to camp. He'd been frightfully civil about things, though, and merely ceased speaking to either Dan or the viscountess for the rest of the hunt. Dan worked especially hard to produce spectacular trophies and dined alone in his tent. He heard later from London that the viscount had hung a portrait of his wife between the mounted heads of a wart hog and a wildebeest, possibly the two ugliest animals in the world.

Safari was devilish hard work at first. Peter never got to fire a gun seriously for a year, except once in a while when they needed camp meat and he had to go out and wallop the odd topi or eland for the pot. It was dirty, backbreaking toil. Peter's job was to supervise the loading and off-loading of the lorries, ruling a mountain of canvas tentage, water distillers, heavy wooden chop boxes, chairs, tables, kitchen utensils, food, drink, and sometimes a portable refrigerator. Once, for a honeymoon couple, they had strapped an enormous great brass double bed, with its feather mattress, on top of the lorry-load.

Peter's chief task was to see to the provisioning of the safari. Peter's job also was to go to the airport to meet the clients, to steer them through customs, and to see them safely bedded down in the Norfolk. It was Peter who took them to Ahamed's and to the Africa Boot Shop to outfit them. Peter was the one who got up before dawn to round up the last of the sleepy, hung-over, elusive blacks, and he came to know the native bazaars as well as Delamere Avenue. He knew every whorehouse, teashop, and drinking saloon that catered to Africans, as he eventually came to know the trails that led from the N.F.D. to the Masai, across the Serengeti and back again to Manyara, up to Iringa and back to Arusha, down to Tabora and deeper down to the Sudan.

Peter drove the lorry and pitched the camp and struck the camp. Peter stayed in camp to protect the white memsaabs from snakes while the Bwana went off to shoot lions with old Dan. In these stay-behind sessions Peter learned a great many things. He learned contract bridge and canasta and that a great many ladies came on safari to collect certain trophies of their own special choosing. He lost his virginity at nineteen, when quite a lovely lady came to his tent one day after lunch as he lay naked in siesta. She dropped her robe in a pool at her feet. Quite as naked as he, she hopped into bed with him and there really wasn't very much that a bloke could do except submit—was there?

Peter accumulated sophistication. He learned the wisdom of trying to avoid the tentative advances of the female guests, at least while the safari was in the field, because sexual tension made extra complications. But there were some, nymphomaniac and otherwise, who could not be put off. Peter was young and handsome and healthy and he was alone very often with the wives and daughters and mistresses of the rich men, usually red-faced and beefy or skinny and paunched and spindly, who came to collect dead heads to put on their country-house walls. In his first year of working for Dan, Peter learned considerably more about women and whisky than he learned of wild animals and their habits. He diminished his shyness gradually and became quite a slick conversationalist. One pretty young wife of a very old, very rich Texas oilman, taught him to do the rumba and the fox trot to the tune of a portable phonograph hitched to the battery of the lorry. Then she taught him quite a few other social niceties without needing any more electric power than she herself could generate on a cold, bright-starred night in the high Masai, when Dan and her husband had gone off to Kandoa Arangi to shoot kudus and had left the little lady in Peter's special care. By the time he was twenty Peter had come to a single conclusion about women, particularly those who were left in his special care.

Peter actually got very little sleep, apart from dalliance. In addition to driving the lorry, he had to keep her fit, and he had to be mechanic to the shooting rigs as well. When they were hunting hard, in rocky country, one of the vehicles was always ailing, and Peter would be up to the dawn, his ears greasy, as he replaced broken spring leaves or soldered a sundered sump or rejiggered a bearing assembly. Crossing the plains in the wet, the lorry was always certain to bog down in the soft cotton soil, and Peter remembered one day when they had made fourteen trips of two miles each, each man carrying some heavy article of the foundered lorry's burden on his head to a point of high, hard ground. Peter walked twenty-eight miles that day, with tables and tents on his head, while old Dan lounged in the shade in a canvas camp chair, drinking gin and telling tall tales to the clients.

Drinking was important, old Dan always said. A bloke had to drink with the clients, else they'd be offended, and anyhow, sitting drinking around a blazing fire with the stars frosty in the sky and the mosquitoes swiftly gone in the sudden cold was one of the finest things about safari. That was the time when you reviewed the doings of the day or the week, the client either bragging or apologizing, and the hunter embroidering the brags and scoffing at the apologies. That was when the boys laughed and sang by their cook fires and thumped drums softly and the hyenas giggled and the lions roared and the advertised glamor of safari emerged to make you forget the dust and the bugs and the heat and the thorns and the snakes.

There was nothing so important as keeping plenty of booze in the camp, Dan said, plenty of beer and soft drinks as well, and keeping the drink cool in the water bags, because when a client came in from a morning in the blazing sun, dust in all his pores and gritting in his teeth, what he wanted most was a beer straight off and then a long cool gin and lime. And at night, when you could see the fires jovially winking and the last bumpy mile on the track took a hundred years, what the client wanted first of all was a stout scotch or a muscular martini before the boys brought his bathi water in the petrol tins, where they'd been heating over the fire.

And the client wanted you to drink with him, to erase the guilty feeling of drinking alone or of drinking too much. He wanted you to drink to celebrate a wonderful shot on a fine head that day, or else he wanted to drink to dull his pain over missing something so easy that he might have killed it with a slingshot. No matter what there was to celebrate, it had to be solemnized with a drink of anything except water. It was especially sticky going in town, because when the client first showed up he was all excited about taking off for the trackless wastes of darkest Affrikka and he was tired from the plane trip, so he wanted to sit and drink to mask his fear and to camouflage his ignorance while he asked questions. The next day he wanted to see the town and he wanted the town to see him, brave in his new bush jacket with the bullet loops. He wanted to be introduced to the game warden and to everybody else as Dan's newest client. He wanted to go dancing at the Equator Club and the Travellers' and the Chez Dave. Then he wanted a last swift one for the road, and maybe let's just stop off at Fort Hall or Narok for a beer, shall we?

When it was all over you all were dear old buddies, and you really must come see us in the States or in Madrid or Canada or wherever. And you must have dinner with us tonight, let's make it a party, how about asking a couple of those cute little air hostesses to come along? And then you would end up singing in one of the back-court cottages at the Norfolk, with the women sweetly drunk and soggy-sentimental and the client's bored wife maybe making a pass at a navigator or one of the pilots, and the client alcoholically sore because the prettiest drunk little air hostess was crawling all over the hunter and paying no attention to the client.

Then there was the going-out-to-see-the-trophies kind of drinking, and the arrangement-of-the-air-transportation drinking, and meeting-the-black-boys-to-give-them-their-tips drinking, and all the good-old-friends-in-the-good-old-bars ordinary drinking, and finally the serious good-by drinking. Then, if you were a very good hunter, the day you pushed one group off at Eastleigh Airport you had a drink in the bar while you waited for a new group to come in the same day, and the boozing started all over again.

The toughest thing about the drinking was that you were supposed to be completely efficient and brightly alert despite it. The trophies had to be found and stalked and killed and skinned. If the client wounded it you went after it to finish it. If the lorry broke down you fixed it. If the game wasn't there you went someplace else until you found it. If the grass was tall you went to where the grass was supposed to be short. You were hired to sit up all night drinking whisky and then to wake up fresh enough to follow a wounded buffalo in the morning. You were never supposed to get lost or be tired or cross or disgusted.

Yes, Peter had learned a lot from his apprenticeship to old Dan. Over the two years of apprenticeship they had had a lot of peculiar clients. There was the queer Englishman who insisted on sleeping in trees, so they had to build him a platform in a tree in every camp and hoist a bedroll up into it. He swam naked in every stream they came to, against all warnings, and bought a thriving case of bilharzia as a result. But he was a jolly good chap and he didn't like to kill things. He puttered with cameras and seemed sincerely fond of lions. Oddly, or rather stupidly, he was completely fearless. He seemed to think that he was living in a large, controlled, airy zoo. When he left the safari he gave Peter a very fine ciné camera and all the raw film that was left over from the expedition.

They were a rare lot, all right. There was the old Duchess of Denton, who cursed like a man and smoked cigars and who had one aim on the safari, which was to eavesdrop lions and elephants and giraffes, especially giraffes, making love. Dan hunted hard, and while they never caught any elephants copulating, they did manage to sneak up on some lions and giraffes. The giraffes were fantastic, all planes and right angles.

There was the pansy chap, a lawyer from Los Angeles, who tried to do all the black boys. Peter caught him with one of the porters, who seemed to think that there was nothing very unusual about it. Peter beat the porter with a kiboko and sacked him, and Dan drove the pansy chap back to Nairobi and refused any payment for the safari.

Funny, the types who came to Africa to keep doing whatever it was they had always been doing in the States or in England or wherever. Peter first learned about lesbians on safari. One, the male part of the show, was a horsy-looking Englishwoman, very rich, who shaved her upper lip every day and who called herself Bill, though her name was Helen. She had a curious rubber contrivance with her. She kept it in a box and made great secret jokes about it with her girl friend. They called the contrivance Lord Derek, and they used to chuckle when they took it out of the box to "give Lord Derek a breath of fresh air." Bill, or Helen, was very jealous of her girl friend, a wispy little thing with enormous sad brown eyes and a weak, petulant mouth. The girl friend made a few tentative motions toward Peter and excited a great deal of jealousy in Bill. The jealousy got so bad that although, God knows, Peter felt nothing but loathing for the girl friend and tried to avoid her, the safari ended in utter disaster, with Dan and Peter eating apart from the women and speaking only in monosyllables when an order to the clients was necessary.

God, but some of them were funny. There was the Yankee book writer who came all the way out to Africa to hunt, and then refused to hunt. He stayed in camp all day long, drinking gin and talking seriously to the baboons who came curiously to visit him. There was the Cambodian prince, a decent little brown fellow, who had a big blond music-hall-type Englishwoman with him, who didn't want to hunt or take pictures or even look at game. What he liked to do was to stay in camp in his tent with the Englishwoman. They made some very peculiar sounds in the tent.

There was the rich spoiled son of a wood-pulp merchant who started the safari with one wife and finished it with another, puzzling the native boys no end. Then there was the cold murderer, who would ask each morning, "How many of what can I shoot today?" This was a Mexican. He shot from the car, over Dan's strong objection. He killed females and cubs and he overshot his license. Once he sloppily wounded a leopard and—Peter could swear to this—old Dan deliberately let the leopard scratch the Mexican up a bit before Dan terminated the leopard. They took this safari back to Nairobi, and Dan turned the Mexican in to the game warden. He was bowed out of Kenya and forbidden a reentry permit.

The types, my word, what types. There was the American female film star who sun-bathed naked in front of the blacks, causing no end of damage to discipline. There was the big, hairy-chested American hero of a hundred motion picture thrillers who was hysterically afraid of everything—mice, bugs, snakes, even the dark. What made it funnier was that they were doing a movie in which the star-bloke played a professional hunter. He and Peter were of about the same size and coloring, so on this one safari Peter found himself to be an actor. He doubled for the actor chap in every scene that needed any contact with animals. The actor won an award that year, possibly for bravery.

There was the rich Michigan manufacturer who ordered Dan to shoot it all and then blandly described how he had shot it all himself. Peter could understand how the man might fake it at home, but to sit on the veranda at the Norfolk, in Nairobi, with Peter and Dan present while he described his imaginary feats of bravery, was just a touch too thick. Especially the part in which the rich man told how he had plunged into the bush after the wounded buffalo—which, as he pointed out, Dan had wounded. In this instance he was correct, for Dan *had* shot it a touch low and had had to dive into the bush after it. The only detail the rich man omitted was that he happened to be reading a detective story in camp, twenty miles away, at the time that Dan dived into the bush.

But they weren't all so bad. There were a couple of chaps who really wanted to know about it and understand it. When they shot it they only shot what was good and they made no show over the killing. They did all their shooting themselves and asked a thousand questions, and neither patronized nor attempted socially to dominate the hunters. These people drank to celebrate and to relax, but they were out of the bed stone-sober before the dawn started to blood-streak the skies. They walked hard in the heat and accepted the tsetse bites and the fine dust settled in the water bag and were very serious about the right bullet weights and the habits of elephants. In two years there were only two of this kind, both young, both rich, and both married to women who seemed to enjoy being married to their husbands. But they were rare, my oath, but they were very bloody rare.

Peter acquired a full professional status earlier than he had ever expected. Old Dan bought a nasty bit o' work with two rhinos one day, a dirty silly accident. He and some client were creeping after buffalo, and they crept right up on top of a breeding pair of rhinoceroses. They were crawling down an old game trail, through the laced thorn, and there wasn't room enough in the trail for two men and two rhinos. Dan and the client bent a barrage on the rhinos and killed them both, but the cow came on wounded and fell on Dan. She broke his leg badly in two places, and the old bones weren't quite up to knitting. He was in bed a year, nearly, and while he recuperated, Peter carried on with the already booked clients. At the end of the year Dan tested his leg sadly and concluded that he was finished hunting. He was too slow and tender-boned to compete in any more foot races with elephant and buffalo. He turned over his string of fifteen Wakamba boys to Peter and sold him the lorry, the tents, and the hunting car on time payments, and retired to be bored on his farm at Nanyuki. Peter was in business himself at twenty.

Peter came on as a personality very swiftly. Dan had tested him on clients, and he was forced to test himself on game. A lot of it he knew; some from Jeff, some from his father, some he knew without knowing that he knew. He was touched with a madness, not a madness to kill, but a madness to learn and see and discover. His lips curved down in scorn at the idea of hunting anywhere that other men hunted if he could possibly avoid it. Mostly he coldly disliked his clients—fat, soft men, or complaining thin men, or fat-or-thin men who liked to kill for no reason but to see death. Nevertheless, he drove himself furiously for those he hated most. He had his secret pockets of game—a pocket near Ikoma in Tanganyika, a wealth of elephant country up on the dry river beds of the Abyssinian frontier, and a certain-sure source of big kudus away past Iringa in Tanganyika. He could produce a lion when there really were no lions to be produced, and the ivory he brought in was always heavy. And when he was angry, when he was offended, he punished himself, driving day and night, scourging himself, speaking seldom, an-

grily seeking a hunter's justification of indefinable prowess for the benefit of strange men he scorned.

Peter cherished a curious ability, mentally, to ennoble the animals
he caused to be killed while despising the humans who killed them. He
permitted no abuse of the beasts. He was of course an honorary game
warden and bound to report game-law violations, but his feelings passed
beyond technicalities. He owned certain pets here and there; a fine bull
elephant that he would not allow to be shot and around which he carefully steered his clients. He was saving this elephant against a day when
some client yet unknown would prove to be worthy of shooting it—saving
the elephant as he saved a certain black-maned lion, a certain fantastically
horned buffalo, a certain wondrous waterbuck.

He had no desire whatsoever to kill anything for himself as a trophy.
When he shot camp meat he never made any sport of it but rode up in
his Land Rover to the nearest herd of Tommies or impalas or topi,
crooked one knee against the windscreen, and walloped it illegally from
the car without trying to dignify it with a stalk. At the same time he
would permit no dangerous game to be shot from the car, no matter how
insistent the client might be. Peter was in love with Africa and with the
animals he saw, the animals which he sought for other men to kill. He
fidgeted in Nairobi after a day or two of wenching and heavy drinking.
He did not feel completely happy until he was back again in the Rover,
his hatbrim backcurled in the stiff breeze, and the dust of the Ngong
Range puffing pink behind him, with the great blue scar of the Rift
beckoning him past Longonot and turning him up toward the high green
hills he loved in the Masai. Or maybe when he crawled past the red
clay hills and wet green Kikuyu shambas past Fort Hall and Nyeri and
on through Nanyuki for the long, short ride to Isiolo, where, apt as not,
you would be likely to see a herd of strolling elephants in the D.C.'s
boma.

The Northern Frontier, past Isiolo, was Peter's very special country. He began to breathe more deeply when he passed Archer's Post,
where the South African airmen had bombed themselves a sweet-water
swimming pool, and he was wildly happy when he turned off to camp
at the Kinya lugger. With the lovely, square-headed old mountain,
Ololokwe, bulking huge on his left, he could curve the jeep around and
aim for the dry rivers, the luggers, that swept new channels for themselves each year as the floods came flashing down, drowning the red-ant-
hill-studded desert in muddy torrents so violent that they slung huge

trees twenty and thirty feet above the river beds and caused the D.C. to put up barriers on the Garba Tulla–Shaffa Dikka road to keep all men out, and in, for the period of the rains.

This was where the hard true life of Africa centered, here on the dry, lava-dusty plains or ocher-wet pits, with the huge knobs of blue-and-red-and-white mountains strewed aimlessly around with no regard for symmetry. Here on the gray, lonesome, heat-shimmering plains with their myrrh and sansevieria bushes, the wild Boran and the painted Samburu and Rendille and the slim, beautiful light Somali roved with their herds of camels and sheep and goats and donkeys. Here lived the Turkana, fierce little black men who went about naked and who wore curved knives as wristlets and who would as soon chop your head as thank you if a question of pride was involved. Here it was *big* enough —big enough for the elephants and the rhinos and the little lesser kudus and the leopards and the lean, maneless desert lions. Here it was big enough for the nomads to drift their cattle over a million square miles of territory that nobody but Peter and God and the elephants really loved. This was the land of the sand grouse pinpricked against a clear well-washed blue sky, whistling as they came to scanty water in the morning. This was where the heat trembled at one hundred twenty degrees at 4 P.M., but where you didn't find any mosquitoes and not many tsetses. This was where the dry river beds were highways of sparkling white sand, islanded with rocks and little green-lichened pools, and where a constant traffic of life surged fretfully in a search for the water that bubbled under the cool sands. On the dry oases Peter could see, in a strip of ten miles, thirty elephants digging earnestly with their tusks for the water that seeped foully under the sandy surface. He could count a dozen rhinos on any morning and follow their trails across a hard-baked plain to the start of their daily twenty-mile walk for water. Why they never stayed on the luggers Peter nor anyone else, not even the Turkana, could explain. But you could spoor them simply by riding along in a jeep, following a big bull by the serpentine bicycle track his penis made as it trailed the ground when the breeding season was on.

This was the country in which the dry river beds were thickly cobbled with the dung of a million animals when it was dry outside on the plains—the sign of cattle and goats, elephants and rhinos and zebras and giraffes and Grant gazelles. The dazzling white sand was a parade ground for the vulturine guinea fowl who ran with their cock-aded heads held high like trotting horses, and where the big, yellow-necked francolin scratched like barn fowl and yelled raucously at sunset. There were always more birds in the Northern Frontier than anywhere else, great hornbills and long, sag-tailed lories, many vultures and slipping carrion kites. The birds kept up an incessant scream, the guineas hoarse, the lories going "Faa-aak, faa-aak," the francolin mournful at nightfall, and always the pleasant good-humored chuckle of the sand grouse as they carved jet-plane arcs in the brilliant blue sky.

With the exception of the nomads, you didn't run across many people in the Northern Frontier. It was all too big and it was always either too wet or too dry. If you knew the way the luggers interlocked, doubling back on themselves, you had a wondrous source of heavy ivory, but a man who didn't know the luggers could get himself lost and die very painfully in the N.F.D. Not many safaris came up this way, because the weather was too unpleasant and the angry red clay pits and dreary gray plains were not picturesque enough for a man who had only six weeks to shoot it all, including pictures. The rhinos here weren't nearly so high in the horn as the rhinos around Manyara in Tanganyika, at the mouth of Mto-Wa-Mbu, the Mosquito River, not half so long-horned as the forest rhinos who grazed on the slopes of Mount Kenya and in the Aberdares around Nanyuki and Thomson's Falls. Beyond the birds and a few Grant gazelles and gerenuk there wasn't much to shoot except the elephants. That is chiefly why Peter loved it so, because there wasn't much to shoot besides the elephants. Most clients didn't want elephants unless they were true hunters who were willing to walk twenty or thirty miles a day through the sucking sands and through the dwarf palms that slashed like swords and the thornbush that clutched and bit at the body.

The immensity of the North Country did something lovely and lilting to Peter's heart. Its very barrenness was beautiful, and its sere heat was happy, healthy. Of all the natives he knew, Peter loved the painted, Masai-like Samburu who roamed with their herds, and after them the ugly, black, squat little Turkana. He actively hated the Somali, but he loved them just to look at the arrogance of them. The women were so lovely with their huge iridescent headdresses, their wonderful small, proudly tilted bosoms and tiny waists and big swaying behinds. And the men so lean, so delicately hawk-faced, and completely treacherous and deadly fast with a knife. They would steal anything, and they worshiped their herds of camels. But they were all part of the North, like its overwhelming nights, when the sky actually took the texture of furry velvet and the stars swung low and melon-golden, not so remote and silvery-twinkly as they were up in the Masai, when the evening cold set in.

Of course a man could love the Masai too, because around the Mara River and the Telek River, up from the Loita Plains, there was country to make your mouth water at its deep-loamed richness. This was all Masai reserve, thank God, and buzzing-full of cattle-killing tsetse flies, so that the people and cattle stayed properly away. But the man who might someday put it into wheat and cattle, after clearing the harsh thorn that housed and nourished the flies, would own a swift agricultural bonanza unchallenged by the discovery of later gold.

This wasn't angry, frightening country like the N.F.D., but soft and beautiful country, once you got away from the alkali dust and the wind-dreary, sere lava plains. This was Hollywood Africa, with rolling downs, now of the softest gentle green, against the background of deep black lofty forest, or long plains rolling yellow-grassed and heavy-headed in the pleasant wind like the ripple of wheat. This country had the pure cold streams, and the hot-water springs around Majimoto, and the wonderful graduated mountains, with Tanganyika off that way and the Rift's scar burning blue behind.

And all, all the animals that God put into the world were on parade. Here in the Masai was where you could see a half million zebras in a day, a half million wildebeests, when the great migrations started across the Serengeti Plain of Tanganyika. Here the bright golden impalas tiptoed dainty-footed in herds of five hundred along the Telek River, its bed brilliant white and green rock-studded. Here a herd of two hundred elephants unafraid. Here the Tommies roved the plains in bands of thousands, and here the protected prides of lions grew as large as twenty or thirty to one family. This was where the very big heavy-bossed buffalo lived, and where the dark-gold leopards fed nightly by the river-banks. This was where you could see a million beasts any day, Tommy, Grant, eland, impala, zebra, wildebeest, all moving out into the center of the plain before the dark-red sunset, moving outward against the menace of the big cats who waited for the violent bloody sunset to die before they nervously whipped their tails, stretched lazily after their siesta, and began to search for the evening's meal.

This was the place where the long-dipping glades were green as in England, and where the acacia flowered in the spring with blossoms as white and fragrant as any English May haw or the dogwood in America. But somehow the Masai was soft country, although its natives were the fiercest and its animals the most numerous. It was a country for women and children and small, awkward, wet baby animals with knobbly knees and unsteady feet. It was not so big and raw and tough and fiercely beautiful as the N.F.D. It was candybox country, created specially for tourists and the movie-making safaris. When Peter was really fed up with clients he and John Thompson would take a Land Rover and a cook and a gunbearer apiece, and they would trek up to the North Country to shoot out their license on big elephants. They would sleep under the intimate stars on doubled blankets without bothering about beds, eating what they killed of birds and small game, drinking nothing, and by and by the foul taste of movie stars and rich, spoiled women and old frightened fat men would come cleanly spat from their mouths, and then they could face another season of commercial safari again.

2

Fred Hall walked into the bar and joined Peter and John Thompson. Fred was a hunter, too, and he was just back from something or other involving a recently divorced maharajah and a French female singer. Fred was a lean, rangy, ugly man who rarely spoke much, except to close friends, when he was drunk, and who was accounted dull therefore. But he was a pure hunter in his heart, and he completed a close corporation with Peter McKenzie and John Thompson.

"Bad, was it?" Fred said. "I'll have the same as you. What did they do especially awful this time?"

"I don't suppose it was actually any more awful than usual," Peter said. "There was this proven son of a bitch and his son. The son was quite a decent chap. But the old man wanted it all, as usual, and in thirty days. You know. Don't care whether it's any good or not so long as it's dead. So the Little Bwana here and I proceeded to toil, and we collected it all. Two elephants, one a hundred, one ninety, two rhinos, two kudus, two buffalo, two leopards—the whole bloody issue. I dragged his arse from the Masai to Tanganyika and back up to the N.F.D. It was amusing, actually, especially in the North. There are ways of saving steps, but I didn't bother to save him any. John and I left them in the hotel at Nanyuki. The father already drunk. I have heard a lot of filthy tongues in my short time, but this man was downright horrid. He treated John and me like we were niggers and he treated the Wogs worse. And do you know, after he shot some mangy old lion or other, he insisted on having the lion's *balls broiled* for his breakfast?"

"Were you still drinking their whisky?" Fred asked, using the classic phrase.

"*I* was. The Bwana John wasn't. Tell him, boy."

"It was first when this visiting gentleman shot the baby zebra," John Thompson said. "Long as he shot it, I thought p'haps I'd use the poor little creature for a bait for some vulture photography he wanted. The birds came down and the hero got sick when the ndege started to poke into the carcass up the rear end the way they do. He'll kill it, sure, but he threw up when he saw what happened to it after it's dead. But it was the lion that did it for me, really."

"Another gin for everybody, Moussa. Lion?"

"An old boy. Really old. We were rattling around in Ikoma and we came onto this old gentleman, see, sick he was and starved and mangy, with his back broken in some recent fight with one of his sons. I judge the old chap'd been helpless there the best part of a week. The maggots had already started on him, and the blowflies were working, and he was skin and bones and really miserable. There were about a dozen hyenas circled round the old chap, their tongues hanging out, just waiting for him to get a touch weaker before they closed in and et him alive. I walked up to the poor old bugger with the .22 and was going to give him the one in the ear to put him out of his troubles, when this four-starred nobleman told me not to shoot. Seems he wanted to *leave* the beast there alive to see how long it would take for the hyenas to eat him."

"So old John shot the lion, naturally," Peter said. "Then he called his client a dirty murdering swine and drank his own grog for the rest of the trip. Oh, it was a charmer, I can tell you. This father chap, at the Greek hotel in Arusha, tried to pinch some young girl off his own son. The girl set up a mightiful scream and the old man took a clout at his boy in the argument, and it was an altogether bloody delightful business. I think I shall get very drunk tonight and behave abominably. John and I've earned it, this safari. And I have a new group of heroes coming in tomorrow. Man and his wife. Young Americans named Deane. His father used to manufacture something or other in Chicago or Detroit or one of those places."

"Maybe they'll turn out reasonably human. The good ones usually follow the bad."

"Say, has the plane come in yet?" Peter asked. "It ought to be Betty's turn to be back from Rome. I could use a little female companionship. Let's walk down to the hostesses' hut and see what Trans Africa Airlines has brought us as a present. As I was saying, I feel like a long, dirty wet evening, and preferably one with a woman mixed up in it somewhere."

"We'll have the road one," Fred Hall said. "Then I've got to nip off. My girl's waiting for me this hour well past at the Stanley, and she'll be in a frightful fit of temper. My shout, men. Here's cheers."

"Cheers. That one bounced. Let's go and scout the livestock, John."

"Right. I hope there's a short one. I am very shy around tall women."

There was a short curvy one named Dottie and a tall lean-legged bosomy one named Betty. Dottie was blond and Betty was brunette. They were just coming out of the hostesses' hut when John and Peter swung through the back courtyard of the Norfolk Hotel, a cobbled arena ringed by cottages. The Norfolk was what might be called an earthy hotel. Its history went back to the old hairy tough days of Kenya, when Lord Delamere wore his blond locks long, as in the pictures of General Custer, and if a bit of a fight brewed in the bar the boys were apt to settle it straight off with knives or pistols, bang on the veranda or in the court.

"Well, the heroes have returned," Betty said. "I believe that we might get fed tonight after all, Dot. Are you chaps rich or are you poor?"

"Rich," Peter said, walking over and kissing Betty. "Come and have a spot in the cottage whilst John and I remove the topsoil. We just crept in from the N.F.D."

"How was the safari?"

"Bloody. How was the flight?"

"Bloody. Everybody sick all over everything, and *the* most monstrous child I ever saw. Betty took her into the ladies' loo and walloped her bottom. She came out screeching, and this one told her mother that she's fallen off the seat and hurt herself. I think I *may* get married, if only to get away from child passengers. And away from Paul Steenkamp. Anybody here want to marry me?"

They swung off to Peter's cottage.

"Paul still drinking as beautifully as ever?"

"Absobloodylutely. You *should* have seen him in Rome. A treat, he was. Got in some sort of argument with a Yankee. Informed the Yankee he was not only the chief pilot of the best goddamned airline in the world but was light-heavyweight champion of South Africa as well. The Yankee said: 'I don't give a bugger if you're bloody Joe Louis,' and downed him. We had a very careful flight next day, due to Paul not being able to see out of more than one eye at a time."

Kamachi was waiting at the door of the cottage. Kamachi was always waiting when Peter came back from safari. He was a big native, an Embu, handsome and purple-black and vastly smiling under his red fez. His big splayed feet were bare under his white kanzu, and he shook Peter's hand in the old classic fashion, seizing him by the thumb and then changing the grip.

"Jambo, you great thief," Peter said. "How are all your whorehouses? Making money? And where are my clothes? The ones you're not wearing, I mean, or haven't sold in the bazaar."

"All here, Bwana," Kamachi said, wriggling like a puppy in delight at seeing Peter. "Villi-villi ginni. Villi-villi barafu. Na whisky na soda. Na majimoto. Na manamouki, villi-villi."

"Seems we're clued up," Peter said. "But he's already taking credit for providing the girls, as well. You'd best watch your step. This Wog has many enterprises. Let's go and sample the gin and the ice he's so proud of, whilst John and I bathe in the hot water he's so proud of. Kwenda, you hyena, and make us some drinks."

"Ndio, Bwana," Kamachi said, making his assent sound like a roll of drums. "I already made them, and your bath is already drawn and your clothes laid out. I knew you were coming in today. Bwana Johnston told me. Chalo has put your guns inside, and your box."

Chalo was Peter's gunbearer and general Number One. He was waiting by the Land Rover parked in front of the tiny veranda of Peter's cottage. Chalo was a Wakamba, a tall, dignified man of some forty years, with filed teeth and enormous holes in his ear lobes. He had tucked the pierced lobes over the top of the ears, giving a strange malproportion to his head.

"All is inside, Bwana," Chalo said. "The guns are clean and I have given your dirty clothes to this Embu baboon to wash. I have counted your suits from the storeroom, and it appears that this thief has stolen nothing in your absence. The whisky is also counted and the tally is correct. You need a new pair of boots, and I have placed the order at the Africa Boot Shop with the little nice Indian who has the wart hog's teeth."

"Good man. Here's a pound. Go and see your wives and try to sober up enough to return from Machakos in three days. We must go again to the Masai. Kwaheri, Chalo."

"Kwaheri, Bwana," the gunbearer said, tucking the money into his tattered khaki shorts and smiling a magnificent cannibal smile. "Be very careful of the pombe and more careful of the manamouki."

"Mind your own bloody business," Peter said, smacking him on the seat of the ragged pants. "I'll look after my own women and whisky, and see you do the same. If you see the Bwana Percival, say him a hello for me."

The cottage was standard for the Norfolk. The girls sat down on the one uncomfortable divan, and Kamachi served drinks, whisky for the women and gin for the men. There were two other chairs and a small deal table and insufficient ash trays in the sitting room. There were two bedrooms and a bath-and-washbowl apart from the toilet. The rooms were dingy but cheerful in a sort of happy, battered way, as if a great many parties had been given there, and the memory of too much drink and too much illicit love had lingered. The guns in their cases were stacked in one corner. The metal ammunition box was placed atop the tin safari boxes. The mosquito nettings were drawn up and tucked into a cone, like an Egyptian's sagging pants, in the bedrooms, and Peter's city clothes were freshly pressed and hung in a closet. The remaining whisky from the safari was grouped companionably like sailors in a corner, with the exception of the opened John Haig and the Booth's gin on the table.

"I'm going to take this gin into the bathroom and clean myself," Peter said. "Big John, you look after the ndeges, and see that you load their glasses. They've got a long way to go to catch us. And when I scream, one of you girls is to come and scrub my back. It's been a long time since I felt a cool white hand."

By the time Peter and John had shaved and the business of the back-scrubbing was accomplished with a great deal of giggling, all four young people were quite drunk and very hungry. The Equator Club seemed indicated, but somehow they stopped off first at the Muthaiga Club and that took time, and then John remembered he had to see Sid at the Travellers' about something or other and that took time, and then when they actually got to the Equator Club all the tables were taken, so they stood at the bar and that took time. They went back to the Travellers' and there were some people there who wanted to buy drinks and that took time. About 2 A.M., after John had thoroughly peeled a South African transient gentleman for some fancied insult and Peter had nearly obliterated two of the South African gentleman's friends and somebody had thoughtfully fired a rifle out the window and the police had come and some strange lady had said something unpleasant to either Betty or Dottie and had had her hair pulled and the best part of her blouse removed, they arrived, still dinnerless, at the cottage at the Norfolk. This demanded a nightcap and quite a lot of singing, during which the night manager came around and had a shoe hurled at him and went off to fetch the manager, who received a chair around his neck. Peter and John took practice swings at each other, momentarily forgetting that they weren't somebody else, and then fell into each other's arms, sobbing eternal friendship. This called for another drink.

Peter woke early in the forenoon with a taste of formaldehyde in his mouth, a shattering pain in his skull, and eyes from which his life-blood appeared to be slowly dripping. He had removed everything but his shoes and his necktie, and was never quite certain how he got his shirt off without removing the necktie. Betty, wearing a brassière, a pettiskirt, one shoe, and Peter's hat, out of some ineffectual groping for decency, was asleep beside him, but wrong-end-to, so that her unshod foot rested across his face. He pushed her onto the floor with a thump and went to look for John, who had achieved an incredible position, with his head on the floor and his knees hooked over the back of the sofa. Dorothy, fully clad except for a skirt, was sleeping soundly in the bathtub, which contained some four inches of water. So far as anybody was able to recall, nothing very romantic had happened to anybody.

"Next time maybe you'll feed us," Betty said as she came out of the bathroom and peered out the cottage door to see if there was a chance of sneaking unseen to the hostesses' cottage. "God, and to think we've got to fly this afternoon. I'm going back to the cottage, with or without witnesses. Will you drive us out to Eastleigh, Peter, after lunch?"

"Sure, if I live," Peter said. "But I cannot live any longer without a cold beer. See you at the bar in half an hour and we'll have a bite of lunch, eh? Then I'll take you out to the drome. I've got to pick up some clients."

3

There are very few finer places in the world than the veranda of the Norfolk Hotel on a bright Kenya morning, with the clouds sailing lazily past, and a dove sounding somewhere up by the museum, and Sucu, the African gray parrot, making rude remarks at the guests in the back court. The flowers are bright around the brick wall, and dahlias and gladioli and the bougainvillaea perky and cheerful. It is cool and breezy on the veranda, but the sun is warm outside, and a steady stream of natives and dogs passes in front of the hotel, across the street from the Community Theater, as they walk down Government Road. The native women are as bright as the flowers in their cheap cotton prints, walking always behind the men, shabby in khaki or cut and resewn blankets. Bonzo, the unbelievable amalgam of bull terrier and other things, is standing always with his forelegs spraddled in front of the door, giving a suspicious stare—from his red eye—to strangers, and beaming at his friends with his black eye with the ring around it.

About elevenish the cars start to draw up, and the taxis disgorge cargo, and a great deal of Nairobi comes for tea or the first gin or the cool beer or the Pimm's cup. The men are mostly in shorts or drill trousers, their legs burned sun-scaly brown. The women, if they're in from the country, are of a uniform, either slacks or lumpy tweed skirts with cardigans and thick stockings. If the women are from the town they're chic in summer prints, with floppy hats and nyloned legs. Most of the men are mustached heavily in the guardee fashion, with the hairs up-curling into their nostrils and getting tangled in their teeth. There is always a great deal of loud laughter in the bar, coming out the window from which Moussa, the bar steward, passes drinks to the porch boys. The bar is cool and dim inside, but its pictures are bright hunting scenes, and there is a long row of clever caricatures of various categories of British armed might in garish uniforms—the Guards and the Black Watch and the Buffs and all the others. There will be some women sitting in the big black, comfortable wooden booths at the other side of the room, but most of the women are on the porch or in the lounge.

Moussa, the pock-marked Swahili barman, knows exactly what his regulars need of a morning, as does his moonfaced assistant steward, Molo. From the reports of the servants on the night before, he knows whether the Bwana John needs a cool beer, or a Coca-Cola before the first beer, or whether he wishes to dive straight into a Pimm's and damn the cucumbers. There is never any need to scream at Moussa or repeat an order. By the time a steady customer is down to the dregs of his drink, Molo is on the way with a fresh one. Moussa took one look at Peter and John as they entered the bar, looking strangely undressed in flannels and blazers, and snapped the cap off two Karlsberg ales, bitter cold from the big refrigerator that stands next to the service window. Peter and John drained the glasses in two gulps.

"Send the next ones outside on the porch," John said, and they strolled out into the sunlight and fell into chairs. They were joined by the manager, a chubby dark man, who was zebra-marked by a few strips of plaster on his face, result of the chair round his neck.

"My bloody oath, but you chaps pitched one last night," he said. "I was lucky to get away with me life. I was down at the cottage to bring you a beer a moment ago, and it looked like somebody'd staged a polo match in it. Are the girls alive?"

"Just barely," Dot said, walking up and sitting down in a chair the white-skirted, red-jacketed servant held for her. She looked very pretty and fresh in her stewardess's uniform, and there were no marks of the dirty night on her bright young face. "I shall have just one Pimm's and no more, and maybe I can survive lunch. Betty wants the same. She's more scars to repair than me. And please, let's not have much conversation. Even my blood hurts."

The boy came with the drinks and Betty arrived, also fresh and smart in her uniform with its perky cap. "God," she said, "I'm going to sleep a week in Johannesburg. Why I ever took up with white hunters I cannot say."

"Well, damn it all," Peter grinned, "you can't expect us to spend our lives chasing wounded buffalo in the bush and then ask us to behave like gentlemen when we strike the city. I mean to say, it's like asking a sailor to perform like a padre when he hits port. We spend ten months a year in the bush, playing nanny to strangers, staying sober, and eating dust. It's thirsty work."

"Speaking of clients and playing nanny," John Thompson said, "don't forget you've got that new bunch due in at two-thirty."

"As if I'm apt to," Peter moaned. "We'll have to eat early. But I think that I shall now try a gin before I tackle the samaki."

"The curry's good today," the manager said, "it's a Madrasi. I had a taste of it meself. And there's some cold pigeon in aspic that's wonderful. Got just a few, so do the buffet early before they're all snaffled. I must be off and see to a few things. Cheers. Last round's mine."

"Jolly decent chap, old Johnston," John said. "Changed hell's own amount in the last year. Fancy him shouting a round two years ago."

"It's the dog's done it," Peter said. "Ever since Bonzo came into his life he's been a changed man."

"You know, you're right," Dottie said. "He used to be the most awful pain. But that damned dog has changed his personality. They've both become human, and I swear the service is better now, ever since Bonzo took to biting the waiters when the meat is stringy."

"Never knew a man *not* to be improved by a dog." Peter laughed. "It's the women that debase the men."

"Lout. Buy me one more Pimm's and then feed me. You still owe us a meal from last night."

Again the pattern in the dining room was curious, the same related people one might see for lunch at the Outspan or the White Rhino in Nyeri, the Mawingo in Nanyuki, the New Stanley downtown in Nairobi, or the Travellers' or the Staghorn in Nakuru. They seemed pressed into design by sex and by age and by usage. At this moment a similar crowd was moving out of the bar toward the dining room in the Muthaiga Club, and one might have shuffled the guests from all the places without noting the difference. They had the look of the earlier Australian settlers. The young men all had ears that were too big and flanged out from sunburned, sort of unfinished faces, with haircuts too close or too long. The young girls were pretty in a rabbity way, and the middle-aged women were definitely dowdy, definitely dumpy, definitely skinny. Their walks, of the older ones, all seemed the same, a sort of lurch, as if their stout common-sense shoes hurt. The older men, in tweed coats and flannels or brass-buttoned blazers and flannels, always seemed to have the coattails hiked up behind, or a gap at the neck, or a wrinkled shirt collar and a twisted tie, usually blue polka dot, that jarred with a green Harris-tweed coat. The hands of all were gnarled and heavily corded with veins. The dress hems of the older women sagged, as the seats of their skirts bagged, as their cardigans wrinkled and bunched, as their blouses bulged out from under the woollies. But the young men were trim in shorts or jodhpur pants, mostly with blazers and a scarf tied ascot-fashion. All who wore bush jackets and country drill seemed comfortable and well dressed and at home in them.

Lunch at the Norfolk is apart from other lunches. Louie, the Goanese steward, stands by the door with his wonderful kind, Hitler-mustached, gold-glinting smile, smart in his white stengah-shifter with the gold buttons and the stand-up collar, the basic niceness of one Portuguese parent and one Indian parent unable to hide itself even when he is angry at one of the black boys. Louie takes you to a table, and the drink steward comes, and always you have the other gin, the other whisky, and then big tankards of beer, because cool beer is as necessary to the buffet and the curry as chips to fish. You have your own table, of course, and the food is included in the hotel bill, so all you do is sign a chit for the extra drink, and the wine steward is very shy and tactful about presenting it, as is Louie when he gives you a chit for extra guests. It is big and cool and dark-shady in the Norfolk dining room for lunch, with the sun coming down hard outside, with Bonzo sitting in his own chair and ogling the pretty girls—girls whom, since Bonzo is a discerning dog, Bonzo will find a way of introducing by tugging at their skirts if he likes you. You know if Bonzo likes you, because if Bonzo doesn't like you he bites you.

The Kenya folk are always a trifle tiddled at lunch. They have been to the bank to arrange an overdraft, and they've had one over the mark with friends in the New Stanley Grill or the Queens or at the Regal, over the theater, and they've sold some crops or been to see the warden to renew the game licenses or to report a rogue rhino or to have the lorry looked over. Or they've been to the big dark store of the Ahamed brothers to buy a new bathrobe, or they've nipped off to the Africa Boot Shop to buy a snakeskin purse or to have some new boots made. Earlier on they would have had tea and cakes in the vast tearoom of the New Stanley, but now they are a little tight and as hungry as hyenas. So they come to lunch at the Norfolk, where a man does not need a coat or tie, whereas the New Stanley, a bit grander and which serves Mombasa oysters, frowns on careless dress. The New Stanley Grill is marvelous, but you simply can't pitch in, and the wine waiter never gets there with the grog.

Peter and John and the girls went inside, and Louie smiled his heavenly-shy-I-love-you hello, and the bar steward brought beer. There was the usual menu card, in its silver clip, which listed soup—always awful, and mostly of barley—fish, always fine, curry and chops and chips, a cold buffet, and a sweet. You never received the coffee inside. There was a table outside on the second veranda where two barefoot black boys in white and red served the coffee. A man could raise many sorts of hell in the Norfolk, but coffee in the dining room he could not get, despite the hell he raised.

Peter had the fish and so did John, but the girls couldn't face it and went over to the buffet. This buffet was a common sight in Africa and was nearly always the same, whether you ate it in Kampala in Uganda or Arusha in Tanganyika, but in the Norfolk it was usually especially fine. Great slabs of underdone red roast beef, cold, lay on delicate green lettuce leaves, and slices of white-fatted, curled-edged pink ham, and great chunks of greenish-mottled brawn and more ham, of York, and purplish-red ovals of salami. There were the little cold pigeons in the aspic, and cold filets of lake fish from Victoria, and crayfish salad from Mombasa. They gave you green leeks and pickled onions and cold beets and cold duck and asparagus with vinaigrette sauce or mayonnaise. There were massive salads of potato and tomato and lettuce and cucumber and radish, and bowls of sauces and mustard-mayonnaise-onions, and a whole fleet of pickle boats. To one side was a nest of cheeses, domestic mostly, but with a decent imported camembert and gruyère and schweizer. A battery of sauces, Worcestershire, House of Parliament, the usual run, stood by the cheeses. A man could live a week off the cold buffet, but a serious eater went a little light on it and saved a mite of energy for the curry.

The curry would be of fish or lobster or chicken or duck, and it would come with the bubbly soft gray chapatties that you ate with butter, or the wispy potato-chip-like chapatties that curled crisply and seemed lighter than air in your mouth, and the mound of white rice, each grain dry and separate, to be topped by the curry and its sauce, hotter than Mexican pepper, and the little peppers, bananas, pickles, coconut, and the chutney that came via a separate boy and on a separate tray. If you could get through another meat course or the anemic sweets of trifle or gritty ice cream you were lucky, but most folk settled for a slab of cheese and a cup of coffee on the porch outside. And then they went off to bed in the cool cottages and slept for two hours.

Peter marched bravely through the entire issue and then went to bring his car round from the back court. He wasn't going to bed. He was going to the airport, to deliver the girls and collect his clients. He belched politely as he swung through the lobby and cut back behind the reception and the gift stall to the inner court where the car would be. It was a vast lunch, and with all that beer, he would have loved nothing better than to flake out for two hours, then have a bath and see who was drinking what in Moussa's bar. Instead, he was going to the airport.

He strolled down to the girls' cottage and collected their overnight bags and piled them into the car. He drove round to the front of the Norfolk and waited for the girls to come out of the ladies' room. He yawned again and cursed clients who always came in after a big lunch. The girls came, and they drove slowly out of the city, through the native bazaar.

"I've come through this quarter two hundred times, and it still gives me the shudders," Betty said.

"Me too," Dottie said. "It's not the stink and the filth so much as the way they look at you—as if you really weren't there. I wouldn't walk alone through here in the daytime, not to mention the night."

"It's not so bad, bar the stink, which always reminds me of how a grove smells when you've driven a herd of baboons out of it," Peter said. "One of you women light me a cigarette, will you? I've a sensitive nose. I've prowled through here at night heaps of times, looking for one of my drunken Wakambas who's not shown up on leaving day, and I've never had any trouble. I imagine I've poked about in every beer-drink, gaming hut, and bawdyhouse in the quarter, and nobody ever stuck a knife in me yet. You hear the mutters as you pass, of course, but it's usually in some dialect I can't understand. Anyhow, most of the shop owners know me pretty well by now, and it would be very bad police business for them if somebody clobbered me over the skull. They walk with me."

"I don't know how the poor sods live in this rabbit warren, though," Betty said. "Here's your cigarette, Bwana. There must be over fifty thousand of them packed into this sink."

"More, I should say. They're always coming and going and changing about. It's awfully hard to find anybody in here if a few keen blokes really want to hide him. They shift and circle ahead of you like bongo in the bush. And you can't hear yourself think, what with the gramophones and the radios going, and the muezzin screeching back aways in the mosque, and somebody pounding drums and playing flutes and singing, all in a couple of acres. They've got no lights, bar a few smoky paraffin lamps and the cook fires. It's really a needle in a—— Whoa!"

4

Peter jammed on the brakes, killed the motor in the same motion, and jumped over the door of the car. He ran back a few steps and peered into first one shop, then another, spoke swiftly in Swahili, and then dashed out of the second shop and whipped into a crooked, filthy alley. He walked back in a few seconds, shaking his head. He got into the car and started off again. The girls lifted their eyebrows.

"What got into you? You really rattled our teeth with that flaps-up landing of yours. What'd you see?"

"I could have sworn it was him," Peter said. "One Wog I keep looking for. I just got a small glimpse of his face, and not much of a dekko, at that. He nipped off before I could get back there, and it's hopeless trying to find him. Besides, you really don't want to miss that plane. The skipper would be cross."

"Any sort of special Wog?"

"Yep. Kid I was brought up with on the farm. Just my age. Named Kimani. He was the son of my father's headman, and we were raised up in the same kraal, more or less. We used to play together."

"What happened to him?"

"Blessed if I know. There was a spot of trouble on the farm, donkey's years back, some mess of superstition, you know, native business. Kimani thought he brought a curse on the house, and there was a big mumbo-jumbo. One of Kimani's little brothers was born upside down, and so of course the old midwives killed it immediately."

"Do they still do that in Kenya?" Betty asked. "They used to do things like that in South Africa, I'm told, but I thought most of that nonsense was finished and done with."

"Still happens out in the country, and in Nairobi as well, I shouldn't wonder," Peter said, steering the jeep around a mountainously loaded vintage Model-T Ford, its top blowtorched off and its interior packed with squirming Indians. "But what made it bad was that about the time of Kimani's curse the Crown decided to crack down on a lot of native nonsense—you know, illegal dancing, circumcision of the women, beer-drinks, baby-killing, spell-casting, and poisoning, all that sort of stuff. So when Karanja's baby—Karanja was the father of Kimani—when the baby was suffocated, the police got wind of it and popped old Karanja into jail as an example. The old man drew five years and one of the old women was sentenced to be hanged."

"Did they hang her?"

"No. They were very old. One of them died just after the trial. The old man—my old man, I mean—put some pressure to bear and got a new trial. The remaining old woman and Karanja were both paroled into my father's care. But I guess they picked up some fresh new germs in the jail, because they both pegged out with tuberculosis about a couple of years after they came loose."

"What did all this have to do with the chap you thought you saw just now? This Kimani bloke?"

"Well, when they put Kimani's governor in jail, Kimani thought that his curse was the cause of the whole thing and that he could clean it up, get his old boy released, if he killed the man that caused the curse. Very involved. The old witch doctor said that the curse came because Kimani had been defiled because my brother-in-law—you've met Jeff—smacked his face for being cheeky one time when we were out on safari. So Kimani went and got a spear and hid out in Jeff's back yard, and when Jeff came out—this was just after he and my sister were married—when Jeff came out to see about a horse or something, Kimani whipped the spear into him and took off at the speed of knots."

"Jesus," Dottie said. "I thought we had the Wog trouble all to ourselves down South. It's worth your life to leave a door unlocked in Joburg or Capetown today. Was your brother-in-law hurt badly?"

"Not very. Spear took him in the shoulder and passed through. Made a nasty flesh wound, but Jeff's tough as biltong. Thing was, Kimani had no way of knowing he hadn't killed him, and he lit out for the high hills. We didn't do anything about police, figuring there'd been enough row already. But I keep looking for him. He was a good kid as I remember him, and smart as mustard. We could use him on the farm—or I could use him with me in the bush. He speaks damned good English and knows a lot about simple car repair and he'd be bloody good with the clients. My Number One is getting a little old and rheumaticky."

Peter turned the car right into a compound which held a series of flat-roofed, oblong wooden buildings connected with covered catwalks. The sign said: "Eastleigh." As they drew into the car-park, one of the girls pointed at a slanting sliver in the cotton-wooled sky and said:

"Well, here comes the tired iron horse, right bang on the nose. We'll get about our business of clearances and things. We'll just whiz into the bar—which is where you'll be, of course—and kiss you good-by until next trip. I suppose it'll be Mickey and Ruth this time. See you treat 'em better than you treated us. My poor head is still killing me."

Peter slapped both girls affectionately on the rump, nodded at the hostess at the reception, and swung off toward the bar. There wasn't much he could do until the plane set down and the first immigration clearance was made, although he knew the customs people better than he knew his safari string. The Indian and the Goanese customs clerks were quite decent, really, and he never had any trouble with guns and cameras any more. The storekeeper who saw to his victualing made out all the correct forms and permits, and it was just a formality to bring the clients' equipment in and out. Also, here they didn't check the bags too closely, for clients, especially the Americans, always came overweighted with cigarettes and whisky and cosmetics and drugs and the other dutiable items.

Peter walked past the information desk and cut across the catwalk and passed through the little bar and waiting room and then through the dining room and into the long bar with the big windows, where you could watch the planes land in front of the signpost that gave all the various distances from Nairobi to places like Addis Ababa and Cairo and New York and Rome and Paris. He nodded to the black bar steward and a few acquaintances, dropped into a chair, and signaled for a beer. He would have his beer, kiss the girls good-by, say hello to the new two, make a date to see them at the hotel after he got his people settled, and then see about getting the clients organized. He'd stand them some cocktails and an early dinner at the Stanley, and then whip off and do the town with the girls. There was never much time in town, and you had to pack a lot of no-sleep carousing into the three, four, or five days you had between getting rid of one bunch and taking on another. He wouldn't bother with those two types he'd left up at Mawingo. He didn't want to see them again. John Thompson wasn't safari-ing for another week, and John could take them to the taxidermist, clear their weapons, and shove 'em onto the plane. John was very good about lending a bloke a hand that way.

The big plane eased down on the runway, bumped slightly, braked, turned, and swung in toward the airport buildings. The uniformed black boys trundled out the disembarking steps, and the small caravan of porters, baggage trucks, officials, and askaris swarmed out toward the plane like efficient ants. The doors opened, the officials entered, there was the usual delay, and then the passengers began to totter down the stairs, carrying their flight bags and attaché cases and topcoats, and wearing the blinking, owlish look of people who have been trapped in a dark stuffy closet and are now tasting fresh light air. Peter had had a lot of practice spotting clients by now. There would be the few Germans first, heading for Tanganyika, who would jostle out ahead of the others. Then the Dutch, going on down South, and then some returning locals, looking eagerly for the faces of relatives. Then there would be some new English —apt as not wearing solar topis and spine pads, under the mistaken idea that Nairobi was steamy tropical instead of being six thousand feet high and twice as cold as Christmas, despite its location smack on the equator. There would be a few assorted bewildereds and some Indians, small and green-gold from being airsick, pushing from behind, the women back in saris, now they were coming home, and the men looking undressed in their British sack suits, when what they really craved were pajama pants and a pair of slapping slippers.

And then there would be the clients, coming out last or nearly so. The first things you would look for were the cameras slung over their shoulders and the mink coat on the woman. If the clients were young the man would be tall, slim, and crew-cut. Blond or brunet, the man would always be crew-cut. The woman would be beautiful, for young crew-cut men with enough money to pay Peter's prices always married beautiful women. This year she would be blond, no matter what the natural hair color was. It was a blond year. And she would be wearing a simple traveling suit of sharkskin or gabardine or some other non-rumplable dress for travel, a tiny hat, and the shoes, bag, and gloves would have been bought in Rome on the way out. The young man's suit would be J. Press or Brooks and would be cut with no padding in the shoulders, and the shirt would be button-down with a knit tie. This applied only to Americans, of course. If the man were English the suit would be cut the same way, from somebody in Savile Row, and the tie would be poplin or rep and have school stripes on it.

If the clients were old there were several possible variations. The man would certainly be fat or else very, very thin. But mostly fat. There were two kinds of old men's wives. One type was as fat or thin and as old as the man, and the two people would look exactly alike owing to having been married to each other so long. But the other type, when the man was fat, the woman would be very young, very blond and tightly curled, very much minked, with a separate mink of another color on her arm, and she would look like either a tart or a shorthand typist, depending on whether the old boy had got himself trapped in a cabaret or in his office. If the woman were young the old boy would be solicitous and flutter about constantly, and the young woman would pout and throw moods and eventually wind up by gently pressing her bosom against Peter's shoulder when they rode in the Land Rover. Then it would just be a question of when she got Peter alone, and under what conditions of moonlight and weather and displeasure at the husband.

There they were. Peter smiled. The crew-cut was blond. The man was six feet two and slim. He carried a covert-cloth topcoat and wore a Rolleiflex on one side, a Leica on the other, the straps crisscrossed over his chest like bandoleers. He wore a brown Cavanagh hat with a black band and with the crown undented on the sides. Shirt, oxford button-down. Tie, black knit. Golden bar across tie, "21" Club. School, Harvard, Yale, or Princeton. Looked a pleasant type, as did the girl. Coat, short honey-brown wild mink. Suit, severe. Either a Balenciaga or a Hattie. Peter knew all the names of the better couturières and could recognize their peculiarities as easily as he could tell a shootable head from an un-shootable head, looking through the sweated glasses in the blurring heat.

This was a pretty girl, dark, but with one blond streak. She had compromised on the season. He couldn't see the color of her eyes, but the shape of the mouth was nice and the face pleasant. They walked purposefully toward the detaining room, and Peter got up to meet them. Dottie and Betty rushed in and flung him a hurried kiss, and while he was paying his bar chit he managed to miss seeing the last passenger to leave the plane.

She was tall and her hair was a deep red-bronze. She had great curving wings of dark brows, and the Kipsigi porter who carried her bag might have said that her eyes were as green as the darting pigeons that flashed through the woods, but he would have been wrong, because the eyes were the color of the reflection of clear water on a green-lichened rock on which heavy copper content had touched a golden fleck to the green of the rock and of the lichen and the water which reflected it. She had a slightly long but very straight nose, and great wide mouth with slightly fleshy but very well cut lips, and a chin that was clean as the prow of a racing yacht. She was wearing a beige suit and a green blouse, and the suède of her bag and gloves almost matched her hair. She had almost abnormally long legs and good square shoulders and a trim top, what there was to be seen of it under the hard lines of her suit. She walked a long-legged, free-swinging stride, and her lips were parted in excitement. She was back in Kenya for the first time in six years, and her name was Holly Keith.

5

Peter winked at one of the passport-control attendants and entered into the forbidden territory. His people were on the other side of the room, which was jammed. The bronze-haired girl had dropped her flight bag and was searching for a match in her purse, her hands full of gloves and passport and landing papers. Her face was turned away from him, but one look at the legs and the figure in the beige suit decided him that the new clients could wait a moment, since they didn't know who he was, anyhow. He dug out the Zippo some client had given him and flicked it near the cigarette which drooped from the corner of her mouth.

"Offer you a light?"

"Thanks most awfully," the girl said, and swung round to face him. The green eyes widened, and the eyebrows flew up.

"Peter McKenzie!" she said. "Peter McKenzie, grown up to be a man and picking up strange women in airports!"

"Good God," Peter said, letting the flame go out. "It can't be little Holly Keith from next door. Not that little——"

"None other. Six years make that much difference? It hasn't in you. And I'll have the light, please, pickup or not. I'm starved for a smoke." Holly puffed deeply and smiled at him, crinkling her eyes through the smoke in a way that most women with green eyes have found effective and unsettling.

"I swear I'd not have known you except for the legs. Nobody else I ever knew had legs as long as you did when you were a filly. Anybody meeting you?"

"I thought the family, but they may've missed my cable. I had to take an earlier plane and cabled them from Cairo. I don't see them through the iron bars, in any case."

"Look," Peter said. "I've got a couple of clients over in the corner. I must just go and get them started. When you get in customs I'll check your bags through to the hotel, and you ride in with me and the clients. We'll book you a room and have some chakula and I'll drive you up to the farm tomorrow if your people haven't shown. Right?"

"That's very nice. *Chakula. How* long since I've heard Swahili. It's a bit nasty coming back after so long and not being met. You run along and tend to your sheep. I'll not have any trouble with the passport people. I'm awfully glad *somebody* I know was out here."

"Right. Take care." Peter turned and headed toward the clients, who were looking nervously around the cheerless room. He bumped into one of the hostesses, whose face brightened. "Peter darling. Did you come to ride us in?" Peter jumped. "Oh, hi, Ruth," he said, pecking her on the cheek. "I'm afraid not. I've got a carful of clients. There wouldn't be room for you in the Rover. See you at the hotel. I must get over to my people." He walked rapidly away, and the pretty little plump stewardess looked blankly after him. Peter, when he was in town, *always* met the plane. Clients or no clients, he deposited the two outgoing girls and collected the incoming crew. Holly Keith saw the interplay, too, and raised her eyebrows, the left higher than the other.

Peter walked up to the clients. He smiled and extended a hand. "I'm Peter McKenzie," he said. "I expect you're the Deanes. I'm your white hunter, come to collect you and your stuff. Sorry I'm a bit late, but I ran into a very old friend and had to say hello."

The Deanes smiled back and looked relieved. The man shook Peter's hand. So did his wife, gripping it firmly.

"Tom Deane," he said. "My wife, Nancy. God, I'm glad to see you. I'm new at this. We had all sorts of ideas about being stranded here with about sixteen cases, all full of guns and cameras and other hot articles."

"Well, if you'll give me your baggage checks I'll just nip round and see to the customs. I can't help you with the passports, but there's no trouble there. Just get in line and hand them to that chap with the turban and the whiskers, and then he'll pass you through into customs. See you in a minute."

"What a very nice-looking boy," Nancy Deane said as Peter walked away, striding largely, slightly pigeon-toed from tracking, his long arms swinging forward of his knees in a peculiar rhythm. "I don't know whether I'm relieved or worried. I thought all professional hunters were old men, bitter from some unfortunate love affair, hiding their sorrows in the jungle. This one looks like a schoolboy."

"Well, he's supposed to be the best there is. Your uncle Jim shot with him out here last year, and so did a guy I was in school with. He may look like a kid, but they swear by him. I'd judge he's about my age, no older."

"He's powerful pretty, honey," Nancy Deane said. "I can see where these jungle nights are going to be a real pleasure."

"None of that Francis Macomber business, friend. You don't go shooting me in the neck. I am no Gregory Peck, just plain Tom Deane from Connecticut, rich but unassuming orphan. Oh, the Beard is beckoning. Let's go get these passports stamped. I want a martini of no less than one quart in size, and with no vermouth in it at all."

"Are you excited?" his wife asked him. "I'm thrilled to bits. Look at all those black savages and Indians and things. It *is* like the movies. I keep expecting to see Stewart Granger and Deborah Kerr pop up in the crowd. Oh, look, Junior, now *there* is what *I* would call a pretty girl, the redheaded one over there."

Tom Deane whistled. "I knew I should have come on this thing stag. I wouldn't be surprised if that isn't the old friend our new teacher had to say hello to."

The babu stamped their passports and they went through to customs, where Peter had stacked a vast array of gun cases and valises on the shelf.

"There's no trouble about the guns if the serials you sent me check. I pay the entry duty, and when you've safely gone they pay me it back. Anything in these other cases you want to declare—tobacco, whisky, stuff like that?"

"No, nothing," Tom Deane said.

"No American cigarettes?" the customs clerk asked incredulously.

"None but a few packs in my coat pockets."

"Very well, sar. But I must look in the one bag. It is my duty. Will you be so kind as to open that one?" pointing to a pigskin traveling case of the square sort ladies use.

He flicked open the bag, looked horrified, and as hurriedly snapped it shut. He was very dark, but he managed to blush under it. "Very good, sar," he said. "The luggage will go round to the hotel in the van."

Peter excused himself and went over to where Holly Keith was waiting her turn in customs. "Come and meet these people," Peter said.

"They seem quite nice. Chat with them a minute and I'll do your stuff for you."

He led Holly over to where the Deanes waited. "This is Miss Keith, an old neighbor of mine come home from abroad, Mrs. Deane, Mr. Deane. Holly here is riding into town with us, if you don't mind a squeeze. You just stroll out to the gharri and I'll be with you in a jiff."

"You've been away quite a while?" Nancy Deane asked as they walked out to the bright sunlight.

"Six years," Holly said. "I was a kid when I left, just after the war ended. I went to school in England, and last year I did Europe. I'm home to stay now, I hope."

"You've people here, of course?" Tom Deane asked.

"Yes. Mother, father, and a little brother who must be enormous by now. My family has a farm next Peter's father's place. I *can't* imagine why they aren't here to meet me."

"I suppose you've known Mr. McKenzie—this Mr. McKenzie—all your life?"

"Well, ever since I can remember. I proposed marriage to him when I was ten or twelve, and got a smack on the bottom for my pains. He was an enormous great boy of fifteen at the time, and he thought I was rather a nauseating child. The only time he ever paid any attention to me was when he needed me to be a tribe of natives or a herd of buffalo or something, when he was playing war games with a little black chap who lived on his farm. My most tender memories of Peter McKenzie have to do with his sister picking cactus spines out of my trousers. Peter was abducting Kikuyu women that day, and I was two hundred and fifty maidens. He dropped me into a cactus. Possibly because I kicked him. I don't exactly remember. It's been ten years and a bit."

Peter came out of the airport.

"All serene," he said. "It'll be a tight squeeze in this Rover. Suppose you take the back, Mr. Deane, and we stow the ladies in the front with me. It'll be more comfortable for them. Those seats are a mite hard."

"Sure," Tom Deane said, swinging a leg over the low rail. "Away we go. Might as well start now calling us Tom and Nancy. We've got the next three months together, and I'm not much of a Mister-man except with people I don't like."

"Me either. I used to call this young woman here Holly, but she's grown up so grand I don't know whether or not I'm permitted a first name. For all I know, she's married, seeing as she's got gloves on."

"No fear." Holly grinned. "I came home to marry you, as I often used to threaten. Since I've seen you, black as a nigger, I think I've changed my mind. However *do* you get that color?"

At the word "nigger" Nancy Deane winced ever so slightly. It was the first time in her life that she had heard it spoken.

"I've been up in the N.F.D.," Peter said. "It's hotter'n the hinges up there now."

"What's N.F.D.?" Tom Deane asked.

"The Northern Frontier District," Peter replied. "The hot country's North here, the cold country's South. We're just a tiny touch over the equator. But there's a hotel near my home where the equator line is supposed to run right through the middle of the barroom floor. You can stand and talk to a friend whilst you're having a drink, with each of you on opposite sides of the equator."

The car approached the native bazaars, and Nancy Deane got her first look at Africa, heard her first African sounds, smelled her first African smells. She seemed stunned. The smell was enough to stun a stranger.

The drive from the Eastleigh Airport to the Norfolk Hotel is shocking to a newcomer. As you drive along Race Course Road you are past the better Indian residences and come upon the native quarter, the squirming bazaars. In the bazaars most of the shops, duccas, are still Indian, but they are smaller and dirtier and more flyblown and more higgledy-piggledy than the ones closer in toward town, with cheaper prices and inferior goods. They sell candy and Kali snuff and cheap cigarettes, bolts of shoddy cloth made in Birmingham for export, castoff clothes, old Army-issue overcoats, nauseating soft drinks, inferior beer, canned foods, tennis shoes, and sticky fly-encrusted cakes. Straggling between are a few shops, shabbier, smaller, and less well stocked, which bear names like Karioki wa Muchiri or Njuguna wa Kamau, indicating that a native has come to commerce. These are shops enclosed by crazy-slanting walls of dented tin from hammered petrol drums, or walls of mud and thatch, or old packing boxes, and they have lumpy earthern floors and dark smoke-crusted interiors. They sell the fifth-hand clothing that comes from the thieves' market or the native pawnshops and that always seem to flap forlornly from clotheslines in the occasional well-guarded muddy clearing. These shops sell dirty pannikins of sickly-sweet tea, and specky rice, and a native beer that is more like gruel than beer. In some of the eating inns you can buy moldy yams and a bowl of mutton or goat mixed with posho, the mealie-maize staple cereal. In the interiors you can see the natives squatting, making a ball of the posho with their hands and then punching a hole in it with a finger to make room for a sliver of meat or a thick and indefinable greasy gravy of rancid fat and God knows what. Some people squat, some sprawl, against the crazy-leaning walls. Some are drunk in the sun, some are merely asleep.

The assorted smells are contested only by the sounds. A hundred languages and dialects fight for supremacy, without victory—Swahili, Meru, Embu, Kikuyu, Wakamba, Kipsigi, Kavirondo, Arabic, Pushto, Urdu, Hindustani, Portuguese, Goanese, Pondichéry French, English, Masai, Somali, Nandi, German, and Greek. There is a wail of children, a blat of goats, a harsh rattle of phonograph, a shrill giggle from one of the filthy huts, a muezzin's prayerful wail, a thump of drum, the smack of a blow and a scream of pain to follow, a mournful chant, an Arab song on the wireless, and the ceaseless static of argument, bicker, bargain, and boast. Frizzy-headed black whores in European dress, but barefoot, spread-toed, flat-arched, laugh and haggle over prices in the writhing knots of people that cling desperately to the corners like the clotted clusters of flies that hang to the blackened strips of meat and over the goats' and sheep's heads in the butcher shops, flies that crawl drunkenly along the mangoes and yams and burst melons and encrust the souring sweets. And always there is a ceaseless, relentless stream of plodding people—people coming in from town or going out to town, crowding the sides of the roads on bicycles and afoot, on sway-backed burros and packed like shrimp in buses and lurching lorries. The women ever bear some burden on their backs—whether food, firewood, or a few pitiful belongings; their necks bow and the carrying strap creases their foreheads.

The smells hang in the air like a low cloud. The smells are inseparable and form one tremendous acrid essence in which the sweetish odors of rotted meat and decayed fruits blend with the sharpness of urine and the dung of animals and humans, mixing with the smell of curry and smoldering cow dung and the sharp nose-itching odor of goats and human sweat and hot sun and strong cheap tobacco and filthy vermin-ridden clothes and untended huts and unclean sickness and rancid cooking fat and drifting hashish and swirling red dust and cheap sick-smelling perfume and rank alcohol and musk. It lies over the bazaar like a dirty cloak and permeates the smallest cracks in the miserable mud walls. It enters your clothes if you pass on foot, or strikes a club-blow in your nostrils as you drive slowly past in a car.

As you come by in a car, as Peter and Holly and the Deanes slowly drove along to reach the town, you are conscious of one thing—a singleness of black expression. There is no curiosity, no active anger, only a great sweeping animal dumb animosity, a massed swing of the heads, like cattle against an enemy, and a frozen stare. Shrill laughter ceases in the small confabbing groups you pass. Talk stops, and the animation ceases. There is only the completely blank look, the look of nothing behind the eyes, no expression near the mouth, nothing. Nothing. The black man in Kenya crouches behind that blank staring wall, and no white man can penetrate that wall when the black man builds it. As your car passes in a puff of dust, the chatter resumes behind you and silence drops just ahead of you.

"You don't mean to say people actually live in these shacks?"

"They jolly well do. About fifty thousand of them, I reckon. They're happy enough. You'll see after you've been out here a few days that these niggers are different to what your niggers are. Yours have been down out of the tree longer. These boys aren't here very far away from the baboons."

Again the word "nigger." It touched a nerve.

Traffic on Delamere Avenue and Government Road thins out past islands on which plum-black native police swing their batons with military precision and savage grace. Their invariably skinny legs look strangely storkish in wrapped blue puttees under wide uniform khaki shorts.

The streets ferment with a fantastic assortment of races and colors. In a single block you may see big, husky, fierce-bearded Sikhs wearing their close-wrapped pleated turbans and carrying the five iron charms—knife, bracelet, comb, bangle, ring—under their smart European clothing. There are high-nosed, delicate Arabs from the coast, the old men proudly bearded and wearing caftans and burnouses. There are many Greeks and Syrians, and small, often beautiful Hindi women with studs in their noses and red religious ceremony daubs on their foreheads. The shops of Nairobi are chiefly Asian, and the names reveal that the followers of Allah, Buddha, and of the Agha Khan have mostly collared the commerce. Sudhoo, Botlivala, Karamji, Patel, Biram Singh, Wali Mohomet, Krishnakarta—the long line leads from Race Course Road through the bazaars, where they are only thinly interspersed with an occasional native name, mostly over a filthy hotel or teashop.

The native parade on Nairobi's streets, especially its side streets and back streets, is motley. Goatskin-caped Masai with spears and ocher-clay make-up swagger arrogantly along the sidewalks. Kikuyu men wearing castoff khaki and old Army-issue clothes, patched and repatched on the patches, nearly always wearing water-soaked and shapeless European hats, walk at the head of their women or squat in clusters on the corners. Here and there you see a country Kikuyu with vast blocks of wood or dangling iron bangles in ear lobes that have been stretched to shoulder level. The women, slick-skulled, wear shapeless cotton dresses of wild greens and reds and purple, and invariably carry a baby in the crook of their arms. The younger Kikuyu are identifiable by the unpierced ears —or if once they had fist-wide holes they now have had them clipped and resewn. But the non-citified Nandi and Wakamba still stretch the lobes and tuck the pierced bottoms neatly over the tops. Many of the strollers are marked by disease and accident—here, perhaps, an old man with no nose, only a red-crusted, angry cavern, he holding out a begging cup or peddling little badly carven figurines; over there a wizened, gray-wooled mzee staggering against his staff and favoring his hideously twisted leg.

The Indians scuttle briskly along, many of the men wearing khaki pith helmets and carrying swagger sticks in an effort to appear English. They stubbornly hold their own, even dominate the footpaths, while the natives—in the white section of the city—move carefully aside. The whites amble carelessly, chattering with each other without regard to their intended direction, sometimes standing in conversation at the crossings, delaying the hooting traffic while they terminate a conversation. There is always a tremendous squawk of auto horns and bicycle bells in Nairobi, always a great bustle on the main streets and a jabber of a hundred different languages and dialects. The city's appearance is as polyglot as its people.

It is rather an ugly, largely treeless city, except for the scabby eucalypti which line its dusty streets, but out toward the edges there is a sudden upthrust of damp green of fir and fig and acacia, of jacaranda and flame, of cedar and palm. The private homes are almost obscenely riotous with flowers.

The city's architecture is fantastic, square white buildings of several stories, slashed by sunlight and shade, and mostly all ugly; here the delicate minaret of a mosque, here a sprawling Indian school of a violent yellow, there a house of pierced plaster in the Arab mood, and on the edges, long, ugly, crumbly-molding green wooden barracks. The suburbs toward Muthaiga and Limuru are rolling and wet-green and lush-forested, as in any good suburb. The better-class white dwellings are snugged by trees and flowers, and the best boast their swimming pools and clipped tennis courts. The richer Indians have their fine homes, too, but not in the white districts. The Indian homes loom square and hideous on the dusty plains on the road to Thika. They sit starkly like yellow boxes, plastered in the front for show, but revealing ugly gray cement block, unstuccoed, behind, and with their plastered porticos carven in Indian scrollwork.

They came into town, and as they drove down Delamere Avenue they passed Lord Delamere's statue. The little man's likeness captured quite a lot of his fabled audacity.

"Who's that fellow?" Tom Deane asked. "Him on the pedestal?"

"Old Lord Delamere. The one that opened up these parts for the white settlers. Wagered his fortune and wrecked his health trying to make this what he called 'white man's country.' Fought England tooth and nail when the Home Office tried to take away the settlers' lands back in '22. Led a delegation to London, a bunch of hairy settlers and a couple of Masai warriors with spears. Told the Whitehall chaps that unless they called off their dogs Kenya was going to do what you people did and bloody well declare war on England. Home Office backed down. England could hardly afford to get mixed up in a war with one of its colonies at that time, and the settlers were dead serious. They were going to kidnap the Governor, just for starters."

"He must have been quite a gent," Tom Deane said.

"He was. My father told me once when Delamere was having some Government red-tape trouble here one time he collected a crowd of settlers and went over and set fire to Government House. Whether it's true or not, I couldn't say. But I do know he used to get drunk and pick fights in the Norfolk bar, and when all the fists were swinging he'd hop on the bar and caper about, and then dive headlong into the mess, feet and fists churning. For a proper baron tracing back to the twelfth century, he was quite a rough 'un."

"It all sounds fascinating," Nancy Deane said. "Is that the Norfolk Hotel there, the red long building down the road?"

"Yep. That's your home for the next couple of days. I've booked you into one of the better cottages. This cottage has two bedrooms and a quite decent living room. You've got so much gear that if we try to put it all in the living room you won't have any place to sit."

6

He turned the car down the narrow alleyway leading to the back court and pulled up in front of a bigger cottage than his own, at the head of the square horseshoe of linked cottages. A shrill voice spoke from a tree.

"Peter's a clot! Peter's a clot! Peter's got a new girl!"

"Damned cheeky parrot, Sucu. My friends teach him all these things to say," Peter grumbled. "Shut up, you gray buzzard, or I'll feed you to Bonzo."

"Bonzo being?"

"Dog. Belongs to the manager. This place is crawling with livestock. Now. You good people just nip in here and look at your new quarters. I suppose you'll want a wash. I see Kamachi standing at the door to greet you. He's a wonderful Wog, and dead honest. I'll just take Holly over and see about a room for her, and then we'll all meet on the veranda for a drink, what? I daresay you could use one."

The Deanes entered their cottage and got a Jambo-Bwana Jambo-Memsaab from Kamachi, while Peter led Holly Keith over the cobbles to the back entrance of the hotel. The manager, Johnston, met them at the reception, on which Bonzo was squatted, both feet on the registry, while he leered with his red eye and lolled his tongue.

"Get down off that registry," the manager said. Bonzo jumped down, walked around the corner of the office, sniffed Holly's skirt, and kissed her hand. "He likes you," the manager said. "But no matter. Your father's just been on the phone. Your cable went wrong and has only just got through to him. He wasn't expecting you until the next flight. He's pranged the car, someway or other, and can't come in until tomorrow."

"Oh," Holly said. "I *am* relieved. I was frightened something awful had happened. Can you put me up for the night? Things are dreadfully crowded, I know."

"Surely, Miss Keith." The manager showed his teeth in a wide smile of purest malice. "I've taken the liberty of moving Mr. McKenzie and

Mr. Thompson in with me. There is not another room in the house or at the New Stanley, either. I've got people sleeping in broom closets."

"But I couldn't take Peter's room."

"Of course you could," Peter said. "We do this all the time. Every time Johnston gets in a muddle he moves me. I've spent so much time in his cottage that people think we're a bit peculiar."

"Well, it's wonderful, and if I may I'll run over and fresh up a bit. What's the number?"

"Ten. The door's open. Your stuff just came on the van and I've sent it round with the porters. Make sure you count it."

"Oh yes, and, Holly," Peter said, "I imagine your father will be ringing through again later on, and why don't you tell him not to be bothered with coming all the way in from the farm? I have to go up to see my guv'nor tomorrow, to collect some clothes and a gun, and I'd love to drive you. Right?"

"Marvelous. I'll tell him when he rings up. Now I must go scrub some of this grime off me. See you in the bar a little later. Thank you, Mr. Johnston. You've been very kind. And so've you, Peter. Ta." Holly ran toward Peter's cottage.

"My word, what a stunner that one's got to be," Johnston said. "I remember her as a little girl, all knobs and knees and freckles. Come along, Bonzo, let's go and buy the Bwana a spot of something."

"If you're reckoning to move in on this, my lad," Peter said as they went down the veranda toward the nearly empty bar, "you have bloody well got another think coming. I staked this one out when she was a child and have just been waiting to see how she'd turn out. This is my own secret country, chum, and you ain't allowed in it. And *not* to go running off your mouth about my carryings on, do you hear, or I'll tell your boss about who tried to force his way into the stewardess's shack one night when he roared home polluted from the Travellers'. But I'll take that drink now whilst my clients tidy."

"What sorts are they? Bloody?"

"Very unbloody, at first glance. But you never can tell. I've seen 'em sweeter than honey in town and at each other's throats, and mine, after a week in the bush. We will see, but I'm betting these are all right."

The manager and Peter were drinking a beer when Tom Deane walked in, fresh-changed to flannels and tweed coat. He had washed and his hair still glistened with moisture. Peter introduced them.

"My God, I feel wonderful, now I'm actually here, but I can't believe it," he said. "Can a fellow get a real dry martini around here? With Gordon's and Noilly Prat? I want a double, at least."

"Martini a maui mbile, Moussa," Peter said. "It'll be right. We had an American purist out here last year, and he clued old Moussa up just dandy. Rooms all right?"

"Real fine. Who do I thank for the flowers and the bottle of gin and the bottle of whisky?"

"Flowers are mine," Peter said. "Old Johnston here provides the booze. Impresses the clients no end. Puts 'em in his debt so's they won't scream when the service is awful and the phone won't go. He gets it back on the bill twice over, anyhow. I say, Tom, what *did* your wife have in that bag that horrified the customs chap so? Snakes?"

"No, Kotex. Actually there were thirty cartons of Luckies stashed under the snowdrift."

"Well, it's damned lucky he picked that particular bag to open, because thirty cartons of American cigarettes would have really tossed the cat amongst the pigeons."

"Oh, we were safe enough," Tom said cheerfully. "She always spreads that ladies' intimate business over the tops of all the bags. Never had a customs man dig under it yet."

"American ingenuity," the manager said. "They think of everything. No wonder everybody over there has a Cadillac."

Tom Deane tasted his martini carefully, and his face glowed. "I haven't had one like that since Ziggy built the last one at Toots Shor's. Can we do this on safari?"

"You can if you want to trouble about a portable icebox. I find the water bags keep the stuff cool enough, from the condensation. Gin bottle's got beads on it in the morning. We have about a twenty-degree temperature drop in less'n an hour. After fourteen hours mucking about in that jeep in a hot sun, you'll drink your gin scalding if necessary and it'll still taste good."

"What do we do when the girls get here?"

"Well, I thought we'd sit here and have a drink and see if Holly's father rings through, and then go downtown to an Indian place I know and buy you a bite. Dining room's closed here now, it's a little late. Then perhaps we'll go and collect some gear; you won't need much, pants and bush jackets and a few odds and ends. You've got boots?"

"Birdshooters."

"The best. But we'll have the little Wahindi make you an extra set, and some mosquito boots as well. Then you and the Mem can seize a little sleep if you'd like, and I'll take us all to dinner at the Equator. There's some music and dancing later, and the food's jolly decent. You can ask me lots of questions and I'll try to answer them as best I can. All right if I ask Holly to feed with us?"

"Of course. But it's my party. I don't get to Nairobi every day. Nancy's dithering around like a sixteen-year-old. She's expecting Gregory Peck to ride up on an elephant any minute. Say, here come the women now. They seem to have timed the entry, a thing I never understood about women."

Nancy Deane had changed into a yellow afternoon frock, and Holly Keith appeared in a lime-green linen suit that subtly changed the color of her eyes.

"What a lovely hotel," Nancy Deane said. "And I think the room boy in the nightdress is divine. What's that you're drinking, Tom? It looks alarmingly like a martini."

"It is. You've got its twin coming. How about you, Miss Keith— Holly? Martini?"

"I think perhaps not. I think rather a gin and tonic, please. Martinis do very strange things to my metabolism, especially when I'm tired. And you'll both admit that the hop from Khartoum isn't a true health cure."

"I just can't imagine I'm in Africa. It's all so *civilized.* I sort of expected everybody to be hairy and armed with horse pistols and a thorn whatdoyoucallit around the yard. But this is like a mountain resort town," Nancy said.

"Very few years ago, when my father first came, all the men wore guns, and every night they shot up the bars. In the old days of this very same hotel they used to shoot the tiles off the roof for fun. And I can still put you in a taxi and show you a lion inside of an hour. As a matter of fact, one of the safari firms had to send a bloke to shoot a leopard out of a hen coop in the native quarter just last night. If the wind's right you'll hear hyenas howling tonight." Peter pointed at Holly with his cigarette end. "I wonder if you remember, Holly, the story your father used to tell about going out into the yard in the dark to harness a donkey, and the donkey let out a frightful roar? He'd tried to clap a bridle on a lion that was raiding the barnyard."

"I heard it often enough, but I never believed it." Holly smiled. "Give Dad one over the quota and his imagination gets rather vivid. But I do remember running onto more than one rhino in the road not more than five hundred yards from the house. Mother writes that you can still hear the lions plainly when they go down to Naivasha for week ends, and a hippo bit a canoe in two the other day."

"I say, I've an idea," Peter said. "I must absolutely stop off at my farm tomorrow, and then too I've got to drive Holly home. If I curse loud enough we can have all your stuff ready by noon tomorrow. Why wouldn't it be a good idea to have an early lunch and drive up to the farm, spend the night, and cut on over to the Masai tomorrow? I can fix all your Kenya licenses in the morning. Then I thought we might go to Tanganyika to a place I know where the grass is short, and collect your lions and leopards and the common stuff there. Are you especially mad keen to shoot an elephant?"

"Not very especially," Tom Deane said. "I'd rather take it sort of easy at first. Like I keep saying, I'm new at this business. But I like the Tanganyika idea. Much of a drive?"

"Two days ordinarily, but there's been a bit of rain and I'm told some of the tracks over the mountains have washed out. Might take three. But the last day's a wonderful trek across the Serengeti Plains, and the wildebeest and zebra migration ought to be starting about now. If you're lucky you'll see half a million animals in a day, and at least fifty lions. Can't shoot, of course. It's a preserve. I thought that if you'd like I'll send the lorry on ahead with the stuff and have them make a camp in a very pleasant spot I know outside Narok, in the Masai reserve. Then we drive leisurely over in the afternoon from my house."

"It sounds wonderful to me," Nancy said. "I'd love to see how real people live out here—not the safari people or the tourists or the town people, but real people who have homes here."

"That's fine, then. I'll get John Thompson—he's a friend of mine —to drive you two up in his car, and I'll take Holly in mine. John and I both have gunbearers, and they'll ride in back of the Rover. We'll put everything but your overnight kit into the lorry."

"What do I wear?" Nancy asked. "To your house, I mean?"

"Pants and jacket," Peter said. "What we'd best dash off and arrange for now. You might take a pair of ordinary slacks and a sweater to change over if you want. It's nippy up in those hills."

A black servant came into the room, tinkling a bell. He carried a blackboard with "Miss Keeth" scribbled on it.

"That'll be your father ringing through," Peter said. "Tell him you'll be home in the latish afternoon. Then go and have yourself a nap. It might get to be late out tonight. I'll knock you up at seven, right?"

"Right. I suppose Daddy can wait another hour or so after six years. Bye-bye, all, till later."

Holly finished her drink and went away to the phone kiosk. Peter called the boy and paid the bill.

"First off we'd best go and get you suitably clothed," he said. "Ahamed does a good job in a hurry, and so does the boot shop. You'll have your duds complete by noon. Let's be off, shall we?"

"Fine. I want to buy one of those wonderful floppy hats that the movie hunters wear," Nancy said. "I want to tie a leopard tail around it to have photographs taken to show the children."

"We just don't happen to have any children at the moment, do we?" Tom said. "I hope."

"No, but I thought I'd take care of the hat, anyhow. You never can tell."

"Oh, one thing," Peter said as they rose to go. "Have you any dinner clothes with you? I thought we'd go to the Equator for dinner, and it's a formal night."

"Oh, sure. I was warned we might need a black tie."

"Well, then, let's go and fit you out for the bush. Kwenda."

"That means what?"

"Let's go. When it's let's-go-in-a-hurry it's 'pese pese.' "

"Kwenda," Nancy said. "Pese pese. I think I'm going to like the language."

7

They went to Ahamed's and were measured for bush jackets with cartridge loops for the big bullets, and pants and shorts, and on Peter's advice they each bought a heavy sweater and two enormous woolly bathrobes and double-brimmed terai hats and two big tin trunks to put it all in. Then they went over to the boot shop and got measured for extra shoes by the smiling little bucktoothed Indian who carefully traced their feet and kept their American boots to model from. Nancy wanted to buy all the leopard-skin slippers and croc-hide belts and zebra doodads and Indian brocade slippers with curly toes, but Peter gently told her that it would be much smarter to do it after they returned. Then they went and collected ammunition from Peter's strongbox and bought pocketknives and flashlights and a few girl-things for Nancy from the drugstore and still had time to pop into the New Stanley for tea, which they decided on to replace lunch. It was nap time when they got back to the Norfolk.

John Thompson joined them for drinks at eight—they all overslept in the cool dark cottages, from varying types of fatigue—and then they met, merry and rested, in the Norfolk bar. Peter placed the girls on stools and the men ringed them round, to fend off the more exuberant types, who had been working at the grog from a little earlier in the day. At eight o'clock the Norfolk bar reminded Tom Deane of San Francisco in the war. There was the same air of shore-leave exuberance from the young bucks in dinner jackets, in dusty shorts, in flannels and tweeds. Everybody smiled widely. Everybody talked too loud. Everybody greeted everybody else as long-lost friends, with a ringing clap on the back, or a cuff on the side of the head, and a roaring invitation to drink.

There was no conversation. There was rather a series of short bursts of sound, such as a ship's anti-aircraft battery makes, the rattle of twenty-millimeters giving way to the sharp clap of the .350s and the heavier boom of the .538s. The noise also reminded Tom Deane of John Dos Passos' old writing device, the camera eye, when all the things people said were crocheted into a tapestry of noise and nobody ever quite finished a sentence. The laughter was full-bodied, chesty haw-haws from the men and uninhibited screams from the women. Peter and John were accosted by at least a dozen, men and girls, all of whom were introduced by the completely idiotic English "Do you know So-and-so," when there was really no remote chance of anyone ever having met before. The circle spread to include the newcomers, all of whom seemed unduly excited over nothing at all. Since each addition demanded the chance to buy a round of drinks, Tom Deane figured that he was about thirty scotches behind the already-paid-for orders.

Holly Keith, sitting strikingly on her stool, soon was discovered as the little Keith girl who had been away to England and my word, what a smasher she's turned out, was besieged by sunburned young men who seemed to stretch well upward past six feet, and all of whom seemed on the verge of proposing marriage within minutes. The smoke thickened with the noise, and finally Peter nudged Tom, who was vastly enjoying himself, and said:

"For Christ's sake let's get out of here. You can't hear yourself think. I've changed my mind about dinner at the Equator. It'll be dull as dirt until midnight, and the food's nothing so very much. We'll feed a lot better at the Stanley, and a lot quieter than here. I'll ring up and hold my table at the Equator and we'll go there and dance a bit later. All right?"

"Sure. Anything you say. But if we don't leave here soon we won't have any women. The competition is a bit stiff, hey?"

"It's due to a shortage of women in Kenya. The veriest hags come out here from England to work, and they're all married off in a snap. I'm told it was the same in America in the early days."

They collected their women over roars of male disapproval and fought a way out into the clean, fresh-washed night air, on which the odor of flowers trembled.

"God, what a crush," Nancy said. "Don't Kenya men do anything but drink?"

"Well, a lot of them work pretty hard," Peter said, steering them toward the car. "And when they come to town they blow some steam. They're goodhearted chaps, most of them, but a little uncurried. They don't drink to stay sober. They drink to get pi— drunk. We have an international reputation for it out here."

Holly said as they drove off downtown to the Stanley: "You know, that's my first experience with masses of young Kenya gentlemen in a bar. They are a bit exuberant, aren't they, after England? The young men always seem so *tired* there."

"I expect it was the war," Peter said. "Here we are. I'm ravenous, as usual."

"You ain't lonesome, Bud," Nancy Deane said. "Those nutritious dee-licious little cucumber-and-tomato sandwiches you gave us at tea do not sufficiently sustain a large-type growing girl. Let us approach the food."

They walked through the long hall, indented on the right by shops which opened on the street, and turned left through a bricked patio to step down into a large formal dining room. A small orchestra played uninspired salon music in a palm-shaded corner. There was a loose knot of people drinking boisterously at the bar, which ran lightly along the room at the entrance but which was contained in a high balcony to fend the noise from the feeders. The people here seemed quieter, better dressed, and considerably older. But again the stamp was apparent. The older men were either sallow from an ancient well-trusted malaria or they were heavy and beef-faced, with purpled cheeks from crisscrossed broken veins. But sallow or purple, the stain of sun overlaid the pallor or the flush. A tall and very correct Frenchified headwaiter bowed and led them to a large round table in a corner away from the orchestra, which was playing something from Strauss.

"If the oysters are fresh, I can recommend them," Peter said. "Fancy some Mombasa oysters after all these years, Holly?"

"I would indeed. The last I remember eating was at the party the day your sister and Jeff got married. *What* a party. *You* got beastly drunk, my lad, at a tender fifteen. You had to go and soak your head in the brook."

"I remember it all too well. It was my first hangover, and I also remember my old man did not give me what-for. I expect he wasn't feeling well enough to make any special point of it."

"Your sister, she's older or younger than you?" Nancy asked, spearing an oyster. "My, but these *are* delicious. Tom's always talking about Sydney oysters. He was in Australia during the last little bit of the war, and all he ever tells *me* about are the oysters. The other men who were in Australia wink and look wise and talk about the girls."

"Never went out with anything but oysters," Tom said. "But tell us about your family, Peter. Big one?"

"Well, there's Elisabeth and Pa and then there's me, and that's all. Lisa's three years older than me. She's married to a wonderful bloke— Navy type like you, Tom—who got blown up early in the war and rushed home early and grabbed Lisa off before the panic started. They've got three kids, wonderful little brutes, and are quite the happiest people I know. Jeff's made a lot of money on the farm. I suppose, actually, Jeff gets more work out of his Wogs than anybody around."

"This word 'Wog'? Where's it come from? I heard it during the war and always thought it was a short for 'pollywog.' Do you think I could have another half dozen oysters? They're wonderful, but not very big," Nancy asked.

"I know about the derivation of 'Wog,' " Holly said. "An R.A.F. chap told me in England. Seems that when the R.A.F. was the R.F.C., the old Royal Flying Corps, in the 1914 war, a lot of it was stationed in Egypt. There was quite a lot of friction between the troops and the locals, so one day the C.O. put out a statement to all H.M. Forces in Egypt. The statement said something like: 'You will hereinafter cease referring to our gallant allies as dirty, thieving coons. They will herein-after be referred to as Worthy Oriental Gentleman.' Worthy Oriental Gentlemen—W.O.G.—Wog."

"I can believe it," Peter said. "When I was up in Addis we had the same sort of directive. It said: 'You will hereinafter cease referring to the King Emperor, Haile Selassie, Lion of Judah, as that "little black bas-tard." You may call him by his full title or not refer to him at all.' So we called him 'Highly Delightful,' out of respect for H.M. orders. Nobody could quarrel with us over that."

"This color thing interests me a lot," Tom said while they waited for the soup. "We've gotten very touchy about it at home. Your attitude out here reminds me very much of the way it works—or used to work —in the South. You sort of treat 'em as not too bright children. You like 'em, sure, but you don't associate with 'em. You call everybody 'boy,' whether they're young or old. You have them in your homes and you depend on them entirely for the success of your work, but you treat them as if they were some special sort of cattle. What happens one fine day when they get tired of being called 'Boy-ee!' and want some of this easy democracy that's being passed out all over the world today?"

"Jesus, I don't want to get tangled up in this one," Peter said. "Every American that comes out here asks me the same thing. In Kenya alone there are six million blacks. God knows how many more from the Cape to Cairo. We are just on thirty thousand whites. Before we came—less than fifty years ago—they were all eating each other and murdering each other for fun. Disease kept the population down and the lions kept the population down and the tribal wars kept them down. All the natural sins and troubles served as a sort of population check. Then we came roaring in and civilized 'em. I'm talking now about the Kikuyu, the people that live in and around the White Highlands here. We threw 'em a pair of pants and said that over yonder was a church where a much stronger God than their Ngai lived. We introduced them to a little simple medi-cine and showed them how to keep their cattle from dying off and told them not to kill each other. We took land from the Masai and gave the Kikuyu the Masai land, and we told them to quit burning down the forests. Wait a minute," Peter said, and turned his head. "Boy! Letti soupi leo, hapana keshu!"

"That means?" Nancy said.

"Told him I wanted the soup today instead of tomorrow. You send one of these chaps off to fetch your hat, maybe, and if he sees a butterfly he forgets the hat and chases the butterfly. You have to ginger 'em up a bit. Do you want to hear any more of this, or shall we talk about lions or sex or something?"

"It'll probably bore Holly, but I'd like to hear a bit more," Nancy said. "Mind, Holly?"

"Not a bit. But I would like to say that we who've been raised out here know just a bit more about the native than the people who *haven't* been raised out here. I used to get so damned sick of people in England, once they'd heard I was East African, reading me long lectures on what we were doing wrong with the native. The only native they ever saw was a drunken American Negro G.I.—excuse me, both of you, I don't mean to be rude—who had collected a couple of Piccadilly tarts and was busy showing London how a military uniform could turn into a zoot suit if you had the necessary money."

"Who reared me, Holly?" Peter asked.

"An African woman."

"Who was my best friend and playmate?"

"A Kikuyu."

"Who was my father's best friend, really?"

"Old Karanja. A Kikuyu."

"And who took care of you as a little girl?"

"Africans. Swahili and Kikuyu."

"Right you are. Now you, Tom and Nancy, are going to trust your lives to me for three months. I have fifteen men in my outfit. More than once your life and mine may depend on whether Chalo and Kidogo and Metheke, the gunbearers, do their jobs right. You've not met Aly, the cook, but next my father he's the finest man I know, and a marvelous chef as well. The headboy, Yusuf, I expect, is the best friend I've got. Kungo, the driver, is the best mechanic in Africa and one of the more decent chaps I ever knew, black or white. Right down to the kitchen mtoto, there's not a man in my string I wouldn't trust with my life or yours, and there's not a man in the string that I wouldn't expect to die for me in an emergency if he had to."

"I'm pleased to hear about the cook," Nancy Deane murmured. "I fancy me vittles. I think I will take the steak now if you recommend it."

"I ordered it for everybody," Peter said. "Two rares, a medium, and one well done. I'm the well done. The South African claret isn't half bad, it's first-class, really. Would you try a bottle of that or prefer the French?"

"Try the local," Tom Deane said. "Get on about the natives. I'm fascinated."

"All I'm saying is that a Wog is a Wog, no matter what you do to him. Kungo's a good mechanic, but if the truck breaks down under certain conditions, it isn't because he forgot to do something essential to preserve its innards. It's a 'shauri a Mungu'—a will of God. Metheke's a good Mohammedan, but he still files his teeth and prays to the old gods. Kidogo, in the bush after a wounded buffalo, doesn't know the meaning of fear. But if somebody tells him that there's a curse on him, he'll lay right down and die on you. Fall sick and wither away.

"I would trust Chalo to offer himself to a wounded lion if it would help me, and he would give the lion his arm to chew. But when I tell him to come back from Machakos at such-and-such a time, it's apt to be a week later, or not at all, if there's any difficulties on his shamba to distract him. I can send him telegraph after telegraph and he will ignore them, because if he doesn't get somebody to read them, then I haven't sent them, see? Yusuf, the headboy, is my complete Number One. He is a master of detail. He runs the shauri. But if an evil omen strikes him he goes potty and throws up his hands. He forgets he's part Arab, and he forgets he's a Mohammedan priest, and he turns right back to being black savage again. I think any one of them would run away, or kill me, or do anything at all, if they got scared enough in certain circumstances."

"My heavens," Holly said. "You ought to go to England and do a lecture turn on the TV."

"Well, I want to get off the subject," Peter said. "It really is a crashing bore. But what the people outside don't know is that the Wogs don't think like us, and they don't react like us, because they are too newly introduced to what we call civilization. I had a friend, an Australian, who was a wonderful white hunter, who quit and went back to Aussie because the blacks drove him literally loony. Frank never could handle them. The thing about the black is that you've got to know when to kick him in the tail, when to humor him, and when to praise him. You can't stretch him beyond his basic powers, and you can't ever *rely* on him in white man's terms. Just when you do, he'll revert completely to his ancestors and do exactly the bloody opposite of what's indicated. Seen it time and time again."

"Don't get off the subject yet," Tom Deane said. "We've still got dessert and coffee coming. I gather that you think the problem out here is that you've tried to 'civilize' them, for want of a better term, too fast."

"You are so bloody crushingly correct," Peter said. "We leave the nomads alone and they do fine, carrying on with the old ways, wearing their goatskins, moving their manyattas—that's a Masai encampment—and, mind you, burning them down when they leave, so as to destroy germs. But we take the Kikuyu, say, or the Wakamba, and teach them how to increase their herds and how to increase themselves, but we don't find any way to absorb them. We change their old crop rotation to money crops and ruin the land. They live bang on the fringe of white civilization, swelling and crowding their properties—and mark you, they've got more land than they ever used before—but it isn't enough. They learn all our bad habits. We destroy every bit of their old logical living because it conflicts with our law, and replace it with bleeding nothing. So now you have, excuse me, please, whores when once there was no such thing as prostitution, and robbers and spivs and sly loafers, because they've become detribalized without becoming decently citified. I *must* be drunk. I never talked this much before in my life."

"You seem to have given this quite a bit of thought," Holly said. "I suppose it started with that business on your farm that I remember, the thing about Kimani spearing Jeff and old Karanja going to jail when they killed the baby."

"Yes, it did, but I don't intend to go into that," Peter said. "There will be a lot of dull nights ahead on safari to talk about that one. But why, please, wouldn't I give it some thought? I just sacked a Kikuyu car boy, a born rogue if I ever knew one. Informed me politely the other day that he wouldn't have to be a car boy much longer. I asked him why, and he said the Russians were coming. He said when the Russians came all the natives in Africa would have a Chevrolet and a radio. Said it was common talk in the bazaars. And I promise you this particular black gentleman don't know a Russian from a boot in the tail, which is exactly what I administered when I sacked him."

"The boot in the tail solves what?" Tom Deane asked gently.

"It salved my feelings for a start and brought this one particular idiot back to reality. The Russians are just around the corner, perhaps, but the boot in the tail is for right now, and an African understands right now. He doesn't understand tomorrow, and he forgets yesterday, because he's got no sense of time. Time means absolutely nothing to him. You'll see a bloke curled up on a road waiting for a bus that isn't due for half a week. He's perfectly happy to sleep there in the dust. The best job you can give the average African is a waiting job. He needs starting to do anything at all specific, but he won't know when to stop if it's white man's orders. We had some Kavirondo on the farm once, the old man told them to dig a well, to dig straight down, and one damned well drowned. When the water came he was still carrying out orders, submerged or not. Boy! Tasama bar steward! I think that it will take at least a double brandy to wipe out the taste of my oration."

"Have you any more sweeping generalities to wash down with the brandy?" Holly asked, smiling.

"Just a couple, and then I either go on the wireless as an announcer or return to being a white hunter," Peter said. "In the African make-up there is really no such thing as love, kindness, or gratitude, as we know it, because they have lived all their lives, and their ancestors' lives, in an atmosphere of terror and violence. There is no proper 'love' between man and woman, because the woman is bought for goats and is used as a beast of burden. There is no gratitude, because it would never occur to them to give anything to anybody else, and so they have no way of appreciating kindness or gifts from others. They lie habitually, because to lie is the correct procedure, else some enemy might find a way to do them damage if they tell the truth. They have no sensitivity about inflicting pain or receiving pain, because their whole religion is based on blood and torture of animals and each other. They think, even the best of them, that nothing's funnier than a wounded animal or a crippled animal. It's a big joke. *I* don't even think that they themselves feel pain the way we do. I've seen 'em with their legs broken and the bones sticking out, and I've seen Masai youngsters half eaten by lions. You sew 'em up with a sail needle and they grin like it was fine fun. I must say they're good to their kids, as a rule, but maybe that's because the female children represent a big annuity for the family, and the males are tomorrow's warriors and day after tomorrow's tribal elders."

The black wine waiter came and poured brandy into snifters, and the black coffee-boy came with his wheeled tray. Holly poured the coffee.

"One sugar, please," Tom said. "You'd say this applies to all the tribes, or just to these—what do you call them—Kyuku?"

"Kikuyu. Mostly the Kikuyu. For two reasons, mainly. They have a reputation amongst the other tribes as crafty, witch-hounded, lying sea lawyers. They were never proper warriors or hunters, but always shifty agriculturists and sneaky murderers, forever out to do the next bloke in the eye. Their system of land tenure is one of the most complicated in the world, and so is the tribal setup.

"For instance, all the agitators like Kenyatta and the other boys that ran the old Kikuyu Central Association—which was banned for subversion at the start of the war—and its present successor, the Kenya African Union, are always screaming about us taking the Kikuyu land. Actually, where they scream the loudest, they never owned that land. The Masai owned it, and we gave 'em a new reservation—you'll see it—and took up land for ourselves.

"The land we actually got from the Kyukes we paid for. But then the agitators say that no one Kikuyu can sell any land at all to anybody, it's a business for the clan, and then it gets to be the business of all the clans. The Kyukes don't say much about the fact that they took most of what they call their own ground from a bunch of wild hunters named Wandrobo, first paying for it by agreement and then gradually forcing the 'Ndrobo out, like the camel that stuck his head in the tent. To understand the clan system you have to understand that every child is his own grandfather, which makes him the father of his father, and his uncle is his brother, and so forth, and it works the same way more or less on the female side. Everybody is everybody else, including his dead ancestor. 'Member, I was damned near raised as a Kikuyu. But the main thing is that they fell smack in the path of our movements out here, so we've had 'em for neighbors, and God knows we haven't helped them any. Now, by damn, I *will* stop. Somebody else talk. I never ran on before like this in my life. I'm winded."

"I assume, then," Nancy said, "that you actually like the individual Negro but only in certain categories, and always as an inferior?"

Peter looked up, almost but not quite angry.

"They damned well *are* my inferiors in the white man's world as we know it out here. I don't mean to be rude, but you've been in Nairobi only half a day. I admire a great many of their skills, and I love the true savage on his own savage ground, and I love a great many things about all the tribes. But I live here, I was raised here, and I *know* niggers. And they bloody well are not ready to sit in the Legislative Assembly. It's a method of thinking for a start. They tried the equality thing once in a trial, letting the elders decide the guilt of a proven murderer. They'd found the murderer literally pulling the spear out of the dead man. The elders acquitted him. They asked why for the acquittal and one elder said: 'It is well known that Kikuyu never murder.' The next one said:

'The accused owed me six goats.' The third one said: 'The accused was my cousin.' Now that is *all*. This is supposed to be a wet bright night in Nairobi."

"My apologies for Nancy," Tom Deane said. "But she took a couple courses of sociology in her senior year in college. Somebody told her sociology courses had no labs."

"Well, I'm curious," Nancy said. "I don't see any point in coming all the way out here without asking some questions."

"Buy her some eland straps," Peter said. "I'm sorry I was B-minded."

"Eland straps?"

"Sure. When a Wog loves his manamouki very much, he gets her some eland straps as a token of affection."

"What is a manamouki exactly? And this business of eland straps, whatever they are?"

"Well, a manamouki is the best word for female in Swahili. It means 'she-thing.' Whether it applies to animal or human, that is what a she-thing is called, 'manamouki.' There isn't any word for sweetheart or fiancée or debutante or wife or loved one. It's just manamouki. And when you care for your manamouki very much, you buy her some eland straps—very strong and supple, from the skin of the big antelope—so that she can carry *more* firewood and potato tops and banana fronds. This way you know the man loves you, because it pains him to think that you've got to make two trips up that long hill, when with the right straps you could carry all the stuff in one trip." Peter grinned evilly. "I think one more brandy and then we'll abandon this dreary monologue of mine for a little more frivolous evening amongst the drunks at the Equator. All the manamouki you see there never heard of an eland strap. It's all they can do to lift their whisky glasses."

"What a magnificently nasty young man you've become, Peter McKenzie," Holly said. "I think I liked you better when you were a thousand Masai moran up from the Loita, on rape and robbery bent, as the poet says."

"It comes of too much association with clients," Peter replied, soothing the sting with a smile. "They come out here in a hurry from a wet night in Harlem or someplace and try to uplift the pore bleedin' 'eathen before they've got their safari clothes delivered. Just you people wait"—he pointed a spoon at Tom and Nancy Deane—"until you've seen the pore bleedin' 'eathen at little closer hand. Especially down-wind, and just after he's mucked up your best blouse because he forgot that fire's hot, even if there's an iron to hold it. Now, if everybody's quite through, I say a spot of noisy nonsense at the old Equate. The band's not bad. Mostly Greeks from Tanganyika. Off, no?"

"This was, by all odds, one of the windiest dinners I ever had," Holly said as she rose from the chair. "*What* a bore you must be in the bush, Peter, if you carry on this way in town."

"In the bush," Peter said, "I am the perfect prototype of the Stewie Granger version of the noble white hunter. I don't talk in the daytime, nor allow others to talk. I am taciturn. I am a man with a secret sorrow. I dye my burnsides white. I drown me troubles in drink at night's fall and speak only of muzzle velocities and bullet weights. You'd love me in the bush, I'm so bloody unnatural, but the clients expect it."

"Well, I enjoyed it, anyhow," Nancy said. "If you can do a rumba as well as you generalize, I am sure we will have a most athletic evening."

"Leave the poor man the hell alone," Tom said. "You paid this, Peter? Then the Equator's mine. Let's go and investigate the sociological aspects of Nairobi night life. They tell me it's much tougher than elephant hunting."

"As a young Canadian client of mine said to me last year, 'Chum, you ain't home yet.' There are more horns and tusks awaiting the innocent bwana wa safari in the Equator Club than ever were seen in the bush. Let us kwenda ourselves away from civilization and go observe life as she is lived in the raw."

The Equator Club was roaring when they got there. It is a restaurant-cabaret, ostensibly private, which is reachable by two flights of long, narrow stairs overlaid by a plush carpet. The plush serves not so much as decoration as a soft cushion for the exuberants who fall, are pushed, or are knocked down the stairs any time after 1 A.M. The cashier is a dour lady and the maître d'hôtel a thoroughly maître d'hôtel type. The band plays mostly rumbas and sambas, occasionally on beat and in tune. There is a bar to one side, foggy with smoke and usually packed six-deep. Food is served at tables round the dance floor and is very expensive for anywhere. On Saturday nights a black tie is obligatory, but most Kenyans having a night out prefer to dress. There is a second bar and a pleasant terrace up another flight, when the samba beat and the shouts of the celebrants become too much to bear any longer.

Peter signed in his guests and they fought their way to a table in a corner, being fairly severely wounded in the process. Peter ordered a bottle of whisky and a siphon, a bowl of ice and some cigarettes, and they turned to watch Kenya at play. The young men were mostly the young men of the Norfolk bar, changed now to white jackets and boiled shirts, and the women wore long skirts with bare shoulders. They were dancing the samba with a singleness of purpose that is nearly indescribable unless one has seen the English doing the samba. The Kenya version of an Englishman doing the samba is roughly as if someone had gotten a covey of kangaroos drunk and penned them all in the same room. Now they leaped, they bounded, they kicked, they bobbed, they jumped up and down in one place and wiggled in the unlikeliest sections of their anatomy.

"I don't know how the poor girls survive it," Holly murmured. "Do they always dance like this out here now, Peter?"

"This is tame. I was at a hunt ball at the Limuru Club last year, and they all had on red coats. They were packed as thick as flies on a Somali donkey. They were leaping up and down in a solid mass. All I could think of was damned souls in hell dancing on a griddle. I was crouched back in a corner, hoping not to get killed in the stampede, and I looked around me at the servants. They all had on red jackets over their kanzus, and they were leaping and bobbing to the music too—doing the war dances. I swear to God, if you had painted the black faces white or the white faces black, you couldn't tell the difference between a samba and a Masai ngoma. Frightful experience. I'd rather go into the bush after a sick buffalo any day."

"I thought all you white hunters were fancy dancing men who break the ladies' hearts on the dancing floor as well as out under the stars in trackless, romantic Africa," Holly teased. "Don't you dance?"

"Sure, I dance. I dance a fox trot and a waltz and I can do a rumba if the music's right, but you don't catch me out there jumping up and down like Masai on the warpath. I ain't got much dignity, but I got too much dignity to do a samba. Also, I'm afraid somebody'll break my leg. Oh, they're stopping now. If the next thing's civilized, after they've cleared away the dead bodies will you do me the honor, Holly?"

"Love to. This seems to be a fox trot. Let's try this one."

Tom and Nancy got up and passed ahead of Peter and Holly to the dance floor, which had cleared considerably. Peter took Holly in his arms and looked down at her. She was a very tall girl, but her amazing green eyes came only to a level with his chin. Her hair was alive in the candlelight, and little sparks of light seemed to dance on it. She was wearing a simple black gown, cut square and low in front, with no shoulders whatsoever. She smelled faintly of some perfume that Peter couldn't identify, although he knew names like Chanel and Tabu and Shocking from dancing with the wives of clients. She smelled a little like a damp spring night in the Masai when the mimosas were in bloom and a careless puff of air suddenly carried the odor faintly to your tent when you lay in bed after a hard day, deliciously weary but not yet asleep. She smiled up at him, and Peter smiled back. She felt amazingly pliant but very soft under his fingers. She danced as lightly as a puffball skips before the wind on the plain.

"I've not had a chance, really, to say anything to you at all today," Peter said. "There's not much to say except that I am awfully glad you're back and that you are the most beautiful girl I have ever seen, and I hope you never go away again. Little Holly Keith from the farm next door. Whoever would have thought it?"

"That's a very pretty speech, sir, and delivered with the assurance that comes with a lot of practice. I suppose you *have* had a lot of practice?"

"With what, baboons? Sweetie, I'm in the bush ten months a year. The women I meet are either all old or all married. Most of them come to Africa and fall in love with the hunter a little bit because of what they've read and what they've been led to believe from the films, but I learned a long time ago from old Dan that romance and safari don't mix, especially when the woman belongs to somebody else. Not little Peter. I smarm 'em, sure, because that's a part of the job."

"I must say you dance extremely well, like an American. You don't hop and crawl sideways."

"I *should* dance like an American. Americans taught me. Lots of times I talk like an American, too, especially after a couple of weeks or months in the bush with them."

"I must say you amaze me a little. That long oration over dinner. Right or wrong, it had some thought in it, and you delivered your message very well."

"Bother the oration. But mind you, when I am working at my job there is an awful lot of time to think. I don't talk when I hunt. I talk at lunch and I talk at dinner, but from the time we leave camp until the time we get back, I don't open my mouth. So you think. You get twelve full hours a day to think in. Speaking of dancing, you're a wizard yourself."

"It's part of my job too."

"What job?"

"Oh, just being a girl. There are as many tricks to it as hunting buffalo. Little things. What to do with what you've got. What to wear with your certain kind of color. Little flatteries. The right perfume. Tricks with the eyelashes. All tricks."

"I must say you seem to have mastered the lot. What do you plan to do now you're back? Work in town? Get married, or what?"

"Peter, I'm a very serious girl. It was fun growing up in London, and fun seeing Europe, and the parties were fine, and some of the people were nice, but it's not for me. There is something sort of sad and sick in the cities that I don't like a bit. Everybody running about and dashing madly and complaining and frightened. Everything rationed and controlled. Every day a new set of crises in the newspapers. Politicians screaming and cursing, and television blatting at you. People always getting married and divorced in the same year. Half the men are pansies and the other half think that because they aren't pansies every woman they meet is panting to hop into bed with them, and they're not so far wrong at that. It sort of made me sick to my stomach. I used to wake up in the middle of the night and think about how the Rift looks just as you go down the hill toward Naivasha, and I couldn't help but cry. All I want now is to go back to the farm with Mum and Dad and the baby and just sort of sit quietly. And someday I hope to find a chap like Lisa's Jeff, say, a chap who loves me, and then I want to get married and have as many kids as we can afford. My, that was quite a speech, wasn't it?"

"Seems to be the evening for it. The music appears to have stopped. We'll go back and then I'll do my duty by my pretty client."

"Pleasant duty, I should think. She seems extremely nice."

"So does *he*. I think this might be one of the good ones. Thirsty work, dancing. I can use a drink."

They sat down. Tom and Nancy were already placed and had mixed the drinks.

"Dearie me," Nancy said. "That must have been quite a conversation. You danced for a full half minute after the music stopped. I must say you looked divine, even without music. Peter, as an old and safely married woman, I must say that when I saw what sunburn and a white dinner jacket can do for a man I *loathed* Deane here, rich as he be. By you he looks anemic."

"Wait'll you see him a month from now." Peter grinned. "You'll have to fight the women off him. They'll be signing him up to do the Tarzan part on the films."

"This ain't a bad little joint," Tom said. "I cast my wicked eye around, and some of these local wenches seem right tasty. I also saw the two hostesses we flew out with in the bar with the pilot and flight engineer. One of the girls keeps looking at Peter, and I have a hunch that she more or less expected to be sitting at this table tonight. Or am I being nasty and suspicious?"

"Actually, you may be right. I love those kids, all of them. They're my kind of people. They're jolly decent girls, and they live a funny sort of disordered life, like mine, and they play hard when they're on the ground. Most of 'em get married to pilots or occasionally to passengers, eventually, but while they're footloose they really try to pack it in during their two days on the ground. I most always meet them at the airport and cart 'em back out again when they leave."

"I suppose they're all crazy-mad in love with you," Nancy said. "I saw that one little girl looking daggers at Holly when you danced."

"Nothing of the sort. We're just good friends. If you don't mind, later on I'd like to ask the four over for a drink. Maybe in my cott—— But it occurs to me I haven't got a cottage now. This woman's ousted me."

"Oh, I'm broad-minded," Holly said. "I'll lend it back to you for a nightcap for your friends."

"Better than that, we'll use ours," Tom said. "It's bigger. And I've got an ocean of booze that this amazing woman of mine seems to have smuggled in." He winked at Peter, and Nancy blushed.

The music began again and Tom reached out a hand to Holly. Peter nodded at Nancy, and they danced. It was a waltz, and a dangerous one, because a Kenyan waltzing is only slightly less dangerous than a bull elephant in the musth season. The glides become ski jumps, and the twirls are cyclones. It is not uncommon in the Equator Club for a man and partner to overshoot a glide and wind up in the bass drum.

"You do this very well," Nancy said from about halfway up Peter's chest, where her head was snuggled. "I can't get over you. I still think you're a fraud, and no white hunter at all. Where are your whiskers?

You got no business waltzing in a dinner jacket. Where are your lions? Where is the woman who ruined your life and drove you off to Africa to face death daily with a grim smile?"

"Blowed if I know. I reckon I'm operating under false pretenses. Where is your chewing gum? All Americans chew gum. Why don't you start all sentences with 'Say' and call us 'youse guys'? I'm told all Americans do."

"That is quite a girl, this little grown-up neighbor of yours. I think she is quite the best-looking girl I ever saw, and that from another woman is an extreme compliment. And she is nice, and smart, and quiet, too. What are your plans for her?"

"I think I'll marry her," Peter said, smiling.

"I think you're serious, too," Nancy said. "I think you're a damned fool if you don't. If she'll have you. *I* wouldn't marry a white hunter any more than I'd marry a sailor. I want my man home with me where I can get some use out of him. When that Deane said safari, I said I'm going too, snakes or no snakes in the bed. I don't suppose you know I'm frightened silly?"

"Mostly they are, at first. And then they either love it and want to come back next year, or they make everybody so miserable they break up the trip. I think you'll want to come back next year. I think you're the type."

"I suppose that's a compliment. Let's do that little twirl again. It's cute."

Tom and Holly were dancing at the other end of the room. Tom bent his head and held her a little away from his body.

"That's quite a boy you've got there," he said. "What do you aim to do about him?"

"Marry him, I think. It's what I came home for, anyhow. At least to have another look at him, now we're grown. He seems to have come along nicely, wouldn't you say?"

"I'd say, not having known him until this afternoon, that he is quite a hunk of man. But how'll you like being a safari widow nine-ten months a year?"

"There won't be any of that," Holly said. "Peter's got a fine farm. His father's getting old. When—or if—I get married to anybody, it's not going to be one of these he's-there, I'm-here sort of things. You don't get married to live by yourself."

"I think you might have quite a difficult time persuading this one to quit the thing he loves to wet-nurse a lot of cows," Tom said. "This lad's at the top of a heap in what I suspect is a very exciting business. I read a piece about him in the *Saturday Evening Post* or somewhere, and from all accounts he's Paul Bunyan in a quiet sort of way. I didn't even know I was getting the same guy until the last minute."

"Well, this is fairly ridiculous conversation anyhow, seeing as how I'm back home less than one day, and for all I know, Peter has squadrons of women panting to marry him. Little girls that grow up next door lack a certain amount of mystery. I can remember plainly some ants getting into my clothes once and Peter stripping me completely naked and smearing me all over with mud. Not much glamor there."

"That, my girl, was yesterday," Tom said. "Thanks for a lovely dance. Let's go back to the bottle, my athletic days are done, and that red-faced gentleman with the fiery mustaches just wounded me permanently with his last swoop."

Shortly thereafter the two hostesses and the two flying types came over. The pilot was a lean, clipped-mustached ex-R.A.F.er with a double row of good ribbons. His name was Michael Something-Something. The flight engineer was named Ralph, and he was a beefy man with a red face and a long, curling blond mustache. He was quite drunk. The hostesses, Ruth and Pamela, looked like all hostesses, in or out of uniform—clean, healthy, neat, competent, and a little buxom. They had a couple of drinks, and Peter danced with each of the girls, as did Tom, while Michael and Ralph steered Holly and Nancy around the floor, which had now achieved a solid concentration of strugglers. It was getting hotter by the moment as the newcomers used up the oxygen. The shouts from the bar were so loud that the band could barely be heard; in its way, a singular blessing. The smoke eddied in long plumes, and there was a short but determined fist fight in the hallway.

"This is really horrible," Peter said to Holly as they struggled off the dance floor. "Let's go over to the Norfolk and have a quiet, cool one on the veranda of yours or Tom's cottage. I can stand just so much of this and then I want out."

"I couldn't agree more," Holly said. "I'm a touch tired still, anyhow. I'm sure the Deanes would like to pack in, and I don't like the way that Ralph person holds me when he dances. I hate being sort of pawed on a dance floor. Or anywhere else, for that matter. Let's go. Now."

The stewardesses, Ruth and Pamela, said they thought they'd go back too, and Michael and Ralph said they'd had it as well. They paid up and went down the long narrow stairway into the chilly night, and when they returned the hotel was nearly dark. Peter drew up in front of the Deanes' cottage, and Tom said:

"That nightcap. Let's have it on the porch. It's nice out. Run over to your cottage and get a wrap, Holly, while I organize a little ice from the night watchman."

"Fine. I'm not sleepy or tired any more. I expect it's the excitement of getting home. Walk with me, Peter. These high heels are murderous on these cobbles."

When they returned from Holly's cottage with a wrap, the flying types and the hostesses had arrived also in a creaky taxi and were sitting on the steps of Tom's cottage.

"Hullo once more," the girl Pamela said. "We were passing by and Mr. Deane asked us for a drink. That Equator Club. I should think another hour of it might've given me smoke poisoning."

The engineer just grunted. He appeared to be slowly simmering over something and had had enough drink to thicken his speech. He accepted his glass from Tom Deane and then turned his back on Peter.

More than mildly exhilarated by the drinks, the cold clarity of the starry night, and his actual presence in Africa, Tom Deane continued to hammer Peter with questions.

"What's the most dangerous stuff, do you reckon? Lions, elephants, or what?"

"Well, it can all kill you if you're careless," Peter said. "But unless there is some sort of dreadfully unforeseen accident, if you hunt it right none of it's dangerous. I promise you, you may see me doing something with buffalo or elephants that'll strike you as the sheerest idiocy, and there's generally a good reason for it or I wouldn't do it."

"Then what's all this I read about wounded buffalo and wounded lions killing people?"

"That's it. They've been *wounded.* The thing is not to wound it. There's no animal in the world that won't run away from man unless he's wounded, insane, is crowded into a corner, or has babies. An old gentleman rhino will charge you if you stumble on him, but that's because he's frightened and rushes on from reflex. He can't see very well, d'you see, and so he runs toward the noise. Actually all he's trying to do is get away."

"Buffalo? I've heard them called the most dangerous."

"Again, only when it's hurt. A buff's a bossy-cow until you hurt him, and then he turns nasty. He'll try to kill you as long as there's the breath of life in him. The only thing I know that'll charge without provocation from a long distance is an old elephant with ants up his snout or a bull in the breeding season or some cantankerous old cow with a new calf. But if you leave it alone it'll leave you alone, likely."

"Aren't you ever frightened?" Nancy asked. "How's your drink?"

"Just fine. Sure I'm frightened. I'm always frightened. I'm frightened when I'm crawling around in the bush after some leopard somebody's just wounded. I'm scared green when I have to go into thick bush after a sick rhino. I'm always frightened when I'm very close to elephants, because you can never tell what they're going to do or when they'll decide to do it. It's good business to be frightened. You stay alive longer."

The flight engineer turned to face Peter. His face was puffed and blotchy.

"And the clients' women? Are you frightened of them as well?"

"Desperately. All women frighten me. Especially other people's women. Bloke gets shot that way."

"You don't have to be frightened of me, my friend." Nancy laughed. "If it was romance I sought, I'd go to Capri. All I want you to do is keep us alive and beat off the snakes."

"You won't be bothered with snakes. They don't hang around the high country much. If you see 'em at all it's apt to be on the roads. They love to wriggle along in the warm dust."

"Is there *anything* you don't know about this business?" Ralph, the engineer, was being markedly offensive.

"Heaps. I learn something new every time out. The day you stop learning is the day you get trod on." Peter was being as deliberately pleasant.

"So this is actually the famous Peter McKenzie, eh?" The engineer swung his head back and forth in a mock amazement. "*The* Peter McKenzie, the one all the little girls on the big planes talk about. Now I can really say I've lived. It'll be something to tell my grandkiddies, that one night in Nairobi when I actually met *the* Peter McKenzie. They'll be impressed no end, I can tell you. I've actually met the famous McKenzie, the handsome hunter, the romantic lion shooter." The sarcastic edge to his voice now was blurred burlesque.

"Nothing to it," Peter said mildly. "Never shoot anything. Just a hired hand. A chauffeur, greasy mechanic, and general handyman."

"I've heard all about you chaps. Go out in the parks and murder some poor animal at long distance and then come back to Nairobi and spend all your time telling each other how brave you are. Pure hell with the women, too, if what I'm told is true."

"Oh, shut up, Ralph," the girl Ruth said. "He's been absolutely *bloody* all evening."

"Happens to all of us," Peter said.

"Tell me very truly," the engineer said with the exaggerated gravity of a drunk who fancies himself a needler. "Speak without thinking, is there any real difference between you and a butcher? I mean, it's all the same thing after all, isn't it?"

"Sure," Peter said lightly. "I do it because I love blood. Nothing is so musical as the groans of a dying elephant. And then I do it for fun, too. I adore going into bush at night after a wounded leopard. I think gut-shot lions in high grass are simply divine. And then I come straight home like a good boy and wash the blood off my hands and steal all the sexy wives away from all my clients. This impresses the clients no end."

Ralph turned to Tom.

"I suppose, like all Americans, you have so much money that you can afford one of these things," he said. "The hire of one of these heroes must come high, especially if you keep him in liquor."

"Oh, sure," Tom said, also trying to hold it light. "I've got pots. All made by my father. I am what is generally called a rich wastrel, and when I couldn't think of anything else to waste it on, I hired Peter. We're hoping he'll break me."

"Why don't you go home to bed, Ralph?" the pilot said. "You're as tight as a newt. For Christ sake, stop being unpleasant. You're a guest here."

"Oh, so now we hear from the noble pilot," Ralph said, pulling at his mustaches. "Over to you. Pilots. Gilded heroes, every one, as well. Sit up there on a soft seat and drive a bus through the skies with George to do it, when they couldn't change a sparking plug on a baby Austin. Pilots. Spend all their time aloft explaining the mysteries of flight to the prettier passengers, and all their time on the ground trying to explain the mystery of life to the prettier stewardesses."

"I say, you *are* in a pretty pet, chum," the pilot said. "I think a little beddy-bye is indicated. All these people did wicked was invite you for a drink."

"Yes, master. Yes, *sir*. The captain has spoken. My regrets, sir. I will button my face." To Tom, "I suppose, like *all* Americans, you——"

"If you don't mind, mister," Nancy Deane said, "would you sort of kind of knock off this 'like all Americans' business? I've heard nothing else in England for the last two months. I'm not *'all Americans'* and neither is Tom. And I'm sick of the sound of it."

"I know. Oh, how I know so well. *Like all Americans,* you're sick of us now we've won the war for you, just because you lent us a little money and managed to roger a good portion of our untidier lower classes when you came over on a week end to see if we were spending it correctly."

"That'll be about all of that now," Tom said. "It's my house here. I think perhaps you'd better buzz off."

"Oh, I'll whip along right enough," the engineer said. "I'll leave the heroes to their heroics and go and inspect the grease under my broken nails." He swung on Peter, suddenly livid with a foolish, unreasoning anger. "Which one of these popsies will *you* do after I'm gone? One of these two air-borne tarts or that with the red hair?"

Peter was sitting on the steps, and the drunken engineer was weaving over him. Peter came up to his feet in one long smooth spring and slapped the engineer across the side of the head with his open hand. The engineer pitched sideways and seemed to soar. He fell in a heap six feet away and was still.

"Christ, I'm glad you didn't hit him with your fist," the pilot said. "I say, I must apologize for this chap. Some pilot or other has just pinched his girl off him, and he's been bloody-minded for a week. McKenzie, would you help me lug him to his room? He weighs a ton. Please remind me not to make you angry at me, ever. He's still out."

"I'm dreadfully sorry," Peter said. "I shouldn't have hit him. But by God I hate rude people, drunk or sober, and especially people who are rude when they're drinking your liquor."

"I'm glad you bopped him," Nancy said.

"*I'm* sorry you hit him," Tom said. "Because I was headed his way myself when you clouted him. I haven't been in a real good hassle in ages. Nancy disapproves. She is raising me to be a lady."

Holly said nothing. The two stewardesses murmured apologies and went off to their cottage. Peter picked up the engineer, slung him over his shoulder in one motion, and said to the pilot:

"Show me his room, will you? No, thanks, it's easier to carry him this way. Show me where he lives and I'll bung him onto the bed. You can undress him or not, whatever you like. He couldn't care less."

"The veriest hell with him," the pilot said happily. "I would like to have socked him myself, but it's dreadful bad for morale, having on your engineers. Also, I think he just might merely have murdered me. He's as strong as a bloody bull."

Peter carried the sleeping engineer over to his room, and the pilot kicked open the door. Peter tossed the engineer on the bed, and the pilot plucked off his shoes and loosened his tie.

They walked together back to the Deanes' porch.

"My word, you *have* got a temper," Holly said. "Do you generally do much of this sort of thing?"

"Rarely. I come unbuttoned very seldom. Again, my apologies, all. What happened to my drink?"

"I fixed you another, sweetie," Nancy said. "Here 'tis. Do you get much of this sort of nonsense from people as a rule?"

"Quite a lot," Peter said, sitting back on the steps. "It's part of the business. Soldier's pay. I've read where the old prize fighters were always having somebody step up and challenge them in saloons. I know our friend the pilot here takes a lot of chaffing from people who wanted to be airmen, proper, and bilged out somewhere along the line. They take one look at a row of ribbons and want to be rude. People are funny. There aren't many of us in my business, so we *are* sort of oddities, kind of freaks. There's always some one special chap who's just a touch tiddled wants to come up and prove something, God knows what, to himself, so he can talk about it the next day. *If* he remembers it."

"Do you always knock them unconscious?" Holly said gently. "It must keep you frightfully busy, and bruised, as well."

"I *said* I was sorry. Please don't rag me. Ordinarily, if it's only me they're going at, I laugh it off and walk away, else I'd be always in a brawl. But I didn't particularly fancy what he said about you and Ruth and Pam, or his entire attitude toward everybody here. A loose tooth'll teach him to keep a slightly more civil tongue in his head. Anyhow, I only hit him with my open hand."

"Well, as the good pilot said, thank God you didn't hit him with your fist," Nancy said. "Or he'd have waked up with no head at all. Probably an improvement on the one he had, at that."

"We've got a busy day tomorrow," Peter said. "If you don't mind, I'll just finish this drink and whiz off to my new quarters in the manager's cottage. Come on, Holly, I'll walk you to the door."

As they walked away Nancy Deane moved closer to her husband and whispered:

"I don't suppose you saw his face just before he hit that awful man, did you?"

"No, because I was lunging over to wallop the awful man myself."

"Well, I saw it. The light from the living room was shining across it. It was fairly frightening. His eyes half closed and I could swear I heard him snarl. He didn't, actually. But he came off those steps faster than anything I've ever seen in my life. It was scary."

"I don't believe I would like to monkey around with this young man very much, especially if there was a woman mixed up in it. I expect he would kill a man very casually. My God, did you hear the sound when that slap of his landed? It sounded like somebody hitting a pumpkin with the flat of an ax."

"You never can tell, can you? I've spent all night wanting to run my fingers through his hair and tell him he was a sweet boy, and then I see him turn into a saber-toothed tiger or something."

"Well, suppose you come and run your fingers through my hair," her husband said. "Maybe it'll be different under a mosquito net. First time in Africa, hey?"

"There wasn't anything different about it at twenty thousand feet when you and I had to share that bunk flying over. Though I have often wondered what sort of dreams the other passengers thought I was having up there in that upper."

"Well, we're running up a very decent collection of firsts," Tom said. "Now what I am really anxious to try is a tent."

"Not me, chum. I like my doings with *doors*. You take the bath first. I've got a couple of things I haven't unpacked yet."

8

Peter and Holly walked to the door of her cottage. She unlocked the door and snapped on the light, standing in the door with the light shining fiery on her hair.

"Well," she said.

"It has been quite a day," Peter said. "I must say once more I'm sorry about that bloke back there. I feel most horribly ashamed of myself. I think I'll say good night now and see you tomorrow for an early lunch. We ought to leave by two, anyhow."

Holly smiled.

"Are you quite certain you hadn't planned to ask yourself in for a nightcap? Or a home-coming kiss that turns into a long struggle for my honor?"

Peter grinned up at her. "If I had, I'm glad I didn't. I've done enough wrong things already tonight. See you tomorrow. Be sure and lock your door, Holly. Been a lot of stealing going on around here lately—young spivs from the bazaars prowling round for whatever they can lift. And I'd drop the netting if I were you. Quite a lot of mosquitoes since the rains. Good night."

"Good night, Peter. I'm awfully happy to be home."

Peter waved and went away to the manager's cottage, where there was a bottle of whisky. He took the bottle and crept quietly round to the stewardesses' cottage. There was a light in the window, and he rapped gently on the door.

The pilot, Michael, was lying on the sofa, his right hand languidly trailing to the floor, where a freshly filled glass rested. His head was in the lap of the girl Ruth, and she was stroking his face and occasionally putting a cigarette to his lips. She was wearing a negligee over nothing, and the pilot had taken his blouse and shoes off. Sitting curled on her feet in a chair, also wearing a negligee, was the girl Pamela. She smiled at Peter and got up, clopping in mules as she went to a sideboard on which a new drink sat. She handed the drink to Peter, then stood on tiptoe, heels rising from the mules, and kissed him on the mouth.

"It took you quite a long time," she said, and led him into the bedroom. She closed and locked the door. Peter looked at the bottle in his hand. "Well, at least I'm glad I brought the bottle," he said. "It looks like another sleepless night."

They drove out from town next day, Peter with Holly Keith in one car, John Thompson and Tom and Nancy Deane in the other jeep. Peter felt like death. Last night with the girl Pamela had been quite a thing, quite a thing, indeed, and Peter felt as if the rats had been at him. She was a sweet lass, Pam, but a bit demanding, and there had been only a scrap of sleep between the demands. Also, the bottle had mysteriously dwindled to an inch. Peter's conscience troubled him—not because of Pam, who, Christ knows, was no virgin and hadn't been one for a good many years—but because Peter had gone and done the exact thing that the drunk engineer had said he would do and for which Peter had cuffed him. He felt a bit awkward when he met Holly, for although he had bathed and shaved and dressed himself freshly in bush clothes, the body scent of the other woman was still grained into his hide, and the marks of her teeth and nails were graven on his back and shoulders. Peter felt guiltily that Holly had a damned good idea that he hadn't nipped straight off to bed. Holly, looking sidewise at him as they drove out and up toward Fort Hall, noticed his lack of ease and quite correctly assumed that if he had spent any time in any bed at all it wasn't his own, because there were puffs under his eyes, which were blood-streaked, and his big brown square hands shook slightly. But with the rather curious unmorality of some intelligent women, she was a bit flattered, a bit piqued, and smally, tolerantly understanding. Flattered obtusely, perhaps, because Peter had not attempted to slake his youthful lust on her as parcel to an evening's entertainment, perhaps piqued for the same reason, and mildly tolerant because she knew that, whichever of the two girls he had chosen, neither represented any threat to her plans.

Holly Keith was twenty-two years old and she had given her first fresh love to a charming young American Air Force major when she was just over eighteen and had been considerably taken down by her ultimate discovery that the young American major, whilst undoubtedly charming, was also a professional seducer and was married to a girl back home, as well. The pain of that one was long dissipated, and there had been two others since, one of whom she had found a trifle silly after a few weeks, and the other whom she discovered to be madly possessive and a frightful bore. Knowing some little thing of men, she would really have thought it rather odd of Peter to spend his short time between safaris without hunting up something pretty to slap, tickle, and take back to the bush as a special remembered solace for the fact that Tom and Nancy Deane slept in the same tent, from which certain sounds would come during the next three months, while Peter bedded chastely at a discreet distance. No, Holly decided, she was not angry with Peter, because she had established no claim. When the claim was suitably staked, she'd have the eyes out of any woman who looked at him crossways.

She glanced at him now. The puff had gone and the slight flush had departed the clear tan of his face, and his eyes had miraculously cleared. He drove along, his hatbrim flapping in the breeze and curled back over his eyes. He drove as swiftly and as carefully as possible, silently and with complete attention to weaving his Land Rover round bullock carts and lorries full of Sikhs; herds of goats and natives on bicycles. He made no effort at conversation. He dedicatedly drove. He drove in the shortest way to reach Nyeri, up the Thika Road toward Fort Hall, where they would stop and have a beer with the Indian in the ducca before pressing on. Holly was happy not to talk, to yell over the roar of the engine and the wind that blew her eyelashes backward. She was much too busy tasting the excitement of being home again, of seeing the new and awful-yellow hotel the Indians had built, of joyfully remembering old sights and eagerly noticing the new. She was not fully happy until they came into the rich farming country, the Kikuyu re- serve, and saw again through delicious memory the rich loamy slopes, the twisting streams and small rivers, the towering cedars, and the small, neat, thatched huts of the native shambas, with their banana trees and yam vines, their herds of goats and fat-tailed sheep, the unbelievable green of fields and the cool mossy dells close to the water and under the fig trees, the spiky-leaved pineapple plants and the broad sweeps of maize. When they stopped off at the little ducca in Fort Hall to have the beer, she could have kissed the Indian for remembering her and welcoming her home and calling his sweet submissive wife to come and see how big and beautiful the little Miss Holly had grown. She had almost cried as they crept up the sheer, winding walls of the enormous emerald valley with its river laughing through it, and she would cry, just a little inside, when she got her first view of Mount Kenya again, if the clouds were high when they came along to Nyeri. Even the fine red dust tasted good on her lips as the jeep bounced over the corrugated clay road.

In the other car, John Thompson was holding a seminar. John's jeep took a different route, a longer one, out past the Norfolk and onto the road that leads past Limuru on the way to Naivasha and Nakuru. He would turn right along about Naivasha and meet Peter and Holly, via Thomson's Falls. The car threaded out of the city, past the schools and the experimental station, past the forests of wattle, and into the Kikuyu reserve that jostles Nairobi. Peter had suggested this route, for the long winding road down the mountaintop to where the Great Rift scar begins, is one of the spectacular short journeys of the world, especially in the afternoon, when the sun glows gold, warm, and then dull red on Longonot, the extinct volcano. It is an excellent hard road, fashioned expertly by Italian P.O.W.s, and the prisoners' little chapel sits sweetly and completely out of character near an abutment which gives a vast sweep to the immense scar of the volcanic upheaval which tore Africa apart; which made the highlands and dried up the huge lake of Serengeti; which formed the crater valley at Ngoro-Ngoro and made the high plateaus and the valleys of Kenya the most beautiful country in the world. On the road out, here too one passes the Kikuyu shambas, bright green against the vivid ocher clay; here too one sees the women toiling uphill with their backs bowed under loads of wood and thatching, the carrying straps cutting into their foreheads. There are some few white farms tucked in between the reserve areas, but not many. This is Kikuyu country and contains some of the richest farming property in Africa or any other country. The altitude drops thousands of feet from Nairobi, but the descent is so gradual that one is rarely conscious of it. There is no sense of Africa here at all, because the forests are heavily treed with black fir and fig and cedar, and a mountain holds the road on the right hand. It could be Germany, it could be Switzerland, it could be Spain or the Pyrenees country of France. It is cold at night, and damp.

Some thirty-odd miles out, John Thompson drew the car to a parking space at the corner of a curve, where the drop was sheer, and swept his hand around him.

"There she is," he said. "It's what we call the M.M.B.A.—miles and miles of bloody Africa. There is no other sight quite like it, I think."

Nancy Deane looked, and felt a catch in her throat. Vastly spread under her was a sea of yellow wheaty grasses undulating in the wind as an ocean rolls. Off to her right was Longonot, the old volcano, with its serried embattlements of blue-misted mountains. Back behind her, now shining red and gold in the warm afternoon sun, were the hills of Ngong, the black-green forests forbidding, and straight before her lay the M.M.B.A.

"On a decent day," John Thompson said, "a bloke can look down this escarpment and see a hundred, a hundred and fifty miles. This valley here is mostly for the white settlers, since we have run out of the reserve. Would you believe it, Peter and I shot ten lions for the Game Department just down there in the last two years? They'd come in off the Masai plains and were raising all sorts of hell with the herds."

"I have never in my whole life seen *anything* quite so wonderful,"

Nancy said. "There isn't anything to compare it to, but it still makes me want to cry."

"The effect is pretty general on everybody when they see it for the first time," John said. "I should hate very much to think I'd never see it again."

"Just where are we now—I mean, where are we from where we're going to meet Peter, and then where do we go to find the Masai country?" Tom Deane asked.

"Down there's Naivasha," John said. "We turn right about there and crawl up some mountains and hit the high country again. Peter's place is up around Nyeri, near a place called Mwega. If we went due north from there we would be heading for the desert and the Abyssinian border. That's where the big elephants are. When you come down to-morrow you'll turn left, you see, just down this hill there, and you'll drive across those dusty plains, eating a lot of lava and seeing nothing but scrub thorns and a very few animals. It's sixty miles of miserable driving, but then you come to a place called Narok, which is where the Masai administration is. Peter'll camp you a few miles, about twenty-five, outside of Narok, on a little river called the Telek, and I expect you'll shoot your leopard there, or a little farther up near a place called Majimoto."

"What does Majimoto mean? All the words sound wonderful," Nancy said.

"Maji—water. Moto—hot. There's any amount of hot-water springs up there. Also any amount of lions coming down out of the closed country now. A couple of years ago we reckoned there weren't more than a half dozen shootable male lions in the whole Masai. Game Department very rightly closed it, and now they're breeding back wonderfully. I expect they'll open it again soon, or at least the fringes of the fly area."

"Fly area?" Tom said. "I'm sorry, John, lad, but we're awfully new here and most of what you say needs some translating."

"It's part of the job," Thompson said, laughing with his little bright monkey-brown eyes. "It's all so simple to us, but I would have to ask you the same questions about anything I saw in New York. Fly area means tsetse flies. There are two kind of tsetses. One kills cattle and doesn't carry sleeping sickness—what do you call it? Some fancy name or other, I can never remember it, but I saw a bloke die of it once."

"It's called encephalitis," Nancy said.

"Well, we have the cattle-killing tsetse here. If you get across the Mara River in the high Masai, you pick up the other kind. There's any amount of man-killing kind in Rhodesia too. Tsetse lives in bush, thornbush. Bush is where you find animals. Game, I mean. Domestic animals can't live in bush country, you see, because of the tsetses. Game also won't live around human habitation—big masses of game, that is. So the Masai is more or less divided into two areas—the long plains where there isn't much bush, and that's where the Masai graze their herds, all the way from here to Tanganyika. It's gorgeous country, a lot of mountains, including Kilimanjaro, but long plains and big forests and, down by Lake Manyara, proper tropic jungle. What say we have a beer? I put some in back before we left. Mala!" this to the car boy. "Toa beer-i, tatu!"

"And all that means, apart from the beer?"

" 'Toa'—take out. 'Tia'—put in. 'Weka'—bring. 'Mupa'—give. 'Hi'—here. 'Fukwa'—fix or do. 'Tatu' is three—'moja, mbile, tatu.' It's simple, Swahili. Upcountry Swahili, I mean to say. Coastal Swahili has grammar and is very tricky, but the upcountry stuff is a combination of Arabic and English and various dialects that the old slave traders made into a kind of baby talk for communication between all the tribes. Here's the beer, a little warm, but still wet."

"Tell some more about the flies," Nancy said.

"Well, once you get past Majimoto, the thick bush starts and the Masai won't drive their herds up into that country, not unless there's a hell of a dirty drought and the herdsmen would finally rather lose a lot of their beasts to fly instead of losing them all to thirst and starvation. Because there's a couple of big rivers in the high Masai and always at least a little water. That's another reason the game thrives there. You never see Masai herds in the fly area unless there's been a dreadful drought. But it is gorgeous country, and I think you'll love it, especially the Memsaab here. Women usually like it the best of all, whilst the men generally fancy the North."

"I've read a lot about these Masai," Tom said. "Is it true they only live off blood and milk? What sort of people are they actually?"

"Peculiar race. They're part of the Zulu-Bantu swarm that came out of South Africa and spread all over the central area. But they are not terribly Negroid, and they picked up some lighter blood, probably Nilotic, somewhere. They're brown-colored, almost red-brown like your Red Indians. They have very fine features, with their hawk noses. They don't kill cattle, because there is some sort of special worship there, in a way like the Hindus worship their herds. Cattle represent real wealth to them. But they do drink blood."

"How do they get the blood if they don't kill the cattle?"

"Simple enough. They take an arrow and plug the tip so's it'll only penetrate so far. Then they whip it into the cow's jugular and drain her, like you'd drain a sump case, and then when the old girl's bled enough, they plaster up the hole with mud and turn her loose to grow some more blood."

"Sounds awful," Nancy said.

"Tastes worse. They take it and mix it with milk and put it into a gourd that's got a mixture of wood ash and—excuse me—cow urine in it. The urine and the chemicals in the ash curdle the milk and blood. They leave it overnight, and the next day it's a thick curd. You'll see all the types carrying a gourd of it as they walk along the road."

"I believe they were supposed to be the fiercest of all the tribes?"

"In the old days, yes. All the other Wogs were scared blue of them. When they attacked a village they killed everybody except the young girls—old men, old women, young boys, everybody. They don't seem to attach any importance to life, not even their own. But they won't work and they aren't allowed to fight any more. They won't civilize, either. There's a school for them in Narok, but it's like trying to put pants on a hippo to get them to come to it. They don't even stay in one village long. They'll build a little temporary thing out of cow dung and clay, if they can find it, and tie some hides or put thatch on the roof, and when it's time to move on they just burn down the village and nip off to where the grass is greener. They take all their belongings on a little donkey and on the women's backs and heads. Up North there's an off-shoot tribe called Samburu and Rendille, close cousins, and they rove thousands of square miles each year, chasing after water and pasturage."

"I find this fascinating. Tell me some more," Nancy said.

"Sure," John replied. "But let's drive on. We've quite a few miles to do yet. Hop in, and we'll whiz on up to the Falls." He backed onto the road and let the car slip into high without shifting. Tom noticed that he never gave a glance to his car boy, Mala, who leaped into the back of the car as it drifted downhill.

"The Masai's dying out. Frightful death rate they have, and not understandable, when you consider that the Kikuyu, who always was a no-hoper and a vegetarian, overcrowded and pretty filthy in his living habits, is increasing by the tens and hundreds of thousands. Here you have the Masai living off the best grazing land in Africa, with nobody to fight and quite a lot of medical attention available, and he just dies. The birth rate drops steadily."

"Must be a reason for it," Tom said. "People don't just die for the sake of dying."

"Wild animals do," John said seriously. "I think the Masai's a kind of wild animal and doesn't fit into this century. All through the history of this country certain original tribes have completely died out. Before the Kikuyu came from wherever they came from there was a race of very primitive dwarfs that lived in caves up around Peter's country, the Ngumbu. You can still see their caves and some remnants of their past. Whether the Kikuyu killed them or whether they just weren't up to competing with an agricultural tribe I don't know, but the point is that there ain't any more of 'em left."

"Oh, sure. It happened to our Indians, and most of the abos—the aboriginals—of Australia are gone, and the hairy Ainus of Japan. I suppose someday some super-race will come along and fix our clock too."

"I don't think we'll have to wait," Nancy said darkly. "Not with these idiots fiddling around with that H-bomb thing. One day some scientist with a bad hangover is going to mislay a beta ray or get his gammas scrambled while he's looking for a shirt stud and blow the hell out of the Stork Club *and* Narok, or whatever its name is."

"I don't know about H-bombs, but I know something about Wogs," John said. "The Kikuyu is perfect for civilization because he always was a bloody townie by inclination, anyhow. But the Masai is a proud professional warrior. You'll see, when you drive up, the men have behinds, pardon me, like women, and are built as delicate as women. They get the big behinds from generations of sitting on them, while the women do the work. Their only job was war, and all they needed for war was a spear, which they throw with a flip of the wrist, and a knife for cutting the heads off their wounded friends. When a Masai is old enough to toddle he gets a spear with a tiny little blade and is sent out lonesome amongst the lions to tend his papa's cattle. As he gets older he gets a spear with a slightly longer blade. When he's circumcised, when he becomes a man, he gets a very serviceable spear and becomes a junior moran."

"What's moran?"

"Warrior. There are three stages of moran, cut into about four or five years each, I forget which. In each stage the spear blade gets longer, so that when a Masai is a third-degree moran his spear is nearly all blade. Then when he finishes his military service he gets married and becomes a clan elder, and they shorten his blade. By the time he's mzee —an old one—his spear blade is damned near as short as it was when he started out tending the herds."

"Well," Nancy said, "if he can't get married until he's put in about fifteen years of being a draftee, he's pretty well along by the time he can go courting."

"Oh, there's no trouble about girls," John said. "Shocking morals these people have. The whole time a Masai is a moran he lives in a big communal house with all the pretty maidens of the tribe. They trade around, all the boys going with all the girls. Since the venereal rate is very high, you'll find the old Masai about ninety-eight per cent venereal."

"That could account for the birth rate dropping," Nancy said.

"The morals of the other tribes are just as elastic," John said. "There *aren't* any morals, as we know 'em. I've an old lion tracker up around the Serengeti who takes his wives on safari with him and hires 'em out at two bob a whack to all the other boys. The girls think it's just fine. The Kyukes have just as much VD as the Masai, and as fast as you cure it they go and catch a fresh case, but they're on the increase and the Masai are dying."

"What's the answer then? I gather the Masai haven't been 'civilized' and are let to live the way they always lived, free to roam."

"It's the business of changing their ways even a little," John said. "If a man is trained to be a killer and you don't give him anything to kill, he is naturally going to waste away. He lives by his spear and isn't allowed to use it. He lives by his shield, and the Government won't let him carry it. His pride of manhood is worn on his head, in a lion-mane headdress, but the Game Department won't let him kill lions. By and by you haven't got a man any more, just a shell, and the breed dies. My grandchildren won't see many Masai, mark my words."

"It's a pity it all has to change," Tom said. "I would have loved to see America in the old days, when the buffalo was on the prairie and the Indians were real Indians and not living on some reservation, and a man could go out and trap a thousand beaver in every stream. It must have been wonderful country then."

"Well, cheer up, sweetheart," Nancy said. "There is still a lot of country out here, and you must remember that when you go back home there is always the TV and the movies to make life worth while. Not to mention Kate Smith."

"They're going to do the same thing to this country that they did to yours," John said. "The people are pouring out here from England to settle. The Hindus are as thick as fleas on a *pie*-dog. The towns are getting bigger and bigger. The Wogs are on the increase, and there isn't any room anywhere for anybody any more. Old John Hunter shot a thousand rhinos at Makueni to make space for the Wakamba to expand, so they could clear the thorn that kept the tsetse a menace, and now the 'Kamba have run out of living room again. One day it'll all be habitation, with the game gone and roads everywhere and the damned Indians breeding up like rabbits. There isn't any game left in Uganda now at all, and they've turned that entirely over to the Wogs. You have to marry a nigger there in Uganda to own land. Yet in this very century the kings of Buganda used to kill thousands of their own people just for fun, and cannibalism was a happy practice. No, Africa's finished as my father knew it. Soon there won't be anything in it but the Wogs and the Indians and the towns. All the game will be dead except for the odd elephant at Tsavo or up at Lake Edward, and I will be a bloody forest guide or something, showing tourists around and explaining the difference between a baboon and a whistling thorn. Too damned many people out here already."

"It always seems to come down to that, doesn't it? Too damned many people," Nancy said. "Sometimes when I'm in New York and go up high in a building and look down at the swarms of people crawling around like ants, each one with his own separate set of problems, I get panic-stricken. Tom's stopped going to the theater. He still loves the theater, but he won't go on the West Side where most of the theaters are because all the people around Times Square give him claustrophobia."

"Don't spoil my day," Tom said. "I do not wish to think of New York for the next three months. What I wish to think of is how far we are from the next town, because I would like a drink of something with more authority than beer; such as, say, namely gin."

"We'll be coming into Thomson's Falls pretty soon now," John said. "There's a fine pub there. We can stop for a snifter and then drive on over to Peter's place. It's not too far."

"Tell me a little bit about Peter," Nancy said. "What sort of man is he, exactly? You seem to be great friends. He fascinates me."

"Everything out here seems to fascinate you," her husband said. "There must be a few other words in today's female vocabulary besides fascinate, thrill, divine, and sheer heaven. I'm going to buy you a thesaurus."

"What's a thesaurus?" John asked.

"It's a rare, three-horned dragon that is rapidly becoming extinct due to lack of usage," Tom said. "Carry on about Peter and the business you're in. *I'm* fascinated, too, seeing as how I'm in his tender care for the next three months. They say he's good."

"I say he's the best," John said. "If I know anything about this business, it's because of what he taught me. I don't know whether you knew it, but I started hunting a good bit later than Peter, and he took me on as his apprentice. Most men in hunting don't want to give away any tricks, they're a frightfully jealous lot, but Peter took me out and showed me everything he knew—all the places, the special places he knew, and all the tricks of the trade. And there are lots of tricks to it."

"What sort of tricks?"

"Oh, little pockets of country that other people don't know about. Getting on with the natives so that they'll look after your interest. Special ways of getting up to certain types of game. When to go where, and why, when nobody else has thought of it. How to find it when it isn't there, and just one special way to outwit it when nine hundred and ninety-nine thousand other ways have failed. Peter's an animal, really, a wild animal, a true wild animal."

"He seems a most remarkably civilized young man to me," Nancy said. "He does a very nice rumba and his table manners are excellent. Also, he's very polite and charming."

"Oh, I don't mean that sort of stuff," John said. "Peter is a gentleman complete in all that sort of business. What I mean to say, he thinks like an animal. He has a talent for putting himself in the animal's place, figuring out what the animal would do, and then doing just the thing to check it. One time I remember we were out after buffalo and the wind changed on us and the buff—must have been five hundred or more—roared down on us in an open plain. There was actually *no* place to go, no tree to climb, not even a bloody thornbush to hide behind. Five hundred buff, weighing about two thousand pounds each, make an impressive sight, I can tell you, when they're coming at you at the rate of knots."

"I wouldn't want to spoil it by asking you what did you do," Nancy said. "But *what* did you do?"

"Charged the herd," John said simply. "Peter took off at the herd, waving his hat and cursing in Kikuyu. There wasn't any place for me to go, and so I waved my hat and charged behind him, cursing in Meru. I speak better Meru than Kikuyu. We must have scared hell out of the buff. They stopped still about twenty-five yards off, glaring at us. Then we let out another whoop and they all turned around and ran away. I don't mind telling you I went off and was sick to my stomach. Peter never turned a hair. He said he reckoned the buff had never been charged before, and there was a first time for everything. Seemed to think the whole thing very funny. *I* didn't think it was funny, any more than I thought it was funny when we got mixed up with half a dozen lions one day and Peter let one come roaring up to his knees without shooting her. I damned well shot the one that was aiming at me, but Peter, he said no, this one had cubs, and he reckoned to give her another foot or so."

"Maybe we better get you an older, more cautious hunter, baby," Nancy said. "This Peter man sounds horribly dangerous to me."

"Contrariwise, no," John said. "I say, would one of you do me a cigarette? Thanks very much. No, old Peter's the soul of caution. It's just that he's more or less memorized all the situations. He knows when to take a chance and takes it, when another man'd be apt to get himself trod on for *not* taking the same chance. Most peculiar thing about Peter is he actually hates to kill things. It pains him, literally. He won't let anybody on his safaris shoot anything just to kill it for killing. He won't allow anyone to shoot baboons or hyenas or even wild dogs for target practice, and they're classed by the Game Department as vermin. He damned near killed me once trying to miss a flock of baby birds that were in the path of his hunting car; slewed her around and ran her onto a rock and threw everybody out."

"Yet he lives off the killing business," Tom said. "Odd. How does he reconcile that?"

"I couldn't say, really. We've mouthed it over a lot, and I suppose that neither of us has the words. Somehow it doesn't seem bad to kill something that you want very badly and have hunted very hard after. This Africa is awfully new, you know, and it's all built on death. The lion kills the zebra and the hyena eats the leavings and the vultures get what's left of the mess the fisi leaves. Then the ants come along and clean up after the vultures, and when the lion's old his son kills him or, worse, wounds him, and then the hyena eats the lion. Before the lion's dead. It goes on and on, round and round. Peter's idea is that it's all got to die sometime, and if you shoot it cleanly and on its own ground, when it's old and well past breeding, then you've only just hastened the process and actually neatened it up a bit. I mean to say, the hyena and the birds and the ants still get their due, and the meat-starved Wogs get their bit, and you've got the hide or horns to remember what it was like that day, and very little's changed, actually, has it?"

"It's a little hard on whichever or whatever you're killing at the time," Nancy said. "I mean, does the lion or the elephant really appreciate that you've done him this enormous favor?"

"Oh, for Christ's sake, Nance," Tom said. "How much time do you devote to the mental welfare of a mink that gets caught in a trap and eats his leg off, when you've come home from Jaeckel's with about ten grand worth of hides draped around your neck? You've got a hundred pairs of shoes and they're all made out of the skin of something. You have to kill it to get the hide off it, and never did I see you sneer at a five-buck filet, either."

"I suppose you may be right," said Nancy. "But I think I'll confine my shooting to birds. Somehow a bird or a fish doesn't excite a great deal of sympathy."

"Changing the subject a little, this Holly Keith is quite a dish," Tom said. "I think I detect a familiar gleam in her eye about our young friend McKenzie. How about that?"

"Couldn't say," John replied. "Up to now old Peter's been very spooky. Any amount of lasses have set a cap for him. He could marry the entire stewardess force of Trans African Airlines if he wished, and most of the fillies in the town, and at least a percentage of his clients. But he's wild. I think he's rather like the Masai. Pen him up and he'll die. And God knows he's seen enough carryings-on to make him a little suspicious of the other sex."

"You keep saying he's wild, he's like an animal," Nancy said. "Just why?"

"Well, we're a reasonably wild breed out here for starters, especially us second-generation types. We were raised in the bush, and we were raised on our own, more or less, let free to run loose amongst the natives and the animals. Just for instance, Peter can *smell*. I've seen him down on all fours, running after an animal, his nostrils going in and out like a dog's. He can track at a run over hard-baked rock, following along the smallest, tiniest little hoof scar. He can follow an animal through grass just by seeing how the dew's disarranged or a blade's bent backward. And he can *feel* things. He'll walk up to one lion and hit it in the face and then drive a mile around another. I've seen him time and time again do the exact opposite of what I'd do in a certain situation, and every time he's right on hunch alone. They tell some tall tales about his father too."

"Tall tales such as?"

"Well, I don't know the details, but the old boy's been out here donkey's years, and he's lived mostly very close to the Wogs. There was some story about witchcraft or something or other. I don't really know. Peter doesn't talk much about his family."

"Speaking of witchcraft, is there any magic you could invoke to move that bar and grill in Thomson's Falls a little closer?" Tom said. "I have a special set of extrasensory perceptions myself, and something tells me that we'll all die of thirst if we don't track some benevolent gin to its lair before long."

"You'd make a jolly fine witch doctor." John laughed. "We are just this minute entering the peaceful, progressive hamlet of Thomson's Falls, and the tavern is no more than thirty seconds away."

They turned and drove to the tavern, in which a cheery blaze was already dancing, for the evening was turning cold.

9

Peter came to the crest of the high hill outside Nyeri, where the road lips a valley of violent greenery, with the Kikuyu shambas printed neatly against the steep slope of the hills. A late blaze of sun had swept the mists from the sky, and Mount Kenya stood clear against the frosty blue to the north, the jagged tooth of her wondrous peak well clear of cloud.

"Would you stop the car for a moment, please?" Holly said. "I'd just like to look at it for a second. It's been so very, very long."

Peter drew over to the wrong side of the road and killed his motor on the edge of a Kikuyu cultivation. The mountain thrust out clear, although miles away, unharnessed of its heavy yoke of cloud, standing sternly black beneath its primly snowy cap, the evening sky brilliant behind.

"No wonder," Peter said, "that the Wogs believe God lives up there. I think so myself. At least, if I were God, that's where I'd want to live. It seems to cover Africa. On one day, I remember, I've been able to see old Kerinyagga up there and then turn round and see Kilimanjaro in the other direction. Fantastic."

"Peter," Holly said, turning toward him. "I'm so *glad,* so very happy to be home again." She tilted her chin. "I'd be very much obliged to be kissed, please."

Peter touched her face gently with his fingertips and kissed her very lightly on the lips. He started the motor.

"I'll be taking you to meet your father now," he said, easing in the clutch. "I'll not be seeing you for three months, because we're off in the early bright. Promise me, Holly, just one thing. Please. We don't know much about each other, but promise me you'll not get married or anything like that until I get back from Tom and Nancy's safari. I think I'm going to fall most awfully horribly in love."

"In that case," Holly said, happy-smiling, "I think I'll have the other half."

This time the Land Rover stalled. Then they went off to the Outspan Hotel, where the father and mother of Holly Keith were waiting to take her home, and Peter drove alone and whistling to Bushbuck Farm.

His father had just fixed drinks for John and Tom and Nancy on the wide veranda when Peter drove up. The old man was the same.

"Well," he said. "Well, well. My wild relation has come back again. Gin?"

"Yes, please," Peter said. "With tonic, if there is any. How are you keeping, Pa? I see you've met my friends."

"Keeping wonderfully," Henry McKenzie said. "Bar a touch of rheumatism and a little reminder of malaria now and again. Yes, and I must say I'm honored. You never brought any clients home before. John tells me young Holly Keith's back."

"Yes, sir. I just gave her to her people in Nyeri. You must go over and see her, Pa. She always had a great fancy for you."

"I believe she's not exactly ugly, or so Thompson here says."

"She's a bloody marvel," Peter said.

"I judged as much. You've still a trace of lipstick on your mouth. Here's the gin. Asante, Juma. Intentions honorable?"

"Hello, Juma, you old reprobate. How are all your wives? No intentions at all, as yet. And that's not lipstick. My mouth's chapped from the wind. How are Lisa and Jeff and all the kids?"

"Usual. Jeffy fell out of a tree; playing Tarzan, he was, like his uncle, and broke an arm. Caroline's had the measle. Young Harry came against a porcupine and lost the battle. Jeff good. Elisabeth still tending the sick amongst the Kyukes and, I think, about to breed again. I say, when you marry this young Keith woman, will you please restrain your reproductive tendencies just a touch? I'm an old man, and worn down from playing horse and such with the kids. Incidentally, soon as you've finished your drink, we'll just go on over to Elisabeth's. Jeff sent a boy with a note asking us to dinner."

"There seems to be a general assumption that I'm going to marry our young friend Holly." Peter smiled at the Deanes. "How was the trip down? John show you all the sights and assassinate my character? He usually does, you know."

"It was gorgeous," Nancy said. "And I think your home is wonderful. I'd like to look around a little in the morning, please, before we go off on safari."

"Surely. John, boy, thanks very much for the convoy job. You're staying on for tea at Jeff's and the night here?"

"No, thanks very much, Peter. I must whiz off when you leave. I rang through to my folks, and they're expecting me. Then I must chase meself back to Nairobi in the morning. I told the Deanes, Nancy and Tom here, that you'd get them the record everything. Don't let me down. They think by now that you're Karamoja Bell, or Selous, at least."

"Nothing to it at all. Very simple: Find it and shoot it. Like the country, Tom?"

"Enough to buy a ranch in it as soon as I can steal the money from the trustees. My God, Peter, it's unbelievable. The sight of that mountain, coming up this afternoon . . ."

"I rather enjoyed it too," Peter said. "It's a very nice mountain on a clear afternoon. Ready to go, Pa? Nancy? You've tidied up from the trip? Then let's go see the rest of the family. So long, Little John, and many thanks again. Do the same for you someday."

Nancy Deane thought to herself that she had never, never encountered before the thing of which she had read and heard so much, so completely brought to fulfillment as the home of Jeff and Elisabeth Newton. The nearest thing to it were her memories of going down in the country on Thanksgiving or Christmas to visit her grandparents, with all the family gathered round, but that had been seen as a child and was subject to childish distortion.

They came to the Newton farm just as dusk brought its startling chill, and entered the sprawling house, being taken directly into the huge living room in which six-foot logs were exuberantly shoving fire up the chimney. Two ridiculous boxer puppies were mixed up in some sort of tangle involving the lion skin on the floor and two babies, causing a slight block to traffic which necessitated stepping carefully. A long bar table at one end was crowded with bright bottles, and a coffee table had been loaded with what seemed to be a banquet but was described by their hostess as a snack, to bridge the gap between drinks and dinner. One whole wall was vivid with books, and there were roses on the long concert piano. The elder son of the house came gravely to shake hands, using his unbroken arm, and the two babies quit the dogs to seize their grandfather's knees. The master of the house, a vast man with a red mustache and an unruly mop of black hair, smiled hello and asked their drink preference before indulging in serious conversation, and when they said "Martini" went off to the corner to do it himself, leaving the reception to the hostess.

The hostess was now a woman of twenty-eight, ripened and comfortably curved by a hearty appetite and the birth of three children. She had a controlled tenderness of mouth that seemed to whisper of a happy secret she would never quite divulge. Nancy thought she had never seen such eyes, huge, violet, and as merry-serene as the mouth.

"I'm so glad Peter brought you along," she said. "We never see very much of him any more, except during the rains, and he never brings anyone to the farm. I suppose he's ashamed of us. Would you like to come along with me, Mrs. Deane, whilst the men get the drinks going? I'm sure you'd like to freshen up a bit. This country is *so* dreadfully dusty at this time of the year."

They went away to the bathroom, and Jeff served the drinks. The children now had established a firm beachhead on Henry McKenzie, the babies crawling over him, and young Jeff, a dark, slim tall boy who looked very much like his uncle, standing between the old man's legs and gesturing with his plaster-cast arm as he described some wonderful happening of the day. The boxer puppies went to sleep against the lion, one resting his chin on the lion's open mouth. Two Gordon setters, brown-ticked against the jet of their hides, strolled idly in from the hall and stretched before the fire, where the male began to snore. Tom Deane went immediately to inspect the enormous buffalo which lowered evilly from the fireplace, and then Tom stood greedily in front of the glass-covered gun cabinet, like a child before a sweetshop, while his host made some joke about the time he took the American Navy into Loch Ewe in Scotland and they kidnaped a Wren. Peter had stolen the two younger children from the old man and was sitting on the floor, surrounded by dogs and children, telling the baby Caroline a fanciful tale about why the wildebeest came to be so ugly.

Some years later Nancy Deane attempted to define what it was about this night that made it so luminous in her memory, because she could remember nothing very particular about it at all. There had been nothing special; no brilliant conversation, no unusual incident. The kids had had their bottoms genially smacked by their uncle and had kissed their mother and father and grandfather good night and had been packed off to bed, together with the puppies, which some savage in a white nightgown and red bolero tucked under an arm. Dinner had been served at a big, heavy-planked table at one end of the room, a simple dinner of soup and vegetables and some sort of wild game with a sweet and a bottle of Chianti. The men had talked Navy and ballistics and crops and weather and lions and dogs and bird shooting. Elisabeth Newton had asked many questions about American women, and what were the new styles like in Paris, seeing as the *Vogues* came so late on the boat, she was always six months behind. Half a dozen times Peter or Jeff got up and went to the bookcase to produce some thick rawhide volume to make a point or quote from a passage. Once Jeff opened the gun case and took out a rifle to show Tom something tricky about its innards. Once after dinner the black boy came and whispered something to Elisabeth, who excused herself and went out into the night with a torch.

"Probably," Jeff said, "to deliver a baby or cure a cancer. She usually needs fifteen minutes for the baby, but the cancer takes a little more time. Say half an hour."

When she returned her husband raised an eyebrow and she said simply: "Colic. Nothing more," and then begged everybody's pardon and went round refilling coffee cups and asking if anyone else wanted more brandy before they switched over to whisky.

When Elisabeth sat by her father he casually rested his heavy hand on the back of her neck, as a man absent-mindedly fondles a well-beloved dog or horse, and Nancy noted that Henry McKenzie had a queer old man's habit of addressing all his statements to his daughter, calling her always by her full name, never by the shortened "Lisa." She noticed that once, as Elisabeth Newton moved past her husband, he rested his hand gently on the curve of her hip in a fleeting caress. She remembered that she and her Tom had taken the center of the conversational stage without being conscious of it; that Jeff had asked much of the peacetime American military and of politics and plans for keeping the Russians at least at bay; that the old man had been inordinately curious about what Texas was like, as if they were talking of Patagonia or Antarctica, and that Peter had said very little about anything. He sat and fondled the dogs and occasionally answered some question that was pointedly asked him, such as how was the new gunbearer working out, or did the Bedford hold up better than the Dodge Power-Wagon, and once his sister asked gently if he was pleased with the way young Holly Keith had turned out, and Jeff winked and asked him his intentions, if any.

When they went home, jouncing along in the fresh cold, under the snapping stars, with the rabbits and the tiny bat-eared foxes scudding in front of the car, with the nightjars and hoarse-screeching plovers leaping grotesquely ahead of the lights, with the large intangible owls swooping ghostily, and with everybody tired, Nancy Deane thought that she had never seen a nicer family. That *was* the word, *nice*. Fresh-come from a world of fashionable psychiatry and the gossip columns, she had been a long time away from Thanksgiving at Grandpa's farm. There was nothing, she thought, chic about Peter's family, nothing madly marvelous, but when she went to bed that night she had a sense of warmth and well-being which she hadn't remembered since her childhood. It was like sitting on your father's knee in front of a fire when the snow swept softly down outside, warm and comfy-snug in your flannel pj's with the feet on them, smelling the fire and sensing the snow and the wind that couldn't get in but that howled furiously in aimless rage, smelling the wonderful man-smell of tobacco and shaving cream and soap and whisky, and feeling the harsh grain of whiskers and the tenderness of strong hands that would never, never let anything hurt you so long as Daddy was there. It was a bunny-rabbit-in-a-burrow feeling, warm against the world, and Nancy Deane snuggled solidly into the small of her husband's back and went blissfully off to sleep in a bed as big as the Polo Grounds, knowing that tomorrow had to be wonderful.

10

They toured the farm and inspected the pigs and saw the new bull calf and had a long, wonderful lunch under the umbrella trees, and then they got into the Land Rover and went off to the Masai. They ate the bitter alkali dust on the way to Narok, and stopped for a Coke and to say hello to the game warden in Narok, and saw the proud, slim, goat-caped Masai with their spears, and arrived at camp on a crook of the stone-studded, tree-hedged, sand-flatted Telek River, seeing the winking lights of the cook fire a long way off, and finally coming into a tiny tent city where the mess tent was already up, a Coleman lantern burning and hissing bright from a downbent branch of tree, the fire fast and noisily alight, a small circle of camp chairs drawn round it, and the melodic hum of African voices blending softly off toward the other cook fire. Yusuf came out to meet them as they alighted from the Rover, his black face shiny in the reflected fire, his white nightgown spotless, his green-and-gold bolero rich in the firelit night, and his smile impudent and happy. There were gin and lime and scotch and orange and beer and Coke and sardines and crackers and cheese and pickles on the side table, under the lifted skirts of the mess tent. From the cook fires drifted a scent of something spicy. One of the porters, dragging out firewood, was singing a song under his breath that was vaguely familiar but for the words. Somewhere was the solid smack of maul on tent peg. One or two of the blacks, shy and apologetic, came up to say something swiftly in Swahili to Peter, ducking their heads and smiling beautifully over filed teeth from blue gums.

"Over there's your sleeping tent," Peter said, pointing. "This is head-quarters, the mess tent. Yusuf is your boss from now on, from here, because he runs the camp. You'll see your personal boys when they serve you at supper. The sanitary tent's that way. It's not very grand, I'm afraid. I live in that little green tent over there. Scream if ever you want me. Would you like a bath, Nancy?"

"I'd adore a bath. I've got lava in my pores and in my soul. Can you arrange one?"

"Sure. Gathiru!"

"Ndio, Bwana," came from somewhere in the dark.

"Letti hi hapa majimoto kwa Memsaab pese pese!"

"Ndio, Bwana. Suria."

"That's the bath being drawn, I suppose?"

"Uh-huh. They heat the water in petrol tins. Then they pour it into a sort of canvas coffin which you'll find in your tent, in the back part. There'll be soap and towels and the boy'll dry your back. Don't be shy; he never looks at you, and it's nice to step out of the tub into a warm towel. I suggest your uniform for this time of day be those heavy flannel pajamas we bought, a robe, and mosquito boots. Then when you're ready to sleep all you have to do is hold out a foot for Gathiru or Kariuki to pull the boot off it, and fall into bed. The boy'll fix the mosquito netting, not that you'll need it now, but for the morning. You'll not be frightened when you see a cannibal staring at you through the nets, will you? It'll only be Gathiru or Kariuki fetching you the morning chai. That's tea. You the bartender or me, Tom?"

"Me. You're the expert on what eats me, and I shouldn't like to tire you. Lovely, nutritious delicious bone-building character-molding gin?"

"Ndio. Without olive, please."

"What are the house rules around here?" Nancy asked, sprawling into a canvas chair and stretching her khaki-panted, ankle-booted legs out toward the fire. "Anybody got a cigarette for a lady?"

"Here. One of yours. I pinched a packet. No house rules. You're the Memsaab wa Safari, the boss. What you want, you scream for. What you don't like, you tell me and I fix. What you wish to eat and what you don't, you tell me, and any little extras we go and buy off the ducca. You're supposed to have fun on this thing. Point of protocol, though. Apart from routine, anything special, you tell me and I'll tell Yusuf. He loses face with the boys if we go over his head. Thanks, Thomas. There is really nothing like gin to fend off the evening ague. Cheers, and a happy hunt to you both."

"Is there any sort of hierarchy, like in the Navy, I mean a chain of command with these boys of yours? I wouldn't want to bitch the detail," Tom asked, handing a cocktail to his wife.

"Works roughly like this. Yusuf's the over-all boss, but he has no jurisdiction with the gunbearers. They're what you'd call elite troop and beyond the scope of a servant. They sneer at Yusuf. They tell him he's a ruddy coward, which of course he is, and the big joke round the cook fire is the plot to get Yusuf off on a buffalo hunt. He's stark silly frightened of the old mbogo. But you can tell the caste system by who eats with whom."

"Who does Yusuf eat with?"

"Eats with the cook, Aly. Also dines occasionally with the two personals, but they sit a little outside the circle. They're in his direct charge. Then you'll see that the gunbearers always eat together, except when occasionally they'll add a guest if they're feeling like company. Once in a while, me. If you're very good, you might possibly get invited. It's an honor to eat with the gunbearers, because, you see, they get first crack at all the best victuals. Fat's highly prized here; the boys are dead keen for it. They think it'll cure everything from gonorrhea—excuse me, Nancy—to impotence. Truth is, they're starved for fats and protein. They'll all have the bellyache after we go and shoot some meat tomorrow. Anyhow, since the gunbearers are always first on the scene when we shoot something, they carve off the fat and the juiciest bits of meat, and so to dine with the gunbearers assures you of the best."

"Who are the poor folks?"

"Well, the porters eat together as a rule, and then the kitchen mtoto —he's the Oliver Twist of the bunch—he eats with the car boy. Whenever we get a visiting fireman in the shape of a game scout or a special tracker, he generally eats with the gunbearers. We must go and shoot something big tomorrow, though. The boys have been lying around town and are fair starved for meat."

"What something big do we—you, possibly, or maybe I—shoot tomorrow?" Tom asked. "There's a little more martini here. Have some?"

"Yes, please. Thank you. Oh, first I thought we'd go out and sight in the guns. Scopes bound to be out of whack, and nothing puts you off so badly as aiming exactly right and having the bullet fly exactly wrong. We'll shove up a target and see that all the guns are behaving. Then we'll go and shoot a Tommy for us. They're that little gazelle you saw coming in, the one with the straightish horns and the black bar on his side. Then we'll go and shoot a zebra for the boys. They're fat as cream, and we might as well start shooting the odd punda here and there, because you'll want the hides, of course, and the boys dearly love the fat. Zebras are a bore, but I'd rather you got started on something that hasn't any importance. You might as well resign yourself to missing a lot at first. The light's very tricky here."

"Christ, I'm resigned to missing without blaming it on the light, tricky or not," Tom said. "I don't know anything about this. All I know anything about is a shotgun."

"Well, we'll do a little shotgunning too. Tomorrow night we'll go, say about five-six, and shoot a pig or so to put in a tree for your leopard —that's no trouble at all—and we'll take the shotty-gun kidogo and collect a mess of guinea fowl and francolin for lunch day after tomorrow. Old Aly boils 'em and serves 'em cold with mustard pickles and mayonnaise and salad, and there is nothing better, I expect, in the world, if you're hungry and there's a beer handy. We're having some tonight, as a matter of fact. Chalo told me he ran into a flock coming down—francolin, I mean—and took the liberty of assassinating a few. I'm afraid Chalo's no sportsman. His idea of sport is to find a troop of guinea running down a footpath and to shoot flat on the ground, aiming at their heads. Oh, Nancy. There goes your hot water. Tyari. That means ready."

"Bathi tyari," the voice floated from the tent.

"I'll go and remove the soil," Nancy said. "You bathing, Tom?"

"Sure. There's more water, Peter?"

"Sure. Soon's your good woman's decent, they'll dump the bathtub and fill it for you. Then I'll have her all to myself whilst you get sanitary again."

"Right. You going to bathe?"

"Yep. When you've finished. I'll just whip into my slightly smaller facilities and take a swift cure."

The African inside the tent, brownly luminous from the small lamp, seemed to show no inclination to leave as Nancy stripped off her stiff new clothes and inspected her new home for the next three months. There were two bunks, canvas cots with inflated rubber mattresses, on which her new striped pajamas and tan robe were folded, and the sheets turned down over the blanket. A rectangular framework held a mosquito netting, still unfurled. There was a table with lamp, a soap dish, and her toothbrush and paste laid out on it. A small mirror was secured to the main pole which supported the ridgepole. There was a camp chair and another bed. Behind, in a sort of alcove, a canvas tub, collapsible, was resting on a strip of brown tarp. A big towel was neatly folded and laid alongside the tub. When Nancy climbed into the surprisingly comfortable tub, the savage walked in and handed her the soap, his head decently turned away. She lay luxuriously in the water, feeling fatigue melt away with the dirt, and only when she shifted her hips was she aware that a small thornbush grew under the canvas flooring. When she was quite clean the boy, head still turned modestly away, tucked her into the towel. The thick furry softness of the new flannel pajamas clung to her body, and her feet slid smoothly into the new red leather mosquito boots that had flaring Russian tops and buckled over the ankles. She pushed her pants into the boots and got into the long, heavy-soft flannel robe the boy held for her, bound a kerchief round her head, and went back out for the dividend drink. The scents floating up from the cook fire now were maddening. The men, when she came, were talking shop. Something to do with one-eighty-grain bullets against two-twenty-grain bullets under beta conditions on the forsteris if the grass was gumbled and the nixtosis all wrong.

Dinner was a memorable thing, when the men had bathed and they'd had the last martini and kicked the fire into a blaze, a horrid-looking old black man bringing a dead tree and dragging it over the center of the fire. The night was really cold now and the stars were lit and dancing, and the symphony had tuned. Hyenas, attracted by light and the smell of cooking meat, had ringed round the camp and were just beginning to sound their various A's. Away off somewhere there was a rumble and a racking cough.

"Your first lion," Peter said. "Old boy's got the rheumatiz, like Pa. The cold brings out the grumbles."

Away down the river there was a steady sawing sound, *hah-hah-hack-huh-hack-huh* sort of sound, and Peter smiled.

"Leopard. I'm glad to know they're hunting about here. Sounds fairish, and a male, I'd say. We'll just decorate a Christmas tree for that chap and shoot him off it when he comes to collect the present."

A shrill cursing followed in the wake of the leopard's coughing, almost similar in sound.

"That's what?" Tom said. "Another leopard?"

"No. Only monkeys—baboons, actually, expressing their displeasure. They're mortal enemies, the leopards and the nugus."

"I don't mind saying I'm excited. I've waited a long time for this. And now to be here, to actually be here, with tomorrow, just tomorrow, right here, I'm goose-pimpled." Tom got up and stood in front of the fire. Somewhere off in the distance there was a strangely abrupt barking. "That's what? Dogs?"

"Zebra. Possibly frightened by a lion close by. Funny to think a horse can make a sound that much like a dog."

"I'm scared to death," Nancy said. "I never heard so damned many different noises in my life. What's *that?*"

"A bush baby. Little soft furry thing, cries like a child. You can see its eyes glowing as big as flashlamps if you'll step over here. They show red in the night. Sad little bugger, what?"

"How long does it take to know all this about it? I mean, what all the sounds are and what kind the trees are and all the rest?"

"Well, Tom, we've grown up with all of it, and so I suppose it's like your knowing about how to get about in New York. I'm sure I would be frightened foolish in London or Rome or New York and perform as an awful ass, not knowing how much to tip or what to order or how to find my way about in tubes. Here I feel at home, and since I've heard hyenas and bush babies and monkeys and lions since I was a baby, I feel comfortable about them."

"What's the chances of one of these things creeping into camp and taking a nip out of you?" Nancy asked. "That tent of mine seems to have very little in the way of protection from any really determined anything bigger than a rabbit."

"No fear. You'll find everything out here more frightened of you than you're frightened of it. I would form the habit of shaking out my boots in the morning, though. Tarantulas and scorpions and such sort of like to crawl into shoes for warmth."

"Good God. What about snakes?"

"Very few up here. You find them more in the jungly country. Might run onto the odd cobra or mamba, but they generally go the other way."

"I don't know about you people, but I'm tired," Tom said. "This has been a very exciting day for me, and I don't want to disgrace myself when we start to shoot tomorrow. I think I'll turn in, if Nancy's ready. I'm beat."

"Fine. Just yell if you want anything, or clap your hands. The lamp's already lit in your tent, and there's a torch on the table if either of you has to use the loo. I'll just walk round the camp and see if all's tidy. Good night, all, and sleep well. If you find anything in your tent it'll be a rhino. Don't move, and the chances are it'll go away."

"Thank *you*, Dr. Livingstone," Nancy said, and went off to bed. She jumped into her cot and tucked the mosquito netting firmly under the mattress, and although a hyena seemed to be about to make her an indecent proposition, judging from the nearness of the noise, and the whole African bush seemed to be conversationally inclined, she went to sleep immediately with a great sense of security. She did not wake until the gray light of early morning, when a cannibal with filed teeth shook her by the shoulder, leered horribly, and said: "Memsaab. Iko hapa chai."

What a curious thing, Nancy Deane thought as she reached out her hand to take the steaming cup of tea, to be shaken awake by a man who only yesterday was eating his uncle, and to have it all seem completely natural.

"Asante," she said, smiling, using one of the few Swahili words she knew. "Thank you." And got up to inspect the day, which naturally must be fine.

11

Kimani had seen Peter just a little before Peter saw him that day in the bazaar, when Peter was driving through to the airport with the two girls. He recognized Peter easily, and he fled from pure reflex. He had been reflexively running for a long time now. He would have liked very much to say a few words to his old companion. There had been a time when, if he had seen Peter in the bazaar, he might have risked stopping to talk with him, just a little, to see what time had made, and maybe he might even have been able to work for Peter, who was a big bwana now and very important. Kimani had heard all sorts of tales about his old friend Peter, because Peter was known all over Kenya and from one end of Tanganyika to the other. But now it was much too late; too late for nearly everything.

From his concealed crouch in a twisting, slimy alley, mushy underfoot with ancient fish heads and rotted vegetables, Kimani watched Peter searching for him and then saw him climb back into his gharri and drive off with the two white manamouki to the airport.

What a different life it might have been except for that bloody nonsense so long ago, Kimani thought, and was surprised to notice that he thought in English. He didn't speak much English any more and thought mostly in either Kikuyu or Swahili. Kimani watched the jeep scoot off in a cloud of red dust, and then he got up and walked out of the alley. He slipped into the throng and let the pressing tide of people drift him to a teashop. His mouth was very dry—dry from the dust, he thought. He would have some tea.

Kimani entered the dark, sour-smelling shop and flopped down on a three-legged stool and shouted for tea. A Kikuyu woman, her hair in peppercorns, one brown breast showing through a rent in her sleazy frock, her belly bulging with child, padded in on bare feet and fetched him a sticky, dirty jelly glass of the heavily sweetened tea. Three Kikuyu men were playing a game with finger-smudged greasy cards in one corner under the unsteady light of a streaked and smoky lantern. The room reeked, Kimani thought, as if a herd of hyenas had just abandoned it.

Kimani was then twenty-five years old. He had thickened. Under a cheap, patched blue suit that was more purple than blue, his chest and shoulders bulked solid. He wore a dirty striped cotton shirt, and on his head an old golfing cap. He owned shoes, tennis shoes with slits cut in the sides to ease his toes. A long white scar creased the side of his face, from an old cut in a knife fight. His nose, once thin for a Kikuyu, had been flattened in another fight, possibly when he was drunk. He couldn't remember what the fight was about. Probably a wager at cards.

"Woman!" he called the slattern. "Bring me food. I am hungry. I have come a long way today."

The woman was immediately suspicious.

"You have the money to pay?"

"Of course I have the money. I have much money." Kimani reached into his pocket and showed a fistful of dirty notes. "When you bring the meat, bring me beer as well. Are there any women available here?"

"I."

"With that great baby in your belly? No. Hapana kapisa sana. A young woman. Preferably one who will not give me a disease."

"My sister, then, perhaps. She is young and clean. But she will want five shillings."

"Send for her. Tell her to bring very much beer. And afterwards I will sleep a little. You have some sort of room here?"

"Yes. But that will cost you two shillings more and you must pay it in advance."

"Take it out of this." Kimani flung her a pound note. "And see that I get some change back."

The fat woman disappeared, and presently another woman entered the room. She was slim and not so very ugly. She wore her hair as long as it could grow, about two inches, and had attempted to curb its crinkles with grease. She had red paint on her face and lips like the white women, and she wore a white woman's discarded cotton frock. She was barefoot, and she knelt beside him to hand him a battered tin drinking can full of yeasty brew. He drank greedily and motioned to her to fill the can again from a galvanized-iron bucket which contained more beer.

"What is your name?" he asked after he had drunk deeply again.

"Kabui," she said. "What is yours?"

"Kimani. I knew a girl named Kabui once, a very long time ago. But she would not now be a whore."

"Kabui is a common name. And not all whores begin life as whores. I, for instance, was a younger daughter who could find no man with a bride price. Also, there was a baby. Where do you come from?"

"Many places. I have just now come from Tanganyika. Before that I was in other places. I am hungry and I am weary and I want a woman and then to sleep. Go and tell that fat hag to hurry with the meat, and bring more beer. Fetch a can for yourself as well. I have a thirst on me like a camel."

The girl went away and Kimani fished a crumpled packet of yellow-papered, black-tobaccoed cigarettes from his pocket and lit one. He watched the loafers playing cards, without interest, and exhaled a great gust of the harsh smoke. God, but he was tired. He had walked all the way from Arusha. Possibly two hundred miles. It was not safe for him to travel the roads, even if he could beg a ride; even if he had money for the bus, and he had plenty of money. But he had to get to Kiambu by tomorrow. He would eat first and use the girl and then he would sleep. He knew a way of ensuring that the girl would not steal his money or send for the police. Unless someone sent for the police he was safe. Thousands of Kikuyu went in and out of Nairobi every day now, and no policeman could find a man who knew well how to hide—not in this rank rabbit warren of Nairobi's bazaar, where the trails doubled and crossed and wound round, encircling each other, and where you could kick through the side of a shanty. It was a long time since he'd been in Nairobi—not since he was a kid. Where *was* that damned woman with his food?

The fat woman came out again and handed him a much-dented tin plate containing some half-cooked pieces of mutton, a mound of posho-meal porridge, a couple of greenish-yellow yams, and some thick, grayish-looking white-lumpy grease in a scum to one side. He ate hungrily with his hands, licking his fingers and swilling down beer. When he had finished he called the woman and sent her out to fetch him some sweets from the store next door. She returned with a stale yellowish pastry oozing some sort of granulated goo from its flyblown crust. When he finished eating he rose and motioned to the girl, who had been watching him silently as he gulped his food.

"Bring the beer," he said. "We will go to lie down now. Where is the room?" The girl gestured with her frizzy head at the black interior of the teahouse, where a ragged, smoke-grimed curtain hung. She drew the curtain aside and walked in ahead of him. A candle flickered on a small table, its flame ending in greasy smoke, and there was a filthy, tattered mattress, stained with urine and other things, in one corner of the room, permanently corrugated on the hard-packed dirt floor. She pointed to the mattress and crossed her arms at the skirt hem and pulled her dress over her head. Kimani scarcely looked at her.

She went to lie down on the mattress, and Kimani took off his pants, stuffing the money first inside his jacket, which he did not remove. Then he flung himself down beside her. This was not very much of a woman, but it had been a very long time since he had had any sort of woman at all, and the memory of those two years in which he had not seen a woman still was hot in his head. He rolled over and covered her body with his own.

When he was spent he reached inside his coat and brought out a pair of stolen police handcuffs. Snapping one circle onto the girl's wrist, he tightened the steel cuff and then locked the other band to his own wrist. Kimani had learned many things in the last ten years, a great many of them practical.

"This way you will not run away with my money," he said. "If you scream I will choke you. Rest beside me now, for I am weary and I want to sleep before we do this again, and then I will leave. I am a generous man and will give you another five shillings." Kimani relaxed, flat on his back, the girl beside him, and almost immediately went to sleep. The girl stared at him with frightened eyes, the distended brown-blotched whites shining in the dark.

When Kimani awoke it was very dark in the room. The candle had dwindled and died in a flat pool, and the girl still lay silently awake beside him. She had not moved. Kimani unlocked the handcuffs, replaced them in his pocket, and took the woman again. Then he got up, pulled on his pants, and flung her a ten-shilling note.

"Good-by, whore," he said. "If you have given me a disease I shall come back someday and twist your neck."

The girl said nothing as he went out of the room, passing quickly through the teashop and entering a side alley. It was quite dark, for which Kimani was grateful. He walked carefully along, keeping to the shadows, and headed out toward the road for Kiambu. When he got to Kiambu he hoped there would be an end to hiding. He felt much better now, rested, no longer hungry, and with that other need quieted. It was not really so very far to Kiambu. He would sleep in the forest tonight, and with luck he would be in Kiambu by dark tomorrow.

12

That day when Kimani had screamed his war cry and had flung the spear at Jeff Newton, he knew that he had killed him when the force of the blade knocked Jeff to the ground. That was good. The curse was now removed and his father would come free of jail. But the English portion of Kimani's upbringing argued swiftly that the killing of Jeff Newton could not be settled by the simple payment of a blood price. The English would surely hang him if they caught him, and so the very best thing that he could do was to run very far and hide cunningly where the English could not find him. Accordingly, he ran like a cheetah until he was four or five miles away. Then he flung himself down, gasping, in a thicket and listened to his heart stop its thudding. He must think clearly now what he must do. One thing, he was very lucky. He had never been made to fill out a kipandi, the working card on which the fingerprints mysteriously allowed men to be identified, no matter what their age or how they changed their appearance, so they could not trap him there. He might run off and hide in Nairobi, but not for too very long, because there were many policemen in Nairobi and someone would be sure to see him one day and report him. He could run away up North, past Isiolo, where the wild men lived and the Somali were, but he did not know the North and he owned no weapons save his panga, and the panga was at the farm, and he did not dare go back to the farm.

So what he had better do, Kimani thought, was to stick to the reserve and the squatter farms and hope that some of the Kikuyu around Nyeri or Fort Hall would hide him on their own shambas, where white men seldom if ever came and where at least he could eat and perhaps beg some extra food and borrow a spear or a panga before he made up his mind where the safest place to go was. Kimani was frightened. He was only fifteen and he had just killed a man and now he could never become a gunbearer and hunt lions and elephants with Peter. But he was glad he had killed Jeff Newton, who had slapped him and put a thahu on the house of his father. And he was happy now that his father would go free. He felt no particular emotion about depriving the Memsaab Lisa of a husband. She was young and rich and could easily find another man, a man who did not go about hitting people in the face. The forest was wet-cold and frighteningly black and full of fearful noises. He did not dare make a fire, although he had matches. He would just have to sit and shiver out the night, because if he moved he might stumble onto a wild animal or a snake, and he had nothing to defend himself with. Kimani, at that moment, no longer felt so much like a proud avenger as like a very cold, miserable, hungry, and frightened fifteen-year-old boy.

Kimani slept occasionally during the night, huddled against the bole of a tree and covered with thick, fleshy fronds. He was up walking before dawn, and he set out for Nyeri, keeping closely to the bush. He of course could have no idea that he had not killed Jeff Newton or that Jeff had decided not to set the police after him. He moved quietly through the forests, freezing once at the sound of voices, but the voices came only from some women out gathering firewood, and soon their gabble drifted faintly from a distance. He avoided Nyeri and headed down the hill toward Fort Hall. There were Kikuyu shambas all along the road, and he would seek food and shelter in one of them. He would not go to one of the richer properties but would choose a poor one. The poorer people would be less likely to turn him away.

He skirted the hills, following patches of forest, until he was well along the road to Fort Hall, and then he cut away from the road and climbed a tall, cedar-clumped hill whose slopes were terraced precisely in cultivation, and where he saw the tiny cooking fires winking on the summit. He walked along one ridge and came out to a clearing, where an old man squatted in front of the fire and women were busy cooking things that smelled delicious to the half-starved boy. As he walked, Kimani decided he would tell the truth. These people, who tended their own tiny plots of yams and plantains, of beans and maize, would not refuse him hospitality nor call the police. In their own small world they hated any white man. Kimani had heard much talk around the fires of Henry McKenzie's squatters' shambas. They did not know Henry McKenzie as he, Kimani, knew him, or as his father, Karanja, knew him. They knew him only as one more white bwana who had taken land from the Kikuyu and would not allow them to keep but just so many goats or so many sheep or cattle because of a shortage of grazing land. There was much talk now about the day when the young men would come back from the war and what they would do to regain their lands. The Kikuyu would band against the white man, and someday, when the war horn sounded . . .

He walked into the clearing and approached the old man squatted before the fire.

"I am a Kikuyu of Mwega. I am running away. I am very tired and hungry. May I stay in your shamba the night and will you give me some food?"

"Of course," the old man said. "Since when did a Kikuyu refuse shelter and food to a kinsman? Rest here by the fire. My wives will bring you food."

He called to a woman, who went into the hut where the cooking stones were and who came out bearing an iron pot with some sort of goat stew in it and handed him banana fronds to make a plate. Kimani dipped into the hot food with his fingers, putting the meat on the leaves. Then the women brought him roasted yams and another vessel, this one filled with a sour gruel. He gobbled like a starved animal, and the women came again with the food. Never had food and fire seemed so warm and wonderful. The old man nodded as he watched the boy eat. He was a very old man.

Kimani looked about him. There were only children and women. There were no young men, not even of his own age.

"Where are all the young men?" he asked. "There are only women and children and old men to be seen here."

"The young men no longer stay in the shambas," the old man said, shaking his head so that his wooden earplugs rattled. "All the young men have gone to the towns to work or have been taken off to the war the Serkali is fighting across the seas. There is nothing for a young man to do on the shambas any more, since there is not room to graze many cattle and the women have grown lazy from the smallness of their goat herds, which need no care, and from the smallness of their cultivation, which any child can stir with a stick and grow whatever crop there is to be grown. If you seek the young men you must go to the cities or else to the white man's war. There is no need for a warrior in Kikuyu any more, because there is nobody we are allowed to fight. What else may a young man do but go to the cities or to the white man's war?" Like many old men, he was garrulous and liked to answer his own questions.

"Are you going to the cities or to join the war?" the old man continued. "You have said you were running away. Have you stolen from a bwana? That is good, if you have stolen, but you do not possess what you have stolen. That is bad. Did you offend some bwana and did he beat you with his stick? Or did you neglect your duties on his shamba and allow a calf to die or a horse to founder?"

"Neither." Kimani spoke proudly now that the skin of his belly was tight and his body warm. "I slew a white bwana with my spear. He struck me in the face in anger, and a thahu came upon the house of my father. A baby of my father was born upside down as a result, and when the midwives killed it, they put my father in jail."

"Were you purified of the thahu?"

"Yes, but my father has remained in jail, and the mundumugu told me that the purification was not complete. So I took my spear and killed the Bwana Jeff, who had cursed me by striking me with his fist."

"You are a fine boy," the old man said. "It is a shame there are not more boys like you to rise and strike down the white man and take back the lands of the Kikuyu once again. Your father will be very proud when he hears what a fine thing you have done, and of course he will be immediately set free now that you have removed the thahu with your spear. *My* eldest son"—the old man spat scornfully into the fire—"drives a lorry in Nairobi. *My* son a truck driver, when at his age I was an elder of my clan and had slain as a njama more Masai than there are leaves on this fig tree."

"Perhaps you can tell me what to do," Kimani said. "I have no wish to be hanged by the Serkali, as hanged I certainly shall be if I am caught. I must go far away to some place where I am not known."

"You will stay here for a while in my shamba with me. It is very simple. When the police come to search the shambas, as come they will, I will hide you in the wood until they are gone, in a secret place I know, and I will tell them many lies, as always. You may bed with my daughter, Mumbi, in her mother's hut at night. She is of your age group and is a fine, comely girl. She will bring you food in the forest."

"I thank you very much, old man. But there will be much talk and the police will come again and again and one day some Kipsigi informer will lead them to my hiding place in the forest, and then I will be taken away and hanged."

"Do not fear, my son. There are many shambas on this ridge, the farms of my circumcision brothers, my cousins and brothers and the relatives of my wives. It is a simple matter to hide you. We can shift you from shamba to shamba and feed you, for you have slain a white bwana with your spear. And one day, when my son who drives the lorry in Nairobi comes to see his wives, when he comes in the lorry, he will hide you in it and take you away. He travels much to Tanganyika and elsewhere. In Tanganyika the Portuguese and Greeks do not care much about kipandis and the personal affairs of people. You will find work in Arusha or Babati or Dodoma. You will be safe in Tanganyika. There are not so many English bwanas there as here. My son will take you in his van. It will be an honor for him to have a warrior in his lorry. And someday, when the war horn sounds, you will come home in honor."

The old man nodded. He clapped his hands, and a wife stuck her head out of a hut. "Send Mumbi, my daughter," he said. There was a rustle from within, and the bleat of a goat, and a girl of about Kimani's age came out. She was wearing a blue cotton frock and was short and fat and shone with oil.

"This *man*"—Kimani swelled with pride, because the old man used the word for warrior, "njama"—"this *man* shares your bed. Tend him well, for he is a warrior and a man."

The girl ducked her head submissively and led Kimani into the hut, which was divided into wattled sections, one for eating, one for sleeping, and one for the goats that nuzzled and murmured and stirred restlessly, their odor sharp and musky, their rustlings soft as they nudged each other. The girl pointed shyly at a bed of skins stretched over poles.

Kimani sank down on the bed, and after a while the girl Mumbi came and nestled alongside him. The fire flickered low, and that night Kimani slept warm.

13

But Kimani did not go to Tanganyika—not just then. He waited for several days, hiding in damp caves in the forest by day and sleeping in the warm hut with the girl Mumbi and the goats at night. His fears eased, and one day, when the old man's son came, Kimani stole away in the back of the lorry, well hidden under sacking. The son, whose name was Muchige, was taking his truck up through Thomson's Falls, then to Nanyuki and to Isiolo in the North. When the old man had told Muchige of Kimani's feat of slaying a white man, Muchige said:

"It is better not to go to Tanganyika. There are places in the mountains where men I know who have gotten into trouble have collected in bands. The Aberdare Mountains are very safe. The forest is thick, and it is easy to hide. There are women there, and little shambas for growing food, and each man looks after the welfare of the other. The police do not often seek out men in the Aberdares."

"How will I find these men?" Kimani asked. "If the police cannot find them, how can I find them?"

"It is very simple. From time to time their women come in to Thomson's Falls or Rumuruti to buy food and tobacco. I will leave a word in the teashops and the market places. I have a friend in Thomson's Falls who will hide you, and one of the women will come and lead you to safety. Get in the back of the lorry now, and I will cover you with sacking. We will not come to Thomson's Falls until after night."

Kimani thanked the old man and said good-by to the girl Mumbi. Then he climbed in the back of the lorry and Muchige covered him with tow sacking. He lay hot and uncomfortable under the coarse cloth, his mouth and eyes and ears full of dust, the truck jolting rudely and bruising his body.

Finally the lorry lurched to a halt, and Muchige came round to the back. "Get out now," he said. "We have arrived at the home of my friend."

It was dark when Kimani beat the dust from his body and jumped over the duckboards of the lorry. It was very dark and he could not see well, but shortly his eyes adjusted to the night and he saw that he was standing in a clay road, a few hundred feet away from which sat a cluster of beehive huts. Muchige pointed.

"Go there and say I sent you to be hidden until you can get into the mountains. My friend is called Njogu. He will understand. Good-by."

"Good-by," Kimani said, and walked toward the huts. He could see now that they were set in a little glade at the edge of dense black forest which rose steeply up the mountainside. As he walked into the clearing a man came out of a hut and challenged him. He was a tall, very thin man with a scrubby gray beard and much gray in his hair. He had a high, Nilotic nose and flat, intelligent eyes.

"What do you want here?" he said, and Kimani saw that he balanced a panga in his hand.

"I came in a lorry with Muchige. He said you were a friend and that I should ask for Njogu. Do you know him?"

"I am Njogu. Welcome. Are you hungry?"

"Yes. I have not eaten since early this morning."

"The women will bring food. Sit down here and we will talk. Why are you here? Have you stolen?"

"No. I killed a white bwana with a spear for cursing me."

"I have heard nothing of any white bwana being killed with a spear. Where did this happen?"

"On the farm of the Bwana Jeff Newton near Mwega. I threw the spear at close hand, and it pierced the chest of the Bwana Jeff, and he fell to the ground, wherefore I ran away. The father of Muchige hid me in his shamba, and I went every day to a cave in the forest."

"I have heard nothing of a murder. Perhaps you did not kill him?"

"That is impossible. I was much too close to throw wide, and the spear went cleanly through his chest. I saw him fall."

"Then perhaps the police are keeping it a secret until they can search all Kikuyu. I must get you away from here in a hurry. I will take you up the mountain myself after you have eaten."

"I have no clothes and no weapon, nothing except these shorts I wear."

"Have you money?"

"None."

"In that case I will give you a blanket. You can pay me later on."

"But how will I get money?"

"They will tell you, up the mountain. Now the food is here. Let us eat and go into the forests. It is not safe for you to be here. Any minute the police might come."

Kimani and the man Njogu ate hurriedly of stew, and then Njogu went into the hut and came out with a blanket and a shotgun. He handed the blanket to Kimani, shouldered the gun, and led off into a winding trail at the edge of the clearing. Kimani wondered about the gun, since he knew that it was illegal for black men to own guns, but he was too polite to ask about it, and also too busy avoiding roots and creepers in the nearly pitch dark. He hoped they would not come across one of the many big forest rhinos that roamed the hillsides of the Aberdare Mountains.

They walked all night, toiling over crisscrossed game trails, scratched by thorns, slipping and tripping over withes and lianas, the man Njogu sometimes slashing through the close-meshed underbrush with his panga. It was bitterly cold, and the underbrush was wet and clammy. Just as dawn grayed the sky, the man pushed his palm backward in the stop sign and made a peculiar warbling call. In a moment the call was answered, and the man repeated his warble, but on a different scaling of notes. Again the call was answered. Njogu beckoned and walked forward.

They came to a small clearing surrounded completely by bush, a clearing no larger than a paddock. Two sketchy huts, carelessly thatched and uncemented by mud, sprawled at the edge of the clearing. The poles and thatch were still green, and the grass in the glade was stiff and high. It had not been trodden flat by use. A heavy squat man, dressed in filthy khaki pants and wearing an old police sweater, came out from behind a hut, and Kimani noticed that he too had a gun, a modern sporting rifle.

"Here is another bird for your nest," Njogu said. "A fledgling, still wet and pinfeathered. But he has killed a white man with a spear and is fleeing from the police. He is strong, even though he is young, and has been sent here by Muchige, the lorry driver."

"Has he weapons or money?"

"Neither."

"We will have to find him some of both. What is your name, boy?"

"Kimani wa Karanja. Of the Bushbuck Farm."

"He whose father is in jail in Nyeri over the affair of the baby-strangling. You have heard of this."

"That is right. A thahu came to me through the Bwana Jeff Newton, husband of the daughter of the Bwana McKenzie. As a result, my father is in jail. So I took my spear and slew the Bwana Jeff."

"When did this happen?"

"Less than a week ago."

"In that case I would not have heard of it. Come, we will eat. Woman! Bring food and coals from your fire. We have a new mouth to feed."

The man, who called himself Adam Marenga, squatted, and rested his rifle against the hut, within hand's reach. The woman brought food in a big kettle, and Kimani noted that it was beef, good beef. He looked surprised as he swallowed his first mouthful. The man saw the look and laughed.

"Oh yes," he said, "we live like the white bwanas here, except that our huts are not so permanent. We move every three or four days. But there are many fat cattle on the farms of the bwanas, and they do not miss one every now and then, because we butcher only what we can carry and leave the rest for the hyenas and the birds. There are many hyenas here," he said, and laughed again. "Most have two legs."

"That is a good gun. It is like the one that Bwana Jeff, he whom I killed, used to shoot when I went with him on safari."

"It is a very good gun," Adam Marenga said. "It should be. It once belonged to the Bwana Turner, who has a large shamba outside of Rumuruti. It is a shame that he managed to lose it, for guns like this are very expensive. Yes, it is a good gun. Good enough to kill an elephant, or a man."

"How can I get a gun?" Kimani asked. "I would like very much to have a gun."

"It is very simple. We will wait until some day the news comes that a bwana has gone to town to drink and carouse with the manamouki at the ngomas, and then we will go and get you a gun."

"Is not that very dangerous?"

Adam laughed. "Not the way we do it," he said. "I think you should sleep now. Take your blanket into the hut, and tonight, if news comes, we will see about getting you a gun."

Kimani went into the hut, in which there was no household article beyond a pile of blankets and a cook pot, and rolled himself in his own blanket. He wondered sleepily how it was that Kikuyu could have guns and live in the forests like the Athi, surrounded by wild elephants and rhinos, and build such shoddy huts while still eating good beef. Beef was rarely eaten by Kikuyu, for cows were wealth and tacitly tabooed except for certain ceremonial occasions. Then he went off to sleep, and when he woke and came into the afternoon sunshine which streamed weakly into the clearing, his friend Njogu was gone. But several other men, mostly young men of eighteen to twenty-five, had joined his new friend Adam, the man with the gun. All these men had guns too—shotguns and rifles. They squatted, smoking and talking, and looked at him curiously. He was quite the youngest of the group.

The men asked him many questions and nodded approvingly when he described how he had flung the spear at the white Bwana.

"It is the lion cub that makes the lion," one man said. "If he can throw a spear he can pull a trigger. He is of our clan. Tomorrow we will see if he can steal, for word has come that the Bwana Riggs of Laikipia has taken his wife and children and left for Nairobi, dressed in their finest clothes. We will go to see if all is well on the shamba of the Bwana Riggs."

14

Kimani, Adam, and two other men, whose names Kimani did not know, rose at dawn and went down the mountain. As he stumbled along in daylight, Kimani marveled that he had been able to walk at all in the night. The trees were packed together like faggots of firewood on a woman's back. Creepers clawed and scratched and bit. The underbrush was so thick that it was almost impossible to see more than a few feet ahead. The men followed game trails, sometimes crawling on all fours. Once they started a rhino, who whooshed twice and then pounded away, crashing in the bush. Again, they came upon a pale green glade in which golden bushbuck fed, and the buck's sharp bark nearly frightened the wits out of Kimani. They came to the edge of the forest just at nightfall and paused inside the fringe of forest. When full night came, Adam turned to Kimani.

"You see there the lights of the Bwana's house burning only in the kitchen. The Bwana is not at home or there would be lights and fire burning while the Bwana drinks gin in his big room. You will go ahead of us to the kitchen and call out softly. The cook will come, or perhaps one of the personal boys. You will tell the cook some tale of misfortune or ask him for employment in return for a meal—anything at all. You will hold him in conversation long enough to be sure that there are not too many people in the house. We will do the rest."

"But what do you intend to do?" Kimani asked. "Why should I talk nonsense to the cook?"

"You are a little fool. We have come to steal—to steal guns, or any other worth-while thing."

"I do not want to steal. It is very bad to steal."

"You will do what I say or we will kill you now. Go and talk to the cook."

Kimani went to the back of the big house, where the cookhouse was. There was a clatter in the kitchen and the murmur of a song. Kimani stepped gingerly up to the back stoop and made the slight cooing noise that some Africans use to establish presence without causing alarm. The humming stopped, and Kimani cooed again. Presently a pot rattled and the cook came to the door. He opened it carefully and poked out his head.

"Nini? Who is there? What do you want?"

"I want to talk to the Bwana," Kimani said. "I have no parents and I want work."

The cook slammed the door and then returned with a flashlamp. He trained the torch on Kimani's face. He saw only a boy shivering in shorts. He walked out into the back yard.

"The Bwana is not here. In any case, you have no right to come to the house. The nearest compound is over there. We have no work for mtotos, anyhow. What can a boy like you do to earn shillingi?"

"I have worked in the house of a bwana, and I know about sheep and cattle," Kimani said. "But now I am hungry and tired and wish to be a——"

At that moment Adam and the other men lunged out from the shadows. Adam took the cook by the throat and the other men seized his arms. Adam leaned his face close to the cook's face and said: "If you make any sound I will kill you." He released the cook's throat and drew a panga from its scabbard and placed its blade against the cook's neck.

The cook's eyes walled upward in terror, showing the whites like a frightened horse.

"Are there any besides you in the house?"

"Only the houseboy," the cook said, his voice husky and frightened.

"Call him, then," Adam said, and pressed the knife blade into the neck flesh. The cook raised his voice. It was higher now.

"Migwe! Come here! Here in the back yard!"

"I'm coming," the houseboy called. One of the men released the cook's arms and stood by the door. When the houseboy came running out, Adam shone the torch full in his face and the other man hit the houseboy over the head with a club that swung suspended from a thong around his neck. There was a meaty crunch and the houseboy fell unconscious.

One of the men picked him up and carried him into the kitchen. They gagged him with a kitchen towel and trussed him with strips torn from the gingham curtains, which they hauled down, rod and all. Adam released the cook, sheathed his panga, and lifted his rifle.

"Lead us to where the Bwana keeps his guns," he said, and nudged the cook in the small of the back with the rifle barrel. The cook moved through the alleyway which connected kitchen with the main house and came to the stout door. It was locked.

"You would have a key," Adam said. "Produce it."

The cook reached numbly under his kanzu and brought out a key ring from his pants pocket. He chose a key and opened the door, and Adam shoved him into the main room. It was very dark, and Adam held the light of the torch low to the floor.

"Where is the place of the guns?" he said.

"Over there, in a case in the corner."

"Give me the key."

"I do not have the key. The Bwana always keeps the key. But its front is of glass."

"Good." Adam flicked the torchlight toward the case. The guns shone black through the locked pane. "Smash it," he said, and one of the men stepped forward and crushed in the panes with the butt of his gun. The glass fell with a tinkle.

"Take only the lighter guns," Adam commanded. "You, Kimani. Take only the magazine rifles. The big double ones are too heavy and do not shoot straight. Ah! There are two pistols, as well. Take the two pistols and the three magazine rifles. Good. You!" to the cook. "Where does the Bwana keep his ammunition?"

"It is in a locked box in the bedroom, in his closet. But I do not have the key to it, and it is very heavy."

"Lead us to the bedroom," Adam said. "Kimani! Take the guns to the kitchen and place them by the door. Put the pistols around your waist. We will wait here, and then we go to get the ammunition."

Kimani ran swiftly away with the guns, stepped over the houseboy, and stacked the weapons at the door. Then he came back and followed the men down the long hall to the sleeping quarters. The cook pointed at a locked closet.

"The ammunition is in there."

Adam nodded to one of the other men. He stepped forward and hacked a panel off the door with his panga. Adam reached in and took out a metal box about the size of a small square suitcase. It was heavy, but not too heavy to be carried. Hanging in the closet was a line of suits and an overcoat. Adam pointed and motioned at Kimani, who reached inside and cleared the rack with a sweep of his arm. One of the other men picked up the ammunition box, grunting, and Adam herded the cook ahead of him, back through the living room and out into the kitchen. The man on the floor was still unconscious. Adam jerked his head toward the guns. Kimani and each of the men picked up a rifle and slung it over his shoulder. Then one of the men stepped behind the cook.

"You do not know our names, you do not know our faces," Adam said. "You came to the door and were struck unconscious. When you regained your senses we were gone. If you say aught else, we will come down one night and cut your throat. Do you understand?"

"I understand," the cook said, whereupon the man behind him struck him at the base of the skull with the knobkerrie and swiftly gagged and bound him.

"I will carry the ammunition box for a while," Adam said. "Divide the clothes amongst you, and let us go away with all speed. We have been very lucky tonight, but it does not do to overtry your luck."

As they stepped through the yard, a dog broke out, barking, from under the house. One of the men drew a panga and sliced him through. He picked up the dog and hung him, upside down and still alive, on a fence post. Then the men ran as fast as they could with their burden, headed for the black silence of the forest. They walked all night but were aided by the torch, which Adam had stuck in his belt. By noon of the next day, very tired from their burdens, they were back in the clearing where the hut was. One of the men crept forward and looked for a signal. It was a sapling, which was broken but not severed, near the hut. Its broken end was pointing straight at the path that led to the clearing and on which the men crouched. The man nodded, and they came forward into the open, throwing down their loads with relieved grunts. One of the men whistled, and presently two women came out of the bush with a load of firewood on their backs. They made shrill sounds of approval when they saw the mound of clothes and the shiny guns. Adam demanded food and the men ate greedily. They had had nothing to eat since they left the day before, and had not stolen from the kitchen because they had no time to waste and no way to carry away food, burdened as they were with guns and clothing.

The men picked over the heap of clothes. Adam chose a gray overcoat and a pair of golf knickers, brightly checked plus-fours. One of the other men seized greedily at a tail coat and a pair of tan slacks. The third man grabbed a rain ulster and a brown business suit. Kimani looked at the remainder and decided on a khaki bush jacket and pair of jodhpur riding pants. The clothing had been made for a very tall man, but thin, so he had to cut off the legs of the jodhpurs and slit the coat up the back to ease his shoulders. But at least now he would be warmer, for he had his blanket as well. Adam kicked the remaining hodgepodge of clothing, which included a pair of tennis flannels, to the women. Kimani noticed later that one woman had made a sort of jacket from the trousers, cutting a hole in the crotch for her head to come through, and using the legs as sleeves. The fly buttons made a neat row down her neck and chest.

Adam did not take a gun but chose both pistols for himself, wearing them crisscrossed round his waist. He told Kimani to take his pick of the rifles, and Kimani selected a .318 because he knew how to work its bolt and to load it, as the Bwana Jeff had taught him. They broke open the ammunition box, forcing its hasp with a panga, and Kimani saw several yellow flat boxes of the .318 bullets and took them, stowing them in his pockets. He wished the bush jacket had a row of bullet loops like those he had seen on the Bwana Jeff and on the Bwana Henry McKenzie. The other men took the other two rifles and the rest of the ammunition, save some boxes of pistol bullets, and went away into the bush. Kimani crawled into the hut and rolled in his blanket to sleep again, but he slept with his gun cradled to his body. Now Kimani had a gun. If a rhino or an elephant or a lion molested him, he would kill it as the white bwanas killed things, and if any other white bwana ever struck him he would take his gun and shoot him. The business of spears was for boys and old men. Now Kimani was a full man, for did he not own a gun?

15

They stayed in the clearing for another day and then moved on until they found another clearing, where the women built another rude hut. They had no more food, and they were afraid to shoot game. So one night Kimani and Adam went down the mountain again, taking the women with them, until they came to a pasture where a herd of cattle grazed in the moonlight. They hid in the shadows until the herd swung close past, and then Kimani and Adam ran swiftly and mingled with the herd, which was alarmed but did not gallop away. Kimani lunged for a heifer, seized her by one horn, and cut her throat with an upsweep of a simi which Adam had found for him in the secret hiding place where extra guns and ammunition were stowed. The heifer opened her mouth to bawl but choked on her own blood, staggered, stumbled, swayed, and sank to the ground. Swinging his panga in a great sweeping arc, Adam scythed through the neck of another, this one a calf, and cut its spinal column. The calf fell in its tracks. They dragged the carcasses just inside the forest and butchered hurriedly, cutting off the hind legs and chopping them off above the knee, to make less weight. They ripped out the stomachs intact, emptied them of grass, and placed within each empty sac the heart, liver, and kidneys. They cut out the tongue and hacked off the rib sections from the calf. They scraped off as much fat as possible and loaded the whole bloody mess into the hides of the heifer and calf, the two women staggering along under the heavier load and the men carrying the smaller one. The hyenas and vultures would finish up the scattered remains, and there would be only a bloody rumpled spot on the ground by the time the birds were seen circling in the sky and a herdsman came to investigate.

They stopped in the forest after several miles and built a small fire, sheltered behind a large boulder so that the flame would not show, and broiled the viscera briefly on green sharpened sticks. The hearts and livers were eaten by the men, while the women roasted long fat strips of the large intestine, from which they had stripped the dung with their fingers while the men were butchering the cattle. They would all eat big when they got back up the mountain to the hut, gorging themselves for an hour or so and then sleeping until they awoke to gorge again. They would not gorge after the first feastings, because in the high cold forests meat kept fairly well and would last several days. It would be strictly doled and a part spread out on bushes to dry into biltong, to chew as emergency rations.

During the next weeks they moved camp constantly, and very often they visited, or were visited by, many other men and women. The camps of all changed constantly and were crisscrossed by a series of tiny trails such as a fox makes. Very seldom were the same trails used. Slowly, through confabs around the fires, Kimani learned the histories of his companions. This one had shot an askari with the askari's own gun when the askari had come to arrest him. Another had stolen money from his master and had gotten clean away. This one, the cross-eyed one, had murdered an Indian ducca-keeper in an argument over a pile of hides. Another had been sent to jail for burglary but had escaped and gone away. That one, the big one with the pock-marked cheeks, had killed his woman for refusing to bring him more beer one night when he was very drunk and angry. He had beaten her over the head with a stick until she died. He was very sorry about that, for she was a good woman as a rule. Adam, who seemed to be more or less the chief of the straggling band, was the only other fugitive who had killed a white man. But that was only a Greek and so did not count as high as Kimani's Englishman. Also, it had happened in Babati in Tanganyika, a long ways away.

Kimani learned that there was a sort of clearinghouse, an underground, for men of this category. It led from the native quarter of Nairobi, in the bazaars, to Arusha in Tanganyika, to Nyeri and Nanyuki and the other larger towns, and circulated through the little shambas of the squatters on white properties. In nearly every big holding there was a certain hut to which a man might go and find food and a way to get free into the hills. Kimani had been very lucky, since he had stumbled on a link in the chain of escape when he first asked food from the old man. The old man did not know about the hide-out in the hills, but his son, the truck driver, was an important fixture in the transportation corps.

There were many women in the camp. Some were the women of individuals, wives legally bought, who had fled with their men. But mostly they were women from nearby white-owned shambas, who drifted in and out, bringing food occasionally, and always news. There was no fighting over the women in the camps. They served as communal property. All a man need do was request the services of the woman of a friend, and the friend would beckon and nod to the woman, and the man would go with her into the hut. A woman was too unimportant a thing to make trouble over. Any woman could accommodate a dozen men in a day without disturbing the bulk of her basic work, since women were made that way. As a result there were several small children and babes in arms, and most of the women bulged in their bellies. Some had been on the mountain for three or four years.

It was one of the women from the white-owned shambas who one day brought news from Kimani's home country. She came puffing up the trail, staggering under a wicker-basket of beans and meal. She was the sister of Djuguna, who had been jailed for breaking into a clothing store in Nyeri but who had escaped his guards.

"Is there a man here called Kimani?" she said. "The son of Karanja, who is now in jail? He who speared the white Bwana?"

"Yes," Adam said, and called Kimani, who was sleeping in the hut. "Come out, Little Brother, there is a woman here with news for you."

"I have seen the man you speared," the woman said. "He came to my Bwana's shamba to eat. He is a great man with a red beard and black hair."

"Then you saw the spook of the man," Kimani said. "Because the man I slew is dead."

"This is not so," the woman said. "My brother, who works as kitchen mtoto in the house of my Bwana, heard all and told me. The man did not die. You struck him in the shoulder, and for a while he could not use his arm, but he did not die."

Kimani could not believe his hearing. He had thrown the spear truly, had seen it strike, and had seen Jeff Newton fall, his breast painted bright with blood.

"Then I have not killed a man," he said. "Did you hear aught else?"

"Yes, my brother heard much. He heard the red-bearded Bwana tell my Bwana that he had not gone to the police and was not going to the police. He said that the entire happening came from a mistake and that he did not intend to do anything more about it."

"He said this, truly? If he said this, then I am free to leave these mountains and return home. I will tell the Bwana Jeff that I am sorry, and then all will be as it was."

Adam spoke up. His voice was harsh.

"You are a fool, a stupid fool. Do you not know that all this is another white man's trick? He rides from shamba to shamba, telling his friends in a loud voice, so that all the mtotos and horse-holding boys can hear, that he has forgiven you and will not set the police upon you. This is nothing more than the usual white man's guile. If you leave here and you go back to the farm, the askaris will come and take you off to jail, and they will send you to the Kingi Georgi Hotel up North to work in the heat and stay in jail for twenty years. You will die long before your sentence is served, as certainly as if they had hanged you outright."

"But the Bwana McKenzie and his son, the Little Bwana, are my friends. Perhaps if I went back . . ."

"You cannot go back. Would you go back wearing the gun you helped to steal? How would you explain the gun? That cook would remember you, and the white police would ask you questions and would want to know where you stayed after you ran away. They would beat you with kibokos and you would talk."

"But if I did not take the gun? If I said I had run away to Tanganyika or to the North with the Turkana and Somali?"

Adam smiled wolfishly.

"You know the way up this mountain," he said quietly. "You know where we live and how we live. You know our faces and our names. You know the robberies we have made and the names of the people who help us. No, little-boy-who-thought-he-killed-a-bwana. You will stay with us for a long, long time. Maybe someday we will *all* go down the mountain. But when we do, we go together, those of us who dare."

Kimani lived for about a year on the mountain. The men and women changed camps always, but grew bolder and sometimes stayed in one place as much as a month. Occasionally a new comrade would come up an elephant trail, led by a woman or by one of the squatters in the nearby shambas. There was always gossip from below, much talk of stirrings in the shambas and of doings in the towns. The war was ending, the people said, the great war across the seas would soon be finished, and then the young men would come back from the labor battalions and there would be changes in Kikuyu. Word was spreading around the shambas of big medicine, and the names of Jomo Kenyatta and Jesse Kariuki and Joseph Kangetha were repeated more often. It would not be long, the runners said, before the big men who had been shut up for the length of the war, the leaders of the K.P.A., the Kenya Provincial Association, would be freed from the detention camps where the Serkali had put them because they advised the young men not to go and fight in the white man's war.

"I bear word," one man said, "that you will not live forever on this mountain as animals hide from the hunter. Someday you will come down to be useful in the new plan to drive the white man out of the country. Even now men come to the shambas to talk of plans which are making in Kiambu and Fort Hall."

The men had little to do but argue around the fires, when they were not raiding for food or weapons, and the raiding was less now, for one day the police had come and had caught some men in ambush and had shot two dead and wounded another, whom they carried away. It was told later that he died of his wounds, without talking. Increasingly, food was drawn from little hidden patches of cultivation which the women tended, and from supplies the women brought from the outlying shambas. Meat was obtained by trap and bow and spear, from small animals, and the old repugnance of the Kikuyu for wild game disappeared. The talk was ever of the white man and the theft of the land.

At first Kimani spoke a little favorably of the white man but was drowned by angry outbursts from the others.

"My father told me that most of the land on which the Kikuyu and the white man now live was once the property of the Masai, and that he remembers well when the Masai made a treaty with the white man and moved from the Laikipia to the South. And that he also said the Kikuyu were paid for any lands that the white men took."

"That is a lie," one young fellow a little older than Kimani said. "According to the old teachings, all the land this side of the mountain Kerinyagga belongs to the Kikuyu. And even if this were not true, land cannot be bought from the Kikuyu without consent of the clan. No one man can sell land."

"Ndemi is right," Adam said. "The land belongs to the clan. It must not be sold outside the clan."

"But my father said that we never used this land before," Kimani persisted. "If we never used it, how can we claim it if it belonged to the Masai and once to the 'Ndrobo and we didn't use it anyhow?"

"That is white man's talk, and it is well known that your father has ever been a great sympathizer with the white man," the boy Ndemi said. "We did not use it because we did not need it, but it was there for us to use. We did not need it because there were not so many of us then, and not so many white men."

"Yes." Another, older man spoke up. "That is so. We had been wasted by plague and pestilence and drought; we were only half our number then. Also, the white men were not so numerous. But they have no land where they come from, only cities, and when the war is finished, all the white men from everywhere will come here and take away the rest of our land and drive us off to starve. I have heard it said many times by learned men in the cities."

"Do you want to be taken away as the Masai were moved, to a land of lions and flies, where cattle and sheep cannot live? That is what they will do to us when they come. They will take us to Abyssinia, where the wild men cut the testicles from their enemies and roast them over fires for food. Or else they will take us to where the Masai live, and the Masai will kill us with their spears."

"But," Kimani said before giving up, "since the white man has come we do not have sicknesses to kill us all, or pestilences to wreck crops. The white man has put up hospitals to care for the sick, and I myself went to school and learned to read and speak English as well as any bwana. Had it not been for the business of the thahu I would be a clerk or a taxi driver or a gunbearer before long."

"This is fool's talk. What good does your knowledge of English do you on this mountain? All the things the white man brought are part of a plot. They wooed us with soft promises and corrupted our clan leaders, who took money and presents and sold off our lands so they could drive in motorcars and buy many wives. Then the bwanas built hospitals to cure us as a trick to gain our confidence. Once our confidence was gained, they gave us schools so that we might learn English and get good jobs. And once we had the schools and hospitals, then we were expected to go to churches and become Christians."

"Of course that is true," the old man said. "We could not learn English without adopting the Christian teachings. And what do they teach? That a man may not marry but one woman and still be a Christian.

That a parent may not sell his daughter for the marriage price, thus assuring himself comfort in his old age. That a parent may not circumcise his daughters so that they be decent women and command a good price. The white man has been very clever. He has separated us through cleverness. First he stole away the land and then he stole away our customs and finally he stole away our God. One day he will fall upon us in force and kill us all."

"These be truths, all," Adam said. "I have heard the same words from the mouth of Jomo Kenyatta himself, as he talked in his school at Fort Hall. Jomo Kenyatta is wiser than all of us, for he has crossed the ocean many times and has attended advanced colleges in the white man's country. He wears white man's shoes and writes learnedly in their language. He lives in a house like a white man. They say when he was across the water he even bought a white wife but left her because she would not work."

"But there are some good white men," Kimani said, "the old Bwana on the shamba where I lived . . ."

"There is no such thing as a *good* white man," the boy Ndemi said angrily. "My father was a very wise and clever mundumugu, and he has taught that there is no sin when you steal from a white man, and that you must always lie to a white man, and that to show fondness for a white man brings a thahu which will rot your crops and kill your children. You should know that well, Kimani. Your father was the pet of a white man, and you were raised as a white man, and now your father is in prison and you will go to prison, too, if they ever catch you."

Another young man spoke.

"I too speak English. I too went to a mission school. And then I went to work in a big hotel in Nairobi. First I started as a helper in the kitchen, and then I became a room boy and finally a waiter. Amongst the waiters were men as old as my father, men entitled to respect. But the white men called me 'boy!' and they called the old men 'boy!' as well. They called us all 'boy!' as I would call up a *pie*-dog. They talked in front of us as if we were not there. They looked through us when they spoke of us as Wogs and blacks and coons and niggers. The white women disrobed in front of the room boys exactly as if we were not present. I thought to steal enough money from the white people in the hotel to go away to Uganda, but I was caught and sent to jail. When I got out of jail I could not get another job because my kipandi had the jail record written on it, and you cannot get a job without a kipandi, and nobody will hire a man with 'jail' written on his kipandi. So I stole again and was discovered but got away and came here."

Having nothing better to do with their time, the men exposed their grievances like sailors penned at sea or old women huddled in a poorhouse. They were bound round by the mountains, trapped in an ocean of blackish-green trees. It was not so bad in the dry season, but miserable, freezing-miserable, in the rains, when the clouds sulked low and black and every blade of grass was sopping and every tree wept streams of freezing water. Then it was difficult to make fire, and they burned mostly punk from hollow logs and shrouded themselves in blankets that never completely dried. From time to time they all got sick and coughed alarmingly. One old man, two women, and three children died.

The rains went and came and went again. Kimani had shot up to full height and had stretched and toughened into a whiplash of a man, heavy-chested, with skinny but powerful legs. Next to Adam Marenga, he was the acknowledged cock-of-the-hill. He had fought once only, with the youth Ndemi, over some lengthy argument, and they fought with knives. The battle was stopped after both had been cut several times and it appeared that one was certain to kill the other. After that they left each other alone, bristling like dogs but, like dogs, successfully avoiding awareness of each other's presence.

It is probable that Kimani became a father several times in his stay on the mountain. Occasionally young women came into camp from the shambas and lay with the men, and the permanent women were used indiscriminately. They paid very little attention any more to the old rules governing sexual behavior. The young daughter of Adam conceived and bore a baby boy when she was barely fourteen. Kimani believed the child to be his, since he had lain with her, with more or less regularity, from the time her menses began. But there was no way of telling, of course. When Kimani was off down the mountain on a raid, some other youth would pass a night with the girl. In any case, it had no importance.

Occasionally one of the men would slip down to the shambas and spend a few nights in the least accessible huts of the ahoi, the tenant squatters on the big native estates, or among the native squatters on the white estates. These men always came back with tales of a growing, mysterious secret society that was being carefully formed against the day the young men would return in the confusion of the end of the war. These young men were called the "Forties" because their coming-of-age circumcision ceremony had taken place in 1940. It had something to do with regaining the land, and returning to the old customs, and driving the white man into the sea. Then each Kikuyu would have ample land for his sheep and the goats and cows, for they would divide up the white man's big shambas, and someday a Kikuyu, probably Jomo Kenyatta, would sit in the halls of Government House in Nairobi. Just how this would work nobody seemed actually to know, but someday the signal would come.

One day a man came, just as the sky wooled with rain clouds and the band was unhappily looking forward to another freezing season in the dripping hills. This man was running hard, panting with excitement. When he caught his breath and a woman brought him a gourd of beer, he called the men around him.

"The war has been over for several days!" he panted. "The English no longer fight across the sea, and our men will be coming back from Dar-es-Salaam and Mombasa, Burma and the other places they have been taken. Some will come back from all the way across the ocean, wise in the ways of the white man. I bring messages from Kiambu and Fort Hall. A man says that it will be safe for you to leave the hills after the rain, and you must go to the cities. The cities will be crowded with returning soldiers and everything will be confused and upset. You can lose yourself amongst the returned people. There is much money to be made, and the white men will all be returning to their shambas, eager to work their crops and cattle again. Many new people will be coming to the towns to live, and many new people will be taking up more land as a soldier's scheme. There is a duty to be performed, and we who know the hills and are violent men have our uses. We must get hold of the new-come Kikuyu who have been away to the wars and make friends. They can teach us much, as we can teach them. Some of us must get kipandis forged—it will be easy, there is an Indian in Nairobi who makes a specialty of providing false credentials—and we must go and find work on the shambas of the white men. There will be much work; in the confusion there will be few questions asked, and everyone will assume that we are returned soldiers. In any case, the white men will be greedy to hire us and will not look too closely at our faces, especially if we seek work far from where we first came."

"This is all very well," Adam said, "but for some of us our necks are at stake. Who is to say that one of our number, if beaten sufficiently, will not betray us and denounce us to the police? If some of us remain behind, who can say whether one of us may not, in fear or anger, lead the police to our hiding places? We may someday need these mountains again."

"That has been thought of," the runner said. "Behind me, more slowly, follows an oath-giver. He has sheep and the sacred githathi stone with him. He will slay a ram and we will swear upon the githathi stone that we are bound forever, or the oath will kill us."

"But we have women and children here," Adam said. "The githathi is never allowed women or children. Its power is too strong. Suppose some child betrays us, or some woman flaps her tongue?"

"That has been taken into account by the mundumugu. This is a new and terrible githathi, and it is applicable to the weakest woman or the smallest child who is old enough to understand the power of the oath. I am told this oath comes straight from Jomo Kenyatta himself, he who is chief of the organization which strives to return the land to the African. I am told he has sat in council with the wisest witch doctors in the land, and that they have sought permission from Ngai to make this oath, and that this oath will certainly kill anyone who dares violate it."

"In the old days," Adam argued, "the githathi was so strong that when a man subjected himself to swearing on the stone he was forced to castrate all his male sheep and goats and cattle and might not lie with his wife for seven seasons, because for seven seasons the stone would kill a man who lied. Now they wish to include women and children as well?"

"It is a new oath, much stronger than the old githathi," the man repeated stubbornly. "It has been consecrated by God and is more adaptable to today than to the old days. Through this oath we will get our lands back from the white man. It is a good oath. I have taken it. Many people have taken it on the shambas. It makes all the Kikuyu blood brothers rather than mere members of separate clans. The old man will come soon now with the sheep and the stone, and the oath will be given. Then, in sixty days, you may leave the mountain and come to the cities and the shambas, taking great care to stay away from where you are known and to keep to the crowds in the bazaars and off the white man's main streets in the cities. And one day you will get another message of great importance. I am going now. When the man comes with the stone and the sheep, give him beer and food and make him welcome, because it is a terrible oath."

And the runner got up and went back down the mountain.

16

In a few hours an erect, gray-haired man, whom Kimani recognized as the man who had first led him to the men on the mountain, came up the path, driving a small herd of sheep ahead of him. He herded the animals into the small glade and squatted by a small punk fire. The women brought him beer, brewed from maize that some one of the women from the farms had brought up. He drank and then said:

"Build an arch of leaves, the size of a small granary. You would not have banana fronds here, so any broad leaves will do. Find thorns and give them to me. Then fetch me here a ram. Ordinarily this would cost you ninety shillings each, but you have been paid for, since they know below that you have no opportunity to get money."

The women hastened to build the arch of leaves, thatched over saplings.

"Leave it open at both ends," the gray-haired man, Njogu, said. "Now bring me two long thorns."

He went over to the ram, which was being held, and with his fingers plucked out the eyes. The sheep blatted horribly. Then he slit its stomach and took out handfuls of the contents, mixing them with water and powders he trickled from a stoppered flask. Then he cut off the penis and the testicles of the living sheep. He tossed the testicles into the mixture, where they floated.

Njogu got up from crouching over the sheep and slashed off the top branches of a sapling, leaving a sharp spear-pointed end. He picked up the living sheep and hung it upside down, kicking and blatting feebly, with the weight of the sheep keeping it pinned through the loins to the slivered sapling.

He went over to where the sheep's eyes lay on the grass and skewered them to two long thorns, which he stuck on each side of the arch. He went round then to the basin in which the stomach contents and sheep's testicles were contained, and took the sheep's penis in his hand. He dipped the penis in the mixture and beckoned to Kimani, who was nearest. Kimani, frightened and unwilling, was pushed forward. Njogu pushed the sheep's penis into Kimani's mouth and then commanded him to spit out the bitter brown mixture, first to the right, then to the left, in all, seven times.

"Get down on your hands and knees and crawl into the hut," Njogu said, walking round to the other end and crawling in himself. He took out a black stone with seven holes in it, representing the seven orifices of the human body, and handed Kimani a length of mokengeria creeper.

"Pass the creeper through the holes and repeat after me the following words," Njogu said. "Now:

"If I am told to bring in the head of a European, I will do so, or this oath will kill me and all my family.

"If I am called by my brotherhood in the middle of the night and am naked, I will go forth naked, or this oath will kill me and all my family, and if I betray my brotherhood, this oath will kill me and all my family.

"If I see anyone stealing anything from a European, I will say nothing, or this oath will kill me and all my family.

"At all times I will say that all land belongs only to the Kikuyu, or this oath will kill me and all my family.

"If I send my children to Government schools, this oath will kill me and all my family.

"If I send my children to mission schools, this oath will kill me and all my family.

"If I am called on to rescue Jomo Kenyatta, I will do so, or this oath will kill me.

"That is all," Njogu said. "Who is next?"

Kimani, stunned by the enormity of his oath, watched in great fear as Adam sucked the bitter liquid and spat it out and crawled into the hut. He watched until every man, woman, and child above the toddling stage received the oath. All the while, the sheep bleated, still not quite dead, and the rain drove down as thunder crashed and lightning split the sky above the sodden forests.

When all the people were sworn, Njogu went over and took down the sheep, which had bled to death. He commanded it to be skinned, and it was partially cooked over a smoldering fire. Each person ate a portion. Then Njogu said: "I have not been up the mountain in a very long time. Where are the other shambas? I will need a man to lead me. *You*"—he pointed at Kimani—"I once led you to safety. You will lead me and the sheep to the other encampments, for everyone in the hills must be sworn."

Kimani went to a hut to get his rifle.

"That is a fine rifle," Njogu said. "Where did you steal it?"

"I stole it from the shamba of Bwana Riggs, there below," Kimani said. "It is a very fine rifle, but I have not yet had a chance to use it. But I have kept it dry, as the Bwana Jeff taught, and I have wiped away the damp with fat."

"You will have a chance to use it very soon, I think," Njogu said. "Lead on, and keep an eye out for elephant. I do not wish to scatter these sheep."

They plodded through the soaking wood, their feet squashing, their clothes wet-clinging. The sheep were no trouble, because the game path was wired round with thick bush, and there was barely room for a snake to slither along the path. Once, when they stopped to rest, Kimani asked:

"What is this brotherhood to which we have been sworn? What is it called?"

"It has no name as yet. It is but the beginning of a blood kinship which will bind every Kikuyu more tightly than a python holds its prey. It will make us one solid force against the European."

"I have heard the name of Jomo Kenyatta many times. I know he is the Kikuyu who went many years abroad to study the white man's ways and who runs the school at Fort Hall and speaks much in white man's council. Is he the chief of this new brotherhood?"

"No man knows who is the chief. Jomo Kenyatta is the head of the Kikuyu Provincial Association, and we are told that the Society of Three Letters and this new brotherhood are one and the same. This would make Jomo Kenyatta our mundumugu, and when I give an oath, the oath is given in the name of Jomo Kenyatta."

"When will the brotherhood be big enough to act in force against the white man? Will it be soon?"

"Not soon," Njogu said, starting to walk again. "We must not act until we are all of one blood and one mind. I have been told that some-day, maybe next year, maybe the following year, there will be a Night of the Long Knives, and when the bushbuck war horn sounds its signal, every Kikuyu in the land will rise up and strike down a white man. Then we will have lands for our own again, and men will not be put in jail for cutting forests and keeping too many goats. Enough talk, let us hurry on. Are we close?"

"Not more than half a mile more. We must spend the night there, because the next encampment is three hours away."

For three weeks they prowled the mountains, going from clearing to clearing, initiating people as they went; initiating and explaining. Of all the people for whom the sheep were slain and the ceremony prepared, only one old man dissented. The old man had watched the ceremony and was outraged.

"This is no true githathi," he said indignantly. "I will not be party to it. A true oath-giving takes place in broad daylight, after much preparation and discussion, and is held in the open, not in a hut, for all men to see and witness that it is just. Women and children and the sucking of an animal's genitals are a profanity, a defamation. Nor will I swear to be a murderer, nor will I swear allegiance to somebody named Jomo Kenyatta, whom I do not know personally, and who lives like a white man with his motorcars and white wives across the sea. I am an old man and I have seen many githathi, and this is more like the ceremony of an evil sorcerer than of a mundumugu. We used to slay evil sorcerers as we slew poisoners, by burning. I will not take the oath."

Njogu drew his panga from his sheath. He walked over to the old man.

"You will swear or I will kill you," he said.

The old man looked at him scornfully. "I do not believe you. If you kill me, my son will kill you."

"Your son has sworn the oath," Njogu said. "He cannot kill me, because we are one in the oath. One more chance, old man. Will you accept the oath?"

"I will not be party to such an indecency," the old man said. "Kill me, and at least I go clean to my ancestors, undefiled by contact with you or your murderer's oath."

Njogu glanced over his shoulder at Kimani and flickered an eye toward the rifle. Kimani slipped the safety catch. The fact that he had not levered a bullet into the chamber escaped him.

"One last, final chance," Njogu said, turning to the old man's son. "Can you make your father take the oath?"

"You must take the oath," the son said. "Else this man is sworn to kill you, and I am powerless to protest."

The old man looked even more scornfully at his son. "Hyena," he said. "Offal for jackals to eat. I will not swear."

Njogu swung the panga. It sliced into the old man's neck, cutting through the spine and nearly removing the head. The old man fell down, blood spurting thickly from his severed jugular. Njogu struck with the panga again, and the head toppled to one side. Njogu picked it up by the hair, carried it over to where the sheep hung upside down, and detached the sheep. He took the old man's head and impaled it on the sapling where the sheep had hung. Blood dripped and clung like a creeper to the tree. Then he wiped his hands and panga in grass. The son stared dumbly at the headless carcass of his father.

"So works the oath," Njogu said to Kimani, who stared, horrified. "Now let us get on with the ceremony. We have another clearing to make before nightfall."

There were no other dissenters on the recruiting trip. The word spread ahead, as if by magic. Conversion was complete, and Njogu, his sheep exhausted, went back down the mountain to his home on the cattle farm of the Bwana Ben Ritchie, for whom he worked as chief herdsman.

17

Kimani strolled the streets of Nairobi, keeping off main thoroughfares such as Delamere Avenue and Government Road, and as he walked he marveled at how many people there were in the world. Life on the mountain had accustomed him to the society of a very few. There had been many people on the shamba of Henry McKenzie, but they were not clustered together like flies on a sick ewe. There had been plenty of space for everybody, plenty of room to work in and much land to move around in. Here in Nairobi people lived in each other's pockets. Here people slept jumbled together into a stinking room. Here there was always the sweetish smell of offal and rotted vegetables. And here there was little or no friendship. If a man intended to eat he must have many shillingi in his pockets. If a man wanted to sleep he had to pay somebody for the place, and if a man wanted a woman, there was none of the old courtesy on the part of a friend, who offered his wife or daughter or sister as a social obligation. If you wanted a woman in Nairobi you bought a whore, some painted slut who counted her minutes in terms of pennies; who was surly and impatient if a man took too long at his task. Also, there was that other thahu.

Kimani was dressed very grandly. He wore an extravagantly cut green gabardine suit and a white man's hat with a red feather in the band. He had a red necktie and bright yellow shoes. He wore underpants inside his trousers, and there were socks on his feet. He had cut the toes out of his shoes, though, and the socks had frayed away from constant wear, so that what he really had on his feet was a sort of spats. Kimani no longer carried a panga. He had a pocketknife with a special mechanism. When you pressed a little button the blade leaped out, bright in your hand.

Kimani had been in Nairobi for six months now and had become very rich. He had shillings always jingling in his pockets and some more non-jingling money hidden in the mattress of the place where he slept. He had another suit and two more bright striped shirts and another necktie. He had a bicycle, and also gonorrhea. A woman had cursed him, had given him a thahu. The thahu was so strong that he wanted to scream with pain each time he urinated.

He was very shy about this new thahu, but one day when he was drinking beer with Adam Marenga both men got up from the grogshop to go and leak in the street, and Adam noticed that Kimani gritted his teeth and winced as he relieved himself. Adam Marenga laughed.

"Oho," he said. "So the little man from the mountains has acquired a city woman's gift. Does it hurt much?"

"Oh no," Kimani replied. "It is doubtless something that I got from some bad food. It is nothing."

"Bad food, bad food, my ass. You have a bug in your bowels that makes pus which comes out through your penis. This little bug lives off women and transfers itself to men, like fleas from a dog. The white mundumugus have a wonderful magic for it. They prick your behind with a hollow thorn full of magic liquid, which comes from the stomach contents of a goat, since it is yellow in color. As soon as your behind is pricked and the pain has gone away, then there is no more little bug in your belly. Come with me. I have a friend who works in the hospital here. He will steal us some yellow fluid and prick your behind with the hollow thorn."

This was the way it always had been since Kimani had come to Nairobi. There was always somebody to do something for you. He had needed a kipandi, for instance, so that if the police stopped him he could produce a working card saying that his name was Chege wa Kariuki and that he had never been in jail. That was how he had got the job as houseboy for an Englishman who lived out in the new housing development on Lower Kabete Road. Adam Marenga had a friend who knew an Indian who could forge a fine kipandi. The Indian wanted five pounds for the job, and Adam Marenga's friend reached into his pocket and pulled out a wad of pound notes, just as a white bwana might have done. He tossed a fiver at the Indian, and so Kimani had his kipandi. He wondered how he would be able to pay back the friend of Adam Marenga, but all the friend did was laugh.

"Someday you will have money," he said. Then he laughed again and winked at Adam Marenga.

Kimani had liked his job with the Englishman. The Englishman's wife was kind to him, and there were two little children, a boy of five and a girl of three, and Kimani spent much time playing with the children. He took his knife and made the little boy a toy spear and taught him to throw it. The little girl loved to ride on his back, belaboring his shoulders and calling him "horsie" while he pretended to buck and rear and prance. It was such a wonderful house, because the cook had a radio that he played all day long, and there were flowers in the garden and the food was plentiful and very fine. There were also, the cook pointed out, a great many things to steal, because the Bwana never locked up his liquor and the Memsaab never counted the sugar and tea and just looked at the laundry, never listing it. As the cook said, the Bwana was rich and didn't know the difference, so if a bottle of gin disappeared after a party, the Bwana thought surely his friends had drunk it. Since spirits were in short supply, a bottle of gin or a bottle of whisky—even the mixed whisky that came from draining half-finished glasses into an old bottle—brought a month's pay in the bazaars. An old undershirt that really wasn't good enough for the Bwana to wear longer brought more money, and you could always say that the laundress lost it. Tea and salt and sugar, if taken steadily, a teaspoon at a time, and cigarettes, if taken only by twos and threes, soon had a way of mounting up. That was how Kimani had got to be rich.

And soon he became richer. One day he met the friend of Adam Marenga in a teashop, and the friend of Adam Marenga said:

"I am told that your Bwana and Memsaab go now to Mombasa to spend the holidays at the beach. Is this true?"

"It is true. I have spent the morning packing their light clothing. They leave this afternoon."

"Very good. Then I will see you later." The friend of Adam Marenga laughed and walked away. Kimani wondered what it was he found so amusing.

Two nights later there was a *cooee* from the back yard. The cook had gone out, leaving Kimani in charge of the house. Kimani walked out into the yard to see who was calling, and there was the friend of Adam Marenga with two other men. He laughed again, because he was a jolly man and he always laughed.

"Now is when you pay me back my five pounds," he said to Kimani.

"But I do not have five pounds," Kimani said. "I bought a suit and I have made a payment on a bicycle to the Indian, and so I have very little money. Perhaps in one or two months I will be able to pay you."

"Oh, it's not necessary to wait that long," the laughing man said. "Your Bwana can pay me for you. Come on, now, and take us into the house. There will be clothes and guns and silver and other things that we can borrow from your Bwana."

"No, I will not," Kimani said. "He is a good bwana, and if you steal from him I will lose my job and then the little girl will have no horse to ride and I will not be able to make more payments on the bicycle to the Indian."

The laughing man laughed again and nodded to one of the other men. The man hit Kimani on the nape with a shot-loaded blackjack. He fell to the ground with a great burst of lightning before his eyes, his knees weak and slack. The laughing man kicked him in the stomach, gently.

". . . *Or we kill you*," he said, chuckling. Kimani got up painfully and shook his head. He led the men into the house. They searched it systematically, taking all the silverware and the two shotguns and the one rifle. They took the radio of the cook and all the whisky and cigarettes in the cabinet, which they burst open. Then the laughing man turned to Kimani.

"You have paid me," he said. "Now I will do a nice thing for you so that your Bwana will not be too angry and sack you." He nodded to the other man, who swung his slung shot again, and this time the light went out in Kimani's brain.

When he came to, his head hurting horribly, a steel band of pain round his skull, he was securely trussed with leather belts, gagged with a tablecloth, and lying on the kitchen floor. The cook found him there eventually, and the police were called. They were very rude to Kimani, but since his forged kipandi was in order and there were lumps on his skull, they finally believed that he had no hand in the robbery and let him go, after beating him a little to make him confess. Kimani had nothing to confess. He just said that some men had come and hit him on the head. The police could easily believe it, because robberies of this type were happening every day. The police said that the war had spoiled the Wogs. They had been so closely associated with the white people that now they knew what a Leica camera or a radio was worth to the Indian fences who ran the thieves' pawnshops.

The English Bwana came back to Nairobi from Mombasa when the police cabled him, and he told Kimani he was very sorry and not to worry, because the stolen goods, bar the whisky and cigarettes, were insured. He gave Kimani a pound in payment for his aching head, and Kimani took it to the Indian as another installment on the bicycle. On his way back home the laughing man came up to him, chuckling. He took Kimani by the hand, and when Kimani's hand came away, there was another pound note in it. The laughing man's eyes veiled as he laughed.

". . . *Or we will kill you,*" he said, and Kimani knew that if he had described the laughing man to the police, when they beat his feet with a kiboko, the laughing man would very likely not have given him a pound. The laughing man went away, laughing. Kimani took the pound and went to give it to the Indian. At this rate it would not be long before he owned his bicycle.

How easy it is to earn money, Kimani thought as he walked over to the shop to give the Indian the other pound. But it is too much trouble to steal things and then have to sell them, when there must be a way to get money without bothering about stealing stuff to sell.

He entered the little ducca where the Indian had the bicycles, and he noticed that when he gave the Indian the pound note the Indian put it in a little iron box with knobs on the front, twirling the knobs after the iron door had swung shut. It was not a very big little iron box. It might be easily carried.

Some nights later Kimani returned to the Indian's ducca. He had ten shillings more, from the sale of filched tea, to pay down on the bicycle. He handed the ten shillings to the Indian, and when the Indian turned to put it in the little iron box Kimani hit the Indian with a wool sock which he had filled with sand. The sock made a soft thump on the Indian's head. He fell to the floor, and the door to the little iron box stood ajar. Kimani reached in and took out much money, perhaps a hundred pounds in notes. A great deal of it was his own money, he thought, as he ran away into the night. *So now I will go to another*

Indian and buy a bicycle. It would not be very smart to take a bicycle from this Indian. Especially since I think I hit this Indian a little bit too hard.

Nobody in the police made much fuss about this Indian who had been hit a little bit too hard. When they found him dead the next day the police sergeant spat and said that was what you had to expect with all the bloody spivs back from the Army and that there were too god-damned many Indians in Nairobi, anyhow, living off rats and taking trade away from the white people. It was a pity about this one, for he was a pretty decent little bloke, but what was a man to do, run every Wog in Kenya to find out who hit one Indian a little bit too hard? A pure no-hoper. The Wogs never talked. They just played stupid and said that they spent last night in a shamba at Limuru, and when you said what shamba and where was it in Limuru, they said the shamba of the wife of the cousin of my uncle, and sure enough, when you went there, everybody said, "Oh yes, Bwana, Kariuki or Karanja or Michege was here all the last night, and we got very drunk and ate a sheep." It was a pity about the Indian, but there *were* an awful lot of Indians in Kenya, and more coming daily, because they bred a baby each year.

Kimani's bicycle not only had a basket, but a bell, as well. The bell made wonderful music, and he only fell off the bicycle a dozen times before he mastered it. It was a wonderful bell and a fine basket and a marvelous bicycle, every bit as good as the bicycle that Peter McKenzie used to have when Kimani was just a silly country Kikuyu boy and did not know how easy it was to make money if a man kept his wits about him and hit the Indian hard enough so the Indian wouldn't talk to the police the next day. Kimani observed with considerable distaste that his trouser bottoms had accumulated grease from the sprocket chain, and so he went to the hole in the garden where he kept his money and removed enough to buy some cyclist's ankle clips to confine his trousers at the foot and to keep them free of grease. He liked the shining clips so well he often wore them even when he was not riding his bicycle. They reminded him a little of the iron war rattles Peter used to wear when they were playing fighting games.

Nairobi was just exactly as the man who came to the mountain had said it would be. The troops, white and black, were back. The airplanes from Khartoum and Entebbe and Addis Ababa were crammed with people. Construction was booming in the town, and there was work for everyone who wanted it. But the work paid poorly, and a man was better to have a little easy job somewhere so that he could do other things in his off moments, and then when he had done enough other things it was silly to keep on working. So one day Kimani went to the English Bwana and told him that he was very sorry but he was going home to work on the shamba of his father and look around for a wife. The Bwana gave him an old suit of clothes and wrote something on his kipandi to the effect that Kimani had been a good and honest servant. The baby girl wept when he left, because now she would have no horsie to ride, and Kimani was very sorry to leave. But a man as rich as he, with a bicycle and money hidden away, should not run and fetch and carry for bwanas until all hours of the night. Also, he did not like to be called "boy!" Kimani was so moved at leaving the little girl who called him "horsie" that he did not steal anything important when he left—nothing except one packet of cigarettes and one of the Bwana's very old neckties.

He went off to the bazaar to live and found a house which was operated by the widow of a distant kinsman. The widow rented her room irregularly to many young Kikuyu, and she was glad to find a steady occupant. Kimani gave her a pound note, and the room was his for a long time. It was a pretty good room. It had a broken mirror and a mattress on the earthen floor to cushion away the cold, and even a rusty chamber pot. He took some money from his hoard and went to the duccas and bought a folding campstool. He pinned pictures torn from old magazines to the wall, because Kimani loved beauty. He sewed his money into the mattress and began to live the life of a gentleman of ease.

The first thing he did in the new easy life was to start a card game. Gradually it became known that gambling was available in the room of Kimani in the home of the widow. Kimani charged a small percentage of the stakes for the use of his room, and the old woman went off to fetch beer and, if anyone was hungry, food as well. There was a slight extra charge for this, and soon Kimani was able to get the widow to move to a bigger house, where he would have a room to live in as well as a room for gambling. He took his pictures and folding campstool and the rusty chamber pot with him. He no longer had to trouble about the bicycle. He got just a little drunk one night and forgot to bring it into the house, and some thief stole it. Kimani thought at first of going to the police but decided against it.

From time to time Kimani would see Adam Marenga, who seemingly had grown very prosperous. Adam said that one day pretty soon he would have some important news for Kimani. He puffed a cigar as he spoke, and patted his stomach. It was getting to be a long time since they had come down the mountain, walking all the way from the mountain to Nairobi and hiding fearfully at first, until they saw that there were so many strange people in town that one face more or less made no difference. It was difficult to believe that once they had hidden in the hills like hunted animals, afraid to mingle with men.

Adam came one day to his room, where Kimani was thinking on the mattress after a hearty dinner the old woman had made him.

"The day of the Long Knives is approaching, Little Cousin," Adam Marenga said. "Soon now the sound of the war horn will be heard. There has been a big decision in Kiambu, a decision by Jomo and some other people, including Jesse Kariuki. There is work for you to do. Much work."

"What sort of work?" Kimani was not especially interested. "I have enough money. I make as much as ten shillings a day from the card games. I now have three women who come here as well, and from their earnings I make another four or five shillings without doing any work. When I need more money I can always steal it, as you taught me on the mountain. Why should I work?"

"You remember the oath you took on the mountain before we left?"

"Surely. I also remember the old man that Njogu killed so needlessly. There was no reason to kill the old man."

"That oath, my young-friend-who-thought-he-killed-a-bwana, is going to make you master of that Bwana's farm one day. That oath has grown, little Bwana-killer. What was once a thieves' pact is now big politics. You come with me. We go to Kiambu to see some men. One is an Indian. One is a strange white one who has come from Addis Ababa. He is what they call a Russian, although exactly what is a Russian I do not know. He smells badly of garlic, they say."

"How do we get to Kiambu? I am not going to walk, **Russian or** no Russian."

"They have sent a motorcar for us," Adam said. "For the love of God, man, this is important. Do you remember your enemy, Ndemi? He is now a very important man in this council we go to visit. Watch your tongue or they will cut it out. You have been chosen for big things."

18

The conference was notable. They went to the house of a very important Kikuyu, a man of much education and travel. He wore a tweed suit and had a short gray beard. They sat like white men on chairs in the parlor of this man, drinking tea, and a servant came to pass cigars. There was the white man that Adam had called a Russian, who had come down from Addis Ababa, where the Russians ran a big trade ducca. There was one Indian that Kimani had never seen. His name was Mr. Dass. The Russian was called a tongue-twisting name that sounded almost like Peter. The conference was brief and to the point. Kimani was glad to see that his old friend Njogu was there, and not so glad to see that Ndemi sat on the right hand of the educated Kikuyu. Ndemi frequently interrupted, and the Russian and the Indian, Dass, and the important Kikuyu gave him serious consideration.

The foreign-educated Kikuyu puffed at his pipe like a bwana and said:

"For many years I have been planning a thing which will return all the land which is rightfully ours to the Kikuyu people. I have planned it through politics and through trade unions and through the friendship of thieves and other men who have gotten into trouble. I have looked for a few good men to help me in the planning and I have found some." He bowed graciously toward Kimani and Ndemi and the Indian and the Russian whose name was something like Piotr and who smelled of garlic, as they said.

"I have men now in Tanganyika and men up North, from Thomson's Falls to Nanyuki to Isiolo, and men over the border of the Northern Frontier. This white man from Addis Ababa is one of us, and he will help us, because he can buy us guns in Abyssinia and will smuggle them to us here in Kenya. This Wahindi, Mr. Dass, will assist us with other guns and ammunition. What I want now is headmen to help me organize for the day when we will take the guns and the ammunition and the knives and every man who can call himself Kikuyu will strike on signal and kill a white bwana. That day is not soon. It needs organizing. I want you to listen now to the white man who comes from Addis Ababa.

Once I spent four years in his country, which was very cold but very well organized. The wa-Russias understand organization very well. This wa-Russia does not speak Kikuyu, but he will tell you some important things in Swahili." He gestured at the Russian.

The Russian spread his hands, tensing his fingers as a man warms his hands before a fire.

"My friend," he said, indicating the foreign-educated Kikuyu, "knows my country and my people. Once, a long time ago, some people like your white bwanas ruled my country. They had askaris to beat the poor people with whips and to tread on them with horses. Everyone save a corrupt few was very poor. The few were like the bwanas here. They took the land and made the people work and killed the people if the people did not obey them."

"What color were these cruel bwanas who mistreated your people?" Kimani couldn't help asking the question. "They must have been of another race."

"Shut up," Adam Marenga said. "Don't interrupt."

"No, it is a good question and one I am pleased to answer," the wa-Russia said. "These people who ruled us were of our own blood, but they were landlords all, and we were only ahoi. So one day we rose up and every man struck truly and at the same time and we killed the corrupt chieftains. We killed them without mercy, and we killed their wives and children, and their mothers and fathers. Now everyone in my country is equal. Everyone has much land to till and there are Ford motorcars for everyone and we dance very much and there are radios and similar things in every home. No man is the master of the other, no man the slave of another. This man"—pointing to the host—"has spent four years in my country. He will tell you that what I say is true."

"It is true. What the white man says is true," the educated Kikuyu said in his own tongue. "You may believe anything he tells you."

"There is one thing I should like to know," Ndemi said. "If he is white, why does he want to help the blacks? Why does he come from his cold country all the way to Kenya to aid people he does not know? What does he hope to get out of it?"

"That is a question which would take much answering. You must understand that the hearts of the wa-Russias are kind and that they wish the entire world to live in the same freedom and riches they now enjoy. Hence they send men all around the world to help people overthrow their masters so that all people in the world may live in freedom and happiness. Also, the wa-Russias hate the English bwanas. The English bwanas were close kinsmen to the corrupt chiefs who trod on the necks of the wa-Russias for so long a time."

"When the wa-Russias help us to gain our freedom, will they stay in Russia or will they come here and replace the English bwanas and make us work as the English bwanas do, and take away our lands for their own interests? Also," Adam Marenga said, "what does the Indian, this Wahindi, what does he want? There are many Indians in Kenya. They do not like the black man. What do the Indians stand to get out of it?"

The educated Kikuyu rubbed his pipe bowl on his nose and smiled. "Mr. Dass will tell you," he said.

Mr. Dass spoke in a high, squeaky voice. He had buckteeth, and he bubbled slightly as he spoke.

"We have had the English foot on our necks for many years in my country," he said. "The sahibs took the money and the land and they treated us like pariah dogs. We could not enter their hotels or their homes except as servants, and they beat us when the mood struck them. They corrupted our rajahs. But little by little our might grew, and now the English are afraid of us, because we are many millions against their few, as the Kikuyu are millions against their few. Soon our country will be free of the English raj. One day the black man and the brown man will rule the whole earth. We are brown men, we Indians. We wish to aid the black man, as the wa-Russia wishes to aid the black man."

"I still don't see what the white wa-Russia has got to do with black people," Kimani said. And this time the much-traveled, well-educated Kikuyu spoke angrily, quickly, in Kikuyu.

"Close your mouth, fool," he said. "The wa-Russia has motives of his own. He is selling guns and he hates the English, and someday he wants Africa for his own. We will only entertain him to use him. Then we will kill him as any other white man. And he knows how to organize. Keep your mouth closed and listen to what he says now, because it concerns the job you will do. Speak," he said to the Russian, "and tell them how you wish this to be organized."

The Russian looked at each man in turn.

"I am told," he said, "that some of you have sworn an oath which binds you strongly in brotherhood, according to the customs of your people. This oath is now and can be your most powerful weapon in the battle against the English. It is signed in your blood; it will kill you if you betray it. This I have been told.

"But any oath is valueless unless it is administered on a practical basis. In my country we have a secret organization called a 'cell.' This cell has a chief and subordinate chiefs and, at the bottom, a mass of people who do what is told them by the chiefs and the sub-chiefs. Such can be possible here with your oath. At the head of all the cells is our friend here. Under him are sub-chiefs for all the cells. And each cell must be run by a man who is dedicated and ruthless in his aim. That aim is to bind every Kikuyu in the country to a blood oath, so that no man dare betray another, so that at a given moment all will arise as one and smite the enemy. So it was in my country.

"Now the man who administers the binding oath is the chief of each cell. There are several things to consider here. One is that the oath-giver must be diligent; thorough. No man or woman or child must be allowed to refuse the oath, otherwise the whole thing is finished. If a man refuses the oath or pleads loyalty to a bwana, he must be killed."

Kimani looked at the gray-headed Njogu. He remembered the day on the mountain when Njogu slashed the head off the old man who would not take the oath. Njogu looked at Kimani and smiled, almost tenderly.

"There is much money in Kenya now, and we will need money to buy guns and ammunition from Mr. Dass and the wa-Russia," the pipe smoker interrupted. "Listen to what the wa-Russia has to say about that. The fees," he added, pointing with his pipe. "Tell them."

"Each oath-administrator of a cell," the wa-Russia said, "must demand ninety shillings from each candidate for the oath. Of this fee, the oath-giver retains thirty shillings for himself and turns in the balance to the central fund. This allows a man to become rich whilst he is preparing to free his country from oppression. More; when a good young man who is intelligent and quick to punish those who do not reason, when such a man comes into view, it is wise to tell him: 'Brother, you must go now and start your own cell. You too can retain thirty shillings.' And when that young man finds another young man of equal talent, then the second young man splits off and starts his own secret clan. If all goes well, one year will see every Kikuyu in Kikuyu-land bound together by an unbreakable oath, one nation united against the English. Also, a clever oath-administrator can get enough money to buy a motorcar."

"But"—this time it was the young Ndemi who spoke—"will people listen to young men—about the oath, I mean—when they know that the young men are not ordained as mundumugu and so the oath might have no significance?"

The well-educated, much-traveled pipe smoker nodded to Njogu.

"Yes," the gray-haired Njogu said. "The people will respect the oath-giver if certain steps are taken. If a man dies for not taking an oath, his brother accepts the oath. If the first-born son of a man be taken to his father, lacking one hand, with a panga poised over the other wrist, that man accepts the oath. Moreover, if this oath be a departure from all the old rules of ancient oath-giving so that a recipient of the oath is expelled from his old customs and societies, does it not then argue that the man is outcaste of his tribe and must depend on his new brethren for strength and support? We have investigated some features of old oaths against the new, as young Kimani here can tell you."

The well-traveled Kikuyu cut in. He pulled at his beard.

"The strength of any society is mutual dependence and much discipline," he said. "Without discipline the structure falls apart, as a hut collapses in a high wind if the foundations are not firm and the ridgepole is not securely fastened to the posts. There is no room for weakness in such an effort as we now will implement. A man must prove his discipline and devotion. If he is asked to kill his father or his brother, if the father or the brother does not accede to the demands of the many, then he must take his panga or his gun and kill his mother or his father. Otherwise we have no organization; all we have is a beer-drink.

"This must be impressed on the people who take the oaths," the cultured Kikuyu continued aside in Kikuyu. "They must be impressed with several things. One is that they become outcaste from their tribal structure when they accept the oath. One is that they have nothing, nothing whatsoever, to protect them except interdependence on each other. One is that they must be strong and harsh; this is especially necessary in the case of some Kikuyu who have an exaggerated sentimental feeling for some white bwanas. There have been cases of bwanas and memsaabs who have gained affection of their servants. To exhibit a sense of stern devotion and disciplined thought, this is most important: A man must kill those he loves to prove that he is not weak."

"He is right," the gray-haired Njogu said. "I know, and Adam Marenga knows, and certainly Kimani wa Karanja knows that the easiest entrance to a white home is from the back yard and through the back door which leads to the kitchen. You will find that very often there is a cook or a houseboy or a headman who is so addled with sentimental foolishness about his Bwana and his Memsaab that he will say 'No' when you come in the night. It is well to allow him to say 'No'—once. Then when you leave one half of his second-born son stuck on a pole outside his hut, he is not apt to say 'No' again, for the first-born is still running about and laughing. In this instance"—and Njogu nodded almost apologetically—"I claim a little firsthand knowledge. Kimani can tell you that after the thieves' oath on the mountain, after just one slight objection was made to the communal good by one foolish old man, we had no more trouble with the oath-taking."

"That is true," Kimani said. "After Njogu cut the head off the old man there was no more difficulty about the oath-taking. Not even from his own son, who stood by as Njogu killed the stubborn old man."

The young Ndemi spoke.

"What is it exactly that you wish us to do now while we wait for the war horn?"

"I want recruits to recruit recruits," the much-traveled pipe smoker said. "I want my strong young men" (he used the old word "njamas") "to go out to the shambas and into the bazaars of the town and organize a brotherhood so terrible that not to be a member of it is worse than being hanged by the Serkali. I want terror, subtly administered in one case, violently applied in another. I want symbolism, and I want three chieftains killed eventually. Waruhiu is one; he, the great friend of the Serkali; Hinga is another. We will choose the third later. When the time comes I want each man in my trust to strike at the English family which he has known most well. But mostly now I want many new members of the secret society, and I want them after a few foolish people have refused to join us and have died rather rudely for the refusal and have been hung upside down with their guts dripping from their slit bellies."

"What he wants is organization," the garlic-smelling white wa-Russia said. "In this way there is much organization. This must be remembered: Those who are with us are bound forever to be with us; those against us die, and as painfully as possible. There must be no weakness. If a white man befriends you, kill him for his friendly weakness, to prove your own strength. If a Kikuyu presents an obstacle to the success of your venture, kill him as coldly as you would kill a snake, but more slowly. And it is best, when this killing starts, to leave behind a sign. This was found to be effective in my country. A strangled cat or a cow with her teats chopped off or a disemboweled dog upended on a fence post makes a good, strong, memorable, effective signature. The organization of terror must ever clutch at the imagination. Mere death is not enough. Symbols are needed here."

"Speaking of symbols," Kimani asked timidly, and frightened, "speaking of symbols, do we have a name, this brotherhood?"

"Yes," the well-traveled, well-educated, gray-bearded pipe smoker said. "We are called Mau Mau."

"Mau Mau? Mau Mau? Meaning what?"

"Meaning nothing whatsoever," the well-traveled man said. "But it is a very short name and will fit nicely into the newspaper headlines."

"What he says is very important," the Wahindi said. "In India much use was made of the newspapers to attract attention to our fight for freedom. When Gandhi-ji went to jail and struck against the raj by fasting, the news was printed in all the papers of the world, and especially in England, where most of the people are softheaded fools, not like the hard men who come here to colonize. The people in England and in America will read of your struggle here, and so will the people of Russia and India. There will be much sympathy for your cause, and one day Kenya will belong to the Kikuyu again. Perhaps the Americans and the Russians will even send guns and money to aid you."

"It is exactly as the Indian says." The wa-Russia nodded. "When the doings of the brave men of the Mau Mau resistance are known, many journalists will come here and the story of your struggle will be heard around the world. There will be much pressure on the Home Office in London, and even a big trade union called the United Nations, which sits in council to champion the rights of free men, will exert more pressure to withdraw the bwanas from Kenya, so that the land may be governed from within by the people who own it."

"Why was this not done before?" the young Ndemi asked.

"That is easy. For many years in the past England was a power in its colonies because of the long rule of cruel, greedy men called imperialists. They made their might and their wealth from grinding men of other colors in the mines and mills and forests of all their properties in other parts of the world. Englishmen who never saw India became rich from cotton and tea. Englishmen who became rich from rubber had never seen Malaya. They lived softly at home and sent brutal overseers to force work from the natives of other lands. But now their day is done."

"I have seen it with my own eyes," the much-traveled Kikuyu said. "You may believe me. England no longer is strong. She was crushed in the war with the Germans, when the German airplanes came over daily and bombed the cities flat. She has lost most of her young men and all of her wealth. She is a weakling now and will not dare oppose us. Moreover, a new body of rulers has come to power, a party called Socialist."

"What is a Socialist, exactly?" Kimani asked. "How is he different from the bwanas as we know them?"

"An excellent question. A Socialist is exactly as we were in the old days. Under Socialists all property is communal, even as the clans once owned all the land. The Socialists work as a unit, each man to his task, and each man sharing the country's wealth. This way there is less work and more cattle for all. Also, the Socialists are men of peace and are horrified by war. Thus they are easy to trick. When we create a great commotion here, there will be a concerted effort by the Socialists to end the killing, and we will have our freedom, even as the Wahindi are getting their freedom."

"It sounds a fine plan," Kimani said. "But what exactly now do you want us to do?"

"As in the old days, there is a plan for everyone, such as when the children tended the flocks and the smiths made weapons and the women tilled the fields and brought wood for fire, as the young men fought and the old men sat wisely in council, drinking beer. There is work here for a mundumugu and work for the mathanjuki and work for even an Athi, for we shall need much skill in the forests and much guile and bravery.

"For instance, you, my young Kimani. There is a special task for you, of which I will tell you in a moment. And you, my young friend Ndemi, and you, Njogu, and you, Adam Marenga. You are all mathanjuki now, as once there were mathanjuki to instruct the young men in tribal lore and in the preparation for circumcision, which bound us as one man in one people and in which lay our strength. You will go forth as mathanjuki, to teach. But now you will teach Mau Mau, as once the old men taught a design for living within the structure of a clan."

"Am I not very young and unwise to be a mathanjuki?" Kimani was disturbed.

"Not for your special kind of instruction," the much-traveled Kikuyu said. "Yours is a very special task. You must go to Tanganyika, to Arusha, where there are other Kikuyu and the Waarushas and other tribes, and you must start your cell there. The amusing thing is that your cell will begin in a cell. You are going to jail. And when you are finished with jail in Arusha, you will come here to Kiambu and report to me. You will spend two years in jail."

"But what good can I do in jail, especially as a mathanjuki?" Kimani was stubborn and puzzled. He did not want to go to jail. "I have been spending the last several years trying *not* to go to jail. I got into all my trouble because they put my father in jail."

"You will go to jail first because I order it, and if you disobey orders you will be killed. Your duty is to go to jail, but for a very important reason. Do you remember the time you spent on the mountain with Adam Marenga and that Njogu led you to safety, and that you hid in the mountains and learned to steal guns and kill cattle and escape the police? Do you remember that you learned many things on the mountain, things of use, and that you swore an oath to bind you as brother to the other men and women on the mountain?"

"Of course I remember. But I did not like it on the mountain either. The mountain was like a jail, except it was much colder and very much wetter."

The much-traveled Kikuyu was patient. He puffed at his pipe for a second and said to Kimani:

"Jail is very important to us. In jail you will meet many men. They will be men who have stolen from the bwanas, and they will be angry at the bwanas. They will be men who have committed acts of violence against the bwanas, and they will all be angry men, eager to learn your teachings. Each man you meet in jail will be your disciple, because you will tell the men of the Mau Mau, and you will swear them to a special oath within the jail. The men will have women and relatives outside the jail, and when each man leaves the jail he will be a mathanjuki as well, and will then swear his people to the proper oath."

"It will be very difficult to give an oath in jail," Kimani said. "The slaughtering of a ram or goat will be impossible to arrange. Also, there are no huts or arches or other equipment. Also, the jailers will be sure to take notice."

"That has been thought of. You will swear the words to the oath, and then you will bind the other men to the oath by a very simple procedure. You know, of course, that in the history of our people sexual relationships between men and men or women and women have always been strictly forbidden, under pain of ostracism from the clan, for to receive the attentions of another man puts you forever in his power and allows him to curse you at will."

Kimani's eyes rolled backward in horror. He could think of nothing to say.

"You know that even if a man spits on you, the possession of his spittle puts him in your power. If he obtains a scraping of skin or a paring of nails, he is your master. This being true, you will practice sodomy whilst in jail, each man in turn leaving his seed in the body of the other man. In this way each man is wholly bound to the other."

"But this—this——" Kimani was overcome by the enormity of the order. "This makes me forever outcaste from my people, my clan, the Kikuyu people . . ."

"We *are* the Kikuyu people. We create our new nation *outside* the old structure. These are new days, needing new methods. When all is over and the white man is killed or driven away, then we will purify ourselves and all will be as it was. This now is for the greater good, and it is necessary that our men be forcibly removed from the protection of the clans, so that they depend only on each other. You remember the mountain. You took the oath. And you took the penis of the sheep into your mouth, an act forbidden by all rules of the tribe. This is similar to that. We *must* be outcaste, and finally we must *all* be outcaste. And the only way to become outcaste is to endure a strong violation of the old rules. You will go now to Arusha. Transportation has been arranged. You will stay there a few days, and then you will commit a crime— some theft or other from a Greek or a Portuguese or an Indian—and you will do it clumsily and will be caught. You will go to jail for no more than two years. You will practice sodomy to bind your people. You will probably have to kill a man or so if they object, but that is easily done in jail, and you will not be caught if you are crafty. Go, now, there is a lorry waiting. Here is ten pounds. More will come to you from time to time. If you bribe some of the jailers, you will be able to get better food and drink, and perhaps you may turn some of the jailers over to our cause. That is all. Go to the lorry."

"And perhaps"—the wa-Russia grinned as the men shook hands all round—"jail will not be so bad. I am told that if you are in prison long enough you come to prefer the society of men, especially young men, to that of women."

"Keep your mouth shut," the pipe-smoking, well-traveled Kikuyu said. "This is no joking matter. Good luck to you. Good-by, and remember that you were never here—or your oath will kill you surely. I can promise this to be true."

19

Kimani went to where the lorry waited. He did not crawl out from under the sacks until the truck had passed over into Tanganyika. He was given shelter in the home of a man on a coffee shamba outside Arusha and the next day went into the city. Kimani found a bicycle shop run by an Indian and beat him up, after first talking long enough to make sure that the Wahindi would be able to identify him. Then he took a bicycle and left it where the police would be sure to look, prominently displayed in a bazaar. When the police saw the bicycle, Kimani admitted ownership and produced a false kipandi. The police took him to jail, and when the Indian came he identified Kimani as the man who had beaten him and had taken the machine out of the door. Kimani was sentenced to two years in jail.

After Kimani had left, the well-traveled, pipe-smoking Kikuyu gave swift orders. To Ndemi the orders were exactly the same as Kimani's, with a minor exception. Ndemi was to commit a crime in Isiolo so that he would be put in the jail for hardened offenders in the Northern Territory. He was to use sufficient violence to get at least two, perhaps three years, and so it seemed best that he get into an altercation with a white man and perhaps strike him or threaten him with a knife. The men in the northern jail would be ripe subjects for recruitment. They were tough men who knew how to use guns and knives, and would be trained to the North, where a man might flee and be safe in the vast reaches of the wasteland. Also, there would be guns smuggled in from the North, guns from Ethiopia, and the aid of some Somali raiders and smugglers would need to be enlisted.

"That is where *you* come in," he said to Adam Marenga. "You will make some arrangements at the Frontier among the Somali. There will be no difficulty in slipping past the guards on the road to the forbidden territory. It is best to join a band of Somali and choose some men. You will have no difficulty. The Somali are always in trouble with the District Commissioner, and there are many men amongst them who hate the British."

To the gray-haired man Njogu he said: "You have known your task for a long time. You will go from shamba to shamba, explaining our purpose to the young men and giving oaths to everyone. You can choose your own assistants from the men you administered oaths to on the mountain. When it is necessary to beat or kill one who draws back from the oath, you know your business better than I can tell you. That is all for now. This parley will be repeated tomorrow night and the next and the next and the next, until our people blanket the country as thickly as wildebeests in migration dot the plains. Only one thing must be insisted on; no man is to act until I give the word, and the word is passed, and the hour set, and the war horn heard. Then shall every man arise and perform his appointed task against the whites—some slaying, some burning, always robbing, and always butchering cattle and leaving your sign. I bid you good-by and good luck."

The Indian and the wa-Russia remained behind for more talk as Ndemi, Njogu, and Adam Marenga went out into the night. Two lorries were waiting to take them to their destinations. Ndemi and Adam Marenga went together in the back of one lorry, bound north for Marsabit, while Njogu headed back toward Nairobi to look for some old friends in the bazaars. His was a vast task and would need many assistants.

The three men in the house talked on into the dawn. It was a tremendous organizational job and would call for a great deal of time, because the uprising could not be functional until the majority of a million and a quarter people had safely been initiated into the Mau Mau ranks, so that no man or woman or even child would inform against another and all would offer aid, according to the statement of the oath. There would have to be very much killing at first to impress the Kikuyu who did not want to take the oath that they would die if they did not accept it. As they rose to go to bed, the educated Kikuyu tapped out his pipe.

"When this succeeds within the Kikuyu tribe," he said, "and when the other tribes—the Nandi and the Wakamba and the tribes of Tanganyika—see what we have done against the whites, they will be eager to join us, and we will stretch in power through Uganda past the Congo. We will hold Tanganyika and extend into Rhodesia. We will go west as far as Ethiopia and north past the Tana River to Lamu. We will flow south and meet our kinsmen as they surge up from the Cape. Africa then will be back in the hands of its own people. Any who resist us will be killed."

The wa-Russia smiled to himself. He was an old hand in this business. He could imagine now how pathetically easy it would be, with the English gone and three hundred different tribes making war on each other, to walk in and bring order out of chaos. It had worked before and would work again. All you ever needed was just a little simple nationalism and a few old customs to pervert, when you dealt with simple people, and they would do most of the dirty work themselves. Of course he did not say these things to his host or to the Indian.

"Good night," he said, and went off to bed.

Kimani did not find his work difficult in the jail. For one thing, he immediately encountered two oath brethren from the mountain and confided his orders to them. The force of the three made it unnecessary to kill anybody. One knifing and a head-bashing or two brought all the men in line, even those who objected violently to the details of the initiation. As time went on there was less objection to the binding part of the oath, and Kimani and the others found that a man might slake his animal appetites on the body of another man quite satisfactorily if no women were available. And so gradually another strong bond, apart from the bond of the oath, was linked to each man. The nights were long and, except rarely, the men were not kept in separate cells, but in barracks. The sounds at night sometimes reminded Kimani of the noise goats made in a hut, snuffling, grunting, and stirring endlessly.

Since practically everybody in the jail was the owner of half a dozen different names, the men gave themselves titles, especially those who had served with the British in the war. They called each other General, and Colonel, and Brigadier, and Major. One Kikuyu called himself Marshal. The majority of the Tanganyika blacks were not so sophisticated and called themselves by the names of Lion, Buffalo, and Elephant.

The talk at work and at meals, and later in the barracks, was always of the day when they would go free and rush to organize their own units. Kimani had told them much of what the Russian and the Indian had said, and they were fascinated. They thought Kimani was a very important man.

"When it is over and the bwanas are gone," the General said one day, "I'm going to buy an airplane and learn to fly it. Then I will fly to Russia to see if what you say is true."

"If the bwanas are all gone," the Major pointed out, "who will teach you to fly the plane, and where will you get it in the first place?"

"Oh, flying a plane is very easy," the General said. "I have had it explained to me. It is much like riding a bicycle. You must keep the wings level so that the plane will go straight and not wobble, and you must press the pedal to make it go fast enough so that it will speed through the air. It is exactly like a bicycle. If you do not go fast on a bicycle and do not maintain balance, you will wobble and fall off. As to where I shall get a plane—why, I will order one from England when I sell my crops and cattle, after I have taken the shamba of a bwana I know near Dodoma, who grows coffee and tobacco and is very rich."

"I do not want us to kill all the bwanas," the Colonel said. "I want one to work for me as my overseer. The bwanas know much of work, and work harder than women. Also, I should like to try out a white woman in bed. They are ugly to look at, with white skin like a dead fish, but they tell me they are constructed differently from our women and have an utter lack of shame."

"What *I* will do when I am rich," another man, he called Lion, "is to buy a railroad, so that I can drive the locomotive. All my friends may travel free, and some I will allow to pull the tail that makes the train scream in pain when it comes to the crossings."

"This is all fine talk," Kimani said, "and I have no doubt that it will all come to pass, but we are not out of jail as yet and the war is not begun, let alone ended. First we must concentrate on obeying orders before we go buying airplanes and locomotives. You, Buffalo, and you, Marshal, go free next week, do you not?"

"That is what the turnkey has told us."

"You are the first of our group to be free. It is your duty to start immediately with your relatives and friends, and it is more impressive if everyone takes the oath together, as in a circumcision ceremony. I will describe to you the oath as it was given to me, and I would suggest that you persuade an old and trusted man in one of the shambas to be the oath-giver. It will have more seriousness that way, instead of coming from a jailbird. You may retain our special feature for the jail for use with the young men if you wish, but I would advise that the women not be told about it. Women are peculiar about such things and might not join willingly if buggery is a part of the ceremony."

"Are there more instructions?"

"Yes, one thing more. As soon as you discover a good man who is diligent and intelligent, send him out to another part of the country to start his own group. Here I suggest that the shambas of the white bwanas are more important for recruiting work than our own shambas. We will not have much difficulty with the shambas of our own people, but the people who work for the bwanas, and especially the squatters, will be more difficult to convince.

"The wise man with the pipe in Kiambu has explained this to me. He says that the squatters, who are afraid of being kicked off the white man's lands, are most likely to resist. But at the same time, they are important, because they are a link between us and the white people. They will help us to steal, once we are brothers. They will burn barns and maim cattle. They will inform of the bwanas' comings and goings and, what is most important, they will hide us and feed us right on the bwanas' shambas if we need shelter or food or refuge. It is especially important, as well, to force the cook and the house servants into the brotherhood. I remember from my raiding days on the mountain, the Number One is always trusted and usually has keys. The Bwana will come if the houseboy or the cook calls him into the yard at night to kill a cobra or to see to a sick horse. The cook will let us in the house, and the houseboys will help us get away and even go away with us. Yes, the men and women on the shambas of the bwanas are the most important of all, or so the man in Kiambu told me."

"Good. I understand. But who was this man in Kiambu of whom you forever speak?"

"I do not know his name. I was told only that he was very close to the great Jomo Kenyatta, that they are as brothers, and that he, like Jomo, also had traveled widely and studied much of the white man's ways in other countries. The wa-Russia seemed to know him very well, and he spoke with great authority."

"He sounds to be a man of much importance. I will do what he counsels when we go free."

20

And so the men went among the shambas of the simple country blacks, and the released criminals went to the cities, where they boasted of their experiences in the jails and as fugitives and found ready ear among the young, rootless men who had left the farms and were clustered in the cities as houseboys and car boys and yard boys—as part-time pimps and spivs and petty thieves and corner loafers. The young men back from the war gave readiest attention to the organizers, for they had worn warm clothing and eaten food from tins and sampled the white man's grog and tobacco. They had been made to do awful things by the white non-commissioned officers, even so far as disposing of offal and burying the dead, a thing of great defilement. They had been kicked in the pants and sometimes struck with sticks, and always they had been shouted at. There was no room on the shambas, and insufficient work to do, and not enough money to buy a wife, and no place to raise a family, save as a squatter on white man's land or a squatter on some relative's land. And relatives, especially the richer ones, were growing more and more unwilling to accept sons of younger brothers and sisters to crowd in on their land. There was little or no skilled employment available to the young men, and only unskilled work of a kind they hated—lifting things, tugging things, carrying things. So the young men hung around the bazaars and at night they stole to sell to the Indian fences. The white households of Nairobi again put bars on windows, and the housewives took to locking up the salt and sugar and tea and to counting clothes, because the old, condoned pilferage had changed into organized robbery. Guns, once left casually in cases, now were locked away, because they had mysterious habits of disappearing the second a back was turned.

These young men took eagerly to the Mau Mau teachings and were initiated in mass groups in shambas just outside the town. Only then did they look more eagerly for work in white houses and for white enterprises. Only then did they start to trickle back to the shambas, to ask for jobs on the holdings of white men, dropping in to visit relatives and friends, and ever sitting around the fires at night, talking in spellbinding fashion of the new day that was coming, when every Kikuyu would be a king.

Always the same refrain was hammered and hammered: "The white man has stolen your land. He has taken your joy from you and surrounded you with rules and regulations. He will not let you keep goats or cut the forests. He is stealing your children away from your authority through mission schools and Government schools. When all the children are educated and speak English they will turn on their parents and scorn them. Also, they will marry as white men marry, of their own accord, and fathers will be cheated of the bride price. Already and for many years the white bwanas have sought to steal your children's hearts and bodies from you. See, the Serkali says that it is bad to circumcise young girls and that young girls may defy their fathers and receive protection from the Serkali.

"They have taken away tribal law and replaced it with a white man's law, where a man who knows nothing of our ways sits on a bench and gives out judgments, putting you in jail or hanging you if he decides he does not like you. They have given you a white man's God and they have told you that to marry more than one woman is not permitted by this God, although when the children go to the mission schools and read in the Big Book, it says often where the favorites of the white God in days long ago had many wives. Their God is a God who always changes his mind, and you cannot depend on him not to curse you.

"They will not let us dance or fight or do anything that we used to do. They do not allow us our simplest ceremonies. They have stolen our pleasure and our law and our children and our God and our land. Where once they were few they are now many, and there is less and less room for us to live in. The day is soon at hand where either the white man must go or we must go. Already the white man is planning to move us to another country, as once they moved the Masai, and they will either kill us by poisoning or sell us as slaves to other tribes, to be used as beasts of burden. But Jomo Kenyatta, the leader of the Kikuyu, and his wise friends are cleverer than the Serkali. They have thought up a way to deliverance."

This was always the talk as they squatted around the fires, drinking beer and eating, the fire highlighting their greasy lips and striking sparks off their black faces. Hands would hook out toward the cook pot and eagerly seize a chunk of sheep or goat, because these emissaries seemed always to have money, and they often brought a ram or some beer for a feast. Then the drums would thump softly, and later hands would clap and men would sing, as they used to sing, but quietly, ever so softly. And they danced again, the old dances, but quietly, and secretly, and in out-of-the-way clearings or patches of pasture.

And old men who had not been active in soothsaying for many years suddenly became popular again, as men brought presents of beer and chickens in return for questions answered from the divining beans ngajé. And among the younger boys and girls, preparations for circumcision, held quietly, were made, and later there were mass ceremonies far from the main house, in the forest or by the river, and the young girl who said no, she would not be circumcised, felt the weight of her mother's hand and the punishment of her father's staff.

Through a miscalculation it took much longer to reach the ears and pique the interest of the simpler natives who still held their tiny farms on the slopes and ridges near the forests and the mountains of the reserves, but the new doctrine roared through the ranks of the squatters and the part-time city workers as flame sweeps a field of dry stiff grasses before the rains. Each white farm soon had its own nucleus of Mau Mau, each farm its own oath-administrator. Initiation ceremonies were held secretly and with a minimum of noise around Nyeri, Thomson's Falls, Kiambu, Thika, Rumuruti, Nakuru, Mwega, Naro Moru, Naivasha, Nanyuki, and Nairobi. There was little opposition. Njogu had done his spadework well. His muscular young men traveled from shamba to shamba, speaking gently, suasively at first; firing the people's imaginations with fine, robust talk, spending much money on beer and sheep for feasts. In the cases of objection, the persuasions were numerous and simple. One grizzled headman who angrily refused to endorse an oath-taking on the farm of Holly Keith's father, and who ordered the organizers away, swiftly saw his huts burn and his sheep savagely mutilated. He went straight to Holly's father, and Holly's father went to the police, but by that time the young men had disappeared; nobody seemed to know where. And one day soon the old headman went into the bush, hunting lost cattle, and two men leaped upon him. They sliced him into small bits with pangas and then stuck his head on a pole over the minced remains of his body. After that, months later, when still other young men came to the Keith shamba, the initiation ceremonies were quietly held with complete co-operation.

Word of the doings came to the chiefs, Waruhiu, Nderi, and Hinga, moderate men who had for a long time been attempting to work out an equitable solution to the mutual difficulties of black and white in Kenya. The chiefs conferred gravely with the police and with the district commissioners and provincial commissioners, and efforts were made to trace the fountainhead of the growing secret organization. But the ancient adherence to oath kept lips tightly shut. Those who had been sworn could not talk on any account. Most of those who had not been sworn lived in daily terror of death or mutilation if they talked, and this apart from their deep-seated natural disinclination to bear witness against any of their race, whether the charge was merely murder or the theft of a pound of tea. And so Mau Mau seeped outward from the cities, soaking through the shambas, and penetrating into the bush, until Mau Mau, still passive and nearly invisible, washed over the White Highlands.

The whites noticed, only gradually, tiny changes in the black people with whom they daily came in contact. In Nairobi the young Kikuyu dandies were seen more often on the large thoroughfares and were a little less eager to move out of a white man's path. Service in the hotels which employed Kikuyu was less smilingly swift and the servants intangibly more sullen and vaguely impudent. The field work on the shambas was performed more slowly. "I don't know what the devil's got into Gathiru—he's positively cheeky these days," was said by everyone in the clubs when the men gathered for sundowners. "Else he's sulky. It must be something to do with the war. I'm told it's like that everywhere these days."

The oaths gradually adjusted to meet special needs. Thousands of young men received a special group oath which ordered a youth to an eventual, approximate military service. The first oath, generally administered to man and woman alike, sometimes was given in three stages—sometimes in seven, according to convenience. The forest oath, which had begun long ago on the mountain to guarantee a protection of secret hideaways, arms, and ammunition, slowly increased in its perversion. Steadily all the oaths went underground, being held in huts for secrecy, whereas formerly all of the differing seventy-some Kikuyu swearings were conducted in the open, honestly, by daylight, or else were considered illegal and unbinding. Under Mr. Dass, the Indian, more Hindus entered into the supply web and active abetment of the underground. Under Piotr, the wa-Russia, more white men came down from Addis Ababa and from across the seas to sit on advisory council. For them especially a third, less primitive, oath was devised, basically political in nature and free of animism. These pacts were sealed by the strangers together with senior members of the council.

The well-traveled, well-educated Kikuyu from Kiambu held a steady communion with his subordinates. He impressed on them the necessity of holding the Mau Mau belowground until he could safely count on a tremendous majority of all Kikuyu, a stout allotment of fighting supplies, and finally some stark, unusual incident that would excite the men to fervor and force them into one blazing frenzy. He already suspected what this event would be. The Duke of Gloucester was coming out to Kenya to confer official city status on Nairobi, in the name of the Crown, and Princess Elizabeth was to visit Kenya with her consort, Philip, for a tour of the country. Among the other places she would visit was Nyeri, where her honorary lodge had been built. This would be violently explosive stuff, since the visit could be attached electrically to the endless Kikuyu clamor over land. The presence of the royal party could easily be sold to the unsophisticated as further sinister intent of the British to alienate more of the Kikuyu holdings, although the pipe-smoking world traveler knew as well as Kingi Georgi that all the lands which had been called Native Reserves and Crown Lands now were permanently held for the Kikuyu under an organization called the Natives' Land Trust, with its ordinance already written on the records, heavily through his own past effort.

The young Mau Mau, the recruiters, and the intended warrior group fidgeted and grumbled constantly.

"What are we waiting for?" they asked each other. "We have arms and knives. We have spread out among all the people in the towns and in the shambas. We are more than ready to rise now. What are we waiting for? Why do we not strike?"

But the pipe smoker from Kiambu was not quite ready. He knew from his daily reports that a good many of the firmly converted Christian Kikuyu and a surprising number of unconverted old-fashioned Kikuyu had not yet accepted his doctrines, even under threat. He knew that the three respected chiefs, Waruhiu, Nderi, and Hinga, were strongly against him. They had steadily conferred with the P.C., and more than once the police had come to break up mass meetings in the outskirts of the towns. The pipe smoker repeatedly sent admonitions to be patient, to wait, and much more grumbling followed. The days stretched always longer, endless for the men with guns and axes and knives, with caves to hide in and secret places in the forests.

21

Kimani sat in the jail, eating his plate of gruel. He had only a few short months of his sentence left to serve. He had done his work. There had been many turnovers of prisoners since he had allowed himself to be caught by the Indian whose bicycle he had stolen. All the men had taken the oath. Not many had been true Kikuyu, but several hundred men of Tanganyika's tribes had graduated as brothers in the oath. At least two of the warders had also taken the oath, and as a result, life in jail was relatively easy. It was one of these warders, a transplanted Kikuyu, who came to Kimani that night as he finished the evening meal. He led Kimani to one side and whispered in his ear.

"Word has come that you are needed in Kiambu," the warder said. "You are wanted in Kiambu urgently. You are to break jail and go there, by walking through the forests and exercising extreme care."

"Breaking jail is much easier said than done," Kimani said. "This is a very stout jail. Did the message say how I was to go about it?"

"Certainly. First, here is some money—ten pounds. There are other clothes at a certain spot in the forest, in a baobab tree, which I will tell you how to find. Late tonight you will pound the bars of the cell and set up a great outcry. I will come to see what is ailing you, and you will moan that you have a tremendous pain in your stomach. I will take you out of the common cell and you will hit me over the head as we pass toward the outer doors. Hit me very hard and bind me with my leggings. Then you will take my keys and let yourself into the jailyard, where you will find the other jailer, who also is our brother, waiting for you. He has stolen the keys to the main gate, which was not too difficult. He put something in the jailkeeper's tea which will give him a very sore head in the morning. It will be morning before your escape is discovered, and you should be far on your way by then. Since your time is nearly up, they will not make too much effort to follow you, since you are a Kikuyu in any case and will probably return home. They will very likely sack me for letting you go, and in that event I will see you someday under other circumstances. Remember. Call out loudly and hammer on the doors. The rest is simple."

"I thank you very much," Kimani said. "But to keep you out of trouble, I had better steal something from you. What have you got that is worth stealing?"

"I have these handcuffs that I bought myself," the guard said. "When you escape, take these. They are a prized possession, as everyone here knows."

"You are my true brother," Kimani said. "I will take the handcuffs, for I have long admired them."

It had been just that easy. He had hit the warder and tied him up and opened the door and gone into the yard, where the other warder had let him slip through the gate, and he had gone two miles to a big baobab tree and there, aloft in a hollow, were the clothes. He had buried his prison garb and put on the other clothing, but the tennis shoes were too small, so he had slashed them with the knife he had also taken from the turnkey when he took the handcuffs. And now all he had to do was walk to Kiambu, but he thought maybe he would stop off in Nairobi first, just for a short time. It was safe enough in the bazaars, and it had been a spell since he had seen a woman. Mau Mau oath or no Mau Mau oath, a man was no true substitute for a woman, not even in jail.

When Kimani reached Kiambu he avoided the town and went deviously round to where he remembered the important Kikuyu's house was. It was late, but there were lights burning in the living room. He went out past the back yard and into a patch of thatched huts. Nobody was awake there. Kimani did not know exactly what to do. It was dangerous to go to the house without first sending a message. He did not dare risk making à mistake that would involve him with the important bearded Kikuyu who smoked the pipe and was educated and well traveled. So he did an intelligent thing. He crawled under the high flooring of a side porch, arranged some flowers to hide his burrow, and curled himself into a ball. He slept until the sun rose high in the sky. There was nobody in the back yard. He scuttled out from under the porch and ran swiftly to a grove of trees, which covered him until he could approach the huts from behind. A few women were going about their early-morning chores. He called to one politely from the cedar grove, stopping at the edge of the clearing.

"I come a long way," he said. "I am hungry. Will you summon your man and ask his permission to give me food?"

"My man is still in his thingira, sleeping," she said. "But I will wake him and ask him if I may give you food. Where do you come from such a long way?"

"I come from Tanganyika," Kimani said, believing as he said it that he was expected.

The woman's eyes widened. She scuttled off to call her man. He emerged blinking and scratching his ribs.

"My wife says you have come from Tanganyika and you are hungry," he said. "What is it like in Tanganyika?"

"It is very tiresome in Tanganyika, especially in Arusha," Kimani replied. "I have had nothing to do for two years, nearly, and finally the boredom was too strong and I came here."

Comprehension lit the sleepy man's eyes.

"We have no food here. I will take you to a place where there is much food, and better food. It is not far. Come with me."

Kimani nodded and followed. They walked a mile or so through the forest and came to a solitary hut. The man hooted and a familiar face poked out of the door. It was Njogu, Kimani's old friend, the gray-haired man who had led him first up the mountain. They exchanged greetings gravely as old friends long separated. Njogu nodded and the other man went away.

"Well," Njogu said. "It has been a long time, little-boy-who-thought-he-killed-a-bwana. Much has passed since then. I have heard reports of you, and you have done well. How was jail?"

"I didn't like it," Kimani said. "It was full of lice and the food was terrible. Also, one gets weary of the society of men. I would rather be on the mountain."

"Well spoken, my old friend," Njogu said. "Because that is precisely where you are going. I will explain as we go, but first you must eat something, because we will have to walk a bit in this forest to meet another lorry, and we do not have much time. Here is much food, with the compliments of the master who lives in the big house back there. It is food from a ducca. He thought you would need a treat after your long stay behind bars. He sends his regrets that he cannot see you, but it is too dangerous. The Serkali is watching him keenly."

The food was excellent, and Kimani ate greedily. There were tins of sardines, and cold tea with much sugar, and a potted red meat, and sweet biscuits, and a sack of candy. He devoured it all and wiped the sweet biscuits into the oil of the sardine tins. He mopped his mouth and turned to Njogu.

"Why did they want me so soon?" he asked. "I had only a few more months to serve on my sentence, and then I could have come free without breaking loose. It was no trouble getting out, of course, the guard was a brother in the oath, but I had to walk all the way in these shoes when I might have taken a bus if I had not been fleeing."

"They need you on the mountain to be a leader. The young men there are becoming weary of waiting for the bushbuck horn to sound and are becoming bolder in their raids on cattle and their thieving forays. They have many leaders, and many leaders are worse than none at all. Each group operates independently of the other, and the men in high council are frightened that the young bucks will do something foolish before we are completely ready. *Your* friends, and the friends of Ndemi, who went North to jail, are proving difficult to manage. They have come from the jails to the mountain, which is a sort of jail, though more uncomfortable in some ways. They itch for action. Their blood is hot. They have guns and nobody on which to use them. They have knives and, like small boys, are greedy for something to cut. Personally I do not care much for jailbirds, with some exceptions," Njogu said politely.

"What is expected of me on the mountain?"

"You will be joined soon by Ndemi, who is coming in from the jail in the North. You two will command the men on the mountain, because most of them know you and know Ndemi and will respect your orders. You will kill whom you must to keep peace, even though they be your blood brothers, for a new oath has been prepared to safeguard forest fighters and their supplies. You will administer this oath jointly with Ndemi. Those who are with you will take it. Those who disagree are ejected from your former brotherhood, and you are free to fall on them and kill them. I will explain the oath to you later. It is quite an unusual oath."

"I had hoped," Kimani said as they walked along, "to have some time in the cities and to take myself a regular woman. I am weary of running away. I am weary of jails and mountains and whores and fellow prisoners."

"This too has been thought of. After the first work is done you will have a very pleasant time on the mountain. Out of gratitude for your work in prison, my youngest daughter, Karugi, has been bought from me by Him"—Njogu jerked his head backward toward the big house—"and she will accompany you to the mountain. You will live with her in a big, dry cave where most of the stolen arms are kept. The arms as well as the men are your responsibility. You have been chosen for big things, my friend. Someday you will be a bwana in this land and drive in your own motorcar. That is, unless you are weak and allow the strong men to spoil it with their impatience."

"I can wait," Kimani said. "How old is this wife of mine that I have never seen? What does she look like?"

"She is just fifteen. She was born thirty seasons ago from the last rains. She is very fat and works hard. She will be a great comfort to you on the mountain. I was very well paid for her. She fetched three hundred shillings and a pair of blankets. That is a very big present from Him on the hill. You should be properly grateful."

"This is very good," Kimani said. "Now I do not mind so much going up the mountain again. Will we have the thirty days allotted for the wedding celebration before I start my duties on the mountain?"

"I am afraid not," Njogu replied. "Your work is most urgent, and these days we do a lot of things from necessity that we never did in the past. But you will find that there is plenty of food now in the hills, and your cave will be warm and dry. You will of course travel much, and perhaps you will have to choose some strong young man to lie with your wife and protect the arms when you are off to visit the other caves and shambas. Do you remember the mountain?"

"I remember every game path and bush in those mountains," Kimani said. "Sometimes I used to feel as if I, not Ngai, made them, I know them so well."

"Do not be blasphemous," Njogu said. "Hurry along now, and save your breath. We are not far from where the lorry will stop whilst the driver looks to see what ails his motor. He will have his head deeply buried in the hood when we climb into the back. It is a closed van, full of furniture, so we should travel comfortably."

22

The mountain doesn't change much, Kimani thought as he walked ahead of his new wife, choosing unerringly the old animal trails which were as familiar to him as Race Course Road had become when he lived in

Nairobi. *And this is a very good woman that they have bought for me.* She is strong and sturdy and fat, and will be warm in the cold nights, when the rain pelts down. I have not had a chance to talk to her yet, but she does not seem displeased to be going off with me. Doubtless her father has told her I am a very important man. And so I am, Kimani thought, or I would not be going up the mountain to organize a herd of thieves and murderers and jailbirds—*as I am myself,* he thought, *a thief and a murderer and a jailbird.* It is just that I have never been caught except on purpose, and that gives them confidence. I wonder what cave they've got the guns in. I will wager I know it; if it's the one I'm thinking about, it is not too bad. "Ho, Njogu," he said over his shoulder to his father-in-law, who walked behind the girl—what was her name?—Kimani had to think for a second; Karugi, that was it. "Is the cave the same one, very high, about ten thousand feet—that I found once when the police came halfway up the mountain and we wanted a new place to hide the guns?"

"That is the one. It is a very good cave with a high ceiling and a dry floor of rock."

"Yes, that is indeed a fine cave. One can stay warm and dry in the back of it and also protect the guns, just as we used to sleep next the goats when I was a small boy. Karugi can cook in the front, and the smoke will drift out like a scattered cloud and will not be easily seen. That is a fine cave. I am very happy about it."

"It is well protected by rocks and trees from the front. Unfortunately there is no clearing in which you might grow any food. But that is just as well. You can send Karugi for food to other shambas, and food will be brought you from the shambas on the plains below the mountains. We do not want raids now. We want much silence on the mountain whilst you and Ndemi train your men into a semblance of order. We want fighting teams as we used to have the raiding teams, two or three or four good men who are used to each other's company and who know exactly what they want to do."

"Why do I always have to work with Ndemi?" Kimani spat, and paused to rest. The girl came up behind him, and her father drew up to one side. It was very heavy going now, and even the men were forced to take some bundles from the girl. She was a handsome girl; sturdy-legged and big-bosomed, with beautiful square teeth like sugar in her mouth.

"Because he is a young cockerel such as yourself. It is a compliment to you both that you hate each other but that you do not let that hatred come in front of your duties. You are both men to be trusted, even with each other."

"If he were not my brother in the oath I would kill him," Kimani said. "I do not like the man, nor do I trust him. Someday he will betray us. I feel it. Let's be moving on."

They walked for two days up the mountain before they came to the cave. They had passed other tiny shambas, isolated, scraggy huts, and were met cautiously by many men Kimani knew. He was greeted as a brother by the men he had sent from the prison. To all he said they would return in a few days' time, and they plodded on. They took no time to sleep; only a short time to rest. It was too wet and cold in the high Aberdares to rest very long; it was much easier to walk and know that at the end there were warmth and protection from the dripping trees and clutching brush.

They came startlingly onto the cave. If Kimani had not found it once long ago by tripping and falling into a wide crevice which was thatched over by packed bush, he might never have known it was there. A bluff of gray stone masked its entrance in the rimrock, in an L shape, leaving only a slim passage between the bluff and the little weedy patio which stood before the actual entry. There was much dense green bush, and immensely thick mountain bamboo clustered all around, like packets of telephone poles. Stumbling through the bush which covered the slanting roof of the cavern, Kimani had literally fallen headfirst into what was now to be his front yard. It had completely overgrown, of course, since he had last seen it, but Njogu parted some close-clung bamboo and showed a low tunnel in the bush which might be crawled through and which led behind the bluff and into the little yard. The entrance proper was a triangular hole about four feet high and three feet wide in the middle. Rocks were piled loosely in front of it as a mask, and these rocks Kimani and Njogu and Karugi removed swiftly. It was dark inside the cave, and Njogu flashed his torch inside. The ceiling was no more than five feet high at its maximum height, and that was close to the entrance. As the cave reached backward it widened in the shape of a funnel and was roughly forty feet across before it thinned again and ran into stark rock. It was possibly a cave in which the Ngumbu, the aboriginals, once had lived. Its floor was lumpy stone and was almost level. The walls had knobby excrescences and some flat projecting planes that streaked the sides like shelves. Stooping, Njogu walked to the back of the cave, and the light of his torch showed stacks of rifles and boxes of ammunition.

There were also boxes of provisions, tins of fuel, and two or three objects which proved to be Coleman lamps. Njogu picked up one of the lamps, lit it, and adjusted its turnscrew. The light flared like phosphorous, hissing, and choked the cave with glaring whiteness. Kimani saw then that there were many, many guns and some few pistols, a big wooden box full of pangas, and a rude bed of blankets folded onto a crisscross netting of leather thongs stretched tautly across a wooden frame.

"This is very good," Kimani said, looking about him as Njogu set the lamp on one of the flat shelf-like abutments of rock. "It is very dry, and if Karugi lights her fire there in the entrance, it will fill the cave with warmth and show no column of smoke at all. The smoke will float out in wisps."

"Yes, it works very well," Njogu said. "There is some firewood back there by the guns, Karugi. Go and fetch some and we will make a fire here, just by the door. It is always cold in this cave, even in summer. You will need always a fire, and Karugi must go every day to search for fuel. Even if the wood is wet, it will dry inside the cave, and you can always be warm. But she must never cut fuel close by the cave. Nothing must be cut or changed within a mile of the cave."

Karugi went to the back of the cave and returned with an armful of wood, some of which she began to arrange in a low-sided pyramid.

"Wait," Kimani said. "There is one thing we must do. We have had no proper wedding. There has been no courtship, no dancing, no ceremonies, no beer-drink, no proper payment of bride price—no nothing but a long wet walk up a mountain. At least we can do this one thing properly. Come, Karugi. Let us go and choose your hearthstones, as my father selected his cooking stones for my mother, and my grandfather before him."

He smiled at Karugi and held out his hand. She smiled timidly back, and together they went out the low doorway.

In the little clearing Kimani straightened up and looked about him. All he saw at hand were the loose cobbles which had been piled up to block the entrance.

"These will have to do," he said. "They are not proper hearthstones from the river, smooth and hard, so as not to crack under heat, but they are all we can manage now. Here, there is a good one, and there, another. I will take them inside and you bring another when you find it." He picked up the two small flattish stones, taking one under each arm, and crawled back into the cave. Karugi followed with another of similar size, and then she arranged them in the correct triangle and laid the fire. Her father produced a match and she lit the tinder beneath the wood. The fire caught, flared, and began to snap. Little flames danced high.

"Put out that light," Kimani said. "It is much too bright, and we must save the paraffin. Also, I like the firelight better in a cave. You do not see so much of the cave, and then it is not so much like a cave as like a hut."

They squatted on their heels before the rude hearth, warming themselves and watching the fire shadows dance on the walls. The cave was now all soft black except for the little circle of golden light and a tiny faltering streak of daylight from outside. Karugi got up, and they heard her fumbling with the huge pack she had carried up the mountain. She returned with an iron cooking pot and a canvas bag of meal and some dried black strips of meat. Then she went back again to bring a calabash of water and some drinking gourds. They had filled the calabash from a spring a mile or so down the mountain. She mixed the corn meal with the water and placed the cooking pot on its short legs over the hearthstones, and then she went again to the rear of the cave and brought back a pannikin and a paper bag of tea leaves. As she put the tea on to boil she smiled again at Kimani.

"I have brought something for the wedding ceremony myself," Njogu said. "Girl, go and fetch my greatcoat. It is back there on the bed."

He took the coat from his daughter's hand and removed a paper-wrapped parcel from a side pocket. He stripped off the paper, tossed it onto the fire, and held up a shiny bottle full of clear liquid.

"Beer is difficult to carry a long way," Njogu said. "This is gin. It is very expensive, but it does the work of twenty times that much beer. We will have a wedding celebration after all." He passed the bottle to the girl, and she poured a third of it into a drinking gourd and handed it to her father. She looked at him from under her lids.

"If you do not wish to live with this man," her father said, "I shall not drink." He was paraphrasing the old engagement ceremony. "I shall pour this drink upon the ground."

"No, Father, do not pour the drink upon the ground," Karugi said. "Drink."

Njogu drank and passed the cup to his daughter, who took a swallow and who then passed it to Kimani, who had a long pull at the gin. It flashed like lightning through his throat but reached his empty stomach in a sunburst of warmth. They sipped at the gin as the meal cooked, and by the time Karugi announced the dinner ready, the gin was two-thirds gone and they were quite drunk. They ate the posho porridge with their hands from the cook pot and chewed greedily at the black leathery strips of biltong. They drank tea which tasted reminiscently of the gin that clung to the gourds, and then when they finished the tea they drank the rest of the gin and became much drunker.

"I will sleep now," Njogu said thickly. "I am drunk, as a man should be at a wedding. I will sleep on a blanket here before the fire. You and I, Kimani, must go some places tomorrow to see some men. We will leave Karugi here to watch over the guns. She will be safe from harm if she does not stray too far from the cave. Take your woman to the bed now, and rest. The bed is small, but it will always be big enough for two." Njogu chuckled and stretched out on the knobbly floor.

Kimani walked in the blackness toward the bed, holding his wife's hand. He cursed when he barked his shin on the sharp corner of a chest of ammunition or supplies. He took off all his clothes and did not bother to remove the money from his pocket. He felt the handcuffs cold in his coat and took them out and hurled them toward the rear of the cave, where they struck a gun with a ring of steel. He felt his way onto the rude bed, naked, and found his wife already there before him. She lifted the blanket to admit him, and he could feel the warmth that her body had already begun to spread beneath the blanket. She drew him to her side, and with a deep, almost sobbing sigh Kimani went immediately to sleep. The girl held him close and presently they both began to snore, their bubbling snores mingling with the chested grunts of Njogu as he lay curled in his clothes before the faintly flickering fire.

Njogu roused early and left the cave to reconnoiter, first calling Kimani to explain his absence. Sleepily Kimani stirred on the bed and then became conscious of the body beside him. It was very warm, very soft, and fitted sweetly into all the curves of his body, held so closely that he could feel the raised welts of his scars pressing into her flesh. The girl was still asleep but came gently awake when he turned her body and buried his face in the soft hollow between her throat and shoulder. She murmured something unintelligible and then drew him to her with arms that suddenly clutched him fiercely, nails biting into his shoulders. As Kimani took her to him he felt, for the first time in his life, a peace so violently tangible that it was almost pain.

23

They left the cave early, Kimani and Njogu, as they once had traveled at the time when Njogu came with the sheep and the new oath, when Kimani was only a boy and had fled to hide on the mountain. Kimani told Karugi to stay within the cave, except to look for wood and water in the mornings, until they returned. "We will not be many days," he said. "There is plenty of food and you will be warm and safe."

Karugi nodded and displayed no emotion as her husband disappeared into the black, dripping bush. When their noise in the bush had faded, she went into the cavern for a panga and a calabash and her carrying straps, to go in search of water and wood. She was very sorry her new husband had to leave her bed so soon, because he was gentle but strong, like a bull, and she enjoyed him very much. She was glad that the important rich Kikuyu had bought her from her father for Kimani to marry, although she would have much preferred a lengthy courtship and nightly dancing and feasting and a month's honeymoon, during which she did no work but only made love and was attentive to her husband. But there would be plenty of time. She was young and Kimani would soon be back. She entered the bush, swinging her panga loosely in her hand.

"That is a good girl, your girl," Kimani said to Njogu as they picked slowly along a game trail that followed the slopes of the mountain, leading downward. "She is handsome and agreeable. She has been very well reared. My father would be happy to take her into his family. I wonder how my father is these days."

"I thought you knew," Njogu said. "He is dead for a long time. He was let out of the jail, but he took a disease of the chest and died on the shamba of Bwana McKenzie."

"No, I did not know. Nobody ever told me in the jail, or in Nairobi before, but then there was nobody I knew to ask."

"He died about the time you went to jail in Tanganyika."

"Truly," Kimani said, "I think there is a curse of jails upon my house. It is possible that in the past some relative aroused the anger of a smith, who cursed future generations as well. The spear with which I wounded the Bwana Jeff was iron. The box for which I slew the Indian in Nairobi was iron. The bicycle I had to steal in order to go to jail in Arusha was iron. And God knows, the bars that hold you in a jail are iron. So I sit now in a cave, freezing in the Aberdares, in a cave which is full of guns, and the guns are certainly of iron. Yes, I think a smith may well have cursed us, because even the argument which caused the Bwana Jeff to strike me when I was a boy had to do with iron guns."

"It is quite possible," Njogu said. "Now be quiet. We come to another hide-out within half a mile. It is best to walk softly. These boys shoot quickly."

They walked on, and when they came to the clearing, Njogu and Kimani stepped into the open, with their guns slung. Njogu touched his chin with his right hand and gazed steadily at the ground. Then he snapped the fingers of his left hand four times, in the bush sign for caution. They waited a bit and heard a rustle in the undergrowth. Then they walked up to a group of thatched lean-tos propped under a stony ledge. One man emerged from a hut. He had a shotgun in one hand and a .22 pistol in the other.

"Oh," he said. "It's you, Njogu, and as I am freezing on this accursed mountain, it is also you, Kimani, my old friend from Arusha. How are things in the jail?"

"About the same as when you left, Joseph," Kimani said. "Where are the others?"

"Wait a minute." Joseph snapped off a single shot from the pistol and then cackled three times in acute anguish, as a hen complains bitterly when she is expelling an egg. Several voices cackled in answer, and shortly men and women began to come into the cleared compound. There were eight men and four women and two children.

They clustered around Joseph and Kimani, shouting eagerly for news. They all shouted at once. It sounded like a tree full of baboons at the approach of a leopard.

"Wait a minute, *wait a minute*," Njogu said. "I cannot answer everything at once. First, those of you who do not know Kimani wa Karanja must be told that he sits high in the esteem of the council. He is a proven man who has done many things, and he knows this mountain as he knows the fingers on his hand. He has been sent here to be chief of the mountain, together with a man named Ndemi, whom some of you know and who will be along soon. Until this Ndemi appears, Kimani is the chief of all the people on this mountain."

A very black man, tall and heavily muscled, stepped forward and shot out his jaw.

"I am called Maina," he said. "I am the chief of this group. They follow my orders, and the orders of no other."

"That has been changed," Njogu said. "There has been too much stupidity running around loose on this mountain, like a chicken with its head cut off. The orders are that you raid no more. You steal no more, and you do not go down the mountain any more. Not until you have been so ordered by Kimani, who will receive his directions from me."

"Who says this? By whose orders do we stay on the mountain? I obey no orders while I am up here."

"You will obey these orders or you will die." Kimani spoke harshly, surprising himself. "But we are not here now to wrangle. Send runners to all the camps you know, and tell the men to come to that big clearing —if it is still there—the one about halfway down the mountain toward the Thomson's Falls side. You know the one I mean?"

"Yes," the man said sullenly. "But I do not know if I will come."

"You will come," Njogu said cheerfully, "or someone will come to call on you, and you will never see that or any other clearing again. In case your rhinoceros brain is able to handle a simple thought, my orders come from Him who lives in Kiambu. Now will you come, you balky son of a Somali donkey?"

"I will come," the man said. "I will come and bring my people."

"Good," Njogu said. "Now you show some faint signs of sense. Send your runners to all the camps on this side of the ridge. We will cut through the draw and see the people on the other side. Kwaheri."

He and Kimani turned their backs and went back into the forest.

"Just what are we going to do with some of these thugs?" Kimani asked as they headed toward the draw in the mountains. "Some of these men will not accept authority from anyone. Not that particular blow-hard, of course, he'll be no trouble, but there will be some who will say no to what we advise, and continue to operate as they please. I cannot spend all day and all night seeing that they do not slip down the mountain to rob people and kill cattle."

"There is a new oath, as I told you, that will swiftly separate the troublemakers from the obedient. It is a very strong oath, the most potent of all so far. It is an oath specially designed for the men of the forest, as I designed the first one long ago. But this is a little stronger and a trifle more difficult to arrange. I will tell you now how it works."

Njogu spoke for a long time. . . .

"It is a horrible oath," Kimani said at last. "It is against all the teachings. It violates every law that my father taught me."

"That is the entire point," Njogu replied. "As you were told many times before, what we do now is to make us outcaste, and then when all is over, everyone is either outcaste or dead. Then we are incaste again and can return to the old good ways I knew as a young man."

"I suppose it is necessary," Kimani answered. "But I hope we do not have to do it."

"You are a very strong and a hard young man. You can do anything that you have to do. Remember, a dead man does not feel pain. There must be other ways to persuade. You will see soon how this works, because there will be one or more to defy us, and many more to sway in either direction, according to the success or failure of the defiance. Come now, let us hurry on. One does not approach these camps by night, and the sun is beginning to fail."

Again they made the recognition signal as they came up to another camp. There was the same cackling and the shot repeated, and when ten men came forth, the reception was identical and the resentment the same. A squint-eyed man said:

"If we do not raid we will die of hunger, and if we do not die of hunger we will die of boredom, and to avoid dying of boredom we will fight amongst ourselves and kill each other."

"Man, you won't die of boredom or hunger either. It is the duty of Kimani here to make you into a trained commando group, like the English bwanas employed during the war. Then you will no longer be a bunch of ragged thieves and cutthroats, living on a mountain, but the proudest spearhead of our attackers when the big day comes. You will be well fed, I promise you, because I myself will organize a flow of supplies up the mountain, and you will send your women down on appointed days to appointed places to fetch the food. And several days a week you will practice commando tactics with Kimani and with the other man, Ndemi, and they will weld you into strong, silent units who attack swiftly, kill, loot and burn, and melt away, losing none of your number. Send out your runners now, and be at the big clearing in a week's time. Tonight we will share one of your huts. We are bone-tired and must rise early tomorrow."

They ate sketchily and then went into a hut, from which two women and a child had been driven.

"You sleep first," Njogu said. "I do not believe anything will happen, but that long-armed nugu with the squint looked at me in a way I did not particularly like. There is no point to having our throats cut. I'll wake you in a few hours, and then you can mount guard over me. Sleep on your rifle. It is not so soft or as warm as a woman, but more dependable as a rule."

"It occurs to me," Kimani answered, "that this is all very fine about teaching them commando, but I do not know anything about commando myself. And we cannot shoot guns very much, or someone will hear us and the police will come and we will have to scatter and hide."

"Do not worry about that," Njogu said. "Go to sleep now and we will return home tomorrow. I will wait with you in the cave until Ndemi arrives, and then I will go with him to talk to the other people in these hills and you can start to work whipping this scum into shape. Your chief duty is to keep them so amused that they won't continue to slip down the hills and call attention to our presence here. Sleep."

The night passed without incident, save cold, and Kimani and Njogu left at sunup to go back to the cave. Kimani was most anxious to return. He wanted Karugi, and he wanted to be dry and warm, and he wanted to squat in front of his own small fire and to pretend that he was not a murderer and a fugitive and an uncertain commander of criminals, but the worthy son of his dignified father and the firm friend of Peter and the eventual successor to his father as Number One on Peter's shamba when the Old Bwana died and Peter became the master of the shamba.

They talked very little as they walked along in file. Talking was much too hard on the breathing at that height, and to stop to rest in the wet was more unpleasant than to keep the blood warm by walking. So it was early afternoon when they returned. Kimani called out softly, and Karugi peeped around the edge of the rock. She looked very pretty, Kimani thought, with a bright cotton scarf tied round her shaven head and her blue dress freshly washed. She had put on some blue-and-red beads as well, and some wire-hooped earrings. She seemed very glad to see them. The fire was blazing, hissing happily inside the cave, which glowed with warmth. Karugi had straightened up the interior, so that the guns and other weapons were off to one side and the provender chop boxes off to another. They were very snug in the cave, like ant bears in a hole, and Kimani breathed a sigh of purest contentment as he flopped down in front of the fire and waited for Karugi to start the supper. If they just had some beer to drink . . .

Karugi came with two drinking gourds and handed them to Kimani and her father. Kimani tasted without looking, and jerked up his head sharply.

"This is maize beer," he said.

"Yes," she answered. "I made it with some meal and some sugar that I found in the provision boxes. It is not very well fermented yet, of course, although I boiled it well and set it early to sour, but it will be better tomorrow. And the next day it will be better still."

"This woman of mine," Kimani said to Njogu, "is a very good woman. I do not see how this can be possible with such a shenzi for a father."

"Perhaps she is not fruit of my loins." Njogu laughed. "I was away from home much before she was born, and I had many circumcision brothers then. Perhaps she takes after the one who is now a preacher in the Christian church." Both men laughed heartily again and drank of the thick, half-fermented gruelly mash. It would continue to ferment in the stomach, extending its effect markedly on the consumer.

After a while Njogu stirred the dwindling fire with his toe and said:

"Can you still throw a spear and shoot a bow?"

"I suppose so," Kimani answered. "It isn't a thing you forget very easily. Of course I have had no real practice in a long time, but in a few days there should not be much lost. Why?"

"Various reasons. For one thing, feeding these people is going to be very difficult and expensive and much trouble, because all the work of it must be done by women. For another, your task, as I have said, is to keep them from being bored to the point of making trouble. For still another, none of these people know how to shoot rifles well, since they have never been allowed guns. We dare not shoot too much, even if we had the ammunition, which is precious and should never be wasted. I had thought to send you up some smiths and some women with a load of iron. The smiths will forge spears and arrowheads—I will send some charcoal as well; this wet wood will never make a decent blaze—and you can start these ruffians off practicing with those weapons. Then you will set them to hunting bushbuck and smaller game on the low slopes, and thus they will train themselves in stealth and woodcraft at the same time. My oath, when they stamp through the woods on their enormous clumsy feet, they sound like a herd of elephants. These be mostly city men and squatter men, and they know nothing of the woods. And for a long time their safety must lie within the forests."

"This, certainly I can do," Kimani said, beckoning to his wife to bring more beer. "All my life as a child and a boy the Bwana Peter and I hunted with bow and spear together. If all had gone well," he said bitterly, "I was to have been his gunbearer and even now might be hunting rhino on these very slopes instead of crouching in a cave."

"Be very glad it is a cave with a fire and food and a woman in it. Those grass huts are bitter cold and wet this time of the year."

"I remember well. Do not forget, I lived up here for more than a year once before. I was never really warm once, not as warm as this, in any case. It is cold and wet at any time of the year."

"Another thing"—Njogu extended his gourd for more beer—"when these men are licked into shape and accept you fully as a leader, weld them into groups—circumcision brothers first if possible, clan members next if possible, and jail members finally if the other things are not possible. Make them work as groups always, with a squad leader, like the English soldiers have. Train each man to respond instantly to what each other man does, each doing his full share. I do not have to tell you how to raid cattle or how to swing a panga or stab with a simi. I do not need to tell you how to approach the house of a bwana quietly or how to strangle a cook in the night. These things you learned well from Adam Marenga a long time ago. But most of these other apes never did anything more dangerous than to rob an Indian or burglarize a Nairobi cottage when everyone was away. They need drill, much drill."

Kimani laughed. "I begin to believe that one day I may be a general," he said.

"That is not entirely impossible," Njogu answered, nodding his gray head. "I see now that my daughter comes with food. Let us eat and then go to bed. I am very tired from the walking, and I presume that the honeymoon, as the bwanas call bedding down with a new wife, has not yet been long enough to tire you."

Kimani grinned, his teeth white in the firelight.

"I will eat first," he said. "A growling belly scares the other thing away, as a lion in the bush startles a young zebra. What have we here? Yams? And a stew? Of what?"

"When I went for water I came across a little shamba which had been deserted but in which yams were still in the ground. They are not very good yams, but they are yams in any case. Then I heard a bleating and saw a baby goat which had evidently strayed away from another shamba somewhere about. I caught the goat and killed it with my panga. There is not very much of it, but enough for tonight and tomorrow." Karugi was apologetic.

"In truth, Njogu, you have given me a magician for a wife," Kimani said, and slapped Karugi on the behind. She giggled, pleased. "She produces beer where there is no beer to be brewed, and when she goes for water she discovers yams and goats. She is warm to sleep with and likes to live in a cave, when she could be dancing with the rich young men in Nairobi. Someday I must see Him who lives in Kiambu and thank Him for buying Karugi from you for me."

"I wouldn't trouble about that if I were you." The old man chuckled again. "She was a present from me to you. I lied about the three hundred shillings and the blankets. He who lives in Kiambu would not give three hundred shillings to save his eldest son from hanging."

"But why should you give me such a fine woman as a gift when she is worth three hundred shillings and more? I do not understand."

"You had been long in jail and, before that, over-long on this mountain. There is important work for you to do here, and I knew you would not want to come alone, without some small comforts and a woman to work for you and sleep you warm at night. I have liked you since you were a very small frightened boy who thought he had killed a bwana and was running away. I consider you as my son. Hence, since you were not actually my son, you could become my son by marrying my youngest girl. Wherefore I gave her to you, and someday you may remember that, when I am old and perchance homeless and you are a rich and powerful man, with a bwana's house to live in and a motorcar to drive. Now we have talked enough. Let us eat. I am hungry as a stork."

"One thing more. Did you also give another daughter to Ndemi? For the same reason?"

"Ndemi? If I were a she-hyena I would not give him a crippled cub. Eat. This goat is very fine. And the yams may be a little moldy from the damp, but they are not entirely bad."

24

They followed the path of a twisting stream which ran silver-bright and softly chuckling down the mountainside, and when they had walked for half a day they came to a big shaggy meadow, now grown over, where some Kikuyu many years ago had burned down the trees to make a shamba—possibly some Kikuyu who had been expelled from his clan and who had taken his family into the hills. The grass waved long and lush, and saplings had started to spear-point the green, where once there had been fertile gardens, and goats and sheep had grazed the edges of the forest. The meadow had filled with people—haggard men and women and children, more than a hundred. Without exception they were ragged and dirty, some clad in tunics made of coarse sacking, some wearing blankets, others dressed in ragged khaki and frayed sweaters and evilly assorted white man's clothing. They were very thin, mostly, and some coughed achingly from long living in the wet. One in particular stood out from the motley, and Kimani recognized him immediately. It was Ndemi, a Ndemi grown heavier, a Ndemi well dressed in bush shirt and shorts, a Ndemi wearing a pistol in a holster round his waist, a Ndemi carrying a rifle. Jail up North had not weakened him. If anything, it had broadened and toughened him. He was no longer slender, and his jaw had squared. He had a smile like a shark. They shook hands. Then Njogu called Kimani and Ndemi to one side.

"You have received instructions as to what you will do here," Njogu said to Ndemi. "They will be the same as the ones I gave to Kimani. Who saw you?"

"Adam Marenga. He is still in the North and is very busy smuggling guns. He told me all; that I was to share command of the mountain with Kimani, and that we were to suppress individual activity in the gangs, and that I was to train the men on my side into competent units. He said I would surely find you here, and that you were custodian of a new oath that would bind the men to our command. That is why I came, to observe this oath, since I want to see what you do when some of the unruly ones deny authority."

"Just this." Njogu briefly outlined the course of action. Ndemi nodded.

"That should do it. It is very strong and well fitted to this particular kind of people. I do not think we should have to kill very many. Most of these people are not well armed, only the leaders and sometimes a lieutenant. Also, they cannot shoot. *I* can shoot, both with the little one and the big one. I hope we are lucky about the boy, else we will have to use a woman. All the leaders have women, but to use a woman is not so strong as to use a son."

"I think we will be lucky. Keep your eye on a squint-eyed big man who has a son, a boy of about seven. I think he will be the first to give us trouble. *And* the last. When I move, you cover me with your gun. Kimani, you array all that are with us behind me. Keep your eye and your gun on the ones who sway in the balance. Then move swiftly to do exactly as I say. . . ."

They walked back into the gathered people, who chatted shrilly in groups, the women off with the women, the men bunched together, the children standing submissively to one side. Njogu clapped his hands three times for attention and told the men to squat. He stood in the outer edge of a crescent, with Kimani to his right, Ndemi to his left.

"You have been told by the runners why we are here. There is no argument. We have been sent to organize the groups into an army of the forests. The men who stand beside me will be solely in command. These are orders from Him of Kiambu. There will be no more raiding, no more cattle stealing, no more robberies. These are orders from Him. You are to be organized into a trained fighting group by these two men. You will obey them in all things. I will see that food is sent, so cattle stealing is no longer necessary. All this you have been told. Next week the men on the other slope will be told the same. Kimani, he on my right, commands you. Ndemi, he on my left, commands the other slope. It will not be so very long before we leave the mountain and you can use what you have learned against the white bwanas. I now ask the leader of each group to take his men, his women, and his children and to draw apart from each other group, so that we may see whom we have to deal with."

The men shuffled their feet and looked at each other. They had been sworn to support each other always, but they were not quite sure about what constituted authority. This man Njogu had the unmistakable air of it. They knew, some of them, Kimani from the old days and from the jail, and trusted him. They trusted Njogu. They did not know or trust Ndemi.

"Hurry," Njogu said. "Form your groups."

"Jump!" Kimani barked.

"Now!" Ndemi said.

The groups eddied and separated until all but two groups had formed apart. One group seemed uncertain and swayed back and forth. The other was firmly decided. Njogu had been right. It was the big squint-eyed fellow with the ape arms. He held a shotgun in his right hand. He stepped forward.

"No man tells me my actions," he said. "I have ten men in my group. Those men obey me. The women of my men obey me, even as does my son. I raid when I please. I go when I please, and I come as I please. I did not come here to be an army. I came here only because there was no place else to go. When we become an army they will send an army against us. As long as we operate separately they cannot catch us. I am taking my group away."

Njogu's arm flashed as a mamba strikes. The panga in his hand swept up in a bright arc and came down with a mighty shearing stroke on the upper arm of the hand that held the gun. The blade bit completely through the biceps and the bone, and the arm hung limply from a shred of skin and flesh. The gun fell to the ground, and the man, with a look of surprise, collapsed after it. He fell so that his shorn arm was bent behind his back, and he gazed stupidly at the stump, at the gleaming white of bone as the dark blood leaped from the wound. As Njogu struck, Kimani and Ndemi focused guns on the men of the squint-eyed man's group. Only one other was armed, and Ndemi stepped forward quickly and jerked the gun out of his hand. Then he smashed the man between the eyes with the butt of his rifle and the man fell unconscious.

Njogu walked over to the man whose arm he had slashed with the panga. He knelt beside the man and made a crude tourniquet with the man's belt and a stick. The blood stopped. Njogu jerked his head.

"Fetch water," he said, and someone stepped forward with a gourd. Njogu took the gourd and slashed water on the wounded man's face. The man opened his eyes, and his mouth formed a bubbling scream of pain.

"Do not die yet, friend," Njogu said. "There is something first I would have you see."

The other groups stared, slack-jawed. Kimani walked among them and collected the half dozen guns they carried, and piled them in a heap near the wounded man. No one spoke. They stared, fascinated, at the stump of the man's arm, at the blood on the ground, at the other man who was still unconscious from the butt stroke. Ndemi then walked over to the group and took the man's son by the hand, very gently. The little boy looked at him with distended eyes. He was a thin, pathetic little boy, his belly bloated tremendously, with wind straws for legs, with white scars on the mottled brown scale of his splintery shins. His nose was runny from the cold, and the overflow coagulated on his lips, and his eyes were as big as Kei apples.

"This is your son," Njogu said, looking down at the wounded man. "I have no doubt he is the pride of your squinted eyes. This is your first-born, and the seed of your loins, and the perpetuation of your clan, your immortality, your life everlasting. Perceive your son."

And Njogu took the panga in one hand and seized the boy's hair with his left. He tilted back the boy's chin by pulling on the hair. The panga swished, and now Njogu held the boy's head in his left hand. The headless body fell twitching, blood pumping from his neck, across the body of his father. The boy's blood surged, bubbling frothy like a flood, onto his father's face, thickly covering his mouth and eyes, and the tiny pathetic body thrashed like a headless chicken on his father's breast.

"These are the ingredients of the new oath," Njogu said. "The new oath calls for the corpse of a man and a boy. We have the corpse of the boy. Soon we will have the corpse of the man. You!" He pointed to another member of the wounded man's gang. "Come here!" He nodded to Kimani. "Hold your gun on him." The man shuffled forward, his eyes downcast.

"Here is a panga," Njogu said, placing it in the man's hand. "Now you may kill me if you wish. Then you will be leader."

The man stood dumbly, the panga limp in his fingers.

"Or"—Njogu's voice lashed like a stock whip—"you can cut the head off your master. Cut! Cut now! Cut me, or cut your master!"

The man looked at the panga as if he had never seen a panga before. Then he knelt and pulled the body of the child off its father's face and chest, dragging it by the skinny legs. The man on the ground blinked up at him through the thick blood of his son. Still tranced, the man swung the panga, and the head of the insurgent rolled off its neck, and the blood of father and son was blended on the damp ground.

"Someone fetch a gourd to receive the blood," Njogu said. "Which is the wife? Which is the mother of the child, the wife of the man who would not take orders?" Automatically the group around the woman parted, leaving her alone, staring at the ground, her hands limp at her sides. She was a skinny little woman with extremely bowed legs.

"Come forward, woman," Njogu said gently, and the woman moved, bandied legs jerking like the legs of puppets motivated by string. When she came up to where her man and her child lay, she stopped, staring down at them. She stared without interest.

"Kneel," Njogu said, again gently, and her knees creaked as she crouched. The other men and women had begun to rock gently from side to side, from front to back, staring, not speaking, rocking and staring, never speaking. Njogu slapped a small, sharp simi in her hand.

"Take the knife," he said softly. "Take the knife and cut off the penis and testicles of your husband exactly as you would prepare a ram for the pot. Leave a good long strip of belly skin so that the organs will be preserved intact."

The woman crouched over the body, her buttocks resting on her thighs, with the knife held loosely, and slowly her hand began to move across the belly of her husband. The knife traced a red perimeter on his groin, below the navel, cutting through the skin and showing an under rim of fat. The knife traced downward around the genitals toward the anus and then traced slowly back again. She placed the point of the blade under the incision and freed the edges of the skin from the clinging fat, lifting the skin away from the fat as the knife retraced the slowly bleeding perimeter. Then she slid the blade in flatly under the skin, held the organs aloft in her other hand, and freed them intact with one slash. Then she fainted and fell forward on her man.

Njogu reached over and picked up the severed genitalia of the dead man and tossed them aside into a bristly clump of grass, which held their weight. Still no one spoke, but now the slow sway had changed into a gentle bobbing of heads, a subtle jerking of necks, a small bending of knees, and the slightest flex of ankles, so that the entire crowd rippled in unison from head to foot, from foot to head, like wheat in a varying breeze.

"Kimani," Njogu said. "Take your panga now and open the skull of the man and the boy. Do it carefully. We need the brains of both. Take out the brains and put them over there with the organs."

As numbly as the woman, Kimani took the panga and split first the skull of the man, making a vertical and then a horizontal cut just above the eyes. He laid back the bone as one would peel the hard shell from a shattered coconut, and scooped out the gray brains. He repeated the operation with the child. Then he carried the brains over and laid them beside the penis and testicles. The slight swaying leap now had increased to a spastic jump, heads bobbing as a snake's head bobs, necks undulating as a snake's throat moves, bodies swaying backward and forward as a cobra's body shimmers, knees backward-bent and locked stiff now, ankles braced, feet flat, and each jump carrying the men and women nearly a yard off the ground. The women began to croon and the men to grunt, gutturally, as a lion coughs irritably on a cold, wet night.

"Now," Njogu said, "now I will take the heart of the child myself," and he bent over the body with his knife. He tossed the still-beating heart over by the other bloody mess. "We are ready to begin," he said. "Ndemi! Scoop up the blood from the two as it mingles with the earth, and put it with the other in the gourd. Move the bodies a little and dig a hole in the earth and line it with mugogo leaves. Then let the blood and earth rest on the leaves. We are ready to begin."

The croon had increased now to a chant by the women, and the bark had changed into full-throated bass roars by the men. The wife of the slain man, the mother of the slain child, had recovered from her swoon and had rejoined the leaping mass. She too began to bob and leap and croon, her eyes hypnotically fixed, staring straight into distance, seeing nothing.

Njogu was very busy. He mixed the mingled blood with the blooded earth and nodded at Ndemi, who went over to the surging throng and took the first man by the arm, leading him, and as he passed the frond-keeled hole where Njogu crouched, he forced the man to his knees by pushing on his head. Njogu took the man by the wrist and slashed it gently with his knife, holding the wrist so that the man's blood dripped into the blood of the dead man and the boy. Each man in the throng followed automatically, stooping and extending his wrist, until all had endured the bloodletting and each had returned to the dancing line. Then the man whose wrist first had been cut came again to the leafy basin of blood, and Njogu commanded him to kneel and sip seven times from the mixture. Again he was followed by another man, meticulously in turn, each kneeling and sipping seven times. Each man returned to the high-stiff-kneed-flat-footed-jumping throng, automatically resuming the rhythm.

Then Njogu mixed the brains of the man with the brains of the child and summoned each man again to taste seven times while repeating:

"*If I am ordered to bring my brother's head and I disobey the order, this oath will kill me.*

"*If I am ordered to bring the finger or the ear of my mother and I disobey the order, this oath will kill me.*

"*If I am ordered to bring the head, or hair, or fingernail of a European and I disobey, this oath will kill me.*

"*If I rise against Mau Mau authority, this oath will kill me.*"

"*If I ever betray the whereabouts of arms or ammunition or the hiding places of my brothers, this oath will kill me.*

"*If I disagree with the order of a superior and argue against it, this oath will kill me.*"

The voices droned on, repeating after Njogu as he catalogued the list of prohibitions. When the last men—Kimani and Ndemi—had eaten of the brains, Njogu took the little boy's heart and held it over the basin in the ground. He took a sharp nail and pricked the heart seven times, then squeezed it with his hand until blood came from the nail pricks and joined the other blood. The men went back to the ranks and continued to leap, and then Njogu stood erect and called for a fire to be made. One of the women came forward and scuffed some grass together with her foot, and another sought dry punk from a rotted log. When the flame was going, Njogu impaled the dead man's genitals on a green stick and roasted them slightly, until the testicles swelled in the heat.

He nodded at Kimani. "Fetch me first the mother of the child," he said. "We really need a dog's tail for this part, or a ram's pizzle, but the man's equipment will have to serve. Perhaps it will be a stronger oath that way."

When the widow came he commanded her to squat, and he took her husband's genitals and handed them to her.

"Place the penis inside you and swear," he said. "Repeat after me: "*If I am ordered . . .*"

When the widowed mother finished the oath she rejoined the dancers, and another woman stepped forward to repeat the oath, sitting on the testicles and placing the penis inside her. She was followed by another, and another, until all were sworn. Njogu stood up again and cracked his stiffened knees with the flat of his hand. He raised his voice in a shout and pointed to the men.

"You will all say together now: *If I ever in my life disobey the Mau Mau in any way and I sleep with a woman, the woman's body will kill me!*"

The men repeated the oath in a swelling roar that rolled over the forest, and leaped higher in their dance.

To the women he said: "Repeat all together! *If I ever betray the Mau Mau in any way and I sleep with a man, the man's body will kill me!*"

The women screamed response as plovers shriek when disturbed on a road at night, and leaped still higher in the air.

"The oath is finished," Njogu said. "We are now as one, and the life of each of you rests in the oath, and in the hand of Kimani wa Karanja, who is your commander and who holds your life. That is all."

He turned to Ndemi. "Walk amongst the dancers now and strike a few. The rest will soon quit and rest."

Njogu sat down on the grass, apart from the bodies. His hands were very bloody, and he scrubbed them carefully with bunches of wet grass. Then he wiped off his panga and the simi, until the blood was cleaned from their blades.

"God, but I am tired," he said. "We were very fortunate here today that there was but one man who dissented and who had a son handy as well. Otherwise we would have had to go down the mountain, some of us, and bring back two bodies from some shamba where everyone has not yet decided to co-operate. I had one shamba in mind, close by, but it would have taken much time and destroyed the effect. Look at them now. . . ."

Ndemi had slapped two men, sharply, bringing them out of their tranced leaping, and each man dropped to the ground, sighed, and fell asleep. It was only necessary to slap one more. The rest sighed and sank to the ground, where they went exhaustedly to sleep, wrung slack by emotion.

Kimani lay on his back, limp, drained, as if by great fright or a very long time with a woman. The sky was blue above the clearing, flecked only by a few white clouds. The sun was beginning to slide behind the hills, but the light was still strong, the air clear. Already the vultures had begun to speck the sky.

Kimani, Ndemi, and Njogu spent the night walking back through the dripping woods, walking slowly. At dawn Ndemi turned off from the trail to another animal path, quartering away.

"I will leave you here," he said. "I will hold my oath-giving next week, when all my men are rounded up. But I think it likely that the word will have spread and we will have no excuse to kill any one of this number. I request permission to go down quietly on one raid, to provide the materials for the ceremony. Are there any shambas nearby where resistance is especially heavy, where I might procure a man and a boy for the sacrifice? And preach a moral at the same time?"

"Yes," Njogu said, looking obliquely at Kimani. "There has been much resistance on the shamba of the Bwana Henry McKenzie. Our members there will tell you whom to take. Do not kill them first, if possible. It is more effective if done on the scene. We will meet you in a week. You have chosen a place?"

"Yes, Kimani can find it easily. He knows it very well. It is higher than the place of yesterday, but it will still be downhill from your cave. You remember, Kimani, the other big meadow? The place where the rhinos sought the sun?"

Njogu arched his eyebrows in surprise.

"You know of the cave?"

"Of course. I was following close behind Kimani the day he found it. I was curious to know where the guns would be kept, in case I ever needed a gun. That was in the old days, when we were only tattered thieves and hungry fugitives, without central organization. From time to time I will come to visit you, Kimani, and you must come and call on me. I too have a cave. Not so good as yours, but good enough for a bachelor."

He grinned and turned, walking swiftly away. Kimani looked with bitter hatred at his back.

"Someday I will kill him," he said. "Oath or no oath, someday I will have his heart for the hyenas."

"You mustn't talk like that," Njogu chided facetiously. "Ndemi is your brother-in-oath and your co-commander. You must always love him like a brother, as if you were circumcised at the same time." He laughed.

They walked awhile in silence, scraping through bush so thick that the morning sunlight filtered through only in patches. Occasionally wild-grape tangles blocked their way and they could see no more than a few feet ahead. Finally they fought their way out to a path that led toward the cave. Kimani, leading, pushed his hand backward. He turned to face Njogu.

"Stop a minute," he said. "I want to ask you something. Did *you* ever take this oath?"

"Of course not," Njogu said. "I don't take oaths. I *invent* them. Someday when it is necessary and someone higher wants me to take an oath *he* has invented, I will undoubtedly have to take one. But right now, no. I am not a cannibal."

"But you—you kill the people and you administer the oath."

"Of course. That is business. That is orders. And they are only people who will not obey and so endanger the Plan. To me it is nothing. *Zaz!* One swipe of a panga; nothing more. Our sheep of yesterday are already with their ancestors. So it was in the old days, so it is today. I am the mundumugu. Until He in Kiambu commands me, I take no oaths—especially one as irregular and improper as this."

"This oath has not yet been consecrated in Mau Mau?"

"Of course not, boy. This is one I made up myself, as I made up the first one. I only look forward to the future. The orders were to bind these animals on this mountain into a solid force. You cannot do this with the milksop little things they do to the people down below, the frightened stupid squatters and the simple farmers. What is pricking a thumb and smearing the blood with millet for seven swallows? What is a sheep's eye impaled on a thorn, a strangled cat, to these baboons? You might as well offer them a sugar teat and repeat the white man's prayer. Mark me well. There will be a day when this Batuni, this forest oath, will be a general practice. For I know the way of men. A drunkard never pleads for a milder potion. The insipid homemade beer progresses finally into white man's gin. So it is with oaths. The finger prick and millet will become Batuni and worse, if we are to win."

"I suddenly notice," Kimani said, "that you made no mention of taking Karugi along to share in the oath-taking. Why? She is no protection to our guns. A child could overpower her."

"She is my daughter," Njogu said. "She does not need blood rituals to be loyal. She has never seen me slay. She is not a criminal and she will never talk, and I will not subject her to these things. Nor would she care to bed overmuch with a husband whom she had just seen eating human brains. We will keep Karugi away from these other rabble and these bloodlettings. She will stay safely in the cave."

"I am very glad of that," Kimani said simply. "I should not have liked her to see what we did yesterday. We will give her the little pricked-finger and millet oath sometime and make her a Mau Mau that way. But tell me one thing more; do you believe firmly in these oaths?"

Njogu looked at him long and seriously. He spoke proudly.

"I am a mundumugu as my father was a mundumugu. I believe in the faith of my father, and my father's father, and in all their old oaths and ceremonials. I do *not* believe in any oaths that are departures from prescribed ceremonial. But I do believe in returning to the faith of my father, in the land of my father, and I will do anything, I will follow anybody, if that can be achieved. I will listen to Him in Kiambu, with his pipe and his tweed coat and his English airs, and I will mingle with clay-faced wa-Russias and filthy pigs of Wahindi, and this vulture dung here on the mountain, if it will bring back our lands and our faiths and our old ways. I will aid and abet Mau Mau and invent vile ceremonies and I will kill you or I will cut the head off my own daughter, finally, if I have to do it to achieve the larger aim. Does that answer you? If it does, let us hurry on to the cave. Perhaps Karugi has found another goat, and certainly the beer has had some extra time to ferment. I am very hungry and tired and cold and thirsty."

"That answers me," Kimani said. "I suppose all these things are necessary if the Night of the Long Knives is to be successful and the white man killed or driven into the sea. I too am hungry. Let us hurry and see what Karugi has prepared for us."

The next week when Kimani and Njogu went over the mountain to the other side, where Ndemi was organizing his men, they found the men assembled as one unit. Ndemi had been right. The word had passed of the other forest ceremony, and no man stood against Njogu when he made his formal speech. But it was necessary to perform the oath in any case, even more necessary now that they all were to be firm in brotherhood.

"What have we to work with?" Njogu asked Ndemi.

"We removed a man and a boy from the shamba of the Bwana McKenzie, your old master." Ndemi grinned at Kimani. "Perhaps that evens things up a bit for all your old troubles, eh? We had very little difficulty. One of our people on the McKenzie shamba pointed out the man and his son. The man has been especially contrary, informing to the Bwana, who runs to the police and who constantly talks against the society, even though he does not know exactly what it is. The Bwana McKenzie is still very strong with his people. He will have to be one of the first to go. But I have told the people here that the sacrificial materials come from your old shamba, Kimani, and so I think it would be necessary for you to cut the head. It will weld you firmly to my band."

"I agree," Kimani said. "I will cut the head. Where is the man?"

"He is tied over there, together with his young son. Here is the panga. Go and do the job."

"Yes, it is an excellent idea," Njogu said. "You must do the cutting."

"I have said I will do it," Kimani said. "What, first, is the name of the man? Perhaps he is someone I used to know?"

Ndemi took a long time to answer. He seemed to chuckle inwardly. He looked out of the corners of his eyes at Njogu.

"Kibarara wa Karanja," he said.

Kimani looked at Njogu and started to speak. Njogu shook his head and looked at the ground.

"The men have been told his name, as they have been told your name," he said flatly. "It is the same name."

Kimani shook his head, as if to clear it, and walked firmly over to where the young man lay bound upon the ground. Next to him was a four-year-old boy. The man gazed upward, and recognition flashed in his eyes. His mouth was stuffed with grass; he could not speak.

Kimani stood over him, and a sob swelled his throat.

"Good-by, Younger Brother," he said, and swung the panga.

25

They went from the sun-glaring-dusty streets of Iringa into the little white-painted, antiseptically clean hotel, into the shabby-leather-furnished lounge, through the lounge and into the bar, with its bright shining bottles of real whisky cradled into brackets and with the automatic silver drink estimators screwed to the bottle tops, so that when you tilted the bottle the float allowed precisely one ounce of the short-supplied whisky to splash into the glass.

"Look," Nancy Deane said. "See. It's real. Ice, actual ice. And red leather stools to sit on. And white people with pants and skirts on. And salted nuts in flat dishes. I want the biggest whisky and soda in the house. Order it for me while I go and investigate the little girls'. I hear tell that since we have been away the flush toilet was invented. I don't believe it, but anyhow I'm going to see."

Nancy had a bandanna tied round her head, against the dust, and over the bandanna was a cocked floppy man's hat. She wore use-furrowed dusty boots, and her khaki slacks and jacket were washed white. The trousers were creased permanently under the knees from endless days of hard riding in the jeep. The seat showed a big patch of sweat from the car's cushions, and there was a big oily spot on one of her pockets where a bottle of bug dope had come unscrewed and leaked. There was another blotch of sweat between her shoulder blades. Her face was filthy with dust, and there was a big white lump standing through the dust on her forehead where a tsetse had bitten her. This was the first time that Nancy Deane had been in white habitation in three months, if you discounted just one beer and a sandwich with the nice little game ranger outside Ikoma, way the hell and gone in the other end of Tanganyika.

Looking at her husband as he crawled up on a stool next to Peter McKenzie and ordered the drinks, it would have been difficult to label him as either client or professional hunter. His face was both as brown and as dirty as Peter's face, and Peter McKenzie's face was very dirty. Both men's clothes were rubbed equally white by rough washing. Both men's wrists were scarred with old tsetse bites. Both their hairy, dust-furred naked legs below the shorts were crisscrossed from thorn and crusted from old bites. Both men wore a smile of completely blissful smugness. It had been one hell of a safari. It had wound up with a bang this morning.

Nancy came back from the ladies' room. Her face was shiny-clean and she had taken off the bandanna and done something to her hair, which was sunburned almost blond now. She walked as a woman bemused, crossing her eyes and staring at her forefinger pointed at her nose.

"Seats," she said. "*Seats*. And they have those little private places where you can go in and lock the door. And there is a string to pull that makes water come out of a tank into a sort of funny white thing made of porcelain. There is a sign on the door which says: 'W.C.—Ladies.' And there are two stone springs with handles that if you twist them water comes out, and one of the handles makes the water hot and the other makes the water cold. I think that this must be the white man's magic I have heard so much about. It seems so funny to go anywhere but behind a bush, with a dozen Africans staring at you. I feel quite weak. Gimme my drink."

"If I live to be a million," Tom was saying to Peter, "I will never forget how that thing looked when we came up onto the donga and saw him standing there on the other side with his head thrown back against that red rising sun, with his nose in the air and those big mule ears sticking out."

"You shot him very pretty, chum," Peter said. "I'm glad. It was the last morning, and God knows we worked for him. It kind of puts a very nice capper on the trip, to get him the very last morning."

"I don't suppose you two built-in bores would be referring to that big kudu you shot this morning, would you?"

Peter grinned. The first scotch in weeks tasted glorious, burning all the way down and hitting with a thump.

"I suppose we have been a bit of a trial."

"Oh, I wouldn't say 'trial.' Inquisition is apter. God Almighty. I sit in camp for a month, reading the same books over and over again, waiting for the joyous moment when I can hear the jeep and see some horns sticking out of the back, so I can associate with human beings again instead of two half-dead-tired, surly, kudu-dedicated bores, who grunt at me, drink a half bottle of gin, shove their food into their ears, and then go to bed so they can get up and climb mountains all over again in the morning. But the horn never sounds for Nancy. I don't care if I never hear anything about muzzle velocity or bullet weight or trajectory ever again. I know more about ballistics than Annie Oakley. I wonder what it'll be like to wear a skirt and have to keep my knees together, like Mother told me nice girls did, one more time? Or what taking a bath that hasn't got fish in it will be like? Or a clean head of hair and unbroken fingernails or riding in a car where the lady doesn't have to straddle the gear box? Yes, I certainly *will* have the other half, Peter. And then I will have the first half of the next round, and then the other half of that too."

"You wouldn't say the old lady's fed up with us, would you, Tom? I mean to say, here she's been three months in lovely scenic technicolor Africa with the self-confessed best damned bird shooter, leopard shooter, lion shooter, buffalo stalker, runner-away from rhino, and martini mixer in all of Tanganyika, and with his noble tutor, who is known from one end to the other as an uncommon fine naturalist, historian, jeep mender, conversationalist, and singer of sentimental songs."

Nancy closed her eyes and moaned tragically.

"If I ever hear 'Stardust' again I will kill myself. Didn't you ever learn *any* other song, even when you were a child?"

"No," Peter said cheerfully. "But I think I do a magnificent job on that one. 'Sometimes I wonder . . .' Sheer beauty."

"Give me the hyenas, every time. They at least have a sense of tune, and as my grandma used to say rather coarsely, you couldn't carry a tune in a slop bucket."

"It seems to me that any girl in her right mind would pay money for the opportunity you've just had," her husband said. "Look at us. Kind, gentle, thoughtful—even give you a gun to take into the bushes so a rhino won't catch you with—you should pardon the expression—your pants down. Feed you, guard you at night, regale you with tales of high adventure every day, ply you with gin, and expose you daily to the wonders of Nature and the glory of God. Plus a little extra personal effort on my part when I ain't too tired. We're handsome, too, in a manly but boyish sort of way. Look at us."

"I see you. That McKenzie's hair has got a covey of francolin in it, plus sticks. And your hair-do is best described as page boy. Stewart Granger and Gregory Peck always shave and have haircuts. You never shave and you smell bad most of the time. My God. I felt something hard stick me in the stomach the other night and felt real sentimental for a minute. I thought, Maybe he *does* care about something except greater kudu, and was prepared to go all soft and sweet and loving." Nancy shook her head. "Junior here was so tired he had gone to bed with his Boy Scout knife still strapped to him."

"And in the wrong bed at that," Tom said. "I was too tired to stagger any farther than Nancy's sack. Wasn't sentiment; just pure fatigue."

"Are you glad it's over?" Peter asked. "Eager to go home?"

"I wish this were the first day," Nancy said. "I have never had such a wonderful time in my life, snakes, bugs, dust, and all. I absolutely loathe the idea of going back to New York again. Me, the White Queen of the Bush, gussied up in a little black dress, listening to the girls in '21' complain about their husbands and praise their new psychiatrists. Those damn women don't know the difference between a .375 magnum and a tinni-kata. They use flush toilets *every* day. That's why there are so many divorces."

"When you get off that plane at Idlewild and ride an hour through that traffic, and then when you cross Third Avenue and smell the stink of those buses and see the poor people sitting on the steps in the heat, in their undershirts, and the kids playing stickball and planning to grow up to be gangsters, I intend to cry all the way home," Tom said. "You know how many *people* there actually are in New York?"

"Drive *me* mad," Peter said. "After this. Remember Nancy that day, after we came up from Ikoma going down to Manyara, when we saw the first motorcar we'd seen in six weeks? Old Nancy got furious. 'What's that damned thing doing here in *my* country?' she said, and I believe she meant it."

"Maybe you'll have better safaris, but you'll never laugh any more than you have on this one, boy," Tom said. "Seems to me everything has been funny. Everything couldn't have been that funny. Even the day the safari ants got up Nancy's pants in the leopard blind. I had heard that there was a certain sort of woman who could get out of clothes in a hurry, but I never really believed it before. Makes me wonder what this woman did for a living before I took her off the streets."

"No faster than our heroic hunter, here, the day the fuzzy brown caterpillar crawled up *his* pants at Manyara. No woman ever screamed that loud at a mouse up her frock. You know, I'm getting drunk. It must be a combination of the flush toilets and the ice. But you know who I'll miss most? Not you apes. Kungo. My hunting partner. Remember the day in Manyara when he went to the local cathouse and we saw him running down the road with all the bad girls screeching after him? I still don't know what he did to 'em."

"Probably didn't pay 'em. But my prize is still that drunken old half-mad skinner, Mako." Peter grinned. "Came to me the other day and asked me for two shillings. 'What for?' I asked him. 'My back is very stiff, Bwana,' he tells me. 'I want to go to the village and get it straightened. There is a very nice fat bibi in the village who smiled at me.' So I gave him the two bob, and in about two hours he was back. 'Did you get your back straightened, old boy?' I asked him. 'Yes, Bwana,' he says. 'But these are a very low class of native here, these locals. They are very ignorant people, Bwana.' 'How's that?' says I. 'Well, he says, 'the bibi only wanted *one* shilling to straighten my back, so I spent the other shilling on beer. That is why I am drunk now, Bwana.' What a people."

"Unless you want to carry me, you better feed me," Nancy said. "Civilization has addled me pretty little head. Food, gentlemen."

"I expect she's right," Peter said. "We've got a hellish long drive to
Arusha."

26

They waited out of the rain, in the hotel in Arusha, and read old papers
while Peter went off to clear the trophies with the Game Department.
Mostly they thought about the trip with sadness, now it was finished.
It had been, Tom Deane thought, the only time in his life in which
he had been completely happy and knew he was completely happy.
There was nothing that he and Nancy did not know about Peter now,
including the one bad love affair when Peter had got himself sentimen-
tally involved with some young thing and had come back from safari to
find another gentleman, a city type, in his bed. Peter knew everything
there was to know about Nancy and Tom, as well. They had lived in
each other's pockets for three months, away off in a land God hadn't paid
much attention to for a very long time. The lorry had bogged down and
had snapped springs, and the food had run out, and the gin had run out,
and the scopes had gone crook, and the Land Rover had consumed bearings, and once some thieves had come and stolen all the cameras. They
had been hot and tired and wet and cold and hungry and filthy and bug-
bitten. Nancy had been often frightened and Tom had been petrified on
occasion, and Peter had got himself lost, and the hyenas had sneaked into
the tent one night and eaten a camera bag. Lions had strolled through
the camp and stolen meat from where it hung fresh-killed in trees, and
in a camp up around the Yaida swamp the hippos had bellowed almost
in the back yard. Elephants strode through the camp, and Tom and
Peter had had to go once into suicidally thick bush after a wounded
buffalo. But in the three months there had not been a single word of
real exasperation, an earnest recrimination, a single serious quarrel.
There had been a lot of chaffing and much sober talk and a great many
completely silly, private jokes, such as the way they always kidded Peter
dead-pan about certain mannerisms and tricks of phrase and of identification of people. They had talked roughly, freely, but without leering or
using smut as a diversion. There was nothing, practically, that Nancy

would say in bed to Tom that she would not say as freely to Peter when they sat around the campfire.

When the men were off hunting hard, hunting buffalo or rhino or kudu, and an extra person was a bother, Nancy either stayed in camp with the black boys or took Kungo and the lorry and one other boy to serve as gunbearer and went bumping off on a bird-shooting safari of her own. Sometimes she would be gone for two or three days, sleeping under a blanket on a pad in the back of the lorry, with the two savages sleeping at her feet. It never occurred to her that it was strange for a young white woman to be camping alone with two complete savages in the middle of the Tanganyikan bush, with lions roaring close by and elephants screaming in the thickets, while her husband was off God knew where doing something idiotic about buffalo.

Sometimes she loafed in camp for days while the men took a basic pack and went off reconnoitering, and she was completely, utterly happy and unbored and knew at the time that she was happy and unbored. Then she wrote long letters home, or read cheap Penguin or Tauchnitz paper-backs, with Yusuf doing her hair for her. She watched the baboons, who came to know her and were very little shy of her, and she loved to watch the ants toiling as they made their mountainous red clay castles. She had one of those hurry-up cameras that develop a picture in a minute, and she took portraits of all the black boys to send back home to their mothers and wives. It was the first pictures most of them had seen of themselves, because while all people on safari made them pose frequently, very few ever sent back snaps. It was a forgetful way people had. The word spread that Memsaab Picha owned a new magic which could make a man's face print on paper in less than a minute, so shortly Nancy and her Polaroid camera became famous with the surrounding tribes, whose people would straggle in every day to plead for a little special voodoo with the camera.

The blacks adored her. Once, when the Coca-Cola supply was running out and there was no prospect of getting more, Yusuf, the head-boy, started to steal a bottle a day. When the end of the supply was announced, the men resigned themselves to a diet of warm gin and an occasional beer. Only after they left camp did Yusuf appear bearing a Coke, cold from last night's condensation in the bottom of the water bag. He grinned and handed it to the Mama, as he called her. "Plenty more," Yusuf said. "I steal very much from the bwanas, save it for Mama." Nancy was so touched that she forgot to tell the men they had a thief in camp, and so drank a secret Coke every day until Peter found out about it over the cook-fire gossip and booted Yusuf unlovingly in the behind. Peter had become very fond of Coke. They unearthed the stolen hoard, and for punishment Peter and Tom drank it all up and didn't give Mama any.

They had captured for her a baby monkey, a shriveled little old man of a beast about the size of Nancy's fist, whom they called Tembo, meaning elephant, because he was so tiny. Tembo loathed Tom and Peter, who were forever teasing him and threatening to cut off his tail. He loved Nancy and clung to her neck like a limpet. The only time Tembo would associate with Peter and Tom was when they moved from one camp to another in the jeep. When Tembo had an urge to urinate he would leave Nancy, leap to one of the men, and void his bladder on their shirts before they could scrape him off. Peter said that he had done a lot of loathsome things for clients before but that he didn't feel that being a W.C. for a bloody nugu was necessarily entered in the articles. Nancy wept when a wildcat abducted Tembo one day. He had been a very dear little monkey.

The whole thing had been just wonderful, both Nancy and Tom kept saying as they waited for Peter to get back from the Game Department with the trophy clearances. All of it. Every minute of it. Nancy was completely in love with Peter, and Tom had developed a massive hero worship that threatened to murder him, because he would do anything at all, no matter what the hazard, to avoid appearing poorly in front of Peter or the gunbearers. In the narrow corner of their lives Peter assumed demi-god proportions. He was as tender with his blacks as a mother, but always with a mother's discipline. He dosed them when they were ill and listened to their troubles, squatting on his haunches at the campfire, and he chastened them when he thought they needed it. They seemed to love him with the blind respectful trust of dogs; they never questioned, never complained, even after many consecutive days of riding high-perched on the lorry-load, in choking dust and searing heat or driving rain and knifing wind. They ran the camp as meticulously as a fine restaurant is run; they pitched it in an hour and struck it in forty-five minutes. When they were out after kudu or buffalo or especially rhino at Manyara, sometimes the hunters would not return until ten, and then Nancy would hear a hushed murmur from the gunbearers as they sat up until three or four in the morning, cleaning guns and repairing the lorry, with Peter himself never going to bed until all was done. The boys would come and sing for her sometimes, and she loved especially one old Wakamba song, a derivative of some ancient Christian hymn, which they just called "Golu, golu." They would accept a half beer each, although it is forbidden to give alcohol to an African, and then they would modestly retire, anxious not to overstay their welcome or embarrass the Mama by taking too much beer and getting drunk. They even asked Nancy to visit their campfire for supper, an unprecedented honor, and gave her choice bits of things to eat which would have horrified her if she had seen them in the original state.

She saw Peter daily in the jeep, in the bush, in the camp, and in the little towns, and she decided she had never known a young man so gentle, so basically clean, so competent at his business, and so completely without pose or pretense. She had seen him find game where there was no game. She had watched his knowledge of animals and grass and weather. She had seen him that bad day with the lion; she had seen him build bridges and fix hopelessly damaged machinery. She had seen him prepare a three-course meal on a wind-racked desert, where there was no wood or water, making the cook fire with petrol and sump oil in a hole in the ground, and draining the jeep's radiator for enough water for tea. She had seen him always quietly kind and really rather shy, and very, very polite always, as a habit and not a mannerism. "Peter?" Always, in answer: "Nancy?" whether she just wanted to ask him to pass the salt or whether he really intended to marry Holly Keith, in which case the answer was always "Yes."

Tom's estimate of Peter was not based so much on the sweeter side but on the utter competence with which he tracked; the almost maniacal concentration on outwitting something which already knew all the answers; the religious dedication to locating the best before any effort was made to hunt it, and then the rejection of it if it had any flaw of shape or length or breadth or thickness. In three months they had shot nothing that was not eaten or, if inedible, was not a candidate for the Valhalla of game, the records of the Messrs. Rowland Ward of London. There had been some very tight squeaks, or so it seemed in retrospect, but the squeaks had been oiled with a foreseen preparedness for just this sort of squeak—twice, with the buffalo, once with the lions, several times with the rhino. They had not yet fired at a rhino. They had run away from forty, because this one was too short in the horn, that one a cow with a wonderful horn but her calf was too young to orphan, another who was pretty good but not quite good enough. Tom had seen Peter drive in the dust, eyes reddened from it, face black with it, from dawn until midnight, spend the rest of the night repairing the lorry, and arise the next day, with no sleep at all, to do it over. He climbed mountains like a hill baboon; he would walk ten miles, leaving Tom under a tree with a book, to verify a vague suspicion.

The trust in which his gunbearers held him was implicit. That day, after the sick buffalo, the boys had spoored ahead like pointers, crouching, halting, noting a bit of scuffed earth here, indicating with a broken stem of grass a berry of blood on a stone or a slash of red on a leaf, circling and sniffing like dogs when a covey of quail is there and the dogs know the birds are there but can't quite nail them. And when the buff had come crashing from behind a bush, where he'd doubled to wait them, the boys took the charge until the buff was hard atop them, and then plunged sideways with their hands covering their heads, while Peter —and Tom himself, although he couldn't believe it now—stood firm and flat and shot until Peter's last bullet picked the eye out of the buff and the great scabby tick-covered destruction sprawled in front of them and winded his last sad bellow.

The gunbearers were something, too, something you couldn't believe. They had no protection but Peter, for they carried no guns except Peter's guns, and of course Tom's guns, and when you reached back to take the gun the black man was then unarmed, but they would still walk into a buffalo herd or a rhino or a whole flock of lions with complete assurance, depending, like small children, on Papa to make it all come right. You never had to look for Chalo or Metheke when you needed a gun, loaded and ready, or if you ran out of shells there was a black hand on your arm with a fistful of fresh stuff. These men rode for hours crouched uncomfortably in the cramped back of the jeep, which was full of guns and glasses and chop boxes and ammunition boxes. When the jeep stuck in a stream, they got out and waded waist-deep into water that harbored, surely, snakes, leeches, and, very likely, crocodiles. The gunbearers were always quiet and they melted into bush like wraiths, in full sight one minute and forever lost to view if you flicked your gaze away.

It was not the shooting, although when the shooting came at the logical end—like this morning when they found the kudu—it was wondrous fine, and then it was thrilling and gratifying to have the boys beat you on the back and call you a firecracker. It was overpowering, the day of the first lion, to have the boys waiting in camp for you and, when they saw the great head with the blood-streaked tawny mane lolling out of the back of the jeep, to beat you with green leafy branches and sing some triumphant song and hurl you about until you were bruised with their affection and sick from laughter. They didn't do it for the money, either; Peter wouldn't allow any tipping on safari.

The finest of it all was getting back at night, tired to tears, lava-filthy and bone-sick from the constant jouncing of the hunting car, feet bruised from stony hills, scratched and hungry and tsetse-chewed, to see the fire a long way off and know that with the fire there was a drink and warm water and clean clothes and hot food and a chance to slump in a canvas chair in the frosty night and watch the sparks whirl upward and mingle with the stars. Then you heard all the noises and talked about that day, or yesterday, or the war, or funny people you knew, or things that had happened on other safaris or that had happened to you before the war or when you were a little boy. Nobody talked gossip; there wasn't any gossip to talk. You just talked sort of lazy and aimlessly. until it was time to go to bed, with the food and the brandy-and-coffee still warm inside you, clean again and snug in your pajamas, so you could die for nine hours in order to get up and do it all over again the next day. The talk was the best of it. The talk and the drinking.

Funny about the drinking. You made a rule without making a rule. If you came back to camp for lunch, if you were hunting close by, you might have one pink gin or a bottle of beer before you ate. Or if you were going to be gone all day you found a bottle of beer apiece in the chop box, with the coarse-grained home-cooked bread and the flat-sliced cold meat and the rock-hard butter and the cold baked beans and clammy spaghetti and the pickles which made your lunch. You ate the lunch under an old baobab or a towering fig or a thorn tree, snoozed a bit, waiting for the heat to drop, and then hunted on until seven, when it got too black to shoot. Then it took you an hour, sometimes two hours, to get back to camp, bouncing along in the grass or on a disappearing track, the wind bitter, every joint with a separate ache, and birds and foxes and rabbits skittering ahead, with Peter swooping the jeep suicidally to avoid running them down.

It seemed then in the last half hour that you would surely die if you did not have a drink, an uniced gin, a scotch with warm water with little wiggly things and dusty sediment in it. Nancy always saw the jeep's headlights a long way off, and when you climbed stiffly down out of the jeep, full of triumph or despair, she would have the drinks ready-made and beckoning and the fire reaching higher than the sagging flap of the mess tent, where the chairs and table and food boxes and the paper-backed books and the sputtering, hissing Coleman lantern lived. Black shadows shifted behind the mess tent as one of the personals freighted the petrol tins full of hot water from the boys' fire to the brown canvas tub with the thorns under it and the fish in it. You took the drink with you into the sleeping tent and collapsed on the edge of the cot with a sigh and let one of the personals haul off your boots and undress you, and when you settled down into the warm, foul water, all the day's fatigue flowed away and peace entered you through the pores, together with the soap. The personal toweled you and helped you into pajamas and mosquito boots and held the heavy robe for you, and when you got back to the fire Yusuf was already dressing the table for chakula, with a checkered tablecloth held firm against the breeze by clips on the corners. And Nancy had the next drink, the really unbelievably, indescribably magnificent drink, waiting. When you had finished that with a cigarette that tasted like all the extra benefits the advertisements claimed, you were happy-flushed with fire and grog, and the soup was smoking on the table. The three personals were dandified in their white nightdresses and colored jackets, and old Aly, the cook, had scored another triumph, even if it was a ten-year-old boar wart hog that he had somehow contrived to alchemize into a six-dollar steak. Nobody made coffee as Aly brewed it over his oven of flat stones. The only trouble with it was that it put you to sleep instead of awakening you, or maybe it was the fault of the brandy that you poured into it. Because after the second cup of coffee with the solid slap of cognac you never remembered getting to bed at all. Suddenly Yusuf was shaking you gently by the shoulder and saying: "Get up, Bwana, it is morning," and thrusting a cup of scalding tea at you, the cup as big as a chamber pot. Your boots were lined by the bed, freshly and moistly dubbined, with the clean bush jacket and pants laid out, the underwear on top, and the thick gray wool socks folded neatly over the top of the boots, and the tooth glass and toothbrush and towel on the little table. You dressed, shivering, putting on the cashmere sweater under the jacket, and then went out to where the fire had shaken down into loosely drifting ash, with a bright cherry core of heat glowing through it, and there would be Peter, having a private attack of malaria in the cold gray dawn, with the wind blasting icily for the last half hour before the sun would rise to smile the cold away and scatter diamonds on the grasses. Peter would always be seated forlornly on a piece of unburned wood, toasting his hands and looking much smaller than in the daytime.

He would say formally, "Good morning, Tom," and you would reply, "Good morning, Peter," and he would clap his hands. The car boy would drive the jeep around and the two gunbearers would climb into the back, and the car boy would give up the wheel. Peter would slide into the front behind the wheel and ease the clutch, and you both would sit, saying nothing, looking, for the hour or two-hour drive to where the hunting was. The sun would creep cautiously up, red or golden, according to the weather, and soon the cashmere sweater would be too hot and you would strip it off and hand it to one of the boys in back. Occasionally one of the boys in back would hand a jar of peramenti —hard candies—over your shoulder to moisten your mouth, and you would hunt on, driving in great circles, seeing all the game there was to see, speaking never except when you stopped for a drink of water from the big-pored canvas water bag lashed to the front bumper. If something you saw through the glasses was a likely head, you got out and stalked it—sometimes a short stalk to an anthill or a patch of bush, sometimes a stalk of which the first five miles was just preliminary, sweating and stumbling and cursing and fighting thorns. When you got up to it to shoot it, you shot, in the later stages, with complete certainty, knowing that you could hold it where you aimed it, and if you hit it where you held it, it would die then with no more trouble . . . except, of course, the day the double-bloody-goddamned telescopes went all the way out and the gun was throwing eighteen inches high and a foot to the left.

But when you shot good there was the handshake and the gunbearers crooning "Oooeee" over the length of horn or color of mane or size of animal, and a cigarette handed round for everybody before you drove on, looking eagerly at everything you had come so swiftly to love. Every baobab, every knobbly butte of clustered green with gold outcroppings of rock, every umbrella thorn, every mottled fig, every sweep of lovely curving hill, every harsh cruel drop of escarpment, every animal and every cloud of weaver birds, rolling and dipping and twisting like a tornado, every flock of guineas pacing, all the lions you didn't shoot, and all the herds you did not molest—all of this was so special that you gazed greedily, anxious to see all of it before anybody else saw it. There was no time for talk and no necessity for it. Talking was for when you got back to the fire and Nancy, if she had stayed behind, and the first drink and the bath and the noisy fire and the hot dinner. Then you talked. You babbled, with all the words you had saved up all day pouring out of you in a great welling rush.

The best day of all was the day after you finally collected—funny how you got to use that word; you never shot it or killed it, you "collected" it—the big thing you were after, because Peter was a purist and wouldn't hunt but the one thing at a time. If it was rhino, you shot nothing but rhino, the same with lion and the same with leopard and everything else except the common game.

The day after you collected it was decreed a silly day. You knew you would be moving on, and so the three of you went out and had a lot of fine foolishness. You took the shotguns and the .22 and shot birds and took pictures and played with rhinos, with the jeep, letting them come up to horn range before you swerved, using the jeep as a bullfighter uses a muleta to turn a bull's charge. You chased monkeys and sang and laughed and chattered and enjoyed the day, hunting nothing, just playing around a land where the horizons were two hundred miles apart and a peak stood as freshly clear at sixty miles as it showed at six hundred yards.

Those were the best days of all, and the days you saw all the things you wanted most to remember later—a lioness cuffing her cubs, giving them a severe lesson in lion deportment; the baby topi that wobbled and staggered, enjoying no more than minutes' freedom from its mother's womb; the wart hogs trotting mock-serious and stuffy-stately, with their antennae tails all stuck high in the air; the zebras wrestling and the hyena away up in the tree where a leopard had taken him to eat him; the mother ostriches playing make-believe wounded and dragging their wings to lead you off from the chicks—chicks, for God's sake, chicks as big as turkeys—and the crazy wildebeests fool-galloping up and down for no reasons, and the two big male ostriches paddling through the lake, and the flamingos settling and rising like an unbelievable pink cloud; the doves calling and all the other bird sounds; that day some hyenas tried to take a piece of meat from some wild dogs, and one of the fisis ran into a tree and knocked himself cold—that was what a man got out of the free days, the holidays, where nothing was serious and you could loose off the shotgun without worrying about scaring away some monster-something that you wanted badly, very badly, for your wall. Those were the fine good days, shining days of blue and gold and green and white, days of warmth and the breeze fresh, days of sheer joy of being there and being alive on that day and in that place.

Nancy was thinking as they waited that she had never encountered such peaceful freedom from the formal fears before. She remembered mingling casually with savages in wild villages where a white woman was a complete curiosity, and she also remembered that she would not walk through Harlem alone or take the dogs into the park because of the muggers and perverts in New York. Or that she wouldn't spend a night in the house in Connecticut alone, by preference, while here she stayed alone with a dozen savages in the butt end of nowhere, in the middle of a zoo which differed only from the Bronx arrangement in that here there were more animals and less bars. In fact, she thought, no bars.

And the difference in Tom, she thought, I wouldn't believe it. He's sweet, but he's always had too much money and no work to do, and it was getting on for that bad time when something worse would begin to happen. Too much time around the late traps in New York and that Palm Beach-Bimini bunch in winter, and the *feria* in Spain where everybody sat up all night, every night, in Seville, drinking manzanilla; the same-people business about Rome and Paris, with everybody drunk and making a flamenco until all hours, all the time. One of these bad days he would be going to get bored with me no matter how much he loves me actually, because when it's right there for you all the time it loses fascination. And that's when some new blonde or redheaded fribbet tells him what a great big wonderful man he is, and unless I steer it very smart, then you run into what the tabloids call a "society divorce," and there I am, alimonied and miserable in my minks, lunching with the girls and cursing all men while wishing to Christ I had the same man back in the same bed to snuggle up to.

But this safari thing and this man Peter seem to have drawn something out of my lad that I suspected he had in him but didn't know exactly what it was or where he had it buried in him. I kid him a lot because he likes it, but there is a hell of a lot of Boy Scout in him that doesn't show when he's lining them up in the bar and listening to Joe E. make special gags for his private benefit in the Copa. I bet from now on he couldn't care less where he gets seated in El Morocco or the Stork —that's if he bothers to go there at all. I really love this Peter, not to sleep with, but to kind of cuddle. I will save the sleeping for Deane for quite a spell. But I love this Peter because when he is in the bush he is very serious and about nine years old in his approach to things, not at all like the brash young bounder of Nairobi, drinking too much and sneaking off with that hostess after he'd left us. I bet his Holly-girl knew it, too, but she's a smart one. Never by word or sign will that particular misdeed arise to haunt the house.

But what I love most about Peter is that he is growing my man up a little bit. I notice Tom has been asking an awful lot of questions about farming out here—what's best, cattle or coffee, sheep or pyrethrum? What do you want to wager, my good girl, that we don't get a proposition made us pretty soon, such as: "Why don't we buy a ranch, sweetie, and spend about six months or so out here every year? We could always get Peter to keep an eye on it for us, and we could bring people out and sort of fool around and let the breeze blow the gin off us for six months a year." I'll get that one any minute now, and when it comes I will say yes, for God's sake, please, yes, and I will be a pioneer woman and love every damned minute of it, especially if I can get me a Yusuf to run the thing and an Aly for the kitchen.

But in the meanwhile, O Lord, I am grateful for small things, such as that Tom is sweeter and gentler and kinder and more humorous and less like a rich man's whelp, less interested in how many drinks he had and how much money he can lose at the races and how many women in the room he could lay if I weren't there to cramp his style. Oh yes, Thomas, I have seen the speculative eye, and you would have been right about ninety per cent of the time. Ninety-five per cent, maybe. You could, too, if I weren't there to cramp your style.

"Let's have a beer, baby," she said aloud. "I wonder what's keeping Peter."

"Some sort of damned nonsense with that half-assed babu in the department, I shouldn't wonder," Tom said. "You stay here. I'll go to the bar and maybe prevail 'em into a Pimm's, if they can spell it in Tanganyika. What a bloody awful lion that is they've gone and hung on the wall. My second worse one looks like the M-G-M bloke by comparison. I promise you, I——"

"Hey, there, Peter McKenzie," Nancy said. "Parse the paragraph. 'Some sort of.' 'I shouldn't wonder.' 'Prevail 'em into a Pimm's.' 'Bloody awful.' 'They've gone and hung.' 'M-G-M bloke.' 'I promise you.' Oh, brother. You walk like him. You talk like him. You swing your arms like him. First thing I know, I'll have to buy an import license to re-enter you into the States. And what's worse, he talks like you do now. What

he would have said after having been subjected to you for three months
is:

"'Yah, he's all fouled up with some bum in the department. Rest,
babe, while I go knock the bar loose from a Pimm's, if they dig it here.
Christ, what a fright-wig for a lion they've stuck on the bulkhead. That
last bum I shot looks like Leo by comparison. Believe me, I——'"

"Oh, all right." Tom laughed. "I've heard you saying a few things
too. Your *a*'s have been getting broader all the time, and that did not start
to be a pun. I'll go and collect the Pimm's, old thing."

Tom walked into the bar and convinced the bar steward that you
could use a pewter beer stein for a more dignified purpose, especially
if you had a slice of cucumber. While he waited for the steward to make
the drinks, he was thinking about a few changes he'd observed in Nancy
since they came along on this thing.

Thank God for this Peter-lad, he thought. Nancy doesn't know it,
but she's dead in love with him in a very strange sort of way, and I
couldn't, as Peter would say, be happier about it. She is seeing a real
man at close range for the first time in her life, maybe, a real good man,
and I am going to come out pretty fair in the end, because I ain't been
doing too bad myself, for openers. Nancy never had a man for a friend
before. All she had was that Long Island drink set and the interior-
decoration pansy set, and for the rest they were all guys like me—too
rich, too frightfully, too idle, too advertising-agency, too Stork, too "21,"
too Morocco, too goddamned-too. They never played anything but lousy
polo or worse tennis, and hung around the saloons and each other waiting
for *Town and Country* to come take a picture of them. And, I suppose,
me.

Here she sees a guy who will slap a lion with his hat or take a
picture of a mama rhino at four feet and who still says *yes ma'am* and
thank you and *please,* and who gets up and bows and offers a cigarette
to everybody when he smokes one, and who is the most real man I ever
met in my life in more ways.

This boy reads a lot and talks soft and is gentle with his black people
and considerate of everybody and is a holy terror when he starts out fierce
about anything. He holds his liquor and he doesn't make passes at other
people's women and he pays his own way and has so much pride that
he'd kill you if you patronized him. He works with his hands and gets
grease under his nails and can come bloody-handed out of the belly of
a carcass, but he still does a neat rumba and plays a damned good canasta.

I reckon maybe this is the first time she ever saw a solid man operating where his father's money and his father's reputation weren't running heavy interference for him. And nobody giving a bloody bejesus about who his important friends are. Up to now I haven't made her ashamed of me in front of him, and that helps me some. All I can say is thank God for that, because I reckon I'd wear it around my neck all my life if I ever let him outwalk me or if he politely didn't invite me to go along on something dangerous like that buffalo. No living person will ever know where my balls were that day, nobody but me. They were in the back of my neck, and they didn't descend for a week afterward. But he asked me to go and I went. They can't take that away. I'll remember it when I'm old. He asked me to go and I went.

There was a fair chance old Nance was going to get too much into that charity-ball-committee routine back in New York, with the girl lunches and the I-hate-my-husband club they have. Poisonous bitches. I used to be always able to tell when she had had one of those girl lunches. I could tell because some one of those slothful sluts with the newest mink would always be divorced, just, or verging. They sit there in the Colony or the Pavillon and spill that corrosive acid all over each other, and then they come home mad at all men and take it out on the husband. They don't have enough to do to keep 'em busy at home, and so all they do is change their hair color every month and go looking for the new little dress shop to buy the new little dress or the new little hat, and then the first thing you know it gets chic to go to the new psychiatrist or to the palmist, she's uncanny, darling, and then somebody discovers a new and simply divine pansy who will do you all *over*, darling, so that all the hair *matches*. And then the psychiatrist tells them that they are repressed and they need a new interior decorator or a new house or a new lover, and whatever was pretty nice you had when it started goes to hell. You fight all the time after the martini parties and finally you clout her or she throws something at you and then the lawyers get together. If it wasn't screwed up badly at first, by the time the lawyers finish gnawing at it and the relatives get stuck into it everything's buggered, and away you go. After that it's only a matter of what you sleep with until you get lonesome for a woman's smell and presence in the house and you marry the first one that throws a kind word at you and the same old stupidity starts again until you get sick of her and fall into the hay with the next one that smiles and then you do it all over again until every son of a bitch you see is related to you by marriage. *Oh no,* said Tom, *I thank you very much, Mr. Peter McKenzie*, for showing the old girl how nice it can be when everybody's being nice all at once, and what she can't possibly suspect is that I am going to buy me a ranch out here next year and come live in it for a good six months a year. We will start to breed some boy-babies and teach them to shoot and ride horses and keep them the hell away from TV and comic books and the other boons of civilization, and maybe I can raise me up an heir or so that won't be a pansy or a filling-station heister, for kicks. *Well, I must say this bastard has taken his time with the Pimm's.*

"Asante sana," Tom said. "They look wonderful." He hooked his first two fingers through the handles of both mugs and carried the drinks back to where his wife sat looking at a year-old copy of *News of the World.*

"God bless us all, cried Tiny Tim," Nancy said. "I thought you'd gone back to Iringa, leaving me lone and lorn with a lot of Greeks. What kept you, Buster?"

"Slow-growing cucumbers, I expect," Tom said, sitting down. "What's that you're reading?"

"*News of the World,*" Nancy replied. "I cannot believe that people actually do the things they say they do in this thing. '*Peer Hits Paramour in Face with Pomeranian. Wife Stands Staunchly By.*' '"*I Loved Him Too Much,*" *Actress Weeps.* "*I Had to Shoot Him.*"' '*Mr. Semmling Can't Remember Where He Buried Last Victim. Possibly Near the Fuchsia, Slayer Says in Dock.*' '*Left Him Because He Slept with Boa Constrictor, Angry Wife Attests.*' God, but it's been nice in uptown Iringa."

"Any sign of Peter?"

"None. Maybe he's pushed off for home and forgot us."

"That I have *not.*" Peter walked into the room. "What's that, Pimm's? I'll just have one, thank you very much. It's still pouring with rain. That Christ-blighted Indian you wouldn't believe. He was going to give me what for about the two lions. *I* pointed out that between the three of us we had thirteen lions on the license. Then he raised hell about the cheetah. Didn't know you could shoot a cheetah. What he really didn't know—and which I certainly didn't bother to tell him— is that the place where we shot the kudu is now a game reserve. They just got around to declaring it closed. We're in the clear, of course, because it hadn't been announced yet. But we're nothing better than poachers."

"What's the schedule?"

"I thought we wouldn't trouble to eat in the hotel, food's lousy anyhow, but drive on outside of town and grab a quick lunch out of the chop box. There's still some corned bully and some cold guinea and beans left. If we don't wait around for lunch, we can be in Nairobi and washed and having one of Moussa's best in the Norfolk before dark. Also, I want to do a little fast business before you go, for which I'll need you."

"We've got a week, and nothing to do but see to the trophies with your man, what's-his-name. That'll only take an afternoon. Nancy'll want a hair-do and anything else they've got at the beauty shop, and that's the crop. What've you got in mind, Bwana?"

Peter dropped into a chair, and the waiter handed him his drink. The bartender was faster this time.

"Holly Keith business. I have arrived at the big decision. As Tom would say, I aim to marry me this here babe. In short, my intentions are ultra-honorable, but I suddenly find myself very shy. I am like that old chap of yours, Miles Standish. I need some character references, because by now Miss Holly Keith will have learned every dismal detail of my short but sordid life. I want us to go down to see her at her house, and I want you and Nancy along for moral support. I am what the man says, on matrimony bent. This is mostly your fault."

"That's quite a lovely compliment, little man," Nancy said. "Just how is it our fault?"

"I'd like to be a touch serious for a second. You people know by now what this life's like, and I've told you enough of what sort of people I deal with, chiefly. Some bastards, some bitches, some cads, some drunks, some queers, some weirdies, very few nice ones. I was pretty sour. But I've loved this trip with you both. And I especially enjoy the idea that people can get married and have fun and laugh and still be fairly old-fashioned about it. Damn it, I don't say it at all well, but what I mean is that you and Tom've made me want to leave this boozing-out-all-night-slap-and-tickle routine I've been mixed up in and get myself a good woman of my own, because I know it's possible. If it can be this good for you people it can be this good for me, and I think Holly's the answer."

Nancy got up and kissed him on the cheek.

"You are a good boy, Junior, and we love you. We will descend on the beauteous Miss Keith even as a swarm of locusts and bespeak your praises in fulsome tone. We will make you out a paragon of all the virtues since love came flying on gossamer wings into your life. In short, we will get you engaged to be married and stand as godparents to your first son, which will probably be at least half buffalo if it takes after the sire. Did I miss a cliché?

"I have known this was coming since the last night in Nairobi, just as I have known that any minute now Deane is going to say: 'Nance, don't you think it would be nice if we bought a ranch somewhere around Nyeri or down at Naivasha, so we can have people out from the States and get Peter and Holly to go off on a fun safari once in a while and grow some cattle and boy-babies?' How far am I off the mark, Thomas?"

"Only on the pigs. Don't *ever* get married, McKenzie," Tom said. "I strongly advise against it. The bloody creatures know everything in advance. I promise you—I mean, honest to God—I just had the thought while I was waiting for the Pimm's. But now that Nancy's said it for me, what do you think of it?"

"Jolly wonderful. I think there's a pretty good property at Naro Moru, near my place, in point of fact. You could have some fun and do some work and make some money, as well. And in between babies we might manage to steal away once in a while and have a little jaunt in the bush. Because I have a dirty suspicion that if this Keith manamouki agrees to my foul designs there will be no more professional hunting for this boy. I will be a farmer, like the old man, and my only chance of ever getting out of the house will be with somebody like you."

"Well, I always wanted to be a milkmaid," Nancy said. "Let's us go away and begin to plot against the chastity of the lovely Miss Keith. I think we better keep it light, though. The heavy hand-holding must wait until after we've gone. Kwenda."

27

They got rid of the home-coming drinking in Nairobi and heard all about Tony Dyer's Frenchman and the buffalo that dumped old Tony and put him onto crutches. They went out to see the taxidermist, and strode through a jungle of impala heads and elephants' feet, leopards' pelts and burlap-wrapped elephant tusks, rhino horns and zebra skins and ash trays made of buffalo hoofs. They sniffed the sharp unpleasant musty smell of the tanning fluid. They watched the assembly line of Kikuyu craftsmen—scraping, dipping, sculpturing, bleaching. There were more than one hundred and seventy-five Kikuyu dwelling on the taxidermist's shamba, all directly or indirectly concerned with the preparation of the hides, horns, hoofs, and heads of dead animals. They fixed the plane booking, and Nancy went off to the beauty shop to get her hair and nails and complexion repaired. There were a lot of hunters newly arrived in town, fleeing before the rains, including one old friend of Tom's, and they had a bright night out on the city, and nobody got slugged. Then they piled into a car and went off to lay siege to Holly Keith. The plot had cooked until quite late on the veranda of Tom's cottage. It was full of what Nancy called Old World charm, Kikuyu-fashion. Nancy reckoned it would appeal to Miss Keith's sense of humor, if nothing more.

And so Tom and Nancy took one Land Rover and went alone to the shamba of the Bwana Keith and introduced themselves gravely to the Bwana Keith and to the Memsaab Keith and to the Bwana Kidogo Keith, whose legs were longer than his sister's. The Bwana Keith was a tall redheaded man with an easy smile and from whom Holly had her hair and green eyes and longish nose and wide mouth. The Memsaab Keith was short and plump and blond and motherly. The youngster had only his father's legs. The rest of him was a carbon of his mother, save the plumpness.

"Where's Peter?" Holly asked as soon as she'd introduced them to the family, and they sat in wicker chairs on the lawn while the son went off to tell the servants to fix the drink cart.

"Coming behind us with John Thompson in John's gharri," Tom said. "He sent us on ahead to parley. Said it was customary in things of this kind. Shocking bad manners if he came himself."

"What's all this nonsense about?" Holly raised an eyebrow. Nancy thought that three months on the farm had not harmed this young woman in the slightest. She was wearing dark green slacks that tapered at the cuffs and fit snugly in the seat, and a cream silk blouse with a light green tie. She had her red-bronze hair pulled high, and she had tanned ever so slightly. She had gained perhaps a pound. She wore jodhpur boots beneath the slacks and looked much more rested than when Nancy had first seen her at the airport.

"What've you been doing since we left?" Nancy asked, ignoring the question.

"Nothing. Just simple wonderful nothing. Riding some with Daddy and flopping about the house with Mum. Sun-baking a little. Haven't been to Nairobi since I left you. I had forgot, clean, how very many interesting things there are to do and see on a farm. I've tended the pigs and midwifed a colt and shot some birds and helped Mum in the garden and walloped young Jerry and read some books I haven't thought of in years. I'm on Ouida now and find *Under Two Flags* fascinating. We play some records and listen to the radio and sleep—you wouldn't believe how much you can sleep. I feel like a filly looking for a paddock bar to kick over. How was the safari? Successful? Fun?"

"More than. I reckon this sunburnt lout of mine never had more fun in his life, and even if I'd hated it I would have enjoyed watching Tom play Indian with that small child, McKenzie. These are not really grown men, Holly. One's about nine and the other ten at most."

"What'd you shoot?" Keith asked. "Just the usual, or did you get something good, especially good?"

"Got a damned fine kudu," Tom said. "Fifty-seven."

Keith whistled. *"Fifty-seven?* Best I ever saw was fifty-two, and he was a monster."

"We lost one Peter said was sixty-two, maybe more. Ran round and round a baobab like a kid playing ring-around-the-rosy. Never in all my life have I seen anything like that one. We spooked him off a road, and when he ran his horns were laid back on his rump, and they projected past his tail. I still dream about him."

"What else?"

"Awful good defassa waterbuck. Not so much of a buffalo. Very big leopard—eight-four, he was. And one very poor lion—the first one, and then a real movie star. Had green eyes and red hair. Reminded me of Holly when I shot it. Hated to shoot it, because it was sort of like shooting Holly. Thought I'd give it to her for a wedding present."

"A *what?*"

"Wedding present. We come to speak formally in behalf of Mr. Peter McKenzie, bachelor, to the parents of Miss Holly Keith, spinster. This, Mr. McKenzie tells me, is customary. Even now he is coming with his father, from whom permission has been sought and granted, and Mr. Thompson, a circumcision brother. Nancy and I constitute the suitor's sponsors."

Holly's father began to laugh.

"How many goats are you willing to pay?"

"That will be decided when the other parties get here. We have arrived at a certain figure, but it is only tentative. Peter says there will be much beer drinking before the final figure is arrived at. I believe there's a hanging clause concerning the first five children or something."

"Just exactly what is all this nonsense?" Holly asked. She was getting quite pink on the cheekbones.

"My good girl, be quiet," Nancy said. "This palaver does not concern you yet. This is an overture only to the parents involved. State the case, Uncle."

"Well," Tom said. "It appears that young Peter wa Henry has observed this girl from afar and finds her comely. He noticed her as a child on her father's shamba, always into some mischief or other, and concludes she is misdirectedly industrious. He badly needs a woman to fetch firewood and dig around the planting on his shamba. Am I getting this right, Auntie?"

"Press on, chum. You couldn't be more perfect."

"Well. We come as the go-betweens. We have observed this young man for the last three months and find him to be reasonably clean, fairly honest, sober, or partially so, and kind. We do not think he would beat a woman much, unless she deserved it. He has signified an intention to be willing to stay home and raise pigs and children."

"And give up air hostesses?" Holly's voice was edged.

"*And* give up air hostesses. Also, he says a thahu has come upon him, and he cannot eat or sleep. He says this thahu can only be removed by the presence of this woman in his hut. So, due to an extreme shortage of honey beer at the moment, we have brought a substitute beverage."

Tom produced a bottle of Johnnie Walker Black Label.

"Tell your women to fetch glasses, please," he said. "No, never mind. Here comes the boy with the drink cart. Holly, mix a drink and put it in a glass. This is part of the formal procedure."

Holly got up and took the bottle over to the cart and poured a two-finger dollop into the glass. She squirted the glass half full of soda and handed the glass to her father. Keith looked up at her and smiled.

"Shall I drink this drink?" he asked. "Are you willing to tend the fields of the young man, Peter wa Henry? Are you willing to leave your home and go to his shamba? If you are, I will drink this drink. If you are not, I will spill it on the ground."

"Spill it on the ground," Holly said.

"Damme if I will," her father replied. "I haven't seen Johnnie Walker since before the war. If you think I'm dumping this drink, even for a joke, you're crazy." He tilted the glass and swallowed deeply.

"As far as I am concerned, you're engaged," he said. "And if you run away, I shall beat you. How many goats did you say she was worth?"

"Peter reckons about forty. But Mr. McKenzie says she is a good and willing worker, and so he is willing to up the ante a little bit. He says a Jaguar sports car, plus the goats. And I forgot to say: a wedding trip to visit us in the States is part of the bargain."

"In which case," Holly laughed, "hand me that glass, quick, Daddy. I want to seal this bargain before it gets away."

Peter came a little later with his father and with John Thompson, and there was a great deal of laughter on the lawn and later in the house, when they sat down for dinner. It had been a silly thing, the formal Kikuyu marriage call, but it bridged six years and three months and solidified an inevitability on a nice basis of humor. Holly thought, when Peter walked her out under the trees after dinner and took her in his arms to kiss her, that there really were worse ways of getting engaged.

They spent a lively week end visiting Jeff and Elisabeth and prowling over Henry McKenzie's farm. The "engagement" was about half serious only, and Peter was very shy with Holly. He clung to the company of Nancy and Tom, with whom he was not shy at all, and only just before the Deanes left to go back to Nairobi for the plane did he speak very seriously to Holly. They had taken a couple of horses and had ridden slowly down along the stream. Peter flung himself off the horse and flipped the reins over the horse's head. He took the reins from Holly also and then held up his arms, and she crooked a knee over the pommel, kicked free of the other stirrup, and slipped down into his arms. He held her for a moment, closely, and he could feel her softness through the thin shirt, could feel the shape of her breasts and the pound of her heart, as you can feel the pounding of the heart of a rabbit or a puppy or any small soft thing you hold in your hand. He lay down then on the short soft grass, under the dappled shade of a fever tree, and when she sank down beside him he hunched his shoulders backward and dropped his head in her lap. His sheaf of hair fell over his eyes, and she smoothed it back from his forehead and tickled his snubby nose with a blade of grass. They sat there, saying nothing, for a few minutes. The doves consoled each other mournfully from afar, and in the growing cool the francolin were beginning to squawk from their perches on the anthill.

"God, I love this country," Peter said finally. "I never want to leave it for very long. And I love you, Holly Keith, although I don't know anything at all about you. I love you in the same way I love the country. I love you like I love the Masai in the spring. I love you the way I love the smells and all the sounds. I guess I just love you, without any practice."

Holly bent and kissed his forehead. Her lips were very cool.

"You *will* marry me? Soon?" Peter looked upward at her chin.

"Not soon. Not for a while. It's not that I don't want to. I've been in love with you since I was six. Or at least ten. But I won't marry any man, no matter how much I love him, who's always away. Perhaps I'll sleep with you. But I won't marry you until you're done with this hunting. And I don't know whether you'll ever be done with it. I don't know whether you'd hate me after a bit if you gave it up on my account. . . ."

Peter took one of her hands and cupped the fingers over his mouth. His lips whispered against her palm.

"I'd intended stopping hunting at the end of a year. I can't stop very well until the rains next fall. I'm booked solid. One very long one, nine months, into the Sudan on a film thing, and I've already accepted the money. The other's short and will be up at the end of October. I can't take you on either—and wouldn't if I could, because I know the people and don't care much for them. If it was Tom and Nancy it'd be different. So I thought this: Let's just be engaged in the old-fashioned way, a long one. We can get married when I finish with the last safari. Tom and Nancy've asked us to come to America to visit them on the honeymoon. You'd like that?"

"I'd love it, of course. They're most tremendously nice people. Go on."

"Well, I'm finished hunting. The old man's been at me a long time to settle down farming. I'm ready, if you'll come along and run me. We can live in the big house with my father or, if you like, I'll build us a wing, like Jeff built Lisa, so we'll have our own new home, whilst still being close to the old boy. He adores you, you know, ever since you were a sprout. And we'll be old and stodgy farmers and get to Nairobi twice a year for a beano and go to Mombasa for the holidays."

"I'd love a wing of our own. Not that I don't love your father. But it's *his* house. I'd rather have something new of our own to start off with. But are you sure you won't hate *not* hunting?"

"I can't say I won't mind it. There'll be times when there's drought or an epidemic and I'll despise farming. I'll start thinking about the North or Tanganyika and curse cattle and sheep. Sure. Then's when we pack a lorry and take a couple of boys and go off someplace. Incidentally, I thought I'd keep some of the string. Yusuf to run the house and Aly for a cook and the two gunbearers as handy men. They know my ways. But to get basic: Yes, darling, there'll be some times when I'll fret and curse, but they won't be very often. But if you don't marry me, nothing's any good, anyhow. I'd hate every minute of everything I ever loved about the hunting."

"You're very sweet. I suppose I'm a pig not to marry you now straight off, but I will *not* spend the first year of my married life away from my husband. It's too much like a week end's fancy fun, and by the time you get back I'll have forgotten what you look like or sound like. It's too much of a hurdle. I'd love to be engaged to you, and I dearly want to marry you, and I'll marry you or just go off with you the second you're back and finished with safari. But marry you I won't until you've finished and done with it."

"I don't blame you," Peter said. "A year's not so long. I'll be back here as soon as I've shipped the Deanes away, and we can start the house. I've two weeks before the long shauri begins, and maybe we can have some fun and get to know each other a little better, to tide us over the long wait. Look, did Nancy say anything to you about me?"

"Just one thing. She said: *'You're a damned fool if you don't.'* I'm inclined to agree with her. Nancy loves you. If she didn't have Tom she'd grab you like a shot."

"I'd grab her right back." Peter grinned. "You look lovely upside down. If you were a very good girl and kissed me properly, I would then allow you to reach into my coat pocket, top left, and withdraw a package. It's for you."

The package was a box. The box contained a ring, a square-cut emerald, a huge deep-hearted shimmering stone. Peter slipped it on her finger and kissed her for a long time, rising from his headrest in her lap and turning her gently so that she lay on the grass, her lips upturned under his, her arms around him, her fingers in his hair. He kissed her gently in the hollow of her throat and on the curve of the shoulder, where the blouse had slipped aside, and the flesh tasted cool and sweet as gardenias. She sat up, shook her head, and held the ring in the air. It was only slightly darker than her eyes.

"Wherever in the world did you get this lovely thing? Not in Nairobi, surely? It's absolutely unbelievable."

"I have a slight confession," Peter said. "I sent to South Africa for it just before we left on safari three months ago. I had a suspicion I might need it when we got back."

"Can we afford it?"

"We can afford it. I'm filthy rich. And even if we couldn't, we could, if you get my meaning. I saw one like it two years ago when I was down in Joburg. Thought it was the loveliest thing I'd ever seen, until I saw you that day at the airport. Then I reckoned that one of you warranted the other."

Holly kissed him briefly and got up.

"I hope I'm not grass-stained. Brush me off. Then let's go show this enormous great thing to the folks. *Nancy* see it?" with a tinge of jealousy.

"No," Peter said, flicking grass from her jodhpurs and giving her a little smack. "Nancy *didn't* see it. I never got engaged before, but I reckoned that no woman wants anybody else to be the first to see her ring. This comes untouched by human hands, save mine and the jeweler's. Up you go."

They rode slowly back, thigh to thigh, the horses nuzzling playfully at each other's neck. It was almost dark, and the sun was crouching red over the hills.

"What a wonderful, wonderful thing," Peter said, reaching out for her hand. "To be young out here with all this country to live in and love you in and to have all the time ahead to do it all in. Come on, I'm too full of spirits to walk. Let's gallop these nags."

He kicked his beast in the ribs and smacked Holly's horse across the withers with his rein ends. The horses lunged, and Holly's hair came loose and streamed red-gold behind her in the fresh evening breeze. When they pulled up, the horses blowing, in front of the house, Holly jumped down and kissed him quickly.

"One thing, my lad, before we go in," she said.

"What thing?"

"No more hostesses. That phase is finished."

They went into the house, holding hands, swinging their arms like children.

28

They were married, Peter and Holly, from the home of Holly's family. Little John Thompson was Peter's best man. Lisa Newton's daughter, Caroline, was flower girl, and Lisa was matron of honor. Jeff Newton stood up with Peter, as Peter, long past, had stood for Jeff when Lisa and Jeff were married. The crowds, the food, the boisterous gaiety were nearly the same, but a little more boisterous now, for all the young men who were not dead were home and mostly married. There had been drought, and the bore holes were dry and the cattle skinny, but it would pass, for the skies were wooling up with angry dark clouds in the Masai, hovering over Ol Donya Rash, Telek, and Lolorok; the sound of thunder was heard, and soon the rains would sweep north, greening up the fields and plumping the cattle. For October, the weather was lovely, more like the times after the rains than the time before, except for the grass that was angled stiff and brown, and the red dust that rolled in clouds.

The year had skipped by for Peter, even though he checked the days against the finish of his last safari. The safaris—the long one and the short one—had been bloody to the extreme. The Sudan was steaming, and he had lost much weight. The clients were impossible, and like all other picture-making safaris, the long one wound up in disaster, with nobody speaking to anybody else. But the movie was made and in the can, and the short safari was unpleasant enough to be interesting. Time slid swiftly by, and before he knew it, almost, Peter was back, the clients tucked onto the aircraft, the bachelor dinner over, and now he was fumbling for a ring.

In the passage of the year Peter had forgotten just how beautiful Holly could be, even though he looked always at the picture she had sent him, and dreamed much, when he drove his jeep along, of that last day on the farm. He was glad now that they had waited. He had written when he could, and it was very seldom that he stopped at a ducca and did not find a long letter from Holly, her back-slanted script faithful to each detail of the new wing's construction, the doings on all three farms, and especially news of Henry McKenzie. Holly was spending more and more time with the old man as she watched the builders and familiarized herself with the farm on which she would be mistress one day. As each day drew the wedding closer, Peter was happier that they had taken the long time.

Now it was all wrapped up in a beautiful parcel. Now all the ends were drawn in and tied in a big velvet bow. Now the hunting was finished. Now the farming would start. Now the girl was in hand. Now there was a round-trip airline ticket for two, gift of Tom and Nancy, for a wedding trip to America. Now gleaming in the front yard was a black Jaguar with red leather seats, his father's wedding gift. Now it was all Christmas. The new wing, in which they would live, was more or less a replica of Jeff's and Lisa's, large cool rooms of subdued green and tawny gold, making a mansion of the big old stone house. And the bride was like nothing Peter ever imagined he would ever own. Lisa had been beautiful, they said, the old people, but my bloody oath, not like this one. This one, with the gold-flecked green eyes under that dark roan, near-mahogany hair, and the creamy skin against the dark curving brows, and the long slim legs under the short, flared, many-petticoated white dress. Men looked with dissatisfaction at their own beloved women.

Henry McKenzie was one solid beam. Now he could rest. Jeff and Elisabeth were firmly welded to Peter and Holly. There were three children in Lisa's house and soon there would be children in his own house again. Peter had come back to stay. Peter had shown sense in his choice of a wife. Peter had not become a drunken irresponsible like so many of the other hunters, and Peter had quit it early. Now he had it all out of his system. It had all been worth it, after all, all the work, all the pain, all the sorrow, all the uncertainty that had marked Henry McKenzie as rock is scored by rushing water. He was a little bit drunk this day, but not so much from the grog as from incomputable happiness. The empire was right there and he had built it; he, Henry McKenzie, all alone with his heavy, broad, horny hands. By God, from now on he would sit on the porch and smoke his pipe and teach the kids all the nice bad habits he could think of, as a grandfather, as was a grandfather's due.

The bride and groom were climbing into the new Jag, the bride even lovelier in a faint gray traveling costume with a green blouse under it, and Peter, for once, with his hair slicked back out of his eyes. They were driving up to Mawingo, outside Nanyuki, for a few days, and then they were going to Nairobi to catch the BOAC for Rome and London and finally New York, where Tom and Nancy Deane awaited them. They were taking two months abroad, and then they were returning with the Deanes for a short spin into the Masai as a sort of farewell safari, just the four of them, and then they would come home and go to work. By that time Holly was almost certain to be pregnant.

The Mawingo, a new and lavish hotel rebuilt from the mansion of a very rich woman and her titled husband, has one particular suite that was designed especially for people in love. It is situated at ground level and is done in white, with a huge fireplace. From the broad window, a rolling green lawn sweeps sharply downward and then flat across and then up again until it blends with the black forests of the Aberdares. At the top of the forests stands Mount Kenya, almost close enough to touch. In the late afternoons, just at fire-lighting time, the mists sweep away and the old snow-capped mountain fills the living room, hugely blue and sternly austere. It is impossible to watch it for very long without weeping a little.

It was just fire-lighting time when they arrived, and the dark mountain filled the window, crowding into the room. Behind the peak lay the softer blue of the northern skies. Again, as when Jeff and Lisa had married, the room was softly filled with flowers, and a barefoot black had laid a fire of eucalyptus logs that cracked and snapped and wantonly diffused their special perfume.

Peter and Holly stood in front of the window with their arms around each other.

"It seems to me," Peter said, "that it is illegal and unjust for anyone to be as happy as I am at this moment. There should be a law."

Holly didn't answer. She turned and held up her face, and when he drew her into his arms he could tell no difference between her body and his body. And suddenly the mountain stood in the window, but the mountain was all alone.

29

For the next year all went smoothly on the mountain. Kimani worked hard with his men, drilling them ceaselessly in the forests, building nuclei from the more intelligent and responsible, then finally awarding full authority to the corporals in charge of each team. The squads were stressed on five-man units. They did not shoot guns, but practiced stealth and swiftness in the forests. They specialized in mock raiding, practicing on each other to see how quietly and surely one group could surprise another, overwhelming the "victim" group in a rush, ambushing or infiltrating. The men, bound by the last oath, were reasonably tractable.

Kimani spent more and more time in the cave with Karugi. She occasionally went with him when he visited another camp, but seemed to take little pleasure in it. She became pregnant, and from the time her belly swelled noticeably, she developed a fixation about the cave. The cave was always warm; it had become more comfortable as women sent by Njogu brought little extra niceties up the mountain; sweets, occasionally, tobacco, and enough meal for beer. Even up to the eighth month of pregnancy Karugi remained lively and diligent in her chores of wood gathering and cooking. When Kimani asked her if she wanted one of the other women to come and help her with the baby, she refused. There was no longer any mysticism or ceremony connected with birth. There was no special maternity hut, no audience for the father to display sugar canes denoting the sex of the child. "When the child comes I will manage if you will help me," Karugi said.

"I will help you if you wish it," Kimani said, well content. It was peaceful to sit warm and eat well in the cave, to sleep and think and remember that there were rain and cold outside. Karugi was always cheerful; always obedient and thoughtful. She was a very good wife.

Almost a year from that day he slew his brother, two important things happened to Kimani. Alone in the smoky cave with his wife, he drew from her body a wrinkled, squalling son, and the mother smiled thankfully as she took the baby from him. Karugi was nursing the child when the word came that a band of young men had come down off the mountain and had killed and mutilated a herd of cows near Kinangop; that a white settler had been hacked to death in the tub as he took his evening bath, and that there had been a massive oath-taking near Kiambu, in a place called Kiambaa.

The next day more news came, this time brought by Njogu. He barely looked at his grandchild as the child pulled contentedly at his mother's breast.

"Come outside," he said. "There is quite a lot to tell.

"The cooking pot has spilled the grease into the flame," he said. "Your friend Ndemi got bored with waiting, finally, and led his men down the mountain. All was nearly ready for the sound of the bushbuck horn, but Ndemi, God curse him for the hyena's son he is, could not wait. He has decided to run the Mau Mau himself, so he has started off on his own, burning shambas, killing that white man at Kinangop, cutting the teats off cows, and leaving strangled cats and disemboweled dogs stuck on posts everywhere he passes. The other itchy young men in the other places have followed his example. The land is in a turmoil.

"The plan is spoiled, for a single big surprise, but the word from Kiambu now is for all to rise and to do whatever can be done. We can expect heavy resistance, of course, and the work will be much more difficult. You must marshal your men today, choose a sector, and start out tomorrow to proceed with the plan."

"But Karugi and the baby? The child is only a day old, and the mother, though well, is weak from her birth pangs. Who will look after them?"

"I will tend them for a few days and then get one of the other women to come and stay until Karugi is strong. Utmost swiftness is imperative, and if we are lucky, perhaps we can salvage something from what that fool Ndemi has ruined in his haste. How are your men?"

"Excellent. They hunt swiftly in packs like wild dogs, and I have not troubled them with any business of guns. Our work can be done more smoothly with the weapons we know; knives and bows and clubs. Time enough for the guns when we are an army."

"That is sound. You should strike swiftly, simultaneously in two or three farms close each other, and then you should fire them and retreat hurriedly. Kill only whites now, and only what Kikuyu are necessary. You have chosen your shambas?"

"Yes, I have chosen them," Kimani said. "Now let us go and see the baby. It is a fine boy, and of course he is named Karanja after my father."

They went inside. Karugi smiled weakly upward, a smile of pride and triumph. The funny little snuff-colored boy burrowed more deeply into her breast, clutching with tiny fingers.

"It is indeed a fine boy and will make a fine man," Njogu said. "But you had better go now. I will see that no harm comes to them."

Kimani bent and laid his hand on the cheek of his wife. He touched the baby gently with his forefinger.

"I will be back soon," he said. "Your father stays with you. Do not worry."

He took his gun and flashlight and a water bottle. Njogu stayed behind with the woman and the child. Kimani looked back just once at the cave before he started down the trail.

This time Kimani was going all the way down the mountain. This time Kimani was going home.

BOOK THREE

MAU
MAU

Peter woke early on the second morning of his honeymoon. His left arm was cramped and numb because Holly had gone solidly to sleep in the crook of it and he had gone off at the same time. He eased the arm from under Holly's rumpled red head and saw that she said something in her dreams, something that made her lips curve delightfully. She stirred in her sleep and crept closer to him. The nightdress had slipped off one shoulder and she had hidden her chin in the hollow of the upraised shoulder, snuggling it in the warm sweet valley. All the scent of her spread through the bed. Such a surge of feeling filled Peter's chest that the sweetness crowded all the way up into his throat and he almost choked on it. He put the pinpricked arm lightly back around her. He kissed the shoulder gently and prepared for another hour's sleep. "Mmmmmm," Holly said again, and lazily flung one arm out to fall on his chest.

The telephone rang. Peter's first inclination was to say oh-for-God's-sake and throw a pillow at it. He wanted to stay where he was warm. But it crowed again and he didn't want it to wake Holly. He slid out of bed naked, shivering in the morning cold, and pulled a bathrobe around his shoulders.

"What is it?" he said irritably, still fuzzed with sleep. "Who? . . . Speak louder. . . . Oh, it's you, Noel. . . . Yes, now I can, quite clearly. . . . *What?* Say that again. . . . Oh, my God. When? . . . Yes, yes, of course. Right away."

Holly came fully awake as Peter listened, and she saw his face turn sick and white under the deep burn.

"What about Holly's people? . . . Thank God for that, in any case. . . . Yes, surely. I'll drop her off at your house. Thank you. . . . As fast as I can drive. . . . Good-by."

Peter turned a new face toward her; a face she had never seen. The nostrils of his short nose were pinched white against the brown of his face, flared like a frightened animal's. His lips were drawn flat over his teeth, and the corners of his mouth pulled downward. White lumps of muscle pebbled over the line of his jaw, just under the ears. He breathed heavily through his nose, and Holly saw his hand shake as he flung the receiver back into its cradle. She sat up in bed, pulling the covers under her chin.

"What is it?"

"There's been trouble. Jeff and Elisabeth and the kids. I might as well tell you. Brace yourself. Jeff's dead. Lisa may live. Two of the kids as well. Dead. Caroline and Harry. House burnt."

"But *what? How?* For God's sake, tell me! *How?*"

"It's horrible. Wogs. They attacked the house last night. Killed Jeff and the kids and cut up Lisa very badly. House is a ruin, Noel says. He was pretty brief. We must get down there right away. Put on anything at all. They came to my house and yours, but thank Christ your people and my father were in Nyeri at some party or other." Peter was dressing as he talked. "Hurry now. We've got to get down there. What a hell of a thing, what a dirty filthy rotten hell of a goddamned thing." He sat down on the edge of the bed and laced his shoes. "I'll go fetch the car. Five minutes."

Peter was back with the car just as Holly pulled on a sweater and buttoned the side fly of her slacks. She left her face unmade, tied a scarf over her head. Peter trod the accelerator, and the Jaguar's motor warmed and then screamed. He drove down the road toward Nanyuki in a way that no Jaguar should ever be driven on Kenya roads. It was too noisy, with the sweep of the wind and the angry hum of the motor, for talk. Besides, Peter was completely absorbed in keeping the car on the road. But Holly could see his lips move as he cursed steadily with horrible concentration. Once, on a long straight reach, after they had surged through Nanyuki, he turned his head and gave her a tight smile and put his hand on her knee.

"Poor old girl," he said. "How absolutely rotten for you, apart from all the rest." Holly smiled faintly at him and covered his big square brown hand with her own. She felt tears prickle in her eyes. From the wind, of course.

So this is the way it runs, Peter thought. One minute you are warm in a sweet-smelling bed with the most beautiful woman in the world who loves you and nothing to do but wake her up, kissing, and then do what you did and want to do as much as ever you can forever. All you

have to think of is Holly's arm and Holly's mouth and then breakfast
and some golf maybe or just loafing off for a spin to Isiolo to shoot some
francolin or watch the elephants and then home to the fire and a drink
and watching her change out of the day clothes and into the night
clothes and then into the bar to say hello to all the people and then
maybe a cinema or a dance and then back to bed. And do it again tomorrow and then Nairobi and then the plane to Rome and London and
New York which I've never seen and Tom and Nancy and that "21"
they always talk about and the Museum of Natural History I always
wanted to see and a trip to Florida to see the other nice ones, the Dev-
lins, and then home again and all your life to make around each other
and now this. This. This goddamned hell-sent *this*. I wonder who and
I will never know why. But who is good enough and I will know who,
oh yes, someday I will know who, all right. Poor little kids. And this
other poor little kid in the shiny new car with me who was going to be
so happy today with her new husband. One lousy bloody telephone
call and it's all changed and buggered to hell and instead of a honeymoon and fun and travel we now mark our anniversaries by the day they
cut off Jeff Newton's head. I won't tell her that for a while, Peter
thought, and took a curve on one front wheel. Damn Jeff for getting his
head cut off on my honeymoon. I didn't interfere with *his*.

Holly's mind was wool-stuffed with the shock. I was going to put on
that new yellow frock he hasn't seen today, she thought. Then perhaps
we would drive up to Archer's Post and if there weren't any Somali
around we would go swimming in the rock pool at Buffalo Springs in
our birthday suits. I was only about half asleep when he took his arm
away and I was going to wake him up pretty soon or he was going to
wake me and it wouldn't have made any difference who woke whom because the result would have been the same. And we would have gone
on to Nairobi and the black dress with no shoulders and just one night
out and too many drinks at the Norfolk and the Equator and then off on
the plane for London, which he hasn't seen, and Rome, which he hasn't
seen, but I could show him, and then New York, which neither one
of us has ever seen but Tom and Nancy would wrap it up and give to us,
and now this. This horrible, awful *this* to remember a honeymoon by.
Never an anniversary ever again when the phone rings but you remember how it was before the phone rang and then how it was after you answered the phone. I hate telephones, Holly thought, and trouble always
comes in the morning when you're half asleep and unfit to handle it.

She put her hand on Peter's leg, lightly, and left it there with fingers touching the inside of his thigh.

"I don't want to go to the P.C.'s house," Holly said as they approached Nyeri. "I want to go with you. They're my people too."

"No," Peter said savagely. "I *have* to see it. I won't have you seeing it. I'm sorry. Noel told me some things about what it was like. You go to the P.C.'s and wait there with Helen. I'll be back as soon as I get the score."

"All right," Holly said, and said nothing more until they pulled up in front of the P.C.'s cottage. The P.C.'s wife was waiting.

"Noel's already gone down. You're to follow straight on."

Peter did not say good-by. The Jaguar bellowed as it settled on the road.

The sun was bright and the sky blue. The rain clouds wouldn't stack up over the Masai until afternoon. A nervous morning breeze stirred the trees and rustled the flowers in the yard. Peter scanned the sky after he left Holly, and as he approached Jeff Newton's farm he saw the blue sky dotted with vultures. They circled lazily, tiny specks high in the sky. As he turned into the lane he passed a lightning-riven tree, dead and leprous-peeling gray, with no foliage beyond a clump of white thorns. Five big griffon vultures sat heavy-bellied in the dead plumage of the tree. They straightened their obscene scaly-snaky necks as he roared under the tree, and took off creakily, their wings flapping harshly. Goddamned ndege, Peter thought. They always know the first of anybody. *How* many kills have I spotted with the birds before and been grateful to the birds for helping me find it. But that was a different kind of kill from this. It wasn't your sister and her husband and her kids. He jammed on the brakes.

The new yellowstone wing of the house was still standing, lonely against the ruin, vulgar-erect among the flowers, like the new house of an Indian. Most of the old house was smoking, roof fallen in, plaster smoke-stained, rock walls standing, but gutted inside. But the new wing was there, stiff among the flowers.

Peter's father, the P.C., several policemen, and Holly Keith's father were waiting for Peter when he drove into the yard and cut the switch, leaping over the door of the Jaguar.

"What happened? What *happened,* for Christ sake?" He turned to his father. The old man shook his head dumbly and gestured toward the Provincial Commissioner. The old man's face was cut in stone.

"We've had to reconstruct it from what we saw. Your sister is still unconscious and hasn't been able to tell us anything."

"Where is she?"

"We've rushed her off to the hospital. She's very badly cut up. Especially her face."

"Where's Jeff? And the kids?"

The P.C. jerked his head toward the barn.

"What's left of Jeff's there. There's nothing left of either Harry or Caroline. Not much, anyhow."

"Where's Jeffy?"

Peter's father answered. A little light was left in his face.

"Thank God for something. He and Lathela, Jeff's 'Ndrobo boy, took some horses and went off into the bush yesterday afternoon. They were going hunting. Wherever they are, they're bound to be all right."

"Tell me what you know," Peter said to the P.C. "Tell me everything you know."

"First you'd best come and take a look at what's left of Jeff," the P.C. said. "Come with me."

They walked back to the stables, from which the horses had been removed. Just to one side of the stable door lay a long stain of dried blood, like an inverted exclamation point, stiff-brown on the green turf. Inside the door a blanket covered something. The form was not that of a man.

"You'd better see," the P.C. said. "That's Jeff." One of the black police snatched the blanket away. What was under the blanket might have been Jeff. The head was missing. Some portions of the legs were there, and some parts of the trunk. You could not really say what was there and what wasn't there, any more than you could say what exact shape the meat that makes a hamburger patty was before it became a hamburger patty. Jeff Newton had been struck more than a hundred times with pangas. There was another blanket-covered form just behind him.

"That's the houseboy," the P.C. said. "He hasn't got a head either. I don't think you need to see him." The black askari pulled the blanket back over the heap of shredded flesh.

"Tell me fast," Peter said. "All that you know, now, while the old man's outside."

"From what we can piece together," the P.C. said, "they came after dark last night and waited. . . . Here, have a go at this flask before I carry on with the details. . . . *There.* The cook was in on it, evidently, because he's pushed off and the Number Two's gone, as well. Somehow, on some pretext, they got Jeff and the houseboy outside, here by the stables. They chopped him and the houseboy, *there*. Then they went into the house. I presume the kids were in the living room with their mother. They probably settled the kids before your sister knew what was happening. We couldn't tell about the kids very much, but they didn't have any heads either, what there was left otherwise of the poor little devils. Here, Peter, have another go at this brandy, man.

"It's hard to say just what happened with your sister. We found her under the piano. One arm was a total loss. There was a tremendous slash across her face and over the top of her head. One leg was pretty well hacked, but the doctor said they may be able to save it. Why they took the heads of Jeff and the kids and the houseboy and left Elisabeth alive under the piano, I couldn't say. Maybe something frightened them. But it was all so very quiet. The squatters didn't hear anything—they *say*. They didn't hear anything and they didn't do anything until after the house began to burn. Then they shoved some people over to your shamba and over to Keith's and found no white people at home. Your Juma saddled a horse and rode over to Naro Moru and finally roused somebody with a car. They came for me. That was after midnight. By the time I got here the old house was a cinder. We sent your sister off to hospital. Then the police went to collect your father and Keith, and here we are. Better come inside now and see the house. What's left of it is not awfully pretty."

They walked away from the stables and back to what remained of the house. Henry McKenzie was sitting under a tree, his head in his hands. Peter did not look at him as he passed to enter Lisa's wedding-present wing. There was no need to open the door. The broad french doors had been smashed in, and only sharp slivers of their glass stuck out from the iron frames. The blood-smell was overpowering, hot, steamy-thick, and sickly-sweet. It was the first time Peter had ever thought precisely about blood.

He had lived with and by blood. Blood was what gushed, black and grainy, from the mouth of a buffalo after a .470 slug ruptured the big arteries and the chest cavity filled with gallons of blood when the aorta was crushed. Blood was of many colors. It bubbled pink from an animal's mouth when the animal was lung-shot. It came reluctantly yellow-green and bily in the red when you gut-shot an animal. It roared out dark red and ropy-thick if the animal was hit in the heart, and it dribbled in pools around the feet of the hurt buffalo when he stood, sick and dying, his head drooped, waiting for you to pass a bush so he could kill you before he died.

Blood? Peter had felt it up to his armpits when he helped flay and butcher a carcass. He had seen it dried and flaky-black under his finger-nails. He had got it on his clothes and felt it crusted in his hair. He had seen it granulated with flies, brown on the ground, artificially stiffening the grasses. He had followed tiny little droplets of it for miles when an animal had been misshot and was running hard while its life leaked out. He had seen it in bright holly-red gouts and maroon slashes on blades of grass, and he had seen it mixed russet-brown with loose dung when the animal stopped to die and the sphincter muscle relaxed. He knew about blood, all right. That he did.

He thought as he looked at the room that it was amazing how much blood anything had inside of it to spill out. Even a well-fed mosquito. An elephant, by the time the Turkana got through butchering it with their spears, left a sluggish lake, a muddy river of blood. The strong sick-sweet scent could be smelled three miles away. The smell never bothered him very much, nor the sight of it, one way or the other. But the Wogs loved it. They lived off it. They doted on it. The Masai drank it nearly neat out of the necks of their cattle. The other Wogs caught it in cups from a dying animal. The Mohammedans, on the other hand, wouldn't eat anything until the halal was made, the knife pushed into the neck or the throbbing throat cut, and all the blood drained out onto the grass. They wiped the knife blade then on the animal's neck. By the time a gunbearer was through butchering a carcass he was as bloody as the carcass, despite what he drained off.

Blood was what you lived off inside you and died by the losing of it. It had all kinds of serious aspects. Bloody was a swearword. Hot-blooded was often a compliment. A blooded horse was a thoroughbred. You killed a man in hot blood, or you killed a man in cold blood. When the moon was red there was blood on it. When you were cold your blood was too thin. A Masai blooded his spear. There was a prince of the blood, and an aristocrat was said to have blue blood. You spoke of bloodlines in the breeding of animals. One kind of dog was a bloodhound. The Wogs said a man who was evil had bad blood. A man who was sick also had bad blood. Blood. Bloody. *Damu.* Even the Swahili word for it was bloody. *Damu*—damn you.

On this last trip he had allowed the client to shoot a zebra, sending the client out with a gunbearer in one of the cars. The man had butchered the zebra horribly, shooting away its jaw, shooting it too far back and too low, and the zebra had run and run, its face bloody, its guts dragging, its hide streaked red from the aimless shooting. The gunbearer had come back for Peter to finish it. Peter shot it, and when they skinned it out he saw it was a female and it had perfectly formed twin foals unborn in its belly. Those foals would have been dancing and snuffing on the plain in a few more days, but now they were dead without being born, washed clean in their mother's blood. A blood bath. A blood purge. A bloodletting. A blood oath. A river of blood. Bloody. For the first time in his life Peter McKenzie was sick in the presence of blood.

The room was soaked in it, swimming with it. It came soggy into his shoe soles. His gaze swung first to the piano. There were bloody footprints stamped across the keys, as if someone had stood on it to reach something. A tangle of wires rose like brambles from the inside of the piano where someone had struck it several times with a panga. There were separate big pools of blood, sticky, coagulated, crusty now. A long slick trail of blood led from one of the easy chairs to end in a thick pool under the piano. The trail was like the blood spoor of an animal, but the prints were handprints and knee prints and there was the long red smeared smudge between. The two Irish setters lay dead, one headless, the other half decapitated, on the floor, red-haired islands lapped by their own blood.

The drapes were partially charred, and one set had been pulled down and was soggy on the floor. The rubber-wheeled bar had some of the bottoms of bottles remaining on it and a rubble of glass prickly beside it, like cactus. Someone had raked the bar clean with a panga. The gun case was smashed and naked of its guns.

The weathered green-gray walls of the room were decorated at intervals with bloody handprints. Books had been snatched from the shelves and the calf-hide jackets of some still smoldered damply in the enormous fireplace. The huge buffalo whose great head threatened from his slope-necked mount over the fireplace was partially without a nose. One stroke of a panga had sheared it off, and the nose still lay in a pool of something else's blood in front of the fireplace. Bloody footprints led out of the room toward the french doors and down the stoop into the patio. Against the polished black of the ebony floors, the blood, even though dried now, made a vivid modern mosaic.

The writing desk had its own artistic design of handprints, like a Countess Mara tie Peter had once admired. Other prints were on the arms of the deep leather chairs. One of the leopard skins had been torn from the back of the divan and lay, bloody-whiskered, on the floor. Another leopard skin still crouched on the other divan, but its head had been sheared off and the divan's back deeply cut with another knife stroke. More bloody footprints led out of the living room through one bedroom and into the bathroom, where the closet shelves had been swept of the medicines they contained. There was blood on the tile, and blood on the shelves, and blood on the lav. One sheet-sized shaggy terry-cloth towel bearing the embroidered initials EMN had been used to wipe blood from big, splay-fingered hands and was crumpled in the corner. Oddly, neither bedroom had been touched, save for some bottles of perfume that no longer rested on Elisabeth's vanity. There were only bloody fingerprints on the vanity.

All the vases and flowerpots that had held roses and ferns and gladioli had been smashed. The flowers were mashed into the blood on the floor, their petals sodden-thick and smeared.

There was a steady high-airplane hum of the big, fat bluebottle flies. The floors and furniture were clustered with them, some too bloated to move. The grounded ones squashed underfoot with a juicy pop.

The wireless had been chopped through its middle. The phonograph had been crushed. Broken shards of records lay on the floor. For no reason at all Peter leaned over and picked up one of the disks. It was jaggedly smashed across its label. Part of its title was left. It said only "—rdanella." He remembered the old song well.

Peter did not bother looking at what was left of the old house. He did not want to see the slashed, headless bodies of young Harry and little Caroline; the little baby Caroline who had been his flower girl at the wedding two days ago. He wanted to be sick. He could feel the bile rising high up in his throat. He did not even bother to go outside the house to be sick. Being sick would not really add any great damage to what was already on the floor.

The police took fingerprints, and the minced bodies of the children were collected—rather, scraped up. They and Jeff Newton and the head-boy were hastily buried in packing boxes close by the flower garden. Peter went to the storehouse for paraffin and sloshed it heavily over all the drapes and the furniture. He took a panga and chopped up some of the furniture in the bedrooms, tore the counterpanes off the bed, hacked the mattresses so that the kapok flowed out, and pulled Jeff's suits and Lisa's clothes out of the closet and dumped them on the floor. He sluiced the whole with the paraffin and then touched a match to one of Lisa's flimsy chiffon negligees. He ran out through the shattered french doors and stood to watch the remainder of the house kindle and burn. The Masai burned their manyattas when they had no further use for them. Perhaps, he thought, someday young Jeffy might want to live here on this land again. He could build his own house then in a different spot.

Peter and his father got into the Jaguar and drove to Nyeri, stopping first at the hospital. The doctor was bafflingly encouraging.

"She has lost an unbelievable amount of blood, and the shock of seeing her kiddies killed must have been fantastic. The right arm is gone above the elbow. We'll be able to save the leg, I think, if she lives. The tendons are badly cut, of course, and she'll always limp. I don't know about the head slash, what it's done to the brain yet. She's under deep sedation, of course, and we will try to keep her knocked out for some time yet. I think she could live if she wants to."

The doctor paused. "*If* she wants to. I think perhaps if I were she I wouldn't want to. However, nothing to do with me, or you. By the way, what's your blood type, Peter, and yours, Henry?"

"Mine is O," Peter said. "Mine's A," Henry McKenzie said.

"She's an O as well. I'll just have a pint of yours now, please, Peter. You know any more O's? It's a difficult type to come by."

"As a matter of fact, I do. John Thompson's an O. So is Lathela, Jeff's nigger. So is Chalo, my gunbearer. I know John's type from his Army dogtag. I had all my boys typed, just against accident. And Jeff's Wog got clawed up by a leopard a long time ago and I was the only one around at the time who could give him any blood."

"That's fine, then," the doctor said. "Come along with me and I'll relieve you of some of yours. Send the Wogs along when you can, and Thompson immediately. The Wogs venereal?"

"I think not, but you'd best run a test on them anyhow. You can't tell with Wogs. They'll be clean one day and four-plus the next."

So Elisabeth McKenzie would live, kept alive by the blood of her brother, the blood of her brother's friend, the blood of a wild 'Ndrobo, and the blood of a Wakamba gunbearer. That was if she wanted to live, which the doctor doubted.

2

The doctor stamped a patch on Peter's arm and gave him a stiff free drink of whisky. Then Peter and his father went off to the P.C.'s house to collect Holly. The P.C. was at home. He had already told Holly the salient details. She was very pale and her eyes were puffed slightly from an earlier weeping, but now she was calm enough. There was nothing much that anyone could say.

"But why, *why?*" Peter said, hitting his palm with a fist. "I can maybe understand about Jeff. He was pretty rugged on his Wogs sometimes, and it's conceivable some boy with a long grudge might do him in. You remember that Kimani had a go at him years ago about that slapping business. But Elisabeth and the kids. I don't understand it. Lisa spent half her time out in the shambas doctoring Wogs. They all adored her. *And* the kids. If there is anything constant in an African's character, it's his love of children. They love their own and everybody else's. What do you think, Pa?"

"I believe I *know*," Henry McKenzie said. "And so does Noel. At least I know some of it, anyhow. It's part of a plan. I think it got started before it was meant to. I think it got out of hand. I think that when they killed Ben Ritchie at Kinangop the other day, when they hacked him in his bathtub, that business was also part of the plan. It's what I think we've all been afraid was going to happen someday. How do you see it, Noel?"

"I agree with Henry," the P.C. said. "The missing-head business tells me that it's more than a murder. It fits in with a great many things. Remember, for a start, the Forties are all back. That 1940 circumcision group was always the tough troublemaking wing in Kenyatta's K.A.U. And they were the boys that went off with the troops, remember. To learn all the bad habits. Also, Jomo Kenyatta's age group was called 'Big Knife,' named after the year the panga was first introduced here for cane cutting. I think that all of these crazy cults have finally settled into one big ugly one, with politics for its broad base. Henry?"

"It almost has to be, if I know anything about Kikuyu. It's been building ever since that lunatic started the Dini ya Msambwa back—

when was it, '44 or '45? Remember, Johnnie Walker and his boys had to shoot about a dozen of that bunch when they were trying to murder the missionary."

"Yes, I remember," Peter said. "I also remember that other bunch—you know, the Watu wa Mungu—that ambushed Inspector Mortimer and his boys. Killed the lot, the Men of God did. And Nairobi said it was just fanatics, like Nairobi always says it's 'just fanatics.' "

"I begin to think that perhaps my old friend Farson was righter than he knew," the P.C. said. "Helen, would you go and fetch the book that Negley Farson wrote a few years ago? The green one. It's on my night table. I want to read these people something."

The Memsaab went off to the bedroom and returned with a book called *Last Chance in Africa*, by Negley Farson. The P.C. flipped some pages until he came to a chapter called "Men of God."

"Farson and I had some arguments about these things when he was out here last," he said. "He was pretty vehement about it. This was at about the time when they killed Dom Mortimer. Listen to a few paragraphs of what Farson wrote about the 'Men of God' and the Dini ya Msambwa and the other cults. If he was right, we have a lovely problem on our hands. Listen."

The P.C. began to read, tracing the paragraphs with his finger.

" 'For some reason—I cannot understand why, unless they do not attach sufficient importance to these cults—top officials in Nairobi like to give out that there is no political significance in these incidents; they are "merely the result of religious frenzy." But people who have had to deal with them, such as some of the more thoughtful Commissioners in the Kavirondo and Kikuyu Reserves, assert that something very much more than politics is involved. They say—and from what I have learned myself I am sure they are right—that these fanatic religious cults which are now breaking out like boils all over the body politic of Africa come from something deep down, some common cause which is poisoning the blood-stream of the black continent, something so deep and desperate in the African's mind, his sub-consciousness, that to look at it for merely its possible political significance, its anti-European aspect, would be taking a superficial attitude. But whatever it is may be as hard to identify as what causes cancer.

" 'Disillusion seems to be the common denominator of all these sects. They are characterised by a sort of blind yearning to get back to the old customs, back to the primitive; yet at the same time they are also characterised by a marked desire to find a new way to God, and that *not* via the white man. Some of them even preach that Christ was a European (a white man), a man of flesh and blood, with, of course, a European's attitude towards the African; and they refuse to accept Christ as the medium between them and God, but prefer the more mystical medium of the Holy Ghost. They are all based on the Old Testament, with its violence, lust and cruelty as part of the Christian religion—a *perversion,* for political motives, of an old indigenous form of primitive religion which has been helped by a natural tendency towards violence and disorder of an immoral nature. They've got a basis of indigenous ancestor-worship, allied to a deep-rooted religion of the pagan *Were* (god); and, superimposed on that, the basic Christian teaching, which, however, has been debased by using the Old Testament texts to appeal to the people —and the whole has been taken as a political weapon. . . .

" 'I have said before that I think it can be shown that too much of the early teaching of the African has been left in the hands of the missions. For one thing, it places too much importance on the part that religion actually plays in the white man's life. It has given him the wrong idea of us. The susceptible African soon sees that we do not follow the teachings of the God that we are trying to get him to believe in. Sensibly enough, he does not doubt that God; he doubts us, and he doubts especially that we have shown him the right way to God. We have deceived him even there.

" 'As a result, the African, whom we have cut adrift, now seems to have lost his faith in everything. I might put it this way: the African has lost his faith in the white man's interpretation of God; he has lost his faith in the white man; he has even lost his faith in life; but he still wants to find his way to God.' "

The Bwana P.C. paused to search for a cigarette.

"That's enough of that; old Neg's preaching a bit, but he's on the right track all the same, and now listen to this about Dom Mortimer. This is what I was looking for. Listen:

" 'When the body of Assistant-Inspector Mortimer was found, one simi slash had split his face across the mouth; another, across his eyes, had laid his brains open; there was a spear wound in his back. The body of a native was also found, hideously mutilated. The wounded native who was the cause of all this was a native tailor who had refused to make a red flag for the "skin-men" a few days before, saying that he had not the time. The Man in Red and his followers had dragged him out of a native hotel—a mud-and-wattle hut—and slashed his hand almost off with a simi. He was not killed, as I had been told at Thika, but he was told that it was "Jehovah's sword" which had cut him, and that he was being marched along the road to execution so that the "skin-men" could "wash in his blood." The arrival of Inspector Mortimer had saved him from that. *God's orders have cut you,* the Man in Red told him.'

"And how about this one he is quoting?

" '*What are you waiting for? Let us wash in the blood of men. What are you waiting for? The time is over.*'

"And try this 'un for games:

" 'It is folly to try to assert that these cults have no political significance. Their aim to escape white supervision, to get back to the past, is in itself political; it means that they are an influence in the reserve which would block the supply of labor from that reserve. And that is about as serious a political platform as any African could adopt in East Africa. When, as the D.C. says in the above report, they can link this with a faith, then they could hardly have chosen a more effective method of self-protection from the normal consequences of non-cooperation with the Government. And each one of these sects is liable to the most murderous flare-ups if the right sort of Prophet comes along. This is exactly what happened when Elijah Masendi was liberated from the Mathari Mental Hospital in 1945 to go back into the Kavirondo Reserve: he had a cult of his own going within six months.' "

The P.C. closed the book violently.

"I'm not going to spend all day shooting quotes at you," he said. "But if you remember that lovely, learned book of our friend Kenyatta's that the Russian wrote the introduction to, old Jomo was mumbling some fifteen years ago about a great uprising to come. We will have to wait a day or so and see if there are any other operations that indicate Mr. Kenyatta's arising has come. If there are, we will shove Mr. Kenyatta into jail, no matter how hard the press howls."

"Shoving Kenyatta into jail isn't going to do very much about Jeff Newton and the kids and my sister," Peter said. "Nor neither some American writer's fine analysis. *We* live here. I know that we can't bring back the dead, and it's silly to talk about it. But one day I think I will find the black gentleman who was responsible for this thing. I will feel much better about it when I find him and his friends. Come on, Holly. Come on, Pa. We're going home."

Peter sent up to Mawingo for their clothes. Holly Keith McKenzie's honeymoon had lasted two nights and a little less than one day and a half.

3

When Kimani came down the mountain with his men he sent one team to Bushbuck Farm and another to the Keith shamba. He was going to attend personally to the shamba of Jeff Newton. He sent another team to the farm of Marian Sorrell and Sally Henderson. That was enough for a start, he thought.

"Do nothing if the bwanas are not there," he said. "*Nothing.* You will be able to talk to some of our people at each shamba before you do anything. You will be able to tell whether the bwanas are in the house. If they are gone away, leave it and go back to the forest, and wait at the oath-taking place. It is no good to burn a barn or fire the house or even to rob it if the bwanas are not there. Obey me, or you will make no more mistakes. Do you understand?" The men nodded.

"*Eeeh,*" they said, and went off in different directions. It was an ill-chosen night. Kimani could have had no way of telling that the Bwana Peter had gotten married the day before and that the entire countryside had continued the celebrating in various towns. His men found the houses dark at Bushbuck and at the Henderson-Sorrell farm and at the Keith property. The owners all had gone to a big party at the White Rhino in Nyeri and were spending the night in town. The raiders drifted in among the squatters, asked the whereabouts of the bwanas, and then faded back into the hills. They were very disappointed, and they cursed. The group at Bushbuck found a herd of milch cows in a paddock near the mountains, so they took their pangas and chopped the udders off a few cows, to express their disappointment. The group at the Keith farm showed their displeasure only by disemboweling Jerry Keith's pet cocker and leaving it screaming on a fence post. Everybody was gone from the women's farm. The cook had gone to Nanyuki to see his family, and the houseboys had locked up and left to attend an ngoma on another shamba. It was a big temptation to fire the house, but Kimani had said no. There was a great respect for Kimani since he had cut the head off his brother.

But Kimani found Jeff and Elisabeth Newton and the children at home.

"Look here, sweetie," Jeff said to Elisabeth after the big wedding party was over and they were driving home next day. "That bunch of howling savages want to throw another party tonight in Nyeri, and I say to hell with it. They'll drink and carry on for another week. Let's us just not go. Jeffy's going off this afternoon with Lathela on some deep secret trek they've cooked up between them, and I want to check him out on the rifles. He's only ten, after all. Also, I'm tired of grogging. We've been to some sort of party for the last six straight nights. Let's us go home and sit in front of the fire and read a book and maybe make another sister for Caroline. She's a bit outweighed by those two boys."

"I admire the intent," Elisabeth said, "and I will co-operate heartily. But I think that the baby-making part is a touch *de trop*. I've been meaning to mention it. Unless the signs are all wrong, we are about to breed again. In, say, about seven months."

"We must be doing something wrong." Jeff laughed and nearly overturned the Rover as he dabbed a kiss at her. "One, two, three, four. Only six more to go, and then I'll give you some time off. What is it to be this time?"

"I have a horrid feeling that it'll be twin boys," Elisabeth said. "I've been feeling awfully seedy, and usually I foal these things like a Kikuyu woman. Just *one* baby couldn't make me as sick as I've been lately."

"I thought you were looking a little peaked, but I put it down to all the parties," Jeff said. "Tell you what. We'll have a nice quiet dinner in the den. I'll run the Wogs off and bathe the kids and fix the supper, and you can put your feet up on something soft and we'll play honeymoon."

"Lovely," Lisa said. "I adore the people, really, but my God, they do get strenuous, don't they? With a few extra grogs aboard, I mean."

"That they do, that they do," Jeff said. "But they don't have many legitimate excuses for it. I reckon they try to make a really good binge last the year, and this'll run to Christmas. Our twelfth Christmas is practically tomorrow, and I am beginning to squeak in the joints. Whiskers getting grizzly too. I suppose it's all this childbearing that's aged me. Must be good for women, like physical jerks in the morning."

They arrived home just at lunch and found young Jeffy and the babies in a state of excitement. The children had been driven home the night before, and Harry and Caroline had been helping Jeffy to pack for his safari since early that morning. Caroline insisted until the bitter last that she was going along too.

Since Lathela, the 'Ndrobo-Rendille-Masai-Samburu, could not drive a car, they were making a horse safari, with one Masai donkey to pack the tent and the food.

"I am going to shoot a lion and an elephant and a leopard," Jeffy announced. "And a buffalo, as well. I am not going to be afraid to be all alone in the night by myself even when the lions roar and the hyenas come into the camp."

"All alone?" Jeff said. "Where'll Lathela be, to leave you all alone?"

"I am the Bwana," the boy said. "I sleep apart from my men. Lathela will sleep by his own fire. He will hand me the gun when I shoot a lion, but he will sleep alone by his own fire. I'm the Bwana."

"Be sure you shoot the lion in the ear," Jeff said. "And when you shoot the buffalo, try to break him down so he won't go into the bush. Now you'd best run off and say good-by to your mother."

The boy ran away. He was dressed in bush jacket and shorts and ankle boots. *Why,* Jeff thought, *in another ten minutes he'll be a man, poor little bugger, with all of a man's problems. He's shooting up like a weed.*

He turned to the grinning Lathela.

"See here, you uncurried cannibal," he said, speaking Masai. "You keep a good eye out for the Little Bwana or I'll skin you alive. I'm giving you a shotgun and the two-two and a little Mannlicher for the Bwana Kidogo to shoot, and a big double which he will *not* shoot. The double's for any special trouble. Hold it close and shut your eyes. But keep him away from anything big, do you hear? Let him shoot a topi and an impala and a Tommy or so, some birds. But stay away from anything larger, or I'll have your tripes for a necktie. Teach him a little tracking as well. It's time he learnt some bush things."

"Yes, Bwana," Lathela said. "I will be very careful with the Bwana Kidogo. Do you think I should allow him to beat me if he is displeased about not being able to shoot an elephant or a lion?"

"Of course," Jeff said. "A dozen of the best. But watch him, 'Thela. I trust you. This boy is my heart, as you are my friend. I would send him into the bush with no other man, except the Bwana Peter. Off with you now, and fetch us back a lot of meat and tall stories."

The safari went away, Jeffy on his piebald pony, Lathela awkward on a fat old mare, and the Masai donkey grumbling under his load. Jeff felt something catch in his throat as he watched the boy sitting his pony so erectly, too proud to look behind him at the house—frightened at the prospect of spending a night in the bush without his father or his uncle Peter, but sitting his horse with his back straight and looking proudly ahead of him. Caroline was sobbing, her black curls tumbled over her face. Jeff picked her up and swung her to his shoulder. "Don't cry, kitten," he said. "Very soon I will take you on a safari all your own, just the two of us. I will be your own personal gunbearer, and we won't even take Mummy, not to speak of those horrid boys. Don't cry any more and I'll tell you a long, long story when we get into the house."

They had finished a dinner which they ate in front of the fire, picnic-fashion, and Jeff was sitting sprawled in a chair with the baby Caroline on his knee. Young Harry was curled up with the Irish setters on the lion skin. Jeff was telling a wild, fanciful story about a time when all the animals ruled the world and all the people were their slaves. Elisabeth was reading on the other side of the fireplace, marking her book occasionally with her finger to smile at some outlandish stretch of her husband's imagination.

". . . But the elephant was very sad because he thought he had changed into a mouse," Jeff was saying, "and so he went to the doctor and asked him for some medicine. The doctor said—— *What's that?* Oh, it's you, Ndegwa. What's the matter?"

The houseboy dipped his head in apology.

"There is a man to see you outside, Bwana. He is by the stables. He would not come to the house. I do not know what he wants. He would not say, except that it is very important and has to do with the Little Bwana who rode off on safari this afternoon."

Jeff came out of his chair.

"Get a torch, Ndegwa. Let's see what he wants. Probably nothing except to say that he saw Jeffy and Lathela and that they are camped in such-and-such a place. Be right back, sweetie. You sit there and think about the elephant that thought he was a mouse, Caroline. So's I won't forget."

Jeff went out the door with the houseboy. They walked to the stables, the light flickering along the grass ahead of him as the houseboy showed the way. The night was chilly, with enough stars but no moon. Jeff had not bothered to put on a coat. When they came to the barn area there was no one to be seen.

"Where's this chap?" Jeff asked irritably. "What——"

Arms shot out of the darkness and seized his arms. Other arms wrapped around the houseboy. Someone kicked Jeff's feet out from under him. Someone struck him on the back of the head. The flashlight rolled to one side, and someone picked it up. The light shone straight into his eyes, blinding him. Then the light flicked away, and the holder pointed it into his own face. The face was only vaguely familiar. Jeff, half stunned, shook his head.

"It is I, Kimani," a man's heavy voice said. "You remember me. I have come back, Bwana Jeff. The last time I made a mistake. This time I make no mistakes."

"Don't be a goddamned foo——" Jeff said as he surged against the men who held him, but something swished as the light of the torch settled back on his face, and he never completed the sentence. As the steel struck his throat there was another swish and a *chunk* and the houseboy flopped headless in the grass, his torso bucking up and down. A wild, red-rolling madness enveloped Kimani and he struck with the panga, struck again and again, slashing away the slap in the face, drowning in blood the thahu on his father's house, washing away the ruin of his boyhood plans, slicing away the cold wet years on the mountain, cutting away the years in jail, cutting, slashing, as he struck and struck again and suddenly found that the crotch of his trousers was wet and the other men had already gone into the house.

Kimani struggled out of the mists of his madness and saw that the other four men had gone already and he began to run toward the house. There was a high scream from the house, and when he burst in the door, putting his shoulder to the glass of the wide french doors, he saw two children, their chests cloven from neck to belly, nerve-jumping on the floor, and Elisabeth Newton dragging herself slowly under the piano, clutching at the bowed piano legs with her one hand. Blood flowed from her as a stream bubbles and rushes down the mountainside. One of the men chopped at her with his panga and then bent to seize her by the ankle to drag her out. Kimani kicked him in the face as he bent over the woman. He looked up, bewildered.

"I did not say to kill children or women," Kimani said. "Only the Bwana. Leave her alone to die, now that you've done it. We must get on."

One of the red dogs hunched painfully along the floor. Its spine had been severed just above the hind quarters, but it snarled and tried to drag itself along by its front feet. The other dog was nearly headless, the head hanging by a string, its neck pumping blood. Kimani flicked the head off the second dog with a negligent motion of his wrist.

He looked around the room. So this was how the bwanas lived these days, he thought, while I live in a cave. In another rush of blind rage he walked to the piano and hacked at the strings beneath the raised lid. He looked upward at the mounted buffalo. He climbed on the piano with bloody bare feet and swung the knife, to shear the buffalo's nose away. He had never killed a buffalo. He looked at the drink table and chopped at the bottles as man attacks a tree with an ax. He drank beer when he could get it on the mountain. He had never tasted real whisky. Only gin.

"You, Kamau," he said. "Fire the house. You, Wainana, help him. Go that way through the passage. You, Mauro, take the guns from the cabinet. You, Karuru, take the heads from the children and the heart from the boy. I will take the heads of the Bwana Jeff and the houseboy. We have other oath-takings coming soon. Hurry, now. We must get away."

Somehow the books in the wall niche offended him. He tore them off the shelves and tossed them into the fire.

Kimani looked at the body of Elisabeth Newton as it twitched, still, under the piano. She is dead, he thought, we do not need her head, and I am sorry she is dead. I am sorry the children are dead, but there is no help for it now. At least I will not take the Memsaab Lisa's head. She was the sister of my friend.

The drapes had begun to crackle with flame in the other part of the house.

"Hurry," Kimani said as the men came back. "Take the heads of the children and we will go away. We can put all the heads in this." He snatched the tablecloth off the table. "Hurry. We have stayed here much too long."

He stumbled over a dead dog as he left the room, and cut at it irritably with his panga. They stopped outside only long enough to pick up the heads of Jeff Newton and the houseboy and place them in the tablecloth. The horses, terrified by the smell of blood, kicked and snorted in their stalls. Kimani scratched a match and tossed it onto a pile of hay, but the hay was wet from the evening dew and the flame sputtered and went out. Then they went away, away up the mountain, and as they left Kimani noticed that the lights in the living room were still brighter than the sparks the new fire was beginning to toss upward in handfuls into the cold night air.

4

The Provincial Commissioner and Henry McKenzie had been sound about the beginning of the epidemic. The pattern shaped and then appliquéd itself swiftly over Kenya. Every other night there was a killing. A white man and his wife were killed, chopped to pieces, in the outskirts of Nairobi, on Lower Kabete Road. Two old bachelor farmers were hacked at dinner, after the soup, when the headboy let in some of Kimani's men. Chief Waruhiu, who had been called the "African Winston Churchill," was murdered at Kiambu. Gunmen shot him to death in his car. An attempt was made, unsuccessfully, on the life of Chief Eliud at Fort Hall. The senior chief, Nderi of Nyeri, was sliced to bits with pangas. Eric Bowyer was cut to pieces in his bath at Kinangop. Commander Jock Meiklejohn was hacked to shreds in his home at Thomson's Falls, and his wife, a medical doctor with a local reputation as a saint, was chopped horribly and left for dead. City Councilor Tom Mbotela, a Kikuyu, was murdered in Nairobi. Chief Hinga was wounded by men who held up his car. He was taken from Limuru to the hospital, and one of the suave assassins followed him in a taxicab. While the cab waited, its meter ticking over, the suave assassin went into the hospital and shot Chief Hinga dead. Some people named Ferguson and Bingley were murdered at a place called Ol Kalou. A family called Ruck was wiped out at Kinangop—father, mother, and little son. The son had been locked in a room. The killers chopped through the panels of the door with pangas to get at the six-year-old boy. The Ngare Ndare police station was overrun and all hands put to the panga. There was a massive raid on the Naivasha police station and a wholesale massacre at Lari. A Seychellese mechanic and his wife and five children were murdered in Nanyuki. A Mr. McDougall was murdered in Nanyuki. A Mr. Beccaloni was murdered in Nanyuki. And hundreds, then tens of hundreds, of Kikuyu were slain coldly for refusing to accept the Mau Mau oaths, for refusing to co-operate in murder plots. The jailbirds of Kimani and Ndemi knew their work.

After fifty-nine "loyal" Africans and some dozen whites were murdered publicly, the Government decided that there might be some particular point to the killings. Britain had already sent a battleship, which aroused great amusement on the shambas, since Nairobi was two hundred miles away from Mombasa, where the ship dropped its hook. Then came the Lancashire Fusiliers, relieved of duty in the Suez Canal Zone, since Britain was giving that up anyhow. The 4th King's African Rifles came from Uganda. The Kenya Regiment was called out. The 6th K.A.R. came from Tanganyika. The 26th K.A.R. came from Mauritius. Fifty native publications were proscribed as prejudicial to the maintenance of order. The Messrs. Brockway and Hale, members of Parliament, arrived in Kenya at the invitation of the Kenya African Union. The Secretary of State for Colonies arrived from England. The Secretary of State left Kenya for England. The Messrs. Brockway and Hale left Kenya for England. The Kikuyu Independent Schools Association and Kikuyu Karinga Education Association, thirty-four schools in all, were closed down.

Jomo Kenyatta and five other Kikuyu were arrested and charged at Kapenguria with running an illegal social organization.

Sir Percy Sillitoe visited Kenya and made recommendations for improved intelligence organization.

D. N. Pritt, Q.C., who had successfully represented Gerhard Eisler, the Communist fugitive from America, was named counsel for Kenyatta *et al.* Diwan Chamanlal, an Indian, arrived to assist Mr. Pritt. L. S. B. Leakey, the son of a missionary, and curator of the Coryndon Museum, was appointed translator. Mr. Leakey had undergone circumcision ceremonies in the Kikuyu tribe, was a tribal elder, spoke Kikuyu as fluently as English, and described himself as a "white Kikuyu." While the trial continued, the murders broke out afresh.

The holiday season came on, and a note was left in a prominent position on a dead African for the police to find. It read:

"Christmas Greetings from Kenya, to: The Africans Communist United. The Africans Government the truth.

"We are now reaching the place of having our self-government because when the Europeans was not present in this country was keeped goats, cows and gardening but in the time we are very angry for Europeans to give the Africans much disturbing and to aim us with guns as a target mind you we are the human beings. Europeans are strangers in this country no doubt we say in sooth this is the Africans Country. The Kenya Europeans government has no United Nations charter. We leaved Athalita Hill and other crowds are leaving Mega Abyssinian boundry we are ready to reach every direction in Africa. We wait to be visited by everyone who wanted us, who goes after a person does not miss him.

"*We are wanting a dozen of heads for the Christmas of this month. We are the Africans Communist Unit.*"

On New Year's Day they had eleven heads. One day later they had exceeded the quota, for they collected two white farmers at one time. Everywhere the teatless cows, the strangled cats, the gutted chickens, the sheep's eyes plucked out and impaled on thorns, the disemboweled dogs spoke the passage of the men of Kimani and Ndemi.

The bands roved widely, striking swiftly, burning, looting, and killing, and then fleeing back to the safety of the mountain. The oath-giving increased, until some ninety per cent of the million and a quarter adult Kikuyu population had taken oath in one form or another. Those who hated and feared the Mau Mau joined up anyhow rather than be killed or see a relative murdered. Some were murdered merely for effect. The hills stank of rotted carcasses, nearly always without heads. A method of preserving the heads for oath-giving had been perfected by Njogu. The blood and brains of victims were saved and dried. Flaps of meat were cut off, largely from the buttocks, and spread thinly on bushes to cure like biltong.

The well-trained bands prospered, because some had learned stealth and precision in Burma with British troops. Others were products of Kimani's and Ndemi's finishing school on the mountains. Some knew woodcraft; others knew city-craft as well. All Kenya began to wear a gun and batten down its hatches in the night. In all the first months of the terror, only one serious setback was received by Kimani's smoothly operational thugs.

The setback was provided, curiously enough, by two women. They were Sally Henderson and Marian Sorrell, who lived on the farm near Peter McKenzie's place. It was the loneliest of all the farms, and when the terror began, Marian's and Sally's neighbors begged them to shut down the farm and go into Nairobi or Nyeri until the killers were quieted.

"I'll be buggered if I do," the big-bosomed, blond Sally said. "No bloody Wog is going to run me off Henderson's farm. He killed himself to make it, and everything I love in the world is in that house and on that farm. Anyhow, it's safer than the cities. Don't you worry about Marian and me. 'Djever see Marian shoot a pistol?"

The lean, short-cropped, blue-jeaned Marian smiled and scratched a match on the flexed seat of her pants. Marian, like everybody else, wore a gun these days. But where most wore .45s and .38s, Marian Sorrell wore a .22 on a .45 frame. She reckoned that was more than enough gun if you could hit anything with it—such as, say, the eye of whatever you were shooting at.

"We won't have any Mickey Mice trouble," she said. "We've got a fine bunch of Wogs on the place. All loyal, I'm sure. We're too high up on the hill for the MMs to organize our Wogs."

The women loved their home. Henderson had filled it with personal treasures that ranged from Abyssinian frescoes to Arab brass from the coast, primitive carvings from the Congo, fine heads and hides and horns, and comfortable sitting-down-on furniture. The floors were spread with thick rugs from Persia and the Gulf; there was a lovely clean-clipped badminton court and a vast lawn which was always glowing with flowers. Sally and Marian had the respect of all their neighbors. You rarely passed there without seeing some young trooper from the K.A.R. or the K.P.R. sitting, brown-kneed and barelegged, on the front stoop, having a beer or a cup of tea with Sally and Marian. They were well past the husband-hunting stage. One was a weathered widow and the other solidly divorced. They laughed as freely and as easily as men, and they always had a new and gamy story to pass on. They were careless with their liquor and prodigal with their food. The last cook had turned out a jewel. He was cross-eyed and limped from a safari accident, but his pastry floated away in a light breeze, and he could take a can of beans and turn it into a symphony. The two personal servants were well trained. They knew each like and dislike of the women. They knew that Marian always bathed first, in order to come back in her pajamas for a nightcap in front of the fire. They knew that Marian always sat next the wireless and that she always tuned the stations. They knew that the girls liked their evening meal smack on the dot of six-thirty and that they always bedded down by ten unless a party was on. They knew that they liked to munch raisins and walnuts as they read or listened to the wireless. They knew exactly what time they always got up; what time they lunched; what time they left for their one day of shopping in Nyeri. The household, roomy and fined down by use, operated smoothly from its eagle's perch atop the mountain outside Mwega.

Sally and Marian enjoyed the friendship of the women as well as the men. They made no motions toward the men of other women. They did not broadcast gossip. They lived in their own house, on their own hill, with its steeply winding but carefully landscaped road, with their two big Doberman pinscher dogs, their cook, and their two house servants. A thirsty man could always get a drink from old Sally; a man with family problems could always find a sympathetic ear in old Marian.

They were sitting one night before the fire, listening to the BBC, munching nuts and sipping beer. Marian was reading. Sally was mending a rent in a pair of jodhpur pants. The two Dobermans, Dolly and Elsa, were twitching in front of the fire as they chased something prehistoric in their dreams. There was no electricity in the house; it was lit by Coleman lanterns and the fire. Out front, in the yard, another lantern burned, by order of the Kenya Police Reserve. If the lantern went out, the night patrols would hurry along to see what was amiss.

". . . *Those are the headlines of the day,*" the voice came from the wireless. "*We return now to . . .*"

Marian got up and snapped off the wireless. She was wearing her pistol. Sally's pistol, a big police .38, was lying on a chair, close at hand. The cartridge belt galled her. The houseboy came in with a jug of hot water, passing through the living room, walking toward the sleeping quarters. He stepped softly because he knew the memsaabs did not like to be disturbed.

"Well," Sally said when the wireless hummed and died. "I suppose they'll never learn. There was no excuse for poor Nanson getting chopped. These people *will* put their trust in Wogs. I'm getting so that I hate to turn on the wireless. Nothing but trouble, trouble, always trouble—trouble here, trouble in the East, trouble in Europe. I think from now on we'll play the phonograph and give the wireless a miss."

"I don't know, I rather like to tune in after dinner and hear what's going on, trouble or no. In a way it makes this all the nicer here. They may have trouble everyplace else, but I know that at night Dolly and Elsa will be snoring in front of the fire and you'll be reading in that chair and I'll be sitting in this one. But Sally, sweetie, you really oughtn't to leave that gun lying about."

"Damn thing chafes me stomach," Sally said. "I ain't a beanpole like you. Be a dear and crack a couple more of those walnuts, will you, before you go to bathe? You're closest."

Marian got up and walked about five feet to the dining table, on which a bowl of nuts and the nutcracker stood. She was cracking a particularly plump nut when a draft came from the front porch and the door opened. Through the door hurtled the biggest African she had ever seen. He wore khaki clothes, filthy, and the legs were tied down by thongs, as men bind their trouser legs to keep them from snagging in bush. He had a long, gleaming simi in one hand and a huge, bulb-ended kerry club in the other. His teeth gleamed in the firelight as he lunged into the room, closely followed by a shorter but very powerfully built man. He carried a simi, too, and his club swung from a thong round his neck. The giant lunged at Marian, his knife hand held low and straight in front of him. The other man went for Sally. As the men rushed forward, the dogs came awake. The dogs charged the men. Suddenly the room was full of screams and curses and growls and grunts.

Marian drew her pistol, knocking over the walnut dish in her hurry to drop the nutcracker and go for the gun. The giant was nearly on her when she fired. But she aimed between his eyes and the bullet smashed into his brain and he dropped across the table. As she fired, a third African ran through the door, and she dropped him on the threshold. Her aim was a bit shaky and she only hit him in the right eye.

She wheeled and saw Sally struggling with the third man. He had forced her backward over a chair, left hand on her throat, simi hand upraised to strike, when Elsa, the Doberman, came off the floor in a smooth leap and took the knife wrist in her mouth with a crunch. The man screamed, dropped the simi, and clawed at the dog. Sally rolled away, and Marian fired at his back. The bullet hit, and the man flinched, grunted, and turned to run for the door, with the Doberman still clinging to his wrist. Marian fired again as the man swung the dog to his right and behind him. The bullet hit the dog in the ear. The dog dropped, dead, and the man stumbled toward the door. Marian fired again at the back of his neck, and he pitched forward, sprawling into the herbaceous border that rimmed the porch.

Sally had gotten up and she had her gun drawn now. There was a scuffing noise in the long passageway leading to the kitchen, and a shadowy figure appeared with another knife glinting in his hand. Sally raised her .38 and fired. The shadowy figure dropped.

Two houseboys raced along the passageway, one heading for the back door. Sally fired again and heard the bullet hit, but the boy went out into the night, with the other Doberman, Dolly, close behind. The second houseboy dashed into the only bathroom and locked the door. The two women went over to the door and shook it. It wouldn't shake. They began to shoot through the door. They heard a gasp and a groan and a thump.

Horrid growls and meaty, crunching sounds and bubbling screams were coming from the back yard. The women reloaded their guns and took a flashlamp and ran across the badminton court. The Doberman would want some washing. Her face and ruff were very bloody, and she had her teeth locked in a neck of which very little remained but bone. They dragged the dog off and went back into the house.

The figure in the hall had been the cross-eyed cook. He would make no more lemon meringue tart. Sally's bullet had taken him squarely in the heart. The huge black man still lay sprawled across the dining-room table, his head crowned by walnuts. The last man to enter was flat on his face across the threshold. He had not moved. The second man still had his naked heels on the veranda, but his head was buried in a mint bed, and the mint sprigs stood bravely past his ears. The wounded boy in the water closet would very possibly not make morning, so Sally decided that he had suffered enough. She walked over to the toilet, blew the lock with a bullet, and then shot the houseboy in the back of the head.

"That seems to be that," Marian said, and burst into tears.

"You're certainly not crying about *that*," Sally said, gesturing at the abattoir. "Surely."

"No," Marian sobbed. "Of course not. I couldn't care less about these dreadful bloody people. It's the dog. I killed the dog. I couldn't help it, I swear, Sally. He swung Elsa around just as I shot. I killed the poor thing, and just as she saved your life."

"Try not to think of it, sweetie," Sally said. "You couldn't help it. What I'm sad about is the bloody cook. Where'll we ever see his like again? The treacherous bastard. Come now, let's drag this carrion out on the porch. Then we'll get some buckets and a broom and tidy up the muck a bit before the police boys come. Oh, my God!"

"What, 'Oh, my God'?" Marian swabbed her eyes and picked the dead dog up tenderly and placed it on the divan. "What?"

"We're supposed to put the lamp out if ever we're in distress, so's the K.P.R. will see it and come to our aid," Sally said. "I completely forgot. Wait a minute."

She unsheathed the pistol and shot casually over her shoulder through the open door. The lamp exploded.

"I guess that'll fetch the laddy-bucks," she said. "You better see that there's enough beer in the frig. The boys'll be thirsty."

Kimani wondered what exactly happened to his best man, the huge Kitau, and to Kami and Karinga, and to the cook and the two houseboys who had been so carefully coached that they had left their shoes waiting, ranged neatly side by side on the back porch, ready for a getaway. It was some days later before a squatter brought him the complete news. The squatter had heard all the details on his Bwana's radio, just before he cut off his Bwana's head and killed the radio as well.

On the twenty-first of October, 1952, a state of emergency was proclaimed in Kenya. By December the casual country had completely lost its lazy charm and had swapped it for an armed irritation. A man looked no longer at his Africans with the old affection, the old tolerance, and occasional impatience. He saw his headboy not as good old Djuguna or silly old Kamau, who's been on the place since I was a kiddy, but as a potential cutter of his head. An African sharpening a panga had once stood as symbol of commendable industry. Now, if you heard the *wheep-wheep-wheep* of steel on stone, you wondered if good old Kungo or silly old Kariuki were merely keeping the tools honed or if he were creating a special shave for your neck.

Arms and ammunition, once so carelessly a part of the furniture in a Kenya farm, now took on a special baleful significance, for a new law had been swiftly passed. If a man lost a gun or it was stolen from him, he went to jail for six months, even if he were the bloody Governor himself. If an African was found in possession of a gun, he was shot on the spot or hanged swiftly. There had been a time in Kenya when a man who wore a side arm was crowed at as a cowboy from the films. Now pistols became chic. You would see a young matron shopping with her small children in an Indian ducca. The young matron would be wearing carefully tailored slacks, neat jacket, and boots. You would notice then that her accessories matched perfectly—suède handbag, suède belt, and suède holster for her pistol. If you went to a late party in

Nairobi or Nakuru, you would see the lovely ladies in their long frocks, with big, beaded evening bags. When a lady was going out for an evening she always checked the contents of her bag—lipstick, powder puff, rouge, hanky, Tampax, mad money, and small pearl-handled evening pistol.

The women were left much alone, in the towns and on the farms, because the men always seemed now to be called off on some secret business or other. Troops crowded the streets and the hotels and the bars. Tanks clanked and grumbled along the roads. And business went briskly forward as usual. Metro-Goldwyn-Mayer came out with Gable and Gardner and Kelly to make a film. Sinatra came to visit Ava. Rich men continued to arrive for safaris. The hotels were bulging. And the murders continued. In London the Mau Mau was still regarded as a brush fire. The killings were reported by the newspapers more as jolly unusual crime, sort of like Mr. Christie, than as a war. Only the settlers were heavily aware that it was already war. And, the people in the Home Office said, *you know the settlers*. Drunken roisterers, all, bad hats and younger sons and retired military types; they've got onto a good wicket where the Wogs do all the work and they drink and chase each other's women. This'll die down, as it always has. Fancy, one thousand settlers demonstrating at Government House. Shocking. Hairy ruffians, the lot. Remember old Delamere? *He* set fire to the mansion one time, in '22 it was, over some such similar nonsense. And the settlers said, over and over in the bars, hitching their guns more comfortably as they drank, if they'll just leave this to us we'll have it over and done with. You can't legislate these people into behaving themselves. Leave it to us and we'll fight fire with flame. *We'll* chop a head or so, and burn a few villages, and have it licked into shape in no time at all. But the bloody Government wants to treat 'em like gentlemen, when all they are is a flock of dirty murderers. Did you hear what they did to the Ruck baby and that thing on poor old Jeff Newton's shamba? I don't have to worry about *my* Wogs, though. They're good boys, the lot, and the houseboy comes and tells me every time there's a meeting. It'll never spread outside the Kyukes. The 'Kamba hate 'em and so do the Nandi and the Masai. It's a tribal thing, and the way to stamp it out is to really pitch into the old Kikuyu and show him a thing or two about terror.

And so it went. Each day a report of another burning, another killing, another wholesale slaughter of the black people by their own black cousins, blood brethren in the tribe of Akikuyu.

5

Tom Deane sat in a hotel in Kampala, in Uganda, in early January of 1953. His room was stacked with cased guns and cameras, safari boxes and square boxes of gin and beer and Coca-Cola. There was barely room in the room for the chair on which he sat and the portable typewriter at which he was pecking. He was writing a long letter home. There was nothing else to do that day, and probably the next. He sipped from a beer as he wrote, slinging two-fingered punches at the little Olivetti portable he had bought on his way through Rome. He had been writing all afternoon, ever since he had driven his wife, Nancy, to Entebbe, to put her on the plane for Khartoum and London, and there was a pile of paper on the floor. He finished the last page just as the sun set. The room was too cluttered to stay in. He picked up the sheets of paper, finished his beer, and went out to the lounge to have a proper drink in a comfortable chair and to read whatever it was he had written. The little lounge was deserted and quiet when he got there. He called a steward and ordered a whisky and settled back in a worn chintz chair to read. The letter was pretty messy, for the keys had stuck and had skipped spaces, but it was semi-legible, anyhow, and he could fix most of it with his pen before he mailed it.

"Dear Mac," the letter said. "I've just shoved the old lady on the plane for Europe and am sitting on my ass in Uganda waiting for something to happen. You being the sporting member of the firm, I wish you'd sort of pass this letter around and give the other people some idea of what the hell's going on out here. It's not at all like the jokes you were making when I took off on this second safari. Things are so unbelievably bad that I have given up all idea of buying a ranch, although God knows you can pick them up for less than nothing now in the troubled areas. Everybody's talking about selling out except a few stubborn, die-hard settlers of the old school.

"I put Nancy on the plane because she was so nervous that she was making *me* nervous, and we were fighting all the time. And Nance, as you know, is not a girl to be very nervous about anything. I'm killing time right now because one of my professional hunters is off being tried for murder—they try them two or three times a week, just as a precaution, fine 'em forty shillings, and let 'em go. The other one has just left us. He's been called up to run a tracking school somewhere in the high hill country. Now Nancy's gone, I won't need a replacement for him, but I also might say that the police have just arrested my lorry driver as a Mau Mau oath-administrator, and so the truck is sitting somewhere between here and Nairobi with nobody to drive it.

"It was an unfortunate time to come, but I had been looking forward to it for eighteen months, and the Mau Mau didn't seem so serious back home in New York. I had read about the slaughter of Peter McKenzie's family and was horrified, of course, but we have those things in America too. I haven't seen Peter this trip. He's off in the mountains with some commando group or other, hunting Kikuyu where he used to hunt rhino. I saw his wife briefly. She's bearing up, like most of the women here, living on Peter's farm with his father and his sister. The sister has partially recovered but isn't seeing anybody.

"But it was damned bad luck that we got here right in the middle of the Christmas massacres. I mean, dammit, man, you don't expect to ride up to the Norfolk Hotel just in time to see a man shoot at a Kikuyu running across the lawn, drop him with the bullet, and then walk over and calmly blow the back of his neck off. That's what Nancy and I and about thirty other passengers saw as we drove up. And I told you about our wonderful room boy from the last trip, Kamachi. The second day we were in Nairobi the Mau Mau cut his *head* off in Government Road, just down a bit from the hotel. I suppose he wouldn't co-operate.

"It was all pretty unnerving, and we got out of town in a hurry. Little John Thompson was our first hunter, and we went straight up to the N.F.D. and it was nice there, like it used to be when I was here before. I wrote you about the elephant and the rhino. Nancy enjoyed it, and the Mau Mau was sort of a brief bad dream. We refused to hook up the radio at night and so missed the gory accounts of most of the killing. Then we went to the Masai, and that was nice, too, except one night somebody came into camp and stole everything they could lay hand to—pots, pans, food, blankets. Thank God, no guns, for they put you in jail for losing a gun. John tried to carry it off that they were just some wild 'Ndrobo—wild tribeless hunters—but we found out actually that there is a big Mau Mau movement toward Tanganyika. That about finished Nancy for the trip—that and her favorite room boy getting hacked. We were going to Uganda to take some pictures and maybe get down to the Congo, but she put that firm foot down and so I am a bachelor for the rest of the trip.

"I don't think it's the violence and the guns everywhere that got to Nancy so much as that one trip we made to shoot ducks. That was when the size of the whole thing hit her. I'll try to tell you about it. I know that all duck hunters are nuts, but I believe I topped the insanity league on that one. We were passing back through Nairobi from the Masai, and I went to a place called Naivasha, in Kenya, for the noble purpose of shooting a few ducks. I went there just after one massacre and, it turned out, just before another one. I very foolishly took Nancy along, still thinking that this place was like it was when I was here before. I guess Naivasha was where it hit me, too, and where my wonderful ideas about buying something out here disappeared.

"It was not as though I were ignorant. I wasn't ignorant even a little bit. I've been in Kenya nearly three months this time. I have been all around the Aberdare Mountains, where they are chasing Mau Mau. I have stayed in hotels where the pansy manager wore a .45 under his tail coat. I have been to cocktail parties where they served shotguns with the gin.

"Jack Ross, a nice guy who is the boss of a safari firm here, is off to chase Mau Mau again, with his head in a beret and a Sten gun slung over his shoulder. Jack owns a farm on Lake Naivasha, in the heart of the Mau Mau belt, outside of Nairobi on the road to Nakuru and Thomson's Falls, where the main and biggest trouble is, and where they had just clobbered a police force. But Jack said the ducks were wonderful.

"You must understand that Jack owns three hotels, quite a few farms, a bank or so, and some other properties. He is not the kind of man you would consider likely to sleep under a poncho at twelve thousand feet and carry a machine gun in addition to the pistols on his hip, but that is the business he is in at the moment, like everybody else, and the other businesses have suffered somewhat. There are about thirty-nine thousand whites in Kenya, counting the military, against more than a million of the Kikuyu tribe, any one of which is likely to be a Mau Mau.

" 'I know your safari is about over,' Jack said to me. 'I know you got that big fine elephant and the rhino and the buff and you have been to the N.F.D. and to the Masai. But I was down to my farm on Naivasha the other day and the ducks are around like nothing you ever saw and I think maybe you ought to go down and have a bash at 'em. I'm sorry

I can't go with you, but I'm the executive officer of a commando that's leaving almost this very minute for some urgent business in the Aberdares, and so I've phoned through to my caretakers to look after you. I'd lock my door after dark if I were you, and you can't shoot after six. The K.P.R.—the reserve police—may be a little trigger-sensitive in that area. Been losing quite a lot of neighbors.'

"Jack warned me not to expect much service down that way. For one thing, murder had run so high among the natives themselves that there was a curfew on the help. You had to lock up the cooks and bottle washers at six, together with the labor force, in a special stockade, to keep them from being clobbered by their cousins. This meant that his caretakers, a pleasant English couple with a couple of the most beautiful blond rosy-cheeked little daughters, were doing most of the work of feeding and running the farm.

"John Thompson, a native Kenyan and possibly the toughest little man I ever met—he's built like a pocket Hercules and is called BIG John by everybody he ever played football against or had a fight with, although he ain't knee-high to a dik-dik—drove us down in his hunting car.

"It's not a long drive down that way. The road is hard-surfaced, turning off right to the Northern Frontier, where the big elephants are, and left toward the Masai and Tanganyika, which is where the lions live. A couple of hours does it. One lovely thing about the Naivasha area is that if you live there you can be in Isiolo in one day, with elephants in your kitchen, or camped up under Egelok in the Masai with the biggest buffalo in the world browsing on your whiskers, and lions in the parlor for cocktails. Or back in Nairobi for the movies, as the case may be.

"Longonot, a volcano, is red in the afternoon sun, with a lake in front of it and big black clouds, at this season, to give it a sinister look. The farmhouse is a simple stone house, smack-dab on the edge of the lake. It is centered in a grove of yellow-and-black fever trees, and the yard is full of flowers. The grass is green. The lake is fringed with papyrus reeds. The mountain changes color to yellow or red or pink or gray or blue, according to the weather. The yard is lousy with dogs—curs, spaniels, African ridge-backs, hounds, and impossibles.

"And this lovely lake, Naivasha, is just loaded with ducks. And the lovely neighborhood is just full of beautifully trained thugs who think it is fun to cut the bags off cows, the heads off babies, and the legs and arms off old people, white and black, who have been kind to them. They also receive a certain simple pleasure from murdering their close relatives.

"We arrived at the farm just in time to see the manager herding his black people off to the compound with a gun. It was really too late to shoot, but we decided to go out on the lake anyhow. Big John was singing a little song as we changed into hunting clothes. It ran something like any children's ditty, except it said: *'Mummy wouldn't buy me a Mau Mau. I have a strangled cat, and I'm very fond of that, but Mummy wouldn't buy me a Mau Mau . . .'*

"This, I thought, was a hell of a cheery way to start a duck-hunting expedition—especially as the lady of the house was busy buttoning up windows, locking doors, drawing shades, laying out pistols, and in general preparing for the cocktail hour. And it was such a wonderful hunting house—big stone fireplace, the usual leopard skins hung onto the backs of the divans, a few good heads, a few good books, and a lot of wide soft places for a man to sit down and wonder what there is about gin that makes it taste better when you're tired.

"We climbed in John's Land Rover and drove a short mile to where the boat was. It had one of those long-handled outboard motors that you bounce up and down to keep it near the surface in the lily pads and shallow waters. You flourish it more or less like an egg beater. It's quiet, and slow. You ought to get one for your boat, Mac.

"It was late in the afternoon and the sun already dropped over Longonot, and the air was getting chilly and brisk. A lot of ducks were rafted out in the middle of the lake, and a few hippos were rooting around offshore, and just a few ducks were trading around in the air, looking for a place to tuck in for the evening. We just chuffed a mile or so down the way and pulled in behind a clump of papyrus reeds and tied the bow painter to the reeds. A flock of Egyptian geese came in low and I loosed off at one, shooting absolutely straight up, and naturally the gun kicked me out of the boat into the cold ooze. Missed the goose, too, or at least I failed to deliver enough damage to slow him down.

"A few ducks came in and I missed some and hit some, and just as a big flock had set their wings and dropped their feet right in front of us, mine host held up his hand and said:

"'No. It's just past curfew time. We don't want the entire Police Reserve and the volunteer night watchers over here shooting us.'

"That's when it really hit me, this Mau Mau business. Here you got ducks flighting in and plenty of shooting light and no limit on birds, the sky full of big black mallards and teal and a cousin of the pintail, and you got to quit. Else somebody—not a game warden—is apt to blow you full of holes because anybody shooting a gun after curfew hours in that neighborhood is either making trouble or responding to trouble, and in either case a lot of hard-faced young men with weapons will come out and shoot you without question if you are just a dim shape in the dusk.

"We chugged the little boat back to the landing. Big John got out and dragged her through the ooze, and we collected the dozen or so ducks and threw them on the bank and then started the jeep for home. Home was locked tight. The hostess answered our rap on the door and met us with a shotgun. Other people have been known to knock on doors, and when the door is opened, the panga and the simi come through ahead of the caller. Pangas are bush knives. Simis are swords.

"East Africa, Mac, is the place where you have all the servants in the world—a headboy, a shoe-blacking boy, a pipe-cleaning boy, three askari boys to keep the chickens safe from stealing, the cook and the cook's assistant and the bathi boy and the soup-serving boy.

"Well, there weren't any servants in this house. The two kids were tucked in and locked in and the living room was closed off and locked, because it was more easily accessible to the front porch, and the dinner was a cold buffet of meat and fish and cheese, and after we had a couple of drinks we served ourselves. The serving boys were all locked up—for their protection and ours. The lady of the house cleaned up the dishes and took them back to the kitchen. Then we went to bed.

"On safari, out in the true bush, I just stagger off to bed when it is time to go to bed, in an unlockable tent. I have no faint idea where the guns are or who's got them or when I saw the pistol last. There aren't any Mau Mau there.

"That night Nancy and I went to the bedroom. I checked my shotguns. They were all there. So was the pistol. So was the ammunition. I checked the ammunition in the pistol. I put the shotgun together and loaded it with buckshot. I put the pistol on the night table, next to the cigarettes, the water jug, the aspirin, the ash tray, and the whisky bottle. Then I picked up the shotgun and herded the old lady down the hall to the bath. When she came out I herded her back to the bedroom and waited for the click of the lock before I went to the bath. The gun went to the bath with me, because a lot of people have gotten chopped in the John.

"When I finished cleaning my teeth I picked up the shotgun and rapped on the door and said in English it was only me, and Nancy unlocked the door and I locked it again and checked the windows—no fresh air allowed—to see if the windows were bolted, and then I laid the shotgun flat on the floor between us and poured a nightcap and read Mr. Leakey's book on the Mau Mau and then turned out the lights and went to sleep and had bad dreams.

"There was a pounding on the door next morning, and first I picked up the shotgun before I said 'Nini?'—'Who?'

"A low voice said in Swahili: 'It's only me, Bwana, Kalufu, with the tea.'

"In the bush, the morning chai begins the day. Usually the ruffian that looks after us comes in the tent and collapses the mosquito net and lets the air out of the mattress and pours a little scalding tea down my chest and says politely, 'Get up, Bwana, the day is here.' Then I put the tea on the deck and don't drink it and go right back to sleep and the same filed-tooth cannibal comes back after a bit with a new cup, which he sets down so I will be free to throw the old cup at him because he has just dumped some cold water on me. It was a joke between us, the morning chai, and a nice way to start a day.

"This day, when the boy said he was there with the tea, I took the shotgun and unlocked the door. Jamming it with my knee, I squinted through the crack. There was nobody there but the boy in the white kanzu and red fez.

" 'Kuja,' I said. 'Come in.'

"And I held the gun on his belly until he had deposited the tea and toast and backed out of the door. Then I locked the door. We had our tea and then I escorted Nancy to the bathroom, the same as before. Mind you, this was a good boy, and a loyal boy, and his feelings were hurt, but he had been taken to the compound last night and let out of it this morning and he wouldn't have been the first boy to be forced to let some accomplices into the lodge to chop the heads off all the nice people, including him.

"We went out to the lake and got into the boat, and the ducks were everywhere. With a proper blind, or even decoys, it would have been murder. But just shooting from the skiff, behind a clump of weed, it was not murder at all. The ducks came just to within range and then darted as they all will do when they see you, and anything I hit had a lot of shauri a Mungu—which translates roughly as God's will—behind the powder. Still, enough of them fell, until we stopped shooting because they stopped flying. It was one of those damned bluebird days when everything with webbed feet lights in the middle of the lake and just sits there, gossiping.

"Big John Thompson is a funny little guy. He said he was tired of this sedentary shooting and we would try another method.

" 'We will stalk the ducks,' said Big John. 'We will try the Mau Mau surprise tactic, as well.'

"So what John would do was creep up on the rafted ducks with the motor muffled and then give her the gun. I would loose off with one barrel at the sitting duck—and any of you guys who have spent money and powder on cripples know that very few distant ducks die when they are sitting submerged past the Plimsoll line in the water. But the copyrighted Thompson-Deane Assassination System, Ltd., worked. Enough shot would ripple the water to make the ducks fly, and nearly every time I would collect one with the left-hand barrel. I question the ethics of this technique, but out here we have so damned few ethics to worry about, since anybody who doesn't look behind him every few minutes is apt to be feeling his neck and wondering what happened to that big hairy bump on the end of it.

"We filled up the boat with mostly black mallards and the pintails' little cousins, and I noted then that a black mallard in Africa is just as suspicious and spooky as his cousin on Currituck or the Susquehanna flats or the Jersey ponds and cricks. A little smaller, maybe, but just as high-flying and sharp-eyed.

"We sweated the boat back, past the lily pads that clogged the egg beater, and stumbled through the mud and went back to the house for breakfast, which was hot, huge, and graciously served, because all the servants now were back from the stockade. With their heads on.

"With the warm sun filling the wonderful room with early-morning light, with the breeze brisk and the lake rippling in front, the flowers waving in the yard, and the dogs playing, and the two bright-haired little girls in their starched pinafores going about the day's duties with the dolls, and with the servants happy and competent now the day had come, with the coffee hot, with the fever trees brilliant and the volcano gleaming—with all the plains behind full of game and grass and primroses—with all these things to make a man happy I got blind furious at the absolute complete stupidity of all of it. There may be reasons why men kill each other that are justifiable, but when they kill little girls and ruin duck hunts and make living one long bloody precaution, when no real rights or real ideals are at stake, then I can get mad. Suddenly you understand why all the old men and the kids are neglecting their business and letting the farms go to hell to hunt Mau Mau, who are perverted fanatics who kill more of their own people, in terms of hundreds, than they kill of the whites. I suppose this sounds like a sermon. Excuse me.

"We dressed in city clothes, which meant a necktie and a pistol. We drove back to Nairobi, with the back end of the jeep full of ducks. We gave the ducks to the kitchen in the hotel and went to check on the news. Somewhere, up around the Fort Hall area, the Mau Mau had lured another farmer out into the compound and had chopped him. Then they had gone to the house to kill his wife. Then they had broken down the door of the room in which his baby was sleeping and had chopped the baby. The next week there was a wholesale massacre down around the Naivasha area we'd just left.

"I got to thinking seriously then about all the foolish things I had done in my life—sometimes at the risks of death and disease and danger. But none of it had I ever regretted, after. Time I had wasted, money I had wasted, and I never begrudged a minute of it or a dollar of it.

"But it occurred that I didn't know how many ducks I had shot on this little expedition, and that only roughly did I know what species. Everything that went to make it worth while had been wasted over a lot of necessary precautions, because a lot of people were running around killing other people aimlessly.

"That's about the size of it. I'm going farther down in Uganda, if Thompson ever shows up from being tried for murder, or if they send another hunter, and if we can get somebody to drive the truck. I never would have thought that old Kungo—he was Peter's driver—would be a Mau Mau, but they say he's an oath-giver. We never worried about him much, because all the other boys are Nandi and Wakamba, and we figured if any heads got taken the 'Kamba would be chopping on Kungo. But he's in jail and I suppose they'll hang him. Strange. Two years ago he was Nancy's shooting partner, and we used to leave her in camp with him and half a dozen of the other Kikuyu. She even used to go off alone with Kungo and the personal boys and spend the nights in the bush with them. But this trip she wouldn't stay in camp unless one of us stayed with her, with a gun. That's why I hired the second hunter.

"This has been much too long a letter, but I haven't got anything better to do. It's raining like stink in Uganda, when it shouldn't be raining at all. Like everything else, the weather's fouled up. Heigh-ho. So much for my Kenya dreams. The only dreams they got out here is nightmares. Give my best to all the gents in the various saloons, and get your girl to make some copies of this letter. That's how it really is in Kenya now, and it's only just gotten started. I'll be back home in about six weeks, I expect.

"Cheers.

"Tom

"P.S. You'll have to wait a bit for those zebra hides I promised you. Some Mau Mau gangs attacked the taxidermist's place again last night, and work is going very slow."

6

Life in Kenya had suddenly become a thing of triggered tension, of constant irritation and irritability, of glum expectance of catastrophe. That was worse than the occasional killings. The killings never really happened to you, of course, they always happened to somebody you knew who must have made a mistake that you would never, never make. But there was no squeaky mouse sound in the night that did not start a man into panicked waking, with his hand reaching automatically for a gun. Doors were bolted, windows locked, shades lowered, lights doused with the same unconscious precision that a man used to devote only to the care of his gun when he was off on safari or in a war.

Now it was all routine. Life suspended at 6 P.M. and crept inside locked doors. Armed askaris, mostly Wakamba and Turkana, patrolled some farms. The Police Reserve and the civilian spotters checkerboarded the country at night, looking in on this farm and that, but *still* the murderers slipped through, to strike and disappear up into the mountains or to absorb themselves in the towns. In a short time every white man in Kenya, from sixteen to sixty-five, was swiftly subject to call up for service in the Police Reserve or special commando duties. Some went into the Home Guards or into the Kenya Regiment. For the blacks, a great many of whom secretly were Mau Mau, the African Special Police was created. Some worked with the white Home Guards. Others, Tribal Police, were employed on their own reserves, and finally someone hit on the idea of reviving an old Kikuyu battle array, the Athegani. This was a special force composed of Kikuyu, Meru, and Embu warriors, some armed with shotguns and rifles, the rest with spears and bows. They operated under direction of the police. The Athegani was recruited mainly through the "loyal" chieftains, Muhoya and Njiri, at the tentative suggestion of the missions. It had been a long time, but now the young warriors had a real enemy to fight, and the scattered bands of Mau Mau were forced to collect into armies to face the Athegani. These Kikuyu guards were not paid for their work; it was enough that they had seized a spear by hand again. They were the men who supplied the guides and trackers, who helped in what was jocularly called the "interrogation" of prisoners, who combined with military and police forces in beats through the forests, who pointed fingers at suspects, aided in arrests, and supplied information obtained, in many cases, painfully. One of the first volunteers for the Athegani was Lathela, the long-time servant of Jeff Newton, the Lathela who had been off hunting that day when the Mau Mau came for his Bwana and who had brooded heavily since. Lathela fitted very well into the Athegani. He was no Kikuyu, but he was a tracker and a spearman and he knew many forest tricks to make people talk when the people did not wish to talk.

It was a time of much movement. The Lancashire Fusiliers had been transported to Kenya in a hurry, to be followed by the Inniskillings, the Black Watch from Korea, the 1st Devons, the 39th and 49th Infantry Brigade. The Royal Air Force came to Kenya and took the K.P.R.'s light reconnaissance planes under a wing, then imported its own bombers and finally jets. The streets were solid with soldiers, kilted, shorted, canvas-legginged, and heavy-booted. Tanks waddled and rattled down the roads.

(It still took London quite some time to recognize that England was at war again. The truth finally struck when, two years from the first murders, Major the Lord Wavell of the Black Watch and the assistant commandant of the Kenya Police Reserve both were killed in a full-scale military operation against Kimani's savage mountain men.)

7

Elisabeth Newton had decided she wished to live. Or perhaps she did not decide it. She was apathetic a very long time in the hospital, and when she finally came out she seemed not to understand entirely that

Jeff and her children were quite dead and her home burned flat. Perhaps the initial shock, perhaps the blow on her head had mercifully dulled her comprehension. Her father and Peter attempted gently, when she was better, to lead her into talking of what had happened. She merely replied that she didn't remember, and turned her face away. She mostly always looked away. The slash on the head and face had left a broad red scar that disappeared in her hair and dragged down one eye at the outer corner, making one whole side of her face grotesque. The severed arm had healed, and after a bit she was able to dress herself with one hand. Her leg gave her constant trouble. The tendons had been so mutilated that the leg had withered and shortened, and she walked with a lurching limp. When they brought her home to her father's farm she spent most of her time in her old room. She did not weep publicly, nor did she join in conversation with the rest of the family. She took to eating most of her meals in her room, as if she realized that the sight of her ruined face was a constant reminder. She especially avoided her young son.

They all lived on Bushbuck Farm now—Holly, young Jeff, Elisabeth, and Henry McKenzie. All thoughts of the honeymoon to New York had of course been canceled by the tragedy. And in any case, every hand was needed now, for most of the young men spent a great deal of time away on secret missions, especially young men like Peter who had been trained in the bush. Overnight Kenya was administered by women and old men and children. Farms went swiftly to wrack, for labor was in increasingly short supply as more and more police raids, more and more wholesale abscondings to the Kikuyu Reserve, more and more murders thinned the labor groups on the farms and made large-scale agriculture practically impossible. Therein lay a source of steady quarrel between Government and settler. At every mention of a wholesale screening, the individual settlers protested, cursing.

"You can't take my Wogs off to a prison camp," they said. "My Wogs are all right. And even if they weren't, how'n hell am I going to run this place of mine without 'em? I'm up in the hills half the time, chasing after Mau Mau. My wife can't do it all by herself. Somebody's got to milk the cows and grow a little food."

It was, possibly, the first time in the history of Kenya that the white man realized completely just how much he had depended on the overabundant labor supply which spraddled out on all sides of him. It was the first time he had truly estimated the degree of his isolation in the human black forest which covered the White Highlands. Despite profane protests and rude demonstrations, the Kikuyu labor forces continued to diminish. The Kenya Police Reserve would come and prowl among the squatter shambas. Acting on information, they'd suddenly select every third or fourth man and whip him off for "screening"—questioning and imprisonment or occasionally execution. There was no yardstick of loyalty to apply to the other, terrified workers. Trusted servants had figured in nearly every white killing. Even the man who wanted to be faithful to his Bwana bent his back before the determined infiltration of the Mau Mau scouts, since in final reckoning a hundred generations of darkness claimed more lobes of native imagination than any current gratitude or loyalty.

Bushbuck Farm was a somber household. Henry McKenzie and young Jeff worked the farm. Holly ran the household, for Elisabeth was of less than no use with the crippled leg and the one remaining arm. Peter was rarely at home. He had gone early into the K.P.R., in some special task force, and would drop in occasionally for a day or so, gaunt and briar-torn, with his eyes haunted and haggard and his hands shaky. Young Jeff had held up remarkably well, considering the first shock. He and Lathela had returned triumphantly from the safari, to find nothing but the ruins of a house and all his family dead or disabled. There was nothing to do but tell him precisely then what had happened, and Peter had told him as gently as he could. Jeffy had not at that time seen his mother. They did not take him to the hospital for a long time. If he was tremendously shocked when he first saw his mother, he managed to control his reaction to her appearance. Lathela was not so easily controlled. He took his spear and headed for the Kikuyu squatter compound which still remained on Jeff's farm, and had to be knocked cold and tied up by Peter to prevent him from wiping out what was left of the labor force.

Now young Jeff was a quiet boy as he worked with Henry McKenzie on the farm. His schooling had been suspended. He went about his chores wearing a pistol on his hip as his grandfather and his uncle and his uncle's wife wore a pistol, saying very little to anyone. When Elisabeth came out of the hospital to her father's home, young Jeff was pale and still. Afterward they seemed to avoid each other by mutual consent. The constant interfamily strain did not make Holly's life easy. It was like living always in a house with a deformed or mentally retarded child. No matter how fine the day, the scarred face of Elisabeth Newton was there to serve as a reminder of things as they once had been. Holly thought from time to time, as she fixed a simple supper after lockup—or when she sometimes took a Sten gun that had been issued to Henry Mc-Kenzie and she herded the labor force to the stockade for the night—that this was rather a poor way for a girl to start a married life. Her husband was almost never home. She rarely ever got to see her parents any more, because night visits were impossible, unless you stayed over the night, and she was needed constantly at Bushbuck. It was no good trying to get to Nairobi or even Nyeri very often, either, because the Mau Mau were firing on cars now, and rolling boulders down the hills, and the roads were booby-trapped, spike-blocked, by occasionally nervous Police Reserves. It was easier just to stay home and play the phonograph after you'd locked everything up and got out the sawed-off shotguns and drawn the shades. It seemed years since she'd been married, and another century at least since the phone had rung that dreadful morning, and it had been just three months. Holly had lost weight. She noticed she was smoking an awful lot and that she looked forward to the curfew time, when Henry McKenzie set out the gin. It was the only happy portion of the old days that still persisted, the fire and evening gin. The late meal was sad and awful. They missed Juma's impudent face and the fine cooking of old Aly, who had come to stay at the farm when Peter had quit his safaris. But Juma and Aly, devout Mohammedan Swahili both and dedicated Kikuyu haters, now had to be shut up with the others for their own protection, since the new restrictions had come in for that area. Too many "loyal" Africans were being butchered, much too easily.

Three months after Jeff Newton's murder Elisabeth came to Holly one morning after breakfast. Elisabeth, as always, wore a kerchief that covered her spoiled face and the down-pulled eye, and a shawl that masked her absent arm. She had a tiny blush of color in her cheeks.

"Holly, will you please drive me into Nyeri? I want to see the doctor."

"What's the matter, sweetie? The leg?" Holly had decided that there was no point in making believe that Elisabeth owned a sound eye, an unscarred face, a strong leg, and a live husband and two children.

"No, the leg's fine. But I think I'm going to have a baby. I *know* I'm going to have a baby."

The poor girl's mad, Holly thought swiftly. She's hung onto herself long enough, and now this is the real reaction setting in.

"A baby? Don't be silly. If there's anybody having a baby around here it should be me, and I haven't detected any signs of it yet. What makes you think so?"

"Please, Holly. I'm quite serious. Before that—before it—you know, before all that awful thing happened, Jeff and I had been talking about another baby."

It was the first time since the killing that Holly had heard her mention her husband's name.

"But after all you've gone through, the hospital and all——"

Elisabeth held up her good hand.

"When we sat beside the fire just before he went out into the yard we had been talking about the new baby. I'd missed two periods and had been very ill in the mornings. I was almost certainly pregnant. Of course I was in a daze most of the time in hospital and didn't know what was going on. But I know I'm pregnant now, despite all that other thing. I want to go and see the doctor."

Poor thing, Holly said to herself. *I've heard of these imaginary pregnancies after a heavy shock. It's some sort of compensation, I suppose, a complete retreat to what she really wants to remember.* "Of course, sweetie," she said aloud. "I'll run and get our coats and we'll take the Jag. It's been ages since I've driven it."

"I know you think I'm mad; that this is something to do with the trouble. It really isn't, I promise you. Feel."

Holly placed her hand on Elisabeth's belly and felt it bulging hard under her fingers.

"It's just not possible," Holly said. "Not with all that loss of blood and the shock and everything. It simply couldn't have carried on."

"Let's go and see the doctor," Elisabeth said. "If there is any chance of the child being harmed I want them to take it now. There are—there are enough odd things about here now without adding a peculiar child. But I want it if I can have it."

Holly felt a blurt of tears start toward her lids, and swiftly turned.

"It's a bit chilly. I'll fetch you that woolly camel's-hair and we'll be off. Maybe even have time for a drink at the Outspan as well." Elisabeth had not left the house since she returned to the farm from the hospital. . . .

The doctor came out shaking his head.

"The nurse is dressing her," he said to Holly. "You know all about this?"

"She told me just today. Is there anything to it, or is it——"

"This woman," the doctor said, "is just on five months pregnant, near as I can make out. Don't ask me why, or how. It's conceivable she was pregnant two months when that thing happened. She's always had very easy babies, and she's as strong as a horse. All I can reckon is that everything happened so swiftly that she experienced no sustained shock at the time. She had pretty fast care, and we were lucky about the transfusions. She didn't weaken herself dreadfully, and she was in a good solid coma for quite a while, and her body must've built itself back. Also, I've always had a suspicion that a little extra something goes into the glands of a woman who loses her husband whilst she's carrying a child. It was very common in the war. The telegram would come and the lady would swoon, and then she would get back up, clean the house, wash her hair, and produce a nine-pound baby. In any case, Elisabeth's five months pregnant."

"I can't believe it," Holly said. "Is there any danger that the child might be—funny? Marked, I mean? It *was* rather awful."

"I shouldn't think so. The child was just a dot when it happened. According to my tests, it's in a perfectly normal stage now. There's nothing to that nonsense of the mother marking the child, as certainly you know, and there's no better blood than the father's and the mother's. She'll need some special dieting to keep her strength up, of course, but if she hasn't miscarried now she's not very likely to, I should think. No, I think she should go ahead and have it. An operation to take it would probably kill her now, psychically if for no other reason. She's got very little left, this girl. Possibly the child would make a great deal of difference—a great deal of difference because the child, at least, won't remember her as she was, but as she is. That's very important to her. Well, here she comes."

Elisabeth limped into the room. Her cheeks were brighter than earlier.

"You see," she said. "I wasn't mad at all. Doctor says I'm a very tough woman and will have a very tough baby. I think we shall need some. And he says I'm to be allowed to have it. Think you can bear another burden, Holly?"

"Of course." Holly kissed her cheek. "Doctor, what about alcohol for expectant mothers? Good or bad?"

"Excellent," the doctor said. "Nothing better. Relaxes them no end. What had you in mind?"

"I thought we'd stop off at the Outspan for a drink on the way back," Holly said. "Neither one of us has been out much lately. How about it, Lisa?"

"I think I'd love to," Elisabeth said, and deliberately rearranged her head scarf. The scar showed striped on her cheek. She put on some dark glasses, which nearly covered the drooping eye.

"Let's go," she said. "It'll be nice to see people again. It's been very poky on the farm. I'll come again in what, two weeks, Doctor?"

"Make it weekly if you can," he said. "Have a good time at the Outspan."

Elisabeth turned and limped out the door, her foot dragging. The doctor rolled his eyes upward and went back into his office, where he allowed himself a very small medicinal drink. His hands were a little shaky.

The women drove past the mottled tanks and the prison compound, pulled into the court of the Outspan, parked the car, and walked through the lobby to the big bar in back. Elisabeth limped, hanging onto Holly's arm. Heads swiveled sharply as they entered. People nodded and said hello. No one approached them directly. They walked into the crowded bar, and a barefoot waiter pulled two chairs up to a small table. "Gin and tonic for me, please," Holly said. "You, Lisa? Rum—Coke, maybe?"

"I think I'd like a whisky. No ice, please, steward. Just some soda. Why are all the people wearing guns in here, Holly?"

Holly hitched her own side arm out of sight under the table.

"I suppose they've got in the habit lately, dear."

"I didn't actually realize it was happening to other people as well. I suppose I thought it only happened to us. I don't suppose it's much good getting myself a gun. I'm still having enough left-handed trouble with a fork."

A whisper had spread through the crowd as Holly and Elisabeth entered. Eyes moved carefully to look at Elisabeth's scar and to see if they could detect the place where the arm was off. From time to time a man or a woman would detach, as if by signal, from the crowd and sidle obliquely over to the table. To say hello, just. Without exception they employed the ancient sickroom strategy of pretending not to see anything that was there to see.

"Hello, darling, how lovely to see you again; you're looking very fit."

"Thank you."

"Well, Elisabeth. Well, Holly. One never sees you about any more. How's Peter and the fam——" Full stop.

"Very well, thank you. Marjorie is well now? I believe it was a boy, this last, wasn't it?"

"That's right. Horrible child. Looks a little like me. Well, so nice——"

"Good-by."

"I say, see who's here. It's Elisabeth and Holly, as I live. Wherever have you been keepi——"

"Very busy on the farm these days, with Peter away and half the boys in jail. Haven't had a chance to get about very much. Do come and see us when you can."

"Well, good-by."

"Cheerio."

Only one woman asked after the children. She left swiftly, hand to mouth.

The crowd was very much as usual, except for the guns. And of course the uniforms. The uniforms and the guns. The pathetically young Englishmen from the Fusiliers, with their North-of-England faces and their sunburned noses and fuzzy chins and pimples, their sub-machine guns slung over their shoulders and their rifles resting against the bar, never far from hand. They drank mild beer and chattered in jarring accent. Even if un-uniformed they stood apart from the settlers as strangers to the country. There was a freshness, a tenderness of complexion, that placed them immediately apart.

The settlers had guns, as well. They carried shotguns slung over shoulders. A few had Sten guns that had miraculously appeared from attics and armoires. Most of the Stens had been liberated in the war and brought home as souvenirs. There was, in fact, a most remarkable array of unsanctioned firearms—Biretta and Luger and Walther pistols from the war, issue Webleys and bartered-for American .45s, even a couple of Jap pistols and three or four Browning automatic rifles.

"My word," Holly whispered over her gin, "the lads *were* a bit sticky-fingered. Look at those binoculars *that* one's wearing. Must have been looted from a German brigadier at least. This looks like a commando get-together from the last war."

The clamor was no less loud than formerly, the men no less red-faced, the women no less weather-beaten, the dress the same, the mustaches as bristly, the jokes no less rude. The flat-palmed pound on the bar and the noisy demands for service had not changed. It was just that the demands were a touch more frequent, the talk swifter, and the drinks disappeared faster. The men drank belligerently, as if they had very little time in which to accumulate a load.

Elisabeth and Holly sat and smoked, not talking, feeling rather than listening to the mosaic of jaggedly fitted conversation, the phrases splintering into and merging with each other.

"We made a mistake when we arrested old Jomo. We could have shot up the whole bloody shamba when we went and found his private askaris posted all round the house . . ."

"The mistake was in going back for new orders. If we'd shot up the place then, there'd have been none of this bloody trial nonsense, with that stinking Socialist defending him and asking for retrials . . ."

"That's what I said at the time. Shoot now and we can always say the bugger was killed in the confusion. Been a powerful damper on the enthusiasm if we'd walloped him . . ."

"You can't say he wasn't smart, though. When we came back, ready to blow the place down, every last single one of his damned bodyguard had disappeared. Out strolls old Jomo as sweet and calm as cream. If we'd shot him then it would've been murder and a fierce great howl. All we *could* do was arrest him."

"If the bloody Government would just leave it to the settlers to settle it as we used to . . ."

"No bloody Wog's going to drive me off my land . . ."

"But, goddammit, Charles, we can't kill a million Kikuyu, and the only way I see out of it is to murder the lot . . ."

"I'm told the Americans used to poison the wells of their red Indians and infect the blankets with smallpox . . ."

"It's the Wogs on the shambas that are the big problem. You can't tell me that every time we make a raid somebody's trusted Number One hasn't tipped off the MMs, and they're already moved when we get there . . ."

"Well, frankly, I intend to give it another year. I've three kids to consider. I made more money last year than I ever made in my life, but what the hell's the future of a coffee shamba if you can't spend the money and can't properly care for the coffee? I'm about ready to pack up, and the missus as well . . ."

"I say, Gunner, what price the old Canal Zone? It may've been dull on Suez, but you didn't have the Gyppos sneaking round your tents with knives so very often. If it's Wogs you want, I'll take the Wogs we knew . . ."

"Another brandy, steward. That's twice I've asked it . . ."

"Did you hear, old Tom got eight the other day? Found 'em squatted in a hut, and turned the old Sten on 'em. Jolly good show, I say . . ."

"Jolly decent effort. A little more of that sort and this thing would cut itself short . . ."

"They say Portugal's nice . . ."

"I was thinking more of Spain . . ."

"Bloody dagos, the lot. Canada, now . . ."

"What the R.A.F. think to do with *bombers* I can't say. They used to miss Berlin and Hamburg. How they expect to hit two grass huts in a bloody rain forest escapes me. I still think that even using that light stuff as spotters is a lot of bumf . . ."

"I see they've called off the R-force. Boys were a touch too direct in their approach to the problem, I'm told . . ."

"One hears there's been a lot of suicides in the Aberdares lately. Wogs found hanging in trees with letters pinned to their coats. You know—'life has become too difficult to bear, good-by, Mum, good-by, Dad' sort of notes . . ."

"I hear they've got a new oath now, fit to curdle your blood. One of the Athegani claims he was at a new oath-giving, and they used a dog . . ."

"Hang the bastard, I say, and hang the Queen's Counsel as well . . ."

"Pity old Delamere and the other old boys aren't around. It never would've got this far . . ."

"Did you hear? They stopped the M-G-M caravan and pulled about half the lorry drivers out. Seems most of them were high up in the organization . . ."

"It's all very well to say that Kenyatta's the head of it, but who's underneath Kenyatta? We don't even know the first twenty subalterns, let alone the top two people . . ."

"Nobody'll ever convince me that the old Indian isn't back of it. It's exactly his smarmy cup of tea . . ."

"Ho, Gawd, Alfie, I thought that when the Germans quit in Libya it was me for 'ome and muvver. 'Ome and muvver were never like this, eh, cock?"

"No, *I* 'aven't tried out any of the locals, but Donald, you know Donald, 'e says . . ."

"I say, that was a jolly good show out of the two old trouts on the hill. I don't suppose the Mickey Mice suspected that they'd been holding pistol practice for the last three months . . ."

"Terribly amusing about old John. They came for him three times during the Christmas week, and each time he'd got so shikkered he had to stop on at the hotel. Saved his head three times, and they didn't even presume to burn down his house . . ."

"If I know old John, the way he felt the day after, it would've been less painful if they'd copped his bean . . ."

"You know the joke now. One's caught the other's piles . . ."

"I say, were you in Nairobi when they blew up the shanty town? They must've had a complete ammunition dump stored in it. Such a blasting and popping off you never heard, when all the hidden ammo went up . . ."

"I see the old Governor's off home, and we're changing generals again. 'Tisn't new generals we need, it's a free hand to run our own shauri . . ."

"I really pity the good ones, though. They're catching it at both ends. We're driving them right bang into the Mau Mau. There's got to be some way to protect them, or we've had them. They'll dive right into Dedan Kemathi's arms . . ."

"And they had a sign hung on the fence: 'Confession is good for the *soles*.' Get it: *soles* . . ."

"Campi a Simba. Now those boys had the right idea, but I hear they've all been whistled off . . ."

"No, it's my shout, Mac. You did the last honors . . ."

"Jomo . . ."

"Plitt . . ."

"Baring . . ."

"Leakey . . ."

"Time, gentlemen, please . . ."

8

The women left the bar and drove home in silence. They would have plenty of time to make the farm before curfew. They had decided not to stop on for lunch. The bar talk, the morbidly curious glances, the array of weapons, all had been depressing. It was the first real concentration of outside talk they had heard, for no one spoke much about the Mau Mau at Bushbuck Farm. There had been too much Mau Mau in the family already.

Holly thought as she drove, giving her full attention to the road, that one time when she was a little girl she had asked her Mummy what it was like to be married. Really married, she meant, having a man around all the time. It had been the day of Elisabeth Newton's wedding, the day when she was flower girl and her Mummy had sent her out to pick some roses for her tiara. Her Mummy was busy with the new baby and with dressing for the wedding and her Mummy had said that she would tell her about marriage some other time when she wasn't so busy.

I wonder, Holly thought, if she could have known or even *suspected that being* married is like what I've had so far, a multiple murder for a honeymoon present, a husband who is never home, and I wouldn't marry him earlier because he wasn't home, and now he's a lot more not home than he would have been not home if I had married him earlier and gained a year. *What is it like to be really married, Mummy?* she mocked herself. *Why, my child,* to be really married is to have to look after a sister-in-law who has been cut to pieces by some strange black visitors, and whose house has been burned down, and whose babies have been killed, and whose husband has had his head cut off. That is all part of the sickness-and-in-health clause, baby. Being married is to have to be a mother to somebody else's child, for young Jeff can't bear to look at his own mother and his own mother can't bear to have him near her. Being married is to see after an old man who is going to die pretty soon, because he has taken about everything a man has to take over a lifetime. Being married is to sleep by yourself because your husband is away, God knows where, doing God knows what, and any day they may bring him in, or mayn't bring him in, with no head on his shoulders. I suppose that's the have-and-to-hold part of it, with emphasis on the until-death-do-us-part part of it.

Being married is shooing the Wogs out with a gun and counting the ammunition and locking up the house and waiting for the time of the month and hoping, hoping terribly, that I'm not pregnant from the few times Peter does get home from his work for a day, because what we need very badly now is another baby. And another baby is what we are going to get almost immediately, because while the outside is wrecked the inside is still indestructible and she is going to produce. She will have a baby begot by a husband with no head. And with the memory of its sister and brother to amuse it with and its big brother who never speaks much and who already feels at home with a gun on his hip. This is the baby we will have in this house, this happy home, if there is a house by the time the baby's born, and if there is a mother to have the baby. And I came home to find some peace and raise a family. God Almighty. I hate her for having a baby. I hate her for spoiling my——

She looked at Elisabeth. Elisabeth smiled crookedly back at her. Elisabeth had been thinking too.

Poor baby, she had been thinking, *poor, poor child.* I had twelve years and she has had two days. There isn't any Jeff any more, but there were a dozen good years of him and all that we had in those years and Holly has had just two days and our thing was a wedding present. She's got me now and Pa and young Jeffy and now another baby and no husband of her own and no baby of her own. I don't know what Peter's doing off in the hills, but it has to do with the people that killed Jeff and my—my—with the people that came—and maybe someday she won't have Peter any more than I have Jeff, and Jeff's other babies, but I have more because there will be another one and there will be something left. She hasn't got anything. There will be something left when this baby comes that won't mind if I'm one-armed and crippled and my face is cut off and the eye is funny. He'll even think I'm pretty and a very special treat for a long time, because children are always fascinated by frea——

But suppose there's something wrong with him, something to do with that thing that happened. Oh God, maybe I oughtn't take the chance. Poor baby. Poor babies, all of them, mine that isn't born and the one that is so tall and would've been like his father, and this poor child that's driving the Jaguar on a trip back from the doctor. This is a trip that we should have made together, but I should've driven the car and she should have seen the doctor. But she has a chance to have something yet and I've had all mine except this, and I'm glad, I'm glad, and I'm going to have it and it will be a good baby. And it'll be all I've really got that's left of him because there is nothing at all with me and little Jeff. Not any more. Not the way I look. To my son I'm a bad dream. It would have been so much better if I'd died. But if I'd died what's left of Jeff would be dead with me and that would be selfish of me. Poor, poor Holly. And poor, poor Pa. Poor Peter and poor everybody. Poor little baby that I've not even had yet. Elisabeth looked at Holly. Holly was driving as fast as she could hold the car to the road, her chin lifted, her hair blowing. She drives like Peter drove, and like Jeff drove, Elisabeth thought. She drives like a man. And I suppose she is the man of the family now. Poor sweet. She's lost weight. She should eat more.

When they came into the yard a Land Rover was parked in front of the porch, and Peter was sitting on the porch with his father and little Jeff. Peter was drunk. He was very drunk. His eyes were bloodshot and his face was swollen. His hair was very long and he wore a navy-blue police sweater under a filthy short-sleeved bush jacket. He looked sodden, as if he had been left under water a little too long. His skin was pale, except for the flush on his cheeks, except for the heavy, black-greenish beard. He had lost at least a stone of weight. It made his puffed face perch oddly on his neck, which now seemed actually skinny. He raised his glass for another swallow as Holly and Elisabeth came up, and his hand shook, and Holly heard the glass rattle against his teeth.

"Hello, *swh*-sweetie," he said. He came stiff-jointed to his feet. "*Sh—* see *whosh*—who's here. The wanderinbridegroom, home from the hillsh —*hills*. Home from the hillsh—goddammit, *hills*—with his hair in a curl. Home is the hunter, home from the *h-i-l-l-s*. See, I made it, I can even say it fast. *Hills.* Frightf'ly sorry I am a *lit-tle* bit *drun-k*. It's the *al-ti-tude* in the Ab'*dares*. Affects man no end when come down fash—*fast*. *Al-so*, also, haven't had 'ngrog speak of *late-ly*. Affects tummy notmention head. How is everylittlething Bushbuck Farm. Give's kish—*kiss*."

Holly went over and lifted her face to be kissed. Peter smelled sour and sick from the—— But she had had a drink too, and she had never smelled drink on Peter when she had had a drink too.

"How very wonderful, darling," she said. "We weren't expecting you. Can you stay long?"

"Can't sh-*tay* very long. Day so. Come for Pa. Need Pa on mountain. Whole mountain need Pa. Pa invited Govvermun request. Hello, Lisa.

No kiss for brother? No kiss little brother? Shbetter. Like in book. Everybody kiss. Kiss blood off hands. Jolly fine book."

"Darling, you're completely done up," Holly said. She looked at Henry McKenzie. The old man nodded. "Come along with me and I'll fix you a bath. Won't take a minute to get some hot water."

"Sh-*stay* here and have 'notherdrink. Send Wogs heat water bathi. Majimoto pese pese boy. Bloody nugu. Suria!" He reached for his drink and knocked it over. "Oh, sorry. Terribly sorry. Cumsy—*clumsy* of me. Where's boy? *Bloody*boy. Kuja hapa!"

Young Jeff got up.

"I took the boys down to the stockade," he said. "Grandpa let me take the big gun. There's some water heating on the stove. I'll fix Uncle Peter's bath." He walked off to the kitchen, the pistol riding easily on his hip.

"Bloody fine man, young Jeff." Peter grinned foolishly. "Jush likesfather. Except young Jeff's got bloody fine head on his sh——"

Elisabeth got up and lurched away hurriedly to the living room.

"Oh, Peter, *Peter*," Holly said. "Darling, you're awfully tired, and the——"

"Sorry, awf'ly sorry," Peter said. "Didn't mean make lit'rary 'lusion. It's just I'm little drunk, see, stopped off have one-two way down and must be hit empty sh-*stomach*. Not mush eat lately. Not very mush anybody eat lately. Mushtoo busy. Liked old clients better. Mush better. These clients hard get net on. Not so hard satisfy once got net on. Getting net on whole problem. Like hunt bongo. All got do is shee-*see* 'em, bang! Bongo."

"I think we'd best go in the house," Holly said. "It's past time to lock up. Also, it's chilly. There's a fire, Pa?"

"Yes, there's a fire," Henry McKenzie said. "I laid it and I lit it. But I don't think it'll do this lad much good. Take him and wash him and put him to bed, Holly. Poor lad's as drunk as a newt."

"Not drunk 'tall. Resent callme drunk. Tired isall. Very tired. Want sit minute front fire. Don't see many fires these days. See poncho sleep under. See one blanket. See canbeans. Don't see fire. Wood too wet burn. Also make signals giveway posish—pos-*t-i-on*. Position. Just tired. Veryvery tired. Don't like have wife think drunk when only veryvery tired."

Henry McKenzie got up from his chair and extended a hand to his son. His son tried to seize it, but his fingers slipped and his hand fell limply away. Henry McKenzie walked round behind Peter and lifted him to his feet, Peter's head sagging forward on his chest. Henry McKenzie nodded at Holly, and she took Peter's other arm, placing it round her neck, clinging to the wrist. Together they walked him to the bedroom— the new bedroom in the new wing that Peter had built for his bride.

"He's filthy," Henry McKenzie said. "I'll peel his clothes off him, if I can do it without a paint scraper. I don't think he's changed them in a month. We ought to wash him up a little and let him sleep, so at least he can wake up clean. Go tell Jeffy never mind about the bath. We'd never get him out of it; he weighs a long ton. We can swab him off a touch here if you'll bring a basin and some towels and soap. Might muck up the rug a bit; not much. Christ! Do you know, the socks have rotted away inside his boots!"

Henry McKenzie stripped the clothing from his son's body, and his grandson came with a basin, and together the old man and Holly washed some of the accumulated filth off Peter. They worried him into a pair of clean pajamas and laid him into the bed. He ground his teeth constantly and beat at the covers with his fists. He cursed, mostly in Kikuyu, but occasionally in English. Then he sighed suddenly, like a man dying, and relaxed. The lines of his face changed, and even under the heavy, knotted beard the face was suddenly the old, young face of Peter Mc-Kenzie. He breathed deeply, and his clenched hands relaxed, and he slept.

They roused him later on, and he came awake as sweetly as a child. He smiled angelically at his wife as she spooned scalding soup into him, and he swallowed it like a good little boy. She placed spoonfuls of milk toast into his mouth, and he chewed and swallowed it dutifully, his eyes tight-closed. Then he made an abrupt sweep of his arm and knocked the plate out of his wife's hand in an irritable gesture and fell back on the pillow.

"*Dowanomo,*" he said, and snored. He slept heavily now, but the muscles of his belly knotted and jumped and the muscles of his arms twisted and crawled as his body jerked under the covers. When Holly went round to check the doors and windows before she undressed for bed, she could hear him grind his teeth and mutter. She undressed in the bathroom, and when she came soft-footed into the room in her night-dress, he rolled off the bed in a single swift motion and tackled her viciously at the knees. His hands flashed up toward her throat, and she struck him, hard, in the face.

"Peter, *Peter!* For God's sake, Peter! It's *me!* Only me!"

His hands dropped away from her throat and his eyes opened, opaquely, blindly. The eyes looked straight at her and never saw her.

"Oh," he said meekly, politely. "So very sorry. Had bad dream. Nightmare. Didn't mean to hurt you. So terribly sorry."

He stumbled to his feet, looked blindly around the room, and lunged on his face at the bed. Holly turned him over and crept in beside him. In the night he held tightly to her wrist and she could feel his body shake with sobs. He sweated heavily, and again the acrid sour smell filled the room. Once he woke himself, sitting straight up in bed, and then he was screaming.

The next morning he came awake early. He looked carefully, suspiciously, at the room, as a soldier might rise up from a foxhole and meticulously check the terrain around him. There was one. The one great big picture of Mount Kenya that he loved. Yes. There that was. The picture was. There was the big wing chair. The green one. There was green chair. The counterpane, yes. Yes it was a yellow counterpane. Yes it was on the bed. There was the chest of drawers, yes that was certainly a chest of drawers. Mmm. The rug on the floor. The little fireplace with the leopard skin next it. Yes. And the bed. Where was the bed? He was *in* the bed. The bed was there if he was in it. The pillow was soaking under his neck where he had sweated in the night. It smelled sour. He knew the smell. But there was another smell not like him. What was that on the other pillow? A head. Oh but what a pretty head. Not like some heads he had seen. This had red hair on it and a lovely face on it, as sweet as any face could be on it, and, much more important, it had a neck on it. And the neck was joined to the torso. That was very important, to have a neck joined to the torso. The headbone is joined to the neckbone and the neckbone is joined to the collarbone. That was a song they used to play at the Equator. The shinbone is connected to the anklebone, and the anklebone is connected to the kneebone, and the kneebone is connected to the thighbone. Hallelujah.

Peter looked at Holly, sweetly softly asleep, and touched his face with his fingers. *Christ.* You could hide a herd of buffalo in the whiskers. His mouth tasted like a rhino wallow looked. He noticed with amazement that he wore striped pajamas. He never slept in pajamas. They didn't have any in the mountains. There was no sign of his other clothes, and just as well, he thought. *I hope somebody burnt them.* He eased himself out from under the covers and went to the window, which was locked. He raised the shade and saw sun. He walked to the bedroom door and saw it was locked and the bolt drawn. He did not really remember that the door had a bolt. He looked at the night table and saw a pistol on it. He stepped on something cold to the right of the bed and saw that it was a shotgun. Then he found a robe and went to the bathroom. On his way he heard a noise in the kitchen and saw that Juma, the headboy, was fussing about with old Aly, the cook. He grinned. He felt better.

"Jambo," he said. "Any hot water and a razor? Bring 'em to me with my chai in the bathroom, and some more water for a bath, as well. I got home late last night. Where were you when I came?"

"In jail, Bwana," Juma said truthfully. "The water is ready. It will be along in a minute."

Peter went into the bathroom and began to shave. The long beard came off easily, softened by the hot water and the shaving soap, but fouling the razor. I look like hell, he thought. I must have been as stiff as a clam when I got back yesterday. I hope to God I wasn't too bad. I don't remember anything about it, except fighting that Land Rover for the last twenty miles. It kept hauling over to the left and trying to climb mountains. Somebody must have washed me a little; at least the topsoil's off. I know I haven't been this clean in weeks.

"Oh, thanks, Juma," he said when the headboy came in with hot water for the bath. "Pour it in now, I'm ready for it."

His face came clean under the razor, and he smiled at himself in the mirror. Then he stopped smiling. His teeth were stained and green-mossed at the tops.

"Jumaaa!" he called at the houseboy. "Bring me some salt and some baking soda. I want to get these teeth clean."

He lowered himself into the bath and gave himself up completely to the hot water. There were some of Holly's bath salts standing in a niche alongside the tub. He dumped about half a bottle into the tub and nearly went to sleep again as the water stroked the kinks out of his muscles and stole away the smell, the sticky-blood smell, the copper-penny smell, the fecal smell that still lingered of himself in his nostrils and seemed to come from his fingernails. There was some shampoo as well; he lathered his head and it came clean under his fingernails—fingernails which, he noticed, had first grown long and now were broken off and dyed with filth and contained the smell. There was a file. He dug and scraped until the nails were clean. Juma came in with the baking soda and the salt.

Peter fixed a mixture in a tooth glass and scrubbed until his gums bled and retreated from his teeth and the teeth were almost white again. He gargled with a mouthwash and dried himself, leaving the bathroom puddled with water, and went back to bed. Holly was still sleeping, and this time Peter really slept, soundly now and without the sweating or the tooth-grinding or the dreams.

Holly awakened perhaps an hour later, and next to her in the bed she saw a man she remembered. He was sleeping peacefully. His impossibly long lashes were curled up on his cheeks—like a baby's fingers, she thought—and he smelled divinely. He was smooth-shaven; his tangled hair had been washed and combed. The one hand that lay on the counterpane was scrubbed raw and the nails short-cut and pinkly clean. He had on no pajamas now, and she could feel his naked body warm-cool and close, not hot and sticky as before. He moved a little in his sleep and she snuggled closer. She turned on her side and eased one arm under his neck, holding the shaggy head closer to her breast. She bent and kissed him gently on the throat. His eyes opened, and smiled, and he was back again. He turned, drawing her toward him, and kissed her. His hands moved over her, and then his eyes opened wide in panic, almost in horror.

"No!" he said. "No! *I can't!*" He hid his head in her shoulder, and once again his body shook with sobs.

9

At first the settlers had their way. After the killings began, meetings were called in the Aberdares District, at Rumuruti and Nyeri and Thomson's Falls. A delegation was sent to Nairobi to talk to the Government about measures. A special force was formed, without official sanction but with implied approval. Its duties were manifold. It was to collect information. It was to dig out, when possible, the oath-administrators. It was to catch as many Mau Mau alive as possible, and it was supposed to induce the captives to talk. It was supposed to kill those whom they could not catch. It was supposed to live out of one poncho and off a can of beans and a tin of bully. It was supposed to sleep under the poncho in the freezing cold and in the dripping wet of the high

Aberdares, living in the close-grained bush at altitudes of twelve thousand feet and more. The armament was simple—sporting rifles, shotguns, pistols, Sten guns, and hand grenades. Knives, of course, and pangas to clear brush and cut firewood when there was any to cut and you dared use it.

It was not what one would call a usual group. Mixed bag was better. Some of it was professional hunters, called off their safaris for duty. Some of it was wild animal trappers, and 'Ndrobo game trackers, and the wild Turkana and Game Department scouts. It was composed of game rangers and members of the Kenya police. The farmers who joined mostly were youngish men with bush experience. The Africans, apart from the Turkana and 'Ndrobo, were safari-hands, gunbearers, mainly, and were Wakamba and Nandi and a few Masai. All were fierce men of fighting tribes. With one exception, no agricultural tribesmen were used in the force. Each white man was allowed to bring a short string of his own blacks. Peter took with him Lathela, the Masai-Rendille-Samburu tracker who was really a 'Ndrobo and who still poisoned himself with hatred over the murder of his master. Peter also took Metheke, the Wakamba who was his youngest gunbearer. He left the older Chalo on the farm to help his father look after the women, but Chalo got itchy when they started locking up the native help and drifted off to his own reserve down around Machakos.

Nearly all the white men owned farms, and they owned them in the Aberdares area, which had been most seriously affected. Nearly all had wives or sisters or fathers and mothers on these farms. Many had joined up, leaving only a wife on the property, to watch the house, the children, and the farm. Some of the men had lost close relatives. All had already lost close friends.

When Peter returned to Bushbuck from the informal commissioning in Nairobi, he called Holly to one side and told her that he was leaving. He didn't say where he was going or for what.

"You can't just leave me here alone with nobody but your father," Holly said. "Your sister's helpless, worse than helpless. Little Jeff is only a child. Your father's feeble. That awful business has wrecked him. I can't stay alone on this farm. I'll go and stay with my parents. Or I'll go to Nairobi. But I won't stay here. I *won't*."

"Yes, you will, I think. God knows I hate to do it to you, but I'd nothing to do with the way things worked out, and now I do have something very much to do with how it'll finally finish. It'll take Christ knows how long for England to get organized on this thing, and in the meantime some of us have been chosen to do a job until the military does get cracking. I'm not asking you to do anything the other chaps haven't asked their women. This is your home. I'm not going to let myself be run off it, and neither are you. You'll stay, Holly, just like the rest of the women will stay. Or else we're finished before we start, you and I."

"What actually are you going to do, then? What's all so secret and takes you away from your farm when a man's needed now more than ever before? It seems to me your duty's plainly here. Your family's already suffered enough."

"That's the entire point. Being on the farm didn't do Jeff any good, or Lisa and the kids any good. The only hope right now is to keep these bastards so busy that they won't have time for much organized raiding. Keep them busy, and weed out the ringleaders, and—— But I'm not supposed to tell you about this. I'm going, very soon, and I want just a few free minutes with you without all this Mau Mau business to muck it up. You'll be fine. Just be careful. I'll come down from time to time to look in on you. We've got the night patrol pretty well organized for here. There'll be a police team on the farm every night. If you keep locked up and watch the guns and don't open up for *anybody* after dark you'll be fine. Come on now, let's have a drink and pretend that I'm just leaving on another safari, which is actually all this is."

"I know," Holly couldn't keep herself from murmuring, "just like another safari. And safari was what you gave up to marry me so you could go away on this thing. I'm sorry. I'll stay. I'll do the best I can. But I'm not much of a pioneer woman, darling, like your mother and the others. I'm frightened out of my wits. I'm frightened even when you're here, and with you away——"

"Can't be helped. Come on now, give us a kiss. It'll be the last I'll have for some time. I must say that I'm not exactly keen on leaving you for where I'm going. But there's damn-all to be done. I've been ordered, in any case. Like the war."

10

When Peter dressed again he folded his city clothes carefully and sent Lathela for his safari box, the old, battered green tin box that had been hammered semi-shapeless by tens of thousands of miles of Kenya's and Tanganyika's lack of formal roads.

He chose from the box the old police sweater with its high-rolled turtle neck, his Birdshooter ankle boots, some gray wool socks, and a plastic raincoat with hood which Tom Deane had given him. Its chief advantage was that it weighed nothing, could be stuffed into a pocket, and when the zipper was drawn it so sealed the body that the trapped heat kept you warmer than a greatcoat. He took a long Spanish knife that another client had given him, and a .44 frontier-model Colt pistol. He took only one rifle, a .416 Rigby with a bolt action. Holly, watching him pack, noticed that when he sorted his ammunition he selected only soft-nosed bullets for the rifle. She also noticed he took neither toilet paper nor underwear. He pulled on the sweater over his naked chest and then dressed in the old shabby-green drill bush clothes, the Birdshooter boots, and the heavy socks. He jammed a khaki beret on his head. He filled a thermos with whisky and piled everything he wasn't wearing into a slick black rubber poncho, on the rough-white underside of which he first spread a single blanket. He drew the ends of the poncho together to form a sack, shouldered the bundle, picked up the gun, and took them out to the car. Then he came back and buckled the pistol round his waist, slid the clip of the knife holster onto the back of the pistol belt, draped his short game-spotting binoculars round his neck, and stuck a carton of cigarettes in the side pocket of his jacket.

"I guess that's the lot," he said. "I'm away to the wars. Don't come with me to the jeep. I don't like those dragged-out good-bys. Nor do I intend to see Pa or anybody else. I'd rather just remember you for a bit. With your hair funny and the way you look."

Holly reached up and kissed him. She could feel the binocular case biting into the soft flesh of her breast. She held him closer, enjoying the hurt of the glasses, pressing herself closer to their hard outlines.

"I'll stay," she said. "Take care and get back soon."

"That's my good girl," Peter said. "Be very careful. For I love you and want you in one piece when I come home soon. Good-by, darling, I'm off."

He ran out of the bedroom, and Holly threw herself down on the bed, which still bore the warm print of their bodies, and pushed her face into a pillow and wept. Then she got up and buckled on her pistol. It was nearly time to take the Wogs down to the stockade and to close up the house. She could hear the angry rattle of the Land Rover and the impatient slipping of its wheels as Peter started it off with a leap. She did not go to the door until the sound had died away, but the raised dust of his passing still hung heavily in the air.

The men met at the farm of Joseph Watson, who owned a small shamba at the edge of the Aberdares. Watson was a big, burly widower. His eyes were perpetually bloodshot from sun and dust. He was just starting his farmholdings, and he had been a professional hunter on the side. He saved his money and had invested every cent he could scrape into his farm. He had a manager, a widower, lame from the last war, who had come out to Kenya from England. They farmed in a three-to-one partnership. The manager's name was Jake Norris. He was a little man with keen blue eyes and a scrubby reddish mustache.

They had built a house, or rather three houses. One was an old settler's bush shanty which they had converted pleasantly into a living-room-dining-room-one-bedroom of rough cedar planks. There was a big fireplace, a couple of easy chairs, and an all-purpose table. Newer, twenty or thirty feet away, was a log dormitory with two double-decker beds and a washstand. Forming the point of a triangle was a combination of kitchen and washroom, with a tin tub and another washstand. The two-holed privy stood away from the other houses, partially hidden by forest. There was a small vegetable garden, for personal use, in back of the clearing which held the little houses, and chickens clucked and strutted in the cleared compound. It was a shoestring farm, constantly in danger of foreclosure if Joseph Watson had a safari cancellation and could not meet his bank payments or buy the fertilizer and farming equipment which kept him steadily strapped. What would happen to the farm now, nobody could say, for Joseph was going off on commando with the rest, leaving old Jake on his own to try to keep the farm going with sparse native help. There wouldn't be any more money coming in for a long time, it seemed as though. Possibly the banks would be reasonable.

Joseph was taking only one native with him—a gunbearer, a Kikuyu named Waithaka. Waithaka was a spare, tallish Kikuyu. He was a fine tracker and, rare for an African, a splendid rifleshot. He had been with Joseph Watson for more than fifteen years, since Joseph was a boy. Waithaka had first taught him bushcraft, and when Joseph became a professional hunter he took Waithaka off his father's farm and signed him on as gunbearer. Waithaka was a very valuable addition to the commando, especially as he was a Kikuyu and proven loyal.

There were not a great many white men at first, about forty in all. They would work in teams, over selected segments of land, as scouts, and as a unit in larger operations. There were some eighty to ninety Africans mingled in the group, and the Africans would work in the teams with their own personal bwanas. The force was directed by a member of the Kenya police, Bill Falconer, a pleasant, blue-eyed, gentle-mannered youngster in his middle twenties. Harvey Edmonds, a warden of the Game Department, was second in command. After that everyone's rank was more or less equal. There was no set plan. The small units would scout on their own until they found Mau Mau concentrations, whereupon a runner would go back and collect as much extra force as was necessary. The shamba of Joseph Watson would serve as a sort of base camp, it being nearest to the mountains, and also planted in the center of the heaviest Mau Mau activity. Jake Norris was communications chief. He laughed when he gave himself the title. The title meant that if anybody had anything to tell anybody else Jake would be there to receive the message, if somebody hadn't chopped him. With a Sten gun and a double-barreled shotgun, Jake reckoned he'd want quite a bit of chopping. While they were passing out titles, they decided to name the Watson farm as well. They called it Campi a Mbingu—Heavenly Camp. That, some wit pointed out, was because they were so close to God— God on Mount Kenya, and God in the Forever, seeing as they were betting their lives that they could bring the true faith to the heathen hordes. Nobody in the gathering had spent very much time in church lately.

"We hunt them like this . . ." the policeman said. And they hunted them like this, but each according to the favorite technique of the hunter. The policeman was a man who was passionately devoted to information. He admired it more than anything else in the world. So the policeman sent his black scouts down to the shambas to see who was Mau Mau and who was not Mau Mau. The scouts were admirable men, all of whom had sworn several Mau Mau oaths and were well abreast of the newest signs and passwords, the latest delicate developments in oathing.

The Game Department bloke was an observer of trends. He had spent most of his adult life checking on the migration of zebras, the changing over of elephant herds from one area to another, the movement of lions, and the incidence of rhinos in certain patches of bush. He was a man of broad view. His curiosity rested chiefly in just how many Mau Mau there were in the hills, where they were dispersed, and what sort of terrain held them. He was fascinated by the habits of all animals—how far they roved, how they followed grass and water, how far the radius of their idle curiosities and necessities extended, and how they would adapt to terrain, shaping it to their wants and remodeling their old habits as the need arose. He would send his scouts to see and tabulate and reckon finally into a likely sum. And he would take an abstract view of it from the skies. From a single-engined monoplane.

Peter preferred to hunt casually, liked to begin aimlessly and allow himself to collide with whatever the day produced, working out a scheme of counteraction as the situation unraveled. He would go out with Lathela to track, possibly with Joseph and his Kikuyu Waithaka and Metheke, the Wakamba, and merely rove. The team might split into halves, according to the need. Joseph was a mountain hunter by preference. He liked to scramble up to the top of a rocky kopje and sit for endless hours, sweeping the hills with his glasses for a minute movement. This was how you hunted kudu and sometimes rhino up North. If you swept your glasses ceaselessly, the sun on an ear flicker, the shiver of a leaf, the rolling of a stone, any movement, no matter how slight, brought your quarry finally into focus. When Joseph hunted, he invariably gave an extra pair of glasses to Waithaka and sent him away to spy on another sector. The man who saw anything first then communicated to the other by flashing a pocket mirror.

The game trapper diverged sharply from the other technicians. He was also a student of animal habit, but in a different sense from the Game Department bloke. The game trapper's name was, fitly, Darwin. He was very famous for his techniques. He lassoed rhinos, using a power wagon and a long noose that payed out from a stick. He knew how to catch baby elephants without shooting the mother, and he could deliver a pair of lion cubs or a baby leopard on demand. He worked much for the films. Any time a movie company came to Kenya, needing animal sequences, they called on George Darwin. He kept a corral of more or less trained animals at his farm on the Laikipia Plain, close to Thomson's Falls. His two especial possessions were a mature leopard and an immensely talented hyena named Buster. Buster was as tame as any dog. He was a magnificent ham actor and had stolen many reviews from the humans who co-starred with him in the pictures. The leopard was named Chui, of course, that being the Swahili designation for leopard, and also indicative of a special way Chui had with anything he set his teeth into, such as hats, boots, or occasionally people. There were many other animals on the farm—rhinos tame enough to ride on, a gross of lions, some baboons and an insolent chimp, and any amount of baby elephants and buffalo.

George Darwin's hunting technique always based itself on the precise spot an animal might be on a given day, at a roughly approximate time. This study enabled him to prepare a pit or a noose or a cul-de-sac which he could control, and so the animal would eventually imprison itself in its own habits. Then George Darwin knew everything there was to know about transporting the animal from its trap or its noose or its cul-de-sac to a stout barrier of logs, where the animal was gentled into at least partial domestication. They said you couldn't gentle some animals. But Darwin had a full-grown oryx, the only fierce antelope, running loose in his yard. He had zebras trained to draw a pony cart. His kids raced ostriches for fun. They hunted medium game with cheetahs, and there were always two or three tousled lion cubs bumbling about the house. The tame-wild buffalo fed with the cattle, and the two mature rhinos wandered loose in the yard. George Darwin could throw a lasso or build a pit or crouch in a tree with a noose in his hand, rig a deadfall or highjack a herd of elephants. All he ever had to know was where the animal was likely to go, and at what approximate time. His bush background was impeccable. He held the single-gun record for shooting elephants on control, and he was born in a wattle hut on the land he now owned. He was a big, stout, beef-cheeked man with a booming laugh, but in the bush he was as ominously silent as a serpent. He spoke fluent Kikuyu, Embu, Wakamba, Meru, and Nandi, as well as Swahili and a touch of Turkana and Somali.

They sat around a fire, squatting on their haunches, in the middle of Joseph Watson's compound, each man plotting his own course. They drank whatever they had brought along, a bottle of gin, a bottle of scotch, a brace of beer. One man, expert with a pistol, decided he was hungry, so he shot the head off one of Joseph Watson's cocks—a cock whose crow skipped an octave and thus was most annoying—and roasted it over the fire, probing into its anus with a hooked forefinger and then clawing the guts clear and ramming a green stick up its behind to grill it over the fire. He had removed feathers and head with one long, graceful stripping motion. He ate the half-cooked fowl without salt. Peter and John Thompson and Fred Hall slept dry and warm that night, because as close friends of Joseph Watson they were allowed first go at the sleeping hut, together with the Game Department bloke and the policeman. The other men rolled up near the fire in their blankets and ponchos. Before dawn the next day each small task group slipped off on its own bent. Only one man went down the mountain. The Game Department bloke was going to Thomson's Falls to stir up his Piper Cub. He wanted to see from up high where the game concentrated and what its movements were. If you swept low in the valleys and barely skimmed the hilltops, you could see a lot of things from a plane that you couldn't see from the ground because of the solid, soggy thickness of the trees and the twined bamboo and the interwoven bush. You could see especially well if your pilot flew the plane with its wings vertical to the terrain.

Peter rose at 4 A.M. and pulled on his boots. He had slept, otherwise, in his clothes, bar the beret. He went out to the fire and warmed himself and then searched among the sleeping men to find his blacks. He had told Lathela and Metheke to sleep close together so he could find them. He nudged Lathela with his toe and noticed that Lathela reached for his spear before he opened his eyes.

"Get up," Peter said. "Where's Metheke?"

Lathela jerked his head at a shapeless bundle wrapped round with blanket a few paces away. Peter walked over and touched the bundle with his toe. Metheke came awake with a panga in his hand.

"Mzuri," Peter said. "Mzuri sana. Kwenda. We go up the mountain. We will make a little reccy. Bring some tea and some beans and beef and your weapons and blankets. Be ready in ten minutes. I go now to have a talk with the Bwana Joseph."

Peter found Joseph Watson having tea with his partner-manager, Jake Norris. They were inside the little hut. A fire danced delicately in the hearth, over which an iron hob stretched a kettle. It whistled sweetly, the steam blending with the smoke, the whistle mingling with the fire's hiss.

"That smells good," Peter said. "May I have some, please?"

"Sure." Joseph poured a tin cupful and spilled some thick condensed milk into it. "Sugar? It's the last you'll get."

"No, thanks, just the milk. Shall we start off pretty soon? It's only about an hour to light, and I'd like to be inside the forest when it comes. We can use the torches at first."

"What are your plans, exactly? Here, try a little brandy in the tea. There's just a drink apiece left."

"Thanks. Wonderful. Oh, I hadn't any real plan. I thought I'd take my two Wogs and slope off tracking. See what trails these buggers are using the most. We've got the warden up top looking down from his plane. Falconer's types will be spreading out through the shambas. What Darwin'll do I can't say, but it'll take him a hellish time to do it. I expect we'll need him more at the end than at the start. I thought maybe we might do a little split-up, if it's all right with you. You take that Wog of yours and go squat on a hill somewhere. Little John and I'll take our people and go see what roads lead to Rome. Here, gimme a piece of paper and a pencil. See, if I take this side and John takes that one and you climb up on that peak there and send that Wog of yours over there —you remember the bluff close the big old sacred fig tree—then we won't duplicate any effort. Any movements you see'll be Mickey Mice. I've a hunch if that bird dog of mine picks up a spoor, the spoor'll coincide with what the warden sees in the plane and what you clue up with the glasses, and we can do something mildly constructive about it. We don't want to be stumbling all over each other, everybody making a pack of noise. How's it strike you?"

"Sounds fine. Where's John?"

"Saw him outside. He'll be along in a minute. I thought we'd take about twenty miles between us and work upward in a sort of loose circle. There's a place I know, very high, a sort of bald spot, where I thought I'd meet John. You know the place?"

"I think. There used to be a more or less straight game trail leading to it, if it's the one I have in mind. Sort of a little crater, very shallow, all on its own? Like an old man's bald spot? That right?"

"Correct. Why don't you give it a couple of days and meet me and John there tomorrow night? Then we can sit down in the lovely wet grass and correlate what we've got, if there's anything at all. Decide then what to do about it. One of us is bound to turn up something. I say, we'd better fix on a signal. Something that can't go much wrong. How about a zebra's bark? There damn well won't be any punda that high."

"Night bark or day bark?"

"Night bark. The jackaly-sounding one. Mystify hell out of the Wogs if there're any about. But a fairish countersign, at that. When you come to the little crater, hang back a bit and bark. If you hear another one it'll either be me or John or an echo."

"Well and good. You'll tell John on the way out?"

"Sure. Thanks for the tea. *And* the brandy. See you tomorrow eve."

"Right. Don't shoot anything that won't go into Rowland Ward's, mind you. No inferior trophies. This isn't a movie safari, you know."

Peter and his men—Lathela and Metheke—scattered out in the wide end of a wedge. Peter took the point and gave his men the wings. They covered their beat like dogs, sometimes crouching, sometimes on all fours, occasionally sniffing. They coursed the interlocking game trails, searching always for a path that seemed extra-beaten by usage, a little less natural portion to the bush. They hunted hard all day. Once they jumped a herd of bushbuck. Another time they started a rhino. Once they heard the crash and the muted-trumpet scream of a forest elephant. The air thinned and the slopes steepened and the breathing came harder. They were in wet bush now; it was never dry, this bush, whether it rained or not. The clouds they could occasionally see below them when they came to a rocky outcropping always kept this bush as dripping-wet as jungle bush, but the difference was that this bush was always soggy-cold, where the jungle bush was steaming-wet.

At noon they sat down to rest and chew on some biltong one of the black men had brought.

"I don't know," Peter said to Lathela. "We must have come up the easy way, or else the hardest way, or else they're smarter than I thought. I haven't seen any track that looked as if a human had passed along it."

"Me neither, Bwana," the 'Ndrobo replied. "Nor Metheke. Perhaps the Bwana John has cut a trail. Perhaps the Bwana Watson has seen something through his miwani mkubwa. But there is nothing here in *these* hills but duiker and rhino and bushbuck. No people: Kikuyu have got big feet. I would have seen some trace of them, as you would have seen, as this raw-elephant eater Metheke would have seen.

"I had no good feeling about this way up, as I often have no good feeling about the Serarua when the elephants have all moved to Lasames or Merille or Seralippe. I think we should work down again in *that* direction. If we cut off the Bwana John it is not important. Nothing lives here but animals, and we do not have any bwanas wa safari to please, eh?"

"Eeeeh," Lathela said. "When there is nothing running up a hill perhaps it is running down. I like the look of that other bush."

"You remember, Bwana?" Metheke said. "You remember that trip in the North with the drunk Bwana who cursed horribly and who ate the stones of the lion? You remember that the rains came strangely and when we went to the Kinya luga there was nothing but dung, old, dried-out dung, and all the elephants had moved off to the plain? You remember we went and camped at Lasames and the plains were newly green and the Rendille were moving backward to seek water, instead of the other way? And we found the elephants grazing on the green plains like herds of Grant gazelles, when everyone else was hunting elephant at Marsabit and finding nothing? And we shot the fine big bull, as easily as you would shoot a Tommy for the pot, the great bull with the huge teeth? And then the littler bull for the drunk man's mtoto? I have that same feeling now. You mentioned a big meadow. I think that if we go to where the big meadow is and walk along carefully we might find some spoor leading into, or up from, or away from that big meadow."

Peter reached over and cuffed Metheke fondly on the head.

"I think you might be right, you runner-away-from-elephants-unless-I-am-there-to-protect-you," he said. "What you think, 'Thela? It's a long trek. And the night is not far off."

"A man can see fires in the night if he climbs trees," the 'Ndrobo said. "I offer you my foot to see, in case you have forgotten." He poked the horned, flat-arched foot with the downcurving prehensile heel out for Peter to look at. "Who walks up trees to hang a leopard bait like Lathela? Who is spoken of by monkeys as a kinsman when it involves trees? I agree with this man-eater from Machakos. I think we should go and search for the meadow. And I will climb the trees."

"Well, it seems we all have the same hunch," Peter said aloud, in English. "Kwenda. We go and find a meadow."

They horseshoed the course and curved down a valley, walking painfully, leg muscles cramping, seizing fast, all the way up to the hips, feet bruising on the loose shale and on the little sharp stones that held a moment, enticingly underfoot, and then shifted to slip and slide in miniature avalanche. They fought the thorn and sometimes cut their

way through close-ordered bamboo, and climbed up high rocky buttes
and down again, rather than circle round them. Night came finally and
they had crossed no trail, sniffed no scent, although the nostrils of all
the men sucked in and out like setters' noses as they probed the air for
scent when the wind stopped its maddening circling and blew occasionally straight into their faces. When they came to any tree that stretched
above its family forest, Lathela or Peter or Metheke whipped up it to
search with the glasses and sniff the wind. Nothing stirred. No plume of
smoke, no swish of bush that was not made by elephant or rhino. They
came finally to a sheer facing of rock, slanting downward from the summit toward the plain. At its highest plane there was a small butte, shaped
like a slightly hollow shield. Peter scrambled up to search the hills
through his glasses, just as the sun sank, and then called down to his
men.

"We'll sleep up here," he said. "It's drier than down below. One
side of the peak kills the wind. Bring all your gear and the food. I don't
think our friends could climb it quietly, if anybody should turn up in
the night."

They ate with their hands from a can of beans, slashed open with
a panga, and a can of corned beef, sliced in half by a panga, and they
drank some cold tea from the neck of the thermos. It still tasted faintly
like whisky.

"It is time to sleep," Peter said. "We must start very early. By my
reckoning that meadow is not too far away."

"Good," the Africans said. "There is a hollow here in this high rock
which will keep the wind off you. We will go apart and find a place."

"Hapana," Peter said. "No. The three of us sleep together in this
hollow, out of the wind. We will keep each other warm this way. Here.
I will take my blanket and yours, Lathela, and put it under us. Then
we will take my poncho and Metheke's blanket and spread it over us.
That way we will all keep warm." He worked his body down between
the two Africans, and the three fitted themselves into the little indenta-
tion in the rock. The Africans, outspanned on the flanks, anchored the
top blanket and the poncho with their bodies, and they pulled the
poncho up to where it formed a loose flap over their faces. Peter zipped
up the plastic raincoat, so only his nose, eyes, and mouth showed beneath the hood. His rifle was cradled in the crook of his right arm. He
had hitched his pistol around so that the flat weight of it fell between
his legs. He pulled his knife around until it lay on the curve of his
groin. He could smell the grease-rubbed Africans, a damp smell like

oiled leather, as the three bodies built warmth on a pebbly bed of stone.

"*Eeeh-ahh,*" Lathela said, pushing a hip deeper into the shaly bed. "This is warmer than sleeping with goats."

"I have not slept with any goats for a long time," Metheke said. "I have been a gentleman gunbearer, working on safari, and had a shelter-half and a mattress of my own."

"Shut up, the pair of you," Peter said. "I hope to God this fishskin shroud I'm wearing is louseproof. But those wonderful Americans. How wonderful they are. I'm as warm as toast in this transparent thing Tom gave me. Funny to think, though, that I'm bedded down with Wogs. Not that they ain't good boys . . ." The men slept, while the rain slashed hard, running noisily in rivulets down the creases of the poncho, draining off into noisy little channels that made tiny streams and eroded, just a bit more, the ancient serrated surface of the rock.

They awoke before dawn, muscle-cramped and bone-bruised by their lumpy bed, but reasonably dry beneath their blankets and poncho, although the edges of the blankets were sopping, where the movement of a body had disarranged the sheltering poncho and the blankets had worked out from beneath their rain-shiny black rubber protection. They got up and stretched and ate nothing, as is the African custom in the morning, especially when there is nothing to eat, although Peter's soul screamed for hot tea and a fire. The guns had kept dry, and Lathela had slipped a leather sheath over his spear blade. The knives were safe from wet and harm in their cases, and Metheke had slept on top of his panga.

They staggered down through the freezing water-dripping bush, stumbling and falling, and made an hour's trek by feel alone before the dawn lit the tangle of trees and the thickets of giant bamboo into a gray semblance of a very poor church on funeral day. There was a little whisky left in a pint bottle Peter had stuck in his jacket when he left Joseph Watson's farm. He had a drink and then held out the bottle to his boys.

"*Asante sana, Bwana, hapana kwa mimi,*" Lathela said, although his tongue flickered over his lips when he saw Peter drink.

"No, Bwana, thank you very much, none for me," Metheke said, although his eyes squinted and his nose twitched at the suddenly released odor of the whisky.

"Don't be a bloody *pumbavu,*" Peter said. "You're all drunkards and we're in it together. Have a little *tembo*"—he used the word for elephant. "It'll make your day." The two black boys carefully estimated the remaining whisky and drank, in turn, licking the last drop off their lips.

Peter saw they had left a fraction extra for him, and he drained the bottle and coughed. God, he wished he had a cigarette, but cigarettes were out on this shauri and he hadn't dared tempt himself by bringing any. He thought regretfully of nine packets of Luckies that he had stashed behind the chair in Joseph Watson's cabin, against his return. *I'll bring some chewing tobacco next time,* he thought. *Or some Kali snuff like the Wogs love.*

"Hey," he said. "Either of you shenzis got any snuff?"

"Ndio," Lathela said. "Ndio," Metheke said. Both men produced round tins.

"Now why the hell didn't I think of *that* before?" Peter said in English. "Mupa." He took a pinch from the first tin offered him and held it to his nose as he'd seen the Wogs do. It tickled pleasantly, and presently he sneezed, a tremendous blast. His whole head seemed clearer. Metheke took out a knife and cut a twig off a bush.

"It's better this way," the Wakamba said, "also quieter," and chewed the twig into a brush. He dipped the spittle-moistened brush into the snuff tin and painted his gums with it. Then he left the twig brush stuck in his mouth, working it around so that it continued to knead the snuff into his gums. The unabsorbed snuff made a fat lump under his sucked-in lower lip. Peter cut a brush and tried the snuff that way. He found that it felt the same way a cigarette felt when you dragged deeply and took the smoke into your lungs, except the narcotic texture was different and you didn't get the optical satisfaction of seeing the smoke float out of your mouth. And the taste was sharper and lighter, as if you had used a powdered mustard on a piece of meat instead of the usual liquid yellow mustard.

They fought on through the bush, until Lathela snapped his fingers as they came to a juncture of two trails. He had frozen over something he had seen. The other men came softly up to him.

"Look." Lathela knelt and pointed at the trail. It was imperceptibly wider at the crossing, as if it had been occasionally used by people who stood and talked. The variation from the game run was tiny, but Lathela knew that animals never stood and talked at the intersection of a trail.

"Take the high trail," Peter said. "I'll work the low. Metheke, climb a tree and see what you can see. Here are the glasses."

Peter went down along the descending trail on his hands and knees, and presently he came upon a thread of wool that had come loose from something and had wedged in a bush. He went on and found another thread. Evidently somebody's coat had gotten snagged. Somebody had been coming up or going down the trail. He turned and started back and heard a sudden *chock,* the slight sound of a tongue popping against open lips, making a minute but carrying noise, like a loose cork popping. That would be Lathela. Peter ran up the trail and found Lathela poised over another thread of the same kind of wool. Peter showed him the two threads he held in his hand. Lathela smiled. It was a happy smile, as a hunting man might smile when he comes upon the strawy kicked-up fresh dung of a rhino, scarred by the big footprints; or the pug marks of a leopard, or the heavy imprint of an elephant's foot in the sand of a luga, or the splayed curved-hoofed outline of a big bull buffalo pressing on wet turf.

There was a slight noise in the bush; Metheke had been up and returned down from a tree.

"About three miles," he said, "down there, there is a big clearing. I cannot see that it is a clearing, of course, but there is a break in the bush as big as my fist and so it must be a clearing. Is that the one you were thinking about? It seems to me it would be pretty close to that old deserted shamba where the rhinos used to come to roll and lie in the sun."

"That would be about right," Peter said. "Lathela, follow the trail up for a mile or so, being very quiet. Metheke, you come with me. We'll meet back here in about four hours. Be careful, Lathela, and *don't* throw that spear at anything. Hear?"

"Yes, Bwana." Lathela turned and was lost from sight as the game trail curved. Peter and Metheke wound down the descending trail. It had been used a lot. Thorn had been chopped, the weathered ends still sharp-pointed from a panga slash. There was an old toe print to one side of the trail. It had not been obliterated by the passage of animals. Here an obtrusive branch had been bent back and wedged under another limb, and it was still caught firmly in place. Men had used this trail. Animals did not wedge branches underneath other branches. Or leave threads of wool caught on thorns.

They came swiftly to the big meadow. They peered from a covering copse of trees and saw no signs of men. Peter sent Metheke to quarter the big grassy opening while he skirted its perimeter. He ran slowly as he looked, and came on one, two, three, four, five, six, finally seven trails, all leading in different directions away from the meadow. More led up than led down, but the one that led down was a bloody great avenue. It had been broadened by many men, men not walking in single file. It was at least two feet wide.

He heard Metheke's finger snap. Metheke was standing erect in the middle of the meadow. He beckoned. Peter ran. Metheke pointed down.

The grass on which Metheke stood was a good eighth of an inch shorter than the other grass. It had been trodden at some former time. There was a pit where once a fire had been made. There were some old scraps of ant-chewed bones lying half covered in the grass. There were some scars in the earth as if it had once been dug.

"A piece of cake, boy." Peter grinned. "This is the town hall, I shouldn't be surprised. All we have to do is run out the trails, and it's easy. Somewhere up those hills are shambas and caves and people living in them. Come on, you snaggle-toothed bloodhound. Let's go collect Lathela and then we'll rendezvous with the Bwana John and the Bwana Joseph. We can just about make it by nightfall."

They walked back up the hill to where the trail crossed, and barked. Another bark answered, and Lathela dropped down out of a tree, where he had been lying on a limb like a lizard.

"A man would be very foolish to pass along here without looking up," he said. "A man in a tree could drop a spear very easily on anything that passed. Especially if it stooped a little."

"What's up the hill?"

"One little shamba. Seven men and three women. Three huts. Also, very much higher, I think a cave. I didn't see the cave. But I went up a tree and there was a little flat smoke on a hill, not smoke that burns straight up from a fire in the open, but smoke that has come out of somewhere. It was lying flat like my palm. There was very little of it."

"What about the men? Could you see any guns?"

"No, Bwana. If they had guns they had left them in a hut."

"How big was the cleared land where the huts were?"

"Very small. No bigger than twice the size of the ground on which the huts stood."

"How about the bush close by?"

"Very thick. Very, very thick. Except for one open space."

"Could you beat it, as we beat for buffalo when they go into a thick place?"

"I think so. If we sent men in from three sides, making noise, we might get them to cross the clear place. The open space is outside the shamba, coming down, and the trail goes through it. We would have to go behind and up top, though, and leave some shooters below. I think a man who is frightened and who runs is apt to run downhill if there are very many of him. If they ran downhill they would cross the clear place, or at least run the edges."

"Uh-hunh. Nice work, Lathela. Metheke and I have found a place which I believe is used for council occasionally. It is the big meadow of which we spoke earlier. But I think our chances of getting very many of them in that one place at the same time are pretty slim. I think we better just work on it pocket by pocket, as they're sure to know we're here when the warden starts slipping around upstairs in that plane. Let's go find the Bwana John and the Bwana Joseph now. It's a long way, that crater, and straight up."

They came onto the little crater at dusk and barked sharply like zebras and heard an answering bark. Peter stepped out into the open and saw that John and Joseph had already arrived.

"We've started the supper," Joseph said. "Which is to say we've opened a can. It seems to be very cold spaghetti. Any luck?"

"Quite a lot. How about you?"

"Nothing. Too much bush. You can't do this one from a hill with spyglasses. But John's found something. Tell him, little man."

"I damned near had to shoot my way out of what I found," John Thompson said. "I was blundering along some bloody trail or other when I ran smack into a Kikuyu woman coming my way. I suppose she was gathering firewood or going for water; there was a stream close by. She let out one yelp, not very loud, and turned to run. But my boy Kamia took off after her like a shot. She tripped over something and we caught her."

"What did you do with her?" Peter asked. "That's pretty important."

"I didn't know what the hell to do with her. I didn't know how far away her hut was or how many people she had with her wherever the hut was. For lack of anything better, we choked her to death and popped her into a tree. Then we went along up the trail and about a mile off we found her shamba. I'd say ten, twelve people, maybe more. I saw four women and the same number of men, and I reckoned that any shamba that had five women—excuse me, there aren't but four now—would have at least double, maybe triple, that many men."

"So you did what?"

"Went back down the trail and collected the poor old girl out of the tree and took her about three miles away and dug a hole and put her in it, right bang in the middle of the toughest piece of bush I could find. I doubt they'll be able to find her. Probably think some animal got her or she just got lost or something. In any case, this is an easy one to knock over. They've stuck the huts jam against a wall of rock, and there's a sheer drop on one side. It's quite a big clearing; I suspect they've lived there a long time. I think we could just walk in on this one, shooting, and there wouldn't be much of a choice of places for them to run off to."

"Well, jolly good show, Little John," Peter said. "We found more or less the same thing, except Lathela says we have to do a beat on it. You were perfectly right about the woman, by the way."

"I never choked a woman to death before," Thompson said. "They're very slippery. But if we'd stuck a knife into her there would have been the usual muck, and somehow there's always that one drop of blood you forget to hide. But I can't say I'd like that choking business as a steady thing. The eyes go horrible."

"Bad business, but it can't be helped. I shouldn't lose any sleep over it if I were you. Well, Joseph, seems to me the drill now's to grab a bit of sleep and whip back down the old mountain in the morning and see what the other chaps have accomplished so far. I expect we could settle the shambas we've found, but Falconer'll have something to say about it, and so'll the others. God Almighty, it's miserable here. Why couldn't these bastards have decided to hole up in the N.F.D., where at least it's warm o' nights?"

The warden, in his plane, had spotted more than twenty small shambas from the air. They reached, he said, spreading his fingers stiffly and far apart, in a radius from the big meadow which Peter had seen. Some could be got at fairly easily if one went at night. Others would have to be beaten by a large force with an ambush planted. They would need more men.

"I have the Masai in mind," the warden said. "It's highly illegal, but I think that if I slipped down to Narok and had a word with a couple of lads I know we might produce a few hundred spears to help us about our chores. Been a hellish long time since the old Masai had a chance to skewer a Kyuke. They'd jump at the chance. I think we could put on a beat that would make the old Indian tiger drives look anemic, and more fun at the end of it."

The wild-animal trapper spoke up.

"I hope when we're beating you'll drive a few my way," he said. "There are a couple of wonderful places to dig some pits, if it's live ones you want, and some marvelous footpaths for trip nooses. One thing's certain. Them as runs have got to run the trails. That bloody bush is so thick you couldn't drive an elephant through it. But I'll have to know what we're using, once I start digging pits and otherwise booby-trapping the trails. Bloody little gain in doing all that work and then finding Peter McKenzie growling at the bottom of some hole, where he's fallen through extreme carelessness."

"You drop me in a hole," Peter said, "and I'll make you prove your ancestor's theory of evolution the hard way. I'll twist you back into a monkey."

"And you wouldn't have to twist very hard," Jake Norris said. "He hasn't got very far to go."

"What's doing in the shambas?" Peter asked the young policeman, Bill Falconer. "Anything from your boys below?"

"Not expecting any reports for ten days or so," the young man said. "I thought I'd let my blokes really get the information stacked up, and when we raid we'll raid big. What I want mostly is the live ones, unlike you bloodthirsty types. These monkeys on the mountain can't live without the native help on the shambas. If we can find just a few—just a very few of the higher-brass lads, the oath-administrators and the transportation buckos—we can start stamping on the source. It's no good just slaughtering these people in the hideaways, although Christ knows they merit it. I want to know *who's* forging the ammunition permits, and who's victualing the thugs on the hills, and who's running the oath business on the farms. I couldn't care less about Jomo Kenyatta up top or the bloke that swings the panga at the bottom. *My* meat is the middle-man—the oath-throwers and the underground logistic types."

"Well, if you don't really mind, Bill," Peter said, "I'm still thinking of myself as the brother-in-law of Jeff Newton and the brother of a girl named Elisabeth McKenzie who hasn't got terribly much by way of a face these days. I will be quite happy to implement an orderly process of scientific elimination and work my careful way up from the bottom until I reach Jomo."

"That's a long task you've set yourself. I believe there's something over a million Kikuyu, and about ninety per cent could qualify as Mau Mau. It'll keep you busy."

"I've got heaps of time," Peter said.

They chose the shamba John Thompson had found for the first raid. They went quietly, only ten men, five white men and five blacks, six men with guns and four without. The only native who carried a gun was the gunbearer of Joseph Watson, the Kikuyu, Waithaka. They arrived at the little shamba before dawn. Joseph Watson and Waithaka crept behind the little island of huts and crawled carefully and softly on their stomachs until they reached the top of the bluff against which the fugitives had foolishly backed their huts.

Facing outward from the huts, the drop to the right was sheer, so nobody would be going that way. Peter and John Thompson and Metheke and Lathela and another white man named Barton and another Negro, a Turkana, took the left wing and spread themselves quietly in the edge of the bush. The policeman, who was bored waiting for intelligence to come up from the shambas, flanked the game trail with another native, a Wakamba askari. The night-long trek up the mountain had been painful, through the black wet bush, and they were happy to flop on their stomachs and wait for the dawn to light the skies. They chewed their lips to keep their teeth from chattering, and shoved their hands inside their jackets, against their flesh, to keep the fingers from freezing. The icy pre-dawn blast attacked their necks and ears. The ground was as wet and cold as snow beneath their bellies.

The sky pinkened, first gray-pink like a dove's breast, and no birds spoke in the early-morning hush. The men lay, their weapons cold under their faces, counting the seconds as hours while they waited for one big noise. The big noise was cupped in the hands of Joseph Watson, who was perched high on the lip of the bluff, within easy stone's throw of the huts. Joseph Watson was of necessity within stone-throwing distance, for what Joseph Watson held in his hand was heavier than a stone. It was colder than the flesh of the hand that held it, so he placed the hand and the grenade inside his shirt, where the freezing serrated metal burned his warm chest like acid. His hand cradled the square-checkered grenade, and his little finger gently stroked the pin. He wanted his hand warm for when he pulled the pin and the depressed flat lever flew up, like a jack-out-of-box, arming the grenade. He had chosen in his mind, already, the hut he was going to chuck the grenade at, although he couldn't see the huts. He was going to heave it at the one in the middle when they stood clear in the morning light. It wouldn't do very much damage, because John Thompson had said the huts were very flimsy, and there wasn't any retaining wall to harness the force of the explosion. Tossing it underhanded into a cave would be a different thing altogether. Joseph Watson hoped someday that he would have a cave to toss a bombom into. Jeff Newton and Joseph Watson had been friends, and he had also been rather more than slightly in love, a long time ago, with Elisabeth Mc-Kenzie. That was before Jeff came home from the war, while Joseph was still away at the war.

The dove's breast of dawn darkened to red and then lightened again to gold. Joseph Watson raised his frosted chin imperceptibly and looked down over the edge of the bluff. There were the huts. Three sodden, pathetic, even, little pagodas of thatch, unplastered, the bamboos that formed the sides hastily planted into the greasy wet earth, the top thatching shoddy. They almost touched, these huts, and Joseph Watson reckoned that if the thing he had in his hand worked properly everybody would be wakened at the same time.

The sun was really high now, gone from red to gold to lemon. Waithaka nudged him gently. There was some gentle rustling noise inside the hut. A woman came out, bending low to get through the doorway and then straightening up painfully. The combination of cold and gonorrhea, Joseph Watson thought suddenly, must be awful tough on the joints. She scrubbed at her eyes with the back of her hand and yawned. Then she walked off from the hut to the edge of the sheer drop and jerked up her dress and squatted down to urinate. As she squatted, Joseph Watson took the bomb out from its warm nest inside his shirt and gently plucked the pin which pressed the arming lever flat to its bed. Holding the lever depressed, although it was now free of pin, he raised his arm, then released the lever, counted to three, and threw the grenade in an easy arc, aiming at the center of the ridgepole of the middle hut. The hut's roof disappeared in the flash the grenade made as it exploded, and the other huts rocked outward, sideways, bits of thatch flying. Joseph Watson then pulled his rifle out from underneath him and slipped the safety catch, his elbows wedged to the ground as he held the rifle prone. He heard the *snick* of the safety of the gun that his Kikuyu, Waithaka, was carrying.

Several figures exploded from the two outer huts. One figure crawled from what was left of the center hut. Another burst out and jumped over the crawler and ran. There was a pall of acrid smoke in the air and the different, clean smell of burning thatch. Some moans came from within the wrecked hut. There were the sharp-upsticking bamboo poles, and the thatch which had blown up and fallen down again on whoever was left inside. The thatch worked up and down as if animals were trapped under it.

The other figures ran. They ran wildly, some limping, some holding themselves where blood flowed and where they had been slightly wounded by the flying bits of grenade. They ran across the green of the little glade. One man ran toward the edge of the bluff, as if he had forgotten that there was no exit there. He came to the edge of the bluff and paused, looking curiously down at the drop. When he turned he darted his head to right and left, as if he couldn't decide where he really wanted to go. This was when Peter McKenzie showed the barest glimmer of a sulphur-match-rubbed sight bead between the rabbit-ears V of the .416's rear sight and squeezed on the center of the man's chest. The chest went away from under the sights and the man was on the ground. Peter got up from his prone position swiftly and squatted on his hams, feet planted firmly, heels flat, and his elbows locked on his kneecaps. Another man ran, ran swiftly as a frightened antelope, and Peter swung the gun past him, leading him with his right eye, centering the rifle vertically with his left eye, and pulled again. The man leaped high, as high as a suddenly shot impala leaps, and came down in a heap.

The woman who had squatted to urinate got up as the blast of the grenade tossed her hut upward, and ran blindly back toward the hut. Joseph Watson let her come closer and held the gun on the middle of her breast and started to squeeze when the gun of Waithaka crashed in his eardrum and the woman clapped her hands to her chest and fell. She tried to crawl, and Joseph heard the gun go again as Waithaka shot her in the head.

Two men and one small boy ran for the trail, and there was the sudden harsh chatter of the machine gun in the hands of the policeman. Bill Falconer held low on the legs and let the gun jump. It was funny to see the two men and the boy fall. They fell in an exactly timed sequence, as ducks drop in a shooting gallery. One. Down. Two. Down. Three. Down. All down, in a descending scale then, the men first, the boy later. Bing, bang, bong. Like a xylophone.

One of the wounded inside the wrecked hut crawled out, humping himself along, dragging with his elbows, and then suddenly lurching upright and starting to stagger without really knowing where he was headed. John Thompson had never trusted himself as a pistol shot. He laid his gun aside and held his pistol in both hands and let the man stagger until he staggered into the steadily held foresight, and then John squeezed off. The .45 roared and the man fell down. Then a woman came running from somewhere, and John had never hit anything running with a pistol. He took a quick snap at her as she ran, and missed clean. Then he heard the solid smack of Peter's big .416 and saw the woman freeze as if she were in a cinema and somebody had stopped the reel. She stood absolutely straight up for one long fraction of a second and then she fell forward, with her belly hitting the ground first, then her face hitting hard.

John Thompson had been close in his estimation of how many people were in the shamba. There were five women actually and nine men. One man got away. Everybody shot at him and missed, although he ran easily and smoothly. Peter jerked his head at Lathela as the man disappeared into the bush, and Lathela smiled a happy, serene smile and went after the man. There were two dead women inside the hut—evidently Joseph's grenade had landed smack into a tangle of sleeping people—and two dead women outside the hut. One woman was wounded by the explosion and crawled out behind the hut and was off into the bush, leaving a clearly marked spoor behind her. They found her later, dead and wedged against a tree.

Of the eight men, three were dead inside the hut—dead enough, in any case, to be worthless as witnesses—and so they sent in Waithaka with a panga. Five were shot as they fled across the open ground. Then of course there was the boy, who didn't count. Peter kept thinking, as they shot, that this was almost exactly the way he and Jeff had shot the buffalo—how many years ago was it?—when they had gone on the safari that time before the wedding. The Kikuyu had run back and forth, addled, witless, exactly as the buffalo had charged back and forth when Jeff had sent Lathela round to let his scent drift down into the herd, and the buff had fled to Peter and Jeff, looking stupidly at each other as the bulls dropped, charging off away from the scent and the noise and then galloping back to the safety of the noise, where there was no scent to frighten them.

When the shooting was over Peter got up and stretched his cramped knees. He reloaded the gun and walked out into the open. The sun was up, high now, and it had gotten warmer. The wet grass glistened in the morning sunlight. One of the men moved, throwing out an arm, and then bucking himself half erect. Peter walked over to him and shot him in the head with his pistol. The man fell flat, quivered, and then lay still, but his outstretched fingers still plucked at the grasses. Peter walked over to the first man he'd shot, holding cold on the chest, curious to see what sort of impact a soft-nosed .416 would make on a man. The man lay on his face. Peter turned him over with his foot. The impact a soft-nosed .416 would make on a man was considerable. The man had no back whatsoever for the space of a square foot. I think I'm using too much gun, Peter thought, before he remembered for a moment that this was a man and not an animal.

Lathela came back from the forests and he was carrying something on the head of his spear.

"Mimi nataka headskin, Bwana!" he cried, flourishing the spear and what he had on the end of it.

"For Christ's sake put that thing down," Peter said. "Throw it in the bush."

And so they hunted. Information drifted in from the shambas, and this information led to concealed villages in deep jungles of bamboo and to caves dug slyly into what seemed innocent stone. Joseph Watson had his chance to lob a grenade into several caves, and he was right about what damage might possibly be done if there were stout walls to control the force of the exploding bomb. Joseph also had a homemade flame thrower now, and it brought back old memories of Burma. He had almost forgotten what a man looked like as he ran flaming, the wind he created by running making him burn brighter and faster until he crisped into a cinder, and tumbled to the ground to smoulder. The flame thrower worked very well inside the caves, as it had worked on dug-in Japanese.

They had built a barbed-wire stockade in back of Joseph's house now, and it held always a dozen, two dozen, sullenly-resigned, gaze-averting blacks from the shambas, denounced and arrested by the spies of Bill Falconer. There was a smaller stockade devoted to women. The prisoners had been used experimentally so far in efforts to elicit social information. Very little fresh news had been extracted from them, although Falconer's police were persistent and persuasive. Several prisoners had died from overinterrogation, but never of boredom. When they died they were taken out and thrown into the bush. Quite a few of the survivors hobbled painfully on sore feet, and several men owned scrotums which were swollen the size of footballs. Beating the feet and tapping the testicles, gently first and insistently later, finally caused the men to writhe in pain and scream from pain and faint from pain. But they did not gossip about their private affairs. What information the police accumulated about the pockets of Mau Mau came directly from the spies, who slept it and waked it and heard it firsthand in the shambas as traitors, and who on occasion went along into the hills as traitors with a load of provisions for the refugees. A Mau Mau membership was a very desirable thing if you were a natural-born traitor and did not take the oath too seriously. Most of Bill Falconer's infiltrators were stout Christians and asked the forgiveness of the white man's God for having submitted to the Mau Mau oaths which gave them entree to the secrets of their relatives. Then they went off to one side and prayed quietly to their grandfathers and to Ngai—begging forgiveness for their double treason.

Peter remembered several incidents apart from the humdrum of creeping up on villages, throwing grenades, flourishing a flame thrower, and sniping at the running men; apart from hoisting a man clear of the ground by a loop around his penis and rocking his head steadily the while to refresh his memory.

One of Peter's more sharply defined memoirs was of a swab-out of the prison pen to make room for more candidates for interrogation. A man called Sloane from Kinangop, who had once been the legal husband of a now dead woman whose child had been taken unborn from the woman's belly and shown her just before the woman died, pleaded for the right to clean out the prison pens. He cursed horribly and tears flowed from his eyes as he walked through the pen with a pistol in one hand and a panga in the other. He became overhysterical finally, and his eyes fixed on nowhere and foam dribbled from his lips. They had to go into the pen and drag him out and tie him down, and then they had to go back into the pen again with guns and finish off what Sloane had started. It was possible Sloane was mad, because he shot himself a week later, biting his rifle barrel between his teeth and tripping the trigger with his toe.

Another memory of Peter's was of the woman who would not talk, an unusual woman who had nothing at all to say. Peter's suggestion, heartily agreed to by Darwin, the animal trapper, was to try a snake. Snakes were abhorrent to a Kikuyu, coming possibly from the legend of the first man, Gikuyu, and his battle with the Great Snake who was now a rainbow and lived with his tail in Thomson's Falls. In the old days, if a pregnant woman saw a snake at close hand, it was her duty to abort herself lest the child have thahu and be born a monster.

This was a young Kikuyu girl, quite handsome, who was the wife of one of the Mau Mau leaders on the mountain. The spies reported that she had been many times up the mountain, carrying supplies, and that she knew the whereabouts of several shambas that they had not yet been able to locate. They had tried pain, which she bore. It was then that Peter suggested the snake.

It was a very little snake, non-poisonous, only about two feet long, just a little green snake with the round head, unlike the flat wedge head of the venomous snake. They stripped the woman naked and spread-eagled her, pegging her arms and legs fast. Then they released the little snake and let it crawl slowly up the inside of her thigh, looking for warmth and shelter. Peter's idea (a sound one) was that if she saw herself symbolically seduced and then impregnated by the snake, she would start to talk at the approximate time the snake's head reached her vagina. She writhed and she fought against the thongs that bound her ankles and wrists. Her body arched and her head tossed frantically from side to side. She moaned. The snake crawled. Once she writhed upward and the snake fell off her thigh onto the ground. Peter picked up the snake and started it up her leg again.

"Which is the way to the shamba of your husband?" He asked it over and over again, and the little snake crawled and retreated, wiggled and crawled and fell off and was put back. The woman screamed, but she did not answer.

"Where is the path that leads to the shamba of your husband?"

The snake wriggled. Finally its head flickered out and touched the scarred inner surface of the woman's body, where the *labia majora* and the clitoris had been removed by circumcision. The woman's body arched once and then was still. The camp doctor raised one of her eyelids and placed a stethoscope to her breast.

"I don't think that was such a brilliant idea of yours, McKenzie," he said. "The woman's dead. You frightened her to death."

The snake now was investigating the moist warmth. Peter picked him up by the tail and snapped his head against a tree and threw the snake into the yard, where the chickens began to peck at him.

There was the time of the trapper, too. They had found a shamba high in the hills and had carefully booby-trapped the trails that led away from it. George Darwin worked carefully and quietly, digging his pits and placing the sharpened ends of bamboo point-upward in the bottom, as the pygmies prepared their traps for animals, covering the tops of the pits with light thatching, earth, and finally leaves, the same leaves which had been carefully saved from the footpath's surface when the digging began.

On other paths he set out snares, trip snares attached to saplings bent double and held by a simple catch. When the noose was tripped by a running man or animal, the sapling disengaged its catch and whipped upward, jerking the captive with it, holding its prey dangling by a foot, high above the ground.

When all was ready the Game Department bloke, Edmonds, took a sub-machine gun and climbed with his pilot into the Piper Cub. They sneaked through the passes, flying low, and when they came upon the shamba, they gunned the plane and flew low over it, the wings tilted vertically. The Game Department bloke sprayed the clearing with his machine gun. As they righted the plane they could see tiny figures diving into the bush, running like hares toward the trails.

George Darwin was happy and proud when they went up the trails the next day to inspect the bag. The snares had caught three men, two women, one little girl, and a bushbuck with quite a decent head. They ate the bushbuck later. It was very amusing, the men and the women and the little girl and the bushbuck all swinging, upside down. Only the little girl and the bushbuck were dead, because the buck had bent his head and the noose had clamped his neck together with one forefoot and he had strangled.

They found five men and two women and one little boy in the pits. One of the men had lit on the base of his spine on a sharpened stake, and it had pierced all the way through him and came out just below his navel. He was alone in this pit and was still squirming on the stake. The others had been only superficially injured by the stakes and had remained quiet in the pits. It was a fine haul, and George Darwin accepted congratulations freely. He got the people out of the pits very simply. He lassoed them and hauled them out. He was deadly with the noose and simply flipped it underhand. It spread as a cobra's hood swells when he rises to strike, and settled sinuously on the necks and shoulders of the people in the pits. They were slightly strangled when they soared out of the pits, but the doctor was there to revive them so they could be questioned later, after their wounds had been dressed.

11

Another thing Peter remembered clearly was the big drive. Harvey Edmonds had come up from a visit to the Masai with a hundred moran. They were dressed for war, ocher-painted, and their (forbidden) lion-mane headdresses and their (forbidden) ostrich-plume headdresses shook and waved in the wind. The buffalo-hide shields (forbidden), bleached white and blazoned with red, white, and blue armorial bearings, rode comfortably on their left arms. These were all senior moran, and their seven-foot spears were six foot four inches of steel blade. They wore leggings of colobus-monkey hide (forbidden) and of marabou-stork down (forbidden) and iron war rattles and the slashing simis in scarlet leather cases. Their hair was plaited and greased and daubed with ocher; they had either clubbed it in a snood or braided it into stiff pigtails that flapped against their necks. They wore their fighting ornaments and bracelets, and their faces, over the basic red of the ocher, were slashed in designs of blue clay and lime. They carried long, thin gourds the size of policemen's clubs, which contained their ration of urine-curdled blood and milk. They held a big ngoma the night before the raid, and their laibons made battle medicine for the first time in a long time. They leaped in the flickering firelight, some of the men jumping flatfooted and straight up as high as four feet off the ground. In a separate ngoma, the Wakamba police askaris had made drums of wet-stretched hide over petrol tins and had revved themselves up to their tumbling, whirling-dervish dances, in which a man may leap into the air and turn himself completely over twice before his feet touch ground again. The tall, lean, hawk-faced Masai, their headdresses shaking from the wooden horns that held the ostrich plumes and the tawny or black chest manes of the lions, rippled their bodies sinuously from seven feet up all the way down to where their flat feet pounded in rhythm on the ground. The shorter, squat 'Kamba whirled and tumbled and thumped their drums, flourishing pangas and short bows. They danced all night, and when morning came they seized their spears and bows and ran screaming into the bush and up the mountain. The policeman, Falconer, ran with his 'Kamba, and the Game Department bloke, Edmonds, ran with his Masai. They knew where they were running to, a forest next the flat green meadow, two sides of which they would flank in a long V whose arms extended to each side of the meadow and whose sharp point was reinforced to build a cul-de-sac. They would wait there until the game appeared.

An Indian Army major (ret.) had organized the beat much earlier. There was a cluster of shambas, pre-spotted by the plane, nestled to the side of a great hill which led down to the open plain of the meadow. There were perhaps sixty to a hundred Kikuyu in the various shambas. The scheme was to collect the lot.

The beat was most easily conducted on the classic lines of a tiger drive, the Indian Army (ret.) chap said. His name was Farnsworth and he had a bad liver which had not improved since he left India for a tea shamba in Kenya. He mustered all the white men and described a square-ended horseshoe of perhaps a hundred beaters. Two long stop lines went out ahead of the solid end of the horseshoe, spread to encompass the hill on both sides, narrowing at the bottom, where the hill drifted into the meadow. The stop lines were checkerboarded with white riflemen and black servants, askaris and gunbearers, carrying extra guns, in some cases, and always spears. The beating line was a double line, solid black in the first file, the men armed only with small drums, pots, pans, pangas, hand axes and hastily cut clubs. The beating line would come in behind the Mau Mau habitation, making much noise as the Negroes pounded on trees with their clubs and axes, as they pounded on their drums and pots and pans, and as they screamed at the top of their lungs. The white men walked behind, also screaming, and occasionally firing pistols. The stop lines moved silently ahead of the beaters. The stop lines' duty was to shoot anything that tried to break through the long sides of the human horseshoe. If all went according to plan, the Mau Mau would be compressed inside the horseshoe and would spill out of the open end onto the plain, where the Masai crouched in hiding with their spears and the Wakamba waited with guns and poisoned arrows.

The Indian Army major (ret.) was a bit of a bore in his explanations, but his house was completely carpeted with tiger pelts and panther skins from the Madhya Pradesh and Assam, and the men assumed he knew his business.

"In a perfect tiger beat," the major said, "one must know the approximate location of the tiger's kill. This is easily determined by (1) the blood trail where the tiger has dragged a bullock or a water buffalo and (2) by the position of the vultures, the carrion kites, and the ravens.

If the birds are in the sky or perched in trees, the tiger is feeding on the kill. When you see the birds come down out of the trees or from the sky, then the tiger has gone to drink. He will not go to bush to den up until he has eaten all of the buffalo or bullock unless he is disturbed. He will eat the animal in two feedings, and he will lie up beside it until he has finished it. He will go to drink at about 3 P.M. on the day following the kill, after the second feeding."

"We've got so bloody few tigers in Africa," one rude man said. "None, as a matter of fact, except what that script writer for M-G-M invented. Could you perhaps confine this beat to people?"

"I've never conducted a beat of *people* before," Major Farnsworth said. "I *do* know about tigers. To continue. If you are satisfied that the tiger is on the kill and has not beggared off somewhere outside the beat area, then the beating becomes unimportant and the stopping jolly important indeed. The tiger will always move slowly ahead of the noise behind him. He moves slowly because his belly is full. If he has never been beaten before he will adhere to the confines of the beat. If he is an old hand, has been beaten and perhaps shot or wounded, then he will do one of several things. He may try to turn and charge through the beaters, in which case one or more beaters are killed. More likely he will attempt to go through the stop lines, in which case one or more stoppers will be killed. Stoppers may prevent this by clapping their hands steadily, not loudly, but steadily, and the tiger will allow himself to be driven along until he comes to the end of the horn."

"What does the bloody beast do when he comes to the end of the horn, as you call it?" Peter asked this question. He had never seen a tiger, and he was curious.

"This would depend entirely on where the shooter was sitting. If, as *I* shoot tigers always, the shooter is on the ground, then the tiger would be apt to spring at or over the shooter. One must be very careful about shooting him head on, for a tiger always leaps in the direction he is facing, and he leaps approximately two and one half times his length, which is generally about ten feet if he is mature. You can always tell if the tiger is mature by the white ruff around his face. He does not start to grow this beard until he is twelve years old.

"But I digress. To reply to your question more fully, McKenzie, the tiger will leap at you or over you if you are on the ground. If you are sitting in a low machan in a tree, he might leap up onto the machan with you and take you along with him. If you are in a high machan he will try to run past you if he sees you. But if you are very quiet he will perhaps walk softly and slowly into an opening and stand perfectly still for as much as a minute whilst he swings his head around. As you possibly know, a tiger has very little or perhaps no sense of smell. It is when he stands quietly testing the surroundings for movement or noise that one shoots him. *Some* people shoot for the head or the point of the shoulder. *I* have always shot for the neck. If you hit his neck on bone he drops and there is no more trouble. If you do not hit the upper spinal column he has only experienced a flesh wound, which heals quickly, and you do not need to follow him into the bush. Also, a tiger is very difficult to kill by shooting him in the head. His skull bones are beveled and the bullet is apt to glance off unless one shoots him directly through the nostrils or low between the eyes. Or in the ear, of course, if he is standing side-on to you. That is about all, I think, except that it is wise to place the tiger immediately in the shade and to skin him as soon as it is feasible. Otherwise, especially if he has just fed, there is a tendency of the skin to slip. The hair drops off in ruddy great patches."

"It sounds very easy," John Thompson said. "What about these man-eaters if it's all so simple?"

"A man-eater is a different color of horse," the Indian Army major said. "He is an individualist. He will not drive. He will not return to a kill. He will not respond to a bait. He cannot be shot with a staked animal or by a person at night. The last real man-eater I encountered had amassed a score of four hundred and twenty-five natives in an area of a hundred square miles. Unless he has died of old age, I presume he is still living off the country."

"Now then," the policeman said. "Since we've played out the Jim Corbett travelogue, as I see it we beat these bloody Wogs into the waiting arms of the Masai laddy-bucks, and the armed file behind the beaters shoots at any tigers—excuse me, people—who try to break through the beating lines, and the stop-line files shoot anything that tries to break through the side lines. And when we force 'em out into the open it's forward the Buffs, damn the torpedoes, and everybody shoots at everybody else, except the Masai, who throw spears, and the 'Kambas, who pot away with those lovely little poisoned arrows. That the drill?"

"That is precisely how I would have said it," the retired major said. "I would suggest that each beater be no more than a hundred yards from the man next him, and that the stoppers keep a slightly closer rank. Perhaps seventy-five yards between each man. And the end of the horn should begin to narrow as the stop lines' first flankers approach the bottom of the hill giving onto the clear space. I also suggest that at least twenty-five men be placed in trees with rifles to bulwark the savages, as we will then be able to shoot at the quarry without catching a poisoned arrow or a spear by accident."

"Sound enough. McKenzie! Will you take some people and trip along with me and my Masai, who sound warmed up enough for anything about now, and climb up some trees and do a sniper bit for us? Try not to infringe on the Masai copyright too much. I think a good old-fashioned spear-blooding mightn't be a bad piece of public relations right now. Remember, I'm the psychological-warfare board here as well as the vice-president in charge of what we used to call murder. Let's have a spot of something, if anybody's got one, and I'll go and collect my spears and we'll crack on."

Peter would remember the day. It was, oddly, a fine clear day, and the sun was bright on the meadow. A brisk wind held, streaming down from the hill and bringing the voices and the tin-panning and the drum-beating and the tree-pounding loudly clear for at least two miles. Peter was sitting high in a big fig, his back braced comfortably against the bole and his legs spread, feet planted on two forks. He had filled the pockets of his coat with bullets. He could even smoke, because in a beat the smoke wouldn't make any difference at all. He listened to the tumult the beaters were making and to the occasional shot from the stop lines. He reckoned that now and again one of the tigers was trying to dash through the stoppers and not getting very far. He waited, and the noise got louder and louder and then there was a heavy crashing in the bush.

He could heard the Masai stir beneath him in their ambush. They were restless in their ambush, but not noisily nervous, for the hysteria of the dancing had left them relaxed. The Wakamba were over on the other side of the V. The 'Kamba were old elephant poachers and they appreciated the value of silence more than the Masai, who fought in the open and scorned strategy. A Masai with a shield on his left arm and a spear in his right hand neither wanted nor needed subterfuge. But then these moran beneath Peter had never blooded a spear in a proper war, and especially they had never seen any fierce game save lions beaten toward them. In a way Peter was more interested in the Masai's reaction to the job at hand than he was interested in the bursting of the game from the bush on the other side of the meadow. They could not skirt the meadow, because the arms of the V reached upward on both sides, and the horseshoe of the beaters and stoppers was steadily holding the Kikuyu in a long and unloving embrace. Peter waited patiently and lit another cigarette. The wind carried the smoke steadily behind him. Lord, how he missed smoking on those long weeks when they were really hunting the hills, when there was no beat on. It is funny what you miss, Peter thought in the tree. I suppose I should be missing Holly terribly, but in one way I don't. Any more than I miss Nairobi after I've had a few days and nights of it. When all's said and done I reckon I'm a bush baby. I never really liked to wear a necktie.

There was a louder crackling in the bush beneath him, and a shout from the other side of the meadow as the game broke cover. The Kikuyu were coming out in twos and threes, like buffalo driven through a patch of bush, with no other place to run but across the open green glade. The Mau Mau men—and my oath, Peter thought, *look* at the guns they have—split as they broached the meadow and attempted to run the edges. There was very much firing now behind the men as they came into the clear. I suppose some of them turned and tried to go back through the beaters, Peter thought. Where are the stoppers?

In answer, the first men in the extended flanks of the beating ring ran out from the bush and, selecting trees, knelt behind them and started to shoot at the Kikuyu who were beginning to pour out of the wood. The Kikuyu who had guns fired them aimlessly, shooting as they ran, comforting themselves with noise, as runners on the outer fringes began to drop from the controlled fire of the stopper flank. The Mau Mau darted wishfully toward the edges of the sheltering bush, and the closer approachers fell. There was no place finally for the mass to move except directly into the meadow.

It was like a technicolor pageant of the battle of Acre he had seen in the films, Peter thought as he rested his rifle carefully on a forked branch and shot one great big man who had opened his mouth to scream a battle cry and who was running straight along in the open. The Kikuyu were specks against the pale cool green of the meadow, with the mountain and the forest bulking black and dangerous on all sides, just like the lawn at Mawingo, he thought, working the bolt of his rifle and changing over to a smaller but heavier Kikuyu who made a fine running target, with only about one quarter of a lead-off angle to compensate for. The Kikuyu bucked when the bullet hit, and Peter could hear the sodden smack because the wind was right. Then he quit shooting and watched.

The Masai had waited long enough. They broke out of the bush beneath him, shields held diagonally before them, spears poised delicately in their throwing hands. The 'Kamba broke at the same time from the other side of the V, and the forces charged inward toward the Kikuyu, cupping them between two gigantic palms. The Masai threw their spears, and the whistle was as keen on the breeze as doves flying or ducks passing high. The Wakamba paused and fired two volleys of arrows and then flung their bows down and leaped into the scramble. The Europeans stopped shooting. They were fascinated by the tableau on the pale green velvety floor of the little meadow, with its heavy black curtains of forest and hill. Also, it was very difficult to see who was who in the scrimmage. Most of the Kikuyu men were dressed in white man's clothing, as were the 'Kamba askaris. Only the Masai stood out distinctively with their heraldic shields and nodding plumes and swaying lion-mane headdresses. They held no spears now. They had only simis, the stabbing swords. The 'Kamba had their pangas.

The Kikuyu lumped finally in one clot in the middle of the sward, as cattle make a battle ring while the bulls face the attackers. A few women and some children trickled out of the forest and ran toward the concentration of men in the meadow. Then the screaming Masai and the 'Kamba rolled completely over the concentration, their onrushing impetus carrying them almost to the edge of the forest. They rolled back again and carried to the other side of the meadow. What they had rolled over now was lying flat on the ground.

Peter saw one Masai warrior killed by a shot precisely through the center of his shield. He saw the impact of the bullet on the shield and then on the man, and he saw the Masai stagger and lurch forward and regain his balance and then dive into a squirming mass of people and cut the head half off somebody—it was actually a Wakamba askari—before he crumpled and died.

He watched some of the Kikuyu run, with arrows showing only feathers as they stood out from their breasts. The men tore at the shafts and galloped as madly as wildebeests. Then the poison flooded the blood stream and they stopped. A man died with one foot upraised to thrust himself ahead. The foot froze in mid-air. It was a good poison, so potent that if you tested it on blood you could see it crawl up the arm, using the blood trickle as a highway, searching always for the heart. It was strong enough to kill a bull elephant in a quarter of a mile's run. It was strong enough to kill a Kikuyu, even a city Kikuyu with white man's pants and a stolen gun.

It was no use here, hoping for prisoners. The Masai went to recover their spears from the bodies of the men and the women and children who wore the spears. The 'Kamba went to recover their arrows—long-throated arrows whose giraffe necks would again be dipped in poison and wound round with soft leather wrappings. Occasionally a body moved and a simi flashed or a panga swung up and down or a club struck with the sound of a bursting melon or a dropped gourd. Peter, sitting in his tree, looked coldly at the tableau and remembered the safari he and Jeff had made against the hyenas. If only, he thought, these people snapped at their own guts and ate each other, it would be so much neater.

He could see the Masai and the 'Kamba moving their own men to one side, away from the dead Kikuyu. A dead Masai—and there were only five dead—looked like a dead lion, Peter thought. The headdress was rumpled and the splendor was spoiled. A dead Wakamba looked exactly like a dead Kikuyu, just dead and sprawled out, but a dead Masai was a magnificent animal from which the life had gone, leaving him rumpled and spoiled, with his mane blood-soiled and all his splendor ruined. The only thing that looked good when it was dead was a leopard. The rest, especially men, just looked dead. And when an animal died it had an orgasm and the sphincter muscle slipped and it was soon surrounded by dung and slop.

Man, but this was a real hunt. There must be a hundred dead ones in the meadow. The vultures would feed heavy from this one. And there they were in the sky. *How* could they know? How could they know so swiftly, and come to the scene so fast? Already some were walking, gravely and bored with waiting, at the edge of the forest, and others sat in trees. It occurred to Peter that he was taking up some room a deserving vulture might fancy, and so he slung his rifle and shinned down the tree.

He walked among the dead, looking at the faces. They did not impress him much as people. The dead slashed children, yes. Possibly the women, a little. But the men, no. He would have been a trifle moved, perhaps, if one of the men had turned out to be Kimani or perhaps Lathela or Metheke or somebody he knew. But there was Lathela, sitting cross-legged on the ground and fretting about a gap hacked out of his spear blade. There was Metheke, blowing his nose as only Metheke could put real emotion into taking a flat nose between his fingers and summoning up an unbelievable force to expel what was inside it.

I never saw a battle and I was never really in a war, Peter thought as he walked among the dead Kikuyu. But I bet you this is how the chaps felt when they saw a lot of Jerries dead or a lot of Japs dead. There in front of me now is nothing but so many hyenas, full of thwarted purpose and their own filth. Look at this sportsman, he thought, gazing down at a Kikuyu who had taken a Masai spear through the guts and then suffered a direct approach from a Wakamba panga, which left him with only half a skull. As Tom Deane would say, dig this character. There will be bloody precious little in the way of Chevvy convertibles and wireless sets for this type when the Russians come and bring the millennium with them. Whatever happened to that silly car boy, that Chabani of mine, the one who informed me once that his first name was *Jeems* and that he was going to study television someday? He thought television was some sort of science.

It was certainly a messy meadow. What Peter remembered strongly of the meadow was how the bodies lay sprawled about in their own shiny-black blood, and how from a distance they did not look like bodies so much as flat excrescence, like a cow pasture seen from a low angle. And how, he thought, that nobody alive in this area gave one really good goddamn about the dead that were there, except the vultures. The vultures were really the only mourners that the heaps of nothing had for the wake, for the Masai were already heading home to the Loita plains and to the Telek and to the big bold, cheerful mountain, Egelok. And the 'Kamba were going back to being policemen at so many bob a day. Because the first fun they'd had in donkey's years was over. And that Peter himself had shot and killed two more men, and the headskins weren't worthy of the taking, since nobody would want to mount one, any more than you'd mount a wart hog for your dining room. He was using too much gun, though. It was getting expensive. The very first time he got back to Nairobo he would pick up that Marlin carbine that Deane'd left. It was a nothing-gun for animals, but on men in bush it would be beautiful. You could hang that peep sight on a running Wog and own him before you pulled the trigger. Also, the ammunition cost about one fifth as much as those Kynoch things for the really good guns. It was a shame to use a really good gun on the filth you had to shoot these days. It was like using a beautiful Rigby or a Westley-Richards or a Jeffery on a bloody wildebeest. I wonder where the hell is Deane, he thought. He's about due out here now for another safari. I know he hired Thompson, but Thompson is here with me shooting Kikuyu. I better ask Big John, he thought. I'm sure Holly'd like to see the Deanes again.

It had been a wonderfully successful sweep, this beat. The Indian Army major (ret.) beamed and preened his mustaches. The beaters had beaten well. The stoppers had stopped beautifully. They all returned to the camp after they had searched the bodies for papers and identification, finding little of value. Some grog had come up from Thomson's Falls, and the hunters celebrated.

"I must say, I *must* say, you chaps couldn't have carried it off better if you were Gonds or Baigas from the Central Province and had been beating tigers all your lives," the liverish major, Farnsworth, said. "Especially the stoppers. Once the game breaks through a stop line, you've really bought it. How many tried to get through, actually?"

"There were a couple of blokes veered off just as we came down to the meadow," one farmer said. "I damned near shot old Warren here. He was in direct line with the Wog, and when I started to squeeze off I was looking Warren right in the chest. So I unsqueezed and let the Wog get clear and then shot at him blind and by some miracle I hit. The Wog, not Warren."

"We had a jolly last-minute do in the beat line," one youngster said. "When we were thrusting them down the hill and they saw that dirty great span of open space ahead of them, any amount panicked and ran back to us. We discouraged them slightly with a volley, but one enormous great nigger came at me with a panga the size of a crosscut saw, and I promise you I was terrified. He was swishing the thing around his head like a bloody lasso. Somebody shot him—I don't know who—and my heart came back down out of my neck."

"Me," another man said. "I remembered you owed me thirty bob from that last gin game. It didn't seem right to let the Wog do you, even though nobody'd care but me."

The men chattered all at once, excitedly.

"*Did* you see those wonderful Masai at work? What a pity they didn't go to fight in the war. They're as good as Gurkhas. We could have shortened the Jap end considerably with those Masai laddies."

"Funny, isn't it, how blood tells? None of the Masai have been allowed to fight since the treaty, and I daresay none of these types ever killed a man except maybe in some private knife fight. But the old laibons had them whetted right up to scratch. They must have been something to see fifty years ago when they went through this country like a plague."

"I hope they don't get any funny ideas from this do," the Game Department bloke said. "It would be a very sweet thing if these Masai and these Athegani they're training into resistance forces got some funny ideas from their success against the Mau Mau and decided that as long as they were in the business they might as well try their techniques on the whites. But, by God, they were wonderful down there in the meadow, like a bloody pack of lion hounds."

"I got the funniest feeling on the beating line. You've hunted bongo, I suppose, and you know how you can track right up to them in bush, and you can hear them stirring in the wild grape, and you think this time, *this* time, I'll get up to them and shoot one, and then there's a *whoof* and the herd bull barks and they all go crashing off in the bush and you've never seen them at all, only heard them. It was sort of like that when we were beating. You could hear the feet scurry and the swishing of the bush, and once in a while some Wog would call out, but you never saw them at all until some of the less eager ones tried to crash back through us as we drove them to the meadow."

"You can say all you want about these gaudy Masai," the policeman said. "But I'll still take my 'Kamba lads. My oath, but I should not like the idea of Mau Mau spreading out to the 'Kamba and the Nandi. Fancy staggering about in bush knowing that one of those dear lads was stuck off in a tree somewhere with that lovely stiff bow and those beautiful arrows dipped in that nice, nasty brown gum. I don't believe there's a white man's poison anywhere that's a patch on what they dip those arrows in, specially when it's nice and fresh and gooey."

"The old Turkana weren't so bad in the close work, if anybody noticed. I still manage to get the shudders when I see how they use those bracelets to chop with. Got a decided advantage over a knife, for you don't have to hold it in your hand. It's welded on your wrist."

"Wonder what's happening in civilization," a man said. "Jake, you've had the wireless going?"

"Nothing very new. One new killing in Nanyuki—John Foulke. Got him in the latrine. Police broke up a big meeting at Thika and killed about a dozen innocent bystanders. Lost one white policeman—your buddy, Bill, I'm afraid. Tony Anderson. Pity. He was a damned nice chap. They've sent out some bigwig from home to defend Kenyatta. Flitt, Plitt, something like that. Got a Wahindi with him as co-counsel. Oh yes. Fifteen loyal Kikuyu and one minor chief chopped at Fort Hall. I forgot that one."

"I certainly hope Admiralty send another battleship soon," a man laughed in a hard bark. "We could use another battleship up here in this bush."

"Only problem is logistical. How are you going to get the battleship transported from Mombasa for use in these hills?"

"Don't be an ass. That's why we built the railroad and let the lions chew up all the workers at Tsavo. So we could ship dreadnoughts up to the Aberdares to hunt Wogs with."

"I always wondered why they were called dreadnoughts. Means 'fear nothing,' and bloody apt, too, 'cause there's never anything near them to fear."

"I suppose we'll all hang someday for this do if the Socialists ever get in. Mustn't go about clobbering Wogs, not if you take the modern view. 'Tisn't sporting. Doesn't conform with the aims of Attlee and the United Nations. Not to mention old Nehru."

"I'm just sorry the Wahindi aren't more directly mixed up in the Mau Mau. Be such a pleasure, *such* a pleasure."

"If we have many more days like this last one, they'll be shoving Mau Mau on license, and it'll cost you an extra seventy-five quid for the second one, like elephant. . . ."

12

The compound was filled again with natives captured in raids below on the reserves and in the white shambas. They were a total loss for information, except one very young man named Moses Wainana. He was only about seventeen, and he did not like to have his feet and testicles beaten. One day, as Joseph Watson rocked his head gently, insistently, fingers gripping the hair and increasing the rhythm to match the insistent tap-tap of a swishy rod on his genitals, the young man screamed and wept like a woman.

"Stop, stop, please stop!" he cried. "I will talk. I will tell you anything."

"Very good, very good indeed. Begin by telling us who was your oath-administrator. What was his name and where does he live?"

"I have forgotten his name, but I would know him if I saw him."

Joseph's voice was soft and soothing, almost a croon. He rocked the man gently by the hair and began to tap on his testicles again with the rod.

"*Surely* you know the name of the man who gave you the oath. *Surely* you remember the name of such an important man. *Surely* if you try hard you will remember the name of the man. *Surely* such a thing as an oath-giving is important and you would ask from curiosity the name of the man who gave you the oath. *Surely* . . ."

"You can stop now, chum," Peter said. "He's fainted again."

Joseph turned gentle, half-closed bloodshot eyes toward Peter.

"Oh, has he?" He smiled. "How dreadful. Let's go and have a beer and let him rest a bit then. I shouldn't want to overtry his strength."

That day a man came to Joseph Watson's shamba. He was a man who sat high in Government. He had some instructions.

"Here is a letter," he said. "It promises a wholesale Mau Mau killing for the holiday season. The killing has already started. Two more white families have been chopped, and any amount of Kikuyu. They are asking a dozen heads for the Christmas season. We think that if there is a reply in kind we might discourage them a bit. Your do in the meadow was one thing. A few Mau Mau heads tossed into native shambas might swerve them from their purpose just a bit. If we could get just one big man to talk, and if we could place a finger squarely on just *one* big oath-administrator . . ."

"I think we may have the man who will talk," Joseph said, "and I think perhaps we have some people here who might qualify for, shall we say, a return of the Christmas compliment. And I think that if our little friend who is resting now saw some of his other friends treated in much the same manner that these friends have been treating some people our little friend here would talk. So . . ."

"I don't want to hear the details," the messenger said. "If I don't know about it I can't talk about it. Do it yourself. I'm off, but something's to be done. You go and do it. Not me."

"The pleasure is all mine." Joseph smiled and his eyes hooded. "We will discourage the Christmas head-taking."

They chose five men at random from the prison compound, all of them men who had refused to talk despite brisk encouragement of one sort or another. They were named Karanja, Kariuki, Mauro, Thuo, and Ngatia, all good sound Kikuyu names. Two were young, Kariuki and Thuo. Ngatia had seventy seasons if he had a day, a kindly-looking, gray-wooled man with the long-drooping pierced ear lobes of the old-time Kikuyu. Karanja and Mauro were youngish adults. They were Forties, members of the circumcision group of 1940. They had been to the wars in Burma. They were non-communicative about their activities since the war had ended. One man, Mauro, came from Peter's farm. He was a cousin of Kimani.

The men were brought out from the compound and thrown to the ground. The young man who had started to talk but who could not remember the name of the man who had given him the oath was revived with cold water and placed apart from the other five men.

"These men will not talk," Joseph said. "Can you remember the name of the man who gave you the oath?" The eyes of the five non-talkers swung balefully toward the young man.

"I cannot remember," he said. The eyes swung back.

"That is unfortunate," Joseph said. "For now we must go into the forest. There are too many people here for any really quiet conversation. Peter, call Lathela and Metheke and my boy, Waithaka. Get the doctor and the policeman and the Game Department. We will take these people a mile or so away, into the forests. Tell the doctor to bring his kit. Tell the Wogs to bring their pangas. And there is a bottle of whisky in my bedroom. Bring it. We may need it."

"Man, you can't do it," the Game Department bloke said. "It isn't a thing a white man does."

"I can do it," Peter said. "Joseph can do it. Lathela can do it. The doc can do what he has to do, which is very simple. Metheke can do it. Bill can do it. A policeman can do anything. If you don't want to buy any of it, don't come."

"I shan't," the Game Department bloke said. "If you don't actually need me I won't come along. I shall go and fly in the plane and see what's left in the way of live game on the mountain."

"We only asked you as a matter of chain of command," Joseph said. "Not as social etiquette. The job's to be done. Nairobi wants it to be done. It's necessary for it to be done. Now and on this day and in this place.

Go and fly your bloody plane. I hope it crashes on a hill and one of the hid-out boys finds you still alive in the crash."

"I'm sorry you feel that way about it. I know it's to be done. But I shall go and fly my plane, nevertheless, if you don't mind."

They walked a mile through a pleasant shady wood, the ground carpeted softly by crinkled brown-and-golden leaves from the tall hardwood trees. It was a tawny afternoon, and the air had the texture of October in a beech forest. Sun slanted through the branches, and the sun warmed the foothills, and as they walked a dik-dik scampered gaily away and stopped to pause and look backward, his four tiny feet firmed together, his true alarm less than his basic curiosity. He was no bigger than a hare, and with his ridiculous two-inch horns, his pert arrogance was amusing.

They came then to a small glen through which a tiny stream slid smoothly over clean white pebbles. There was watercress in the stream, and on the sides of the stream there were white sand and a soft green lichen. Boulders carelessly strewed the slopes of the hill leading down to the ferny glen, and some tiny button flowers peeked up through the green, close to the moist protection of the rocks.

"What a lovely place for a picnic," Peter said. "I'd love to take off my boots and go wading. I haven't washed my feet in a couple of weeks. Look! See the little trout."

Joseph Watson gestured with his Sten gun at the six men, who, shackled together, were being prodded along with spears by Lathela and Metheke and Waithaka.

"Cut that one loose," he said, gesturing at the boy who could not remember his oath-administrator's name. "Put him over there and tie him to that tree. Let him sit comfortably. I want him to watch. The other blokes go on the ground. Well, Peter? Doc? Bill?"

"Well," the men said. "I suppose we have to start somewhere."

"We'll start with the old boy," Joseph said. "Old man. Will you talk? Will you tell us who administers oaths on your shamba at Fort Hall?" The old man said nothing. He closed his eyes.

"The light hurts his eyes," Joseph said. "What a pity. Perhaps I can fix that. Lathela! Waithaka! Hold his head still."

Joseph Watson took a long Swedish knife out of a sheath and looked at its point, felt the edge on his thumb, stropped it on his boot sole. Then he took his left hand and pulled the old man's eyelids wide apart. He aimed the point of the knife precisely and dug out one eye.

Blood gushed from the socket. The old man screamed and his body plunged. Then Joseph Watson went to the other eye, pinched it open between his fingers, and picked it out with the point of the knife. The old man screamed once more and fainted. Blood washed down his face. Joseph Watson went over to the stream and scrubbed his hands.

"Waithaka," he said. "Get me two long thorns and build me an arch of leaves. Not a very big one. Any size will do for this ceremony. We probably won't need it anyhow."

The Kikuyu gunbearer brought the thorns. Joseph Watson took the two eyes and impaled them carefully on the thorns.

"Look," he said. "This old man would not talk. So now he has no eyes. The old man would not talk. Will you talk? Will you talk, Karanja?" He flourished the thorn-pierced eyes in front of Karanja's face. The man said nothing. He was a member of the Forties, and a circumcision brother was with him as witness.

"It would be much better to talk," Joseph Watson said. "Talk. I would prefer that you talked."

Karanja swung his head slowly around and looked at Joseph Watson. He did not talk. He looked at the ground.

"Lathela," Joseph Watson said. "Use this knife. It is very sharp."

"No, Bwana," Lathela said. "If you please, I would prefer my knife. It is duller. I was the man of the Bwana Jeff."

"Very well."

Lathela took his knife and bent over the groin of the man Karanja. He cut off the genitals in three slow-sawing motions and tossed them into the man Karanja's face. The man Karanja did not scream before he fainted. He looked at his blood-gushing groin with a detached amazement. Then he fainted.

"We progress," Joseph Watson said in Kikuyu. "We continue to progress. But I believe we need brains and a heart as well. You," he said to the young Thuo. "I believe we need the heart of a young man for this oath to be really binding. Will you talk now, or will you give your heart to make the oath more binding? See your friends. One would not talk, and now does not see, and we have his eyes for the oath. The other would not talk, and now we have his breeding organs for the oath. Will you talk or give your heart? It is for you to decide. I would prefer to have you talk. I am fond of conversation."

The boy Thuo looked straight ahead. Joseph Watson shrugged.

"Metheke," he said. "You are a skinner. Cut me the heart of this man, as you have often taken the heart and liver from an impala or a Tommy. We will need it to roast over the fire."

"Kill him first, Bwana?"

"No. The oath will be stronger if you do not kill him first. Take the heart still beating from his chest. See? A little slit under the ribs and then you can reach in with your hand. No, a longer cut. That is good. Now, the heart."

The young man Thuo screamed, screamed again and again, the screams ringing through the wood. The Wakamba's hand came out of the incision in his stomach, under the ribs, and in the hand he held the heart, which kicked and throbbed. He hauled it nearly clear of the body and then slashed the arteries that held it to the body with his knife. He tossed the heart onto the ground, where it still quivered.

"Cut his head off before you wash your hands," Joseph Watson said. "We will need the brains for the oath. What happened to the doctor? We may need him to preserve some life in the first two."

"The toubib ran away through the woods," Metheke said, walking over and picking up the heartless man's head in his left hand. "He left his sundouki, his kit, behind. It is there by the man with no balls."

"Take all three heads," Joseph Watson said. "They are dying, anyhow, the other two."

The three living men sat while Metheke cut the heads from the castrated man and the blind man. The boy who could not remember the name of his oath-administrator put his face in his hands and his shoulders jerked. The other two men, the very young man and the other Forty member, sat impassively. The young one, Kariuki, now drew Joseph Watson's attention.

"Behold," Joseph Watson said. "You have seen many things. You have seen the heart of a boy and the brains of a man and the eyes of an old man and the testicles of a young man, all of which will go to make a strong oath, stronger than the oath you swore to. But we need many more heads for this oath. Any head that does not talk is useless to its owner. Will your head talk, or will we take it and send it back to your wife on your shamba?"

The young Kariuki said nothing. "Please," Joseph Watson said, "I beg you to talk. What is the name of your oath-administrator? Who is the chief oath-administrator for Nyeri? Tell me and you will not lose your head."

A crow called loudly, and the call was answered. Somewhere, far away, a dog barked.

"Perhaps you would like it if I let out your guts and hung you upside down on a stick, as you leave the dogs and cats as your sign?" Joseph Watson's voice was pleasant. "Or shall I be merciful and saw your head off very slowly? Or would you like some little safari ants and a bit of sugar on your face? Or would you save yourself some great trouble and talk? I have a tremendous curiosity. Will you talk?"

The man stared glumly at his feet. The ankles were swollen. He looked at his feet without curiosity. He said nothing. Joseph Watson turned to Peter. "Your turn," he said. "Make it very slow."

Peter took a pair of pliers in his left hand. Lathela forced the man's mouth open with a stick. Peter reached in with the pliers and seized the tongue of the man with the pincers. He pulled the tongue out of the man's mouth, until it was stretched flat and stiff. It was a very long tongue, sharp-pointed, and it joined to the man's throat far back from the teeth. Peter began to cut, very slowly, across the stretched surface of the tongue. The man's eyes rolled in agony and he choked on the blood that flooded backward into his throat. Suddenly the tongue came clear, and blood spurted from the man's mouth. Peter took the tongue and placed it with the other things. His stomach heaved, and there was the coppery taste of pennies in his mouth.

"You see," Joseph Watson said, "now here is a man who could talk but would not talk, and now he has nothing whatsoever to talk with. Soon he will have no head to think with, so he cannot use his brain to regret his stingy speech and his absent tongue. How much simpler it would have been for everybody if he had only talked."

The slope that reached down to the stream had become toboggan-slick with the blood of the men, and a tiny trickle ran down away from the soaked ground and clotted in the cold stream. The little fish surfaced and struck at it as they might strike at a grasshopper. You could see them clearly through the red film of the blood in the water. The sparkling sand alongside the stream was dyed bright red and soggy now.

"And so," Joseph Watson said, "we come to our last hero. Mauro, is it? Good. You remember the Bwana Peter, I suppose? You should. You ate the food of his father on Bushbuck Farm, and you remember nothing but kindness from the Bwana Peter, is not that so? So I shall let the Bwana Peter repay you for the gracious way you received his kindness, the way you repaid the kindness with extra kindness. Do you remember the Memsaab Elisabeth, the little Memsaab who was so good to you when you were a little boy? Who tended your mother and your sisters? Ah, yes, I see you do. You would not recognize the little Memsaab now. Her appearance has changed somewhat. I do not suppose you know who changed her appearance for her, and who killed the Bwana Jeff, and who killed her children? And if you knew, of course you would not say."

"Yes, Bwana," the man Mauro said suddenly. "Yes. I will talk. Do not kill me, Bwana, I will talk now."

"No," Joseph Watson said. "It is much too late. I have lost interest. Peter, do not hurry when you cut his throat. Go about it gently with the panga. It is not a very sharp panga. I cut some firewood with it this morning."

The man rolled his eyes upward at Peter McKenzie as Peter took him by the hair and pressed the panga blade against his throat.

"You will kill me, Little Bwana?" the man said. "You will kill me?"

"Yes," Peter said, and tears flowed down his face. "I will bloody well kill you. I will kill you now." He sawed steadily with the knife, and after a while the head came free in his hand. Then an uncontrollable nausea washed upward inside him and he went to the stream and vomited. He bathed his head in the cold water and when he came back his face resembled the face of his father that day when he had come to the home of Jeff Newton.

"And so you see," Joseph Watson said to the only remaining Kikuyu, the boy Moses who could not remember. "So you see. Any number can play at Mau Mau if there are enough knives and eyes and heads and other things. This eyeless head, this tongueless head, this balls-less body will all go tonight to certain shambas. These other heads will be rolled like balls into other shambas. And we will leave *you*, my friend, stuck on a stick like a dog for the birds to peck at while you are still alive, as our secret symbol."

"This will happen to you now unless you remember," Peter said. "Unless you remember the name of the man who gives the oath."

"Speak, dog," Lathela said, and flicked his panga at him contemptuously. The panga sliced a tiny piece of flesh from one finger.

"Speak now," said Metheke, hitting him in the face with the back of his hand.

The policeman whittled one end of a large wooden match very sharp and shoved the needle end under the man's thumbnail, the point buried in the flesh. He lit another match and fired the match that protruded from the thumbnail. "Talk," he said. "Or I will give you nineteen more of these, one for each finger, one for each toe. Speak. Who gives the oaths?"

"I will speak," the boy who could not remember said. "Do not burn me. I will speak. I remember now, I remember."

"The name?"

"His name is Njogu. He works on the shamba of the Bwana Ritchie, he who was killed. He is an old man, very thin, with white hair. He is my uncle, the brother of my mother. He has always given the oaths, here at Thomson's Falls and also up the mountain. He has given oaths in Nyeri and Nanyuki. When other oath-givers are sworn, it is always my uncle who swears them." The boy's head dropped. He had betrayed his oath. Now the oath would kill him. The thought crossed the minds of the white men at the same time.

"I should say," Bill Falconer said, "that in this case the oath was right. He has betrayed his people and the oath will certainly kill him."

"Not before I am ready to allow it to kill him," Joseph Watson said. "What we want of him now is a little pack-mule service. I think it might be very impressive for the other boys in the bull pen if he sort of had to carry the trophies back."

"I'll send some of my good men and true down with the trophies tonight," the policeman said. "I know just where I want them left. Bloody messy business, no?"

"It is a bloody messy business," Joseph Watson said. "It is a horrible business. But there may be some people who will say, twenty years from now, that a handful of white men and some few loyal blacks saved Kenya, whilst Whitehall was trying to make up its mind whether or not kilts were suitable for outdoor wear in heathen Africa. You might think of that, young McKenzie, when you wake up screaming one of these nights. I find that this thought, accompanied by whisky, quite often sends me back to sleep, and sometimes even the dreams are better."

"Come on," Peter said. "Let's get back. Did you say whisky?"

"By God, I forgot the bottle," Joseph said. "Here. Have a pull. Waithaka! You and Lathela and Metheke take these bodies off in the bush. Bury them fairly deep. Our little talkative man will carry the heads and the other stuff. I think he should be quite impressive as he goes back into the compound. So they cut heads, do they, for their oath? By God I'll show them head-cutting on an assembly-line basis!"

The men were silent as they walked back in the pure brisk air of late afternoon, the Kikuyu who had finally remembered staggering along ahead of them under his awkward bloody burden. He stumbled and fell several times. He was helped courteously back onto his feet and his tumbled cargo reassembled. It was true that his breeched oath would kill him. His head was found outside the compound next day. It had been removed from his neck by fingers and fingernails.

That night Bill Falconer and a body of twenty men went down to the shamba of the late Ben Ritchie. They were greeted politely by the man they sought. Njogu was exceedingly suave. He could not imagine, he said, how the white askaris could have made such a tremendous mistake in identity. No man abhorred the Mau Mau's evil work more than he. Of course he would go willingly with the bwanas. He hoped that the bwanas would soon discover that he was innocent and would perhaps allow him to work with them in their camp, of which he had heard much. Remember, he had lost a bwana too, and his heart was foul with rage.

They took him back to camp and popped him into the prison pen. Tomorrow they would see how he reacted to persuasion. The other men in the pen already showed signs of budding loquaciousness. The boy who had finally remembered had been *quite* impressive as he staggered into camp under a burden which continued to leak and soil him thoroughly with what was leaking from the burden. Before he died, that was.

Peter McKenzie washed his hands again and again. They became raw from the washing, but he could not rid himself of a smell that had crept into his nostrils and lived there. He had not minded some of the other business. The shooting was quite impersonal. So, in a measure, was the interrogation. But that last bit by the stream in the forest . . . horrible. Even in the best cause it was horrible.

Yet he considered the men with whom he was associated. There was the Game Department bloke. No finer man lived in Kenya. He loved his animals so fiercely that if he had his way the entirety of Africa would be converted into a national park, with shooting disallowed except on Government control. He cherished a wife and three children. He owed no man money and went regularly to church when there was a church to go to. If Peter had not already owned a father he would have been proud and pleased to have the Game Department bloke for a father.

Look at the policeman. Peter had attended school with Bill Falconer. A decenter chap you'd never run onto. Peter had thought once quite seriously of Bill's sister, a pretty girl named Eileen, but the Holly business had fixed that. But there was no man he trusted more. There was no man he'd rather hunt with or drink with than the policeman. And unlike most policeman, he had no deep-dyed streak of cruelty. He was a kind man, a good man, and a happy, pleasant man.

Then consider Joseph. Now there was the big surprise. Most people who knew Joseph figured him to be an old maid. He was precise in his ways, and he rarely swore, and he did not drink very much or smoke at all. He counted his pennies and put every cent into his farm. He had never wenched. To this day Peter did not know that only shyness had kept Joseph from courting his sister. He was a prime pain on safari, old Joseph. He wanted everything laid out neat and performed on a prissy schedule. But he was a good and sincere hunter. Nobody could possibly imagine that he was such a wild shenzi about this Mau Mau business. Peter shivered.

"He really likes it," he said aloud to himself. "He actually, truly likes it. He enjoys questioning them. He loves that hand-grenade business. And he liked what he was doing this afternoon. He enjoyed every minute of it. You can see it in his face and in what happens to his lips. He plucked those eyes out like you'd pick a plum."

God Almighty, forgive us, Peter thought. Look at me. A bloody-handed murderer, as bad as the Mau Mau, maybe worse, because we do it absolutely coldly. Come home from a hard day's work. The little woman says brightly: "And what did you do today, dear?" And you reply: "Nothing very much, sweetie. Cut the balls off one chap, some stranger or other. Plucked out a few eyes and hacked off a tongue and oh yes, I almost forgot. We also chopped five heads. What's new with you? The new cook improving, or shall I cut off his h—— Shall we sack him and look for a new one?"

And what would I like for Christmas this year? I wonder. A new pair of pliers to pull out tongues with? A new panga to cut heads off with? That other panga's losing its temper. Or perhaps a portable rack like they used in the Inquisition? Something to pull them completely apart with. Maybe Joseph could hook it up to his generator. Jesus Christ. And just yesterday I was a blushing bridegroom off for America. I wonder how this old oath-giver we've flushed will respond to suggestion. I've a hunch we can't break him down with pain. And I've a hunch he's the one we're supposed to break. Well, we will see. In the meantime——Oh Christ.

Peter put his face in his hands and wept. The hands still smelled of whatever it was they smelled of.

13

The old man Njogu resisted the most persistent efforts to shake his almost frivolous assumption of innocence. He had been accused as an oath-giver by six of the shabby men in the prison pen after Joseph Watson's clinical afternoon by the stream had destroyed a certain amount of self-confidence among the prisoners. Njogu, under intense interrogation, was able to smile and remain aloofly dignified, although certain extra efforts by Lathela and Waithaka would have been sufficient to stir most tongues into garrulousness. Not even the business of the safari ants and the molasses or the threat of death and an exquisite additional variety of pain was able to destroy the old man's almost serene composure.

"There's no point to killing him," Joseph said one day after a particularly strenuous session in the little glen. "And if we carry on much longer this way we'll have to kill him. There's got to be some other way to get inside him. Peter, do you reckon your old man would run up here for a few days and work him over? He knows more about Kikuyu than most. Didn't he play about with witchcraft a bit in the old days?"

"They always said so. He was very close to old Karanja. I used to hear quite a few tall tales about him when I was a kid. I could shoot down to the farm and bring him up here for a few days if you'd like. He might think of something. We wouldn't lose by trying."

"Good. Hop in your gharri and go and visit the home folks. Come back tomorrow."

So Peter had gone home to fetch his father and had gotten drunk on the way and had made an unholy show of himself, and now he and his father were driving back to Campi a Mbingu. The old man asked very few questions as they drove.

"He's an old-style Kyuke, is he? Not one of these city types with a mission education?"

"No, sir. He reminds me quite a lot of old Karanja. Dignity spread all over him, and very brave. We've tried about everything in the book on him, including water down the nostrils and a lot of stuff that that Waithaka of Joseph Watson invented. Funny about Waithaka. I have had the feeling that this was one man Waithaka wanted to see dead. He worked harder than Lathela, and we have had to tie up Lathela at night, or we wouldn't have any prisoners left. No, sir. You won't get at this chap through pain or fear."

They drove into Thomson's Falls.

"Stop a bit," Henry McKenzie said. "Who here would have a gas mask? One of the old ones? You know, with those great glass eyes and the snout?"

"I suppose one of the ex-soldiers might have one stuck away in his kit. There were a lot of old 1914 nose bags issued at the start of this last war. Let's stop off at the pub and make some phone calls. I could use a drink. Look."

Peter held up his hands. They were shaking.

"You had quite a load aboard last night," Henry McKenzie said. "And it wasn't all liquor. What have you chaps actually been up to in that camp?"

"I'd rather not talk about it," Peter said. "I try not to think about it very much, especially when I'm doing it. Here. Here's the pub. Order us a drink, please, and I'll get onto the phone."

When they drove into camp, Henry McKenzie had added a mirror and a picture frame to his gas mask, a horrid black rubber contrivance that looked like a demon's face.

"What are you going to do with all that junk? And those kiddies' fun masks you also invested in?"

"I don't really know yet. But I'll need some few other things. I'll tell you later, after I've had a look at this Wog. Has Darwin still got that tame hyena, that one who works on the films?"

"Who, Buster? I suppose so. He'd be over at Darwin's farm."

"Good. Send for him and get me some goats as well. I may have to make a little medicine."

They took Njogu to a spot in the forest near one of the sacred fig trees under which the old Kikuyu used to leave sacrifices to propitiate their God. A very old Kikuyu from a nearby shamba, a mundumugu of the ancient days, was a standoffish member of the group. He wore a gray monkey-fur cloak, and his ears were plugged with wooden disks. He carried a bag of magic. His name was Muchiri, and his face under ceremonial paint resembled a weathered persimmon. He sat on his heels, apart from the other men.

Henry McKenzie walked over to the grassy slope on which Njogu lay bound. He squatted beside Njogu and spoke very softly.

"You are not a man like these animals that rove the hills and eat brains and otherwise vilify themselves." Henry McKenzie spoke as one old-timer to a friend of equal mellowed standing. "You are a man as I remember men from my youth; a good man, and a man who desires the old days back again. The old days will not come again so long as men rob and burn and murder and turn this country into a ngoma for the hyenas."

Njogu said nothing. His eyes were bloodshot and indrawn, wary. He had no fingernails on one hand, and the fingers were purple-raw and hugely swollen.

"Here is a mundumugu of your faith and years, this man Muchiri. He is a man of God, a man of good faith, a man as your father was a man when first I came to this country. He has with him a sacred swearing stone, the githathi that all men awed, whose power is so strong that a man might not lie with his wife for seven seasons after swearing on it, and who must straightway castrate his male animals, lest thahu be passed through either woman or beast. This is the true oath: *'If I lie, this stone will kill me.'* This is not the filth by which men now copulate with living animals and even use the menses of prostitutes in an oath cere-mony. This is not a Mau Mau oath. This old man can cleanse you of your oath to Mau Mau, if you have taken one, and reaffirm you in your father's faith."

The man Njogu said nothing. He looked straight ahead. He had no interest in whatever it was he saw.

"If you die now as a result of your oath-givings in the Mau Mau, you will not live in the hereafter as a man. I have a powerful medicine, as powerful as the medicine that makes planes fly through the air, that brings voices from one side of the ocean to the other, that sends sounds crackling through the air and drives ships beneath the sea. If you die with the stain of Mau Mau on you, you will prowl through eternity as a *hyena*."

For the first time feeling shimmered over the thin tortured face of Njogu. He touched his dry lips with his tongue. He spoke.

"I do not believe you," he said.

Henry McKenzie appeared not to have heard him. "A hyena," he said dreamily. "Fancy, a hyena. Eater of filth and carrion. A broken-spined skulker and ripper-off of the udders of cows. An animal so vile that even his droppings near a hut bring thahu. An animal so vile he breeds upon himself; one year male, another year female. A stinking unclean servant of death, to whom Kikuyu throw the bodies of their dead kinsmen sometimes before they are completely dead, in order to avoid a curse, so that the curse may go from the dead into the body of the hyena. Into *your* body, Njogu. I *will* do this thing to you. And we will kill you to be a hyena. Will you be cleansed and then swear your purification on the sacred githathi stone? Or will you die and become a hyena?"

"I have nothing to be cleansed of," Njogu said. "I have not taken any bad oath. I will not take an oath."

"Very well," Henry McKenzie said. "You've given many. The guilt is the same. You are polluted. See here what I hold in my hand. It is only a mirror, a simple mirror one buys in the duccas for ten shillings. Look in the mirror. Now you see a man, is it not so? You see yourself, Njogu, as you have seen yourself each morning when you wash your face in a stream. Now then. First I shall make you dead by my magic, and I will revive you and show you yourself as a demon hot in hell. You will feel the licking flames and you will see yourself as an evil spirit. Then I will quench the flames and bring you back to this life again. Then I will ask you again to swear. If you do not swear, I will change you then into a hyena. After I have changed you into a hyena, then I will change you back into the demon. And finally I will make you into a man again. That is your last chance. If you do not consent to talk I will change you once again to a demon and finally to a hyena, and you will eat the foul flesh of your wives and children throughout eternity. Eternity is a long time, Njogu."

"I do not believe you," Njogu said. "I am not a fool. I am not a child. I am not a Mau Mau. And I will not take an oath."

"Very well. Behold, you will die now and become a demon in hell."

He nodded, and Peter stepped swiftly in behind Njogu and clapped the gas mask over his face, pressing in the little button which cut off all oxygen to the rubber mask, which clung to the contour of Njogu's face. He suffocated, taking a little more than a minute to lose consciousness. He moaned and fought inside the mask as the air within was consumed and his lungs began to burst. Peter knew that the claustrophobia itself was the worst of it. He had tried on the mask and had been able to endure only fifteen seconds before he ripped it from his face. Njogu made horrible noises inside the mask before he collapsed, his body jerking, his legs kicking. Henry McKenzie nodded again. Peter took the plug out of the mask. The doctor administered artificial respiration. Njogu began to breathe inside the mask. He sat up. Lathela and Waithaka brought torches of fat wood, impregnated with oil, which they held outside the range of Njogu's eyes, slightly burning his body. Then Peter placed the mirror in front of Njogu, and Njogu saw himself now as a demon, a long-snouted, black-faced, goggle-eyed demon against whose horrid visage danced the flicker of flames. Lathela and Waithaka held the torches closer to him, and there was a smell of singed flesh. Njogu screamed inside the mask, and then Henry McKenzie pressed in the plug again. The flames roared higher, and Njogu watched his demon's face move and shiver and dwindle in the mirror. He suffocated and passed out again. They withdrew the button from the mask once more, and again the doctor gave artificial respiration. Henry McKenzie beckoned, this time to the wild-animal trainer, George Darwin. Darwin grinned and walked forward with a full-grown hyena on a leash. This was Buster, the actor in many films and the pride of George Darwin's menagerie.

"Stand that awful beast there," Henry McKenzie said. "And when our man recovers, be sure that the hyena is standing close enough so that our man can smell his stinking breath. Then, Peter, reach over Njogu's shoulders with that empty picture frame, and hold it in front of him so the hyena's head and shoulders are enclosed in it. I want this Wog to think he is still looking into a mirror."

They whipped the mask off Njogu's head and placed the hyena. Buster stood solidly, grinning, tongue lolling, eyes greedy, his more-powerful-than-a-lion's teeth shining between jaws that could shear off a thighbone of a zebra or take off a man's head in one snap. He was no longer Buster, the ham, who used to accept bits of meat from Clark Gable and Gregory Peck. He was now Fisi, shuffling, stinking, crafty symbol of darkness and death. Njogu's eyes came open and he shook his head. His eyes cleared of the red mists and he looked and saw himself truly as Fisi, the hyena. Buster yawned, raised his chin, and attempted a running scale of calliope notes as George Darwin waved a piece of meat at him from behind Njogu's head. Fisi roared and lunged, and as he lunged Peter slipped the gas mask back over Njogu's face, pushed in the plug, and once again Njogu blacked out. When he was revived the flames danced again about him, and he saw himself in the mirror as a demon. His breath was extinguished again, and this time, when he came to, the gas mask was off his head and he saw himself as himself in the mirror. He was bleeding at the nose and mouth, but it was himself he saw in the mirror. The flames and the demon and the fire and the hyena had gone away.

"Will you believe me now?" Henry McKenzie asked. "Do you remember aught of your trip into the other world? Did you see yourself become a demon? Did you see yourself as a hyena? Did you feel flame and smell sulphur?"

Njogu moaned. Tears flowed down his cheeks, tears of weakness and old pain and tears of fear, a black man's basic fear that has not yet been dispelled by logic. The world lurched about him. When it steadied, he looked around and saw only the trees and the grass and the flowers, the sun in the sky and the sacred fig tree and the men who ringed him round, watching. He heard a bird call. A tree frog croaked. The demon was gone. The hyena was thinned into nothing.

"It is not true," he said. "I saw nothing. I saw no hyena. I did not become a demon. I know nothing. I will not swear."

"Very well. We will try it again. This time you will see more demons, and you will become the hyena again. This time you will be a hyena quite a long time. This is your last chance. While you are a hyena, you will consent to talk, or you will be a hyena forever."

He turned to Peter and spoke in English. "Ready now with those Guy Fawkes masks we brought along, that we got off the kids in Thomson's Falls."

This time when Njogu became a demon he saw his demon's face surrounded by horribly grimacing red and white and black faces of other demons, shimmering and dancing and bobbing next to his own black demon's face. He felt puffs of flame—and searing heat—because the men behind him were adding gunpowder to the torches now. Then Buster was led up and Njogu became a hyena again. Buster sat on his haunches like a big dog and smiled cheerfully at Njogu. Njogu fainted, without help from the gas mask. When he regained consciousness, Buster was gone.

Njogu's voice was very faint and husky, for his throat was thick with his own hemorrhaging.

"I will take the true oath now, Bwana," he said. "I believe it. Then I will tell you what you want to know."

"First we will purify you of your Mau Mau uncleanliness," Henry McKenzie said. "Old man. You, mundumugu. Come with your goat and get on with the work of purification. Then you will give the liar's oath. We go away now. Only Kikuyu will stand as witnesses."

The old man hobbled forward, leading a black he-goat. The white men went away. Waithaka and another Kikuyu askari stood as witnesses. The old man brought the goat close to where Njogu lay on the ground, took a sharp knife and split the goat's nose, sprinkling powdered lime on the cut. He then took the knife and dug a hole in the ground and covered it with the leaves of the mubogo tree. He filled the hole with water and sprinkled a powder in it, a different powder from each of three small flasks.

He took the goat by the forelegs and steered it around the leaf-lined pit so that it left a trail of blood on the ground. He chanted loudly, commanding the unclean thahu to leave Njogu's body.

He then took the goat's right forehoof and dipped it into the water in the hole. He held it to Njogu's mouth and commanded him to suck it. He sucked the hoof and spat to the right. Then he sucked the left hoof and spat to the left. The witch doctor chanted: "Vomit, vomit, vomit out the thahu."

He dragged the goat behind Njogu's back and nestled its bleeding nose beneath each of the man's armpits. Then he draped the goat on Njogu's back and cried: "Let the thahu be like a load on the back that is cast off as I cast off this goat."

He then threw the goat on the ground with its legs spraddled in the air and slit its belly. Opening the stomach with the point of his knife, he scooped out a palmful of the half-digested contents and flung the mess into the basin. With a small sharp stick he pinned the edges of the stomach together. Then he tucked the bulging stomach back into the goat's belly.

The mundumugu took two bushbuck horns from his medicine bag and dipped them into the dark liquid in the leaf-lined hole. He pushed the horns into Njogu's mouth, commanding him to spit. Each time Njogu spat, the mundumugu chanted, "Vomit out, vomit out, let the thahu be vomited out.

"If the thahu came from the arms, from the feet, through the navel, through the mouth, through the nostrils, through the anus, through the penis, let the thahu be vomited out. If it came through the roof, if it came from the milk of the breasts of a woman, let the thahu be vomited out. If it came from the hut, from the shamba, from the earth, or from the sky, let it be vomited out. If it came from the dung of a hyena, if it came from a curse, if it came from a snake, let it be vomited out. Let it go away and be dissolved in the mists. If it came from unclean oaths or evil association, let the thahu be vomited out."

Then the mundumugu strangled the goat until it was nearly dead, and skinned it while it was still slightly alive. Then he broke each of its legs. He opened it again, holding preciously a tiny bit of life, and cut strips from the stomach, cut off the testicles, cut out the eyes, and finally removed the heart. He made circles of stomach skin and slipped them over the reedbuck horns. He festooned a strip of gut over Njogu's shoulders like a wreath and tossed the goat's eyes into the basin, together with the testicles and heart. Once again he soaked the horns in the bitter mixture and commanded Njogu to spit seven times. Then he took the strips of intestine from Njogu's shoulders and buried them at the foot of a tree. Thus again the thahu had passed into the intestine of the goat. He buried the eyes separately under another bush. Then he prayed, his eyes cast upward toward Ngai in his home on Kerinyagga. He stirred three fresh measures of white chalk, black ash, and red powder, and smeared them onto Njogu's nose, between his toes, and on his neck and navel. Then they slightly roasted the flesh of the goat and ate it.

Njogu was now cleansed and ready for the truth oaths. The first oath against lying was the ordeal of the goat—another goat this time, a spotted he-goat. The mundumugu bound his legs and smeared ointments into the goat's ears, eyes, and nose. He handed a knobbed club to Njogu.

"You know the words," he said. "Repeat them."

Njogu struck the goat carefully, taking great pains to break one bone at a time.

"As this goat's bones snap, may my bones snap if I lie. As this goat's skull is crushed, may my skull be crushed if I lie. As this goat slowly dies, may I die as slowly if I lie. As this goat is broken to pieces, so may I be broken to pieces if I lie."

When the goat was quite dead, clubbed to a jellied pulp that swished inside its skin, the mundumugu picked the goat up and flung it into the bush for the hyenas to dispose of.

"That is all for today," he said. "In the morning we make the oath of the githathi. I am too tired to do more today."

Njogu was led back to the compound and shoved into a hut apart from the Mau Mau prisoners in the pen. The prisoners were uncleansed. He was tied up and placed on a new mat. The doctor came and smoothed salve on his burns and on his ruined hand. He was brought water and left alone. In the middle of the night he screamed, and the guards came to see what the trouble might be. There was a panga slash in the new mat beside his ear, which had lost one lobe.

"Some man came to kill me," he said. "He struck once and then took fright and ran away. It was a tall man, but I could not see who he was. He ran into the forest behind the Bwana's hut."

The night watch counted the prisoners and they were all in the pen. Waithaka, the gunbearer of Joseph Watson, checked off the askaris and reported all on hand and asleep except those who guarded the compound with rifles and shotguns.

"It must have been some shenzi sent from the forests to kill Njogu now that it is known he is going to speak," Waithaka said. "I think I had better sit in his hut with him this night."

"I have a better idea than that," Joseph Watson said. "Bring him into my house. *I* will sit up with him tonight. I want him alive in the morning."

So Njogu went to spend a night in front of the fire of Joseph Watson's hut, and as he lay in the dark on the worn rug before the fitful fire he thought many things, and liked nothing of what he thought. The next day he would be purified and oath-bound and he would talk. Then he would be dead. But to be dead one way was better than being dead another way and coming alive permanently as a hyena.

The next morning the old mundumugu took the captive Njogu to the sacred fig, where he had built a small arch of leaves. He had the black githathi stone with him, hidden under his monkey-hide robe. He crawled into one end of the arch of leaves, and Njogu crawled into the other. The old witch doctor handed some lengths of the mokengeria creeper to Njogu and commanded him to pass the creeper seven times through the seven holes in the sacred stone. Each time, Njogu swore:

"If I tell a lie, let the symbol of this oath kill me. If I falsely accuse anyone, let the symbol of truth kill me." The witnesses who stood around stuffed lengths of the creeper in their ears, so terrible was the power of the old oath, administered in the old way. When the ceremony was over, a goat was killed after first being castrated, and the old mundumugu took his stone, accepted some money from Henry McKenzie, and went away. Njogu was returned to the place of questioning.

". . . And *now*," Joseph Watson said, "*and now* we will hear some truths. Let us start at the beginning. . . ."

Njogu had much to say, his tongue finally loosened by the oath. The chief oath-administrator for Nyeri was the District Commissioner's confidential clerk, he said. It was he who had been issuing the ammunition permits. The oath-administrator for Thomson's Falls was the lorry driver of Fred Hall's safari group. He had given these people the oaths, as he had sworn the men on the mountain. The head oath-giver for all the Mau Mau, a purely honorary position, had been the well-traveled, well-educated Kikuyu of Kiambu, who was now on trial in Kapenguria. That was well known, of course, but he did not know the men directly under the man who was on trial in Kapenguria. He, Njogu, had given the oaths for most of the Aberdares District in the beginning. Now he had many assistants. He looked up and pointed. He pointed at Waithaka, Joseph Newton's gunbearer. "That one," he said. "I gave the oath to him, and he has since become an oath-giver. Let him deny it, but watch his face to see it as he lies."

Waithaka's lean black face turned sick and gray. He staggered and almost fell. Joseph Watson got up from his squatting position alongside Njogu.

"Is this true?" he asked Waithaka. "Is what this man says true?"

Waithaka stared, speechless.

"Did you try to kill this man in the hut last night?"

Waithaka's lips moved, but no words came.

"Where did you give the oath to Waithaka?"

"On your shamba, Bwana. In the clearing behind your sleeping hut, there where the spring flows. Whilst you traveled to Dar-es-Salaam last year. He may deny it if he wishes, but you see he does not deny. You see his silence."

Joseph Watson turned and looked at the faces of the other white men, of the black askaris. He gazed beyond them to the prison pen where other men sat behind wire.

"Waithaka," he said softly. "You are a fine gunbearer. You taught me the ways of the mountains and the forest. You have been my friend. Tell me that this man lies."

Waithaka looked at his feet.

"Waithaka. You are a gunbearer. Go to my house and fetch me the bundouki mkubwa, the big double rifle. I have bullets for it with me here. Fetch it in its case. I wish to see if you have kept it clean."

Waithaka turned and walked away as a man walks in his sleep. The men watched him enter the cabin and emerge with a battered brown calfskin case in which Joseph Watson kept a Rigby .450 No. 2 heavy double rifle. Waithaka knelt at Joseph Watson's feet and unstrapped the thick stiff leather straps, then clicked open the metal catch of the case. He took the gun out in sections, barrels first, the once-blue tubes now worn silver-brown by much handling, the forepiece snapped to the barrels. He unsnapped the forepiece, looked into the barrels, blew through them, and snapped the barrels onto the stock. Then he fitted the walnut forepiece to the underside of the barrels and clicked it into the stock. He rose and handed the gun butt-first to Joseph Watson. Joseph Watson broke the gun and peered through the barrels, snapping them back into locked position. He handed the gun again to his gunbearer, Waithaka. He took two large brass-cased bullets from the loops of his jacket and twiddled them in his fingers like large cigarettes. He jerked his head at Waithaka. "Come with me into the forest," he said. Waithaka reversed the gun, gripping it by the barrels, the stock riding behind him as he balanced the weight of the heavy gun by the barrels on his shoulder. Joseph Watson walked away in long, unhurried, mile-eating strides, his gunbearer just a bit ahead and to the right of him. They disappeared from sight in the woods. Perhaps five minutes later the waiting men heard the heavy boom of the .450 No. 2. Presently Joseph Watson came out of the bush, carrying the gun himself. He still swung one big burnished bullet from his fingers.

"Let us get on with the questioning," he said, and squatted down again.

All the men had some particular question to ask. Who was responsible for the Gray killing at Limuru? Who had done the job at Thika? How long had the training been going on? How many Mau Mau did Njogu believe were seriously in the movement? How many men were there on the hills, and by whom were they led? Peter McKenzie had a special question.

"Who led the attack on the shamba of Jeff Newton? Who was responsible for the wounding of my sister and the deaths of her husband and children? Who?"

Njogu dipped his head.

"You know him. He is the husband of my daughter. He is the son of your father's friend. He the friend of your childhood. His name is Kimani—Kimani wa Karanja—and he is one of the leaders of the men on the mountain."

There was a mad shriek and a flash of shiny movement. Lathela leaped upon the old man, had taken his throat in his fingers, and was biting at his face. Peter hit the 'Ndrobo on the skull with a pistol butt and pulled him off the old man. He dragged Lathela to one side.

"Somebody sit on him when he comes round," he said. "He was very fond of his Bwana and his Memsaab and the kids. Better still, snap some handcuffs on him, one of you policemen. Else he'll tear this old boy to bits."

"Could you lead me to where Kimani hides, old man?" he said gently. "Could you take me to Kimani?"

"If he is still in the cave where he has lived with my daughter I might be able to take you. But the men on the mountain are scattered since your raids. Also, my feet will not be fit for walking for a long time. I do not think I will live to see that cave again. I am very weary and I think that I shall die soon."

The old man drooped his head. Njogu was past questioning until he had recovered some of his exhausted strength. Peter lifted the man's face by gripping his hair and pulling the chin upward. The old man's eyes were closed.

"I think we've had this chap," the doctor said. "I think yesterday and today and all the days before have been a little too much for him. Let's check the heart." He put his stethoscope to Njogu's chest. "Not very much doing there. Let's stretch him out and maybe he'll come round. But I doubt it."

The doctor was right. Njogu died quietly in the night. But at least he would not become a hyena. He had been purified, he had taken the githathi oath, and he had returned to the first principles of his fathers.

14

Njogu's revelations had been considerable. A massive roundup of the oath-givers came about swiftly. A new ruling making oath-giving punishable by hanging was made law, and the gallows creaked. Police and troops swept down on shambas, and many planters suddenly were indignantly without the services of cook or herdsman or Number One. The whites largely refused to believe that any of their pet Africans might be guilty of complicity in Mau Mau. They swore tremendously and complained to the provincial commissioners and to the members of the Assembly. But the cooks and herdsmen and headboys were taken away and did not return. Whole lines of lorries were stopped and searched at the roadblocks. One moving picture caravan suddenly found itself stagnated, for most of its truck drivers had been identified as prominent Mau Mau. There were also many other disappearances from the shambas. Men who had not been picked out by police suddenly disappeared, sometimes with their women, often with what they could steal. They went up into the hills, and the bands grew large again, approaching the size of armies now, one hundred to three hundred grouped closely, and always on the move. The striking police forces would find ashes warm from fires; huts still containing fragments of food. Somehow the mountain men, the forest men, always seemed to have advance information when a strike was planned. They slipped quietly off into the bamboo and the thorn. The Mau Mau communications system was improving. At the same time a wave of revulsion soaked the British newspapers and heavy pressure was placed on the Home Office to make an end of the brutality. New generals were appointed. The command was dissolved. The settlers were reproved. The starched English military took over.

Then the terror settled comfortably into almost a homely routine. Peter and his father returned for a time to the farm. There was much work to do if any farms were to be operated even partially. A tremendous drought was dehydrating the land. They had missed one complete seasonal rainfall, and the earth blew away loosely in pink gusts. The bore holes were dry up top and muddy at the bottom, and the cattle shambled thin, loose-hided and sick. Men watched the skies for the plumped-up rain clouds more carefully than they watched their house servants in the daytime; as carefully as they locked their doors and latched their windows at night. Rich white bwanas hand-worked in the fields again, and on the smaller shambas their womenfolk worked with them, driving tractors or dipping cattle, as the shortage of native labor increased. Thousands upon thousands of Kikuyu were swallowed into the reserves; more and more were slipping off into Uganda and to Tanganyika. The Kikuyu labor force eroded like the land. The help was replaced to some extent with Kipsigis and Merus and Embus, but they too received pointed attention from the Mau Mau infiltrators. What the settlers had dreaded most began to happen. The poison seeped and spread to the neighboring tribes—first from fear and physical intimidation, then partially from admiration for audacity, finally from the African susceptibility to secret societies. The Wakamba, who had always scorned the Kikuyu, took votes on whether to embrace Mau Mau. The vote-taking was equal to the ultimate oath. Only the Masai and his northern cousins could be certified as absolutely aloof. They roved their own parched lands and continued to live with their herds, proudly apart, as they had always lived proudly apart.

Everyday living for both the blacks and the whites had become vastly complicated. There were designated trouble areas where a man was shot swiftly by the police patrols just for the accident of being there. Mostly the shot men were black, but several Europeans had near squeaks with itchy-fingered youngsters who fired at the rustle of a bush. Limitations on all movement increased. The roadblocks were huge upstanding spikes or bouldered barriers, and every car was stopped and searched. It was forbidden, even to the safari firms, to transport a Kikuyu outside Kenya. For a Kikuyu to be found in possession of a gun by day or night, or even a panga at nighttime, resolved into a hanging or extinction on the spot. A man who ran in panic or misunderstanding from the command "Halt!" was swiftly shot. Or at least shot at. Merely to be black and at large was dangerous.

The many innocent suffered heavily from both sides. Loyalty to a white man called down a sweep of Mau Mau on the black man's shamba, killing and burning, killing first by scores and finally by tens of scores. The rapid growth of the Athegani, the armed resistance groups, and the presence now of full-scale task groups of British military of necessity shaped the straggling Mau Mau murderers into excellent disciplined armies. The names of Mau Mau "generals" began to appear in the public consciousness. Dedan Kemathi was the most famous. Other leaders took their names from Russian propaganda and past military experience. There was a General China, a General Burma, a General Korea, a General Suez, a Field Marshal Kaleba. One portion of the Mau Mau army infiltrated to Tanganyika and set up extensive guerrilla operations from Kilimanjaro to Arusha. For the first time Tanganyika felt the edge of the Mau Mau panga.

But the killing of the innocent, by both sides, and the slaughter of native police and the massacre of the Athegani turned a brisk harrow in the loam of resentment. The native shanty towns of Nairobi had been dynamited and burned, leaving thousands without homes. In one year 150,000 Kikuyu were arrested. Sixty-five thousand were released, mostly to unemployment. The others were tried, sentenced, and either jailed in the majority or in the minority hanged. Jomo Kenyatta and four associates went to jail for seven years for the sin of operating an illegal social organization. The euphemistic shortness of the sentence did not bother many Kenyans, for Jomo could always be tried again as the prime oath-administrator and hanged when he finished his sentence, if he lived to finish it. In any case, control of Mau Mau had fled Kenyatta's hands when the first violence slipped its leash. Mau Mau's political direction shifted to purely criminal hands, where first only its implementation had been handed to the thugs. The face of Kenya wore an expression of sullen fear, for Kikuyu men and women were being—and many more would be—relocated from Nairobi and other towns and shipped up North to detention camps; some were being transported to islands in the Indian Ocean; some were being penned in hastily thrown up detention camps for screening. City business lost or was forced to discharge, for expediency, most of its clever trained Kikuyu help.

White people in the streets and bars spoke knowingly of military operations with H.Q.-beloved names like "Epsom," "Carnation," "Ratcatcher," "Primrose," "Bluebell," and "Wedgwood." The Mau Mau "generals" and "field marshals" began to leave jeering notes of their intentions and achievements stuck in cleft sticks or pinned to the bodies of horribly mutilated men. The simple little brush fire had flamed into a war that now cost three million dollars a month to operate, and the incomes from farms and businesses had been slashed by billions as depleted labor forces and compulsory military service for the farmers made large-scale land operations impossible. Two hundred thousand Kikuyu had been employed by four hundred farmers. Now the farmers, white and black, employers and employed, were in the hills, chasing each other with guns and knives.

As resentment against the Mau Mau increased inside the Kikuyu tribe, the generals and the field marshals conferred and recognized the necessity of more and stronger oaths. The point was ever more, now, to weld the Mau Mau more firmly by increasingly horrifying and loathsome oath-takings. All semblance of the original tribal symbolism had disappeared, and now the oath-takings were simply orgies of obscenity, black masses employing the most basic revulsions. The oaths were numbered, each competing for horror and obscenity. Military Intelligence copies of documents taken from a raided terrorist camp in the Aberdares read precisely as follows:

"General Nderitu says that when a gang has had an action and when Security Forces are not close on their heels they will take away a dead body. Then at their leisure, in the Forest, they cut open the head and remove the brains, the brains are then dried in the sun and ground up and bottled. The heart is cut out and dried. Blood is drained from the body and dried in the sun and then ground up and mixed with brains. Steaks are cut from the dead man's buttocks and dried in the sun then folded up for easy carrying.

"In each Batuni or Company there is a particular man who acts as the butcher. This human flesh is usually taken from an enemy, but if one of the gang has done something to merit death he is killed in the Camp and cut up for Oathing. In each Batuni there is an executioner who performs the killings when disciplinary measures are necessary. A spear, simi, or strangling rope is used.

"Dedan Kemathi has given orders that all Oath Administrators are to think up the vilest methods of giving the Batuni Oaths. When an Administrator has thought out and performed a particularly revolting method, he is to pass his methods on to his brother administrators. In this way the varied oaths are produced. General Nderitu says that there are seven oaths only, but having reached number seven you return again to number one but it will be administered in a different way."

15

Kimani accepted all the major oaths and invented a few of his own. Nothing bothered him very much any more. He was called "General" now. He lived on in his cave with another woman, for his wife Karugi had gone down the path one day to visit another shamba and had never returned. Shortly the white men had attacked that shamba and killed everybody in it, but when Kimani went later to dig up the carcasses for identification, he was unable to find Karugi's body. Maybe one of the white men had run across her on the trail, or perhaps some wild animal had taken her. It was easy to get another woman, and he needed one to look after his young son Karanja, who was a crawler now. This woman was named Kabui, as his childhood playmate had been called, as had also been called the prostitute in Nairobi. This present Kabui sometimes served as a ceremonial prostitute in the oath-givings, but she was not a professional whore and she tended his child well and looked after his other needs. But she was not like Karugi. There would never be another wife like Karugi, so gentle and jolly and willing and thoughtful.

Life was generally dreary, as always, on the mountain. It was livened considerably when they raided, but the gangs were forced to shift constantly. Kimani had perfected one fighting technique which gave them some basic security. This was an organized delegation of men from distant areas to do the personal work of isolated killing. For instance, Kimani would organize a raid for the Mwega area. But he would not send his own men. Other men would be called up from Nairobi, strangers to the co-plotters on the farm, and would suddenly come in the night to do the actual shooting and burning. Then they would return speedily to another area, and so there was less possibility of involving Kimani's own supply lines in the foothills. When the police came, no matter how urgently they questioned the squatters on the farm of the killing, there was nothing that the squatters could tell them about the killers.

There was not so much panga work any more. There were plenty of guns, coming in from up North and cleverly circulated by a few Indians. The men knew how to use the guns now, and in a big operation, such as an attack on a jail or a brush with the Athegani, you had to use guns. There wasn't the time or the compressed space for close work with knife or club. Kimani never went along on anything but big operations any more. He sat in his cave and drank beer and played with his son, when he was not at a council meeting or shifting his troops.

He wondered occasionally about Peter McKenzie. He knew Peter was in the mountains, and once he thought he saw him when he was skulking away from a raiding party, but he couldn't be certain. But he had heard of the techniques of the Campi a Mbingu, and he thought he smelled much of Peter in what he had heard. Especially about the business that had canceled the visits of old Njogu up the hill to sit and gossip and play with his grandson. Kimani missed Njogu more than anything or anybody. He had become very fond of the old man, whose daughter Karugi had given him a son and who had gone down the trail one day and had never come back. I don't know who's winning this thing, Kimani thought in his cave. Kemathi and Kaleba and China say *we* are, and soon all the British will leave Kenya and we can all come down off this accursed mountain. I don't know. It seems to me that if they were going to leave they would have left. But they come every day with more and more soldiers and planes, and now those things that leave a silver streak in the skies behind them. Maybe nobody will win and we will just go on this way until we are all killed. Kimani called Kabui and demanded more beer. Sometimes it was very depressing in a cave. *I miss old Njogu,* he thought. *They must have been very clever to get that one to talk.*

16

There was a loud unnatural gaiety among the whites when they went occasionally to the towns now, as their nerves, strung taut as banjo wires, twanged and broke in sudden release from the twenty-hour tension of the isolated farms and the houses on the outskirts of towns. Not that it was as physically safe, possibly, in the towns as on the shambas, but there was more company to be frightened in. Nairobi seethed with soldiery, noisy young men who held cocktails as casually as they carried their shoulder-slung machine weapons and who seemed to regard the entire campaign with detached amusement. Bloody silly do, they thought, to bring a man all the way from Korea to chase some barefoot Wogs up a mountain and down a mountain. They thought it shocking that Major Sir Brian Mannering should have been done in by some tattered savage. *Lèse-majesté,* old boy, a gentleman deserves a better fate than that. With the Japs in the last one it was just a bit different; even the sneaking round in jungles and hauling them out of holes was different. This Mau Mau job was a bit for an exterminator, not a soldier. They should've left it to the bloody old settler in the first place. But I must say the beer's better here than at home. Pity there's not more women, though. These popsies aren't bad, but there's not enough of them to go round. That smashing redhead, for instance, the other day in the Norfolk. Married to some horny-handed settler, and he keeps her stuck off on a farm somewhere when *that* one, now, would be *something.* No milkmaid, she; more Mayfair than farmeress. What's the old joke from the last war? You remember, Monsarrat wrote it in that navy book of his. Oh yes. "She suffers from marital thrombosis. Her husband's a clot." Kind of clot who'd shoot you. "Clot" was a word you heard frequently.

But it was very gay, as wars tend always to be very gay, and the cogs of control were completely slipped in Nairobi, where the ratchets had never been very deeply grooved anyhow. The tempo of the drinking increased daily, weekly, monthly. The romances flourished wildly, like weeds in the wet. Men would go up into the Aberdares on police work —because every man was called now for some sort of commando or special police patrol, even if it was only tracking for the soldiers or surveying the danger areas at night—and when the man came down the hill he would notice that some blond-mustached young subaltern in the Buffs or some captain of Inniskilling had a more than casual way about the house—a too certain knowledge of where the grog was stored, a too *easy* approach to the bathroom or the kitchen. You kept meeting a great many strangers in your own home and in the homes of your old friends, and when you took your wife or your girl into the Norfolk or the Stanley for a quick one, it seemed as if you were always having to bob up to be introduced to some Pommie popinjay with a swagger stick under his arm and a pipe stuck out of his garter tab on the stocking tops. There was a party somewhere every night, and the parties started with elevenses in the morning and never quit until it was time for tomorrow's elevenses to cure the shakes. There seemed to be more fist fights and louder music and a great many occasions of wives suddenly shrugging away from you

in bed and speaking too rapidly about a trip back to England or to Capetown, they hadn't seen Mum in ages, and anyhow, it wouldn't matter
because you were always away on some top-secret boy scouting in the
bush. Of *course* one knows a lot of people. One can't just always sit home
crouched over a shotgun, waiting for somebody to walk in and chop your
head off.

Yes, Nairobi was quite a sight to see these days. You could spot
the settlers, especially the farm boys, by the way they wore their liquor
and their side arms. There was nothing delicate or sophisticated about
the way they drank or packed a gun. They went for the swill, and when
they finished the swill they fought and passed out or just passed out.
And they wore their side arms not so much as weapons but as a shooting
license. The young buckos were beginning to enjoy themselves hugely.
A Sten gun gave a bloke more dignity than being scratch at golf or a five-
goal man at polo. They talked loud and large in the towns when they
came back out of the hills. With many, Mau Mau had become a sport,
an easy exit from the unending labor of crops and cattle.

It was possibly the women who most markedly showed the strain
—not so very much the leathery old girls or the very, very young ones,
who dashed giggling about with the pick and choice of the soldiers—but
the young matrons and the middle-agers. Some of the women in their
middle thirties had been married fifteen years and had half raised families
without ever really getting to know their husbands very well. Some husbands had been posted away for six or seven years in the last war or had
been taken prisoner early. Some of these same men had been recalled
when the fighting started in Korea. And now under the Mau Mau they
might as well be off in bloody Burma, for at least the Wogs here used
to be tractable during that war and you had service in the house and a
bit o' fun with the neighbors from time to time. Now all the home folks
were clots. All they talked was Mau Mau, Mau Mau, until you felt
you'd scream.

Now it was always strain, tensed nerves, and untethered tempers. If
you had kiddies you fretted double for each child. The women checked
their calendars eagerly. The tension put everything off, and a pregnancy
was regarded more as tragedy than not. God knows there was enough to
do that was unpleasant without having to throw up while you did it.
But the nerves bred a constant gnawing discontent, and you lost weight
and looked very chic, especially in the cities, and the discontent turned
the more attractive husbandless women eagerly to experiments they might

not have considered in another time. The hopping-into-bed was more frenetic even than in the old days when every third man was a disgraced younger son of a lord and the parties ran on for weeks. Somehow it became distasteful to be deeply in love with a man whose hands came to you bloody during his infrequent returns to the house or to the farm. It was easier to laugh and be gay and dance a lot and sit up very late at the clubs and occasionally totter into bed with some comparative stranger, who had no meaning for you, who would be gone this year or next, and whom you remembered only dimly even next morning, unless he happened still to be there in the bed. It was not a new experience for war; what made it ridiculous was this was no war, only hoodlumism magnified all out of proportion. Yet it was damned trying to come home in the afternoon from shopping and find that your nursemaid had been hauled in by the police as a security risk, or the kitchen boy had been taken away, leaving the dishes dirty in the sink. So apt as not you just let the dishes sit there and went and had a gin and then rang up some young guardsman to come and help you baby-sit.

But Nairobi and Nyeri and Nanyuki and Nakuru were more fun than the lonely farms. There was never any single moment of accepted safety or mental ease on a farm any more. The odds were a thousand to one, maybe better, that if you were careful nothing would ever happen to you. But the necessity of being extra-careful while you went about the simplest chores of living and labor was what dropped that stone of weight off you; was what made you sharp with the kids and impatient with the old people and frigid to your husband when he did get home. One needs peace for love, peace and relaxation and dalliance. In Kenya on the farms there was no peace and no relaxation and no dalliance. If love meant rising in the night and unlocking and locking doors in order not to run the risk of making a baby, then many women whose bodies had grown accustomed to their husbands took a simpler, more basic step toward the avoidance of baby-making. They slept with their husbands, but they rarely did anything more than *sleep* with their husbands. Which was generally just as well, quite all right, with the husbands. It was difficult to prowl forests by night and kill by day and then come home to pretty pillow-talk and a slap and a tickle. A bottle of grog and a little solid sleep in a clean bed, for a change, were preferable to a lot of hanky-panky. It was only when a bloke got into town, once in a donkey's years these days, it seemed, that suddenly little Prue Something or little Joan So-and-So looked alarmin' fine, and if there were enough grogs in the evening a man might wind up making a damned fool of himself and wondering next day what had led him to it and why, since he'd much better bed fare at home. Kenya nerves, they said. Always Kenya nerves. Whether they blamed it on the altitude or slackened morals, it was Kenya nerves. Well, now they had altitude, the visiting troop, *and* the Mau Mau to make Kenya nerves.

17

Peter and Holly bickered almost constantly when Peter was home. Peter was not home much. When the commando finished he of course was taken up in special police work and was gone again for two weeks, three weeks at a time. They sent him up North, because he knew the North, to see what was going on with the gunrunning. He went as special scout and tracker on various military and police raids in the Aberdares. They sent him to Tanganyika to see what the Mau Mau diversions of troop amounted to. Peter became very vague about how much time he spent anywhere. He always seemed to have come home via some bar or other in Nanyuki if he were driving down from the North, or Nairobi if he were coming in from Arusha, or just any pub at all if he had been combing the mountains. There were plenty of pubs in Nanyuki and Naivasha and Nyeri and Nakuru and Kusumu and Fort Hall.

It was never that Peter was anything but silly and sometimes sad when he drank. It was actually better for everybody if he was a little drunk. Because when he was coldly sober he was nervous and wary and uncomfortable in the presence of anybody, whether it was Holly or his father. He had a maddening way of disappearing. He would be there one moment and when you looked again he would be gone on some fancied errand that never quite got explained. Odd, too, that he displayed very little interest in either young Jeff or in his pregnant sister. Maybe not so odd about Elisabeth. She was coming on for seven months gone and was not very appetizing to look at, even if she had owned an unscarred face and two arms and two legs of the same length.

Holly did not like Peter to be drunk when he touched her, and it seemed that Peter never touched her except when he was drunk. The old man, Henry McKenzie, stared at his son from time to time and shook his head and said nothing at all. He said very little to anybody, in any case.

Peter, drunk, took several shapes. Sometimes his eyes went frighteningly wild and he would beat his closed fists on a wall or on the floor or on his knees. Sometimes he would sit and stare and open and close his hands, stretching his shaking fingers wide apart and watching them curiously. At other times he would insist on standing, his eyes blurred and unfocused, body weaving and speech nearly incoherent. Sometimes he would be teetering on the edge of unconsciousness but would draw on some inner reserve, literally pack himself together, and then think up something to do that involved immediate motion. He had two auto accidents in this sort of state; once he took a curve on the wrong side of the road and smacked the Land Rover into a tree, breaking Lathela's collarbone and raising a large lump on his own skull. Another time he ran the Jag off the road and was found by the K.P.R. next morning, soundly and blissfully asleep, with the Jaguar nearly undamaged by collision with a field of pineapple. But mostly it seemed he hated to sleep. He would stay up, inventing any excuse not to go to bed. It was as if he were afraid to relax, to drop his guard, to let sleep steal away his power to resist. Holly remembered a short story she had read once, a story by Rudyard Kipling, in which a man would punish himself with spurs to prevent himself from sleeping, because something horrible stole into his soul when he slept. Peter, she felt, was using grog as a spur. He was roweling himself with gin.

Certainly his appearance had changed. He would come back from a Mau Mau safari underweight and haggard, but in a few days his face would puff and his eyes would pouch and he developed a flabby overhang of fat on his belt line. His dark face never seemed to tan any more. The brilliant blue eyes were muddy and evasive. His speech was either very loud or almost incomprehensibly soft and blurred. He sweated constantly when he slept, winding himself in the wet sheets, thrashing at the pillows, and when they attempted anything at all he was very nearly always impotent before they finished, mumbling an apology and going off to snore and curse in his sleep.

Holly hated her life. She hated the iron bars newly set in all the windows. She hated the daily presence of Elisabeth, with her scarred face and untactful bulging belly, and her crippled leg and her amputated arm. She hated Father McKenzie, who never really said anything to anyone, but who drifted about looking mistily at yesterday with his washed-blue eyes and an unshakable air of resignation. She hated young Jeff, who never spoke very much, either, and who wore his pistol casually, as he wore his blue jeans, who had shot up to be a weedy six-footer and was starting spots on his face. Little Jeff practiced with the pistol daily. The front porch was stacked high with targets, the bullets mostly centered in the black. Holly had to speak sharply to him on several occasions about leaving the targets littered there.

Old Aly was becoming a total loss as a cook. There was never much game in the house any more because nobody had the time to go and shoot it, and Aly was a cook, primarily, of game. Also, he had prided himself in the evening meal, and the evening meal was no longer possible, owing to the curfew and the herding off of all blacks at 6 P.M. Aly's rheumatism pained him. Aly missed the little kingdom which had been his as a safari cook. Aly finally was becoming another crippled guest-in-the-house. And Juma, damn his slanting Swahili eyes, was not much better. Juma was a coward. Juma was a cultured, reading-and-writing Swahili from the coast. Juma did not like Kikuyu, nor did he like the low-caste Negroes with whom he was penned nightly in the protection stockades. Juma had Arab blood and was a Mohammedan priest; black heathens offended him. Also, Juma missed the brightness and gaiety of the old life, when he personally ran the household of the Bwana Mkubwa, wearing his red or gold or green vest over the sparkling white kanzu, with a gold-embroidered red fez on his head and the guests making jokes with him. There was much gray in Juma's steel-wooled hair now, and he hated this picnic living. There hadn't been a proper party or a decent meal served at Bushbuck since he couldn't remember when. Everybody just went around looking sour-faced and speaking sharply to everybody else, especially to him. There was no pleasure in serving food with a flourish if nobody payed attention to the flourishes. And the Bwana Peter was always drunk when he was home and never ate anything. Juma sulked. Aly burned the toast and let the soup get cold.

It seemed to Holly McKenzie that she had inherited all the troubles of Kenya. The kitchen was a mess. The food was awful. The house was mussed and dusty unless she found time to boot Juma in the tail and make him clean it properly, which, she knew, was beneath his dignity, but it was beneath her dignity as well to have to kick his behind to make him conscious of duty before dignity. The sheets never got washed properly any more and the ash trays always needed emptying and you ran out of cigarettes at odd moments. She had to take the car and do the shopping, and old Patel never seemed to have whatever it was you went after that day. It was always tomorrow, Memsaab, and how is everything with Master Peter? She was tempted on several occasions to give him a very short, very rude answer.

Of course she knew that what was wrong with Master Peter was not Master Peter's fault, nor was it her fault, but only the fault of something that had happened and wrecked everything for everybody. She knew vaguely what Peter did when he went away and why he drank as constantly and as morbidly as he drank; she knew all this. She was sorry that Jeff Newton had had his head cut off on her, Holly Keith's, honeymoon, and that they hadn't got to America; and that little Jeff was an old man at eleven, with his gun; and that Elisabeth had got herself impregnated by her husband just before she had no husband, and that Elisabeth was a fright to look at every day; and that Father McKenzie was beginning to dribble more food down his front and that his mustache was always untidy; that her husband was drunk and ineffectual in bed and that Aly had rheumatism and Juma was unhappy and the food was awful and the house was always mussed. She also knew why it was they locked doors and took shotguns to bed and jumped at a floor squeak. She understood it all. She forgave it all. But she hated it. She hated it, goddammit, she hated it and hated them and hated all of it, because she was only twenty-three and she was having to deal with it and suffer through it and be unhappy with it. She was only twenty-three and her honeymoon had lasted two nights and now her husband came home to grind his teeth and sweat and stumble and stagger and lose erections and forget he'd made a bloody botch of bed. She had to live with it but she didn't have to like it and she hoped Aly's rheumatism killed him or that a Mau Mau got him when he went to the chicken coop, if he served another meal like that lunch yesterday. She was damned well fed up with pioneering at this point, Holly Keith—who did not now think of herself as Holly McKenzie—said. She needed a change and by God she'd have one.

18

They had suffered one more attack by the Mau Mau on Bushbuck Farm. A band of thirty-odd men came down the mountain and overran the native shambas. They came in force at ten in the morning, after the Kikuyu workers had been herded from the stockade and were going about their various businesses in the fields. Peter was away on a commando. Young Jeff, Henry McKenzie, Lisa McKenzie, and Holly McKenzie were all in the house having coffee when the screams began in the squatters' compound and the sound of gunfire cut the bright morning air.

"Doors!" Holly shouted, spilling her coffee. "Jeff! Get the guns! Father McKenzie! Windows! Come with me, Lisa! I'm locking you in your room! Juma, Juma! Close up the kitchen! Get busy on the windows, jump!"

Holly dragged Elisabeth from the living room to her bedroom, pushed her onto the bed, and locked the door from the outside. She threw the key into a big earthen jar which stood in the hall and which held a towering fleshy-green plant of elephant's-ear. She raced back to the living room and saw Henry McKenzie sliding the latch bolts, slamming down windows. She heard other slammings and clickings coming from the kitchen. Little Jeff was sitting on a sofa, surrounded by guns. He was methodically sliding back the bolts of rifles, squinting at breeches, checking the loads of shotguns. He handed Holly a big ten-bore. "Buckshot," he said. "Here's another dozen shells." She took the fat yellow shells and dropped them in the front pockets of her frilly apron.

"Grandpa," Jeff said, "here are the .500s. You've got your own bullets. Watch the hind trigger on the No. 1 gun. It's got something gone wrong with the sear again. I've got the .470s." He got up from the sofa and placed boxes of ammunition on the coffee table—extra .500 packets to one side of a silver bowl of roses, extra .470 packets to the other side, next to the polished rhino-hoof cigarette box. Then he took a carton of shotgun shells over to a window seat. "Here are the rest of the shotgun shells, Holly," he said, and then drew his pistol, spun the chambers, and shoved the pistol back in its holster.

"Everybody on the floor," Henry McKenzie said. "I'll go and check the kitchen and lock the boys in the pantry." He returned in a moment. "All serene in the kitchen," he said, and got stiffly down onto the floor. They lay on their bellies and listened to the screams and to the gunshots. Then there was a new scream, this time a scream of horses. The stables had been fired, obviously. They lay on the floor for half an hour, and then guns roared closer and bullets began to thud against the stones of the house. Young Jeff raised his eyes up to window level. He took the barrel of his gun and knocked out a pane, resting the big double rifle against one of the iron bars that made a grill outside the glass. Bullets from outside spatted against the glass, sending a fine-glass shower over young Jeff's head. He shook the slivers from his hair and raised his eyes cautiously again, squinting down the rifle. A flash of a running body appeared, slipping from a thick hedge to the bole of the towering cedar that commanded the lawn. The runner disappeared behind the cedar and then poked a gun around its edge. Half of a head appeared over the barrel of the gun, a head bisected vertically by the tree trunk and horizontally by the gun barrels. The half-face fired, drilling a hole high up in the still unbroken glass and crashing into the sideboard in the room, breaking a decanter. Jeff shot, the reports of the two guns almost merging. The man behind the tree pitched out from it and flopped on the soft green grass. Jeff fired again at the thrashing body. The bullet hit with a soft whunk and the man jerked and lay still.

"Got that bugger," Jeff said, reloading. Henry McKenzie was shooting at something now, two thundering explosions from the huge-barreled .500, blasts that shook the fixtures of the locked room and filled the air with acrid yellow-smelling cordite fumes. No other men appeared in front of the house. Some straggling shots were fired from behind the house, and they heard china crashing in the kitchen. There was a final popping from the native compound, and then there was a loud silence, punctuated by the screaming of the horses. Jeff and Holly and the old man remained on the floor for another ten minutes, and then they heard the sound of motorcars.

Three jeeps filled with police reservists drove into the yard. The police sergeant waved his askaris toward the Africans' compound, where the horses screamed, and then stretched his gun above his head with both hands and shouted.

"You can open up now!" he yelled. "They've all pushed off. Any damage inside?"

"Not much," Henry McKenzie shouted back. "Holly, go and see about Elisabeth. Jeff, go and let the Wogs out of the pantry. We'll leave the house locked whilst I go down and see about the damage."

"Wait for me, Grandpa," young Jeff called as he raced toward the kitchen. "I want to see where I hit that chap behind the tree. Wait for me!"

Holly rapped on Elisabeth's door. "It's only me. Are you all right? It's all over. Let me in."

"I can't. You took the key and locked me in."

"Of course. I forgot. Are you quite all right?"

"Couldn't be finer. The baby hasn't stirred."

Holly ran off and dug the key out of the potted plant. She fumbled the key into the lock with shaky fingers and saw Elisabeth sitting calmly, annoyingly serene, in an easy chair, with a pistol still held in her left hand, its barrel resting, pointing downward, on her swollen belly.

"They've gone? What flushed them?"

"Yes, they've gone, the police have come. Someone heard the shooting and alerted the K.P.R. Do you want to come out or stop on here?"

"I'll come out. I could use some of that coffee we started. I'm a bit nervy. It's not nice being locked in and not knowing what's happening outside. Is little Jeff all right?" Holly thought at that moment that it would be easy to strike Elisabeth, baby or no baby.

"Of course. He's outside now with your father and the police. Most of the action seemed concentrated on the Africans. And the stables."

"Oh, the poor horses. I could hear them. Horrible. But I heard you shooting. Did you kill any of them?"

"Young Jeff collected one, I believe. Your father fired a couple of times, but I don't think he hit anything. Come on. We'll go and have Juma warm up the coffee."

Young Jeff was out to the tree and looked at his first dead man. He was a very big man. Jeff's shot had glanced off the outer edge of his cheek. It had smashed the bone but sheered off to the ear and the man had lurched outward from the bullet's shock. The second bullet had taken him low on the neck in the back of the head. "The gun's throwing left," little Jeff said to his grandfather as they looked down at the dead Kikuyu. "I swear I held solid on his nose. We'll have to sight her in." He touched the body with his foot. "Ugly bugger, isn't he?" Then he turned and ran swiftly to a clump of willows. Henry McKenzie could hear his grandson being violently ill. Then he heard weeping and more retching, and he motioned to the policemen to come away.

The stables, dry from the long drought, had flared like petrol. The horses were a dead loss, poor brutes. So were half a dozen of the squatter women and children. Most of the squatter huts had been fired. There had been no men in the compound when the killers came. The men had been off working in the fields. The raiders had shot or slashed four women and two children and set the stables alight and had evidently lost their courage about the big house when the guns began to return fire. It was a pity about the horses. It was a pity about the people. Now the squatter men would not be wanting to work in the fields if their wives and children were getting killed in broad daylight. It was the first daylight raid the Mau Mau had made in that area.

Somehow the fact that the raid had come by day unsnaffled the checkrein Holly had been wearing on her nerves. Now the days would be as bad as the nights. Now you couldn't drink a cup of coffee on the porch at noon without expecting screams and gunshots. The fact that the K.P.R. had been close and one of the Africans had run off to fetch it when the first shots sounded was just blind luck. Next time would be different. Even if there wasn't a next time Holly would be waiting every day for the next time. In any case it was nearly time for Elisabeth to go to town to the hospital. The baby was in fine shape, the doctor said, but he couldn't say when it would come. It might come early; it might come late. It was a big baby. But it would be a good idea to move Elisabeth closer to immediate medical attention. It would be just too terribly tragic if the youngster whimsically decided to arrive in the middle of another raid. There were complications enough without that.

"We're going to Nairobi," Holly told Peter when he came in two days after the raid, filthy, bone-weary, and trembling-sober. "I can't stand any more of this. Your sister's apt to have her child any minute. I just can't bear any more of it, and I specially can't bear the idea of having to midwife a child in the middle of a Mau Mau raid. Or of having your sister have the thing when she's shut up in a room and I'm lying on the floor with a gun. Or any more having to lock up the cook in the pantry . . . Or gun shells in my apron pocket—or just being here alone." Holly sobbed.

"You're not exactly alone," Peter said. "There's Pa and the boy and Lisa and the Wogs. . . ."

"I'd rather be alone than be here with them. You're never here.

Can't you understand what it's like, seeing them all every day? It's like going back to the scene of an accident every morning. Every time I look at Lisa it's like looking at the wreck of my own life. The hell with Kenya if it means this. I'm going to Nairobi. If they cut off my head there, at least your sister'll be in the hospital where she can be looked to. And maybe I'll be drunk when it happens. God knows I've had enough instruction in *that*, lately."

"But you can't just walk off and leave Pa and the boy here on the farm. I can't stay, you know that. One just doesn't walk off and leave everything to the Wogs. It's what they're after."

"The hell one doesn't walk off and leave it to the Wogs!" Holly's voice now lifted nearly to a scream. "*I'm* going to walk off and leave it to the Wogs. The goddamned Wogs can have it. If your father wants to stay he can stay. Little Jeff can stay or go, I couldn't care less. You can stay, but I'm sick of it, sick to death of it, and I wish to God I'd never left England!"

"You're just upset. You'll feel better tomorrow. Here, let me get you a drink. It'll settle you down."

"I don't want any drink to settle me down. And I won't be less upset tomorrow, because tomorrow I'm not going to be here. Do you want to drive me and Elisabeth in, or will I take the Jaguar?"

"I *can't* drive you in. I'm due back at the Falls tonight. There's a thing on, and I'm more or less running it. You're really going?"

"Yes, dear, I'm really going. And I'm staying. And I'm not coming back to this. It's your family. It's not mine. You look after it."

"*Your* family," Peter said, "won't be leaving their home."

"You're so wrong, dear. They've left it. They're going back to England. My mother isn't a pioneer woman either, like her daughter. She's half mad from worry over Daddy and Jerry. *Both* of them are away about three quarters of the time. She's going straight on to home—to England—with Dad to follow if he can find anybody who's ass enough to buy it. If not, it can sit there and rot. I suppose Jerry'll stay on here and play cowboy with all the rest of his chums. He's got to where he looks naked without a Sten gun."

"I don't suppose there's any more I can say, sweetie, if you're dead set on leaving. What'll you do in Nairobi for a place to stay? Flats are difficult to come by."

"I'll find something. I don't want much, so long as it's near a police station. I'm putting Elisabeth in the hospital. I'll go and stay with Elspeth

Warren or somebody until I can locate some digs of my own. Somewhere, I hope, close to the center of the town. I'd as lief stay on here as in Kabete or Muthaiga."

"I never really thought you'd quit," Peter said quietly. "I never thought you'd chuck it in. I thought you'd stay and see it out. I thought it would be a point of pride, if nothing else."

"Point of pride be damned. I don't want to be proud. I don't want to be proud like Elisabeth, walking around with a dead man's baby inside her and her face cut to pieces. I don't want to live my life remembering what it's like to see my babies butchered. I don't want to wear a bloody gun as costume jewelry, and be brave, and noble, and cope, and wash dishes, and lose two stone from fretting, like Diana Masters did, and I don't want to go to bed every night wondering if I'll see the morning. I don't want to *not* go to the bathroom when I want to go to the bathroom because I'll have to unlock doors and take a gun with me. I don't want to spend every month being terrified that I might be pregnant. And I most especially don't want to be married to a man that's slowly being torn to pieces by what he's doing. I'd rather be a widow than that." Holly slammed her hand flat on the table and got up and walked off to her room. She closed the door with a crash. She went to her closets and began to throw clothes on the bed.

Peter went over to the bullet-scarred sideboard and poured himself a big dram of scotch. It burned the lining out of his throat going down, but it was warm and reassuring in his stomach. Women, he thought. Jesus God, women. I can't blame her for being edgy, but everybody else's edgy too. She hasn't got a copyright on it. I'm edgy. I have a right to be edgy. The whole bloody country's edgy.

He walked out into the yard. His father, fingers meshed behind his back, was pacing up and down on the lawn. The brown wrinkly-horn handle of his pistol was shoved forward on the belt to make room for the big hands clasped in the small of his back.

"Pa," Peter said. "Pa."

The old man looked up mildly.

"So she's packing up, eh?" he said flatly. "Poor child. I don't blame her. Surprised she stood it as long as she has. The McKenzie family certainly hasn't brought her any luck. We don't seem to run much to luck in this family. Certain kinds, yes. Other kinds, no. As if there was a thahu on the whole bloody lot of us."

"Pa," Peter said sharply. "If please for Christ's sake you don't mind,

I don't need any talk about thahu ever again in my whole life. Please."

The old man swept his eyes around the bone-burned fields, the long blue hills, the weathered stone house, the ancient trees that shaded the lawn, that clustered close to the little stream. His gaze included the charred stables, the mossed gravestones on the hills. He twitched his shoulders in a funny little shrug.

"I suppose it's been worth it," he said softly to himself. Then:

"Peter. Son. I know quite a lot of what you blokes have had to do up in the hills. I know what you've been through in terms of—of dirty doings. I know what that sort of thing can do to the insides of a man. I know why you're all drunk when you're down out of the hills. I know everything that your wife's had to cope with. For her, I promise you, in many ways it's been worse than what you've been saddled with, and in many ways worse than all that Elisabeth's had. Because Elisabeth is absorbent, spongy, like me. She can soak up the lot and still walk off from it. Also, she's about half mad, really. She doesn't feel things as keenly as Holly feels them. There's a fuzz on her brain that protects her. She's never quite come out of the first shock, baby or no baby."

Peter started to interrupt. The old man held up his hand, pushing the palm gently toward Peter.

"Wait a minute, boy. Just one more thing to say. One day this mess'll be over and some sort of sanity will come back. We'll have to give in to these millions of Wogs a lot, and we'll find ourselves as white guests in the big black house. But there will be some day when the black Governor of Kenya will make a speech and he will thank blokes like you for keeping this lovely land at least on the fringe of decent living instead of giving it up and chucking it back into the bloody savagery we took it out of. I don't mean to lecture. It was a damned rough country when I came to it and it is a damned sight rougher country now, and in some ways everyone's had to do a great many dirty things that needed doing for the last fifty years.

"I don't want to meddle in your marriage. But I strongly advise that you send Holly to Nairobi. We've money, plenty of it. I advise also that you send her off to England with her mother if she wants to go. Send her to Spain, send her to France, and when you can, go after her wherever she is and take her off to America to start that honeymoon all over again. But if you love the girl and want to keep her you'll have to let time wash the blood off your hands and the smell of it off your body and the memory of it out of her head. For you've already lost her, else, because you never had time enough to really know her. She's more English than Kenyan, and she's had one hell of a bad do from this country and the people in it. Elisabeth's mine, and she's yours, and so we can both look at her. But to Holly she's just a constant horror, delivered fresh like milk, daily."

"Holly just said almost the same thing, Pa." Peter nodded. "I guess it's a little like safaris used to be. Some women think dust and bugs and heat and cold and snakes are funny. Or at least necessary. Others keep thinking about lifts and bath salts and cinemas and television and night clubs. Right now, today, this truly isn't a country for gentlefolk. I'll send Holly to Nairobi. She's going, anyhow. I can't go with her because I've got to leave tonight. Would you do me a great favor and leave the bloody farm to run itself for just one day and see the girls settled in and let poor little Jeff, poor little bugger, go and see one cinema? But mind you bring him back to the farm, Pa. His place is on this farm until he's big enough to go into bush with the rest of us. If you don't raise him up a man we've no hope here. He's eleven years old and already he's killed a man. He has to know what made it worth it, and he won't find that out in Nairobi, not by a bloody long chalk. All the spivs aren't black in Nairobi."

Henry McKenzie put his hand on his son's shoulder, tenderly. It was the first time since Peter was a boy that the old man had made any real gesture of tenderness toward him. Henry McKenzie dropped the hand abruptly.

"You're a very good boy, son," he said. "I think it will all come right one day, Holly and the rest. Let's go and have a drink now. Then you go and tell Holly good-by and then whip off fast. It's no good staying on to stretch it, for as far as you both are concerned you are saying good-by today. No matter how often you see her as long as this thing continues, it's just a stretched-out painful good-by."

Poor little kid, the old man thought. Poor little Peter. One day they'll give him a hero's medal for being a bloody murderer and losing his wife and wrecking his life, and by the time he gets the gong he'll probably be too far gone in drink to appreciate it. Poor little boy who is a man.

"Let's have the drink," he said. "It's about the right time of day for it." The two men walked together into the house. It was the first pleasant drink Peter could remember for quite a long time.

19

Elisabeth Newton lay in the hospital bed and tranquilly regarded the mound of her belly under the starched sheets; the flowers banked around the scrubbed white room. There was a small radio on the night table and one chair for visitors. It was wonderful just to lie there, relaxed. The sisters were very kind. Everybody was very kind. It was wonderful that everybody was so kind. It was so nice to have someone always in the chair, except when she needed the bedpan, and then whoever was in the chair handed it to her and then went outside, taking his gun with him, to stand against the door.

The hospital was situated in a thickly wooded outskirt of Nairobi, quite close to the scenes of several Mau Mau raids. But it was the best hospital in Nairobi. Even though one chieftain, Hinga, had been followed into the hospital at Kiambu and shot to death, there was still a feeling of great peace and safety about a hospital. It was part of what made a person believe everything a doctor had to say; what made people submissive to the bullying of nursing sisters, who woke you up at gray dawn for no reason whatsoever and who always referred to the patient as "we," as if the sister had the same complaint. "How is our baby today?" the sister always said. "Why aren't we eating our nice dinner?" Someday, perhaps, she might say: "Why are we so sad because our husband had his head chopped off and our other babies were killed?" But Elisabeth wouldn't think about that now. She would think about the new baby, who would be a fine boy and look exactly like Jeff, and who wouldn't mind the scar on his mum's face or the fact that she had only one arm and limped horribly. Elisabeth smiled at the man in the chair. She had only just met him, but he seemed a nice man, sitting there reading a newspaper, with his shotgun resting across his thighs, the muzzle pointing toward the door. All the men were nice.

Most of them were Peter's friends and old friends of Jeff. They were funny. A man would sit for four hours, talking with her if she wished, remaining quiet if she wished, always with a shotgun or a rifle across his knees or resting close to hand against the wall, always with a pistol strapped round his waist. When the four hours were up there would be a knock on the door and another man would come in, bringing his gun. The man in the chair would get up and gesture to the new man.

"Oh, do you know John Barnes?" he'd say. "This is Mrs. Newton. You know Peter, of course, Johnny. Well, I'm off. Anything doing at the Norfolk?"

"Nothing very much," the new man would say, sitting down. "I'm glad to know you, Mrs. Newton. Jeff and I were great chums before the war. I'm from down Mombasa way. Is there anything I can get you?"

She would say yes, please, she'd like to ring the nurse for some ice water, and would he like a drink of whisky? There was a bottle about somewhere. And he would always say no, thank you, Mrs. Newton, not on duty. And she would wonder for a bit if this was something new the Kenya Police Reserve had thought up, hospital duty. They had every other kind of duty. That was what kept Peter away from home so much and what made Holly so sad that she cried quite a lot. But these men were all so nice. Like this chap, Mr. Barnes.

"What is your business, Mr. Barnes?" she asked politely.

"I'm in the automobile business in Mombasa," he said. "Or at least I was. Nothing very much going on at the moment. I'm in the K.P.R., like everybody else. We've been working lately around Thika. My wife's running the shop whilst I'm away."

"It's so terribly nice of you to come and see me. Everyone has been so nice. I must say it's a little odd, though, waking up in the night or early in the morning and finding a perfectly strange gentleman in my bedroom. I suppose the neighbors would think it quite odd if this were anything but a hospital."

"Yes, ma'am. The sister said you weren't to talk too much. It's almost time for your pill and a nap. I'll just get the pill for you, shall I, and then you sleep a bit."

It was so wonderful to be looked after so well. Even though the men were a little rough-looking and usually smelled of whisky. They wore shabby khaki and often needed a shave, and they were generally big and hairy, with sun-baked faces and crisscrossing wrinkles on their necks from much time in the sun. A few had beards that came down to their chests. Some were past middle age, some practically boys. But they all had guns and they all sat quietly in the corner, and it was a great comfort. Lisa wasn't embarrassed any more about asking for the bedpan. The men would either call the nurse or, if she knew them at all, would pop it under the covers and then go out to the corridor. Then they would come and take it from her and set it outside in the hall for an orderly to collect. She liked the men much more than she liked the sisters. They were so kind, so gentle, so *comforting*.

20

Elisabeth's strange array of male nurses caused quite a lot of joking at the Regal Bar, at the Queens, at the New Stanley and the Norfolk. But it was gentle joking, because most of the professional hunters, farmers, and policemen from Eldoret to Mombasa were involved in it. It had started out when John Thompson said over a beer to some mate in the Regal: "I say, Peter McKenzie's sister's come to town to have a baby. You know, the poor girl who was in that early head-taking. Jeff Newton's wife. Seems she was pregnant when they hacked old Jeff and killed the kiddies. They slashed her up pretty grim, too. But she kept the baby, somehow. I think it's the least we could do if we stuck a sentry-go on the old hospital. This lass's had trouble enough. Least we can do is give her a little peace of mind whilst she waits out the mtoto. Anybody agree? Another beer, please, steward."

"I'm on," his mate said. "There're always enough blokes passing in and out to do a little maternity patrol. You go on over, Johnny, and I'll relieve you. What's the go? Might as well cut it into four-hour watches. It'll mean somebody will have to stay sober for the twelve-to-four and the four-to-eight."

So it had started. Peter's hunting friends, men like David Sheldrick and Andy Holmberg and Harry Selby and Fred Poolman and Tony Dyer and John Sutton; Jeff's old Navy cronies, farmers from the Aberdares area, Game Department blokes, voluntary reserve policemen in town for a week end's beano—even some of the foreign safari clients— all had a shot at baby-sitting Peter McKenzie's widowed sister who was having her baby and mustn't be disturbed by anybody, especially the Mickey Mice. Conversations took on a peculiar tone.

"One more, old boy? Another double gin for me, steward."

"No, thanks awfully, old chap, I really mustn't. I've got the midnight-to-four at the hospital, and I don't want to go out there slopped.

If anything happened on my watch, half the able-bodied men in Kenya would be after me with guns."

"I say, Donald. There's a couple of girls on the veranda that seem to have been giving me the eager twinkle. Shall us?"

"No, I'm afraid not—not right now. Old Andy's out there with a frightful hangover, and I promised I'd relieve him so's he could have a couple of spots before the bar closed. Devilish poor business, this hovering about a sickroom with a thirst. Hospitals make me damned well nervous even when I'm drunk. Ta. If the wenches'll listen to reason, I'll meet you here in four hours. Do your best, and I'll share the bar bill."

"Look, David, dear old boy, don't you think you've really had enough?"

"Of coursh *not*. I'm stony sh-*sober*. 'Nother one all round, eh?"

"This one's hopeless. You'll have to take the late shift, Michael. I'll sober this type up and deliver him in the early bright, if I have to kill him. We mustn't do anything to disturb Wilbur."

"Wilbur" was a name that the guardian ruffians had bestowed on the unborn child, for no very good reason except that they had to call their godbaby something, and Wilbur seemed to be an apt name for a child who had not yet emerged to inspect the woes of life. Wilbur he became, and Wilbur he would remain, no matter what sex he was or what name they gave him.

Every day one heard in the bars and the hotels:

"I say, Ian. *You've* been out today. What's new with Wilbur?"

"Doctor says he thinks inside of a week now. But his mother's been having some sort of kidney complications. Bloody little brute may come any minute, or again, he might stretch his wait out for ages. I'll be jolly glad to see him whelped. He's getting to be a dreadful nuisance. My love life *and* drinking life are both going to hell, waiting out this damned child."

Later in the day, at the Grill:

"What's the gen on Wilbur? Any fresh news?"

"No, afraid not. Little blighter's being very stubborn. *I've* suggested salts."

As the days passed along, the guardian ruffians reduced their conversation. There was no question now of anyone having to warn anyone else about sobriety or promptness in relieving the watch. The retiring watchman would enter a bar and call for a double anything. The men clustered at the bar would all turn and jerk their heads in question.

The man who was diving headfirst into his drink would shake his head. Then the men would turn and go back to their searching appraisals of women, weather, Mau Mau, shooting, football, women, polo, elephants, lions, weather, women, Mau Mau, and women. Never in the thorniest history of Kenya did so much concentration attend one single event. No royal accouchement ever received such tense anticipation.

"I swear to God, if that damned baby isn't born soon, we'll all be dead. You can't drink before you go on duty, or not very much, and you can't drink while you're on duty, so you try to pack it all into the other sixteen hours, which means no sleep. Such a contrary little bastard *I* never saw. Any fresh news?"

"Hapana. He's stubborn, old Wilbur. He doesn't want to stay inside the boma, but he refuses to come out. But boy, you ought to see him kick. I shoved a teacup onto his mama's tummy for a second today whilst I lit her a cigarette, and damn me if the little bastard didn't kick the saucer off her belly button."

"Well, bung-ho. I must nip off to the Aberdares. God, what a relief. I fancy Mau Mau any day over that stone-faced head sister at the hospital. Every time she looks at me I start re-counting my sins. Where the hell is Peter, by the way? Why doesn't he come and baby-sit his own bloody sister?"

"He'll be down shortly. That thing he was on is finishing, or's finished. Incidentally, don't forget to tell the chaps up there that all's well with Wilbur. They'll be keen to know."

"That gives me an idea. There's no reason why a bulletin on Wilbur can't go out on the safari news after the BBC, is there? Along with the Mau Mau and the conflicts at home and the other news. Why don't one of you chaps nip off to the broadcasting station and arrange with the program bloke to shove a little Wilbur gen into the late domestic news?"

"Jolly fine idea. Here, steward. We've sprouted a genius in our midst. Fix him another gin and hold my chit. I've an errand to run."

The Nairobi radio station customarily first put on the late BBC headlines, then an expansion of the news, then the headlines again, then the domestic news, and finally a special broadcast for safaris, since there was no other way to relay urgent messages to men in the bush. And so that particular night John Thompson, gone off again on short safari with Tom Deane, during a slight lull in John's military service connected their portable radio to the battery of the lorry and switched on the late news. The French had collapsed another cabinet, and Eisenhower had done something, and the fighting in Indo-China was roughly the same. The Russians were opposing something in the Security Council. Another American aircraft had been shot down by MIGs. Four men were kicked to death by terrorists in New York's Central Park. The United Nations was *squawk*, but another session to be *screech*. The headlines were repeated, another riot in Tunisia, the divorce of a movie star, the Queen today left for *squawk*. We return you now to Kenya for the domestic news. Another Mau Mau killing was reported from Nairobi when forty armed Kikuyu overran *screek* police said action speedily taken new roundup Mau Mau suspects Kiambu police crackdown new drive Aberdares Home Secretary says *squawk* General Erskine Sir Evelyn Baring *scree-eek*.

"For Christ sake cut it off," Tom Deane said. "I'm sick of it. Same everywhere. Trouble, trouble, trouble, and it's raining in Uganda. It's like a bloody soap opera."

"Wait a minute," John Thompson said. "We've had all the other pain. Maybe there's a message for us. Won't take a minute."

The radio screeched and squawked. ". . . That ends the home news," a girl's voice said. "Stand by now for the safari broadcasts. Attention, Joseph Watson, John Howard safari, Northern Frontier. There is an urgent cable forwarded for you at post office Isiolo. Repeat: Joseph Watson, John Howard safari, there is an urgent cable for you forwarded post office Isiolo. Attention, Bunny Allen, M-G-M safari. There is cable for Mr. Gable waiting Narok post office . . . Repeat, there is a cable . . .

"Weather report: Rain moving up from Tanganyika, reported light falls in southern Masai. Raining hard Uganda, but no rain yet reported Marsabit south to Archer's Post . . .

"Attention, all safaris: There is nothing new to report on Operation Wilbur. Nothing new to report on Operation Wilbur. Mother doing fine. Child still unco-operative. That is all of tonight's Kenya news."

"Well, by God, at last we get something constructive in safari broadcasts. I thought the bloody child would be passing out cigars by now," John Thompson said. "When I was in town two weeks ago the doctor said it was a matter of minutes. He'll weigh a young ton if he doesn't get born soon."

"Well, John-o, I think we'll pack up and leave tomorrow." Tom Deane yawned. "Maybe we can get back in time for the baby's arrival. It's no good our sticking on. Maybe there aren't any rains anywhere else, but even the hippos are complaining here. We'll check out with Ken tomorrow and shove. Between the weather and the Mau Mau, I think I've had safaris, and especially Uganda for picture-taking purposes. Christ, listen to that rain. . . ."

Joseph Watson listened to the broadcast alone. His client hated radios and had gone to bed. Joseph would have to drive Mr. Howard down to Isiolo tomorrow. That was the trouble with important clients. They always had somebody sending bloody nuisance cables to them. But nobody cared much if the client was rich enough. This client really didn't want to hunt. He wanted to go back home and talk about hunting. It was all right with Joseph. He needed the money. After that do with the commando, the till was scraped clean, and Joseph Watson needed a safari badly. He was lucky that this one fell into his lap. There would be enough money to make another payment on the farm and send a little extra to Jake to buy some fertilizer and seed with. If Jake was still there on the place with his head on. If the farm was still there. My God, Joseph Watson said, I hope it's over soon so I can go back to farming. I can't do safaris very much longer. Nerves rotten. Old Howard doesn't know it, but I led him away from a very big elephant today. But the boys know it. They know it and they know why I ducked the old bull. I know what they're saying around the fire right now. "The Bwana's lost his stomach," they're saying. "The Bwana is afraid." And they're right. I used not to be afraid of elephants. I used to play with rhinos. And now I lead my clients off from the big ones because I'm afraid to tackle it. Oh well. This old boy'll be going back pretty soon, without his elephant, and then maybe I can organize a photo-taking safari up in the Masai with some keen bird fancier. I wonder what's keeping Jeff Newton's baby from being born. Everything's messed up. Raining where it shouldn't and not raining where it should. Between the Mau Mau and the A-bomb and the flying saucers, nothing makes much sense any more. I wish I wouldn't dream so much. I think I'll see what kind of pills old Howard's got in his medicine chest. Maybe if I slept well I'd stop shaking. I can't even stand watching a boy skin out an antelope for the pot any more. I don't mind shooting it, but I don't like to see it dead and I can't stand the blood. Well, some pills. Maybe some pills will do the trick.

Joseph Watson got up from his camp chair and went to the medicine chest and chose a pair of red capsules. He swallowed them and washed them down with half a glass of whisky and went off to bed. The dreams persisted, and he was sweaty and shaking again when he awoke. Maybe the malaria had come back, but this wasn't the time for it, and it was hellish hot and bone-dry in the N.F.D. He hoped they wouldn't run across any more elephant today.

Peter heard the broadcast from the pub at Nyeri during the lull when all the men clustered before the fire and stopped their chatter to hear the news. It was Peter's first day out of the bush, and he was heading down to Nairobi.

"What's all this Operation Wilbur business?" he asked the man next to him. "Something new the Army's cooked up in the way of an operation that won't come off at the last moment because somebody's buggered the details?"

"My oath, chum, you *have* been away," the man said. "That's your own nephew they're talking about. Half of Kenya has been baby-sitting your sister in between police raids and other small chores. Wilbur's the tag they've hung on the chee-ild. Where've you been, Peter, not to know about Operation Wilbur?"

"Busy," Peter said. "Well, cheers. I've got to make Nairobi tonight, and I don't fancy a breakdown on these roads. The gay lads will be popping away with guns at the cars?"

"Sure. But nobody's bothered to tell Kaleba about lead-off angles yet. They still think that if you point a gun at something when it's moving, the bullet will hit it. White man's magic. Good trip, lad."

Peter went out into the chilly courtyard and roused Lathela and Metheke, who were sleeping curled up in tattered overcoats in the back of the jeep. "Let's get on," he said. "It seems we're having a baby."

In a way, the great paternal pride of half of Kenya in the unborn baby of the dead Jeff Newton was easily understandable. This would be a sort of symbolic baby, like the little tad who wears a top hat and diaper to celebrate New Year's. Here's this poor girl hacked to pieces, you see, with her husband in bits in the yard and the other kids clobbered and the house burned down, and she still hangs onto the baby. She'll have it, Mau Mau or no Mau Mau, emergency or no emergency, drought, rain, hell, or high treason, and it'll be a bloody good baby. It takes more than Mau Mau to lick this breed. Mau Mau or bloody Japs or Germans or the Russians tomorrow. As long as women like Elisabeth Newton will have babies like this one, everything's going to be right. Well, cheer-ho. I must just whip off and check in for the bedpan detail.

Elisabeth was not allowed much company, for there were complications, and she was better off to stay quiet with just her watchdogs. Holly came once a day and brought flowers three times a week and chatted briefly. When Holly came, the man on watch would generally leave the room and smoke in the hall while the women talked. They never talked long. Holly could find very little to say to Elisabeth about the baby. They talked a little about the apartment Holly had found.

"It's quite nice," Holly said. "I'd hoped for something closer in, but this is in that new block of flats down by the traffic circle, and the rooms are quite large. There's a big sitting room and three bedrooms, one quite tiny, and a jolly decent kitchen, and a very keen police patrol. I've found a servant, a Kikuyu named Solomon Something-or-other. They've had him through a security check, and he's been a hundred per cent cleared. Not a bad cook-cum-housemaid, either. I thought it'd be best after the baby comes if you stopped on with me for three months or so. It'll be a little difficult to go back to the farm until you're strong."

"I want to get back as soon as ever I can," Elisabeth said. "I hate thinking of Pa and little Jeff there all alone. Any news of Peter?"

"Yes. He rang through today from Nyeri. He's all right. He's coming down soon, he says. They keep nipping in and out of the Falls and all round about. It's very big military, people dashing about in the forests and leaving messages shoved into hollow trees and I don't know what all. Father McKenzie rang through as well, and he says everything's fine with him and little Jeff on the farm. He'll be coming in soon, he says, for the baby. I'd best run now. I don't want to tire you. I'll just go and call your watchdog."

"They're sweet, these men. It's a sort of odd nursing service for an expectant mother, but I like having them here. Especially in the absence of a husb— Especially since Peter and Pa can't be here very much. Thanks so much for coming, Holly. I can't wait to see the flat."

Holly went into the hall and nodded good-by to the watchdog, who was leaning against the wall by the door, scraping at his nails with a hunting knife, whistling under his breath. He watched Holly appreciatively as she tip-tapped down the corridor on high heels. McKenzie better spend less time with the Mau Mau, he thought. I'd not like to leave that running loose forever in this town the way it is now. Then he took his rifle from its rest against the wall and went back inside.

"Anything I can get you, Mrs. Newton?" he asked.

"Yes, please. The bedpan, if you don't mind. Thanks awfully."

The man slid the pan in under the bedclothes and went back into the hall again. I hope that little bastard hurries up and gets himself born. Fancy me slinging bedpans at my time of life, he thought. He waited until he heard Lisa's "All right, please," and went back into the room. Now dammit, the man thought. Her sister-in-law just left, and she waited for her to leave before she asked for the pot. Strange. He sat down in the chair and began to read his newspaper. His relief was due in half an hour, and he hoped to Christ he wasn't late. He could certainly use a beer to wash that iodine-y hospital stink out of his nostrils.

"Everything all right with Wilbur, ma'am?"

"He's awfully lively today. I think he's threatening to break out momentarily."

"Jolly good. The chaps'll be glad. There are some who are hanging about, won't leave town until they see how this turns out. It's sort of like those things they have on the wireless. You know. The Yankees call them cliff hangers or something."

"It is rather like a radio serial, the whole thing." Elisabeth smiled. "Would you mind dreadfully calling a sister? I'm not actually feeling very well."

"Of course. Let's hope this is the break-through."

He went off to call the sister, and when he returned his relief was standing by, with his sub-machine gun slung over his shoulder.

"Oh, say, Bill," the relief said. "I'm to tell you that you're wanted in Kiambu. There was a big do up there last night, news just came down, and you're called, laddy. You're to nip straight off tonight, if possible. What's with the problem child?"

"He's highly restless. Looks as if we may squeeze him out into the open shortly. By God, he's stubborn, is old Wilbur. I hate to miss the big event. Be sure and have it put on the wireless, will you?—sex, weight, name, and the rest. I'm off. Thanks for the message."

When the man Bill got back to the Norfolk he walked into the bar and was besieged, first by the manager, then by the drinkers.

"Still reluctant." He grinned. "But showing signs of claustrophobia. Maybe tomorrow. What's this about Kiambu?"

"The Ms touched off a mission early today. Killed the priest and a couple of helpers. Dirty great mob of them, in daylight. They've gone to ground, but the C.O. reckons he knows where they're headed. Dirty big drive on, and you're in it, chum."

"Well," the man Bill said, "I'm not in it until one of you slackers has stood me a gin. Who's got the duty tonight?"

"Kiambu or hospital?"

"Hospital, fool. Kiambu'll take care of itself."

21

Apart from the daily trips to the hospital, which she dreaded, Holly McKenzie was enjoying Nairobi a good deal. She had stayed a few days in a tiny cottage on the hotel grounds and then quite by accident had blundered onto a flat. It belonged to some friends who were going to England on a long home leave, and they were delighted to let her have it for six months. It was a nice flat, gay with chintz, comfortably furnished, and owning, as she had told Elisabeth, a very keen night patrol. It was wonderful to go to sleep again in a big bedroom with the loo adjacent, without having to lock anything but your front door and your bedroom door. Holly steeped herself in just being alone. There was a big blond-wood radio-phonograph and stacks and stacks of fairly recent recordings. There was a whole wall of newish books, bright and cheerful in their jackets. There was a soft white rug on the living-room floor and a nice large fireplace and an oversized sofa and huge, quilted chairs. There was even a chaise longue in the bedroom.

The husband, Eric, had showed her the liquor cabinet and suggested mildly that he'd taken inventory and it came to so many hundred shillings, and if she'd like to pay him it would save her the trouble of victualing her own bar. Holly wrote him a check and they had a martini, very cold from the ice cubes in the vast humming frij, to seal the bargain. Then the people went away to catch their boat at Mombasa and left Holly alone, to beautiful, wonderful solitude and female frippery. She wore a negligee in the house and did her face and started to repair her hands and fingernails. She went and had her hair done and bought some clothes, not that she needed any clothes, she still had an unused trousseau, but she couldn't bring herself to wear the trousseau clothes. She didn't want any more reminders than she already had. So she had a dressmaker come round and ordered herself a complete new outfit. Henry

McKenzie had given her a check for a thousand pounds when she came in from the farm. "Secret," he said. "Don't tell Peter."

She had the Jaguar, the wedding present, and so her transportation problem was nothing, and some angel had sent her this Solomon wa Whatever, and Solomon was divine. He slapped around barefooted and sang a little in the kitchen, mission songs, of course, and spoke a decent English on top of his Swahili and his Kikuyu, and was security-checked besides. For the first time in several months Holly McKenzie began to feel something like the girl who had gotten married and had gone away to Mawingo. There was the daily trip to see Elisabeth, of course, body-bloated, brown-blotched, and stringy-haired from the baby. But at least she was not *in the house.*

Naturally Holly knew people. Diana came to call and so did Helen and so did Florence and Beth and Charlotte. Holly was young and she was very lovely and she got asked out a lot for dinners and lunches and cocktails or dancing, always to fill in for some young Captain Alastair Something or Vyvyan Something or Flight Lieutenant Something. Any number of Peter's old friends saw her at the Equator or the Stanley and said, well, see who's here, if it isn't old Holly, as I live and breathe, how's Peter, and why don't you come along with us? We're going to whip off to the Muthaiga for a spot of something and then on into the early. And so Holly had a fine time, especially after the farm. She practically stopped reading the *East African Standard,* and when the wireless changed over from the BBC world report and came to the home news she switched off the wireless and cut in the record player. She had people by for tea and in for cocktails and occasionally for meals, and she managed to keep her virtue intact without actually fighting for it. Although there were a couple of gentlemen, one from the Black Watch, the other from the Buffs, who had been a little too persistent after a good-night kiss or two and who had to be read off sharply.

The English troop loved her because she was an old Londoner, not so bloody chapped-lipped-square-handed-competent as the Kenya wenches, old boy, and she's been inside a theater and knows a few things apart from bloody cows and sheep and rinderpest and Wogs. But nothing doing there, so far as I know. I promise you, I had a ruddy good go at it and got nowhere. I understand she's married to one of these frightfully worthy local types who spends all his time up in the hills, coursing the Wogs. Shouldn't want him angry at me. These boys are very basic these days. Never saw such a flock of basics. I suppose colonists are all alike, no matter where you find them. These chaps out here might even be Americans. They're so bloody *earnest.*

22

Peter had come in only once since Holly had left the farm. He came, sober, into the flat, and she saw that he had a box of clothing with him.

"I stopped off at the farm and collected some stuff," he said half-apologetically. "A dinner coat and a decent suit or so. I thought, now you're here in Nairobi, we might be going out a bit, and you wouldn't want me looking like a shenzi. Where's the bath? I could do with a bit of a wash. I must say you were lucky in finding this."

Then for a few days it was very pleasant and quite a lot of fun, like it might've been. Peter drank very well and behaved properly. He looked clear-eyed and handsome and neat in his blue blazer and flannels for daytime and his dinner jacket for night, and they went to bed and made love and it was better. Not a great deal better, but some better.

The thing that baffled Holly about Peter was that he didn't seem to be very emotional any more. He didn't cry or sweat up the bed or cling tightly to her hand or groan and curse in the night, as he'd done at first. He seemed to have a close hobble on his behavior. He seemed—not cold, but what was the word, what was it exactly?—detached and indrawn and very, very cold and elaborately casual. The fresh boyish niceness, the brattish spontaneity had gone away somewhere and left a hard-shelled man she didn't know. When they went to bed he made love competently, never impulsively or sweet-little-boyishly. *He treats me as if I were some sort of project,* Holly thought one of the nights when Peter had gone off to sleep and she lay awake on the pillow by his side. *He sort of copes, as if I were an elephant to find or something to track in the bush.*

I could understand him better when he was horrified and nervous and drunk and cried and sweated. But that's gone and he drinks his whisky as if it were medicine and he doesn't get drunk and when he laughs it's too loud and there isn't any reason for it. Also, I don't care for his way with Africans any more. He doesn't joke them or even abuse them. He doesn't even see them. That other noon in the Norfolk, when poor old Moussa made some joke or other, and Peter just looked through him. I don't know. I don't know him at all.

They had some people in one night at the flat for drinks, and it was pretty noisy. The talk got around to Mau Mau and to England's home policy, and there were a few of the British soldiers there, a Captain Morrison from the Inniskillings and some major who was staff to the general. There was a lot of talk and some drinks, and the staff major was talking very learnedly about something to do with tactics, and Peter just got up and looked at him. He got to his feet and looked at the staff major again as if the staff major weren't there, as he'd looked at Moussa, as if everybody in the room had gone away.

"Balls." He said the word very precisely and walked to the door. They heard the roar of the Jaguar as he brutalized it into gear, and when he came back the next morning he was very drunk and had not bothered to remove a good portion of the lipstick that was grained into his lips. He packed and left swiftly, not bothering to say good-by.

There had not been very much Holly could do to salvage the party after Peter had said that word and left. There was never very much that anybody had ever been able to do when somebody said that word and got up and walked away.

"What a surly sod that one is," the staff major remarked to the captain as they went away from the apartment. "I still don't even know what it was I said that made him angry. What was I talking about, tanks, jets, or attrition, or something? I'm sure I can't imagine what boiled him off."

Neither, actually, could Peter as he drove in the early morning up the Thika road, heading for the mountains. He seemed to be cheesed off at something all the while. Somehow every time he saw those yacht-club British troops he got angry. They seemed to think that this was a bloody house party and that they'd all be back off it when the other guests got bored with it. In any case, they didn't have to live here. In any case, they hadn't done what he and Joseph and John and the others had done and were still doing when it was necessary—except now it had to be done very carefully because the bloody Government would run you if you rumpled a Wog's hair when you tried to coax a little truth out of him. Kill him, yes, that's fine; that's commendable. But none of this "brutality" business. Look what they did to that Pommie captain. Had him up like a bloody criminal for being beastly to the Mau Mau.

Fine bloody thing if they find out half what we were up to in the old days—and then Peter stopped thinking, shocked, because the old days were much less than half a year ago.

23

Wilbur was being difficult. He announced his arrival by a series of false labor pains, and that started promisingly and then ceased, while Wilbur coyly retreated to the status quo. Elisabeth was very ill. By reckoning, Wilbur was about two weeks overdue, and the false labor weakened her considerably, physically and psychologically. Henry McKenzie and young Jeff had come into town and were staying in the flat with Holly. Henry McKenzie took one of the regular security watches himself, the early one, from four to eight. He sat solidly in one corner, in the dark cold of the early morning, listening to his daughter's breathing, a gun resting its barrels against the inside of his thigh, pointing up and backward under his arm. He sat in the dark and thought. He thought about all the things old men think of, mostly of the pleasurable things, very little about the painful parts. He thought that soon he would be dead and planted on the hill next Caroline and the other children. He thought that death might be pleasant, certainly relaxing, but that he did not want it to happen to him for a very long time. He thought it would be nice to watch young Jeffy grow up and to watch this baby grow up, as he had planned; it would be nice to have some peace again and things going better with Peter and Holly, and their kids shooting up like weeds around him.

He would like to see the country again as it was when he first came; uncluttered, unmechanized, with the Wogs simply savage and the horizon limitless. He thought about the new life that pulsed in his daughter's belly, his lovely daughter, Elisabeth, scarred and crippled and maimed, inside and out, but still capable of producing a scrap of hearty life to begin the cycle all over again. He thought about a day he once spent all by himself under a cool mimosa grove in Tanganyika, where no white man had ever been before him, and where the elephants were tame and friendly, and where the sun came through the patches in the green umbrella tops and dappled the ground with flecks of gold. The mimosa were spaced with the tall palms with feather heads. There was a light sweet breeze and complete silence in the grove. The ground was yellow-packed with clean straw. A dove called somewhere, far, far away. There was a dim crash, also far away, where some big animal, an elephant or a rhino, had taken fright and moved swiftly. A little river flowed slowly down at the edge of the clearing, and he could hear an occasional gurgling splash as a croc slid into the stream. The air was lovely with the little white blossoms that smelled like tuberoses. He had lain on the clean yellow straw, packed where the elephants walked, and gone softly to sleep. He had dreamed then that he had died and gone to heaven. When he awoke and looked about him, the delusion persisted, and he had thought, for just a few seconds, that he was still in heaven. That's what the country had been like in those days, he thought as he sat in the uncomfortable chair with the weight of the gun pressing on his leg and the steel of the barrels burning cold through his trousers on his skin.

He heard his daughter moan in her sleep, and then she came awake with a soft, muffled little scream. Her body writhed. He snapped on the light. Her eyes widened in horror for a second, and then she relaxed. She was perspiring heavily, he saw.

"What is it, Elisabeth?"

"Oh, it's you, Pa. I suppose I had a dream. But please call the sister, and perhaps she'd better call the doctor. I think that this time young Wilbur is serious." Her body arched upward as a spasm of pain seized her. "I'm sure he's serious," she said, and bit her lips white against the mottled sallowness of her face.

And so Wilbur was born in his grandfather's presence, as Wilbur's mother had been born in her father's presence, except that this time Wilbur's grandfather and Elisabeth's father stood outside the delivery room with his gun, chewing his mustache and fumbling his pipe as he listened to the noises coming from inside the delivery room. The noises, Henry McKenzie thought, were much the same as his wife, Caroline, had made on that one long-remembered wild, wet night when he had delivered her of the woman who now made the same noises inside the room. But this time the labor was brief. Wilbur had been a long time making up his mind. When he got it fully decided he came with a burst of speed, like a charging buffalo, as if angry at having been confined for so long.

Wilbur was born fighting mad. He opened his mouth wide and howled his indignation. He was a big boy and weighed ten pounds. He had long black hair already and was as wrinkled as his grandfather. He was bright red in color and had feet on him that already looked too big. His nose had been broken somehow in delivery and was mashed against his cheek. One eye was bloodshot. He clenched his hands into fists and struck out at the world. He opened his mouth again and screeched.

"By God," Henry McKenzie said to one of the sisters. "He cries *bass*."

"He's a fine boy," the sister said. "I hope he doesn't grow up to take after most of his honorary uncles. Your gel's fine. She's knocked out, dead tired, but she's fine."

"By God he *is* a fine boy," Henry said. "Look at his ears. Just like mine."

"We'll fix that," the sister said. "They have ways of fixing that these days. You go home now and get some rest."

"I can't," Henry McKenzie said. "I haven't been relieved. The relief isn't due for half an hour. I'll stay here with my gun."

"Well," the sister said, and patted the old man on the sleeve. "I'll find you a little medicinal alcohol to celebrate your grandson."

"No," Henry McKenzie said. "It isn't allowed on watch."

Wilbur's natal day will possibly be remembered in Kenya long after the Mau Mau have been forgotten. When the relief came Henry McKenzie went to the Norfolk Hotel and saw to it that the bar opened early. Telephone calls were made. It was estimated that the bills for breakage in the Norfolk, the New Stanley, the Regal, the Queens, the Travellers' Club, the Muthaiga Club, both Equators, and the airport bar almost approximated the cost of a week's Mau Mau campaign. A special bulletin was broadcast which said that Operation Wilbur had been successfully terminated, that the weight was ten pounds, and that no name had yet been selected. This inaugurated breakage in all the better water holes of Nakuru, Thomson's Falls, Nyeri, Noro Moru, Kiambu, Thika, Fort Hall, Naivasha, Nanyuki, Eldoret, Kusumu, and Kinangop. John Thompson, passing with Tom Deane through Kampala in Uganda, heard the radio flash, and the trip back to Nairobi was delayed another day. One of the few white people who did not know about Wilbur was Wilbur's uncle Peter, who was high in the Aberdares, hunting.

All children who are formally born get peculiar presents. But Wilbur's array was startling, even for Kenya in a time of crisis. Wali Mohammed, the metalsmith, found himself besieged with orders for christening mugs. All were to be mounted in wart-hog tusks. Cables were sent to the firms of Rigby and Westley-Richards in London, demanding almost immediate delivery on small double rifles. It was estimated later by some statistically minded drunk that by the time Wilbur was a year old he would have taken delivery of about forty-three weapons of assorted caliber, a gross of stag-handled hunting knives, one Land Rover, and an entire remuda of variegated livestock, ranging from horses to ridge-back hounds. It was fortunate that Wilbur had not been born a girl, because the only gift that a female Wilbur might have used was an advance order for ten gallons of christening water from Buffalo Springs at Archer's Post outside of Isiolo in the Northern Frontier. Even the christening mugs had a rather masculine design, apart from the wart-hog-tusk handles. To a man, the orderers had specified that all mugs be made outsize—"just big enough to hold a decent Pimm's," the shoppers said.

Wilbur's rattles were old Kikuyu and Masai war rattles. He received a bassinet which was built of teak mounted on four rhino feet. He received a leopard rug to wrap, as the donor said, a proper Baby Bunting in. None of this bloody rabbit-skin stuff for our boy Wilbur. Two lion cubs created quite a problem in the hospital and had to be taken away to the Norfolk, where a room was rented for them until somebody could think of a place to keep them until Wilbur was old enough to play with them. All considered, Wilbur had received an excellent start in life by Kenya standards.

Some days later, when the wrinkles had smoothed out of Wilbur's face and his bright ocher coloration had faded to a more formal pink, his broken nose reset, and the blood clot cleared from his eye, the question of name was discussed.

"I wanted to call him Peter," Elisabeth said. "But I can't. Wilbur's a horrible name, I think, but the poor little fellow is stuck with it. His name is Wilbur Newton, and he'll have to use Peter for the middle name. Even if I called him something else, he'd still be Wilbur for the rest of his life." So Wilbur became Wilbur officially, and this fact, too, was recorded and broadcast on the radio.

Elisabeth gained strength quickly. Her eyes had brightened, and she seemed to have lost much of the stunned, almost childlike simplicity and vagueness that had afflicted her during the time since the—since the accident. She was ready to be discharged from the hospital when Wilbur was two weeks old and approximately, as one of his uncles reported to the boys in the bars, a foot longer and twenty or thirty pounds heavier. "I swear to God," the uncle said, "he's already started a mustache." Holly was firm in insisting that Elisabeth come and stay in the apartment for several months. Elisabeth was firmer in her refusal.

"No," she said. "No. Thanks awfully, Holly, but I'm going home with Pa and little Jeff. I want to go home."

"But how'll you ever manage with the baby? I mean, you're——" Holly stopped on the word "crippled." "I mean, you're weak yet and the baby needs——"

"We'll manage with Juma and Aly and Pa and Jeff and me. It's only one baby," Elisabeth said. "I'm going home with Pa."

And so Wilbur Peter Newton went home. A stranger seeing the escort might have thought possibly that a column of troop, or a shipment of bullion, or at least a dead politician on his way to the cemetery was passing by. Henry McKenzie reckoned later that Wilbur's home-coming to Bushbuck Farm cost him just on four hundred and twenty pounds in whisky, gin, and beer, and that the breakage, when totted up, would bring the total to at least five hundred quid.

24

Holly went back to the flat. At least she'd done her best. She had made her offer. She was willing to take the baby on, and the mother on, and look after the pair until the child was creeping. *But* at her flat in Nairobi. Not on the farm. And now she was relieved. She had made her offer. She had done her best. It wasn't her fault if Elisabeth and the rest of the family had that mad fixation about a bloody farm. And certainly she had been saved a lot of trouble. Elisabeth to cope with and a baby always primary in the interests of the house would have made the flat impossible for all the things she loved about the flat. If they wanted the farm they could go and live on the farm. What she wanted was not to go and live on the farm. What she wanted was a drink. She went over to the sideboard and looked over the room again. It *was* a nice room. It had a lovely record player and a lovely bar in it. It had a lovely sofa and a lovely pair of chairs and lovely books and lovely ice cubes in the lovely frij in the lovely kitchen. There was lovely gin on the lovely sideboard.

She poured herself a slap of the gin and spilled some tonic into the glass. The ice bucket was empty, and she yelled for Solomon to fetch some ice. She sat down in a chair and kicked off her shoes. When Solomon came with the ice cubes she tonged a couple into the gin and tonic and took a drink, a long drink. She lit a cigarette and inhaled and noticed that her hand had fallen on the French phone on the side table where the glass sat. She dialed a number and a voice answered.

"Major Martin, please," she said. "Mrs. McKenzie calling. Thank you."

She waited, kicking her stockinged foot up and down, drawing on her cigarette. She blew a ring and poked the coal of the cigarette through the hole in it. She could hear the phone being lifted again on the other side. A different man's voice spoke.

"Oh, hullo, Jock," she said. "It's Holly, here. I'm awfully bored and I dislike drinking by myself. If you're nearly done in the office why don't you dash by for a drink, and I'll make you a supper. Unless you'd rather go out somewhere."

The receiver hummed with the man's voice.

"That's wonderful then. In an hour and a half? Bye-bye."

Holly took her drink with her into the bedroom. She opened the clothes closet. She looked at her frocks. She wondered what she had better wear, and decided on green. Then she naturally chose the little black sleeveless one.

When Peter came down from his hunting on the mountain again, he stopped off at the farm. Nothing much had changed about the farm except that Holly wasn't there and young Wilbur was. Young Wilbur was a month old and had taken over the management of the house. He screamed, and everybody dropped everything. He sulked, and the household stepped softly. He commanded, and everyone obeyed.

The change in Lisa, Peter thought, was fantastic. She still limped but did not seem to drag. She talked animatedly again and made jokes. She did a heavy share of the work, even with one arm. The old man, too, seemed sprightlier than before. Young Jeff was out of the house most of the day. He was off supervising the labor force and was rarely off a horse. Young Jeff was coming along. He was still weedy and spotty on the face, but he was beginning to show signs of soliding down into the kind of man his father had been. Since the arrival of Wilbur, Peter noticed, there had also been a marked change in Jeff's hesitant manner toward his mother. The first night at supper, Peter heard Jeff say "My father" two or three times. He was no longer abashed in the presence of Elisabeth. This one will be all right, Peter thought. Now he isn't all that's left of the wreck any more. He's his own man. Without thinking, Peter said: "How'd you like to ride into Nairobi with me for a few days, Jeff-o? Be a change. Young Will here can take over your work outside the house, if what he's mumbling in his cradle is Kikuyu. He seems to run the inside pretty well, as it is."

"I'd love to, Peter," Jeff said. It wasn't Uncle Peter any more. Just Peter. Well, fine. Very good. Well *and* good.

"Fair enough. I want to see Holly. Anybody got any ideas about her plans? She still insist on staying on in the flat?"

"I really don't know." Elisabeth spoke carefully. "She seems very happy there, much more so than here. I should say that she would stay on. At least for a while."

"I don't know." Peter smiled. "I'm told I'm a married man. But it seems to me I married Jomo Kenyatta and Dedan Kemathi and all the other boys instead of Holly. I feel like a visitor when I see her. Which is bloody seldom. I don't suppose I ever knew her really well."

"Would you like a brandy with your coffee, son?" Henry McKenzie got up from the table and wiped his mustaches. "Let's take it in front of the fire, if it's not too much trouble, Elisabeth?"

"I'll get it," Peter said.

"No, it's my shauri," young Jeff said. "We have a division of labor around here when the Wogs are shut up for the night. Mum can do a lot of things with one arm, but she can't manage a coffee tray."

Well, damn me, Peter thought. Well and bloody well done. So now they talk about Jeff *and* mention the arm. Bloody good show.

"In any case, I can find the hooch," Peter said. "I shall pour the hooch. Do we crook the little finger these days or just slosh it on?"

Everybody laughed, although he had said nothing funny. It was jolly fine they are laughing now, Peter thought. Jesus Christ himself can't measure up to the miracle of this baby. Wilbur. *What* a name. And it's apt. He looks a little like a baby wildebeest. Maybe we'll start a new strain in Kenya. A baby Wilburbeest. Joke.

"We'll drive in tomorrow, Jeff," Peter said. "After lunch. I'd like it very much if you would show me round the farm in the morning. I've been gone so much I don't know whether we're growing alfalfa or what."

"Well, we grew a pretty good baby," Elisabeth said. "Put the coffee here, Jeff. I'll pour if you'll manage the sugar."

Now it's jokes, Peter said. I will just be go to hell, as Tom Deane'd say. I'm sorry I missed him, by the way. I imagine he's chuffed off for the States. Pity about his safari being bitched. Oh well. But jokes in *this* household I cannot believe. I'll try something. Maybe I'll collect a rocket, but I'll try it anyhow.

"Look, Lisa," he said. "I think that damned scar of yours is just a touch more noticeable than necessary. You don't *have* to wear it around like a bloody badge. We aren't exactly poverty-stricken. Why don't you go off to England next year, when young Tarzan is able to stand your absence, and get a really good plastic surgeon to see if he can't fix it?"

Elisabeth looked at him levelly. She smiled.

"Pa and I've already discussed it with the doctor in Nairobi. He thinks that a skin graft will practically remove it. I thought I'd go next summer, possibly, but I'll take the baby. And Jeff as well, if things have quieted down to where you can spend more time on the farm and help Pa."

"Somehow I'll make the time," Peter said. "My end of this business is about finished, anyhow. Another six months, perhaps, and we'll have it pretty well under control. I hope. Well. If nobody minds, I shall shoot off to bed. I'm dog-tired. As usual. Night, all."

It seemed peculiar going off to bed alone in the new wing, in Holly's room. He had spent very little time in this room, which still was a woman's room, still had closets packed with clothes, still smelled obtrusively female. He had never slept in this bed without Holly in it beside him. The sheets were freshly changed, of course, but they were soft sheets and still smelled faintly of perfume. Well, lonely bed or no lonely bed, Peter was tired. He would sleep. The dreams weren't so bad any more. A businessman eventually quit dreaming of business.

Peter was never after quite sure why he asked Jeff to ride into Nairobi with him to see Holly. He wasn't ever sure how he knew that it would be a good idea for somebody to be with him when he went to Nairobi. Peter still operated by hunch, and the hunter's intuition had sharpened during his work against the gangs on the mountain. There were days when Peter felt that they would turn up a nest of the carefully hidden men. There were other days when he felt as if it were no use going to the trouble of a long, careful stalk because the men would be flushed when they got there, dispersed widely after a warning from some spy from the shambas. When Peter and young Jeff climbed out of the Rover at 6 P.M. that day in front of the apartment Peter felt the special hunch muscles twist in his stomach. He felt the same swift-sink-ing-elevator feeling he used to get just before a lion's tail shot out into a stiff bar and the lion charged; just before an old bull rhino dropped his flag and thundered blindly straight ahead. It was the same feeling that operated so strongly now in this hunting of men, some intangible thing that made him go to that hill instead of this hill, the same thing that caused him suddenly to backtrack and circle and discover that sixty yards ahead he would have stepped smack into a carefully planted ambush. The stomach muscles unknotted, and Peter walked up to the apartment door and pushed a key into the lock. Jeff was walking just behind him.

And there, of course, there it was. There it had to be. Just as he knew it would be, there it was. The finish of it was there in full sight. Not that there was anything wrong at all—much, except everything. But Peter McKenzie lived in his nostrils and eyes and in his stomach, and what he saw marked a plainer trail than a series of signposts.

A blond man with a short mustache was sitting on the divan with a glass in his hand. He was a major in a staff uniform, with a row of damned good ribbons—D.S.O., Military Cross, ribbons for Crete and Africa and the France-and-Germany. He wore his blond hair long over the ears, brushed back without stickum. He had a crescent scar on his cheekbone under one eye. The eyes were blue. He was a slender man, but tall, more than six feet, to judge from the length of leg that was draped casually over the arm of the sofa and the ankle of which he had been bouncing gently up and down. The shoe was burnished. He had a good batman, this major, for the tropical uniform was beautifully ironed. The major was alone in the room. As Peter entered, the major set the drink on the coffee table and dropped a copy of an old *Life* magazine beside him on the divan and got gracefully to his feet. The major had a spare body that was made for the wearing of clothes, for his uniform fell into place in a single ripple of elegance as he rose.

That was what made all the difference. This man cared for clothes. That was why he would not ordinarily be sitting in a lady's lounge with his shirt collar unbuttoned, the tie slipped down no more than an inch, the buttons of his tunic unbuttoned so that the jacket gaped as sloppy-comfortably as any husband's jacket ever gaped when he got home for the first drink after a hard day at the office.

"Oh, hello there," the major said. "I imagine you're Peter McKenzie. Holly's back there, dressing to go out. I'm Jock Martin," and held out his hand.

Jeff Newton saw Peter's hands drop to his sides and the fingers curl upward, as if in tense supplication, as the long flat muscles of his arm bulged backward in his jacket. Jeff Newton saw the bulge and the stiff upcurling fingers and two white knots appear under Peter's ears at the corners of his jaw and the body bend forward just slightly as Peter made a small noise in his throat. So Jeff Newton did a very intelligent thing for an eleven-year-old boy. He swiftly drew his pistol and, taking it by the barrel, he hit his uncle Peter with the butt on the base of the skull, and Peter lunged forward on his face, taking the glass and a siphon and a silver bowl of roses off the top of the table with a shattering crash as he dived unconscious, headfirst, into the divan.

"I imagine you had best clear off," Jeff Newton said. "He won't stay unconscious very long, and I expect he won't be happy to see you still here."

The major slipped his tie upward against the unbuttoned collar, buttoned his jacket with one hand, and reached his cap and swagger stick off a table by the door.

"I expect you may very well be right, young man," he said. "Thank you very much. I rather imagine I'll pop along. Good-by."

The major went out the door as Holly McKenzie came into the room. She was wearing a cocktail dress, but her mouth wasn't made up. She took a swift look around and clapped the back of one hand to her unmade-up mouth and then took it away. Peter was still sprawled over the coffee table, with his head burrowed into a pillow. Jeff still held the pistol by its barrel. He flipped it, caught it by the butt, and shoved it back into the holster.

"He's all right," he said. "I had to tap him with the gun butt. He was going for your major, and I thought I'd better give him a headache rather than let him in for hanging. I'm leaving here now. Throw some water on him and pull his ears, and he'll be right. And tell him I'll be waiting for him at the Norfolk. Here are the keys to the jeep. It's parked outside. Good-by, Holly." Young Jeff walked to the door. His eyes were very old and cold. "I shouldn't imagine he'll beat you," he said, and went out into the hall, closing the door gently behind him.

There was really nothing to say, although Holly tried. She soaked some ice water into a towel and wiped Peter's face and then pulled gently at his ears, and he came up out of the sofa pillows with a start, shaking his head and touching the egg on the back of his skull. He looked at Holly as if she were a new and interesting insect.

"Jeff walloped me?" he said, feeling his bump. "Would you get me a whisky, please? I suppose your soldier took off. Intelligent of him. Smart of Jeff, too, to bung me with his gun. I suddenly got awfully angry. I'm sorry, truly. I think I might very well have killed that chap." He explored the lump on his head with tender fingertips.

Holly brought him a drink, and he drank half of it in a swallow.

"I don't suppose it's any good my telling you that there was nothing between Jock and me," she said, sitting down on one of the wing chairs. Then she got up. "Excuse me for a moment," she said, and went off to the bath. When she returned she was wearing lipstick.

"There actually isn't anything, you know. He's taken me about some. He's quite a nice chap, and he drops in for a drink now and again."

Peter held his hand up and spoke wearily.

"Leave it, Holly. It doesn't make any real difference. If there's nothing as yet, there would have been something soon. I can recognize a man who's at home in another man's house. Pukka soldiers don't slop about with their neckties loosened and their jackets unbuttoned in a house they're just visiting. Let it go. Drop it. If it wasn't this bloke it'd be another."

"What do you want me to do, then? I can't have this sort of living, with you striding in and killing people in the parlor, so to speak. We're finished, Peter. I don't suppose it's either of us's fault, any more than you can blame a pilot for that last Comet crash. We were finished that day in Mawingo when the phone rang, I expect. What exactly do you want?"

"Nothing at all, really. Mark you, Holly, I am *not* blaming you. But I'm not blaming me a dirty large hell of a lot, either. I didn't ask for this mess we've been mixed up in. But the mess is here on top of us and it has to be coped with and I live here and I will by God cope as long as I've anything left of me to cope with. You're not marked for Kenya, Holly. Some are, maybe, and some aren't, and you're one of the ones that aren't. Elisabeth is. Some other women are. It's nobody's right to say who is and who isn't, as some people don't like horses and other people are afraid of dogs. Go on back to England and leave this bloody mess to the copers. Your family's gone away now?"

"All but Jerry. He's being called up soon for the Kenya Regiment. Some South African has bought the farm. Mother's gone on ahead to London, and I expect Daddy'll be leaving inside of a month or so, when he's tidied up."

"Then go on back with him, for Christ's sake, back to where you belong. You want a divorce? Do you want to marry this chap?"

"I don't know. I really don't know. Actually he's got a wife. Back in Kent somewhere. I'm all of a muddle. I don't know. Oh, Peter, *Peter,* how sorry I am about it all. *Why* did it all have to work out this way?"

Peter got up. He looked around the flat at the lovely sofa and the lovely chairs and the lovely drapes and the lovely phonograph. He looked at the lovely Holly sitting there with her eyes a lovely red and her lovely mouth dragged down sadly and noticed that she had put lovely lipstick on it since she first came into the room so now it too was a lovely red. He felt deflated, dehydrated, as after a long game of football or polo. He felt shrunken and his head hurt like the very hell where that cheeky young bugger Jeff had walloped him.

"Look," he said. "I don't know. I don't know anything about anything any more, any more than you do. This has all been a little too swift for me. All I know is that we never had a real good go at it and I am most awfully sad about that. But so long as it has been bitched to hell I don't see, either, where there's much hope or much chance to haul it back together under the circumstances. I've still work to do; you've still time to pass. I don't particularly *like* to be coming home and finding strange gentlemen lounging about in the living room. If it *were* my home, which of course it isn't. My home's at Mwega."

"It's not fair, it's not *fair!*" Holly cried. "We had such a beautiful chance and now it's all ruined. It's not fair!"

"Nothing's very fair right now, except maybe Elisabeth's baby. He's fair. That's fair enough. I say"—Peter's eyebrows jerked upward—"you wouldn't be sort of pregnant or anything like that, would you?"

"It's a thing I've been spared," Holly answered. "No. Not pregnant. Not by you or anybody else."

"That's a mercy then. I should make an unholy great clamor about a child. Well, sweetie, it's like this, as I see it. We're married, and with all my worldly goods except my guns did I thee endow. So's if you'll decide on an allowance through some solicitor and Pa, I'm sure you'll be well off for cash. I'm sorry. Also, I'm off. Take care. And if you want a divorce I'm almost certain I can find time to supply the necessary grounds."

"So it ends up like it always ends up in the books," Holly said. "I'm dry-eyed now but presently I will go away and cry. I won't cost you very much money, Peter. And I won't do anything about the divorce. Another marriage is one experiment I don't think I care to make for a while."

Peter kissed her on the cheek.

"I'm off now. I won't make any fuss about your major. I'm sorry I started to go for him. You can call it Kenya nerves." He grinned with the corners of his mouth down-pulled. "Be brave, be happy, be full of cheer." And was gone.

And the worst part is that I'm glad it's over, Holly thought, and went into the bedroom to weep. But I think I could have loved him so and been such a good wife if all this mess hadn't happened.

And the awful thing is I'm relieved, Peter thought, because all along I saw it on the wall. Maybe I always was a bachelor. And I am bloody grateful to that little blighter Jeff. I must really have tossed my jockey there, to make Jeff decide to hit me that fast. Fancy the flap if I'd clobbered the major type. Him and his pretty decorations all nice and dead in the living room. Ah, well. But I didn't think she'd do it so fast. Really I didn't. I should have known. God knows I met enough of them on safari and off it in the old days.

Peter drove to the Norfolk, and from the road he saw young Jeff sitting on the veranda drinking a lemon squash. He parked the car in back and went in through the rear entrance and walked through the bar and nodded at Moussa and went out to the front porch, where Jeff sat at an iron table with his lemon squash. Peter dropped down on a chair and looked at the boy. He smiled as one adult to another.

"Thanks, asante sana kapisa, youngster. You saved everybody a great deal of trouble. But Jesus, did you have to hit me so hard?"

"There wasn't very much time, Peter. I just sort of swiped at you without thinking. You don't have any way of knowing what you looked like. If I hadn't smacked you, I think you might have killed him."

"I'm certain of it. Look, chum, if it's all the same to you. This wasn't really anything more than my terrible temper, which ranges from ferocious to horrible all the time. Actually there was nothing at all wrong with the bloke being there where he was. You know how it is; you're tired and nervy and cross and suddenly somebody does that one extra thing and then's when you kick the dog. I'd appreciate it a great deal, I'd be very grateful, if we just forgot this one. Holly's going home to England for a bit whilst this Mau Mau mess settles down. I'll tell Pa and your mum about it myself. It's all finished, I think, with Holly and me, but I shouldn't like it broadcast. She wouldn't be the first girl to find it a bit rough out here and dart off to England. It's just I don't want any point made of it. So we'll share this one between us, eh?"

"Of course," young Jeff said. "I say, *Uncle* Peter?" He stressed the "uncle."

"What?"

"Would you mind awfully if I had a beer?"

Peter looked swiftly away. There was a hot burning behind his eyes. His brain raced backward, eleven, twelve, nearly thirteen years ago. He was sitting under a flat-topped acacia on a plain with the father of this baby—this man—who sat now with him at the iron table on the veranda of the Norfolk Hotel. He had just taken his first public, adult-sanctified sip of whisky with the father of this man. Peter blinked his lashes rapidly and built a smile into his mouth.

"Jeff," he said, "it is always a pleasure to have a drink with an old friend, whether or not he's related to you. Boy! Letti hi hapa sasa beer-i kwa Bwana!"

25

And so that was how the stick floated, Peter thought as he drove away from Bushbuck Farm. He had dropped Jeff off. He had had some drinks with his father. He had had some more drinks without his father, from a bottle. He liked the phrase, that's how the stick floats. It was a phrase he'd picked up from Tom Deane. Tom explained it was what the old mountain men of America used to say. Something to do with beaver trapping and the general direction of current events. There she floats. Thar she blows. They went thataway. We'll cut 'em off at the draw, pardner.

It works out simply to the fact that I who once had a wife now have no wife, Peter thought precisely. I who was a professional hunter and am now still a professional hunter but for no dough. Damn that Deane. He corrupted my speech. Deane and whisky corrupted my speech. I quit professional hunting because it was no job for a married man, and my wife would not marry me unless I quit professional hunting. So I quit and got married. Check. So we had a little tragedy around the place and something called Mau Mau came into our lives, and I—he who was no longer a hunter—had to go away and become a hunter again, but still for no dough. The trophies were terrible. There wasn't any money in it, but it kept you away from home. It kept you out of the bars. The new wife of my bosom did not care for it at home when her husband was off being a professional hunter of people, and for this you certainly couldn't blame her, because the people her husband was hunting might slip down the hill someday and make her some new identification marks for her kipandi. Or cut off her head, perhaps, or burn down her bedroom, or whatever. So the lady didn't like it and she didn't like the sight of a sister-in-law who reminded her of a honeymoon that was cut short—excuse the word "cut"—out of painful necessity. So now this day I have no wife and I am still a hunter. But for no dough. And just a bit, just a touch, stinking.

Peter quit his silent thinking and formed his thoughts aloud as he shoved the Rover hard into a curve. It was a way he sometimes had when he was alone and especially if he was drunk.

"Now, so long as I am a hunter and working for no dough," he said aloud, "I'm allowed at least one trophy for my troubles. I never used to shoot any trophies for myself. In the Mau Mau thing I have shot only wart hogs and camp meat, so to speak. I think now I want to go and find me a fine trophy. I've lots of time to find it in. No home worries at all. None. Just so long as everybody else has got something to remember the beauty of the day by, I want a special souvenir for me. Something for the wall. I will see if I can't find my old boyhood chum—General Kimani, if you please—General Kimani, and ask him why he had to go and get slapped by Jeff Newton so that he started off the whole god-damned string of events that wound up with me not having any wife because Kimani cut off my sister's husband's head. I will collect old Kimani and hang him on the wall so that I can point him out to the guests as the beginning and the end of all my troubles. I don't know anybody else's got a general on the wall over the fireplace.

"Lathela!" he shouted over his shoulder to the man Lathela in the back seat. "Pass me the bottle. I find I'm dry, and the dust is heavy. We need rain, but I can't wait."

Lathela handed him the half-empty bottle of John Haig on which he had been working. Peter took a drink, coughed, shuddered, and handed the bottle backward over his shoulder.

"You ever see a general's head on anybody's wall?" he asked Lathela in English. "I wonder if you'd mount a general looking down or with his neck twisted to the right or left. How much headskin would you take from a general, a real true general, chum?"

Lathela made a polite noise. He hoped the Bwana Peter wouldn't drink very much more. The Bwana Peter was drunk, and when he was drunk he quite often drove off the road into ditches. It would certainly be a shame to spoil such a nice afternoon. The Bwana seemed very upset about something. But then the Bwana nearly always seemed upset about something, except when he was in the bush. It was only when the Bwana was both upset and drunk that he drove the car off the road. Since they were passing a high hill with a sheer drop on the near side, Lathela certainly hoped that the Bwana would drive the gharri off the other side, where there was only a field, if the Bwana felt like driving the car off any sort of road today.

"It would give a sitting room a nice homey touch." Peter was still talking in English. "Stick him smack over the fireplace, and of course you'd have to leave quite a bit of headskin. I *must* be mad. Where would you hang his medals if you didn't leave some headskin? But then I don't suppose Kimani's had any formal medals given him as yet. Heads are so perishable. Medals'll have to wait a bit until the campaign's settled down a bit more. What is the arm patch? I wonder. A strangled cat? In a way it's a pity I didn't collect that major. He had some medals. He had heaps of medals. I could have put his head on the other side of the general's head, and then if I was lucky I might have managed to bag myself a lieutenant colonel, and we could have had a museum group. Although I never liked groups. Rowland Ward make them, and they still clutter up the place like a museum. No, I won't put any competition up on the wall with my general. He'll have the wall all to himself. I think I'll mount him in a sneering sort of mount, with just the one corner of his mouth curled over his front fangs. Just one corner. I think a wide-open-mouth mount is corny."

It was drunk-talk, of course, but the next morning when Peter woke he woke on the bitter dregs of the foolishness and thought again about Kimani. In a land and in a time of symbolism Kimani made a very acceptable symbol. The spoor was clear all the way, the pitiful path that had turned a paradise into an abattoir. Kimani, Peter thought, was the black half of it as he himself was the white half of it, and the whole thing senseless. Whose fault all of it was didn't make any real difference now. You couldn't blame children for playing with matches and burning down the house, and you couldn't blame the man that made the matches, either. But after that you tried to keep the matches out of the reach of the child.

Take Kimani, Peter thought. He started out as a good kid with a fine father, but they civilized the outside of him and forgot all about his inside. They slapped a coat of paint on him, and that's supposed to hide the fact that his insides are just as roaming with demons and full of darkness as his grandfather's insides were. All this business of thahu was just as real to Kimani as a tree or a rock or a bushbuck. So the chain of events starts, and civilization takes over and good-kid Kimani becomes a thug and then a murderer and finally a Mau Mau general. You multiply him by a few thousands, and every one of those boys hidden out in the hills is another Kimani for about the same reason, one way or the other. They weren't Kikuyu any more and they weren't white men either. They were civilized enough to want cars and radios and to use guns and stealing to get cars and radios, when every one of them was still a naked savage underneath the spiv suits and the yellow shoes. We educated them and made them want things and took away their old securities and then didn't give them any other securities to replace what we'd taken. We gave them wants and didn't give them any way to gratify the wants. We took away a God they understood and tried to shove a white God into them and it didn't take, because a white God was like a white man, which meant that the white God would drink in the Norfolk, where they couldn't go except as servants, and the white God would clap his hands and yell "Boy!" when he wanted something done.

So now all the old ceremonies have been jazzed up to spell Mau Mau. All the old cattle raids and healthy battles between men whose business and pride were fighting were forbidden and now they get their rocks off with Mau Mau. I can't believe that there's a man up that hill who really started out as a "bad" man, any more than Kimani did or I did. And I am just as bloody a murderer as the men I kill. And I started out as what the women call a "nice boy." The only trouble was that we both believed that the same land belonged exclusively to us, and all of us were well trained to hunt.

The settlers hunted animals for food and sport and exterminated animals that threatened their land. The Wogs hunted animals for food and each other for sport and exterminated whatever it was that threatened their land. So then we develop a few superficially educated political damned fools like Kenyatta, who plays neatly into the hands of the Russians and the Indians, and who whips up his people into a fine religious frenzy and then loses control when the gangsters take over and his holy war suddenly isn't a holy war any more but a bloody aimless shambles without any point to the killing. We kill the Wogs, and the Wogs kill us, and the Wogs kill each other, and agriculture stops, and terror grows, and the bloody Russians and the Asians sit on the sidelines and laugh, like hyenas waiting for a sick lion to grow weak enough for the hyenas to walk in and gobble him. The people looking on laugh like hyenas laugh, because it is very funny to see a lion crawling with maggots, his spine broken, slowly starving. It is very funny to the vultures, too, circling slow in the sky for the lion to convert to carrion. It is always funny to see predators preying on each other, like that time I saw the hyenas fighting the wild dogs over a chunk of offal.

When I hunted animals I never minded leaving bits and tatters of hide and flesh behind for the birds and the jackals and the hyenas to eat. Nature's law, I used to tell the clients. It's the African way. Life-builds-on-death routine. Kill a zebra, take the hide, the boys eat the fat and some of the meat, the hyenas get their whack, and so do the birds and the little bat-eared foxes. Everybody's happy but the zebra, who is now just scraps of carrion which will enrich the soil to make more zebras fat for more lions to eat and more people to kill, and there she goes all over again. It takes on a slightly different perspective, though, when the carrion becomes men, and the birds and the hyenas become men. Yet what the hell can we do but fight fire with fire? We can run away and leave our homes that we made. We can run away and leave the land in a mare's-nest, with all the Wogs fighting each other and the jolly old Russian free to walk in and grab Africa, just as he's grabbed every place else where he planted his poison. Or we can hang on and try to kill enough of these buzzards all the way up from the bottom to those silly jailbirds and elevated bad-hats that call themselves "General," for Christ's sake, General and even "Field Marshal." Some snot-nosed cow watcher runs off to Nairobi and learns how to steal and wear pants and now he's a field marshal. I would love to catch me a field marshal and give him to old Lathela to play with. I would love to catch me a general, even. I think that if we collected enough generals the colonels might start to fight with the majors over who was going to take the command. Maybe that idea I had about collecting Kimani last night was sound, drunk or not. We haven't really collected many of the top brass since Mau Mau quit being a gang and became an army. I even hear they got a "rest camp" for the valiant military Mau Mau over by Kilimanjaro, where they send themselves on compassionate leave. Maybe I will safari-off and look for old Kimani or one of his associate brain-trusters. I'll have a word with the head office.

26

So Peter went to Bill Falconer, the police chief under whom he worked, and invited him to ride into Thomson's Falls for a beer to cure Peter's hangover. They had proper base camps now, outside of the Falls and Nanyuki and Nyeri and Fort Hall, proper barracks with tanks and air strips and all the other pukka drill.

"I'd like a little time off from the regular stuff," Peter told Falconer. "I haven't told anybody yet, Bill, but I'm pretty well shot. Nerves shaky as hell. Holly's left me. I'd appreciate it if you didn't mention that to anybody, but she's packed up. She's off to England."

"That's a damned shame, Peter," Falconer said. "That's a very rum go. But it's happening to a lot of the chaps. This isn't much life for a woman here now. Constant strain and the men away. My old lady and I fight *all* the time when I'm home. Any chance of patching it up?"

"I doubt it. You had some chance to start your marriage. I was married two days when the hell cut loose. I don't see how you can blame a woman for not liking the kind of life Holly's had from the first day of her marriage. Hell, man, all she knows about me is that I'm always off in the bush killing people, and all she knows of happy home life is Mau Mau raids and my sister dragging around with half her head cut off. The only baby Holly's had any contact with wasn't even her own baby. It was a dead man's. No, there's bloody small show for Holly and me."

"Well, if you want some time to go back and make a final stab at it, I can easily spare you from this next do. One of the other boys can track for the soldier lads."

"Thanks. But I don't want the time off to go to Nairobi and start screaming at Holly. I want to go off into the bush on my own with Lathela and just disappear. There is a family matter I want to attend to. You know that Wog, Kimani, who's billed as one of the top "generals" now? The lad from my farm that old Njogu told us led the expedition that chopped Jeff? He's been bothering me a lot lately. We've not had much luck with the high brass. They always seem to be off somewhere else when we make a sweep. We collect the sergeants and the subalterns. I'd like just one crack at collecting my old childhood playmate. The son of a bitch has singlehandedly mucked up my life and most of my family's as well. I think I know how to find him if I'm given the time. He's got to have a well-hidden cave if he's a general. You don't find caves by blundering about with a lot of heavy-footed soldiers crashing through the bush like a herd of elephants. Give me a couple of months. If I can't find him in that time I'll come back and go back to teaching the soldiery the difference between a track and the King's Highway."

"Well, sure, Peter. Go and course your Wog. I hope you kill him painfully, but it would be very nice if you brought him back alive."

"I don't think there's much chance of that. I'll bring you his head instead. As much as anything else, Bill, I want to get back in the bush on my own again. I feel now like I used to feel at the end of a long and difficult safari with a herd of stinking clients. I've a very bad taste in my mouth. I think perhaps a bit o' time hunting with Lathela will recharge my batteries. If it's all right with you I'll push off this afternoon. I'm not taking much, about the same kit we used when we first scouted the operation."

"Let's have another beer. Steward! Beer-i mbile. There's hell's own number of men in those hills, chum. How you'll reckon to haul one man out of one hole, I can't say."

Peter grinned and reached for the fresh beer.

"There may be hell's own amount of men in the hills, but I know hell's own amount of holes in the same hills. You never hunted anything but people, Policeman. If you'd hunted animals as much as I have, you'd know you first have to turn yourself into the precise animal you're hunting. You have to imagine that you're a sick old bull with hundred-and-thirty-five-pound ivory and that you've kept those teeth in your skull for a hundred years by being smart. There are only so many special places for a big bull to be smart in. It's the same with leopards. I never had any trouble getting leopards. It's just a matter of choosing the one particular tree that you'd love if you were a leopard, and then deciding whether you'd adore to find some dog, some baboon, some wart hog, some Grant, or some impala hanging in that tree you would love to sit in. Don't forget, I was the lad who dug out the Old Man of the Douma after everybody else'd had a shot at him for years."

"That was that enormous great lion with the black mane hanging down to his knees like a skirt, wasn't it?"

"The very same. *He* lived in a cave too. I took along a drunken old lion tracker named Kibiriti, a Waikoma bucko, and we went out and sniffed and peered and thought and made medicine and played hunches, and one day we came onto a cave and there was the Old Man, for God's sake, asleep in front of the cave in the sunlight. He'd been there so long he didn't even bother to hide his tracks going to it or coming away from it. The cave was so obvious that you wondered why nobody'd stumbled onto it. Kibiriti and I backed off, and the Old Man never quit snoring. We went and retrieved the client from the Grummetti campi, shoved him back up the hill the next day, and there was the Old Man, still snoozing in his favorite sun spot. Client walked up like you'd walk up to a topi, walloped the Old Man in the ear, and the old gentleman never woke up. He flopped over like a dirty big dog with all four feet in the air, and that was all there was to the Old Man of the Douma."

"You figure this Wog of yours has been run to earth for so long that he's got sloppy?"

"Something like that. From what I've been able to get out of interrogations, he's been on and off that mountain for ten years, ever since he whipped that spear into Jeff and took off for the high timber. He would have found a hidey-hole somewhere. Very few people would know about it. He'd be extra-careful about telling many people about it, because for some reason or other he would like that hole better than any other. He'd be happy in it. He'd never allow any large concentration of people near it. He'd probably have some women in it, and all the comforts of home. He'd leave it less and less except to plot with the other big shots. In police work, you know damned well that a man can hang himself with his habits. He drops into little careless habits without being aware that he's making a pattern. All animals do it. A man on a mountain is more animal than man if he's been up the hill long enough. I'll find him. It'll just take some time to sort him out. Between this animal Lathela of mine and myself, we'll sort out the son of a bitch all right. Sort him out and kill him and fetch you his headskin. And if we can collect him, I reckon I can collect China and Kaleba and Kemathi and the other boys the same way, whilst you polish off the middlemen and search the shambas. The big boys have stayed snug too long."

"Apt to find they've checked in at the hotel as M-G-M extras." Bill Falconer smiled. "Well, crack off, then, boy, and very good hunting to you."

"Thanks, Bill. I think I'll just go on back to base now and collect my wild man and some chow and a little gear. Thanks."

They finished their beer and walked back to the jeep. They nodded to a man with a bandaged arm, a man who wore a tweed jacket and who had a shotgun slung over his back. With his good hand he held a leash attached to a monstrous Alsatian dog.

"You hear about that one?" Falconer asked as the tweed-coated man went into the pub. "Bloke named Charles Phillips, got a little shamba not so far from here. A gang went for him the other night, and that monstrous great wolf created an amazing diversion. The beast spoilt the first rush and they only just nicked Phillips. He shot his pistol hot and didn't bother to reload. He scooped up a panga one of the boys had dropped and actually beheaded the cook with the panga. Case of poetic justice or something. Mild-looking little bloke, ain't he?"

"Why," Peter asked, as they got into the jeep, "why does it *always* have to be the cook?"

Bill Falconer didn't bother to answer. They drove out through the circular court and roared down the road for camp, passing a long line of troop-crammed carriers on the way. The lorries raised a considerable amount of dust.

Peter and Lathela walked carefully up the mountain and settled on a hill where they could rest quietly and look around and think. At first they did not attempt to hunt. They did not want to hunt. They weren't interested. They wanted to sit quietly and think about what they might hunt and where they might hunt it. They built a tiny fire in a shallow hollow indented in the side of a rocky butte and sat outside the hollow, letting the rocky walls bounce the warmth outward, and they talked much at night. They always ate together now and slept together for warmth. The proper formal business of Bwana and man had all gone away, had gone a long time away. Peter thought of Lathela now as a completely talented and trustworthy hunting dog who lay at your feet and slept in your bed and would find any game he was asked to find, who would die fighting in front of you, and who would never question anything you did up to and including the killing of him if there was a sound reason for it. In the bush Lathela accepted Peter conversely, for in the bush Peter was able to do most things as well as Lathela, some things better, but very few things worse. Peter couldn't climb a tree as well as Lathela, or swarm as swiftly up a steep uneven ladder of rock. But then Lathela couldn't shoot as well as Peter, either.

"Listen to me, nugu," Peter said the second night, after they had swept some country, traveling separately, spreading out like bird dogs searching a covert. "What would you do if you knew these mountains very well and wanted a safe place to hide, no matter how much activity went on around you? A permanent place, I mean, not just a place to spend a night or so."

"Bwana," Lathela said, squatted on his heels, his thighs braced against his lower legs, so that his knees nearly framed his face. "Bwana, I have hunted many things. I have found that men are more difficult than bees, but not much. I have hunted kudu, and I have hunted bongo, and all the other hill animals. Let us consider a moment. Suppose we go to Tanganyika and we hunt kudu at Kandoa Arangi. What do we do? We go and sit on a hill with the glasses and we look, we look all day, every day, and when we see a kudu flick an ear we walk many painful miles up the mountain until we come up to the kudu, or to where the kudu might be likely to go, and wait a long time, and then we shoot a kudu.

"Or let us say we are after elephants. We do not walk a million miles asking other elephants if they have seen any very good elephants lately. We drive up and down the dry river beds in the gharri, and from time to time we may see a track. If it is a heavy track, and a bull's track, we follow it, walking in the heat and through the thickets of palmetto, and finally we come up on the elephant and he has only one tusk. So we do not shoot that elephant. We walk another twenty miles back to camp. We ride up and down the river bed again until we find another big footprint, and maybe when we walk a very long way to track this print down to the animal that makes it the elephant has two big tusks and so we shoot it. We cut away the tusks and go back to camp, and the camp boys dance and sing and wave wands in celebration, hoping for money." When Lathela said "camp boys," he spat.

"Now if we were to be hunting kudu up past Iringa on the Ruaha, we do not trouble very much about the glasses. We merely ride the roads, do we not, and very often we see kudu on the roads. We go also to the licks, where the salt is crusted on the rocks and where a kudu may come to drink the water and muzzle salt at the same time. Or we go down to the bank of the river where grows that strange shrub which drives the kudu mad. Or we go each day and see if there are any kudu feeding round a shamba in which a death has occurred so that all the people have gone away and the old crops grow wild. There are many ways of hunting kudu in the mountains. There are times of the year when the old bulls are away from the young bachelor bulls, waiting high in the hills by themselves. There are other times when each old bull takes his harem of cows and works low to the river and frequents the licks. There are times in the rutting season when an old bull is apt to be as stupid as a calf, and blunders about with his hearing closed to noise and his nose closed to scent, his neck swollen and his balls rolling around where his brain should be.

"There are many complications, as you know, to hunting. There is the time when the lion will refuse to come out of the thorn, and so you must kill a topi and leave the topi for the hyenas and birds to work at, and then the lion becomes angry and rushes out from the bush. I have not hunted sable, but I am told that it is best around Tabora when the grass is burnt flat and the food very scarce and the sable must come to the low country for food. But I have seen klipspringers in the Masai in one valley on the lower Mara where there are not supposed to be any klipspringers. I have hunted through the high hills of Tanganyika, up by the Kiteti wood, and you know that all the desert animals are congregated there, the oryx and the long-nosed rhino and the gerenuk, even, although oryx are desert animals and so are gerenuk, and you would not expect to find them up in the hills by Kiteti, away off in Tanganyika, where everything except the Rift as it ends and the lake as it begins is swamp. But there they are, for some reason I cannot explain."

"You are taking a very long time to answer my question, chum," Peter said. "What you are getting around to is exactly?"

"I would not hunt this man as I would hunt kudu. I would not hunt him as I would hunt elephant or lion or leopard or klipspringer or kudu or even bongo or buffalo. I would hunt him as I would hunt a wildebeest if there were only one wildebeest in the world. I would hunt him as I would hunt a topi or anything else stupid. I would hunt him as a *man*."

"By God, I think you may be right, Lathela. In other words, we hunt him by guess and by hope and by dumb luck."

"Yes, Bwana. But only remembering that a man is not very intelligent, and so a man is apt to make more mistakes than an animal. So: a rhino will walk twenty miles each day to a water hole. Will a man? No. Especially if he has a manamouki who does not wish to walk that far to a water hole. Is a man intelligent? Yes. So he looks to find a safe place to hide that is close to a water hole or a spring.

"An animal has a thick hide and he does not care much about weather, except perhaps the lion, who does not care for it when it rains and pains his joints. But a man cares much for comfort. So a man would certainly want a place where he could be warm when it is cold and dry when it is wet. And which is near to water, which he must have to live, and which also is near to fuel, which he must have to cook his food."

"All right, all right, I follow," Peter said. "Teach me my business."

"Yes. To continue. What food does the man eat? He cannot cultivate a shamba, not now. If he is a big man and an important man he will want good food and much meal sent in to make beer of. He will not want to share his good food with the common men or allow them to know that he drinks beer when they have no beer. He certainly will not want to let them know where his hiding place is. But the hiding place must be *close*—it must be close to water. It must be close to where he can get food. It must be reasonably close to where he can find fuel. It must be close to where the other men are that he does not want to know where he lives. It must be a place where his women and possibly his guns can be hidden safely. Hence it must be a cave. Hence it must be a cave that is hidden so well that it is a trick to find it. Hence it will need luck to find it, but I have always thought that a man walking down is luckier than a man walking up. And that a man who wishes to run, runs down instead of up. And that a man is always willing to climb to get to a place he likes but is not willing to climb to get away from it. And finally, Bwana, a man stays closer and closer to a place he likes, as he gets older, and sends people to do things for him. It would seem to me that what we do is go up high and hunt down; that we watch to see how many people move to do what for somebody who does not appear to thank them for what has been done. It seems to me that we start at the top of the hills and search down, always remembering that there should be no trail leading to a hiding place, but that somebody will make one, without knowing that he has made one."

"I wish I had some whisky to offer you, friend," Peter said. "I just said the same thing to the chief of police. And I am nowhere such a fine hunter as you, Lathela. We will hunt as you say. We will hunt humans and not credit them with too much intelligence, eh?"

"That is right, Bwana," Lathela said. "I think we should sleep now and go hunting in the morning as one might hunt a man who, if he is not at the Norfolk Hotel, would possibly be in the Regal bar over the theater where you spend so much time."

"Oh, go to hell and put out the fire," Peter said. "I want to go to sleep."

"It is just as well that I was not hunting you, Bwana." Lathela laughed softly. "This is the ninth time you have used this place to sleep in, and you always make a fire that casts a small glow as you would see if you go over yonder on that hill and climb a tree."

And so they hunted Kimani as they would hunt a man, bearing in mind that a man leaves his habitation to attend to the daily wants of nature, and goes well away from where he eats and sleeps, and goes always to the same place. If he is living long in a place he will make a rough latrine. So Lathela and Peter kept their eyes downcast to the ground, looking for a trail which would lead to excrement. They looked always for a trail that led round to water or to fuel, led round to where the water or the fuel was, but which stopped abruptly on the back track. They looked for lightly trodden paths that threaded into thickets of the mountain bamboo or tight-packed trees and died suddenly without explanation. They searched for trails leading up the mountain, that dwindled and disappeared without reason. They looked for trails creeping down the mountain, trails that began without justification and then wound down to mingle with other trails.

Peter never smoked in the bush now, and he was not drinking, for there was nothing to drink. His nose developed its old animal keenness, and as they hunted, circling out and crossing back on each other, their nostrils sucked in and out as they tested the wind. They were able in that way to smell each other sometimes for half an hour before they met. Lathela wore the shooting binoculars now, and he scurried up trees more easily than they could press through the dripping, tight-clenched bush. They had run out of food in a few days; Lathela now made snares for small game, and they both whittled bows and arrows, tipping the arrows with the metal from cartridge cases, split first and then flattened and honed sharp with Peter's oilstone. They fed off small game from the snares and an occasional bushbuck or duiker they shot with the arrows. They ate tuberous roots and some berries, and they were seldom ever able to cook the meat. It was too wet to make biltong, even if they had the time or the sunshine. Peter's liver was squeezed clean of poisons; as his mind was squeezed clean of his past experience with the Mau Mau, of his troubles with Holly, of his memories of the massacre. Nothing lived in his head now but Kimani, and he did not think of Kimani as Kimani, but as quarry. He thought of him as impersonally as a man might regard a difficult problem in chess or mathematics. X plus K divided by C to the third power equaled a cave. The cave equaled Kimani. Peter lost more than a stone of weight. His body was as spare as a whalebone quirt. He gave no thought to the freezing nights and soggy-dripping days or the cold, hard, wet ground on which he slept. His mind, heart, soul, and body were compressed into hunting.

Sometimes they allotted themselves sectors of hills and slopes and forests and spent a week apart fine-combing the ground. They found many caves, sometimes with people living in the caves. They came across many little shambas and marked them all with red checks in their minds for future extermination. But they avoided contact with the gangs and did not have to kill anyone. There were very many people on the mountain, because the trackers were constantly leading troops of soldiers up to the little pockets of concentrated people, and daily the planes were bombing, and men fled before the raids.

On several occasions they spotted tiny clearings which had been used as impromptu latrines. They spotted little clearings which had been cleaned of fallen logs and chopped out for dead bush. They became excited and followed the habit trails to where each might end, and then they sifted every inch of the bush, spreading every branch, inspecting every stone, as a man would sift ashes for some small valued object in the ruins of a hut. Two months passed swiftly, and there was still no sign of Kimani.

One rain-pouring morning Peter slid out from under his poncho and stretched his aching muscles. He looked about him at the dismal sea of dank black-green bush and gray-outcropping rock and suddenly felt the old stomach twist of excitement. It was the same old surge of the hunch muscles in his belly, with the same down-dropping, fast-falling upward rush of stomach to the throat, burning of face and tautening of neck skin, so that the hairs prickled separately. He turned to Lathela.

"I think our luck may be changing," he said. "Yesterday I found a porcupine quill. Today I feel a monkey in my belly. I think today we might find him."

"Let us hurry then and find him and kill him," Lathela said. "I am sick of these mountains, and I believe we have covered every foot of them. Let us hurry before your luck goes."

"Come with me today," Peter said. "We will hunt together."

It was Lathela who found the tiny clearing no bigger than a rhino wallow where brush had been cleared, stroked slanting with the blade of a panga. They had passed and missed it every time. It was Peter who found another clearing where a huge, fallen log had been cleaned of its punky insides, and there were nail marks and knee marks on the floor of the logs, where someone, someone small, had crawled inside to claw out the punk. It was Lathela who ran upon another clearing, backed by rock on two sides, so that a man on his morning business would have his back and one side protected as he squatted down with his gun. The clearing was cobbled with old dung, as the white sands of the dry river beds are cobbled when lack of water forces the elephants and rhinos in to the lugas from the dried plains and they come in throngs to leave their droppings. Some of the droppings were fresh—a day past. It was Peter who heard a sweet whispering behind a green-mossed ferny rock and who found the tiny spring which bubbled and chuckled and sent a tiny stream of water down a hillside to disappear and die in thick wet bush. The basin of the spring had been scratched round. It was just deep enough to immerse the lips of a water gourd. Small beaten paths led into each clearing and to the spring. All these paths backtracked, to be lost in bush. But as the trails ended there was other sign. Again, a sapling had been pushed so frequently aside that it had lost resiliency and leaned misshapen in a way no wind would warp it.

Here there were branches with leaves slightly bruised and then brown-crumpled on the edges from passage. Here a stone, its wet side jostled by a hasty foot, there an upturned slab of mold on cold wet ground. These little signs led nowhere except into the infinity of the bush, but they screamed that the person who used the little trails adopted caution at the end and went each day along another path—scraping, perhaps, the bark of a tree or wearing it shiny with a repeated rubbing on the tender scars of the earlier bruises. Here was spoor; here was sign. It was easy to triangulate the clearings and the springs and to fan out, pushing each sapling aside, looking carefully around each tree. They worked from up to down, then they worked from down to up.

And finally they found the cave. They found it by accident, as Kimani had found it himself in the long, long ago. They were prowling carefully down a long slope of hard rock, loosely grown with bush, when Lathela, out well ahead, stepped into some low bush and almost disappeared. He crawled back onto the shale and pushed Peter backward with his hand. They walked backward as a man might walk backward when he nearly treads on a sleeping rhino, for a hundred yards, softly, toes placed first and heels gently seeking the sod. Then they turned and walked silently half a mile before Lathela stopped. During the time they walked Peter had not questioned Lathela.

"Bwana," Lathela said. "There is a cave under that lip of rock. I almost fell into it. There is a little yard, no bigger than a small room, which is behind a big shield of stone. I smelt old smoke when I slipped, and a tiny smell of cooking fat. Outside the shield of rimrock there is a big stand of bamboo. I believe that we will find tomorrow that all the little trails from the little clearings will spread like the fingers of your hand, and the palm of that hand will be the bamboo. They have left the bamboo as a ring of spears about that little entrance into the rock, and they go a half mile, at least, through the bamboo before they head to water or to firewood or to empty their insides. He has been very clever, to stay hidden all this time. But I do not believe that any man could find this cave without accident. Maybe your porcupine quill found the cave for us. I placed my foot forward carefully and my toes groped for the ground and suddenly I felt myself fall. If I had not seized the bushes"—and Lathela plucked some thorns from his palms—"if I had not caught myself on the thorn, I should have gone tumbling down into the entranceway to the cave."

"How will we watch the cave to see if our man is the man in it?" Peter asked. "You can't see anything from up top. There aren't any trees nearby that you could spy from. From what you tell me, the whole thing is masked by the stone shield and the bamboo in front and the bush on top."

"We could do one of several things. We might go to where the man visits in the morning, but I think he will go in the dark, and that is no good. We could hope to find him coming out through the bamboo where the other trails cross, but that could take a month. I think that the man Kimani must come out and sit in the little paddock between the rock shield and the entrance to the cave. A man needs air if he lives in a cave. Once in a while there is some sun. Perhaps he has a habit of sitting outside the cave door. We could creep close to where the rim of the rock drops, at night, and sit there very quietly and see. He will not hear us through the rock roof of the cave if we come very, very quietly at night and sit there and freeze until we hear him stirring as he comes out of the cave entrance and goes around the corner of the rocky shield and then goes out through the bamboo. We can get as close as I got, and that is on the very edge. If anybody heard me when I missed my footing, they would think it was an animal. But we should not return for several days. We would not want to frighten him, and he will be wary if any sound was heard when I stumbled. He might even change his place of living. A man like Kimani would have many different places to hide. In any case, we could go and hide in that big tree near where you saw the spring. We could see if a woman comes there for water, and we could watch the way she disappears when she leaves the little trail."

"I think not. We could make one mistake and frighten her and she'd take off and we've had her. I think this is the one we've looked for. If it isn't Kimani it'll be another snug little bug worth squashing. Is there any way we could chuck a bombom into the cave?"

"No, Bwana. There is only a little yard, as I said. If we crept through the slit in the rock the force of the bombom would blow us backward. We must sit like nugus over the top of the cave and wait for the leopard to come out of his hole. That is best. When he comes out into the sunlight he will come bent over, and then he will straighten up and stretch his arms and possibly stop to scratch. Then if you stand straight up perhaps you can shoot down. That might be difficult. There is much bush on the slope of rock that makes the roof of the cave."

"How would *you* do it?"

"I would sit in the bush over the entrance to the cave. I would take a knife and cut a little peephole in the bush during the night, so that I might see a little. And then when the man comes out of the cave I would shoot if I could shoot, or if I could not shoot I would jump down on his back and kill him in the little yard with a knife. Or something. Perhaps a pistol."

"But we have no pistol. You know we left the pistol in camp, to make the load lighter, since a pistol is only good on farms and in cities."

"So then if I could not shoot him with a gun and if I could not throw a bombom into the cave—and we have only *two* bomboms in any case—I would jump on his back as a leopard waits by a water hole to leap onto an impala."

"Muzuri. So we will give him a night or so and then we will go and crouch in the grass, eh, and wait for him to come out. It'll be bloody cold, waiting."

"We have been cold before, Bwana. A little more cold will not kill us. It would have killed us already if we were going to be killed by cold."

"We'll wait, then."

27

The waiting was as miserable as all waiting can be, and was triply miserable since it was done squatting in dripping, clammy bush, with a wild wind prowling through the bush and each hair on your hand collecting its own particular tiny freezing drop of moisture. They waited each night for a week, creeping onto the rocky bush-covered roof of the cave after midnight, squatting on the edge of the slope, peering through a tiny tunnel that they had softly sliced through the bush. The woman came out regularly. Peter sighted on her as she came stooping, backward, out of the cave, and found that if he waited until she slipped just through the slot in the rocky shield he could hold her in his sights for a second and command a shot at the upper third of her body and a clear view of her head. She had to turn her body sideways to squeeze through the slot in the stone, and as she turned she faced the top of the hill that roofed the cave.

Several times she came into the open veranda and brought a child. They could not see her or the child, for they sat motionless too far back from the drop of the rock to see her when she rested at the entrance to the cave, waiting for a tiny faded flicker of sun to wash her threshold feebly. But they could hear her talking to the child. Once, then again, Peter heard her call the child "Karanja." His heart skipped, for while there are only so many names in the Kikuyu language, Karanja would certainly be what Kimani would call his son, since the grandfather's name automatically passed to the first-born. Peter wondered what the baby looked like as it cooed and gurgled in the little stony courtyard beneath the bush where he and Lathela crouched, waiting high on the hill. Obviously the child's father was away, probably on some mission or other, for the woman went alone for wood and water. I suppose she ties the child into some sort of crib when she's gone, Peter thought.

They stayed each night from just after midnight to about ten in the morning. When the woman went off to the spring, they wriggled backward like snakes and disappeared swiftly in an opposite direction from the watering place, from the fuel places, from the latrine places. They waited two weeks, and still there was no Kimani.

As they waited in the freezing wet, in the low thorn and dripping mountain gorse, Peter thought a great deal about Kimani. He recalled, in the boring dark wet night, each exact detail of the warrior's battle they had had that fine day on Bushbuck Farm before they had gone off on safari with Jeff Newton. Peter could project it brightly in his brain, like a cinema, as he squatted freezing on his heels and waited. He replayed it as a man might play, over and over again, a favorite song, until it stood out sharp and clear against his memory. It was only kid games then, of course, and little Holly Keith was only two hundred and fifty Masai maidens to be ravished and carried away to a life of shame. The little Kikuyu girl was named Kabui. There was Mister Mac, the goat. Whatever had happened to Mister Mac? There was his sister Elisabeth, who had broken up the war games. How had it gone, so far away, however had it *gone?* That day he remembered, when he had killed the Tommy with the spear. That day so different from this sitting in the sopping bush waiting for a man he didn't even feel sure was the same Kimani to come back to a cave. But how, now, it fitted so strangely into place.

The night passed slowly, and nothing stirred below. Then, just as dawn diluted the black sky, there was a rasp of clothing against the rock below. Peter felt Lathela's hand tighten on his arm. There was another scuffing sound of clothing on rock, and then a crackling in the bush outside the shield of rock and the sound of a man picking his way through the bush. Both Peter and Lathela knew it was a man, since they were thoroughly familiar with the woman's sound, and the woman never left the cave this early, in any case. Peter turned his head slowly and looked sidewise at Lathela. In the dim streaky light Lathela nodded. It was a man, gone away into the forest to relieve himself. He would relieve himself and return, to sleep again, possibly, or to eat, or to collect his gear to leave the cave. So he had come to the cave yesterday, very late in the day or early in the night. And it would be light enough to shoot when he returned, if it was the man they sought who returned, and Peter's belly told him it would be the man he sought. His right hand automatically caressed each detail of the rifle's curved trigger, the knurled safety catch that flipped crosswise over the breech, stiff-locked on safety now, the trigger rigid under his finger, the steel hot-freezing in his hand, the wood warmer and pleasant to the touch.

It was quite full light, the sun showing red when they heard a rustle again in the bush, the rattle of a bamboo as it was shoved aside and sprang back against a neighbor. Then there were sounds of footsteps returning softly and with assurance, and then a swaying in the top of the bush close by the rock that guarded the cave, and then the sound of fabric brushing against rock again.

Kimani came crabwise through the slot in the shield stone, and Peter's rifle went up under his eye. The fore sight rested in the hollow of Kimani's throat, its bead barely showing through the deep V of the iron rear sights.

A thought flashed through Peter's mind. *So this is how he looks now. I wonder if I have changed as much. I wonder if time has done that to my face as well.*

It was Kimani, there was no mistaking him. But the jaw was brutally heavier, the eyes habitual slits, the nose broken, scar-slash on face, lips turned thinly down and locked at the corners, deep grooves running from nostril to mouth like gullies, wrinkles slicing across his nose between the eyes and gouging furrows through his forehead. A man with no smile for the morning or any other part of the day. He had a gun slung over one shoulder, a .318 that had belonged to Jeff Newton. He paused a second as he slid through the slot in the rock, and looked directly into Peter's eyes, searching the top of the cave for motion and finding none. Peter closed one eye and his finger softly squeezed the trigger. It stopped squeezing for no reason at all that Peter would ever be able to explain. It stopped just before he stroked it into releasing death in a soft-point bullet just below Kimani's Adam's apple. Peter laid the gun aside carefully and drew his legs taut under him, easing his knife out of the sheath. It was the long Spanish knife that had been honed thin and incurving like a butcher's blade.

"Kimani!" Peter screamed, and leaped.

The roar of Peter's voice and the crash through the bush were loud as thunder in Kimani's ears, the leap through the bush louder than a herd of buffalo stampeding. Peter's surge carried him eight feet straight down the side of the cliff face and halfway into the little courtyard. He hit the ground on one flat-spread hand, his knees and his toes, his joints loose to take the shock of the jump. Without rising he lunged forward again and dived straight for Kimani's legs as Kimani moved away from the stone wall and half clawed the gun from its sling over his shoulder. Peter's left shoulder smashed into his legs, and the shock carried Kimani backward against the stone of the rocky shield, the gun slipping loose and flying off to one side, where it landed with a clatter of metal on stone. Kimani's back rammed against the rock, and Peter's forehead drove into the rock as his head and right shoulder plowed past Kimani's knees. The knife darted from his hand. Both men were stunned for less than an eighth of a second, and both reeled away from each other, each losing the other. Peter's short haziness persisted perhaps one sixteenth of a second longer than Kimani's surprise. Kimani had dragged his knife out now. He turned and dived for Peter with knife hand high as Peter moved from the wall and crouched, shaking his head. The woman inside the cave heard the noise and rushed to the entrance, coming out stooped with a panga in her hand. Lathela, standing erect at the lip of the cave's roof, heard the woman coming and saw the flash of the panga. Lathela speared her through the shoulders just below the neck as she stooped, coming out of the cave. She went flat on her breast onto the shaly ground, pinned by the spear, and one hand flung the panga ringing away. Lathela picked up Peter's gun and sighted it on the back of Kimani, but decided not to shoot. This was the Bwana's shauri. He was not supposed to shoot. Else the Bwana would not have put the rifle aside to jump like a goat and make a fight with only a knife. It was the Bwana's shauri. He would watch it.

When Kimani dived for Peter, Peter turned completely over and kicked out with his feet, catching Kimani a glancing blow in the groin and deflecting the downward swish of the knife, which bit into the ground beside Peter's ear. Kimani's heavy body crushed down on top of

Peter, and Kimani jerked the knife clear of the pebbly ground as Peter's left hand found Kimani's wrist. Peter's knife glittered on the ground, six feet away.

Peter's thick legs locked round Kimani's waist, his ankles crossing behind and gripping each other firmly as his shoes chocked into each other as he pulled Kimani's body close, holding Kimani's belly to his belly, spreading past his hips Kimani's knees, which searched for Peter's groin. Kimani's left hand flashed to Peter's throat, and the fingers bit into Peter's neck. Peter's right hand took Kimani's left wrist. The men no longer thrashed. The pressure was slow and evenly exerted.

Peter's eyes were bulging and his breath closing in his throat when his right-hand pressure on Kimani's choking hand began to loosen the fingers on Peter's throat. The left hand fought the knife away from Peter's breast. The knife dipped down and touched flesh, cutting shallowly once, twice again, before Peter's left hand forced the knife wrist out to the left and slightly backward, turning the wristbones against the inflexible foundation of the elbow. At the same time the choking hand left Peter's throat and the fingers spread from the enormous pressure Peter's right hand gave the wristbones of the choking hand. Peter forced extra pressure into his left leg, as it gripped the small of Kimani's back, and bent his body ever so slightly to the left, carrying the knife hand more and more to the left and around backward, twisting it ever so slightly more upon itself. The men breathed harshly, grunting, the breath whistling through their flared nostrils, grunting deep in their chests, as they fought each other's wrists.

Peter gripped Kimani's surging body harder with his legs, slightly relaxed his tension on the knife hand, and forced a tremendous leverage up and over the right hand of Kimani, and heard the elbow crunch and go. He dropped the dead arm, which flapped, and as Kimani's breath whistled and he screamed sharply once, Peter's right hand went up to the throat that now poised over him and sank his thumb to the knuckle into the little hollow of the neck. The men looked into each other's eyes as Peter gasped breath back into his lungs. Kimani's eyes bulged, bloodstreaked from the distended veins. Peter held a steady backward pressure now on the knife hand, not forcing, but holding, as the wrists locked, darted like birds, back and forth, swooping in, pressing backward. At the same time he increased the leverage of his left leg and harnessed his right shoulder muscles behind the long flat biceps and sent a ripple of extra effort down along his tensed forearm into the choking wrist. Kimani's mouth opened and his tongue crept slowly past his teeth, as an animal emerges from its burrow. Peter squeezed. The knife hand weakened. Peter squeezed again on the throat. The tongue came out more, hesitantly, and the knife hand gave an eighth of an inch. Peter squeezed. Then he slightly retracted his left hip, rolling a little more to the left. Then Peter really squeezed, and wrenched the left leg as he squeezed, shoving, to the left with his right knee. The knife dropped out of Kimani's left hand, and Peter heaved again and flopped him over. The knife was under Kimani's back and Peter was on top of Kimani now, with a knee in Kimani's groin and both hands fastened to the throat. Kimani's unbroken hand clawed at the hands on his throat and beat at Peter's face. Peter buried his knee deeper into Kimani's groin, and Kimani beat his legs wildly past Peter's back. The knee that bit into Kimani's groin now crept high up on his chest, and Peter hunched his shoulders close to his neck and took a deep, sobbing breath and squeezed. Kimani's tongue came all the way out past his teeth, and the eyes suffused in blood as the tiny vessels broke. There was a slight crick and then a sharp crack, as if a man had trodden on a dry stick, and Kimani's body went limp. Peter took his thumbs away from Kimani's throat and pulled his fingers out of Kimani's neck and wiped them on Kimani's shirt front.

Peter stood up and looked down at Kimani. He touched the bruises on his own wrists, the sharp hurting points where his back had been scored by tiny rocks, the long bloody smear of scraped skin where his head had crashed against the stone, the deep bruises in his own throat. Then he saw the woman dead on the ground in front of the cave entrance, with Lathela's spear all the way through her and Lathela standing still on top of the hill with Peter's gun in his hand.

"Very good, Bwana," Lathela said. "It is good to kill an enemy with your hands alone, especially when he has a weapon."

"Why didn't you jump down here and rap him on the skull, you silly baboon?" Peter walked over and picked up his knife and stuck it in the sheath. "I lost this bloody knife right at the start. Were you going to let him kill me?"

"Of course, Bwana. I would not interfere in a personal matter. When you did not shoot and laid the gun down I knew you would kill him with your hands. You *wanted* to kill him with your hands."

"Well, come on down here and collect his headskin. You can pack it in the poncho. We need to take it back. And throw me the little torch. I want to have a look inside this cave." Lathela tossed the flashlight and slid down the hill, holding the rifle high in front of him. Peter went into the cave, sweeping the light ahead, stepping over the dead woman and pulling the spear out of her back as he stooped to enter the cave.

He straightened up and flashed his torch around. Its beam picked up one of the pressure lanterns on a shelf of rock. Peter went over and lit the lamp so that again the cave was flooded brilliantly white.

"So this," he said aloud, "this is Kimani's home." His voice boomed in the cave. A thin hiccupping wail came from the rear of the cave. Peter walked over and saw a little brown baby squirming in a packing-box cradle, its top crossed with straps to hold the infant in when its mother had to leave it to go for wood or water. The child was just on a year old, Peter thought as he looked down at the baby, who bawled now at the top of his lungs and fought the restraining straps with his brown fingers. The bawling made a lot of noise in the cave.

"So this is the home and that is the family," he said, again aloud, and prowled, stooping, about the cave. There were many guns, oiled and clean, standing in stacks in the back. There were wooden cases of ammunition, including one box of hand grenades, modern ones. There was a mattress from a double bed, and a mound of blankets. There were tins of food and a case of yellow-paper cigarettes. There was a three-stone cooking hearth in front and a row of pots and pans. There was a cured side of beef hanging from a thong on a spike driven into the wall. There was a pile of garments, greatcoats and suits. There were only a few women's clothes, but there was a case of snuff tins for her comfort. There was a gourd that swished when he picked it up, and Peter wrinkled his nose as he sniffed it. Half-fermented pombe. Bugger does himself well, I must say, he thought.

Lathela came into the cave and pricked his ears when he heard the baby wailing.

"Oh, that must be the child that came out with the mother into the little yard," he said. "Shall I knock it on the head? It is of no use to anyone."

"Yes, do," Peter said. "Poor little bugger's got no future."

Lathela went over to the cradle, slashed the restraining straps with his knife, and picked the baby up, holding it upside down, one hand encircling the tiny ankles. Lathela looked around for some sort of anvil.

He saw a rocky outcropping and walked over to it, swinging the child from his right hand, ankles held close together, the child upside down and screaming. Lathela swung the child backward like a pendulum.

"Wait!" Peter's voice was sudden, sharp in the cave. "Don't kill it. Wrap it up in a blanket and bring it outside."

"Yes, Bwana." Lathela swooped the child gently forward, caught him by the back of the neck as the head came up, and transferred him to the crook of his left arm. He snatched a blanket from the floor and took the child out into the sunlight. Peter walked over to the box of grenades and selected one, studying it as it lay in his palm. It was standard Army issue, metal-checkered and simple, with the pin poked through the arming lever. He put the grenade back and went out into the little court. The dead woman lay there, sprawled on her face. Kimani lay there. He had no head where the blood puddled. Lathela had the baby in one arm and in the other hand he held the black rubber poncho, now gathered into a sack which held a round heavy object.

"Go on outside the rock with the child and that thing you've got in the poncho," Peter said. "I will bring the gun and your spear." Lathela disappeared through the slot in the rock. "Go about fifty yards away and get down behind a big rock," Peter called.

Peter went back into the cave and tugged at the box of hand grenades. He dragged the box forward to the fire pit, just inside the entrance to the cave. He tilted one end of the box and dragged it onto the largest of Karugi's cooking stones. Then he lifted the other two cooking stones and made a nest of the three. Then he took one of the grenades and wedged it between the cooking stones, resting it flat on its side, with the arming lever on top and the ring of the tripping pin free and pointing toward the door. He tugged at the grenade and saw it was firmly wedged by the hearthstones. He fished into his pocket for the ball of strong cord he always carried and made the free end fast to the tripping pin with a bowline knot. Then he loosened the pin gently in its socket and walked backward out the door, paying out the line before him as he walked.

When he came out into the open he backed across the little courtyard, lifting the line gently over the dead body of the woman, leading it around the headless body of Kimani. He picked up his rifle and Lathela's spear and edged sideways through the slot in the rocky shield. He dropped the coil of line and took the gun and the spear to where Lathela waited with the baby, crouched behind a boulder some fifty yards away.

Peter walked back to the shield of stone and edged through the slot again. There was a rubble of loose boulders, and he rolled half a dozen over to the entrance to the cave and stacked them on top of and around the dead woman until the entrance was blocked. Then he led his line through a crack between the boulders and went out into the courtyard again. The flies had already come, with the weak sun that streamed its lemon light into the pebbled courtyard.

He slipped out through the slot, carrying the limp line in his hands, and walked about twenty yards away until he found a big boulder. He lay flat on the ground behind it and tensed his cord. When the cord was taut he pulled hard. There was a roar, and then a bigger roar, and then a deep rumble as rocks fell within. Peter dropped the string and walked down the hill to where Lathela was waiting with the baby and the other burden. The baby and the burden were resting on the grass. The baby was crying.

"You know how to make one of those slings the women use to carry children in on their back?" he asked Lathela.

"Surely, Bwana. I can make one out of this blanket, easy. But surely it would be simpler to knock it on the head. What shall *we* do with a baby?"

"Make the sling and tie it on my back," Peter said. "I will hold the baby whilst you fix the blanket."

Lathela handed him the little boy, who now had stopped crying, although his nose was running and his eyes were bright with fright. His face was shiny with grease. He had never seen a white man before. Lathela folded the blanket and draped it over Peter's shoulder like a toga, with a loose fold to make a pouch.

"Give me the child now," he said, and stuck the baby feet first into the pocket in the toga. Then he drew the gathered ends of the blanket tight and tied them in a knot round Peter's middle. The baby was wedged, warm and secure, against Peter's back. His head peeped out of the cocoon just under Peter's left armpit.

"Let's go," Peter said. "You take the rifle and that thing in the poncho. I'll carry your spear and the baby."

They began to walk, sliding through the clustered bamboo for a mile, walking and crawling carefully because of their burdens, until they came finally to a broad game trail where they could walk easily and erect, going downhill. The wood was soaking, but there was some sun that occasionally pierced downward through the dense green treetops, making little yellow puddles of light on the ground. A monkey complained bitterly about something, and once Peter heard a bushbuck bark. As they walked lower down the mountain a duiker scampered across the path, and the sun shone brighter. Peter glanced sideways at the fuzzy black head under his arm, then ahead at the steady-striding figure of Lathela, who walked in front with the gun balanced barrel-end forward over his shoulder, so that Peter saw only the checkered metal butt plate and the wood of the stock. Slung over the other shoulder was the poncho with its round burden, the burden humping against Lathela's back, as the baby shifted against Peter's back.

They walked all the day and finally came to the low slopes which prefaced, lime-green, the deep rich green of farming country. The baby was crying constantly, fretfully, and Peter thought that they had better feed it something pretty soon. It had already wet through the blanket several times. Peter wondered what he would do with the baby; why he hadn't let Lathela kill it. It would have been so much simpler, poor little bugger. The baby stopped its crying and began to whimper like a puppy.

I suppose it's actually *my* baby now, Peter thought. It's about all I've got. I'll take it home to Elisabeth and let her raise it up with young Wilbur. They can play together, and maybe someday I will teach them both a few of the nicer things I know.

They came out onto the flat now. Over there, a mile or so, would be a road. You could tell there was a road there because a long caravan of Army vehicles kicked up a steady slip stream of dust. Peter would hitch a ride with one of the lorries. They would be heading back to the base camp where his clothes and his jeep were. He wouldn't stop for more than two drinks after he had delivered one of his burdens. He would take the other burden home and not tell anybody whose baby it was that he carried, like a Kikuyu woman, slung in a sack on his back. But he would certainly have to feed the baby something pretty soon.

GLOSSARY

ahoi — tenant farmer or share cropper
Akikuyu — a man of Kikuyu
asante — thanks
askari — police or soldier

barafu — ice
baridi — cold
bibi — young female, woman
biltong — jerked or sun-dried thin strips of meat
boma — thorn enclosure or formal title of District Commissioner's compound
bombom — grenade
bongo — large member of bushbuck family, very wild antelope who lives on highest slopes of Kenya mountains
Boran — wild and very savage nomadic tribe of North Frontier
bundouki — gun
bwana — white master, title of respect

chai — tea
chakula — food
colobus — black-and-white monkey

ducca — any general store, mostly run by East Indians

Embu — members of Bantu race, quite similar to Kikuyu in appearance, tradition, and agricultural background
Engai — God Almighty, as opposed to separate gods

fisi — hyena

gharri — car

githathi — oath of honesty so potent that to breech it brings death
gituyu — small forest rodent with sharp teeth

hapa — here

iko — is there, or there is, according to inflexion

jambo — hello
ju — up

kahura — special circumcision dance
'Kamba — member of the Wakamba fighting tribe
kanga — guinea fowl
kanzu — long white robe worn by servants, like old-fashioned nightgown
karibu — water bag
kibiriti — matches
kiboko — hippo; or, more popularly, a lash or switch made of either rhino or hippo hide
kidogo — little
Kikuyu — either a man of the Kikuyu race or the country in which the Kikuyu live
kipandi — working permit bearing fingerprints, which all "civilized" Kenya Africans must have; identity card
Kipsigi — members of Bantu race, quite similar to Kikuyu in appearance, tradition, and agricultural background
kishoto — left
kisu — knife
kuisha — finish, through
kuja — come
ku-lala — to sleep
kulia — right
kwaheri — good-by
kwenda — come on, or let's go

lala — a nap
letti — bring
lini — down
Loita — the broad volcanic plains leading to the High Masai country

manamouki — female, either animal or human

manyatta — Masai village

marabou — carnivorous stork, which lives off carrion

Masai — fierce fighting tribe of Bantu origin which lives in southern Kenya and Tanganyika

mathanjuki — wise man, instructor, especially for circumcision ceremony

maui — rock, stone

mberi — straight

mbile — two

mbogo — Cape buffalo

mbuzi — goat

memsaab — African corruption of memsahib, meaning lady; opposite of bwana

Meru — members of Bantu race, quite similar to Kikuyu in appearance, tradition, and agricultural background

mingi sana — very many

mkubwa — big

mokengeria — shrub used in sacred ceremonies

moran — Masai warrior

moto — hot

mtoto — baby, animal or human

mubagé — sacred beans used in magic divining

mukongogo — a type of tree

mundumugu — wise man, witch doctor

Mungu — Swahili word for God

musth — male elephant's breeding period, when elephant is rendered mad by excretion from glands in head

mutu — man

mzee — old man; term of respect

na — and

Nandi — one of Kenya's best-known warrior tribes

ndege — bird; airplane or people who fly airplanes

ndio — yes

ndofu — elephant

'Ndrobo — wild detribalized hunters who can be of any tribal derivation

Ngai — other spelling for God Almighty

ngoma — dance

nini — who
njamas — Kikuyu warriors
nugu — monkey

panga — large bush knife, very much like a South American machete
papaya — yellow-fleshed, black-seeded, tree-grown melon
pese — hurry
pie-dog — any masterless cur in the state of semi-starvation
piga — shoot, hit, or commit
pombe — booze
posho — mealie-maize flour
pumbavu — idiot
punda — zebra

Rendille — nomadic pastoral tribe, close cousin to Masai, which roves Northern Frontier of Kenya
risase — bullets

safari — journey, a walking out
Samburu — nomadic pastoral tribe, close cousin to Masai, which roves Northern Frontier of Kenya
sana — much, very
sasa — now
semama — stop
Serkali — Swahili word for British Government
shamba — farm or area of cultivation or group of huts
shauri — business, act
shauri gani — how are things going?
shenzis — wild men, shaggy
simba — lion
simi — short two-edged stabbing sword
sjambok — whiplike staff
Somali — dark Aryan pastoral race of Mohammedan faith which inhabits the Northern Frontier of Kenya up through Somaliland
soupi — soup
sundouki — box or suitcase
suria — obscene word for extreme hurry
Swahili — trade language, baby talk used in Central Africa to communi-

cate between different tribes; also formal name of a coastal race of bastard Arab/Negro derivation.

tasama — look for
Telek — river in the Masai country
tembo — elephant
terai — wide double-brimmed hat
thahu — curse
thingira — Kikuyu bachelor hut into which no wife may intrude
tia — put in
tinni-kata — can opener
toa — take out
Tommy — small golden gazelle about the size of small pointer dog; named after famous explorer, Thomson.
Turkana — very savage primitive tribe of hunters who inhabit the Northern Frontier of Kenya
tyari — ready

veldschoen — raw-calf bush shoes, first worn by the Boers
villi-villi — likewise; as well
wa- — common Swahili language prefix to most tribal and proper names in Kenya. It means simply "of," so that the 'Kamba tribe is called Wakamba and a Hindu is called Wahindi. A man's full name would be Karanja wa Kariuki, meaning Karanja (son) of Kariuki (father)

Waikoma — savage relative of Masai, found close by the Serengeti desert in Tanganyika
weka hi — put it here
wattle — long thin tree used extensively for tanbark, hut construction, and as money crop

Kwenda tasama Tommy na letti hi pese pese bloody nugu. Go and look for the Tommy and bring it here in a hurry, you bloody baboon.
Letti ginni kwa Bwana pese pese. Bring the gin for the master in a hurry.
Toa bundouki mkubwa kwa Bwana Kidogo pese pese na tia risase. Take out the big gun for the little master in a hurry and put in the bullets.
Kata hi ya tumbo. Slit the stomach here.
Martini a maui mbile. Double martini on the rocks.

Letti soupi leo hapana keshu. Bring the soup today, not tomorrow.
Letti hi hapa majimoto kwa memsaab pese pese. Bring the hot water here for the lady in a hurry.
Letti beer-i kwa Bwana. Fetch the beer for the master.
Iko hapa chai. Here is the tea.